BOOKS BY JULIAN DUTTON

Keeping Quiet: Visual Comedy in the Age of Sound

Water Gypsies: a History of Life on Britain's Rivers & Canals

REVIEWS OF WATER GYPSIES

'A comprehensive and enchanting social history,' - Camden New Journal.

'This is a beautiful book. Julian Dutton grew up on the water, and he's the perfect guide to the life aquatic. There could be no better or more informative guide to a history of life aboard,' - Samuel West.

'Wonderful... Essential reading,' - Nautilus Telegraph.

'Love the book! Super-informative facts and history,' - Thames Path National Trail.

REVIEWS OF KEEPING QUIET

'A custard pie in the face of those who say slapstick is dead, by the go-to writer of British visual comedy,' - Harry Hill

'A must-have item for all fans of comedy as it fills a distinct gap in the bookshelves. Highly recommended!' – Dick Fiddy, British Film Institute.

THE PARADE'S GONE BY

FURNIVAL BOOKS

EVERYDAY LIFE IN BRITAIN IN THE TWENTIETH CENTURY

From the Diaries of Thomas Sibley 1878-1974

First published 2023 by Furnival Books

British Library Cataloguing in Publication Data.

A catalogue record for this book is available from the British Library.

ISBN 9781399958325

For My Father, Rex Kidman Dutton
1925-2016

CONTENTS

FOREWORD I

ACKNOWLEDGEMENTS III

NOTE IV

INTRODUCTION VII

Chapter 1 The Belle Epoque 1

Chapter 2 Zeppelins Over Wanstead 207

Chapter 3 This Happy Breed 323

Chapter 4 The Last Dance 388

Chapter 5 The Enduring Flame 466

Chapter 6 Brave New World 568

Chapter 7 Blue Suburban Skies 672

I

FOREWORD

'... the truth of anything at all doesn't lie in someone's account of it. It lies in all the small facts of the time. An advertisement in a paper, the sale of a house, the price of a ring.'

Josephine Tey, The Daughter of Time

This book is the story of everyday life in the twentieth century, inspired by the diaries of a man who lived from 1878-1974. My father discovered the journals in a musty old chest at an auction when I was a boy. If you like the idea of being a time-traveller then you may like this book, for it is an eyewitness, day-by-day account of the lives our Great-Grandparents led.

The story of the twentieth century has been told many times and we are familiar with its broad strokes - Edwardian England, the Great War, the General Strike, the Blitz, Rationing, Rock & Roll, the Sixties. This book tells this wider story but shifts the reader's gaze from the political, economic and historical to the local, colourful detail of ordinary family life.

Thomas Sibley was a travelling salesman born in London in 1878. He kept a diary for every day of his life from 1900 to 1972. When he was born Jack the Ripper was prowling the streets and when he died the Moon landings were already old news. His journals are the equivalent of cine-film of everyday life in Britain in the twentieth century: he describes the streets, shops, cafes, music halls, cinemas, boarding-houses, seaside towns, food, drink, visits to the doctor, holidays, illnesses, Christmases, births, marriages, deaths.

II

This book is not a biography of Sibley - it is our national story told through the saga of three generations of an ordinary family. The diaries are used as stepping-stones, each entry akin to an artefact discovered by mudlarks on the Thames foreshore, acting as gateways to the wider world.

Sibley may have had a walk-on part in our national life but his story has epic moments. His father was discovered drowned in the lake in Victoria Gardens, Hackney in 1901. He pressed his young lover Annie against a wall in Ullin Road, Bow, and kissed her deeply. In 1915 he saw Zeppelins turn the sky electric white above London. In 1920 he swam in the sea and watched the minstrels on Brighton Pier. In 1941 while his wife lay dead in his front parlour a German bomb tore his house apart. On his deathbed in the 1970s he took up his diary from 1900 and read of his younger days, when he rode a carriage through the streets of London with the fire of youth in his eyes.

History comes most alive not in the anecdotes of the great, the good or the famous but in the beautiful triviality of the ordinary - how our Great Grandparents spoke, thought, loved, how they spent their days at work, their evenings at play. And perhaps the perfect expression of social history comes to us from the diary. For it is only when we move our gaze from the broader pageant to the intimacy of the individual do we hear and feel the true beating heart of our national story.

III

ACKNOWLEDGEMENTS

My grateful thanks are extended to David Sibley, Great-Nephew of Thomas, for permission to use his Great-Uncle's diaries as the basis of this book, and to Thomas' grandson Howard Ringwood, and nephew Professor Alan Millard, for their memories.

IV

NOTE

This is a history of British life, but readers will see that London looms disproportionately in its pages. In the most profound way Sibley's history is inextricable from that of the capital city of his country, and in the unfolding of his life he *becomes* the city and nation: in telling his story we reach that moment where individual, capital city and country become so enmeshed they are indivisible.

Human life is chaos, and moreover the city is chaos, all form projected onto a fitful disorder by a mind that craves pattern, regularity and repetition, lest we be engulfed by pandemonium. So the only structure I have imposed upon the narrative is chronological. Just as ordinary people's lives jump from holiday to work to drinking to love to despair to family tragedy, so too this history aspires to mirror this crazed kaleidoscope, this jumbled admixture, and the only architecture I have adhered to is that of the human lifespan.

Why *The Parade's Gone By?* In an age of new ideologies, religious decline, revolutions both technological and political, warfare of such dimensions as had never been seen before, an explosion of cultural achievements in all realms of artistic endeavour from music to art to architecture and literature - such an age can only be described as possessing the nature of a parade. Parades are a display of collective spirit, embodying celebration, nostalgia, identity. Yet the twentieth century was also an era of iconoclasm, impatience, curiosity - and ultimately unease, when in Yeats' famous phrase, *'the centre cannot hold.'* We lost much and gained much in this century, and it befits our spirit to dwell for a time in the presence of a person who moved through its horror, love and pageantry with a steadfast, ordinary soul.

Illustrations: all photographs have been sourced from the public domain, or are ephemera contained in Sibley's diaries. Where possible all accreditation has been ascribed. It is regretted that there is a paucity of photographs of the Sibley family, as many of these are lost, but I am grateful to Professor Alan Millard & David Sibley for providing the ones that exist.

INTRODUCTION

Russia Lane, Bethnal Green, East London is a smart residential thoroughfare of mostly 1970's public housing. Neat brick apartment blocks sport metal balconies overlooking a well-kept playground, a friendly corner shop squats at the junction with Bishops Way, and young plane trees burst from swollen ruptures of tarmac stretching gold leaves to a milky London sky.

There is a buoyant air of friendliness and community here. To stroll along the pleasant streets of Bethnal Green today it is hard to countenance that a century and a half ago the district was one of the direst and most notorious in the capital - a dark shamble of rotten dwellings, marshy wastelands, filthy cottages, dilapidated boarding houses haunted by sunken-eyed prostitutes and murderers (the London Burkers, a gang of cut-throats that eked out their miserable existences supplying cadavers to the London Hospitals, operated out of a tumbledown house of horror stuck on the late brick-field north-east of nearby St. Leonard's Church); later in the century, the neighbourhood became famous as the haunt of Jack the Ripper.

Bethnal Green was even home to the infamous mountain of filth that inspired Dicken's 'waste heap' in *Our Mutual Friend.* The real hill was in Nova Scotia Gardens, that same aching expanse of waste as where the Burker's house stood, where drugged victims would be held head-down in the well until their struggling bodies expired. Towering above passers-by, this scarp of darkness became a symbol of all that had been abandoned by London - literally the rejected effluence of the city surrounded by the waste of a similarly abandoned humanity. When Dickens' friend the philanthropist Angela Burdett-

Bethnal Green, 1882. The streets where the five year-old Thomas Sibley played, a few hundred yards from the Ripper murders.

Coutts asked him where she should establish her welfare institution the writer replied without hesitation *'Bethnal Green.'* The first ventures of the great chronicler of the London poor Henry Mayhew were made into the dark streets, alleys and courts of this parish, his horror-infused articles later published in the *Morning Chronicle*. Body-snatching, murder, eight-to-a-room poverty and bleak surroundings pepper the history of this dark, grimy pocket of the East End.

It was into this ghastly maelstrom of deprivation, violence and gaslit horror that Thomas Sibley was born.

When Thomas Sibley was born Benjamin Disraeli was Prime Minister and the Zulu War was still two years away. Thomas Hardy had just got into his literary stride, the steam plough was a source of wonderment, and the telephone, wireless and aeroplane were rudimentary blueprints in a workshop.

When, at the age of 94, he made his final journal entry, the television viewing public were already beginning to tire of the Moon landings, the Beatles' Sergeant Pepper album had faded from the charts, and Edward Heath was in his second term as British Prime Minister. Military establishments in the United States had begun to develop what would evolve into the world-wide-web.

Sibley's life spanned the last quarter of the nineteenth and most of the twentieth century. He lived through much of the most tumultuous social and technological change the world has known. And every day from the age of twenty-two to ninety-five he painstakingly recorded the events of his life, and the lives of his family, in neat copperplate handwriting in a series of Letts Diaries spanning the years 1900 to 1972 (the final two years, probably through illness, are un-chronicled). He lived his life mostly in London, being born in the East End of the late Victorian era, then following the pattern of many aspirational hard-working citizens he moved gradually to the suburbs - first Wanstead, then to a large, comfortable house in Ilford, Essex. He lived a solid, respectable life, raised children, pursued a job as a travelling salesman, belonged to his local Baptist Church.

On his death in Ilford, as happens with many, his property scattered; his son had died, and the gatherings of a long life became detached from the Sibley family and drifted out into the ether. Amongst the effects dispersed thus were his collection of diaries, so carefully written. This precious record, along with all his other belongings, vanished.

Until one summer in the late 1970's.

My Father, when he retired from his work in the television industry, pursued a late-flowering job of buying and restoring antiques. His speciality was furniture but occasionally he would return from one of the many auctions he visited with an armful of curios. One Saturday he came home carrying a chest. Inside were sixty-odd volumes of hard-back journals, all slim Lett's Desk Diaries, the first forty red buckskin, the wartime volumes of necessity cheaper, the 1960's & 70's volumes the more familiar navy blue. There were a few missing volumes but mostly it comprised a complete record of the writer's entire life from the age of twenty-three in 1900 to his death in 1972. Anyone born in the twentieth century and who kept a diary as a youth will recall Letts diaries, usually bought in W.H. Smith, with their tables of currency converters, calendars, and global time charts.

I began reading. The entries were largely of a uniform length. Each began with a record of the weather of the day: each detailed his daily routine, the people he met, the places he visited, the family members he encountered. These were not great events he was recording, but small, one might say even trivial, incidents, the everyday phenomena of an intensely ordinary life.

I quickly realised this was no Samuel Pepys involved in great affairs of state, no diarist writing for the public with one eye on posterity. Sibley achieved no great status in his life, fought no great battles, performed no heroic deeds. For most of his life he worked as a travelling salesman, journeying back and forth across London and the rest of the country plying his wares.

(The company he chiefly worked for, the British Drug House, operating out of a small warehouse in Graham Street, Pentonville, was to grow into the now gigantic Merck Corporation).

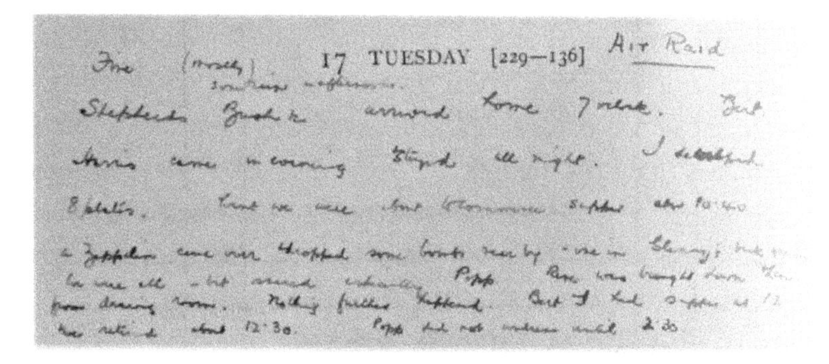
17 TUESDAY [229—136] Air Raid

A Zeppelin raid, August 17th 1915.

He married, raised a family, cultivated his garden; he attended the funeral of Queen Victoria, cycled down to Crystal Palace in the heyday of the English Edwardian Summer, huddled round the first Edison phonograph with his family, (being *"much amused by the sound of our voices,"*) bought his first car in 1927 - a Morris Oxford which he drove home proudly after two or three lessons - listened to Chamberlain's historic broadcast of 1939 declaring war on Germany, was bombed in the Blitz, and watched Dixon of Dock Green on his first television set in the late 1950's. Bank Holiday outings to Brighton, charabanc trips to the Cafe Dreamland, Margate; arguments with his young son in 1909 for '*running into the pond after his boat,*' fights with the War Office over compensation for bomb damage; Christmas parties in the 1920's.

His life was not without drama: he found his drunken Father drowned in the lake in Victoria Gardens, Hackney, his house was bombed in 1941. But for the most part his life was a series of quiet moments, no less significant for that. The untimely death of his son, a move from the East End of London to the more prosperous suburban Ilford - these were Thomas Sibley's epic moments.

Gradually, as I read, the diaries began to exert an alchemical affect. Each entry grew in importance, becoming a vivid snapshot of the actual hours in which Sibley was living and breathing, until suddenly it struck me like a bolt of ice-cold lightning: these *were* epic diaries, these *were* episodes of an extraordinary pageant, which by very dint of their smallness become giant; the small brush-strokes of this apparently ordinary, stolid, English lower middle-class life assuming the stature of a grand chronicle of the twentieth century.

There is a reason Shakespeare's minor characters are as well-known and as well-loved as the Lords and Kings that people his plays. The heroic or tragic heroes when set beside the Falstaffs, Nyms and Bardolphs assume, in their grandness and posturing, a skein of artifice. It is the more lowly participants of his dramas, with their everyday concerns, foibles and very-human lusts and delusions, who seem more *real*. Falstaff embodies the history of England no less more vividly than Lear or Cymbeline.

This book, then, is a history of Thomas Sibley's England from 1900-1972, a chronicle of one family's life and how they rode the tide of the most dramatic century in the history of humankind. It tells the story of how the DNA and mindset of the Victorian era extended into the space-age of the late twentieth century. It does not - could not - contain an exhaustive mining of his journals in their entirety (some journals are indeed missing); his entries, thoughts, commentaries, are rather used as markers through the years; the minutiae and detail of a vast painting that illuminate the wider events on the national and international canvas.

Sibley's was the life of an Everyman, a London Leopold Bloom.

Statesmen, royalty, historical figures, all assume walk-on parts in his life: glimpsed over the heads of a crowd, ranting on podiums, recorded as mere background detail in the landscape. It is Sibley himself who is centre stage, preferring to record how much it cost him to buy two currant buns and a bottle of lemonade at a Lyons Corner House in 1910 to debates about the League of Nations or the Problem of Germany.

And this is just as it should be. We have a surfeit of the memoirs of Generals and Prime Ministers, actors and broadcasters, pop singers and sportsmen. History comes most alive in the wills, the court rolls, the diaries, the interviewees of Mayhew, Defoe and Dickens. To get a proper feel of what it was like to live in late Victorian England I want to know what they had for dinner, how they amused themselves in the evenings, what they talked about with their friends, what the streets and buildings smelt of; their reaction to an unwanted pregnancy; their family arguments; their first kiss; their illnesses, their purchases, their disappointments, their triumphs. And all this Sibley offers us; intimate snapshots - sometimes seemingly petty but never less than compelling.

For in the process of reading these volumes, something peculiar happens. His diaries begin to add up to something greater than their constituent parts; in T.S. Eliot's words, they become something *'rich and strange, universal and impersonal.'* One of the fruits of reading his work is the growing awareness that the everyday flotsam of Sibley's life is the story of all our lives. *'Only connect,'* said E.M. Forster - and Thomas Sibley truly does connect. He omits nothing - supplying us, for example, with painstaking details of he and his wife's illnesses. This is not the sanitised apologia of a guilty general or a seven-times married actress: these are the warts-and-all jottings of an ordinary man so obsessed with the ordinary that they become, by transmutation, extraordinary.

Sibley's life is, to be sure, a vivid portrait of what it was like to have been born in late Victorian England: he was shaped by his times, as we all are: his poor upbringing in the East End of London, his discovery of Self-help and Evangelism, his acceptance of his lower-middle-class status. And yet, more powerful than this, his diaries tell us that all our lives, throughout history, have always been the same - whether we are an Iron Age farmer, a Medieval clerk or an Edwardian travelling salesman. For we are all governed by the natural cycle of the seven ages of man - our rites of passage, our fears, our lusts, our ambitions, our fights with our parents, our desire for a mate, our impulse to better ourselves, our acquisitiveness, our boredom, our jealousy, our love.

Why did he start his diary ? - and, more importantly, why did he continue it, from the age of twenty-three to ninety-four ? He began it prior to discovering religion, so it cannot have been Christian zeal or a sense of 'vocation,' a desire to convert. It was certainly not meant for publication. It was simply a man talking to himself; recording the often humdrum and sometimes dramatic events of his day with a painstaking regularity.

I believe that his diary-keeping gave Sibley's life order, structure and purpose. In a sense, he created himself through them - became Thomas Sibley, Diarist. Such conscious creation of self often derives from a need to escape suffering. Certainly his childhood and upbringing to the age of sixteen was hard. His Father drank regularly and was probably an alcoholic (as evinced by the simple scarcely-cryptic note '*Pere d. -*' which occurs on many pages of the early diaries). His Mother - from the outset of the first volume - is ill. Yet from the time he leaves school, the young Thomas is never out of work. He is on a constant search for self-improvement. He is a driven man. One of the chief characteristics of the diaries is his energy and determination: his working hours are phenomenal - right up to his late eighties he is still doing his rounds as a salesman. This dynamism and sense of self-purpose betray an unconscious reaction to suffering and deprivation. He has, quite simply, hauled himself up by his bootstraps. He has witnessed hardship in both his immediate family and in those of his neighbourhood - the Bethnal Green district of London at the time of his childhood was one of the poorest in the country - and he is determined not to let his environment defeat him.

At the beginning of the diary we find the young Sibley behaving just like any young man anywhere, at any time. He *'mouches down the Bow Road'* with his brother Bob and *'pays a visit to the Plough.'* He goes off to the Holborn Town Hall dance on Saturday night and gets two girls *'very lively and saucy with wine.'* He tumbles into bed at midnight or later and gets up at six the next morning to go to work. He takes strolls with his girlfriend along Ullin Street in Bow - a notorious place of convenience for spooning couples - where there is much *'inspection of her red dress.'*

He takes Bank Holiday trips to Brighton, where he flirts with another young girl staying at the boarding house. He dabbles in smoking, having the odd 'puff' here and there at the People's Palace.

As the diaries progress we watch him develop into an earnest young man determined to make his way in the world. His conversion to Christianity provides him with strength and purpose, and the keenness and enthusiasm with which he supports his family never wavers across the years. He suffers setbacks and tragedies; his triumphs are the minor achievements of a minor life. And yet, at the age of ninety-four, when we read his final entries as he lies bedridden in hospital, Thomas Sibley's life assumes a kind of poignant, epic grandeur, as - even when on the danger-list - he faithfully records each pain and discomfort, and in a moment of prescience begins reading his own diary of 1900 - that far-off morning of his life when the sun shone on the Empire and he was a young man with a brightness in his eyes - right up to his final day when he wrote: *'Nurse Crump came. Washed, and sat in chair. Had a meal of veal, beans, baked apple and custard,'* - then closed his eyes forever.

CHAPTER ONE

THE BELLE EPOQUE 1900-1910

Morning broke rainy and foggy on January 1st 1900 as a young man caught the train from Bethnal Green to Liverpool Street. At some point during his day's work as a salesman for W.J.Petty Ltd., a pharmaceutical firm in Gracechurch Street (he later switched to working for Davy Hill & Co.) the twenty-two year old bought a diary from one of the many stationer's shops in the City. Or perhaps he'd received it as a Christmas present. However he acquired the journal, when he retired to bed that evening Thomas Sibley opened the crisp newly-bought notebook in his gaslit upstairs bedroom in Stanfield Road, Bow, East London, and with a fine-nibbed fountain pen wrote his first entry.

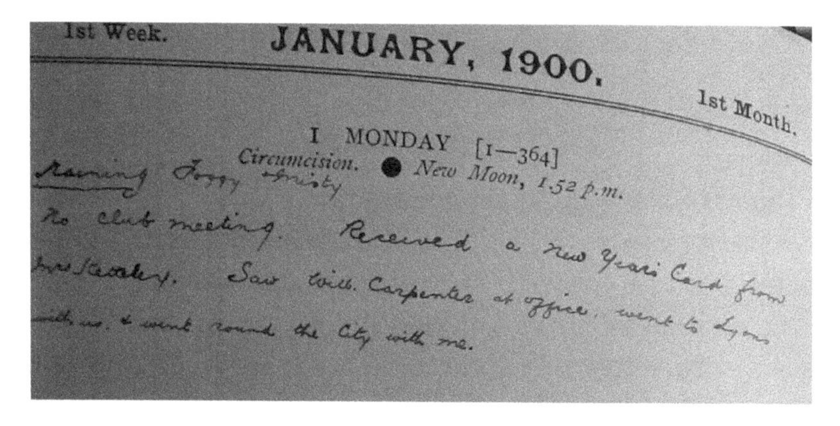
1st Week. JANUARY, 1900. 1st Month.

I MONDAY [1—364]

Circumcision. ● New Moon, 1.52 p.m.

Raining Foggy Misty

No club meeting. Received a New Year's Card from Mrs Keatley. Saw Will. Carpenter at Office. went to Lyons with us. & went round the City with me.

It was to be the first of thousands. As the rain beat on the sash window of his little home and he carefully listed the names and addresses of his brothers, his employer, his sweetheart and his friends in the front papers of the Lett's Diary, he could not have conceived that one hundred and twenty three years later his life story would form the bedrock of a narrative history.

6, Stanfield Road, Bow, London. In the upstairs bedroom the young Thomas Sibley began his diary.

Thomas Sibley had already travelled far, in mental terms, from his inauspicious beginnings in an East End tenement. From the outset we hear the voice of an assured, aspirational young man fully involved in his community, but possessed of a restless energy that would thread through his life as through a stick of rock. His journal begins:

JANUARY 1900.

1st Monday Raining, foggy and misty. No club meeting. Received a New Year's card from Mrs. Kettley. Saw Will Carpenter at office.

Went to Lyons with us, and went round the City with me.

From the outset Sibley is making his stamp; his intentions clear, purpose straightforward. No preamble, no statement of great intent, merely a spare, utilitarian recording of cold hard events. At first glance only a few meagre sentences promising to yield little fruit, yet from these scant thirty-two words we learn he works in an office, is a member of a club, eats in one of the most famous restaurant chains in British history, and that there are two supporting characters in the drama of his life: a Mrs. Kettley, and a Will Carpenter.

How did he arrive at that momentous moment of deciding to record his life? He already had twenty-two years behind him. What of the world of his childhood before he became a diarist?

Number 6, Russia Lane, where he was born, is now gone, but would have been a grim slum. He was one of five brothers, the 1881 census recording his father William Thomas, his mother Susannah, *nee* Bridges, and his four brothers Henry, Edwin, Thomas and Robert. Thomas was the second youngest. His father William was a joiner who had moved from Hendon in north London a few years previously, probably for work, as Mill Hill and the northern environs of the capital at that time were not the teeming towns of Greater London they are today, but more rural outposts. In the Russia Lane of 1881 when Thomas was 3 years old they rubbed shoulders with brush-makers, milliners, a cab-proprietor and a nurse. These were semi-skilled jobs, proving that whereas only a few decades earlier one could have spotted from the upper rooms of the houses in Russia Lane the enormous mountain of waste in Nova Scotia Gardens, the neighbourhood was making valiant efforts to appear, while most certainly not 'middle-class,' at the very least aspirational. The borough was still officially the poorest in London, yet when Sibley drew his first few breaths in 1878 the area was at least showing signs of improvement. This was an effect of both the influx of skilled labour and social reform. For centuries a silk-weaving parish, by the time of Sibley's birth the industry was in decline and weavers were under-employed. Occupations such as tailoring, furniture making and coster-mongering replaced it but none were prosperous, sweated labour was prevalent, and much of the population was caught in a downward spiral of poverty. A modern analysis has placed Bethnal Green as the second poorest London parish in 1841, the poorest by 1871. Into this malleable district, then, the young Thomas Sibley emerged, to play in its streets and alleyways, observe its rites, customs.

The very name of Sibley's place of birth, Russia Lane, itself betrays its origins as a place of settlement for the migrant populations of Russia and Eastern Europe, predominantly Jewish, fleeing pogroms and persecution. Tellingly, abutting the bottom of Russia Lane was Palestine Street, and a Jewish School was founded nearby in the 1880's. And it was this migration of largely skilled labour and tradespeople, along with dynamic philanthropy, 'muscular Christianity,' that actually rescued the district.

And what of the wider England at the time of Sibley's youth? What was Sibley's world? By dint of his very birth in the capital city of the British Empire the twenty-two year old was inheriting the Earth: London in 1900 was a pliant, flexible muscle, or more appropriately an organ, absorbing migrants from all parts and disgorging those who wished to travel and work across the globe. The world, perhaps, had never been freer, before or since: with no need for passports an enterprising individual could on a whim journey to Australia, America, Europe, the Far East. Quite simply, Britain was the industrial powerhouse of the globe. Its empire was at its zenith, its technology unrivalled. Britain's exports of coal and steel to the continent alone was a source of its supremacy. London, the trading and financial hub of the nation, had grown to such a degree that Victorians had begun to call it 'the metropolis.' The capital's population had expanded from 2.3 million in 1851 to 4.5 million in 1911, and as other cities grew a certain Patrick Geddes had to coin a new word for the phenomenon, *conurbation*, to describe the tentacle-sprawl of Salford, Liverpool, Manchester, Sheffield, London. If all its suburbs were counted, then the true figure of London's people swelled to 7.3 million. This vast organism was fuelled by coal, powered by gas, and connected to the rest of the country by the railway, which for the first time in British history had created a nationally-integrated economy.

And into these pulsating conurbations and urban centres had poured first huge swathes of Irish migrants, driven by the fierce depopulation of their home country by dint of the famines, then towards the end of the century by large flows of Jewish settlers fleeing the persecution of Russia and Eastern Europe.

This was the milieu in which the young, mewling Sibley first blinked: a nation at the very apex of the balance of power, mirroring the equivalent ascendancy of northern Europe: the British did not name it such like the French but there is no doubt the United Kingdom was living through its own *Belle Epoque*. Yet at the heart of this wealth and power existed vast pockets of human flotsam and jetsam, a grimy underclass of casual labour, seasonal unemployment, sweat-shops of the exploited: and below them, pools of humanity who had slipped completely through the net for a whole forest of reasons - lack of luck, lack of skills, drink: the battering storms of circumstance. Such were the variegated parts of each city and large town in England - a mixture of the skilled industrial class and the truly poor.

By the latter part of the nineteenth century the forces of Victorian social improvement were having profound effects on the amelioration of conditions for the poor. In Bethnal Green sprang up refuges for prostitutes, orphanages, cultural institutions for the dissemination of church teachings: even the prototype for the Museum in Kensington was moved to Bethnal Green for the 'promotion of knowledge of the arts and sciences' amongst the poor (the building is now the Bethnal Green Museum of Childhood). Thomas Sibley's part of the East End was slowly attempting to haul itself out of the mire by its bootstraps.

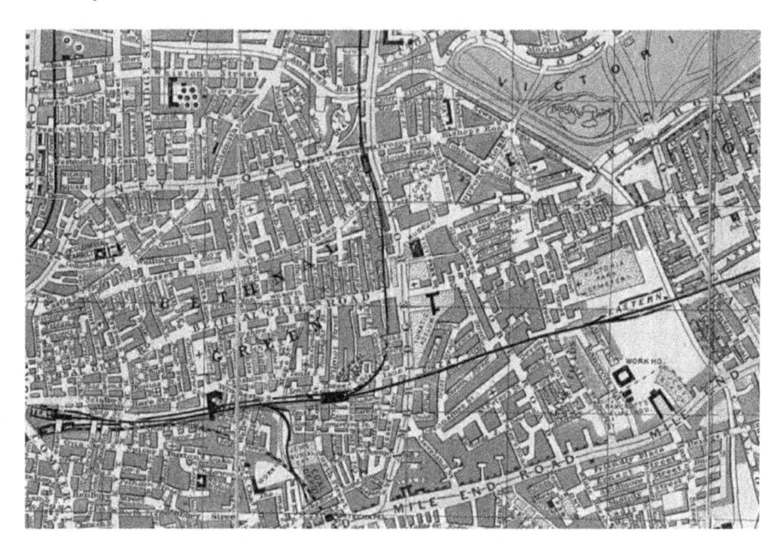

Thomas Sibley's Bethnal Green of the late 19th century.

Closer to home, had Sibley commenced his diary at the age of ten there is little doubt he would have recorded the most infamous events of the time: the 'Jack the Ripper' murders. The ghastly deaths of young women between April 3rd 1888 and February 13th 1891, variously known as the 'Whitechapel Murders,' and the 'Leather Apron murders,' have gone down in grisly and harrowing folklore. They took place only a stone's throw from where the Sibley family lived, in the streets and alleyways where the young Thomas spent his formative years, so these horrors must have cast a shadow over their lives and the lives of their neighbours. The Victorian popular press spun these tragedies into melodrama with *grand guignol* pictures of the murder scenes emblazoned across all the weeklies and dailies such as *The Police Gazette* and the *Penny Illustrated Paper,* so it is difficult not to conclude that the murders would have held a grisly fascination for young people, especially ten year old boys at the local schools. The Ripper's first victim, Mary Ann Nichols, was found only a mile from the Sibley's doorstep, in Buck Row, a narrow lane forking off from North Street, now Brady Street. In the coming weeks and months a further four canonical victims were discovered; the horrific killings continued to 1891, though investigators are in dispute as to whether these other murders were perpetrated by the original 'Ripper.'

That there were horrendous homicides in other parts of the country at the time there is no doubt, yet there is a dreadful inevitability that the most famous slayings in the nineteenth century took place here in Bethnal Green, the capital's poorest borough. In its dark rookeries and courts, where 3d given for a bed for a homeless person was more often than not spent on alcohol (which had, indeed, been poor Mary Nichol's fate, for on her final night, August 31st 1888, she had spent her last coins on drink so found herself wandering the streets alone) there was deprivation as severe as anything in human history. One only has to glance at the map of 1882 to see the symbols of hardship and suffering - the lunatic asylum just south of St. John's Church, the workhouse near Russia Lane itself, the almshouses for poor old folk fronting the Mile End Road. Terrible sights and scenes of everyday poverty must have impressed themselves profoundly on the mind of the young Thomas as he went out and about with his parents, perhaps venturing with his father to a place of work where the elder William was working as a joiner on a house, or stopping off with him at one of the many taverns on the way home.

Were the Sibleys representatives of their environs? That they were an aspirational family is without doubt: by 1891 when Thomas is 13 his elder brothers William, Henry and Edwin are now all working as commercial clerks. His father now is listed in the census as a 'carpenter,' - possibly having broadened his profession from joinery which is focused on the making of furniture, fixtures and fittings.

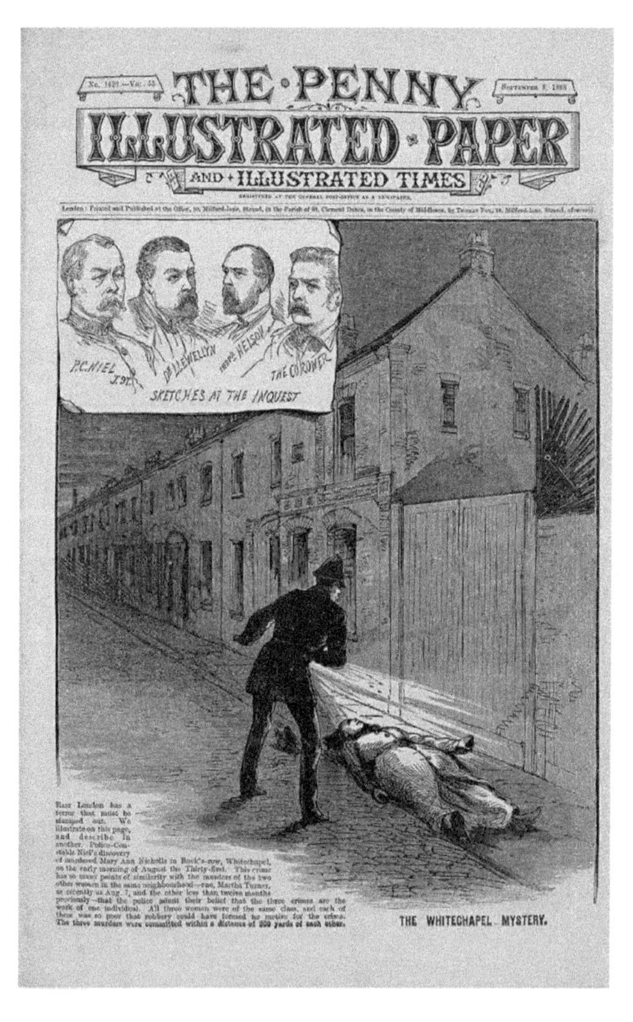

THE PENNY ILLUSTRATED PAPER AND ILLUSTRATED TIMES

East London has a terror that must be stamped out. We illustrate on this page, and describe in another, Police-Constable Niel's discovery of murdered Mary Ann Nicholls in Buck's-row, Whitechapel, on the early morning of August the Thirty-first. This crime has so many points of similarity with the murders of the two other women in the same neighbourhood—one, Martha Turner, as recently as Aug. 7, and the other less than twelve months previously—that the police admit their belief that the three crimes are the work of one individual. All three women were of the same class, and each of them was so poor that robbery could have formed no motive for the crime. The three murders were committed within a distance of 300 yards of each other.

THE WHITECHAPEL MYSTERY.

In 1891 they have moved from Russia Lane and are living just around the corner in Robinson Road. Was this an advancement? The remaining terrace today that stretches along Robinson Road speaks of modest respectability - two-up-two-down homes of typical mottled London brick, with no front gardens and tiny yards at the back.

A family living in one room, Bethnal Green, 1890. It was from deprivation such as this that Thomas Sibley sought to escape.

But these were not slums, for by the 1890's the area is up-and-coming: nearby is a Congregational Church, a Jewish School; there are public baths in Cambridge Road, and the green expanse of Victoria Park is a mere five minutes stroll away, with its fresh air and ornamental boating lake, in whose cool waters Mr. Sibley senior was wont to swim every day.

Thomas's mother Susannah was born in 1841 in Bedfield, a small village in mid-Suffolk: losing her bricklayer father before she reached the age of ten, in 1851 her mother was working as a dress-maker. Between 1861 and 1871 Susannah - now also a dressmaker - moved to London: certainly by 1868 we know she has met and married Thomas's father, William. This migration from country to city is the principal feature of demographic flow in the second half of the nineteenth century: the extraordinary expansion of the metropolis was commensurate with the mechanisation of farming, the industrial growth of London and the consequent employment prospects, and the swelling of particularly the 'East End,' into which poured not only migrants from the villages, towns and farmlands of Essex, but from oppressed communities from overseas.

Thomas's father William himself had done his own share of migrating, but from a locality closer than his wife's Suffolk roots; to wit, Hendon. The son of a wheelwright, his wife was four years older than him. They quickly set about raising a family.

Between the time of Thomas's birth and the year he began his diary, then, the family had inched their way not so much to outright prosperity but modest *betterment*. We have marked their move to the slightly more respectable Robinson Road just round the corner from Russia Lane, and by 1900 we find them in Stanfield Road in nearby Bow, representing another gradual, but significant advance. Number six, where they lived, is still an attractive end-of-terrace London brick house that - remarkably, given the wholesale development of the district in recent times - has long outlived its optimistic occupants of the turn of the nineteenth century. The reason for their move to a slightly more comfortable dwelling is clearly the advancement of the Sibley boys, all of whom by 1900 are now working.

Given Thomas Sibley was born right in the middle of what Jack London called *The People of the Abyss*, how did he escape?

A powerful engine of Thomas's flight from the poverty and deprivation of the locale in which he found himself must undoubtedly have been his schooling. He would have attended

St. John's Church of England School, a very short walk from where he lived in Russia Lane. Built in 1843, the school was as its name indicates a 'daughter' of its church, the nearby St. John's. His elder brothers William, Henry and Edwin would have attended the same school, and having brothers would have given his socialisation into the world of education a certain edge.

6, Stanfield Rd., Bow, London - the house where Thomas Sibley began his diary.

Given their later friendship in adulthood, the family was clearly tight-knit: his elder brother Edwin was four years older so would have been a senior pupil at the same time for a few years, and having a brother Bob two years his junior would also have imparted a quality of protectiveness to Thomas. No matter what the educational standard or status of their pupils, all schools are tough, and that there was a 'gang' of Sibley brothers would have given him a mettle and capability not afforded to the solitary only child.

Thomas's school day would have begun at 9am with prayers, followed by a long day on the school bench until 5pm: reading, writing, arithmetic, and for older pupils the acquiring of a fine copperplate handwriting style which became, quite literally, the signature of every state-educated pupil of the late nineteenth century.

Of the intervening years between his schooling and the commencement of his diary in 1900 aged 22, we have no record, apart from his own mention, on his 88th birthday, that he 'left school in 1891, aged 13. Did he further his training? Did he study book-keeping, and other clerical skills? This is highly probable, for in 1891 when Thomas is 13, his elder brothers William, Henry and Edwin are all commercial clerks, and nine years later when he makes his entrance on the public stage of his journals he too is engaged in full employment in the City in clerical work, clearly having followed his brothers into the burgeoning world of the administration of commerce. But Thomas must have been made of slightly different mettle than William, Henry and Edwin, for shortly thereafter he becomes a commercial traveller; betraying perhaps a certain restless energy, a keenness to avoid a sedentary office life.

By 1901 his brothers Henry and Edwin have moved out of the family home at number 6, Stanfield Road, Bow, to the more prosperous suburban Leytonstone - but his eldest brother William has moved back in, sadly already being a widower at the age of only 32. His younger brother Bob, aged 20, is still in Bethnal Green, with whom Thomas 'mouches,' regularly including visits to their local pub, The Plough in Bow Road.

A late Victorian National School Classroom.

It is in this familial context that Thomas, for reasons we will discover, begins the great adventure of his interior life, and makes the momentous decision to commit his entire life to paper.

First - there are diaries themselves. The volumes of the early years are scarlet buckram bound and printed by that stalwart of the British journal manufacturer, Charles Letts Ltd., founded in 1796 and still operating today. Beginning as a producer of trade-specific stationery products for book-keepers, insurers and the like, the original founder John Letts saw the possibilities of a mass-produced journal for the 'common man', so in 1812 the famous Letts Diary was born. From the outset its advertising slogan was *'Use your diary with the utmost familiarity and confidence. Conceal nothing from its pages nor suffer any other eye than your own to scan them,'* - and by 1850 the company was selling thousands to Victorians of all classes, eager to commit their lives to paper.

One such customer was Thomas Sibley. The burgeoning of this 'diary mania,' of which Sibley was merely a part was perhaps inspired by the publication, in 1875, of Samuel Pepy's famous journals. There had been partial earlier editions of Pepys, in 1825, but most of the diaries had been decoded and presented in the latter part of the nineteenth century, and for the first time the world was proffered a glimpse into the life and mind of a man who, although moving in the high circles of state and government, nevertheless peppered his journals with such ordinary, everyday ephemera and incidents that some, through Victorian circumspection, had to be excluded.

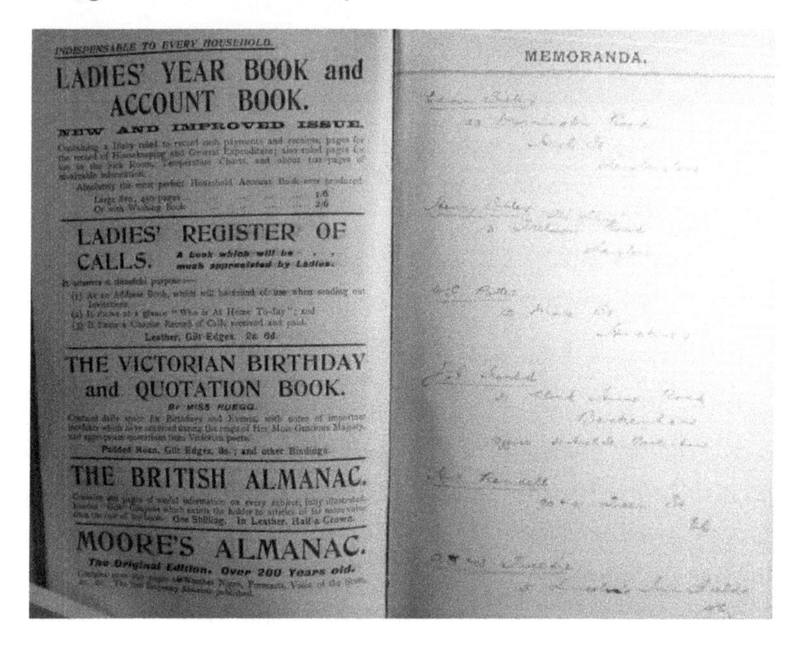

INDISPENSABLE TO EVERY HOUSEHOLD.

LADIES' YEAR BOOK and ACCOUNT BOOK.

NEW AND IMPROVED ISSUE.

LADIES' REGISTER OF CALLS. A book which will be much appreciated by Ladies.

Leather, Gilt Edges. 2s. 6d.

THE VICTORIAN BIRTHDAY and QUOTATION BOOK.

THE BRITISH ALMANAC.

One Shilling. In Leather, Half-a-Crown.

MOORE'S ALMANAC.

The Original Edition. Over 200 Years old.

MEMORANDA.

Yet there were enough left - details, for example, of his illnesses, his irritations, his feelings - that must have appeared so fresh and new, that they struck the reading public as an illumination of a bygone age never before encountered.

We have seen his very first entry from January 1st. His week continues:

2nd Tuesday. Rained until 1 o'clock. Evening fine. Saw V. at S.B. Went with her to Alice's. V. had the giggles and was in a cantankerous mood, which gave me the pip. Took dancing shoes from Alices. Gave V. cq wallflower. Caught 11.18 back. Passed a restless night.

3rd Wednesday. Raining. Miserable day. Went to Bull Wharf and saw 6 cases of opium weighed, and gave man (Webb) 2/6. Had a hot bath. Dropped collar into bath so had to go home without one. Bob and I wandered about Bow Rd. and visited "Plough." V and A went to see Lu at Stratford and arrived home at 12pm.

4th Thursday. Rained slightly, dry most part of evening. Saw V at S.B. Saw Mrs. K. at door & had a chat, during which Alice appeared. Had a jolly walk with V & A round E.I.Dk.Rd, & left A. at her home. Paraded Ullin Street with V. for an hour. Caught 11.33 back. Enjoyed myself immensely. Had sheep's heart for supper.

5th Friday. Dry most part of the day. Worked late. Wrote Fred Amlot telling him I could not play football Saturday. Bob and I mouched down Bow Rd. and visited the "Ph."

6th Saturday. Dry. J.C. won (Old Palmerstones) 2-1. I did not play. Bob & I left Lyons 3 o'clock, walked to Holborn Town Hall & visited Viaduct & met Mabel; arrived home at 5. Bob, Alice, V & I went to Holborn Town Hall dance. Bob & I had three drinks then met girls in train at Bow. Cheated Railway company out of girl's fares. Danced and had 4 wines, played hunting for sugar. Made the girls very saucy and lively on wine. Cabbed it to Broad Street just in time to catch last train. Rode home 1st class. Squeezing and kisses with sympathy and sugar were the chief enjoyments. Had a fine time. Grandmother went to Infirmary.

One page of simple entries, indeed, but a snapshot of the whole world of a young man in London at the beginning the new century. Here we have work, play, love, irritation, happiness, misdemeanours, a family circle, an extended family, sweethearts, club associates, the illness of an elderly relative -

in short, a palimpsest in shorthand of all human urban life in 1900.

The little world which Sibley inhabited was, as we see, not so small - his immediate territory of course is the East End, with his girlfriend living in Poplar ('S.B.' being South Bromley railway station, now called Bromley-by-Bow); he clearly works in 'The City,' knocks around with Bob his younger brother, has a busy social and sporting life, plays football on a Saturday and is an enthusiastic member of a private dening club, The Trojans. But his urban village is extensive - he walks from his work near Liverpool Street to Holborn Town Hall, later visiting it for a dance with his brother and their girlfriends.

This is a new, exciting London Sibley is enjoying: Holborn Town Hall, now a Grade II listed restaurant and offices fronting a choked High Holborn, had not long been built at the time of Sibley's dance: designed in the French Renaissance style in 1894 by William Rushworth, it opened as a library but clearly by the turn of century was being used for licensed entertainment - certainly, in the young Sibley's case, for the consumption of 'four wines.' Before he and Bob pop to the Town Hall - possibly to buy tickets for that evening's entertainment - they 'visited Viaduct.' This is the Viaduct Tavern on the corner of Newgate Street and High Holborn, still serving City workers a hundred and twenty years later.

Earlier in the week Sibley had paid a visit to Bull Wharf and *'saw 6 cases of opium weighed,'* after which he 'gives man (Webb) 2/6d.' It's not totally clear whether Sibley is buying the opium, or a portion of it, or paying Webb for some other product. Given the close connection in the sentence between object and verb and the fact that he doesn't mention another product that might be the object of his payment, it would appear he is indeed purchasing the narcotic.

Built in 1894, Holborn Town Hall, on the left, was a magnet for London's men-and-women-about-town.

By the time Sibley bought his opium at Bull Wharf in January 1900 one was meant by law to provide a name and address when buying any narcotic, so there was some regulation, but otherwise opium, heroin (the brand), cocaine and morphine were all pretty easily obtainable over the counter at a pharmacy. The addictive nature of all these products were becoming known, and would be restricted from 1912 on as a result of the International Opium Convention. But Britain was a reluctant signatory, and for years opium continued to be delivered alongside normal cargo. In the 19th Century travellers to Norfolk were asked if they wanted to lace their pints with opium, to ward off the malaria that flourished in the Fens. In short, it was a totally acceptable drug to buy for medicinal purposes, whilst possessing known risks. Given his grandmother is 'in the infirmary' it might well have been bought for her.

Bull Wharf was one of the many docks lining the river-front between London Bridge and Limehouse, approached via Upper

Thames Street, a short walk from Sibley's place of work. At this time he is a clerk in an office in Gracechurch Street, at 'D.H. & Co., Ltd.,' (Davy Hills Pharmaceuticals, the business Sibley remains in all his life).

London's wharves in the late 19th century.

On the same day as he buys the opium, he has a 'hot bath':

3rd Wednesday. ….Had a hot bath. Dropped collar into bath so had to go home without one.

Public baths had spring up all over London, and indeed the country, ever since the Baths and Wash-houses Act of 1846. Having made the connection between hygiene and disease, and with cholera still making sporadic outbreaks in the capital, the Victorians set out to tackle the problem of personal cleanliness by encouraging accessible bath-houses catering for every class. Town councils and parishes funded them through the rates, and by 1900 there were hundreds, so Thomas would have been spoiled for choice. As he was down at the docks that day he may have sampled the Glasshouse Baths, or the newer wash-house that opened two years previously in Cheshire Street, Bethnal Green.

His stipulation of a 'hot bath' indicates he has paid extra, for one could obtain a cold plunge for as little as a penny. There were many tiers in the services offered by public baths, much like the 'gold, silver and bronze' of a car-wash today: the basic public cold bath for the aforesaid penny, more for private ablutions, warm, hot, with the summit being a luxurious session with carpet, chair, mirrors and combs. The private bathing was in compartments, with taps operated by the user - the cheaper service was manually serviced by attendants.

Victorian public bath house. One penny for a public bath, twopence for a cubicle.

The ultimate in luxurious public bathing, however, was the Turkish bath, which had grown in popularity in the late nineteenth century. But these were expensive; according to an article in *Living London* magazine of 1901, a stint at the famous

Hammam in Jermyn Street, St. James, cost four shillings.

That Sibley was one of the many millions of beneficiaries of Gladstone's free education for all in 1870 there is no doubt. More well-known as Forster's Education act, it made schooling more or less compulsory between the ages of 5 and 12 or 13. As the Standard Exam for these new local authority schools consisted principally of reading and writing and basic arithmetic, this had the immediate effect of creating a vast new reading population beyond the upper and middle-classes. Evidence for this is the proliferation of popular magazines, the first of which, *Tit-Bits,* founded in 1881 by George Newnes, reached a circulation of 700,000 by 1900.

Whereas in Dickens' time there might be one person in a street living in a poor district able to read, and so narrate from the popular mid-Victorian weeklies to his neighbours (*Our Mutual Friend's* 'He do the police in different voices,') by the end of the century, whilst illiteracy was by no means abolished there was a whole new lower-middle class of literate, numerate workers able to fill the thousands of administrative jobs created by an industrial pre-digital economy.

Such was Sibley, as were his brothers. From profoundly working-class artisan roots, their father a joiner and their mother a dress-maker, they all ascended to positions of clerkship. In Sibley's case it is clear he works in or near Gracechurch Street, but the stop-off point of his shortish commute is Liverpool Street, and his company was 'D.H. & Co.'

Davy, Hill and Co. was a pharmaceutical wholesalers made up of A. S. Hill and Son founded in 1755 and Davy, Yates and Co founded in 1760. Sibley would remain with this company - with brief interludes - throughout his life, as it passed through various incarnations via amalgamation and takeover, first by the British Drug Houses in 1908, thence gradually expanding decade by decade until its partial sale to Glaxo in 1967 and its renaming as BDH Chemicals. The company still exists as Merck Ltd., a vast multi-national.

As a commercial traveller Sibley was earning pretty good money, evidenced by the surplus income with which he makes regular purchases - on January 30th he 'bought pair of boots from Cleggs, Elephant & Castle,' on February 13th a pair of gloves for his girlfriend for Valentine's Day, and on March 5th he 'orders from Bult's, a fancy vest and a pair of trousers.' These last two items cost him 14/6d each, a total in today's terms of around £100 - certainly a comfortable shopping spree.

Sibley was undoubtedly a beneficiary of the Liberal Age of the late Victorian and Edwardian era: along with Britain's supremacy as an industrial power came a related evolution of its commercial strength, and as a consequence a huge white-collared commercial class was created, a commuter class of self-driven, ambitious members of the former working-class seeking to 'better themselves.' Acres of suburbs were built to accommodate this rising class of shipping clerks, insurance clerks, Civil Servants, and Educational administrators, and dormitory towns such as Croydon expanded to meet the advance.

Underpinning the rise of this huge commercial lower-middle class was Samuel Smiles' philosophy of individual striving as expressed in his famous work, *Self-Help*. Published in 1859, its influence extended from the period of mid-Victorian liberalism to the end of the century and beyond, and along with the optimism and 'self-improvement' philosophies of American writers such as Emerson, Phineas Quimby and the Christian Science of Mary Baker Eddy, Smiles' *Self-Help* became the manual for a generation; an antidote to the fatalistic pessimistic doctrine of Karl Marx, whose central tenets of oppression and class-conflict had fed into the burgeoning trade union movement but had failed to win over the vast swathes of the British population - much to his chagrin.

Samuel Smiles (1812-1904), creator of Victorian Self-Help

The Liberal - or 'Whig' - view of history, as epitomised by that great Victorian historian Macauley, presented a macrocosmic bedrock of this doctrine of individual effort. The Whig analysis of historical change rested on the belief that human society is on a constant path of steady, indefatigable improvement, that liberal civilisation itself is on a 'mission.' With the macrocosm, so too with the microcosm: the individual citizen must make his or her way productively, through the acquiring of knowledge and the enhancement of one's moral nature - and in pursuing those noble individualist ideals, one brings prosperity and advancement to the whole of society.

Despite the fact that Lord Salisbury's Conservatives were in power during the time of the early diaries - 1895-1906 - it was the Liberal mindset of the age which clearly infused the young man Sibley and allowed him to blossom. Perhaps the very act of purchasing a diary towards the end of 1899 was part of this desire for individual development: stemming from a decision to instil order, purpose and drive into his life. No one keeps a diary for every single day of one's life without harbouring the notion that it is of significance. Sibley's journals do not appear to be created for pure vainglorious notions of posterity but for *self-development*, a record of his material and spiritual evolution.

From the beginnings of the diaries Sibley is clearly experiencing itchy feet at his place of work and is scouting around for a better place of employment. It is not known how long he has been working at Davy & Hills Ltd., but on Friday March 16th 1900 he seems to experience some kind of epiphany, a burst of pro-activity that he records in the following entry: he has '*bought 5 quires of writing paper with address printed in Gracechurch St.,*' and declares that he has been '*embracing opportunity's (sic) thoroughly and thoughtfully for some considerable time,*' which perhaps indicates he has been changing jobs for a while since leaving school in a quest to improve his situation. Determined, he buys the headed paper to launch his marketing campaign. As much as anything, this diary entry has the power of a declaration of intent, smacking of the impulse of a 'to-do' list - by committing his desire to paper, and ordering the headed stationery, he is setting the wheels in motion:

March 16th. 'I decided to write after two situations to effect if possible an improvement in my financial standing and future prospects. Therefore wrote to 'Export' Box 3433, (export clerk), and to 70/220 C & D (assistant representative) and pondered and wrote and pondered.'

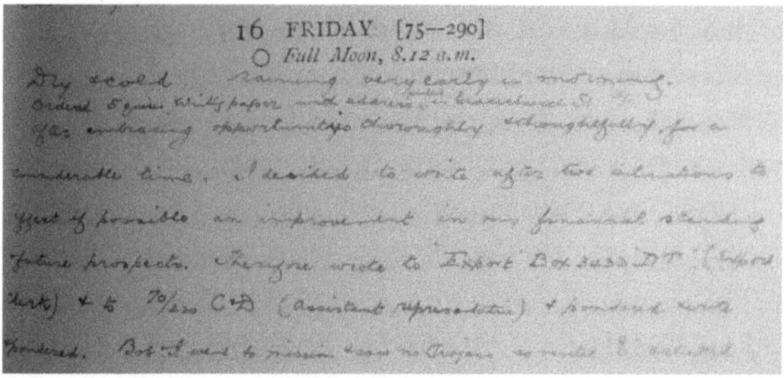

This is the self-driven Sibley in action, a true representative of his age, whether of liberal 'self-help' or conservative 'social Darwinism' cannot be known, but as New Historicism tells us, the background influences of the age cannot but have an effect on the individual citizen. We know he is clearly a reader - on a visit to a work colleague's house in February 1900 he is 'shown Aristotle's works.' The lower middle-class were often voracious readers who, while not having had the classical education of the public school, were nevertheless devouring the popular classics of the age through serial publications, magazines, and complete books.

The suburban homes of this growing army of clerical and commercial workers were filling with modest libraries, comprising every branch of printed literature from technical manuals, directories, collections of Dickens and Shakespeare to Mrs. Beeton's Cookery books, and bound volumes of *Household Words.* At this stage Sibley had yet to 'find religion,' - that lay ahead. Indeed, for all the talk of 'self-development,' in the first year of the new century we find him quite the pleasure-seeking man-about-town in pursuit of fun, entertainment, women and drink. His moral evolution was clearly still tinged with the true soul of most twenty-three year olds throughout history, that of the lotus-eater driven by his impulses. Apart from clothes-buying, much of his surplus income at this time seems to have been spent on entertainment.

The East End at the turn of the century, while comprising poor though up-and-coming districts, nevertheless provided a feast of cheap fun for all classes: theatres, taverns, boxing in rooms above pubs, slideshows, primitive cinematic shows (in March 1896 the Lumiere Brothers had premièred their magnificent film displays prior to a national tour). And music halls -

The Genesis Cinema, still in Mile End, was once Lusby's Music Hall & later the Paragon Theatre - one of the many places of entertainment for men-and-women-about-town in the East End of the late 19th century.

A contemporary of Thomas Sibley, a Mr. C. A. Brown, born in

Mile End in 1887 so nine years younger than our hero, wrote down his memories of the area at the age of 91 for *East London Record*, no.2 (1979). His picture-painting provides a vivid snapshot of Sibley's immediate stomping ground:

'Between Mile End Gate and the famous music hall known as the Paragon (formerly Lusby's music-hall) there was the area known as The Waste. On here was an open market, with itinerant traders of all types - baked chestnut barrow, hot baked potatoes, the toffee maker, the old clothes man, the negro sword swallower, jellied eels, cheap jack crockery, the whole lot was just one confusion, illuminated at night by countless flaring Naphtha lamps which frequently conked out, and released a cloud of paraffin vapour over all and sundry. In one spot were rolls of sheet lead belonging to the builders merchant shop. I often wonder how long sheet lead would lay safe without protection on that spot today. The same stretch of pavement contained also the ancient almshouses of Trinity House, the Great Assembly Hall, and the ancient weather-boarded hostelry The Vine Tavern.

'I saw the pageantry and procession of the visit of Queen Victoria to the People's Palace, we had a fine view of this cavalcade from the front windows of our house, that was in 1897. It was a wonderful institution, then a place of learning and culture, a beautiful winter garden, and yet, inconceivable as it may sound, it housed a circus, a huge marquee on the space in front of that majestic building. I have a vivid picture in my mind of that spectacle. A lady dressed in immaculate male evening suit, complete with top hat and a silver cane, dancing on the back of a lovely piebald horse, as it galloped round and round that magic circle. Also a large swimming bath where incidentally we kids were taught to swim from school. Our instructor used to begin the lesson with the ominous words - 'you will swim or else,' *and we did.'*

The two principal venues mentioned by Mr. Brown - the

Great Assembly Hall and the People's Palace - were of major importance to our young hero Thomas Sibley; he spends many happy hours with his friends and girlfriend at these remarkable communal buildings. His diaries in his younger days contain numerous references to evenings out at one or other of these splendid places, and often both. The entry for February 15th 1900 - 'Went to assembly hall and saw limelight pictures of Battles of the South African War,' is one of many hundreds of visits.

The Assembly Hall was built in 1886 by the philanthropist and evangelist Frederick Nicholas Charrington of the wealthy brewing family, who famously renounced his inheritance following a Damascene conversion on the Mile End Road - he witnessed a poor woman pleading with her husband outside a tavern to stop drinking and give her some money for food. Glancing up at the tavern he was stricken by the sight of his own name, *Charrington,* emblazoned above the pitiful scene - after which he devoted his life to improving the lot of working people through temperance and Christian teaching. A pioneer of treatment for alcohol dependence, Charrington even bought Osea Island off the Essex coast and made it a centre for the treatment of addictions.

With its foundation stone laid by no less than Lord Shaftesbury, and opened in 1886, the Assembly Hall became a hub of socialising for the common people of the East End. While obviously observing temperance, with its 'book saloon' and 'coffee palace,' it provided refreshments and a meeting-place for young and old, with lectures, shows, exhibitions, and of course the regular evangelical sessions, with Charrington himself at the forefront.

It was only a short mile's walk from Sibley's house, so he would perambulate there regularly with his younger brother

Bob or, more often, with his girlfriend, 'V.' On Thursday 15th February he takes 'V' to the Assembly Hall to see *'limelight pictures of British Battles of the South African War.'* This is an extraordinary record of one of the earliest visits to what would become cinema. What Sibley describes as 'Limelight Pictures' were one of the first forms of projecting moving images, via a projector in which the film - probably 70mm - was illuminated by limelight.

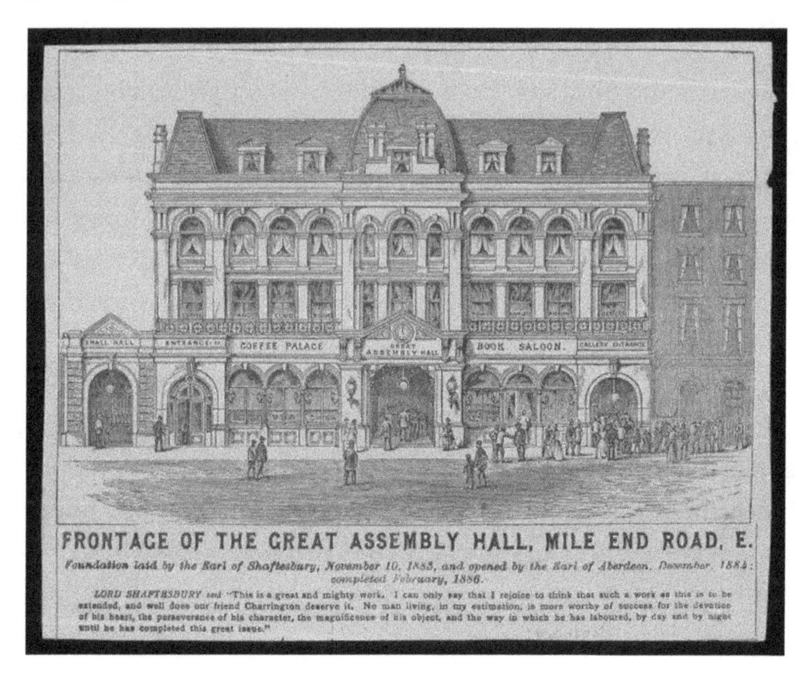

The Great Assembly Hall, Mile End Road - a magnet for young people of the East End.

The film industry in Britain was only just beginning to burgeon at the time Sibley and his girlfriend witnessed those scenes of the South African war, meaning they were present at the emergence of a growing phenomenon that in the last five or six years had slowly begun to proliferate in theatres and halls up and down the country. In France Georges Melies was the most famous producer of fictional works for the screen, but Charles

Pathe had only begun to make newsreels in 1900. In England in 1894 Brit Acres had enjoyed much success with his films of sporting events such as the Henley Regatta and the Oxford v Cambridge Boat Race, and a film-maker called Charles Urban, who had moved to England from the U.S. in 1897, was making his mark with his travel documentaries and, later, science and natural history films.

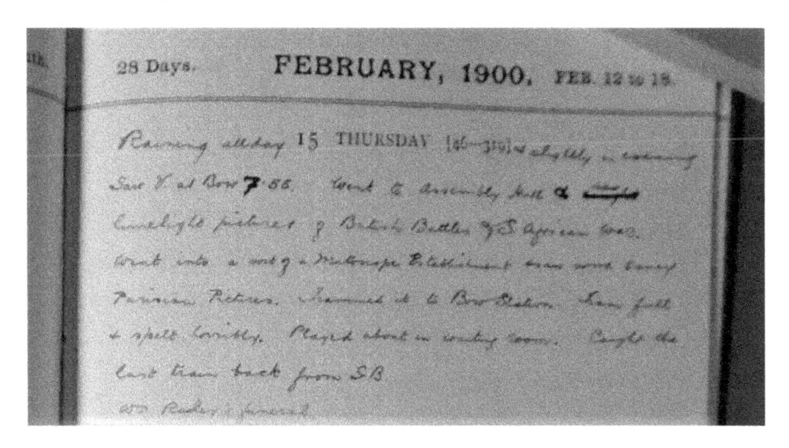
28 Days. FEBRUARY, 1900. FEB. 12 to 18

15 THURSDAY [46—319]

Raining all day [illegible]
Saw V. at Bow 7.55. Went to Assembly Hall [illegible]
Limelight pictures of British Battles of S. African war.
[illegible]
[illegible]
[illegible]
last train back from S.B.

In 1900 Sibley witnesses the growing phenomenon of Limelight Pictures, the precursor to cinema.

What Sibley and his sweetheart witnessed was in all probability one of Charles Urban's works, footage from the Second Boer War (1899-1902). We think of the film industry in its flowering phase as being principally drama and comedy, but in its early days its greatest and most popular successes were reality-based - Urban's *Unseen World,* for example, ran for an extraordinary nine months at the Alhambra, Leicester Square in 1903, the principal attractions of which was close-up footage of flies and cheese-mites. These spectacles would have been wondrous to the late-Victorian observer, and one can only imagine the spellbound faces of Sibley and his escort as they sat in the darkness of the Assembly Hall, Mile End, that winter's night in 1900 and watched the flickering images of British soldiers fighting the Dutch guerillas in the Orange Free State.

Urban's company motto 'We *put the world before you,'* encapsulates the profound widening of his audience's gaze as they witnessed these never-before-seen vistas of geography and nature. Charles Urban went on to form his own company and moved to Wardour Street, establishing Soho as the home of the British film industry.

Clearly not satiated by the visions of Urban's proto-cinematic wonders, on the same evening Thomas and 'V' 'went into a sort of 'Mutoscope establishment and saw some saucy Parisian pictures.' It was certainly an evening of contrasts - the Assembly Hall was a fine and upstanding venue the presentations of which were in total harmony with the evangelical aims of its founder Frederick Charrington, a far cry from the titillation of what became known in Britain as 'what the butler saw' emporiums.

Charles Urban, pioneer film-maker of the early years of the twentieth century.

An American invention, Mutoscopes became a craze in the late-Victorian and Edwardian eras and beyond, right up to 1971 when decimalisation rendered them largely redundant as the penny slots were too tricky to convert. One wonders what Charrington would have thought of the two youngsters as they sampled the surreptitious delights proffered by the crank-machines. Certainly there were many who railed against their pernicious influence. A letter to the Times in 1899 heartily denounced the '*vicious demoralising picture shows in the penny-in-the-slot machines: it is hardly possible to exaggerate the corruption of the young that comes from exhibiting under a strong light, nude female figures represented as living and moving, going into and out of baths, sitting as artists' models etc.*'

A trade advertisement for the Mutoscope - or 'what the butler saw' machine, a craze throughout the late-Victorian and Edwardian era and beyond.

The Assembly Hall was only one of several regular haunts of Sibley and his companion, 'V.' A few weeks earlier we find them paying a visit to the Bromley & Bow Institute, where they see the company of famous music-hall star Marie Lloyd:

Jan 13th Dry & Freezing. JC drew with Chingford Elmsed 0 -0. Went to Bow & Bromley Institute and saw Mme Lloyd's company. V & I enjoyed ourselves. Saw C.L.I.V. in morning. Saw the last of Kaffir and Ernie. About 30 Trojans outside Salvation Army Q.V. St.

The Bow & Bromley Institute.

The Bow & Bromley Institute was a large hall built above Bow Railway station in 1850 for entertainments, lectures, and other gatherings. The records state that in 1887 it became part of East London Technical College, but as Sibley still refers to it as the Bow & Bromley Institute in 1900 one must assume it remained under that name for years afterwards. He mentions *'Mme Lloyd's'* company - this can only mean the great music-hall performer Marie Lloyd. Whether she performed that night or not isn't clear: theatrical records state that in February of 1900 Lloyd appeared in the pantomime *Cinderella* at the Crown Theatre in Peckham, where she was supported by such star turns of the day as Vesta Tilley, Kate Carney and Joe Elvin.

Conceivably the show in Bow two weeks previously could have been a try-out. Once again, the Bow and Bromley Institute is a favourite destination for the courting young couple, for the very next Saturday they make a return trip:

Jan 20th. Evening very foggy. Nelson gave a month's notice to leave. J.C. beat Clove 1st 4 - 0. Slow game. V & I went to Bow and Bromley Institute and saw an exceedingly good company; a handsome impersonator, & a thought reader, also a mimic were the chief artists. A densely thick fog came down at 10 o'clock. Man stepped out of train at S.B., thought it was station, and got injured. Saw Misses Lyall & Snowdy. A woman pretended she had lost herself, approached me at S.B., but was repulsed.

And thus we find Thomas Sibley at the beginning of his long adventure in the new century; a pleasure-seeking young man-about-town and an Englishman with a sense of restless energy, determination and will-power. Floundering slightly, but clearly infused with a *brio* that hints at his remarkable journey to come. Ahead lay marriage, war, death and family tragedy - but in these early scraps we have glimpsed a kernel of the strength in Thomas Sibley that suggests to us that he might overcome any challenge he meets with a fortitude forged in the hardship of his youth.

Hardship that occasionally took its toll on mental health: at the turning of the year in early 1901 his sweetheart 'V' (in the diary she morphs into 'Annie' then her nickname 'Poppy') succumbs to what can only be described a frightening anxiety attack, causing much consternation among her family and friends. These episodes were to recur throughout her life, and her undulating general health as the century progressed becomes a dark and upsetting leitmotiv of the Sibley chronicle. By 1901 both Sibley and his sweetheart have joined the Baptist Church: both from that moment on embrace the purpose-driven life, but a setback certainly seems to have occurred by January 10th of that year when Thomas writes solemnly of going '*down to Annie's and discovering her in a pitiful condition. She is suffering from hysteria which has flown to religion, which is the worst subject possible.*' For one who had a few months earlier embraced the Faith himself, he shows a liberal understanding of the rare mental dangers induced by a too-extreme obsession of religiosity.

The relationship of Annie and her diarist till then has been quite a passionate affair for a young courting couple both of whom still live with their parents, he in Stanfield Road in Bow and she in Poplar. They meet up to three or four times a week and stroll in the evenings: mainly on Bow Common, or in Ullin Street - one of the narrow back-streets of jerry-built houses that crammed the East End until the redevelopments of the 1950's and 60's. Ullin Street still exists, much of it having spared the ravages of the wrecking ball: the Victorian church of St. Michael's, though now long since converted into apartments, nevertheless still casts its London-brick shadow across the street's entrance where Thomas and Annie were wont to amble in those far-off Edwardian summer dusks.

Thomas had a packed social life, for to be young in Edwardian London 'twas very heaven. In addition to his perambulations on Bow Common or Ullin Street with his sweetheart, in August 1900 they ventured further to Hampstead Heath, finding a '*dark spot,*' and having to ask a passer-by the way back as they were '*going in the opposite direction.*' In March they made one of their regular visits to the entertainment at the Bow and Bromley Institute, to see the 'O.J.O. Minstrels,' who performed a '*very laughable sketch.*' The People's Palace in Mile End road was a regular haunt of Sibley and his sweetheart; on Saturday October 13th 1900 they see the 'Follies' there, during which performance the '*recitation The Pool of Blood nearly killed me with laughter.'*

In May he and his brother Bob make a trip to the Royal Agricultural Hall in Islington to see the 'laundry exhibition,' and on May 26th to Earl's Court for the 'Woman's Exhibition.' The whole of the capital's machinery of commerce and entertainment was a pageant freely available to all mere yards from ones door: this was an age of unfettered cultural and economic confidence, and England, particularly Edwardian London, never missed an opportunity to put on display the fruits of its power and influence.

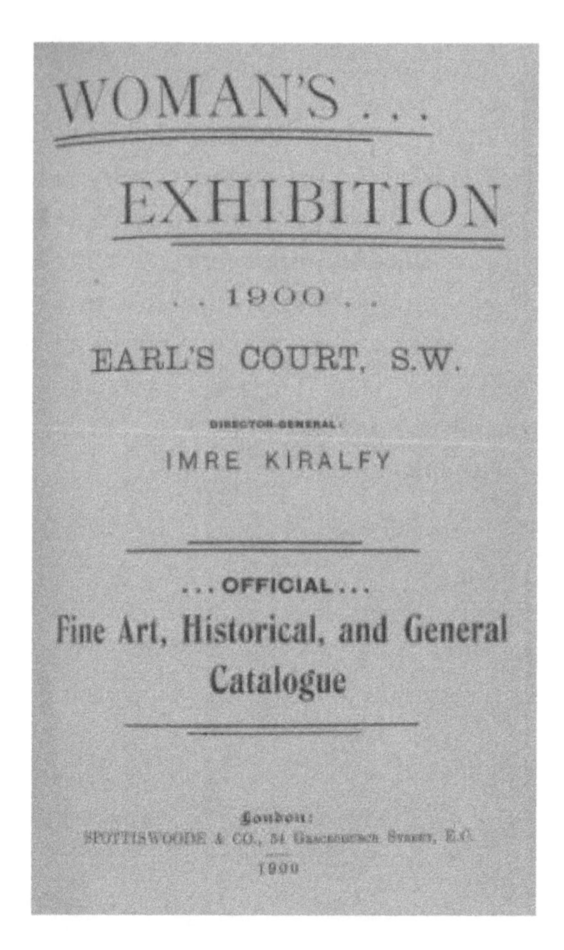

WOMAN'S . . .

EXHIBITION

. . 1900 . .

EARL'S COURT, S.W.

DIRECTOR-GENERAL:

IMRE KIRALFY

. . . OFFICIAL . . .

Fine Art, Historical, and General Catalogue

London:

SPOTTISWOODE & CO., 54 [illegible], E.C.

1900

The Agricultural Hall, now the Business Design Centre, was a major venue for national events: built in 1861, it hosted the Royal Tournament from 1880 and Cruft's Dog Show from 1891. Earls Court was a prime exhibition centre from 1887 prior to its construction of the art deco masterpiece in 1935, and on a fine Saturday afternoon on May 26th 1901 *'Bob and I went to Earls Court to see the Woman's Exhibition. Lovely grounds,'* - Sibley's somewhat niggardly diary entry that belies the notability of the event. The whole affair was produced as a flowering of the late-Victorian Woman's Movement, spearheaded by the upper and upper-middle class, and staged by the major impresario of the age, Hungarian emigre Imre

Kiralfy, renowned as the producer of the White City Exhibition of 1908.

The introductory article to the Exhibition in the catalogue presents a rich and detailed portrait of the event:

'During no period in the world's history has the progress of woman's work been so remarkable as in that of the present century. Although this advance is fully realised, and several attempts have been made to illustrate the progress of woman's work, there has never been an Exhibition dealing adequately with this great subject. The advance of woman in the fine arts, in education, in refined and beautiful workmanship, in inventions, her studies and devotion in nursing, and her softening influence, which has penetrated into almost every profession, elevates the nineteenth century in the memorable record of the world's history. It is an apparent fact, particularly when we turn to literature, that the work by woman during the last hundred years greatly exceeds anything accomplished by her in all previous times. It is, therefore, but fitting and just that woman's work should be represented in a worthy manner, at the close of this century, by a commemorative Exhibition, the first of its kind ever held. ...Nothing is more interesting than to trace, through all its vicissitudes, the lengthy course of laws and customs which have slowly raised woman from a condition of abject slavery to a position of social and civil equality......The day is passed when Woman, inspired by the necessities of a barbaric or warlike age, could repudiate the weakness of her sex, and contend with man on the field of battle. Christianity and civilisation have taught her to renounce such ideas, and to assume another and a more glorious duty...The new mission is symbolised by the name of Florence Nightingale, its originator, its apostle, and its example. Words can scarcely express the great debt of gratitude we owe to this lady, who, by her generous and heroic labours, has given up her whole life to the promotion of humane work, to the amelioration of the condition of our soldiers,

to the improvement of hospital organisation. ....Royalty has had many bright representatives in history, but it remained for this century to give birth to the noblest of all – Victoria, the greatest and most honoured of Sovereigns. ...Her monumental work and mighty influence have not only benefited the one-fourth of the women on earth over whom she rules, but all other nations over which it is spread. No sooner had she ascended the throne than a complete revolution for the advance in education, science, and culture took place which resulted in the great progress of literature, arts, industries. And legislation which have glorified her reign and made her era unparalleled in history.'

Grandiose hyperbole perhaps, and typical of the public discourse of the age, but not so exaggerated as to bear no relation to the truth: with exhibits including inventions, designs, textiles and object-d'art, the event was a panoply of female British civilisation and a striking reflection of the emerging social and cultural power of early twentieth century women.

Periodic trips to Brighton were naturally a feature of Sibley's days off, as indeed they were for a large number of Edwardian Londoners, the Bank Holiday as strong a fixture of the calendar as Harvest Festival. On August 6th 1900 he and 'Vi' head off to the south coast for the day, the rain not diminishing their enjoyment of a concert show on the West pier. During the show Sibley pops off to visit friends - Mr. Kirby, Teddy, and 'dear little Maud,' leaving Vi on the balcony and rejoining her later where they 'finish the performance together.' The following Sunday, the 12th, finds him once again in Brighton. Vi does not join him this time as she 'is going to Witham with her Dad,' so he spends the day once again with the mysterious Mr. Kirby and Maud, who was *'very pleased to see me, and very sorry I couldn't stop.'* Mr. Kirby he describes as a *'short man with a rather boozy look and rather common. He is in the fur trade.'* Clearly not to Sibley's liking, Kirby *'of course walks out with Bob*

& I, worse luck.' As ever with these snapshots of ordinary lives, it is what is left out that tantalises. Because the diaries have been begun in his 22nd year, one is 'jumping straight in,' so to speak, with minimal exposition or back-story. My guess is that Kirby was a regular occupant of the boarding-house at which Sibley stayed, and Maud was one of the staff who had clearly taken a shine to the young salesman. In the Edwardian era holiday-makers were wont to stay at the same boarding-house year after year: it was 'your place.' Proprietors, staff and regulars would become lifelong friends, forming bonds across the years.

Brighton, 1900

The resorts of the East coast were as popular destinations as Brighton - in September of 1900 Sibley's sweetheart Vi (Annie) and her family spend five days in Southend, and Thomas rushes down after work on Wednesday Sept. 12th to join them. He's doing well - he buys a First Class ticket for seven shillings - the equivalent of £38 in 2023 - and *'gets a good seat.'* Further evidence of his growing relative prosperity is that later in then month he *'gets his photographs done at Taylor, 6 for 12 shillings and sixpence.'*

As ever the great historical events of the time take second place to the personal. On May 19th, the Relief of Mafeking receives a mere passing mention in the diaries, while his evening perambulations with his girlfriend are granted reams of effusive sentences. 'Twas ever thus: social life becomes one's centre of gravity while the macro-political is a drama enacted on a stage if not physically then mentally distant. Later in the year, on October 29th, he makes a passing mention of the vast procession of the C.I. V. (Cyclists & Infantry): '*...CIV procession - grand sight,'* - which was one of the great victory parades of the war - but then swiftly moves on to talk about his mother's illness.

When Sibley commenced his diary the Second Boer War had been raging for six months as the British Empire battled for control of the Orange Free State and the Transvaal. Early setbacks had shocked the British forces, resulting in the besieging of Ladysmith, Kimberley and Mafeking. This was one of the first international wars to be covered extensively in the press, so its presentation on the stage of public consciousness was far-reaching and powerful. Indeed, reporters from the four London papers – *The Times, Morning Post, Daily Chronicle* and *Pall Mall Gazette*, were inside Mafeking itself, their dispatches slipped through the Boer lines by native runners who carried them to a telegraph office fifty miles away. The redoubtable garrison commander, Baden-Powell, later to achieve fame as the founder of the Boy Scout movement, received his first flush of celebrity and acclaim as for seven months he withstood the assault of 5,000 hostile Boers and the concomitant hunger of a protracted siege. Despite the obvious hardships undergone by the inhabitants, life at Mafeking during those seven months was not without distractions: by mutual agreement there was no fighting on Sundays, when everyone relaxed, picnicked and played cricket and polo.

Robert Baden-Powell & his staff, the victorious defenders of Mafeking.

Despite being enacted in a far-off land this drama echoed back to the Mother Country; indeed, the rise of the popular press ensured that in 1900 events that took place in the empire became domestic events, romanticised in the retelling by journalists and writers and then by proxy in the taverns, inns, pubs and parlours across the whole of England. (It has been observed by Andrew Marr in his *The Making of Modern Britain* that ordinary citizens of the Edwardian era were actually better-informed on current affairs than our current generation are by the internet: mass literacy had created a vast popular press).

Through these means Baden-Powell's seven-month conflict assumed mythic proportions, a siege of Troy in miniature - so Sibley and his friends could not help but be caught up in the Mafeking saga: it spread like fever. On Friday May 18th Thomas, after he'd finished his day's journey as a salesman, *'took a stroll'* at 9.30 with his younger brother Bob: he notes that the *'news reached London from Reuters,'* but *'unfortunately I did not hear about it until Saturday morning.'* So while the rest of the capital amassed in hysterical crowds in Trafalgar Square, and indeed across the country, Thomas spent his evening sat on a bench on Bow Common with his sweetheart Vi and *'had two hours spooning.'*

London crowds celebrate the Relief of Mafeking, May 1900.

The next day after work he receives a letter from 'V' saying she *'could not go to Earls Court on account of her ma's illness'* so once again after work he perambulates the city with Bob and this time *'gets mixed up in the patriotic crowd.'* The Mafeking celebrations were prolonged and nationwide, from factory yards in Manchester to village greens in Twickenham, continuing late into the night and the following day with fireworks, parades and parties. In London, of course, the frolicking was busiest: Sibley's use of the phrase *'mixed up'* in the patriotic crowd conveys a seething mass, united in ecstasy. For the country - despite the various divisions of the age - possessed a unity that transcended any enmity of class or social inequality, and events like the Relief of Mafeking were its perfect expression.

It is difficult to countenance in our disparate, cynical era the profound bond love of country instilled in the populace, but the Edwardian age clearly was infused with a commonality of spirit and social glue that melted barriers, and the Mafeking phenomenon was one such catalyst. Its effect rippled into the future: Mafeking was a victory, to be sure, but one of the unpalatable truths laid bare by the Second Boer War was that the British Army had become unfit, its weakness in comparison to the sturdy Boer exposed. James Barbary in *The Boer War (Penguin, 1975),* observes that 40% of the army suffered from a plethora of poverty-related illnesses such as rickets. It was perhaps this that led the star of Mafeking, Baden-Powell, to write *Scouting for Boys* in 1905, the bestseller that formed the basis of his invention of the Scout Movement in 1908. The sons of the British Empire - and daughters, for the Girl Guide Movement began not long after - should be fit, strong, beneficiaries of fresh air and exercise, their city pallor banished by expeditions in the green meadows, woods and hills of the British countryside.

We have noted the importance of the Great Assembly Hall, Mile End, as a fulcrum of both entertainment, social life and spiritual education in the lives of East Enders, and it is this vortex that exercises perhaps the greatest influence over the formative character of the young Thomas Sibley and his sweetheart. What salvation existed for those inhabitants of the East End who were not defeated by it?

Baden-Powell's Scouting for Boys, published 1908, became a handbook of citizenship & self-instruction for a generation of Edwardians.

Londoners wore their city like a garment - for many it weighed them down, crushed them: some, like Sibley, sought escape. In tracing his narrative as a microcosm of the city it is difficult to retain in the mind the awareness of the deprivation and suffering of those around him.

A Mile End rag market, from Jack London's People of the Abyss, 1908.

The London of Sibley's formative years was the London of Jack London's *People of the Abyss,* the author of that grim work describing his territory as a *'human wilderness of which nobody seemed to know anything,'* and going on to paint a grisly portrait of not just the region of the city he was exploring but the entire capital: *'Nowhere in the streets of London can one escape the sight of abject poverty, while almost five minute's walk from any point will bring one to a slum; but the region my slum was penetrating was one unending slum. The streets were filled with a new and different race of people, short of stature, and of wretched or beer-sodden appearance. We rolled along through miles of bricks and squalor, and from each cross street and alley flashed long vistas of bricks and misery. Here and there lurched a drunken man or woman, and the air was obscene with the sounds of jangling and squabbling. At a market, tottery old men and women were searching in the garbage thrown in the mud for rotten potatoes, beans and vegetables, while little children clustered like flies around festering piles of fruit, thrusting their arms to the shoulders into the liquid corruption, and drawing forth morsels, but partially decayed, which they devoured on the spot.'*

And so he goes on. Whilst not challenging the veracity of Jack London's encounters one must make allowances for his *grand guignol* hyperbole in focussing purely on the hellish side of his visit to Britain's capital. After all, he had a publisher's remit to fulfil. He was a writer on a mission, and his quest was plainly to seek out and depict the underclass of which he had heard so much. And he found it: but what one seeks one will find, and his unrelenting images of decrepitude, whilst accurate, were demonstrably selective. He was writing in 1901-1902, the first two years of Sibley's journal, and was lodging in the doss-houses and poor homes of Whitechapel. So he was tramping the streets of Sibley's very own district: they may even have rubbed shoulders.

So suffering there most certainly was, and an underclass of derelicts, thieves and prostitutes: we have seen in an early entry from January 20th 1900 the young Sibley being approached by a streetwalker at South Bromley station: *'A woman pretended she had lost herself, approached me at S.B., but was repulsed.'* But a balance must be struck between the almost salacious accounts of 'dark and dismal London' that had become a genre of journalism in itself ever since Mayhew, but which was nevertheless shot through with a negative special pleading - and a brighter portrayal of the age as one of high employment, good wages, unlimited opportunities, free education, and freedom of movement. The truth plainly lies somewhere in between.

That there existed opportunities for self-advancement is evinced by Sibley himself - who, the son of a joiner, had trained himself in clerical skills and become a pharmaceutical salesman. But material progress was clearly not enough, for during 1900 he along with his sweetheart Vi is converted to Christianity, and from then on his every day becomes a step forward in a purpose-driven life.

The momentous day is October 21st 1900, which Sibley describes as *'the happiest day of my life.'* They had been regular attendees at the Assembly Hall in Mile End to listen to the various speakers, but clearly something special happened on that fateful autumn evening when they settled into their wooden seats in the vast hall to hear a certain Mr. Vine. The subject of Mr. Vine's sermon is not recorded, but the efficaciousness of his oration is beyond doubt, for Sibley writes in his best copperplate and with a simplicity that belied its significance, *'V & I were converted and received the Holy Spirit… Mr. Vine prayed with me in the inner room and I gave my soul to God. Rather quiet afterwards on account of the great change. Prayed long and earnestly when I reached home.'*

While not wholly out of character, Sibley's Damascene moment is not without surprise. Up until that moment he is a fully-rounded, red-blooded Edwardian man-about-town, who clearly liked his drink, his personal possessions, his women and his social life. Only the day before his conversion he is playing football up at Stamford Hill with the reserve team for his club the Trojans, despite having a bad cold: *'I elected to play although feeling weak… borrowed a pair of boots which were unhappily too small… slipped about manfully… lost 2-0. Did not see V as she was attending to an ill friend, so Bob and I went to the Alhambra, then had supper in Fleet Street.'* This is not quite a lotus-eater, but one who clearly enjoys the good things in life, the fruits of his hard work as a self-made lower-middle-class Londoner.

There is something deeper and more profound at play here. Sibley is a discreet diarist in that deeply personal problems or traumas are hinted at rather than made explicit: his are the writings of one who wishes to conceal the entries from members of his immediate family. He is still living at home at Stanfield Rd. Bow, and though his mother is now bedridden there is his father and brother Bob to hide his inner life from, lest they stumble upon his journals. Peppered throughout the early diaries are references to *'Pere d…'* - hardly a code worthy of Samuel Pepy's cryptograms but nevertheless sufficient to conceal references to 'Father drunk.' At times it is 'Pere very d.,' and the phrase becomes more and more frequent until it becomes almost a daily occurrence. On March 2nd he writes *'Pere no money, so sober.'* His father William is now 55 years old and there are references in the diaries of his work as a joiner drying up: the phrase *'Pere no work,'* also now occurs with solemn regularity.

The issue of drunkenness and its relation to Sibley's conversion is rooted in the linkage between non-conformism and the temperance movement; in urban environments of dense working-class populations the two things were inextricable, as the missionaries of the Baptist Churches and the Methodists sought to wean victims off the bottle and 'take the pledge.' Nowhere was this partnership between drunkenness and the temperance movement more visible than in London.

'Taking the pledge' - to abandon drink - was a keystone of one's spiritual progress, and in the days following his conversion Sibley and his sweetheart Vi become quite evangelical in attempting people to do likewise - on Sunday November 4th, a mere 13 days after their own submission to the Faith, Sibley writes that *'Vi tried hard to get Miss Loydall converted and take the pledge, but failed. A friendly lady also tried but without success.'* Whether he tried to persuade his father is not known - it seems likely, given their co-habitation and the evident distress it must have been causing the family.

A STREET PREACHER AND HIS AUDIENCE.

A temperance preacher in the East End of London

Alcohol in the nineteenth century had become a vast mass-produced commodity, and consumption in London in Victorian and Edwardian times was ubiquitous, with round-the-clock quaffing in hundreds of gin palaces, beer houses, dram shops, restaurants, pubs and private clubs. As Thompson & Lummis state in their *Family Life and work Experience Before 1918, 'The true role of drinking in Edwardian Britain was… humdrum. Beer was the basis of leisure. It took the place which later became filled with cigarettes and television. Children would fetch jugs from the pubs for tired parents to relax at home at the end of the day. At funerals, at weddings, at harvest, at the initiation of apprentices, at ordinary work breaks, a glass of beer would be exchanged.' (Thompson P. and Lummis T. 1970/2009. Family Life and Work Experience Before 1918 (1870–1973).*

This was not wholly a new phenomenon of course - the eighteenth century had had its gin laws as a response to the perceived problem of reckless dissipation that culminated in Hogarth's famous *Gin Alley*. But the huge population increase of

London in the latter half of the nineteenth century fuelled the problem, resulting in a Parliamentary Enquiry in 1877 that investigated most cities across Britain. Evidence was bandied to and fro, with some regional committees presenting proof that there was a majority of 'non-reckless' drinkers in the working-classes who far from frittering away their wages on alcohol were actually prudent savers: in Preston magistrate Charles Roger Jackson even produced evidence from the Preston Savings Bank which detailed the employment status of depositors to make the point that not all men's wages were drunk away at the weekend. Most were mill workers, followed by plasterers, railwaymen, policemen, labourers, shopwomen, workwomen, milliners, book keepers, clerks, shopkeepers, tradesmen, farmers, gardeners, spinsters, widows and married women. When asked for the point in presenting this evidence, Jackson replied that it was to show that money was being saved and not spent on drink and that not all of the working classes were frittering their wages away on drink every week but that some, arguably the more 'respectable' sections, were either abstaining or drinking moderately. *(Thora Hands, Drinking in Victorian & Edwardian Britain, Palgrave Macmillan, Open Access, 2018).*

Was William Sibley of this class? His son Thomas certainly was, an industrious salesman of the clerical and commercial sector who by dint of his innate ambition and work-ethic, perhaps instilled in him via his schooling, was clearly looking around at those in his immediate surroundings and thinking, *I will not succumb and join the defeated.* The link between his father's drinking and his conversion is implicit.

In the days following, the solemnity and significance of his conversion seeps through on every page. On October 22nd he writes *'felt the wondrous change. God being with me I felt a different fellow. Happy to know I was saved.'* And on Tuesday the

23rd he visits his sweetheart Vi at her home in South Bromley, Poplar, where they talk earnestly about their recent huge life-event.

A parenthetical word about South Bromley - the '*S.B*' - where Sibley's sweetheart Vi lived: it refers to the part of Poplar that was once divided into all the 'Bromleys' of the compass. South Bromley is now a little-used name (although still recognised by older residents) for the south-eastern part of Bromley-by-Bow, which has been sliced and diced by communications improvements over three centuries. The railway station where Thomas would so often meet his lady-love in the 1890s and early part of the 1900s opened in 1884, and stood at the end of Rifle Street (off the western edge of the map below), at what is now the north-east corner of Lansbury Square, closing in 1944. The construction in 1770 of a short canal called the Limehouse Cut separated South Bromley from its parent and the locality thereafter evolved as an extension of Poplar. From the mid-19th century, factories were established beside Bow Creek with workers' housing further inland on what had formerly been Bromley Marsh. Between 1864 and 1885 David McIntosh laid out compact but sturdy terraces to the east of St Leonard's Road, some of which survive today. A mission chapel was built on St Leonard's Road in 1861. This was soon replaced by St Michael and All Angels church, which could accommodate a thousand worshippers. It has since been converted to flats.

Here, in Vi Kettley's little house at 191, St. Leonard's Road, she and Thomas would sit in her front parlour and canoodle and chat, once her father had gone upstairs. More often, though, they would perambulate the surrounding streets and parks, venturing sometimes as far as Bow Common half a mile away, or down to 'the pier.' The identity of this pier is imprecise - it could be Limehouse Pier, Northumberland Wharf or Blackwall Pier, one of several jetties that have long since been demolished to sink without trace in the murky Thames when the big ships left the capital. Most often their favoured haunt was Ullin Street, a small lane that still exists today, where much intimacy took place. Perhaps it was a chosen place for young courting couples.

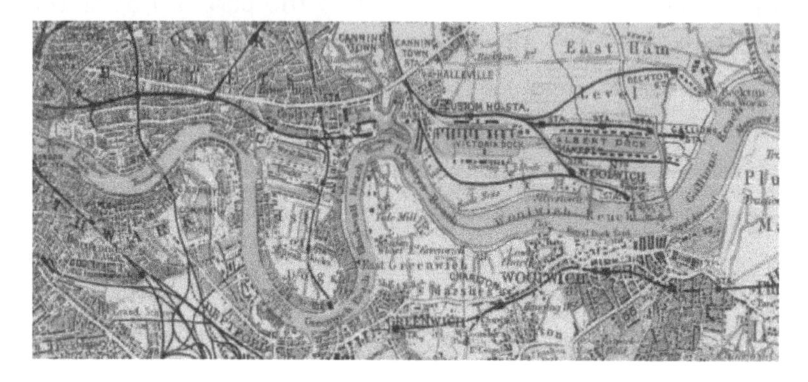

London docks, 1900

Between 1900 and 1910 London's docklands were the fulcrum of the Empire, and Thomas and his sweetheart would have found themselves in a seething, bustling place of jangling harnesses, creaking ships, the shouts of lightermen, the laughter of stevedores. Since the West India Act of 1799 the vast expansion of the docklands was compared to the engineering feats of the ancient Egyptians, with foreign visitors astonished at the magnitude. The French poet Verlaine, on a visit in 1872, and gasped at the sight: '*The docks are impossible to describe! They are unbelievable! Tyre and Carthage all rolled into one.*' By 1930 the docks employed 100,000 people: by 1980, at the end of our story, the wharves had all but fallen silent and seven hundred acres of docklands and the Isle of Dogs had become a derelict landscape of empty warehouses, rotting jetties and the ghosts of sailors. The move to deep-water container ships that dragged trade to the sea docks of the East coast may have been written in the stars, but was very far away when Thomas Sibley and his sweetheart kissed as they gazed out across old Father

Thames.

On the evening of October 23rd 1900, though, courting is secondary to their considerations of the momentous spiritual change they have undergone. '*Saw V. at S.B., went on pier, and had a most happy evening, but brimful of the wondrous change. God's will be done. V. entirely changed and most happy. We are a changed couple both for the lord and his works. Mrs. Kettley as expected cried for joy and is dying to see me.*'

Thus begins Sibley's twentieth century: he is an earnest young man, though not without humour; ambitious, in love, with one foot in a family that seemed to represent the old, working-class world, and fortified by a bold dream of the future. It would not be too fanciful to describe young Sibley as a microcosm of the country itself as it eased into its new century.

This may have been a *Belle Epoque* but it was no *Pax Britannica*. Britain was involved in a colonial war in South Africa, was beginning to sense the mighty power of the American economy rumbling on the horizon so was engaged in a furious debate about its trading links with the world outside the Empire; imperial preference, the rise of Trade Unionism, the nascent women's suffrage movement - these were the broad strokes being applied to the national canvas while in a corner of East London the Sibleys bustled about in the game of survival.

And so Sibley's decade unfolds thus:

1900

Nov 24th Met V at Bow at 4.10 and journeyed to Mr. Creed's at Leytonstone. After a little trouble found house. Two of Creed's nieces turned up unexpectedly. They were nice only very awkward, being a trifle lenient towards the lower order. Had tea then amused ourselves all evening. Played draughts, tiddly-winks, louda. Enjoyed ourselves immensely.

Nov 30th … Received hamper from Ted containing fowl, rabbit, apples and vegetables, not forgetting sausages.

Sat. Dec 1st. Davy Hills & co. Company dinner. Bob and I hurried home from football, dressed and rushed off to the London Tavern Fenchurch St., arrived 7 o'clock. Had a very good dinner and concert. Saw the old faces.

Dec 4th. Mr. Kerwen got in by 21 votes - Borough District by-election. Mr. Dix nearly went off his head for joy.

Throughout his life Sibley was an enthusiastic participator in the democratic process, unerringly voting Liberal. The period 1905-1915 was of course the last great flowering of Liberal England, nourished by the great liberal quartet of Henry Campbell-Bannerman, Herbert Asquith, Winston Churchill and David Lloyd George, whose combined legislation transformed Britain into a free trade, compassionate powerhouse providing its citizens with National Insurance, working rights, and free healthcare for all children.

Dec. 7th Chelsea journey 5 orders arrived Earls Court Station 4 o'clock, & journeyed to WJPs. Met Trussell for the first time. Has been travelling for Manners Hopkins, also used to be at CJ Hewlett's. Heard about Lipton Verney's husband, worked in the lab. Described him as a great hulk.. Heard startling news about Lusted. Poor Petty to be summonsed for libel. Caught 11.32 at Wimbledon and rushed to catch 12.30 at Liverpool St. Got on bus luckily. Got into bed 1.30.

Dec 8th V & I had a very long chat at SB about past events and V told me a great deal confirming and putting things right anything exaggerated and wrongfully told.

Dec. 9th V had a great deal to say, chiefly about Charlie Stott.

Dec 12th Miss Hopper would not sign the pledge.

The mighty Liberal quartet of Campbell-Bannerman, Asquith, Churchill & Lloyd-George, whose policies dominated Britain from 1905-1915.

Dec. 5th. ... visited Taylors and bought away 2 photos.

Dec 6th ... Went to GAH and saw Mr. Nokes give a talk on the Paris Exhibition. The pictures were grand.

An early twentieth century lantern slide projector. The 'Magic Lantern' was a popular form of pictorial and instructional entertainment before the age of the cinema.

Dec. 14th Mrs. Bowyers wrote about Bates owing so much rent.

Wrote to Mrs. Bowyer telling her if Bates does not pay to go to the station and to give him a written notice. The rent to be 5/- in future, come 1901.

Dec. 16th … Tram broke down so were transhipped.

Dec 17th Went to Davy Hills and got some perfume. Harry, Bob, Father & I had a long chat about the war and its complications.

Dec. 18th Delivered two forceps to Dr. Welpey.

Dec. 19th I purchased a Lady's Companion, 15/-. Also bought some brushes… Gave V the Lady's Companion as Christmas present. She was very pleased with it.

Dec. 22nd … played St. Paul's FC… got half stunned by ball striking back of head… Gave perfume to Mrs. K & V.

Dec 24th … Bought for myself gloves 3/- 6d, cigarettes 1/- 5d ha'penny.

Dec 25th Got up at 9.30 and went to GAH, & heard Mr. Harrison. Had dinner at home then journeyed to Mrs Kettley's. Had a lovely tea then a quite enjoyable evening. Played Mr. K & Will at draughts, made a noise on organ, & helped to sing a few hymns. Had a hearty supper and caught 11.17 home. A very happy Christmas. Annie in great form both singing and playing.

Dec 26th … departed for St. James Street & played football. Other club only turned up 6 strong so lent them 5 men & had 10 ourselves. Beat opposing team 4-0. I got muddy ball each side of face. Two stingers. A lovely sight I was. Caught 11.19 home. Uncle Fred was there but happily did not stay long. Went to Mrs. K's. Mr & Mrs. K. went to Virginia's to tea so Annie and I had it all alone. Annie spoilt me. Annie & I spent a lot of the time enjoying ourselves. Will came round for pickled onions as they had run short. They returned at 11 o'clock so I could catch the 11.17 but I preferred to walk.

Amateur football then, as now, was a popular weekend pastime for young men, with teams springing up spontaneously amongst friends and, more often, workmates, as factories and workplaces gave birth to clubs. The most famous of these was Arsenal F.C., that began its life as a motley gang of labourers and engineers at Woolwich Arsenal armaments depots on the south of the Thames. It appears from the diaries that Sibley was a member of a team called *The Trojans*, playing mostly in East and North London, even at White Hart Lane.

Dec 28th. Gale of wind caught umbrella and smashed stick. Nothing else injured. Took it to be repaired in Roman Rd.

Alexandra Park F.C. in 1904 - one of many local clubs whose fixtures were friendlies with similar scratch teams across London.

Dec 31 Went to Watchnight Service at GAH. A huge gathering. 225 pledges taken. Annie and I walked home. Saw her safely indoors abt. 1.30, spoke to Mr. K then proceeded to stroll home. Arrived safely 2 o'clock.

1901

Jan 2nd. Ordered trousers from Smith's Cheapside 11/-.

Jan 3rd Annie & I went to GAH, saw some dissolving views. Onions in evidence. Had to take frequent smells of Annie's scented handkerchief.

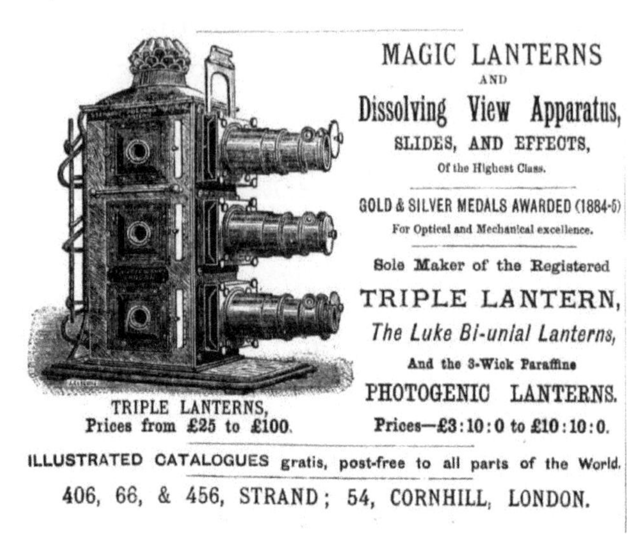

Dissolving Views were a more sophisticated form of Magic Lantern technology in which one slide, much like in cinematic dissolves, melded into the next, manually operated by the projectionist.

Tues 8th Collected trousers from Smiths Cheapside and bought diary at Lett's, 1/-.

Jan 10th Went down to Annie's and discovered her in a pitiful condition. She is suffering from hysteria which has flown to religion, which is the worst subject possible.

The subject of 'hysteria' in women in the nineteenth and earlier part of the twentieth century is a complex and problematic one; an umbrella term collating a melange of symptoms ranging from anxiety to mania to hypertension.

Before modern psychiatry - which no longer designates 'hysteria' as a specific mental condition - treatments included rest and sexual massage, the latter of which Sibley does indeed administer to Annie in later entries in his diary, and which doctors themselves administered to female patients in the nineteenth century. During the growth of psychoanalysis with Freud and Jung, 'hysteria' was relegated to a pseudo-term, its symptoms divided into mania, paranoia, hypertension, schizophrenia, delusion, etc.

Jan 11th Went down to Annie's and found to my joy that she was much better. Took her a few grapes. Although very weak and fears not quite gone she was very much improved and I felt that my prayers had been answered. Annie and I had a very pleasant evening and I left religion alone as much as possible. Did as much spooning as possible to keep her attention from religion.

Jan 15th Walked through R.A. Dks (Royal Albert docks). Policeman chalked on my bag. … went to Tabernacle… felt very apprehensive regarding Annie and was certain she would be bad again having started too soon. Went home sad in consequence.

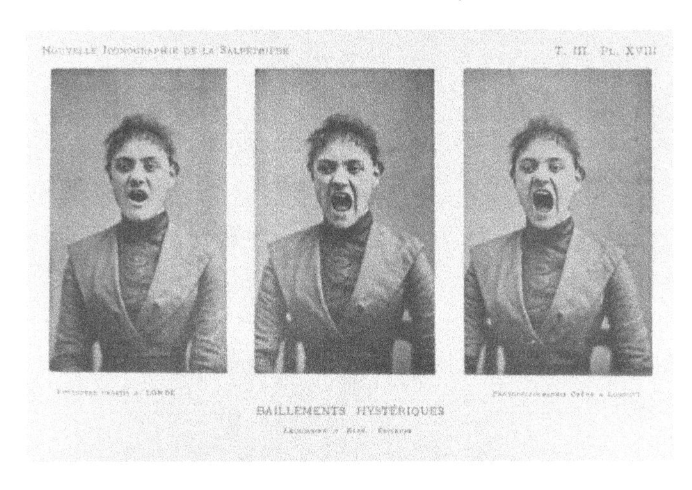

A woman suffering from a condition of supposed hysteria in the 19th century, a diagnosis which became redundant with the birth of 20th century psychoanalysis.

Jan 16th … went to GAH (General Assembly Hall, Mile End Road). *Annie however came on bad and had to be hurried home.*

Went indoors with her and she became hysterical and cried a good deal, and I had a job to leave her and catch last train. However, calmed her a little.

Jan 18th ... Hackney journey. Used Dr. Hurst's dumb-bells which were on the table and he saw me and evidently did not like it. Asked if 'they were mine?' Poor old chap.

Jan 19th First intimation of the Queen's illness.

Jan 21st ... hurried to Leytonstone to hear Dr. W. J. Grenfell's lecture... gave a lovely lecture on Labrador and the Mission to Deep Sea Fisherman's work. Saw Grenfell afterwards and said a few words. Heard rumour that Queen was dead.

Jan 22nd DEATH OF HER MAJESTY QUEEN VICTORIA, 6.30 at Osborne House. Age 81. Reigned 63 years. ... went to GAH and heard in there that the Queen was dead. Dead march was played and a most pathetic scene took place. People gave way to tears. Saw Mr. K at door shutting up shop but did not go in.

Jan 26th On account of Queen's death, no football was played. Pere d. (drunk), naturally.

Feb 1st Pere sober for a wonder.

Sat 2nd Queen Victoria's Funeral. General holiday. Mr. K. returned from funeral, and Annie and I went to Loughton, walked around High Beach and lost ourselves. However, managed to extricate ourselves by knocking at a house & asking the way. Went to the City and got something to eat at the Swiss Restaurant, Liverpool St.

The cliche 'end of an era' has scarcely been more apposite than for the death of Victoria, whose reign spanned the birth of modern Britain, its movement from semi-agricultual quasi-manorial nation to imperial and industrial powerhouse. Mourning took place across the world, for this was of course the death of an Empress. Not since the demise of the greatest Emperors of Ancient Rome had such scenes of grieving and adulation been seen, stretching from Cape Town to Carshalton.

Queen Victoria's Funeral procession, Feb. 2nd 1901.

In London the outpouring was at its fullest height, as thousands thronged the Mall and the streets around Westminster. As the great and good wound their way to Westminster Abbey and thence to Windsor - it was the largest gathering of European royalty hitherto seen in the capital - Thomas Sibley, instead, chose to take his sweetheart for a walk in a forest.

The woods must have been cool and empty that day. High Beach is a village in the Uplands of Essex, in the heart of Epping Forest. A popular refuge of city-dwellers and courting couples, it was reachable by a short horse-bus ride and was a pleasant getaway. A network of paths threading their way through the ancient woodland was laid down following the Epping Forest Act of 1878, allowing Londoners to pursue walking as recreation and escape the stifling crowds and industrial pollution of the city. Sibley and his young partner were beneficiaries of the burgeoning rediscovery of the countryside, begun with the Commons Preservation Society that became the Open Spaces Society (the Council for the Preservation of Rural England would be established in 1926).

Epping Forest 1900, a rural refuge from the teeming, polluted city.

Here Thomas and Annie wandered in the quiet green spaces, far from the leaden sadness of a city in mourning. But perhaps their conscience pricked, they then caught the Central London Railway to Liverpool Street for a Saturday tea at the Swiss Restaurant. In 1901 the area around Liverpool Street was far from the acreage of steel and glass it is today: it was a thoroughfare of shops and offices - fishmongers, umbrella makers, tobacconists, solicitors, fancy goods merchants, hatters, tailors, cigar importers and boot-makers. It was also a haven for hungry travellers alighting at the recently expanded Great Eastern Railway Station. With 600 trains a day the district was a place of constant crowded pavements and jostling crowds, on February 2nd 1901 the throng exacerbated by the Royal Funeral;

perhaps Thomas and his sweetheart were seeking out the sense of community from the sad faces, the air of collective gloom. The 'Swiss Restaurant' was perhaps the Moretti Brothers establishment spanning number 11, 10 & 8 Liverpool Street, one of the many cafes in the City run by immigrants.

Feb 4th Went to GAH. Went with Alf & Will to Victoria Home in Whitechapel Rd. who took two men there. Horrible place it seemed all full of rough and dirty men, but a Godsend to many. Lodgings 6d and 8d per night.

Thomas' visit to a lodging house for the homeless was a voluntary descent into the social abyss of his neighbourhood. This was a far cry from the elevated pageantry of the royal funeral only 48 hours earlier. Only few years after the notorious Ripper murders had exposed the deprivations and degradations of the East End to the world, the social philanthropy of the late Victorian age was accelerating: the Victoria Homes had been founded around 1886 by Granville Augustus William Waldegrave, Baron Radstock, in partnership with other trustees, setting out to provide a better grade of accommodation for itinerant labourers and the homeless than that available in lodging houses, with higher prices and a Christian mission.

Taken over by the Salvation Army in 1918, we have a detailed description of its interior and of the men who were obliged to use its well-meaning but dubious facilities: *'in the front block, a ground-floor reading room (with billiard tables by 1903), basement dining hall and upper- storey dormitories; and in the back range, a ground-floor reading room (a chapel from 1903), basement dining hall with kitchens to the west, and elsewhere dormitories. An enclosed yard was used as a recreation ground.'*

Victoria Home Whitechapel prior to its demolition in 1993. Taken over by the Salvation Army in 1918, Thomas Sibley visited this lodging house on Feb 4th 1901.

The Edwardian era was the age of explorers, and just as there was a huge appetite to investigate hitherto-unknown regions of the world, so too was there a missionary zeal to investigate the darker corners of an uncharted Britain. In 1897 the British Weekly sent a reporter into the Victoria Home, Whitechapel, and a somewhat pleasant and optimistic impression was the result: '*The men behave remarkably well, and many of them form friendships and club together their means both for food and lodging, so that when one is out of work his neighbours help him. The most comfortable-looking room in the Victoria Home is the large hall where the men can read the newspapers, and where meetings and services are held, but the whole house is bright, cheerful, and well-warmed, and the men I saw seemed thoroughly comfortable.*

Recitations and music brighten the winter evenings.' ('Working Men's Homes in Whitechapel', The British Weekly, 8 April 1897 (LSE Booth Archive, B227, 161-2).

Homeless men in the Whitechapel hostel in 1897. An officer hands them printed hymns.

A rather less favourable portrait had been painted five years earlier by a Daily Telegraph reporter of another lodging house nearby: *'A notice, painted in bright colours and big-faced letters, advertised that you could have a comfortable shelter for 2d. The money is taken by a man in a small recess to the left of the passage. In return for it he hands you a metal disc. This you give up to a man stationed at the foot of the staircase. You notice that the walls, ceiling, and floor of the corridor are clean and brightly and tastefully pinked out with colour. The staircase mounted, you gain admission to the first floor of the shelter. The sight is a startling one. You catch sight of low-pitched rafters with lines of pillars supporting them. There are gaudily illuminated text scrolls on the walls, rendered more vivid because of the dark background of mural colouring. The scene below you next invites and demands attention. You are standing on a platform; on your right are layers upon layers of folded skins. Each lodger takes one, you mechanically do the same. Immediately beneath you, far away to the front, and deep to your left and right, ranged in regular lines, are some 150 coffin-shaped boxes, touch to touch one with the other, and with the floor.'*

'Coffin beds' in a Whitechapel Lodging House.

Such was the fate of many of Thomas Sibley's peers, who comprised a fateful admixture of the temporarily unemployed, itinerant workers from the countryside yet to find a place on any social ladder, and the dismal lot of the permanent long-term homeless. These vast hostels, often founded by wealthy philanthropists, were a feature not just of London but of many towns and cities in Britain and were gradually replacing that grim but well-meaning stalwart, the workhouse, though those last vestiges of the Victorian Poor Law were not wholly phased out until 1948.

Feb 5th... Annie very bad, same complaint, and her mother awfully upset. She was ill with a very dull headache which made her think she was either going mad or going to die. She told her mother she was going to join the Salvation Army and wear the bonnet. Mrs. K said she should not. Mr. K. has had the pip of this religious hysteria.

Feb 11th .... At the club, Heyward apologised after a fashion to Bourdon. Heyward acknowledged he was a contemptuous person during a short argument with me.

Feb 13th Bob went to Kings Dancing Academy.

Feb 14th Went to club and did some work on squad. Boxed Bourdon and accidentally made his nose bleed.

Feb 19th Earls Court journey... had dinner in Lyons, Brompton Rd.

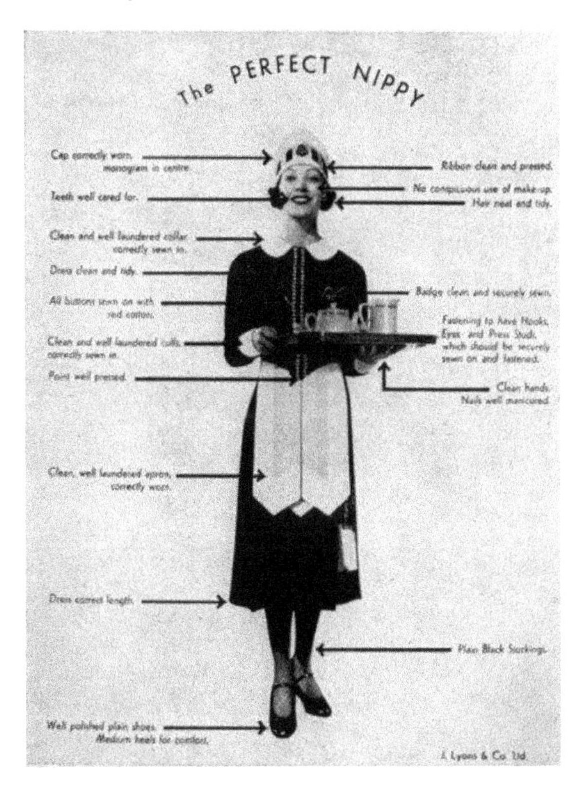

The 'Nippy' was a regular sight of the Lyons Corner Houses right up until the 1970s.

Lyons Corner Houses were a ubiquitous feature of the British retail landscape for decades. With their elegant interiors, their state-of-the-art chrome tea and coffee-making machines, and their famous 'Nippies,' - waitresses attired alike in classic Edwardian servant-wear - they became part of everyone's communal life right up to the 1970s.

Founded in 1894 by Joseph Lyons, the son of an itinerant watch-seller from Kennington, Lyons' first teashop opened in Piccadilly, London in 1894, and from 1909 they developed into a chain of teashops, with the firm becoming a staple of the High Street in the UK. At its peak the chain numbered around 200 cafes. The teashops provided for tea and coffee, with food choices consisting of hot dishes and sweets, cold dishes and sweets, and buns, cakes and rolls.

Feb 23rd … walked through tunnel to Blackheath and back.

Entrance to Blackwall Tunnel, Poplar, London.

Officially opened by the Prince of Wales on 22 May 1897, the Blackwall Tunnel became a major artery of the body of the capital, connecting southern flow and northern flow of traffic from the coastal county of Kent to Essex, Suffolk and beyond:

accelerating the pulsating passage of goods from the southern ports of Britain. With its northern entrance at East India Docks, it replaced the ferry as a means of crossing this wide stretch of the Thames, and remarkably it was for the use of pedestrians as well as traffic. Built for horse-drawn transport, its twists and turns were designed not only to avoid subterranean sewage systems but also had the benefit of preventing the animals from bolting once they glimpsed daylight: its cavernous depths were illuminated only by incandescent lighting.

Feb 24th GAH ... Annie took a girl home. Had to listen to a lot trouble connected to 5 girls or so. Not comforting or edifying to wait about in the cold while the woe is being expatiated.

Feb 25th Milder. Fine. Blackhurst Heath, Loughton, Epping & Stratford journey. Arrived home for dinner 4 o'clock. Finished work 8.30 & had tea. Harry & Bertha came. Had to leave hurriedly on account of father being very much boozed. Went to club but no squad. Came home with Bob after visiting 'E.'

Feb 28th Ordered 'Today' to be sent to me weekly by woman at Coborn Rd. Station. Went to Dr. McCleans and got more medicine. Discover that Annie likes medicine. Had a hot bath. Finished evening by sticking foreign stamps in album.

March 2nd Maida Vale journey, 2 orders. Arrived home 12.15. Went to Highgate and played for reserves against St. Mary Magdalene, lost 3-0. Ground a long way from station and very hilly. First team beat new court 7-3. Arrived home 7.45. caught 8.30 train to S.Bromley. We did not go out. I was tired and pleased to rest. Spent a very pleasant evening with Annie. She was not very bright but fairly jolly so enjoyed myself. Had some cocoa and biscuits. Caught last train home. Pere no money so sober. Will borrowed 2/- 6d.

March 5th Mrs. K very queer and worrying herself over her children.

March 6th Annie and I went to Dr. Dunlop's. Annie got some medicine for her nerves.

March 7th GAH (General Assembly Hall, Mile End) Saw dissolving views on a 'Trip to the Continent.'

March 9th City journey, 2 orders. Got an order on Hovendens and went there and bought razor and chat. bag. Ordered suit from Bulls 55/-.

March 15th ... tried on suit at Bulls. Bought wool vests and satchel at Hope Bro's. Ordered trousers at Smiths. 14/-. Bought a cake of French almond rock. Tore A's silk blouse.

March 16th ... did not play football. Caught 3.30 to S.B and had a little tea. Annie & I then hurried off somewhere and eventually found ourselves in Crystal Palace. Walked about the grounds. Visited parrots and fish and monkeys etc. Had a very interesting conversation with a parrot. Saw a good match of Rink Polo.

March 19th Westcombe park journey. Went on free ferry for first time. Saw Annie in evening. Mrs. K said she had to to have a 'stimulant.'

March 20th Spoke to Mr. Canning. He advised me to keep A. away from meetings.

March 21st Annie thoroughly examined in the new Hospital for Women Euston Rd. She had a rough experience and a complete over-handling which she did not appreciate. Mr & Mrs. K. went but had to wait outside hospital. Mr. K. visited Red Lion St. & left Mrs. K. who very nearly fainted. Mr. K came back at an opportune moment. A. had a lot to tell me... Heart weak through anaemia. Got to visit once a week. Gave Mrs. K. satchel for birthday.

The New Hospital for Women, Euston Road, was founded by the physician Elizabeth Garrett Anderson and opened in 1890.

The first hospital in Britain with only medical women appointed to its staff, in 1918 it became the Elizabeth Garrett Anderson Hospital and continued to have only female medical staff until its absorption into a larger hospital in the 1980s.

The New Hospital for Women, Euston Road, and the hospital today.

March 22nd … went to Wigmore St. in afternoon. Went to see Dr. McDonald but saw crowd outside with ambulance so did not go in.

Hurried to Hall and was baptised - may the Holy Spirit rest and abide in me - was my prayer before entering water. A. unexpectedly met me outside.

March 23rd Went to S.B. in evening and saw Annie. Stayed indoors. Rather cold so had Mr. K's coat to keep us warm. Stays discarded, so Annie rested in peace for an hour on couch. Enjoyed myself immensely.

March 28th … Annie very jolly and much better… I was privileged to explore the regions deep down and we playfully enjoyed ourselves. My manipulations were deep and interesting.

March 30th … bought pair of glace kids boots in Queen St.

April 3rd … went to Allenbury's cricket club meeting and concert. I was elected vice-captain. WJP(etty) and Butler Harrington were there. Solomon in great form. Solomon & Graves a trifle squiffy.

April 4th Did not do any business. Felt very much off of the last night. Practically had nothing to eat all day. Fitted on suit at Bulls & paid £2.15/- & left it to be sent on. Went to Gower St. Station & waited near new hospital for women to see whether I could meet Annie. She did not turn up by 6.50 so went home.

Sibley's life is shot through with sartorial self-awareness, not to say ambition, and his diaries are liberally peppered with clothes-purchases, for both himself and others. In 1903 kitting oneself out was more than mere utilitarianism, it was a statement of social standing. Just as Bernard Shaw said that anyone in England who opened their mouth to speak immediately gave away their social status with their accent, so too a person's attire was a cypher for their class. Sibley was a twenty-something professional with his eye on the future. His world was his customers as a travelling salesman, and his own idealism as a man of faith: he dressed for both. The cost of his fitted suit?

His £2-15/- in 1905 was his equivalent of our £290 in 2023, a not unsizeable sum.

The Edwardian era was the age of the dandy, the swell, the knut, the man-about-town, all demi-humorous soubriquets for a swaggering well-dressed young man. With its origins in the late nineteenth century, the quirkily confident, preening, smartly-clothed man had become such a 'type' as to be satirised on the music-hall stage - indeed, the 'dandy' and the 'swell' became a persona for many successful performers:

'The dandy as the mock upper-class 'swell' rose to prominence in music-hall entertainment of the later 1860s. The subject position of music halls, especially in the West End, was that of the upper-working-class or lower-middle-class male, and the parodic aspect of the music-hall dandy therefore had a considerable appeal to socially aspirational young men in the audience who worked as clerks, or in other positions in which they might nurture hopes of a professional career. Many of them had a desire to be fashionable in dress and would put on their 'slap-up toggery' for a Saturday night out, or a Sunday jaunt. There were several performers associated with the swell, but pre-eminent among them were George Leybourne (1842–84) and Alfred Vance (1839–88). It was Leybourne's song 'Champagne Charlie' (music by Alfred Lee), first performed at Princess's Concert Hall in Leeds in early August 1866, that first generated huge enthusiasm for the swell. Yet, Charlie was a double-coded dandy: he might have displayed admiration for fine clothes, wealth and status, but he subverted bourgeois values by celebrating excess and idleness, boasting that he was 'a noise all night, in bed all day, and swimming in champagne.' (Derek B. Scott, The British Dandy on the Popular Musical Stage 1867–1915).

Sibley, of course, was no dandy but made of more earnest stuff: seemingly his frivolous days were over now he had settled down with Annie and was carving out his future with a determined single-mindedness that resembled a straight-ploughed furrow.

Men's fashion in the Edwardian era was influenced by the 'dandies' of the stage.

He wore his suits as a uniform of his social soul - upper-working-class or lower-middle class prosperous, agile, upwardly mobile. He was leaving the humbler artisan's world behind him, and he had the suit to prove it.

April 6th Saturday … Annie's face and neck came on bad, the nerves in the face and neck extremely painful. Rubbed her neck with oils. She laid down and gradually became better. A. became larkish later on so I feelingly and admiringly approached the beautiful P.o.L. & left her in a perfect state of disorganisation.

April 9th Had a ride on the new electric tram at Shepherd's Bush for the first time.

On 4 April 1901, the London United Tramway Company opened London's first regular electric tram service on a public road, so when Sibley took his first trip on the 9th it was merely five days old. This was the golden age of the electric tram. The first public tramway had opened in Blackpool in 1885, and between 1900 and 1907 the national tramway mileage doubled.

A postcard of the new electric tram at Shepsherds (sic) Bush, 1905. The new automatic vehicles quickly established themselves across the capital, spelling the decline of horse-drawn traffic.

In the ensuing years, encouraged by the Light Railways Act of 1896, tram and rail services were transforming patterns of settlement in Britain's cities and enabling working people to move out to the suburbs. The census returns for 1901 show, for example, that the population of Middlesex and Surrey had grown by over a third since 1891, while that of the county of London had fallen. Londoner Charles Masterman wrote of his childhood, *'When I first went to live in Camberwell in 1900 our sole communication with London...was a few erratic horse omnibuses and lines of slow-moving, two-horse trams...Now we have fast lines of electric trams, brilliantly lighted, in which reading is a pleasure, hurrying us down from over the bridges at half the time expended under the old conditions...Family after family are evacuating the blocks and crowded tenements for little four-roomed cottages, with little gardens, at Hither Green or Tooting.'* (Charles

Masterman in circa 1906, from Lucy Masterman's C.F.G. Masterman 1939).

April 10th Annie became fidgety and larkish so got tickled. Made her very lively with my encroachments and I persisted, kissing &c, the p of l.

April 13th Sat. Met Ted at ABC Broad Street at 3.20. We went to the Sth. Kensington Museum in afternoon. After we were turned out we had tea in ABC Sth Kensington & then tried to get into Egyptian Hall but found it too crowded. Paraded down Strand. Ted bought in the "arcade" a Dolly - a few remarks from girls as they passed. After looking in bookshops & c. we journeyed home.

An ABC tearoom, 1901. Along with Lyons Corner Houses, they democratised the British High Street.

AERATED BREAD COMPANY, LIMITED.

No Gratuities Allowed.

LIST OF PRICES.

No Gratuities Allowed.

	Per Cup.
Tea	3d.
,, (small) ...	2d.
Coffee	3d.
,, (small) ...	2d.
Cocolate	3d.
,, (small) ...	2d.
Cream	1d.
	Per Glass.
Milk ... ... / Soda and Milk / Soda Water	1½d. *large* 3d.
Lemonade (from fresh Lemons)	2d. & 4d.
Lemon Squash	3d. & 6d.
Egg and Milk ...	3½d.
	Per Bot.
Ginger Beer (stone or glass) ... ... / Sparkling Limado / Lemonade	2d.

Bread or Roll, Brown and White (Special Quality) ...	1d.
Crescents	1d.
Pat of Butter ...	1d.
Bread and Butter (2 slices)	1d.
Buttered Toast ...	2d.
Milk Cake (toasted, buttered)	4d.
,, ,, ,, (half)	2d.
Tea Scones ...	1d.
,, (toasted, buttered)	2d.
Egg (Boiled) ... ... / ,, (Hard Boiled)...	2d.
Poached Egg on Toast	3d.
Crown Cake...	1d. & 4d.
Madeira Cakes ... / Fancy Pastries ...	1d. & 2d.
Milk Cake (half 1d.)	2d.

	Per Plate
Roast Beef	6d.
Pressed Beef ... / Ham ... ... / Tongue (Finest English) / Brawn	4d.
	Each.
Sandwiches (Ham, Tongue or Beef) ...	2d.
Rump Steak Pies (hot)	3d. & 4d.
Melton Mowbray Pies	6d.
,, ,, (half)	3d.
Beef Rissoles ...	2d.
Potted Ham and Tongue	2d.
Smoked Ham and Tongue	2d.
Jam (various)	1d.
Biscuits (various)...	1d.

1d. Each.

Queen Cakes (Plain or Currant).
Buns (Plain or Currant).
Ginger Bread.
Rich Seed and Sultana Cake.
Sponge Cake.
Lunch Cake (Seed or Fruit).

2d. Each.

Pound Cake (Seed or Fruit).
Ginger Pound.
Dundee Cake.
Genoa Cake.
Mince Pies.
Bath Buns.
Empress Cake.
Shortbread.
Jam Sandwich
Lawn Tennis Cake.

1900. Sep.

Nowadays the only evidence that ABC's - from 'Areated Bread Company' - ever existed are the occasional faded signs descried above renovated shopfronts, but for decades the tearooms rivalled Lyons Corner Houses as the most popular eateries of the Edwardian era and beyond. Founded in 1864 as an offshoot of Dr. John Dauglish's innovative bakery empire - he eschewed traditional bakery methods with a radical pneumatic process that rendered kneading redundant - the eateries sprang up across the country and were, like Lyons, symbols of a democratised High Street, providing cheap meals and refreshment to the masses, including permitting lone women as customers for the first time.

April 17th .. ominous possibilities of Annie slipping from God as she seemed to like being with her step-sister who is a very ungodly woman.

Friday May 3rd Met Annie at Bow and walked to Common. Some fellow was trying to commit suicide in Grove Road by throwing himself in the canal but his wife or girl wouldn't let him. Went to Ullin St. St. Michael's Bazaar. Bob went.

May 4th Caught 2.30 train to Homerton. ACC got beaten by St. Barnabus on a wretched long-grassed pitch at Hackney Marsh. I made 3 after batting for about half an hour.

May 6th Went to club. Fred Amlot brought his air-gun up and we had some shooting. Charles Bourdon capped it by shooting the Queen and smashing the glass to the picture.

May 9th Mother returned from Eastbourne.

May 27th Whit Bank Holiday. Met Annie at 8.7. train and went to Boxhill. Walked in Boxhill Park. Had a miserable dinner and tea in Dorking. We then journeyed to the top of Box Hill and had lovely views of the surrounding country. Went into wood and laid down until 7 o'clock. Picked a few wild flowers on the way down. Had a very crowded train going up. Had to sit on Annie's lap. Two fellows in corner had a musical taste and kept singing. Arrived at S. Bromley 10.55. A delightful day.

Box Hill Surrey, 1903 - a popular rural escape for Londoners.

Easily reached from Waterloo, Box Hill in Surrey was a popular Bank Holiday destination for weekenders in the warmer months, seeking respite from the teeming streets of the metropolis.

May 30th thurs. Mr. K. went to Witham for the day on his machine.

Weds June 12th Caught 9.15 at Waterloo, picking up Butler, WJP & CJP on the way to Kingston. Had two boats and commenced about 10 o'clock rowing down the river. Had lunch at 1 o'clock at a secluded spot which we discovered, and a jolly good feast of cold mutton salad and bread with pasties & pineapple chunks &c. We then proceeded on but dropped in for some rain. Finished day about 6.30. Had haircut at Mr. K's. Annie came in as I was undergoing the operation. She came in shop & protested.

Admirers of that classic work of humorous late-Victorian fiction *Three Men in a Boat* cannot fail to note that the young Sibley and his three chums Butler, WJP & CJP (the latter two presumably the two Petty brothers of chemist's wholesalers W.J. Petty & Co., chose pineapple chunks as a comestible, just as George, Harris & 'J' did on their memorable boat trip on the pages of Jerome K. Jerome's masterpiece a few years earlier. One hopes that Sibley & Co. had better luck opening the tin and did not have recourse to attempt to smash it open with an oar.

While still a working river, by the early twentieth century the Thames had for some decades become a place of pleasure, courting and retreat, with young men escorting adventurous maidens upriver in slow-moving craft in the hope that the dappled sunlight in the low-hanging willows on the banks and the warm breeze might lull the heart and instil in their lady-loves lofty romantic thoughts.

Sibley would have seen the Thames in its Three-Men-in-a-Boat heyday, catching it before the urbanisation of Greater London changed the first 15 miles of its landscape forever. In his memoirs of 1926 Jerome K. Jerome wrote: *'There were lovely stretches then between Richmond and Staines, meadows and cornfields,'* a paean proving that by the 1920s things had all changed utterly: *'At first, we used to have the river almost to ourselves; but year by year it got more crowded and Maidenhead became our starting-point. Sometimes we would fix up a trip of three or four days or a week, doing the thing in style and camping out.'*

For Sibley and his chums on that far-off day sunny day in June 1905, the river would still have been crowded, yet they found a secluded spot for their lunch, where presumably they could bond as work-mates over their potted meat sandwiches - superiors and inferiors rendered, albeit temporarily, equalised by the levelling balm of nature.

June 14th Annie and I had usual tickling. Practised new kissing.

June 22nd Woke with a shocking cold in my chest. However, saw Dr. MacClean after journey so got some medicine...1.50 to Cromer.

Had a very comfortable journey down, arrived at Cromer about 5.30. Left bag at station and went in quest of lodgings. Fortunately with God's help found comfortable ones with Christian people: Mrs. Lambert, 'Ladysmith,' Alfred Road. Had a lovely walk along picturesque cliffs.

By the beginning of the 20th century pleasure boating on the Thames was a national pastime.

By 1901 more and more working-class and lower-middle class were embarking on holidays: no foreign trips yet, but this was the glory days of the British Seaside Resort when weekenders would descend in charabancs on Brighton, Blackpool and Paignton. For East Londoners like Sibley the Essex coast was the usual destination, but occasionally the more distant charms of Norfolk and Suffolk lured him and his sweetheart. In those days the coastal towns were crammed with boarding-houses, usually managed by widowed landladies or retired couples.

Cromer, Norfolk in 1900, as it would have looked to Thomas Sibley on his first visit in 1901.

June 23rd After tea went to Baptist's Chapel and made acquaintances. ....Days following... Overstrand, Lion's mouth, Roman Camp, Sheringham, Telbrigg Hall, (Felbrigg Hall?) Had a stroll with Minister. Walk along East Cliffs - too many Flying Butlers for enjoyment - had to knock them down with my stick & hands. Read poems. Road Moffat's adventures as a missionary. Some touching poems. Accidentally met Mr. Wrightman and went with him to a Christian Endeavour meeting. Had a jolly walk afterwards.

Cromer, while a fishing town, had grown as a tourist resort from the beginning of the 19th century, and by 1900 boasted the famous pier and Pavilion Theatre. In 1883 the London journalist Clement Scott named the stretch of coastline, particularly the Overstrand and Sidestrand area, 'Poppyland' and the combination of the railway and his writing in the national press brought many visitors. The name 'Poppyland' referred to the numerous poppies which grew (and still grow) at the roadside and in meadows - the inspiration, of course, for Thomas Sibley naming his sweetheart Annie 'Poppy' from that time on in his diaries. While they strolled the cliffs King Edward VII was playing golf at one his favourite courses nearby, the Royal Cromer Links. The popularity of North Norfolk at this time had been noted in the London City Press in a report dated 5th September 1886: *'The public are greatly indebted to railway enterprise for the opening up ofthe East Coast. More bracing air and delightful sands are not to be found in any part of England. The only drawback is that the country is rather flat. Thisremark, however, does not apply to Cromer, which bids fair to become the most popular watering place, it being entirely free from objectionable features.'*

July 11th Went to Davy Hills to see whether Ted was going to cricket, but he was not. Saw his latest baby.

July 15th Annie went to Greenwich Park with Miss Holden and they both got very much stung with mosquitoes. Annie's foot very bad and she would scratch it. Took Annie gloves, Bryno-haemoglobin & smelling salts.

July 16th Bryno-haemoglobin makes Annie feel sick.

July 20th Met Annie at Bow 2.30 and went to Stamford Hill to

Trojan Sports. Father, Mother, Dena, Bob of the family there. Father was introduced to Annie, though partly drunk. A nice introduction. Sports went off alright. I did not enter. Bob represented family but did not win anything.

July 24th Annie had some coca-Bryon which made her lively.

July 29th Packed Annie's things in bag. Vinnie arrived with her baby and I refused to nurse it.

30th Finished packing Gladstone. Managed to get everything in.

31st L&SE Rlwy collected Gladstone to convey to Gosport.

AUGUST

1st At Annie's, Vinnie was there with her three children. Fearful noise and bad behaviour was all I found with the children.

No sooner had the couple returned from Cromer, it seems, they were off to Gosport with their friends Claud and Maud Mills.

August 3rd … bus to Bank, electric rlwy to Waterloo. 12 o'clock train to Portsmouth Harbour. Nice little boy in train who Annie liked. Swim in Stokes Bay, Southsea, Brocklehurst…Mrs. Mills upset as she didn't think I liked her child enough to look after it.

6th Went to Privett… found a nice spot… evening stroll near soldier's encampment… very dark gloomy path… came to desolate place near Stokes Bay… animal running around that terrified Annie. Cowes by boat from Southsea…

7th Mrs Mills in a worrying state. Unfortunately I upset Annie (who was very unwell and nervous) with a thoughtless remark that I said jokingly.

8th …Cowes… had a long walk and had our sandwiches. Annie

afterwards gave way to tears because of last night. Annie got frightened at some waves. I spent a grievous and heartbroken night.

9th Went into Annie's bedroom and kissed her. Mrs. Mills, Claud, Annie & I went to Portsmouth.... Mrs. Mills wanted an expensive hat so Claud & I waited.... had some lemonade & sweets. Bought Annie smelling salts bottle 3/- 6d. After waiting 3/4 hour they appear. Annie told us all about Mrs. Mill's good hat, the cheapest she could get. Annie very gigglish in consequence. We had a lovely tea in Stoke Road Dairy.

10th Annie spent evening turning Mrs. Mills' hat... I sat & smoked and watched her.

His 'thoughtless remark' having soured things between the engaged couple, they re-bonded over mutual fun over Maud Mill's choice of hat, and their holiday continued untroubled.

Portsmouth Harbour 1900.

11th Caught 2.45 train from Portsmouth Harbour, got into

Waterloo 5 o'clock. Had tea at ABC Broad Street. Found that Mrs. Williams had broken a blood vessel.

15th Met Annie in E. India Dk Rd. Mrs. Williams wants to go away for a week or so and & Annie to mind house, children & Mr. Williams while she is away. I strongly objected... Mrs. K didn't mind her going. Mrs. K. 'up the stick.'

The slang 'up the stick' meant pregnant, so changes were afoot in the Kettley household. And further big life-events were unfolding:

August 19th Engaged to Annie. Mrs. K. & Annie went to East Ham. Met them in St. Leonard's Rd. Annie will not be going to stay at Mrs. Williams while she is away. Annie went to see her Aunt Marnie (corpse) who had just died. I asked Annie to become engaged to me and she consented. Went home happy and praising God.

23rd... Annie had to mind Vinnie's baby which has been usual of late. Too much of a good thing. Annie quizzed me a little over what she said if her mother were to die.

24th I gave Annie a serious talking to with regard to her faith in me & c. and that she loved her ma best. Her love was too little towards me.

25th Annie and I had a serious chat. She has got not the faith in me that she ought to have.

30th Walked down Mile End Rd. with Annie and looked in shops & c. Saw Mr. K shave a drunken man.

31st... asked Mr. K for consent to become engaged to Annie and he cordially sanctioned it.

Sept 4th A & I went to Roper's Mile End Rd. & selected

engagement ring which has to be made smaller. Left a deposit. Ring ready Friday.

Mile End Road, East London in 1899. Whilst an impressive street of shops and workshops, the clap-board houses and horse-drawn buses still gave Mile End a touch of the Wild West.

Mile End in East London then, as now, was a long broad High Street, established in Roman times as a thoroughfare from the City proper to the villages, fields and farmsteads of Essex; but by the early twentieth century Greater London had swallowed up the rural parishes such as Tower Hamlets and Bow. As they strolled that September day in 1901 Thomas & Annie would have passed James Frances' Lamp Warehouse, John Patterson's Rifle Range at No. 15, David Fichbein's Tobacconist's shop at 23, and of course the familiar General Assembly Hall, proprietor the Hon. Frederick N. Charrington, philanthropist and evangelist of brewing fame - not to mention the fruiterers, stone carvers, coach builders and dozens more artisans workshops, wholesalers and retailers. Numerous Jewish shops pepper Kelly's Street Directory of 1901: Joseph Silk, fishmonger, Augustus Viegand, Baker, Levy Mondschein, furrier - Roper's Jewellers is not listed, but may have been a stall within an arcade. However, there is listed a Robert Roper, auctioneer, at number 58 Mile End Road, which is perhaps where the Thomas and Anne solemnised their engagement with the purchase of a ring.

Sept 6th Gave Annie ring which was much admired, also Bryno-Pepsi, CLO and emulsion pills.

Sept 7th 3.20 to Hendon. We walked to Edgware and went over cottage. Called in and saw Aunt but did not stay long. Went to see Mrs. Bowyer and she paid me £2 9/-/11d.

Part of Sibley's financial ambitions was the ownership of a small cottage in Edgware, which he let out to tenants of varying reliability; over the years he seems to experience much difficulty in obtaining any rent from them at all. The origins of his possession of this property is unknown, though as he has relatives in that district it appears to have come from his father's side, who was born in Hendon.

Sept 12th Annie very unwell - neuralgia in head & face.

Sept 13 Harry's baby practically dead, will only last an hour or so.

Sept 14th President McKinley dies of wounds.

In a grim foreshadowing of the assassination of Archuduke Franz Ferdinand, President McKinley's death was at the hands of an anarchist. Anarchism, while possessing historical antecedents in the Levellers of the seventeenth century and the Utopian communities of the early settlers in America, blossomed - if horticultural fertility can be apposite as a metaphor - in the late nineteenth century and early twentieth century. Britain's liberal immigration laws led to many foreign anarchists and revolutionaries settling in London, from Marx himself to the Latvians who were behind the infamous Siege of

Sidney Street in 1911.

President McKinley b. 1843- assassinated 1901.

In 1907 Joseph Conrad's prescient novel of terrorism, nihilism and anarchy, *The Secret Agent* was published. Fuelled by the counter-cultural tracts of Marx, Proudhon and Bakunin, cells of nihilist radicals formed in urban centres. While mainstream politics between 1900 & 1920 continued to offer the British electorate a binary choice between Conservative & Liberal parties, in February 1900 Trade Union delegates founded the Labour Party in London , and its bedrock of socialism marshalled and nourished fringe elements of the left that fed into minor outbreaks of radical action, some of it violent.

While Thomas Sibley was plying his trade at the chemist's and doctor's surgeries, a certain Vladimir Lenin was a fellow Londoner, using the hospitality of the British capital to foment revolutionary activity in his homeland of Russia.

Lenin lived in London in 1902, formulating his philosophy of unrest and discontent.. Three years later in 1905 the first - unsuccessful - revolution broke out in Russia.

15th Mrs. K. still upset with Annie. upset also Vinnie, and Mr. K anxious about me. Had some brandy but did not get better.

22nd Work people coming Monday to do up parlour kitchen and wash-house.

23rd Bought slippers for Mrs. K. Bought myself a pipe. Went to East Ham with Annie to fetch Bert. Tom Williams causing a commotion for bringing drunken men and women into the house. Mrs. Williams came back from Southend, left the 4 children next door and went back to Southend. A & I bought Bert back with us. Work people in house.

24th Chelmsford journey. Dined at a Temperance Hotel Chelmsford.

Sept. 26th Annie, Vinnie, Bert Williams & I watched pictures (limelight) from window which were being exhibited outside church opposite. Had a chat with Mr. K. on religion. Mr. K. believes in self-righteousness. Had to sleep walk Annie.

Temperance Hotels sprang up all over Britain in the late 19th early 20th centuries, promoting sober living to weary travellers.

Oct 3rd Mother & Annie went to Opthalmic Hospital City Rd. Annie's eyes suffering from weak nerves. Annie told me all about her adventure with the saucy doctor. When A & I were upstairs Mrs. K. was overcome at the foot of the stairs and lay there until Mr. K. tried to get indoors and couldn't. Annie let him in the shop door. Mr. K. swore at Mrs. K. and got her upstairs, and left her in the bedroom cuddling the floor.

The Ophthalmic Hospital at City Road, London.

Founded in 1804 in Moorfields near the present day Liverpool Street Station, the original Eye Hospital treated returning soldiers from the Napoleonic War suffering from an epidemic of trachoma. The hospital Annie Kettley visited in 1901 had been opened in 1897 by the Prince of Wales and was a state-of-the-art treatment centre, with air-conditioning, advanced microscopy, and central heating.

Sat 5th Mrs. K did not say much to me about Thursday. Bert went home. Mary Ann sent an ungrateful and practically insulting message.

Oct 7th Bought bowler hat from Cork Hat Co. 8/- 6d.

19th Annie had a tooth out but it only made the other teeth worse. She had a wretched time. She wanted me to stay all night but I couldn't very well.

By the early 20th century by far the most common bodily affliction for the majority of the populace was tooth decay. While dentistry had made significant advances in terms of the invention of anaesthesia, drilling, and teeth straightening, when Thomas Sibley paid his visit, extraction was still the most prevalent solution.

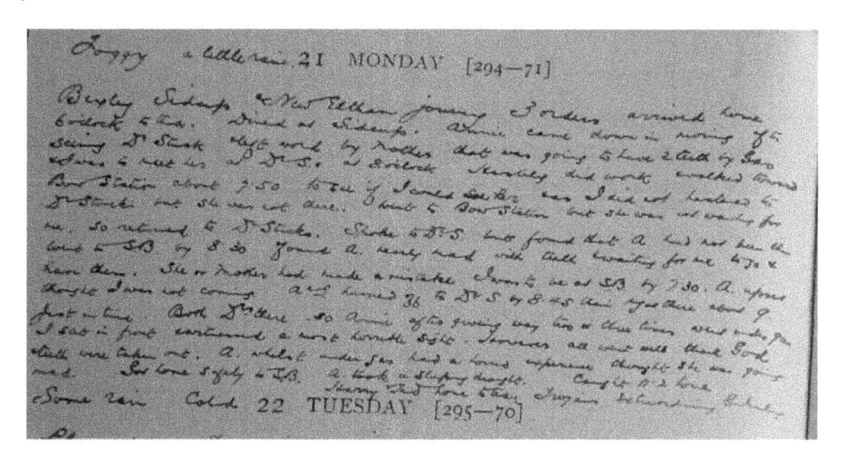
Foggy a little rain 21 MONDAY [294—71]

Some rain Cold 22 TUESDAY [295—70]

Nov. 4th Blackest fog known for many years. Found it was so foggy I could not see an inch before me so cancelled travelling. Lent Mother £2. Will said he had his pocket picked of £1 so could not give mother anything.

Nov. 21st. Annie had been out and had trimmed a hat for Mary Clarke. I told her I might go to Davy Hill's dinner, and she said she considered a Christian ought not to go. We had words but made no headway. I told Will he was dishonest and was ashamed of him.

Nov 28th Told Annie I had resigned Trojans and had given up football. She was delighted.

In the late nineteenth and early twentieth century there was a crusader's movement to wean men away from football, associated as it was in the social mind with exuberance, intemperance and excess. Evangelicals spoke out against it, and especially in Wales the men of rural villages were warned that a love of the game would lead to moral ruin. Sibley, it seemed, soaking up the teachings of London evangelicals at the General Assembly Hall in Mile End, fell prey to this sober crusade, and hung up his football boots forever.

Dec 4 Heard from Edgware that Mrs. Bowyers was dead.

Dec 5th Annie came to tea got here 4.25. Showed Annie everything we had interesting and she duly inspected my office. Waited until Father came home. Ted came down about 8.

Dec 7th Mother has slight diabetes which is dangerous. Went to Maguires to have teeth stopped. He said it could not possibly be done as flesh had grown the hollow of the tooth. I told him to take the back one out. He injected cocaine and pulled out the tooth in 4 pieces. Nice job.

Dec 16th Father had to come home ill brought on by excessive alcoholism.

Dec 20th Bought Mrs. K a shirt but lost it. Annie and I went to Chrisp St., a china shop, to see if it had been left there, but without avail.

Dec 23rd Saturday. Annie and I went to City. Went to Sunday School Union to buy Mr. Creed a card… A&I then walked up Oxford St. Went in Lyons had tea then went to Hyde Park and returned by tube.

Sibley's use of the word 'tube' indicates the relative rarity of his use of the underground network: his travels were mainly by overground railway. While the Central Line had opened in 1900, it had not yet reached the East End, let alone the distant reaches of Ongar and Epping in Essex. Yet the tube was inexorably transforming the life of Londoners. 1900-1910 was the transitional age between horse-bus and motor traffic - but with the internal combustion engine still in its nascency, despite the vehicle licence plate being introduced in 1904 with Earl Russell queuing all night to obtain the very first issue - A1 - it was the electric underground train that led the field.

The London Underground at Marble Arch, 1900. The 'tube' would become the principle means of cross-city travel for most Londoners by 1910.

Dec 25th 10.4 to Leytonstone. Took Winnie & Wilf toys &c. Ted and I went to Baptist Chapel. Caught 1.37 to Bow Rd., arr. SB 2.5. Spent afternoon chatting with Mr. K on religious matters. Spent quiet evening upstairs. Caught 11.2 home. House empty. Father, Mother & Bob went to Harry's for dinner. Mother stayed there all night. Father & Bob got home about 2 o'clock.

Dec 30 … arr. At Annie's 8 o'clock, found she had been in bed all day with her head bad. However she was much better in the evening & was playful, plenty of tickling &c ad lib (2).

Dec 31 Annie unwell & grievous. We had a long chat about last night. However, left her in better spirits & confidence strengthened which seemed broken. Caught 11.2 to Bow and went to GA Hall and to Watch Night Service. Mr. Nokes & Mr. Harrison spoke. Splendid service. Took about one hundred and fifty pledges. I spoke to 2 old women and to a poor young girl. Chatted with plenty of friends. Got home 1 o'clock much happier than when I started.

1902

As the new century progressed, the old order was slowly falling away - the imperial Boer war ended, Balfour the Liberal was elected Prime Minister, the new King Edward VII was crowned, Harry Jackson became the first criminal to be convicted by way of fingerprints, the *Hound of the Baskervilles* was published, and Bernard Shaw's *Man and Superman* was first performed. A new, modern spirit was emerging - cars were becoming faster, electric trains were skimming hundreds of feet below the pavements, and vegetarian restaurants opened in metropolitan streets.

Meanwhile, life went on in the little barber's shop at 191, St. Leonard's Road, Poplar, as Mr. Kettley, father of Sibley's sweetheart Annie, took on a new assistant as business picked up in the hair-cutting trade:

Jan 1st Annie tried to coax away my grievous thoughts and nearly succeeded. Mr. K's new assistant started work.

Sat Jan 4th Heard Will had got drunk and upset Father Mother & Bob at tea. Cheeked Father and nearly got his head punched. I offered a special prayer for Will's conversion.

5th Went to GAH in morning and heard the Boy Preacher (God made manifest in a child), and was astonished at him. Surely a miracle from God.

Jan 1st. Thomas tries to convert Will. Father mad drunk and tries to fight Bob.

As Thomas Sibley's purpose-driven life in his embrace of faith begins to grow, his family's descent into alcohol-induced anguish deepens. Both father and son are now in the grip of the demon drink, and Thomas - at this stage of his life at least - sees it his mission to help.

14th Ted & I after a very hard struggle got Will to go to GAH & sign the Pledge. Will went into Inquiry Room but would not give his heart to God. Annie stayed with Mother & Father, who came in very drunk. Annie had his company. Father wants to sign the Pledge.

20th - 24th Feverish cold. Too ill to do work, but get up, light fire in office and go for sharp walk for 2 mins.

Jan 31st Mother very ill. Annie came and looked after her afternoon and evening. Ted & Li came also Harry. Mother cooked some fish for supper.

Feb 2nd Heard that mother had kidney disease and would not last long. Had a grievous day.

Feb 3-6 Mother dying in bed. Annie stays all night with her. Visitors trooping in and out to say farewell. God bless Annie for her kindness.

Feb 6th MOTHER TAKEN TO REST. 11 o'clock in morning. Bermondsey, Rotherhithe journey, 7 orders, arr. home 4 o'clock. When I arrived home I found that my dear mother had been taken to glory - dead to the world but alive in Christ. I prayed and cried. Annie had hysterics and felt very ill. Tried to comfort Annie. Father broken-hearted. I looked at the body where my poor mother used to be. Thank and praise Lord that he has taken dear Mother to his home, and there I shall meet her when my time is come, and I know Annie will. May her death save Father, Harry, Will, Bob and all others who witnessed her illness last.

Feb 7th Mile End journey 7 orders, dined at May Tree Rstnt., arr home 3.30. Father made all arrangements with regard to funeral - it will be Tuesday next. Mrs. Smith & Bertha looking after washing etc. - what an untold blessing to us. Annie came round about 5.30 with a severe cold in tooth. Took her to Dr. Hastings & had it out. Annie fainted when she came to. In worse agony.

Feb 11th Tues. MOTHER'S FUNERAL. GOD IS LOVE. Mother is in heaven. A most sorrowful and mournful day. I did not go to business. Uncle Harry came and brought a wreath which showed his respect, but I wish it had come without the curse of strong drink. Mr. & Mrs. K. kindly sent a wreath which Annie brought… Father, Will, Harry, Ted, Bob, Bertha, Li, Aunt Polly, Dena, Annie & I followed to the grave. Funeral at 12.30, back at 2.15. Poor Annie, she suffered greatly through grief. Mrs. Smith stayed at home and prepared dinner. Heartbreaking scenes at grave and at service. God giveth life, and he taketh away.

12th Annie and I had a basin of gravy soup between us and tried to be cheerful. Father helplessly drunk and went to bed in his clothes.

FEB 22nd Sat. Redeemed gold chain 18/-11d at Roman Rd.

In 1900 there were more pawn shops in London than pubs.

Half a pound of tuppenny rice,

Half a pound of treacle,

That's the way the money goes,

Pop goes the weasel!

The seeming jollity of the Victorian rhyme (in which a weasel & stoat=coat is pawned in order to obtain a few pence for treacle and rice) disguised a brutal truth, that for the poor of the capital pawning items was often a regular, if not weekly necessity.

In the early 20th century the pawnbroker was the first port of call for those in need. (Living London, 1901).

Sibley wasn't poor, yet had clearly 'popped' a gold chain perhaps the previous year (if goods were not redeemed after a year and a day the ownership was transferred to the pawnbroker). A common sight in the early twentieth century was children sent round the back of the local pawnshop to avoid the scrutiny of neighbours when items had to be exchanged for much-needed cash.

Pawnbrokers have never disappeared but their heydays were understandably in times of economic downturn, with anything from bundles of clothes, bedding, boots and shoes, to items of jewellery, handed over the counter to lurk, expectantly, on a shelf until redeemed, if that day ever came.

24th Dined at YMCA Canning Town. Dena did not go to school because of party at Mrs. Hawarden's. Caught 7.45 to SB and found that Annie had gone to Harry's although she said she would not go if it rained. Went to Harry's and got there about 8.40. Annie seemed to rejoice at my having had any trouble and made me out to be cross. I retaliated and said she'd been flirting as she had had some violets given to her by a young fellow in the train. Annie did not like it. But it was tit for tat.

27th Will has agency for coal. Gave Will order for 1/2 tone of coals.

28th Annie came in afternoon and did work and made puddings.

After his mother's death, Annie is clearly now doing domestic work for the Sibley house. This was not merely a favour but a necessity - running a house in early 20th century was an arduous, lengthy affair, from wash-day when clothes and bedding would be boiled in a copper, to hanging and drying, shopping, cooking, and cleaning. We shall see in the future years how Thomas & Annie were themselves able to employ a housekeeper: this was often the case even for working-class folk - it was more common than hindsight might indicate that humble families were able to employ live-in maids.

MARCH

3rd Father a trifle muddly.

6th Annie here doing work, scrubbing &c. Had a heartrending letter from Liza about Will. Liza asked me to take photo from Will's room and letter, which I did. Wrote back a sympathy letter with plenty of scripture in it promising to meet her on Sunday.

7th Will came home in afternoon and soon missed photo. He was told I had it. He came and asked me. He was brokenhearted. I was very stern and nasty to him. I told him he had refused God and therefore he would be brought down more still. He was frightened and I told him to pray. He did so in his room and came back to me to pray for him. I did so, and Will also, and he gave his heart to God. I was happy.

8th Had tea in Lyons Oxford Street.

Sun 9th Went to Hampstead via Camden Town. Started 10.6 at Bow, arrived at Hampstead 11 o'clock. Liza there to meet me and we went for a walk on the Heath. Liza told me about Will, what a week he had spent, so deranged he did not hardly know her. Borrowed under threats 14/- 6d. With Bob Boyser and his drunken wife. Put matters right with Liza, through Grace of God. Will sent her a letter confirming Christ had saved him. Will is saved God be praised. Will write to Liza in a week to say all is well, and then Will can see her. Will, Dena & I went to Hall. Will gave in his name for membership.

Weds 12th Liza's photo back.

13th Wrote to Liza to say Will was truly converted and wished them every happiness in their reunion.

18th Liza wrote to me thanking me for my services. Wrote to Liza and gave to Will to include with his letter.

24th Father said he was going to give notice so I said I did not care a jot. He had spent 23/- and it had upset him.

31st Easter Bank Holiday. Started for Brighton 9 o'clock arr. 11. (Annie & I) went for a long walk on downs by race course. Afternoon windy but sunny and warm so enjoyed ourselves.

Brighton racecourse, high on Whitehawk Hill by the South Downs, had been a leisure spot for both fashionable and lowlier society since the early eighteenth century, but its heyday came with the arrival of the railway in 1850 from which time hordes of hatted Bank holidaymakers would descend on the south-coastal saucy mistress of a town and sample the races that overlooked the sleepy blue sea. For a three-day ticket costing 10/-6d visitors were treated to seven races at half-hourly intervals.

Bookmakers bustle to & fro on a busy Bank Holiday at Brighton Races in 1905.

But Sibley's thoughts were elsewhere than betting when he returned with Annie to their accommodation:

Got back to Hove 4 o'clock and washed. The attendant was talking down religion &c so I tackled him with the Holy Spirit strong within me and won the victory and stilled his tongue. Had tea at SC Gunnery. Had to wait a long time through the slowness of a thick but good-looking waitress.

APRIL

4th Father came in at six o'clock and cried, said he was mad and would have no more drink.

7th Went direct to Annie's. Miss Lydall there to tea and when I arrived at 7.50 they were conversing in the dark over the tea things. Spent a musical evening then went for a walk down E. India Rd.

8th… Bob trying to go to S.A. as a clerk.

12th Father & Dena went to Ted's but he was out. Ted had gone to the Zoo.

14th Annie spoke to Mrs. K about having me to lodge with them. She did not object.

15th Annie spoke to Mr. K. and he poo-poohed the idea as there was no room.

16th Had a letter from Bob saying he had been accepted and had signed on and was at Woolwich A.S.C. (Army Service Corps). Wanted 5/- as he had no money. Annie came down and was surprised to hear about Bob. Bob came in about 11. Mrs. Rose gave Bob £1 so Bob repaid me. Told Vinnie that she could have my piano for £6.

The departure of Sibley's younger brother Bob to South Africa with the Woolwich Army Service Corps proved to be a heroic yet short-lived affair - the Boers surrendered but a few weeks later on May 31st.

The Second Boer War, 1899-1902, was a costly imperial enterprise involving imperial troops from Australia, Canada, India and New Zealand as well as British. By its end Britain had spent £200 million, lost 22,000 troops and more than 400,000 horses and mules. In many ways a bitter rehearsal for the Great War, only Britain's technological might took it to victory over the guerilla tactics of the Boers, plus a scorched earth brutality that prefigured the 'total war' of the 1939-45 conflict.

19th Caught 2.19 Moorgate St. to Hendon and got to Aunt Polly's about 4. Visited my cottage and found agent (Alfred) in a pub, being directed there by his niece. He was boozy but had a chat with him.

24th Man came round and saw piano, asked him £8. Told Mrs. K Albert may not have piano. She thought it mean. Heard that Mr. Harrington was leaving & I was to take over some of his journeys.

25th Mr. - came round and said his brother would not take piano as it was iron-framed. Mr. Clarke decided to buy bureau and drawers off father for 30/-. Told Albert he could probably have piano but it would probably be £7.

26th Told Vinnie Albert could have piano for £6 10/- and he could take it away when he liked.

27th Thanked Mr. & Mrs. K for offering me a room.

29th Spoke crossly to Will about leaving Dena alone in house.

30th Will moved out at 6.15 to 18 Teviot St. Albert collected piano and took glass and picture for me & left at Mr. K's. Father sold 6 chairs, a carpet & a rug, which were taken away. Harry & Bertha came. Annie sorting out odds & ends. Dena went to Bertha to stop for a night or two. Mrs. K said she would charge 12/-.

MAY

1st Took some small things to Annie's. Caught 10.47 home. Place in a great muddle.

2nd Annie and I went to Commercial Rd., Collins, and saw desk. Ordered it, £2 17/- 6d., paid 5/- deposit… Bertha wild about Will asking her to mind Dena for a week.

The travails of young Dena - the daughter of Sibley's dissolute brother Will - were only just beginning.

4th Father and I alone in the house. Had a mutton chop each.

6th Aunt Emma and her son-in-law came with a truck and took away all she could get. She took a fancy pepperpot off mantleshelf when no one was looking. I wrote to ask her to return it at once. Carman came and cleared off a lot of father's rubbish, couch &c.

The casual purloining of relatives' property may resonate with many; yet the idle pocketing of a pepper-pot by his Aunt had not escaped the gimlet eye of the shrewd Sibley.

7th … took a few things in a bag to S.B. My desk came and it is liked very much.

Friday 9th. Bob's farewell. Harry, Will, Ted, Father, Li, Bertha, Annie & I, there and wished him success. Father got muddly.

So, a mere two weeks prior to the surrender of the Boers, young Bob Sibley embarks for South Africa. And Thomas himself was on the move - slightly closer to home, in that he was disembarking to St. Leonard's Rd., Poplar, the house of his sweetheart's family.

12th Told Reeves to move my things tomorrow. Father and Mr.

Barby made a muddle of business and neither knew what the other was doing.

12th WENT TO MY NEW HOME. Bromley & Poplar journey, 4 orders. Hurriedly did work and packed up my property and generally prepared for removal. Reeves moved my things when I was out. Annie and I went to SB by train to get there before furniture. Annie left her umbrella in Bow so had to go back for it. Reeves did not turn up, so went in search and found him in St. Leonard's Street by Bromley Station. Got things in alright. Chest of drawers knocked about and glass broken. Paid Reeves 4/-6d. No 15 helped to get things upstairs &c. Had a good night's rest in my new home.

191 St. Leonard's Road, Poplar today is one of the few remaining Victorian stretches in an otherwise re-developed neighbourhood. Mr. Kettley's barbershop would have been situated downstairs front of course, and the young Thomas Sibley's bedroom would have been upstairs, along the landing and a suitable distance from his fiancée Annie.

14th … caught 8.45 train to Bow and saw Father, Will, Harry & Bertha coming out of Father's new home.

19th Whit Monday Bank Holiday. … Mr. K. & I went for a walk to Greenwich Park and Blackheath. Visited Naval Picture Gallery, & returned home by ferry & rail.

29th … got to 811 2.30 and and found Mr. Lister there showing instruments as arranged. Learnt some valuable information about sundry instruments. WJP told us some bad news about the firm.

31st PEACE DECLARED. (Treaty of Vereeniging).

By 1902, the British had crushed the Boer resistance, and on May 31st of that year, the Peace of Vereeniging was signed, ending hostilities. The treaty recognized the British military administration over Transvaal and the Orange Free State, and authorized a general amnesty for Boer forces. Sibley's brother and chum Bob arrives at an apposite moment:

JUNE 1st … Bob arrived in Cape Town.

2nd … People in a hilarious condition on account of peace. Another 'Mafeking' in the City. Numerous fights in Poplar in consequence of the 'merry' surroundings.

3rd … people still 'upset' over peace, and little boy processions numerous.

Crowds throng Mansion House in London to celebrate the surrender of the Boers in May 1902.

8th… Peace thanksgiving at St. Paul's - King &c.

10th Vinnie's baby George pulled my cocoa on top of him and stung his face badly, but nothing serious.

11th… Barking & Grays journey. Grays children's fete on.

12th Annie & I went to Harry's (63 Harrowgate Rd.) in evening, arriving there about 8.40, stayed an hour. Had a look at Harry's garden, which is very good and large.

14 Annie & I went to Leytonstone & saw Ted & Li.... Ted & I had an interesting chat about worldliness.

16th.... went direct to GAH to Sunday School Anniversary. The Duchess of Warwick gave away the prizes. My class had 6 prizes.

Sunday Schools were a rich thread of social and spiritual engagement from the late eighteenth century until the 1970s, when they all but vanished, or morphed into after-church children's activities. Set up originally as a means of providing education and food to poor children in urban centres in the 1780s, like much of the voluntary sector the movement had grown organically and locally until the Sunday School Society was founded in 1785 by Baptist deacon William Fox. Its progress was rapid - by the mid nineteenth century nearly half a million children were attending.

United Sunday Schools' Treat in 1921, in Crowland, Lincolnshire, England. Children and adults generally marched separately, singing hymns, accompanied by bands, banners and tableau, this ending at a location, often a local farm or significant business, where the children would sit for a special tea.

Funded by subscription, each Christian denomination fashioned their own version of 'Sunday School,' the Anglican becoming the basis of National Schools following the Education Act of 1870. Sibley became involved in Sunday Schools all his life. This was more than teaching scripture to young people - it was sports activities, drama and civic unity. Many alive today still remember the Sunday School parades of their childhoods at Whitsun, the plays and songs performed to locals, the trips to the seaside. Many football clubs still prominent today grew out of Sunday Schools.

One who had slipped through the social safety-net that organisations such the Sunday School provided was William Sibley, brother of Thomas, whose descent is painful to read:

16th contd.... Arr. home 4 o'clock, unfortunately met Will by St. Michael's church, intoxicated. Addressed a few impressive words to him & left him. Wrote him a strong remonstrative letter to turn, aid and encourage him. May God bless my letter to him & my prayers. ... ... Took stock of instruments. Annie helped me until nearly 11 o'clock.

19th ... Annie returned with some terrible news concerning father & Will. Annie visited Will's & found him intoxicated in his room. After finishing work I went to post, then went to Will's room and searched it but he was not in. Met him in street drunk. Gave him a strong talking to & walked him up and down Teviot Street. Gave him some soda. Went with him to his room & talked to him for half an hour. Prayed with him and left him in tears.

20th Father came round about Will and waited about for him. Will went out early and nothing has been seen of him since. Went to post and called at Will's, & accidentally met a Pearl Superintendent. He wants his money and books.

Sat. June 21st. HOLIDAY IN CROMER.

22nd Had a lovely walk in the country. Annie afraid of horses.

24th Had a long and most delightful paddle. Annie felt giddy at first but afterwards got used to it and thoroughly enjoyed it. Spent evening on cliffs and had some rollicking fun. Bad news about the King. No coronation.

Originally scheduled for 26 June of that year, the coronation of Edward VII had been postponed at very short notice because the King had been taken ill with an abdominal abscess that required immediate surgery. But royal matters were far from the young Sibley's mind as he holidayed on the north Norfolk coast with his lady-love.

25th Had a long walk through Northchupp's Avenue to Sidestrand, saw the landslip.

The landfalls at Overstrand near Cromer had clearly been famous for years, if not centuries, where locals and visitors would gather to watch the cliff collapses: remarkably, the British Geological Survey only began studying this erosion in 2001.

26th Had a letter from Ted with news from Will. The news was better than I expected. In evening Annie & I walked to East Runton. Saw the villagers keeping up the holidays with "overingbacks" & dancing.

27th Had my first swim and got into difficulties. Cut my feet and bruised myself on the rocks and stones.

The young couple's summer holiday was one of discovery in other ways than mere rambling, yet was not without its difficulties:

30th … went to ferns and rested. Had a spree together and enjoyed ourselves. After dinner returned to same place but.. were disturbed by two hulking yokels who were too curious. So we left our pleasant retreat. Saw Beacon Bonfire &c.

2nd Went through same woods (Runton) & on to the Roman camp. We found a nice cosy place in tall ferns and heather & had a splendid time. Special scenery was viewed with surprise especially by Annie. … both felt remarkably well.

3rd I went for a fast walk to Sheringham. Annie stayed indoors and trimmed Mrs. Lambert's hat.

5th Poppy and I went to Roman camp. … much better and lively… I nearly got torn up.

7th Adjourned to ferns and had a skippish time. Had a yokel watch us curiously from a bush nearby. … Went to Roman camp in afternoon and hid ourselves from the public, but I could see my Poppy. Back to tea with ravenous appetites.

12th Bade goodbye to Mrs. Lambert and journeyed to London by 2.35 in a corridor car. The lavatory came in useful. A fat farmer got on at Norwich & amused us. Arrived home at 7.20 and found Mrs. K in a deplorable state.

18th Will came to see me to borrow 6/- to pay rent &c. Has nothing to do and is of course half-stewed.

21st Monday. Will came round pennyless (sic) so I lent him 5/-. Poppy & I went to father's but found him out. Met him in Medway Rd. boozed. He was nasty and nearly abusive. Spoke against mother so I left him. Heard that Will was drunk Saturday night. I was upset. Looked about for Dena. Father saw us and came out again to us. Saw Dena and she said Dada had been drinking on Saturday. Called round at Will's but he was out. Poppy & I waited & saw him. Told him what we had heard. He denied it and told other lies. Discovered he is not a Christian and left him. Wrote to

Liza and advised her to give him up.

22nd Will came round for me to pray for him. As he had had drink and I knew he was lying, I was compelled to refuse. He admitted he was not converted and not saved. I told him all I could and he left.

23rd Met Will drunk in St. Leonard's Rd. & followed him nearly to E.India Rd. & then back to oil shop in Teviot St. Waited for him then had to stop him going in the St. Leonard's Arms. Will resisted but Poppy & I got him indoors. Poppy & I then returned home.

24th Poppy called at noon on Will's landlady and heard Will was always drunk, and had filled her up with abominable lies - somebody owes her £2 17/- he has paid no rent. The money I lent him he wasted on drink.

28th Poppy was in such agony she came into my room and got into my bed. Will came round and asked me to pay the rent but I refused.

29th Went to Dr. Dunlop's private house & while he got medicine Mrs. Dunlop played & Miss Dunlop sang 'Wipe those tears away.'

AUGUST

9th CORONATION DAY. Clacton-on-Sea... returned by 7.20, arr. home 10.20. Mrs. K. had too much of usual. People about drunk & mad. Plenty of illuminations.

11th Mr & Mrs. K., Arthur & Mr. & Mrs. Williams went for a drive to see the illuminations. Police would not let them through so they saw but little. On return about 10 o'clock the horse fell down. Mr. W. ran for his life. Mr. K. led the horse and Arthur pulled the trap to the owner. They got back about 3. Mrs. K & Mrs. Williams walked home from Limehouse.

While fanfares filled the streets, Mr. Kettley in his East End barbershop was entertaining himself and his customers with his new-fangled gramophone player.

Once again collective national joy swept the country as a new monarch was crowned. The Edwardian Age, though short-lived, created modern Britain.

24th … Mr. K. had his gramophone at work.

25th Mr. K. had to go round to Vinnie's in morning to get Arthur off stairs who was drunk and asleep. Vinne could not get down with baby. Arthur in an awful state, & sat swearing & cursing all the morning in Vinnie's kitchen. Poppy went round and had some. Vinnie upset & frightened out of her wits.

28 A friend of Mr. K's came in evening with Gramophone and plain wax &c for us to sing into. Mr. K., Arthur, 'guest,' Poppy & I sang. Had some fun. Heard our voices which caused great merriment. Got to bed late.

It is testimony to the speed and suppleness of late-Victorian and Edwardian manufacturing that an invention of a few years previous - that of recording on first tin-foil then wax paper, cardboard and finally cylinders - had by 1902 become a mass-market product available to many at low cost. Edison's first fumbling attempts in 1877 with his hand-cranked low-quality *'Mary had a little lamb'* warbling had a few years later become Alexander Graham Bell's more sophisticated wax roller, and with pre-recorded and 'plain' - ie. empty and recordable - cylinders cheaply priced and available, a new household entertainment had opened up: that of hearing one's own voice for the very first time.

SEPT.

Sunday 7th Piggott the impostor started his astounding claim that he is the Messiah, at the Ark of the Covenant, Clapton.

This is the extraordinary story of the deeply eccentric Reverend John Hugh Smyth Pigott, who along with his mentor the Rev. Henry James Prince (1811-1899) had founded a fringe and frankly depraved millenarian sect, first in Somerset and then London, involving Messianic prophecy and dubious sexual practices. In the evening service of Sunday 7th September 1902, at the 'Ark of Covenant' in Clapton, Pigott announced himself as the second coming of Jesus Christ and declared his predecessor Prince a harbinger for his coming, just as John the Baptist had been for Christ. His claim was reported in the newspapers, which created public curiosity and gave him the desired publicity. The service of the following week of the 14th of September attracted a large and mainly hostile crowd. Pigott was attacked and heckled inside the church. Thousands were heard yelling and uttering threats at him while he was escorted away by the police.

With apocalyptic rioting going on a few miles away in north Hackney, the Sibleys turned to their new gramophone for entertainment and distraction:

11th Arthur amused himself with gramophone in kitchen.

25th … went downstairs and sang into gramophone. I sang 'Blessed assurance.' Mrs. K. had a turn and did a little yelling. Plenty of fun.

If the drunkenness of his brother were not enough, Thomas now has to absorb the shock announcement from his dissolute father that he was going to marry a certain Mrs. Smith.

27th Went to Harry's in afternoon. Father, Dena, & Mrs. Smith there. Heard that father and Mrs. Smith were going to get married in about 3 weeks. I was surprised at such disgraceful news. Mother only been dead 7 months and I vainly looked for the love Father had towards her. I am certain that father, Harry, Bertha and Mrs. Smith will rue the day.

OCT.

2nd Mr. & Mrs. Weatherburn (Will's landlord and wife) came round and told us how Will had sold all his furniture for 30/- and decamped without paying her a farthing although he owed 28/- for rent. Popp and I went round and saw that he had left a sack of clothing & a lot of Dena's clothes and keepsakes, chair, stool &c. We had permission to go round one night and take away Dena's toys &c.

3rd Poppa and I went round to 18 Teviot St. and collected Dena's toys &c. Came back, put them into two bags and parcels, and took them to her at Bertha's. Found Harry, Bertha, Mrs. S., Dena & Pinky in the midst of a fried fish supper. Did not stay long.

The sad flight of Will Sibley from his problems left his young daughter Dena as the principal casualty, yet it is testimony to the kinship of the wider family that they rallied to help. Alcoholism has always destroyed families, so it would be invidious to portray the early twentieth century as more peculiarly prone to its deleterious effects than any other age: but what marks out the Edwardian response is that in the months ahead the Sibleys - particularly Thomas - never ceases to attempt to instil in his brother the template of personal responsibility. In Thomas' eyes, it is solely Will's fault and he is salvageable. Time would tell whether Thomas was correct.

9th Poppa had been looking at houses in Manor Park with Mary-Anne. Had a look at Popp's list of wants for our home… Poppa excited as she expects to be able to be married soon after Christmas.

10th Poppa and I visited Chrisp St., purchased a sheepskin rug & mat. Saw a nice carpet we liked at Neaves.

18th Mrs. K. gave us a white quilt as a wedding present. (In) Old

Street we ordered a suite of drawing-room furniture at Beadman's, £10.10/-.

Sibley's evident growing prosperity mirrored the nation's. Between 1875 and 1900 real income - for both working-class and middle-class British citizens - had risen by approximately a third. Working hours were still long - Saturday mornings were still part of the working week - but it is generally agreed that in the first decades of the twentieth century Britons of all classes had more disposable income than at any other time in history. This is baldly evidenced in the growth in the purchase of manufactured goods: people were buying more bicycles, pianos, newspapers, fancy goods, and more holidays were being taken. Notwithstanding Will Sibley's problems, overall there was a decline in the amount of income spent on drink.

For Sibley, house-purchase was a long way off, but his growing income as a dynamic travelling salesman meant that he and his fiancée could plan with confidence for an imminent wedding, and that meant furniture, décor, and clothes. But as the up-and-coming salesman prepared for his wedding and looked forward to a bright future, conversely the travails of the widowed William Sibley Senior were about to get worse.

29th Heard father had been moved about 3 weeks, and had last Saturday gone to Mrs. Lambert and asked to be taken back.

30th Father Died. (Only 8 months and 3 weeks after poor dear mother). About 8 o'clock in Victoria Park bathing lake poor old deluded father met his death by drowning. God have mercy on his soul.

31st Mile End journey, 10 orders, arr. Home 3.30. dined at Whites. Will here when I got home and told us terrible news of father. Father had been found drowned in Victoria Park bathing lake at 9 o'clock last night. Will still boozy. Gave him tea and a whigging.

Poppa and I went to Harry's and heard proper details. Father was not married to Mrs. Smith but had been on the drink. Yesterday morning he went out and took his bathing drawers (cut down pants) and a towel with him. He must have knocked about during the day and in the evening when dark went for his fateful bathe. His body was found near the diving board and his clothes were on the railings by the side. It appears to have been an accidental death and all I can hope is he looked to God before death choked him. Harry has had the trouble of viewing the body &c.

A great and sad blow.

FOUND DROWNED IN VICTORIA PARK.

Dr. Wynn Westcott held an inquiry at the Hackney Coroner's Court on Monday respecting the death of William Thomas Sibley, a carpenter and joiner, aged 58 years, who was found dead in the bathing lake at Victoria Park on Thursday night. Deceased formerly lived in Harrogate-road, South Hackney.

From the evidence of a son it appeared that deceased left home on Thursday between nine and ten o'clock in the morning, and never returned. He had been in the habit of bathing.

Edward Dyer, a London County Council constable, said he was on duty in Victoria Park on the 30th October. He was patrolling the lake at night, and saw a man's wearing apparel hanging on the railings. Thinking there was someone in the water, he went for assistance, and found a man in about five feet of water near the middle diving-board. Artificial respiration was used, and a doctor sent for. The man had a pair of bathing drawers on. A clean towel, which had not been used, was found near the clothes.

Dr. Hirst, of Victoria Park-road, deposed that death was due to drowning.

The deceased's son said his father had often told him that he could cross the Park at any time, and that he often had a "dip." He had lived in the neighbourhood about forty years, and knew every inch of the ground.

The jury returned a verdict of "Accidentally drowned while bathing."

The death of William Sibley in Victoria Lake, 1902.

NOVEMBER

1st. Poppa and I went to Harry's. We... perused father's papers &c. ... Inquest to be held Monday morning. Will of course boozy. He seems to be getting weaker in intellect. Poor father. I had hoped for a better end.

The death of the head of a family is often a time of unity and coming together. Sadly for the Sibleys this was not the case, for reasons of a certain insurance policy.

4TH. Went to Harry's... Bertha called me into her bedroom and asked whether Ted & I intended keeping our insurance money from father's policy. I said yes. She then started saying it was shameful and unbrotherly. I told her not to waste her breath as I did not countenance her interference and walked out.

It appears that only Thomas and his elder brother Edwin had taken out a life insurance policy in the name of their father. This was not to the liking of their brother Harry or - more significantly it seemed, to Harry's wife Bertha.

6th Thursday. Father's funeral. Had dinner & got ready. Caught 1.49 to Homerton. Funeral started 2.20. Very sorrowful & melancholy day. Poor father in his last resting place. Got back to Harrowgate Rd. 4.30. Harry spoke about Ted & my insurance and considered we were doing a shabby action & it was our duty. Did not agree with him, so left it as it was. Wrote Ted in evening and told him Harry's views, & sent him cheque (from Prudential) to cash. Ted left funeral at Stratford. Royal Standard requires all our signatures, will not pay Bob's until they hear from him.

After the funeral, the division of the assets:

8th Saturday. ... caught 4.30 train to Harry's. Ted & I set to work and divided father's things. Of the principal things Will had 'watch,'

Ted 'chain,' Harry 'bedroom glass,' I 'father's bed,' Bob 'clock.' After dividing tools Harry mentioned money but Ted & I would not share policy, but took no part in other divisions. Will, Harry & Bob had £3.5/- each. Harry of course not satisfied. Bertha bad friends with me. I took home some tools and got back to S.B. 11 o'clock. Told Popp I expected to be back about 8 so Popp was very cross.

10th ... we drew lots for mother's two rugs.

20th ... Popp & I went to Leytonstone & saw Ted& Li. Li informed us of a few of Bertha's thoughts and remarks which were not very flattering to Popp or me.

26th Will came round and asked me to sign a paper to have father's tools sold, and of course asked for a loan. He said he wanted a license for peddling, and that he had purchased some jewellery. I promised to buy him a license if he showed me some of the jewellery but would not give him a penny.

Peddling was the life and blood of the streets of London and had been since medieval times. Indeed, the city's first shops were in essence street-stalls, with goods tumbled out onto the pavements and only taken inside at night. For centuries every market-place and highway in the capital, and across the country, were full of the cries of the hawker, huckster, higler, chapman, packman, or costermonger, selling anything from ice-cream to crumpets. Since 1225 a license had to be obtained, and still to this day it is a requirement.

29th ... Popp & I walked down Mare St. then took a tram to B.G. (Bethnal Green) Rd. Had a chat with Herbert at the shop in BG Rd. where he works. Inquired the price of a fender. Saw plenty of Rabbis. Will came at tea-time and I gave him 5/- for license.

DECEMBER

5th.... Popp & I went to Vespers & C. in evening and booked bedroom suite £10.15/-.

18th. Went to Leytonstone & visited Ted. Mr. Digby came and we had a long chat on Roman Catholicism &c as our views differed. Mrs. K helpessly drunk & had to be put to bed by Mr.K.

23rd. Bromley & Poplar journey. Saw man at Cardale's with a fractured skull.

25th Christmas at Ted's.

26th After dinner Popp & I had a walk to New Oxford Street.

New Oxford street, London, 1903.

In an early act of development as social engineering, New Oxford Street in London's West End, was built between 1844 and 1847, partly to break up the St Giles rookery, a notorious slum, by demolishing some of its most obnoxious alleys and tenements. Prior to its construction it had been *'one dense mass of houses, through which curved narrow tortuous lanes, from which again diverged close courts... The lanes were thronged with loiterers, and stagnant gutters, and piles of garbage and filth infested the air.' (John Timbs, Curiosities of London).* In its place rose this splendid thoroughfare of temples to shopping:

30th. Had a surprise! The first wedding present. Helena sent us a handsome dinner service. Wrote & thanked her and sent a bottle of perfume. Mrs. K nasty about it, evidently jealous. Mrs. K had too much of course and was not pleasant, so we beat a hasty retreat upstairs. Packed service in box in my room.

31st. BANNS PUT UP.

1904

Sibley's journal of 1903 is missing - a momentous personal year in that he and Annie (Poppy) were married. As 1904 commences we find Sibley and his elder brother Edwin (Ed) attending a further education college in the City, studying a range of subjects from science to Greek.

In the wider world through 1903 Edward VII had been proclaimed Emperor of India, the government had rejected the idea of imposing penalties for drink-driving, and in certain corners of London rebellious ideas were beginning to stir: at a congress in the capital the Russian Social Democratic Party split into two faction, the Bolsheviks being led by an obscure malcontent called Vladimir Lenin; and while in Manchester Emmeline Pankurst was founding the suffragette movement, Polish-French chemist Marie Curie was awarded the Nobel Prize.

Momentously, across the Atlantic two brothers called Orville and Wilbur Wright had made the world's successful flight in a petrol-powered aeroplane. As the world improved, so in his own way did Sibley. Having left school at 13 - as was the normal age for the working and lower-middle class - he nevertheless possessed a thirst for knowledge which drive him to enrol with his elder brother Edwin in a further education college in the City of London.

The momentous flight of the Kitty Hawk, the first sustained flight by a manned heavier-than-air powered and controlled aircraft, Dec. 17th 1903.

JAN

4th … Did work and went to College.

5th …Went with Popp to Pummell's Temperance entertainment.

6th … A spritualist who often goes to Ridley Hall (London City Mission), Upton Lane, asked if I could prove Christ's virgin birth. I declined to argue with him.

26th Popp, Li & I went to Leytonstone to look over a house.

FEB

Feb 1st Went to college and returned to Manor Park with Ted & the Fotheringhams. Sang in the train. Gave a tract to a girl on the train.

6th. Ted moved to Leytonstone. Went to Ted's new home and gave them a minor help. Li (Ed's wife) *does not like the new home.*

13th Went to W.J.P's (Petty's) and there had lessons on splints and trusses &c. WJP wrote saying my appearance was not so smart as heretofore.

16th Did examination... could not finish when time limit was up.

20th Sent order for 5cwt of coals - 20/- South Yorkshire Coal Co., 741 Romford Rd.

Coal was the lifeblood of the nation's energy. Sibley paid the equivalent of £97.00 for his 5 hundred-weight of coal, which for the majority of the populace coal was delivered by a vast network of horse-drawn and - later - motor lorries.

Coal - the lifeblood of the nation.

27th Saw P.W. Howard's lecture on the advantages of the knowledge of Greek. We went and ordered a bookcase & coal-vase from Roberts &c.

MARCH

5th Roberts sent bookcase & coal-vase. Went to Greek class 6-7.

While Sibley ploughs forward in his purchasing, there are rumblings at the offices of W.J. Petty Pharmaceutical Wholesalers where he works:

13th WJP expects there to be an alteration in travel for firm. WJP would engage a qualified man to do all the county journeys and London would be divided in four. Took Popp for a short walk in E. Wanstead to look at empty houses. Went to Greek class.

16th RECEIVE NOTICE TO LEAVE. WJ Petty gave me notice to leave. Was a surprise - but praise the Lord he knows and hath prepared.

A bombshell for anyone at any time, losing their job, But Sibley forges on regardless, wasting no time in pursuing other avenues beyond W.J. Petty's.

17th Wrote to Easterham for a YMCA secretaryship.

18th Ted sent me C&J supplement and I wrote after two places.

21st Saw Mr. Ettman and stayed to dinner at the Mildmay Medical Mission to Jews. Many doctors promised to give me orders if I represent another firm. WJP wrote and said I'd better finish on Thursday and he would settle up by giving me £25 (rate of £42 a qtr).

24TH FINISHED WITH WJP PETTY. In Daily Telegraph saw advert for a representative in India, to represent ceramics. 3rd advert. It seemed to flash across me that this is the Lord's way of taking me to the foreign field. Wrote to Warrington after the appointment.

25th Had a letter from Corbyn Stacey & Co. to call and see Mr. Stacey at 11.30-1.30. Took Popp with me and saw Mr. Stacey at 2 o'clock. Wanted £150 plus £4.10/- a week expenses. Left it with him. Went and saw Mr. WJP and settled with him - £25. We parted good friends.

Here is a confident young man who knows what he wants and who lays down his demands surely and straightforwardly to a potential employer. Sibley's request for £150 per annum was the equivalent in 2023 of £14,599 - not a fortune, but more powerful in real terms than today. It is testimony to the near-full employment that existed that there were plenty of positions to go after in the clerical/sales sector; Britain was producing roughly 40% of all world manufacturing, and it needed armies of people to sell the products. Sibley follows up his applications with a personal act of symbolic renewal:

26th Had a good clear out - burning papers, clearing out desk &c.

APRIL

7th Li gave me a note from Ted saying Aird had died and there was a vacancy.

8th Went to Davy Hill & Co. in morning. ... Nothing decided yet because of no time.

9th Heard from Crossfields & Co. saying there was no vacancy and they had decided on their representative for India. Went to Greek class.

16th Saw Mr. Millard (at CJ Hewlett's) at 11.15. He offered to start me @ £2.2/- per week to do my connections and take over other ground. Left it until next Thursday before deciding. Wrote to 9 firms during afternoon.

Hewlett's was but one of dozens of manufacturing chemists

and wholesalers that had sprung up in the second half of the nineteenth century as a result of the huge advances in pharmaceutical treatments for illness. Many of those earlier foundational companies exist today - Pfizer, Merck, Glaxo - that began as small family enterprises in the USA, Europe or modest laboratories in London backstreets, with warehouses backing onto canals. Since Thomas Beecham established his drugs factory in St. Helens in 1859, and Wellcome and Burroughs opened their offices in Snow Hill in 1880 and their first factory in Bell Lane Wharf in Wandsworth, Britain became a major force in the industry - a far cry from the poky little apothecaries and medicine shops of the early 1800s.

The Royal Pharmaceutical Society had been founded as far back as 1841 but regulation was minimal, and it was not until 1908 with the Poisons and Pharmacy Act that the industry that Sibley worked in all his life was monitored with any legal strength.

Monday 18th ... Found that Vinnie had been confined on Sunday. She has a beautiful nurse.

19th Received telegram from Ted saying go up and see Davy Hill & Co. I went and interviewed Mr. Jacks and Mr. Hill about 3 o'clock. Popp went with me. They said they would write tonight and let me know.

20th PRAISE THE LORD. 'He remembered his promise.'

Had a letter from Davy Hill in the morning saying they offered me the job at £125. I went and accepted the appointment. Got some samples and looked about generally and had a chat with Collins &c., and got prices from Charlie. Ted & I went and bought a bag for me at Beauforts, 10/11d. Left at 4.20 and went to Hewletts. Thanked Mr. Millard for his kindness.

The firm of Davy Hill & Co. had an illustrious history, reaching back to the eighteenth century: 1755 and 1760 respectively, the firms of A. S. Hill and Son, and Davy, Yates and Co, combined in Davy, Hill and Co. Once he has his foot in the door of his new employers, Sibley is off like a greyhound from the slips. Fired up by his faith and the dynamic doctrine of self-help, he starts a new - and long - chapter in his life.

Thursday 21st April FIRST JOURNEY FOR DAVY HILL & CO.

Plaistow journey, 3 orders, arr. home 4.30. Did work then went to Ridley; Mr. Haslett spoke on South America.

22nd ... Popp had a woeful tale of those at Poplar, asked to have Georgie for a week & consented.

23rd .. Wrote out a list of my customers to have circulars sent. Went to Greek class.

Sunday 24th... Mr. K and Albert brought down Georgie at 5.

26th Grays & Southend 5 orders. Harding at Grays and Butler at Southend. Exciting competition. 'If God is for you, who can be against you?' Got on very well.

MAY

8th. Sunday. Had class in chapel. Missionary from Madagascar here.

11th Went to the Chemist's Exhibition.

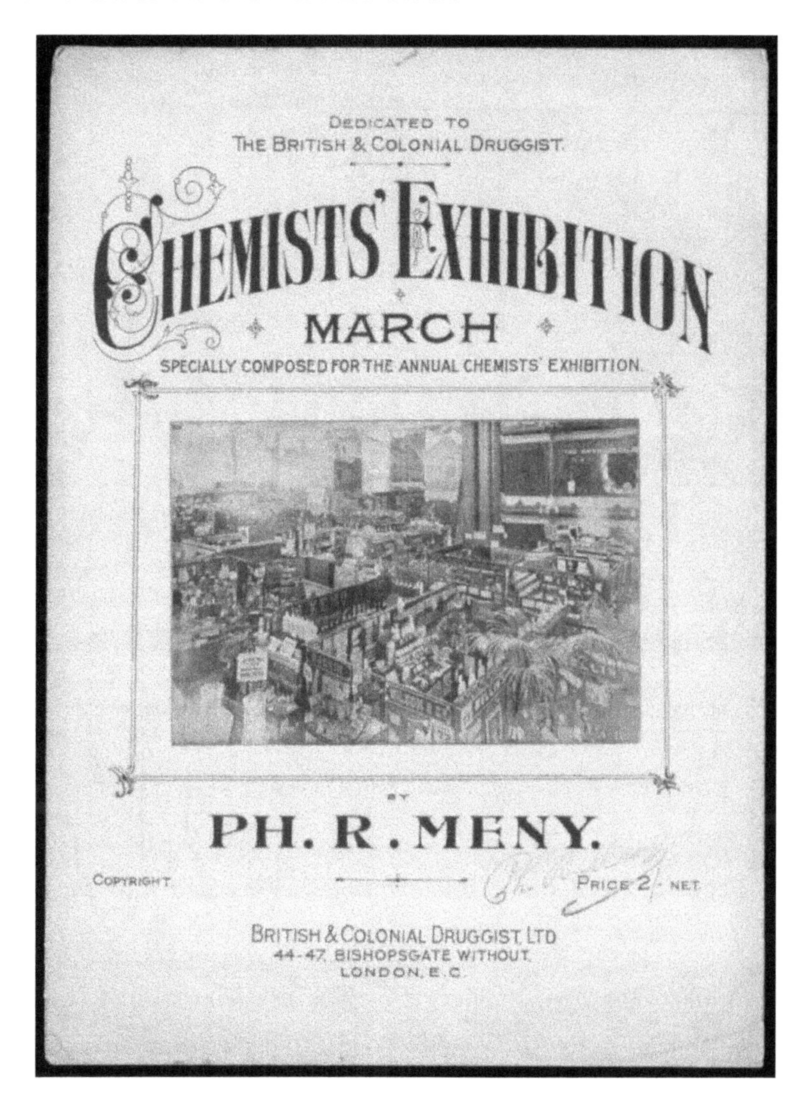

The Chemist's Exhibition became a lavish annual affair, a demonstration of industrial and retail might, one which even merited its own specially-composed march. Sibley's new firm, Davy Hill & Co., would have had a stand proudly situated among the hundreds of others.

21st Holiday. 9.20 London Bridge to Hastings. Walked round the town and secured lodgings at 10 High St., Mrs. Newbury. Didn't care for the appearance of them - very worldly.

Hastings in the early twentieth century was already a bustling holiday resort.

22nd Whit Monday. Had a walk on cliffs and visited Castle Caves. Popp nearly had a fit in the caves.

26th Received rent from Mr. Alford £5. The council did not require any of my land.

JUNE

22nd Popp taken ill (as if a miscarriage). Wired to firm saying I could not do journey to Bayswater.

23rd In morning I went to Mary Anne's to ask her or Mabel to run round for a girl, names and addresses given from Registry Office. After some bother a girl from registry office was sent. We engaged her - sleep out - @ 3/- per week. 24 Cranmer Avenue, East Ham.

28th Popp gave Florrie notice to leave.

The army of domestic servants in the employ of the upper-middle and upper classes in this period is well known: what is less known is that the working classes and the lower middle also had recourse during the early twentieth century to a 'live in maid.' In Sibley's case he employed the services of Dr. Barnados, the charity for orphaned children, part of whose mission was to assist their charges into secure employment on reaching maturity: this often meant manual work for boys, and domestic service for girls.

JULY

6th Went to Tent Mission and heard Mr. Olney and Mr. Spencer Johnson the converted comedian.

After experiencing a 'worldly' landlady in Hastings, the Sibleys have better luck in Littlehampton where they spend their August Bank Holiday weekend.

Littlehampton beach, 1905.

Saturday 30th. Caught 10.20 to Littlehampton. Secured lodgings with a Christian lady. After tea we strolled about the town. Popp bought a blouse.

AUGUST

1st Went to sea and after a lot of waiting managed with a nice young fellow to secure a bathing tent (full of holes). Popp disappointed because of not having shrimps. Caught 7.50, arr. Home 12 o'clock.

2nd I had some oysters for supper.

7th Went to Leytonstone. Spent most of time speaking to an old soldier (not in age) who had come down through drink.

9th … Bob & Bessie came to tea and stayed all evening. Amused ourselves all evening with Ludo &c. Bessie is fair and about 19. Her people are in America.

11th .. Went to Walthamstow & on the way spoke to Mr. Morgan whom I knew at Speyer Schwardt & Co., 13 years ago.

12th … Met Butler at Grays who apparently thought it a shame I was discharged. Told me that Harding (my successor) had been sacked.

Sunday 21st Went with Popp to King's Own Mission Essex Rd.

30th Tues. Arr. home 6.30. Dena waiting about for us & Will at Woodgrange Park Station. Dena went for her father - he came - they had tea. Dena left (here) until Saturday when Will was coming for her. Dena occupied Sarah's (who is to come) bed.

SEPT

3rd. Will came to dinner as asked but as he was not going to take Dena away I did not let him do stamps as mentioned. He wrote my advices. Will went after tea. Sarah Colvin was brought here in afternoon by a lady.

It seems that reaching out to assist his alcoholic brother Will was still an option for Thomas, as he apparently offers him piecemeal work for cash, and looks after Will's daughter Dena. The Sibley's had evidently just employed a live-in maid Sarah Colvin, so Sibley was evidently doing well in his new position at Davy Hill's. But family troubles are not far from the surface, as it becomes clear that Will is unwilling to provide as a father and take care of his daughter.

7th. Heard that Davy Hill's had received the army contract.

8th… Finished writing my essay, 'Study the Scriptures.'

10th Sent Dena to Hampstead and went to Seven Kings. Will sent Dena back.

12th Will here concerning Dena. I told him he must take her away… Will went, without Dena. (Will) Asked Annie - Poppa - for 6/-, unsuccessfully.

13th Tuesday. Li & Popp took Dena to workhouse Leytonstone but were told that an order had to be give by the Relieving Officer, 285 Shrewsbury Rd., & then she would be taken to Hampstead, Will found, and be made to pay 5/- per week or prison.

Workhouses in Britain in 1904 were a refuge for the homeless and destitute, providers of ample, if austere and manual, employment; and free healthcare for pregnant women and all in need. It was a last resort, to be sure, and Sibley's intention to leave Will's daughter in the workhouse was very probably meant to deliver a potent message to the neglectful father. But settling Dena in proved more tricky than they might first have thought, as there was some doubt as to the borough she resided in, Will obviously having engaged in a flight from his rented accommodation in Hampstead. Thomas, together with his brother Ed and his wife, set out to track down their errant sibling.

14th Relieving Officer came & inspected Sarah's bedroom &c. He advised me to take her (Dena) and leave her at Will's address or see the relieving officer at Hampstead.

17th Saturday. Took Dena to Hampstead - met Ted, Li, Winnie at Leytonstone on Station. We went to 26 Fleet Rd., Kentish Town, a paper shop where Will had letters sent. We then went to Hampstead workhouse, saw porter & attendant, and was directed to the private address of the relieving officer, Wheatley - 40, Well Walk. Saw him, who told us to apply at Manor Park. We however sent Dena to the workhouse and came home.

The forbidding entrance to the former Hampstead workhouse. This is the alleyway Thomas Sibley and his brother would have trod as they attempted to find accommodation for their niece, Dena, on Sept. 17th 1904. (Attr. Ceridwen).

Admission to workhouses was the rung below going 'on the Parish,' which was a welfare provision by Poor Law Guardians: before claimants were given tickets to exchange for essentials such as bread, milk and margarine, applicants were subjected to rigorous means-testing, with officials visiting their homes to ensure that all objects of value had been pawned.

Once in the workhouse, inmates were clothed in baggy brown or grey uniforms; husbands were separated from wives, and only allowed to eat together on Christmas Day. Cleanliness was a huge obligation in order to avert disease - hence the huge boiler-house chimney in the above picture of the workhouse at Hampstead. Despite widespread condemnation, workhouses persisted right up to 1929, when the Dickensian 'Poor Law Guardians' were replaced, and their duties taken over by the rather less forbidding County Councils.

Inmates at Crumpsall Workshouse, 1895.

24th Saturday. I went to office at request of Mr. Hicks. I (was) told that Symonds had accused me of spreading tales of his failures &

that he was leaving &c. I repudiated same.... Mr. Hicks said he did not believe that I would do such a thing.

29th (At Chapel) had a long chat with a man named Jim Bull, who would not decide because of his mates. He works at the G.E. railway with Syd Smith. I went and found Nigger who lost himself in Halley Rd.

30th Catford journey, 8 orders, arr. home 7.30, two hours late. Popp in tears - thought I was lost or killed.

OCTOBER

14th Gave Sarah (housemaid) a talking to for standing on my desk.

Sarah was not the only one to cause trouble in the Sibley household in the autumn of 1904 - their dog had to be put down:

17th Nigger taken to Wardale's to be poisoned.

But was this the end of the redoubtable hound? Apparently not.

18th. Heard that Wardale had not poisoned Nigger... he had got out of their garden and gone.

26th Ed Baptized. Praise the Lord.

NOVEMBER

6th Sunday Popp, Sarah & I went to Pritchard's Congregational Church. I took the sacrament.

The Sibley's social life mainly revolved around their church-going, but dinners with friends at home was not uncommon. Mr. & Mrs. Creed were to prove regular dining companions, along with their son Leslie, who clearly took a shine to the

Sibley's new maid, Sarah.

29TH … Mr. & Mrs. Creed & Leslie here to supper. Leslie & Sarah were fast friends.

DECEMBER

8TH … Met W.C. Potter on his bicycle in Kingsland Rd., had a nice chat.

Weds 21st… Took Christmas presents to K.C. Hoop at St. Peters. Too foggy to do evening journey.

23rd. Popp & I bought a turkey in Green Street. Afterwards I went to Studs and purchased a bottle of ginger wine.

25th Sunday School. Mr. Server spoke then hurried away to death bed.

29th Went to Mr. K's in evening and took some Christmas pudding. Received some in return.

31st. Popp & I went to Stratford and bought a small clock, 6/-6d, for John & Emily as a wedding gift.

1905

JAN

8th Sunday… Went to B.G (Bethnal Green) workhouse with Will Warwick. Visited Poplar workhouse with S.Smith & his young lady.

11th Sent off my paper to Christian Community Memorial Hall. Saw Ted at office. Called in at the Royal Free Hospital.

12th John & Emily came to tea, also Li, Ted, Bob. Bob visited D.H & co and secured himself a berth £80 p.a. Bob had to listen to a spiritual conversation. However he enjoyed his tea and we prayed for him before leaving for Harry's.

13th Friday. Went to Scripture Research Society meeting at 68 Fleet Street, arriving 3.30. Mr. P.W.H's paper read.

19th. Hoxton journey. Sarah had a "stupid" day - evidently not well - a cold. Met Trussell near Dr. Arthur... had a chat about things in general. W.J.P is working one short. Trussell doing fairly well.

23rd. Hornsey journey. Met Arnold (of Mallinsons) at New Barnet. He is travelling. Arrived at College too late for 'Logic' lectures. Had tea in Lyons.

FEB

5th Sunday. Went with S. Smith & his girl to Poplar Workhouse. I spoke and had a blessed time.

7th Whilst at Wardales got Jones to pull out a molar (upper). The Lord answered prayer according to Ephes. III 20 & His presence and grace was so manifested that I felt neither pain nor nasty sensation - I was filled with praise and joy.

10th Friday. Went to Scriptural Research Society conference... St. Thomas' church Westminster. Mr. Mercer there - he of course got mixed up in controversy - on particular redemption.

22nd... Went to Albert Hall via Hyde Park to hear Mr. Torrey & Mr. Alexander. Too crowded so went into the top balcony, but could practically see and hear nothing. Returned disappointed. Spiritualistic journal 'Two Worlds' given to us outside the Hall, caused much amusement.

Visits to huge evangelical events became over the years a staple of Sibley's social engagements. Reuben Archer Torrey was a writer, pastor and evangelist from Hoboken, New Jersey; in 1902–1903, he preached in nearly every part of the English-speaking world and with song leader Charles McCallon Alexander conducted revival services in Great Britain from 1903 to 1905. Charles McCallon Alexander was a native of East Tennessee, was a popular nineteenth-century gospel singer who worked the evangelistic circuit for many years.

TORREY-ALEXANDER MISSION, ROYAL ALBERT HALL.

Over the course of his ministry he toured with R. A. Torrey and John Wilbur Chapman, most notably. When Sibley watched him sing in Febrauary 1905 McCallon had not long been married to Helen Cadbury, daughter of the Cadbury Chocolate Company president. She toured with him on the evangelistic circuit and together they spread The Pocket Testament League around the world.

It is clear that the cultural current along which Sibley was being drawn was the swift stream of purpose-driven Christianity. There were many other cultural currents at work at this time, of course - political, ideological, scientific, humanistic: but these were currents outside the everyman's orbit. As an antidote to the relative squalor and deprivation in which he found himself as a youth, he had settled firmly on religion; a deeply felt, interior engagement incorporating an almost austere sense of duty. This was perhaps the most visible and 'performed' solution evident to the poor in the East End.

There were fringe political groups - socialists, fledgling communists, even anarchists - who were offering alternative outlets to the disaffected in British urban society - but it was the peculiar nature of Britain's supple society and the flexibility of its establishment that these ideologies never took deep root or manifested in any particular political efficacy: they were largely dalliances of the intellectual classes. George Bernard Shaw - a leading member of the largely middle-class Fabian movement - expressed doubts that the new Left thinking - whether Marxism, Socialism, Fabianism, or the doctrines of the new Independednt Labour Party - would ever win over the British working classes. He was right. They never did.

Reuben Archer Torrey, 1856-1928 *Charles McCallon Alexander, 1867-1920*

This is not to say radical thinking made no headway: filtered through the main political parties, in particular the Liberals led by Henry Campbell Bannerman, major progressive social and economic changes were to be implemented in the ensuing years.

As for the cultural currents of art and literature, the Edwardian Age was a fulsome one of popular novels, magazines, and poetry. Across the English Channel there were disturbing rumblings of a new visionary Modernism: for now Britain remained relatively untouched by it, until perhaps the Post-Impressionist Exhibition in London in 1910 that introduced the New Art to an often bewildered populace.

Nevertheless, despite maintaining its roots in a somewhat conservative literary and visual culture, Britain in the first decade of the twentieth century was producing a fresh literature that has stood the test of time and which faced, in its own way, the modern world head on. The Edwardian age has perhaps unfairly been portrayed as an age of literary whimsy, escapism and fantasy - largely because of the huge shadow J.M. Barrie's *Peter Pan* casts, along with the imperial stories of Kipling and the first adventure stories of John Buchan. But there was a harder realism seeping into the cultural view of ourselves: late Victorians such as George Gissing had already embraced the emergent realism of French writers like Flaubert and Guy de Maupassant, and Somerset Maugham had taken up the baton of novel-as-realistic-depiction with *Liza of Lambeth* in 1897 and his later novels. H.G. Wells was moving away from his late-Victorian fantastical science-fiction masterpieces *The Time Machine* and *The Island of Doctor Moreau* to more social-historical portraits, *Kipps (1905)* and *The History of Mr. Polly (1910)*, and in 1905 John Galsworthy produced *A Man of Property*, the first of his mighty portrait of the twentieth century upper middle-class, *The Forsyte Saga*. The satires of Oscar Wilde had cast an influential shadow, and there were rumblings of a new style of realistic drama emerging with Harley Ganville-Barker's directorship of the Royal Court Theatre in London between 1904-1907, where he introduced the theatre-going public to the ice-cold radicalism and intellectual rigour of George Bernard Shaw.

The works of H.G. Wells, Bernard Shaw and John Galsworthy brought a harder-edged realism to Edwardian literature. Wells had moved away from science-fiction in Kipps and The History of Mr. Polly, Bernard Shaw was flourishing at the Royal Court, and John Galsworthy's first instalment of The Forsyte Saga - A Man of Property - was published in 1905.

All these currents cannot have passed Sibley by: working in the greatest capital city on Earth he cannot fail to have watched the first cinema billboards go up - Cecil Hepworth's ground-breaking short film *Rescued by Rover* was released in 1905 - and he was a regular visitor to the book-stalls round St. Pauls and the City. We will will learn later of his voracious appetite for literature, but as he establishes himself as a young newly-married man his energies and appetites are evidently focused on constructing an inner determination and purpose-driven life, one which he derives from his religion. He would become an avid visitor of galleries and purchaser of books from the famous Foyles bookshop, especially after it moved its poky quarters in Cecil Court to its brand new HQ in the Charing Cross Road, but in his twenties and early thirties he is - very much like the majority of the population - too busy earning a living to indulge in the dalliance of culture. Not out of snobbery or anti-elitism - he was, after all, enrolled in a college of Further Education - but out of simple animal necessity.

MARCH

1st. Heard from Eliza Poyser this morning asking me to take Dena for a short time. I wrote back at once and refused.

6th Ted moved to Rotherhithe.

13th Prizes distributed at College. Ted took 2 prizes for me and 4 for himself.

15th … Went to Chemist's Exhibition at Covent Garden Theatre, saw Petty & his brother, also… Rockford, Holloway & others.

18th Prince & Princess of Wales visited East Ham to open Technical Institute (College). Sarah allowed to go out to see them and stayed out all afternoon.

In 1891 the East Ham Local board formed a technical instruction committee to organize evening classes in chemistry, mathematics, the use of tools, building, cookery, shorthand, and 'ambulance'. In 1895 this committee appointed a full-time organizing secretary, and in the same year suggested the building of a technical institute. It was eventually agreed that this institute should be built beside the new town hall, and that the Essex county council, which had from the first been associated with the committee, should share the cost of it. As well as running its own evening classes the technical instruction committee provided scholarships for East Ham pupils attending secondary day-schools and evening classes outside the district, and the technical college, opened in 1905 by the borough council and the county council, was designed for use as a secondary day-school as well as an evening college. This college, which stood beside the town hall in Barking Road, included carpenters' and plumbers' shops, a building department, and a clinical laboratory. The first principal, W. H. Barker, had charge of both day and evening departments, and some of the teachers in the secondary school also taught evening classes.

23rd Met Mrs. Creed at Manor Park Station - she is living at 2 Second Avenue. She was in black - lost her mother and father-in-law. Mr. Creed is collecting the rates in this district. Popp started labour at 4 o'clock.

24th BABY BORN at 6.15pm. Woolwich journey 3 orders arr. home 6 o'clock. Popp in labour in night and grew anxious as nurse (Mrs. Scott) lived so far away. I went for her at 2.35 - called Sarah up to see to fire &c, and caught 2.56 to Maryland Point. Called nurse up at 3.10 and waited for her. We walked back home. Popp in hard labour. I laid down and snatched a few winks but practically had no rest. When I came back from journey Dr. McKettrick was in the house tending to poor Popp. I prayed earnestly for the deliverance. Praise the Lord he gave stringth and safety. After confinement Li came. Doctor had some tea with me... I went up and saw poor dear Popp and our fine boy. He is fat and looks well. Praise the lord for his love.

East Ham Technical College, built 1905.

Childbirth at home was a common affair in 1905, healthcare being very local and home-based. The birth of Sibley's first child, Leonard, has all the perennial hallmarks of births before and since; the anxiousness, the snatched naps, the bitten nails, the pacing. But factored in of course was the additional anxiety of maternal survival. In the period under consideration the maternal mortality rate was declining year on year but in 1905 it was still approximately 40 per 1000. The reasons for the mortality were multiple, mainly involving infection.

But with their newborn 'fat' and his wife 'getting on well,' much of that anxiety was thankfully dissipated on that momentous day in March 1905.

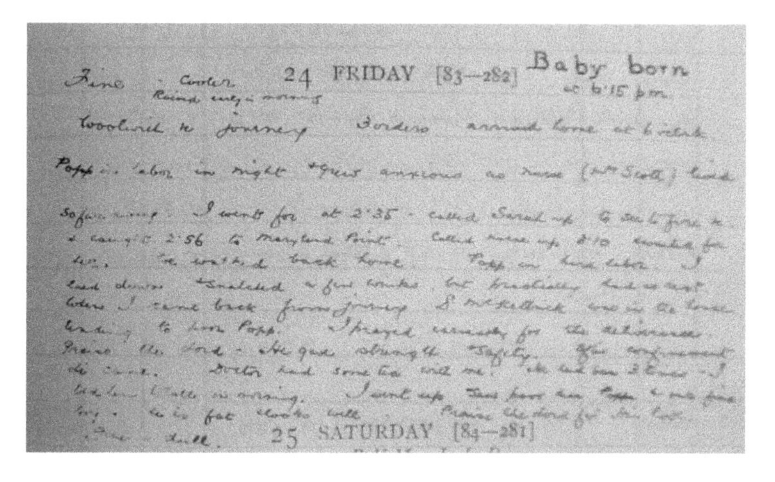

24 FRIDAY [83—282] Baby born at 6.15 pm.

25 SATURDAY [84—281]

25th Saturday. … Mrs. Moulton came in and saw Popp. Popp getting on well, and baby. I did a little digging and many odd jobs.

28th Mr. & Mrs. Kettley came in afternoon and stayed to tea. Popp received for baby 10/-, & nurse 2/-. I kept Mr. K. company most of the time.

29th Ted & Li came to tea. Baby had a long crying spell so did not make things very pleasant. Li brought babe a nice bib.

APRIL

6th … Helena came to see Popp. She stayed some time. Heard all about Fred and his wife, of their secret marriage and child. Helena gave a nice bib to baby.

8th… Popp in parlour today. Popp bought baby's bonnet, veil, cot &c. Having them sent - a selection.

21st I went to Mrs. Raiments at 12 Disraeli Rd., Romford for 'Ridley Hall' bath chair. Walked with Kathleen to Upton Lane. Got bath chair. … took Popp out in afternoon, and Sarah carried Leonard.

22nd … Bath chair gone. Mrs. Piddy came for it for her husband.

25th Gave kitten a dose of flea-powder.

28th … Visited Whitechapel Picture Gallery.

29th Saturday. Bought mail-cart at H. Haycorn.

MAY

2nd … Leonard very cross all day. Better in evening.

10th Had a chat with Miss Brook, Silchester Rd., who said she was choosing her husband. Had a long chat with Mr. J.C. Buske who preaches good works, although a vagabond.

22nd 'Open air' testimony to Jews. A noisy opposition.

23rd. Hertford & Ware, 3 orders. Country beautiful.

24th … Went to John Duncan's and stayed all evening. John's cockerel flew at Popp and lodged on her back. Popp screamed and very much upset.

29th Monday. After classes went into 'open air' Flower & Dean St. and started speaking to the Jews. Great opposition mostly from children & women. Stone &c thrown - many bruises. I got a stone on the forehead, and hat aimed at & knocked off. My silk hat a centre of attention for missiles.

Flower and Dean Street, Spitalfields, had been home to most of Jack the Ripper's victims.

By the first decade of the twentieth century Spitalfields in East London had become home to a large Jewish population. From 1881, mounting persecution in eastern Europe and Russia led to the arrival of thousands of Jewish immigrants. They made their way to tenement houses already occupied by a considerable Jewish working-class community. By 1901, parts of Spitalfields had a 95% Jewish population. The area around Flower and Dean Street contained a wide range of dwellings, from slum properties and cheap lodging houses to newly-built model housing for the poor. Connecting to Brick Lane in the east and to Commercial Street in the west, Flower and Dean Street was fronted along most of its north side by the flats of the Nathaniel Dwellings and along half of its south side by those of the Charlotte de Rothschild Dwellings. The religious needs of the residents were met by a wide range of places of worship within walking distance of Flower and Dean Street: from the grand Ashkenazi synagogue at Duke's Place in the City of London (destroyed in the Second World War) to the Great

Synagogue in Fournier Street, Spitalfields (once a Huguenot chapel and today a mosque).

Despite these places of Jewish worship Christian evangelicals saw the inhabitants of Spitalfields, Aldgate and in particular Flower & Dean Street, as ripe for conversion, which was why on a May morning in 1905 Thomas Sibley braved the understandably hostile Jewish crowds and took a stone at his silk hat for his troubles.

JUNE

14th … Babe still very ill. Popp in despair - faith seems only in name. Painters whitewashed ceilings in kitchen and wash-house.

16th. Woolwich journey. Saw a Lascar on top of a mast - he would not come down. I heard he had been up there for hours. Read next morning that he attempted suicide by jumping off into the docks.

'Lascars' was a term given to any sailor or crewman of Asian origin, mostly Bengali but also from Somalia and Yemen. A common feature of merchant ships for centuries, by 1891 there were 21,000 Lascars working on British vessels. While many British sea-captains made an effort to learn their language to give them instructions, treatment of these sailors was not always as it should have been, and some were exploited or abandoned at ports to fend for themselves. Was this the fate of the sorry Lascar Sibley saw that June morning, swaying atop a mast at Woolwich, an act of desperation at the brutal conditions of his employ? Had he heard he was to be let go, and was without a berth? Whatever the outcome of his despairing plunge into the Thames, many Lascars did end up being looked after in Christian charitable institutions in ports across Europe and Britain. We can only hope that this was the outcome of this sorry episode.

23rd*. Folkestone. Long walk on cliffs before breakfast. Climbed into a window of a disused fort and inspected the structure. I had my first swim. No bathing machines being used but a bathing-house with a safe enclosure for non-swimmers. … Sarah had a bathe after I had had my swim.*

24th *I put Leonard's foot in water. He cried.*

25th*… when I returned I found Leonard had had a fit. Had a nasty one in my arms after tea.*

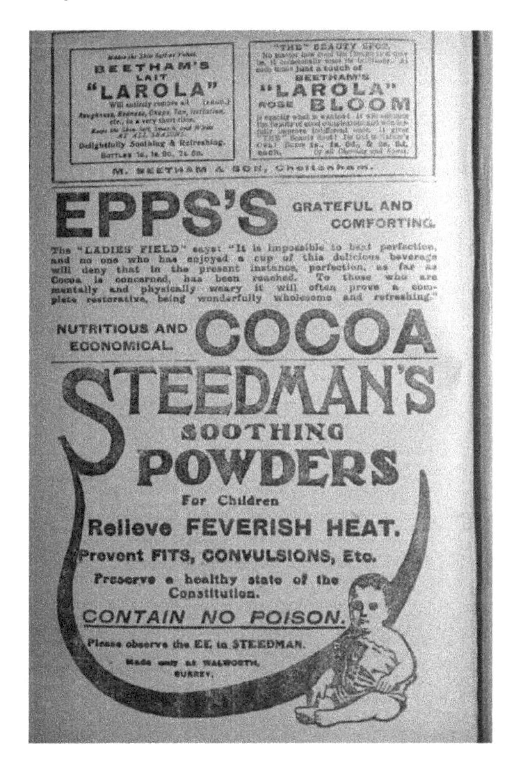

A medicinal advert from 1909 proclaiming cocoa as an antidote to children's convulsions.

26th*. Leonard very queer in night. He had some more fits during the day. Doctor sent for at 1 o'clock but as he did not turn up we took Leonard to see him in evening - S. Larkin, a customer of D&H & Co. He did not understand the case - prescribed Misc. Bromide &*

chocolate calories (?). Leonard did not have another fit - praise God.

27th. Popp lost her gold brooch - a present before marriage. Popp & Sarah found some small mussels on the iron work of the bathing-house. But in the enjoyment Popp carelessly left her gold brooch on the beach.

6th Li, Popp went to Ridley in evening. Sarah out for the evening. I looked after Leonard while they were out. Sarah came back - her Uncle escorting her - at 9.45. Her Uncle apologised for her lateness.

JULY

But Sarah's apology was not sufficient to assuage Sibley's high domestic standards, for the very next day -

8th. Sarah received notice.

He wastes no time in securing another live-in maid to assist in the household work:

13th. Mrs. Bond & Maud came to see (Popp) re. her situation. Sarah upset when she saw the new girl.

14th Bought a trilby straw hat in Woolwich. Sarah went after a place in Leytonstone and found it after an hour's search.

21st Maud Grover came & stayed with Popp during afternoon & some part of evening. Sarah had a day out at Miss Lister's garden party.

25th Tuesday. ... Brakes started for Trent Park Barnet - Mr. T. A. Bevan's estate. 7 brakes in all composed the party of the Christian community. Arrived at 12 o'clock and had an hour's look around before dinner. Mr. Bevan has a magnificent house & grounds... Had some cricket, then a row in the lake. Short open air meeting. Mr. Bevan spoke.

Trent Park House, Barnet.

Trent Park was a formidable country house outside London, domicile of the Sassoon and then the Bevan families. Perhaps its most extraordinary era was during WW2 when it became a prisoner of war camp - albeit a luxurious one - for captured German officers.

Seduced by the opulent surroundings and treatment received - well-stocked libraries, lavish food and a full staff of servants - the high-ranking Nazis were unaware they were being listened to by an underground eaves-dropping station in the mansion's basements. Largely staffed by German-Jewish emigres and refugees employed for their knowledge of German slang and colloquialisms, released documents in the 1990s revealed that the intelligence gathered at Trent Park resulted in British foreknowledge of the V2 rocket in both its development and whereabouts, thus preventing a catastrophic endgame in the German's favour.

AUGUST

3rd. Mr. Beck told me to leave umbrella in shop as it was wet and asked me to come inside. Mr. Umbrella maker nearby came in and stole it. Beck and I went to his shop but of course he denied it. Beck bought another for me for 2/-, promised to give me 5/-. Had a day's heart-searching from the Lord who shewed to me why He did not bless our marriage.

The Trent Park spies, listening to oblivious Nazi Officers in their lavish living quarters above. The intelligence gathered very probably led to a foreshortening of the war.

4th Maud Grovey came. Wired for Maud who came dinner time to stay. She worked well and place soon looked straight. Leonard not well so anything but a happy home.

7th Popp in bed expecting a miscarriage.

8th Popp very queer in bed, losing a lot of blood but no miscarriage.

Maud had a lot to do to see to baby &c.

9th... Popp against me, as the cause of the trouble. This makes matters worse.

10th Dr. Wright told me that if Popp had a bleeding Placenta, great care was necessary. Sometimes doctors recommend abortion as the quickest and safest plan.

The casual diagnosis that a termination may be the best course belies our perhaps too simplistic perception that before its legalisation in 1967 abortion was an underhand, secretive never-mentioned process. There must have been many doctors who practiced it for the health of their patients.

17th Hoxton journey. Had a vegetarian dinner - not a sufficiency.

18th. Holidays. Took Popp, babe and Maud to City. Leonard had a screaming fit in Lyons.

31st. We went to Purfleet by the 2.14. Visited the Botany.

SEPT.

1st. Train late coming home. Probably on account of the Great Eastern smash at Witham - Cromer Express.

2nd. Saturday. Popp upset because I would not go and get meat. A nasty cutting asunder of the spirit. (We) went to photographers to see photos of Popp & baby. Not good, so decided to have another sitting.

6th Mr. Howard wanted to see me at College Hall. I was offered a deaconship for the (proposed) church.

8th Went to college in evening. Mr. Howard told me of a report from Ilford concerning my preaching. Mr. P.W.H. said my special talent was for believers. I was to be careful of Keswick, mysticism

The aftermath of the train crash at Witham in September 1905, in which 14 died. With more people travelling by rail than ever in the nation's history, rigorous safety regimes were paramount in the age when the motor car was still a novelty.

10th Sunday School inaugurated. I am secretary.

21st Went to office in afternoon. Saw Mr. Hill. He spoke to me of my bad accounts. Got a sample of our Infant's Food.

25th Went for a walk with Popp in afternoon. Saw a house, 108 Shrewsbury Rd., to let, 10/-. Had a look. Popp liked it and wanted it, so we went to see the owner at Ilford, 49. Seymour Gdns. Landlady was out so left name & address. Had soda & milk at Ilford.

So in September the Sibleys are on the move again. Perhaps the new surroundings might serve to heal the rifts in their marriage. They have their eyes on Ilford, in 1905 still not the sprawling salubrious suburb it later became, but one upon which keen-eyed developers were beginning to focus. In many ways the huge tide of Victorian house-building was a step backwards: the eighteenth century housing in the early 'subarbes' of Richmond, Twickenham and Stepney, with their generous plots, spacious rooms and high ceilings, were what the suburban villas of the twentieth century aspired to recreate. In between those two eras was the rapid and monstrous explosion of the Victorian age, with its cramped quarters, single-skin walls, threadbare niggardly backyards, common pathways for tradesmen, and the constant sound of neighbours voices.

This is what the aspiring lower-middle and middle classes, with their increased incomes and their ambition, sought to escape. They wanted space, fresher air, better sanitation, and room to display the new grander furnishings they gazed at in the windows of department stores and furniture warehouses. But in many ways this bubbling demand was not yet being satisfied.

29th Mrs. Cooke called on Mrs. Rogers and got satisfactory references & then came to Popp and accepted us as tenants, leaving key.

30th Dug up flowers and took them to Shrewsbury Rd. and put them in the ground.

OCTOBER

3rd. Evening spent packing and taking some things round to Shrewsbury Road.

7th MOVED TO 108 SHREWSBURY RD. Chasebro' moved us.

9th Kept busy in evening laying linoleum.

17th ... Took a ginger-coloured stray cat from Creed's who had daily fed it &c.

18th The King in the Strand opened the new route to Oxford Street - Kingsway and Aldwych.

108, Shrewsbury Road, Forest Gate, London. The Sibleys moved here in Ocober 1905. Not quite the large suburban villa they aspired to, and more Forest Gate than Ilford, but they were slowly moving East.

19th Penny in slot gas laid on. ... Went to office and Mr. Hill mentioned to Ted about my general appearance, & not dressed smartly enough.

Found Popp had given away one my best boots for an ornament.

Had a short argument with one of the long-haired brethren in High Street, E.H. (East Ham).

NOV

6th Had a ride on tricycle with Ling in Commercial St.

21st Extremely foggy - black and thick.

22nd Mr. C. Hill that Davy Hill will amalgamate with Hodgkinson Clarke making a Limited Co.

It wasn't just the Edwardian suburbs that were beginning to

expand - right in the urban centre of the city there was still room to sweep away parts of the narrower Victorian highways, widen its arteries, and allow a smoother, more rapid flow of ever-increasing traffic. The construction of Kingsway and the Aldwych ploughed through a patchwork network of ancient streets dting back to 1500 - Little Wild Stret, Clam Market - tenements and theatres to create one of those broad, pleasant tree-lined boulevards redolent of Haussman's Paris. A more impressive metropolitan grandeur, but a touch of medieval London was lost forever.

Old London: in 1905 a swathe of the medieval city was swept aside to make way for Kingsway and Aldwych. Little Wild Street, shortly before demolition.

24th Constable called in this morning to see me. Scared Popp & Maud. He came again in evening and asked me about Mr. Law who was seeking a peddler's license.

25th Bob & his girl - Miss Striver - came unexpectedly to tea. Popp in a flurry. I got ready to go to Conference at College Hall - however the Lord gave me to testify to Bob & Miss Striver.

The new Kingsway, and a new London - broader, metropolitan. The capital had entered the twentieth century.

DEC

6th Started out at 7 o'clock for Dartford County Court. Met Drake (of Belvdere) at Dartford who arranged matters with me. I was called before Judge to state what means (the) defendant had for paying, and I did not refuse to take the oath.

11th. A dense fog all over London & suburbs all day. Bus conductors had to walk in front of their buses for safety &c.

1906

JAN

5th. Called at Belvedere in evening and saw Dr. Hill. He was enraged at firm for summoning him and for obtaining £1 judgement in excess.

13th... J. Bull & confrere chatted on the elections - Liberals.

16th Liberals winning easily.

17th. Nothing but talking election.

The Liberals under Henry Campbell-Bannerman won a landslide victory in January 1906, with the Conservatives losing half their seats. A new age of progressiveness had begun, culminating in the extraordinary People's Budget of 1911 in which Lloyd George and Winston Churchill laid down the foundations of the modern Welfare State.

19th Popp heard from Kathleen who sent her book on the Song of Solomon, by Hudson Taylor.

20th Romford voting. Mr. Creed & I chatted the election. I gave my vote to the free-trader Bethell.

This was the beginning of Sibley's lifelong allegiance to the Liberals.

22nd… the Lord blessed the book on 'Song of Solomon' for me, 'I am my Beloved's,' 'His desire is towards me.' Praise Him it taught communion by the teaching of the union of bride & bridegroom. Joy manifested.

25th Mr. Groom when here left a book written by Mrs. Boardman. I read some of it and the Lord opened my soul to receive: it continues in a marvellous way what the Lord was teaching in the S.of S.

FEB

3rd .. Arr. home 1.30. Nursed Leonard for an hour or so, then did work.

8th. A severe thunder and hale storm (sic) burst over the country at 3 o'clock. I was in Lyons so did not hear it.

9th. Popp queer in evening. Thought she was going to be confined in the night but I did not get up and we both went to sleep.

13th Popp & I were silly enough to argue this morning, which broke the spiritual ties for a time. Alright when I came home.

22nd Mr. Hill favouring Hitching above me in making calls where two are calling. Ted advised me to cultivate chemists, leaving out many of my doctors.

25th Maud fetched Mrs…-, who stayed all night. Nothing happened.

26TH Popp not confined but expected any hour. Nurse remaining. I am not enjoying the chair bedstead.

MARCH

3rd. Maud took Leonard to her Aunt's in afternoon.

7th Met Hitching in office and we discussed journeys and men in question. Mr. Hill interposed and said journeys were to remain as before, so that concluded our meeting.

8th Had to go to office to with an order for lymph as could not get through on telephone.

17th Did some digging in the garden. Chatted with Mr. Smith next door.

22nd… Popp delivered this morning, praise the lord, though she was kept waiting 10 days.

That a sad miscarriage is perceived as a common tragedy - though one must be careful not to infer normalisation from a bald diary entry - proves its ubiquity. This was an all-too prevalent event in couple's lives until midwifery became more advanced as the century progressed. As ever, Sibley's solution to personal tragedy is to work:

APRIL

13th.. Went into garden and finished digging and set some flowers &c, made things in general look ship-shape. Maud went out for the day. I took Leonard out to Romford Rd. and bought some sweets &c.

21st Had a chat with Bull on spiritual things. He is unorthodox, not believing in verbal inspiration. Bought some wood and flowers and had a chat with a Trojan. Made a barrier for the foot of stairs.

Married life brought with it new obligations and exclusions, so Sibley may have felt a pang of nostalgia on meeting an old fellow Trojan Club member, the old football club from his single days.

25th. Weds. Met Ted at the ABC Mansion House, & we went to the Chemist's Exhibition, Royal Horticultural Hall St. Vincent's Sq. Westminster. Saw W.J.Petty & his wife 2 daughters. CDP is travelling for Hewletts. Spoke to Mr. Holloway and numerous others.

26th Bob is growing a beard because of his face.

MAY

11th. Wrote to Mr. W. Alford 21 Coombedale Rd. East Greenwich for settlement

12th. Maud's machine was brought and the manager gave her a lesson.

The identity of this 'machine' is shrouded in mystery, but one infers that it made Maud's domestic work easier.

16th Purchased three of Hudson Taylor's books. 18th Bermondsey, Balham &C. Called on Truman Waterloo Rd. - who was ill with gout and was nearly drunk - full of tales which I brought to a close.

25th Wrote to Dena, & packed up her Bible &c.

28th Heard from Mr. Alford, said he could not pay me rent, out of work &c. Received rent (5/-) from Seviour.

JUNE

4th Bank Holiday Monday. Ted & family came in afternoon. Had tea in garden and enjoyed ourselves as far as possible. Popp very weak but... she was enabled to get down. Mrs. Gardner came for me to help her to get her to the college but I was unable to just then. Ted and I went to the College conference.

7th Mrs. Finlayson came to tea with her baby boy. Popp & I with Maud & Leonard went to their house in evening. Popp went in her bath chair.

11th Burnham. Walked from Southminster to Burnham - a splendid walk.

13th Heard from Dena. She says her Uncle Bob is married.

14th. Went to office and saw Mr. Hill. Bob not married - Dena misunderstood his letter.

19th Wore light suit for the first time.

20th Very hot. Went with Popp & family in Recreation ground for an hour or so.

JULY

9th Southend journey. Had a walk along the front. A crowd of day-trippers there.

21st Saturday. Took Leonard to Wanstead Park. He liked the ducks & fowls, and also partook of milk and sponge cake. Enjoyed the outing.

AUGUST

1st. Chiswick. Called in Queen St. Boot Shop & inquired after some brown boots leather lined - cheapest 15/9 so did not purchase. Mr. Seviour wrote saying could not pay rent this week.

13th Holidays. Up at 4.45. Started for Margate, Maud, Leonard & I. Poor Popp remained at home not being able to come. Li coming to stay with her in the morning. Train got in at Tilbury 9.40, & 'King Fisher,' G.S.N. & Co. Turbine, at Margate 12.40. Bought Leonard a spade & pail, then had a swim. Had sandwiches & cakes, then paddled. Had tea at 4 o'clock. Bought a teapot. Boat started at 5.30 and arrived at Tilbury 8.20. Exciting race to catch 'Kohinoor,' all but reached Tilbury first but had to wait. … Reached East Ham 9.30. We witnessed a thunderstorm from the boat - escaped it. Popp glad to see us home safe. Praise the Lord, he gave us a splendid time.

Alford sent £2 - water rate overdue

The Bank Holiday 'boat trip to Margate' was a staple of the London holidaymaker in the Edwardian period.

The SS Kingfisher, built in 1906 by Messrs. Denny of Dumbarton for the General Steam Navigation Company. She was reputed to be the first turbine passenger steamer operating on the Thames, running a service between London, Tilbury, Southend and Ramsgate.

Mrs. Seviour - 7/-.

14th. ... Went to see Mr. & Mrs. K & Vinnie. ... Mr. K has arranged a waggonette for Thursday. God willing Mr. & Mrs. K & our family will have a drive.

16th Mr. & Mrs. K arrived at 1 o'clock in a nice waggonette suitable for 5, and we went for a drive to Theydon Bois via Barkingside, Hainault &c. Had photos of trip taken on the way. Experienced a very heavy shower. On arriving at Theydon the horse fell and grazed its knees severely. We had tea at Dossums (?) and a walk. Policeman would not let us return with the horse with cut knees. Popp scared. Another horse not being available, we returned by rail. Parted company at Stratford & arrived home 9 o'clock.

17th (At 9.30) Mr. P.W. Howard (& I) started for Romford on college tricycles. We had a collision with some stones near Ilford to escape a van. Only a shaking. Continued on to Chadwell Heath where we had a puncture. .. After two tries, mended the puncture.

Started again for Romford. We found the tyre had gone down again so took it to a Bicycle Repair shop, left it for an hour until 1 o'clock and went and had luncheon. Mutton chops, 1/-6d for 2. Found the tyre was not yet repaired, so returned at 2. Tyre could not be mended so we were forced to buy a new one 4/-. Chain (fell) off at Chadwell Heath - man put it on, 3d.

(Chain fell) off again at Ilford. We put it on ourselves.

Met Popp at Shrewsbury Rd. Tired out.

The most famous bike of the age, the Rover, invented by James Starley. His development of the differential gear revolutionised cycling. Starley bicycles are still made today in Coventry.

Sibley's first excursion on wheels was evidently not without its travails. Bicycling had of course flourished in the late nineteenth century and had by the 1890s become something of a craze. This is when the first 'Safety Bicycles' had appeared, ie. with chain, brakes and pneumatic tyres. The paralell evolution of the tricycle was interesting, as it was often looked down on as a resort of the more timid cyclist. But it was not without its fans. 'Tricycles Coming to the Front' declared a headline in *The World of London* reported as far back as 1878: *'There is quite a rage for tricycling this season at Brighton. Owing to the marvellous perfection attained in steel work, tricycles are now produced, combining great strength with extreme lightness. The mode of propulsion having also been greatly improved, they have become a fascinating and exhilarating means of exercise and locomotion. Ladies have taken to them, doctors do their visits on them, and tradesmen circulate their goods by them.'*

Cycling itself of course had a huge impact on the liberation of women from the more cumbersome fashions of the Victorian age, and even gave rise to the Rational Clothing Movement, in which wide flowing dresses gave way to trousers and simpler upper garments.

18th Went to Edgware, took Leonard. Saw Mrs Seviour, Mrs Holloway & Mrs. Shelley (aunt Lizzie). Mrs. Seviour out of work was the explanation why no rent was sent for 2 weeks. … Leonard a good boy. Had some milk and cake in Hendon.

20th 'Kingfisher' to Margate. Had a swim.

21st Took Leonard to Recreation ground for an hour or so. Leonard made friends with 2 respectable girls. Took Leonard to Wardales to get some HCN for 'Ginger.' (Cyanide). Mr. Triggs preferred to kill it for me. Went thro' rec., Leonard had a run, met the same girls & Leonard played with them. Names Winnie & Dolly Swain.

Sibley's paternal attention to his young son refutes the received perception that men were not 'hands on' parents in the early twentieth century. Throughout his chronicles, Thomas is deeply involved in childcare as a matter of course.

22nd. Took Ginger to Wardales & Triggs killed him using HCN in a syringe. I bought it back and buried it. Leonard helped me stamp down the earth on him. Had haircut.

Having acquired a taste for travelling on the SS *Kingfisher*, Sibley gives his father-in-law Mr. Kettley a well-earned break from his little barbershop in Poplar.

23rd Met Mr. Kettley at East Ham, caught 8.24 to Tilbury. 'Kingfisher' to Margate. Had a lovely swim. Saw Miss Kellerman finish the swim from Broadstairs to Margate. Went to Broadstairs by tram and watched the Swimming Gala - aquatic fete. Walked round coast to Margate - 6 miles. Went to arcade. .. The Kingfisher arrived late. Stormy voyage off Margate. Heavy swell, the boat rocked about.

Annette Kellerman was an Australian swimmer and a huge star of the Edwardian era; not only was she the first woman to publicly advocate the one-piece female bathing suit, she was also the first actress to appear nude, in *Daughter of the Gods, 1916.*

Annette Kellerman, the first woman to wear a one-piece bathing suit.

24th Friday. Mr. Heward & I started for Romford. ... Mr. Hewards left me and when gone a number of factory girls came up. I gave them a text or so but they were up for a spree. One got on the tricycle, one wrote on the board &c. But they went at 2 o'clock.

25th Took Leonard out in morning and went round Forest Gate near flats, trying to find a suitable house. Went over a weird house, also another 14/-6d per week.

27th. (Popp) visited the house in - Rd. Thought it was haunted. Horrible house.

28th Popp found a house in Whyteville Rd. she liked. We went round & saw it and agreed to take it. 12/6d per week. Wrote to landlord Mr. Tunstall 17 Vernon Rd. Leytonstone.

SEPTEMBER

7th Moved to 51 Whyteville Rd.

Balham 8 orders, arr. home 6 o'clock. Finished packing then waited for van. Arkle who moved us came round about 8.30. Got in Whyteville Rd. 11.30. Mrs. Smith gave me a cup of cocoa & biscuits. Got to bed 1.30.

The restless Sibleys move again, this time to nearby Whyteville Road, still in Forest Gate.

8th Spent afternoon putting flowers in ground and putting up shelf for gas ring. Popp, Maud busy, place looking a little better.

11th Catesby's sent lino this morning.

12th Mr. Ling called when I was out, desiring to be put up for the weekend. Coming round tomorrow to see me.

13th Met Ling in tram, told him it was very inconvenient to stay with us next weekend.

17th Had some tea with Mrs. Watt & her two nieces. Mrs. Watt gave me a large William pear, 11oz.

24th Mr. AC Triggs pushed an envelope in our box at 10.30 on which was written 'Dear Brother, Just passing. I hope to be able to call on you tonight.' And on back - 'I am doing very bad indeed.'

25th Wrote to AC Triggs concerning non-payment.

28th Yom Kippur.

OCT

4th Ed came in at 6.30 and we went to the Cass Institute and I received my first lesson in chemistry. Got on fairly well.

This relentless quest for self-improvement was characteristic of the age: further education institutes were blossoming, providing a need for those who'd perhaps left school early and not had the opportunity to attend university. In truth, these colleges were in effect the universities of the working and lower-middle classes. Classes at the Sir John Cass Institute in Jewry Street, Aldgate, had begun in January 1902. Courses covered aspects of Science, Arts and Crafts, Commerce, together with practical tailoring and cutting for the boys and Domestic economy for the girls, including Cooking, Laundry work and dressmaking.

7th Sunday. Popp & I took Leonard to college without dummy, & he was troublesome all the time. Glad to get out.

11th Had a fearful rush to get to the Cass Institute by 6.30 - motor bus broke down by Stepney Station, jumped off & just caught train to Fenchurch St. & managed to arrive in time... Had second lesson in Chemistry.

23rd. I heard a knock at our door at 7 o'clock in the morning. I answered thinking it was Maud, and went to get tea, but there was no one. A death summons?

26th Heard from George (Mr. Kettley) saying that Vinnie's girl had died - diptheria - a sudden blow. Wrote to Vinnie & Albert.

27th Went to mother's (Mrs. Kettley) in evening. Vinnie & Albert there. A sorrowful scene.

NOV

*6th Met Mr. D**k at Law Courts & went with him to the Royal College of Surgeons. We inspected as time would allow the different parts of the human frame beautifully preserved, showing veins, muscles &c., also skeleton's diseases exhibited in large variety. Would take me a week to see all. I had an hour & a quarter.*

12th Dena wrote asking if she might stay Friday night with us.

13th Wrote to Dena to say she could come.

14th Leonard had an accident - tumbled down cellar stairs. Had another fall in Maud's bedroom and cut his chin.

16th Friday. Dena supposed to have come to stay overnight but did not, being prevented.

20th Tuesday. Went to Charing Cross Hospital to meet Dr. Oeth(?) to go over museum. He did not turn up so saw Mr. Pearce… Saw Dr. D. but he was busy. Found my card, said Thursday. Leonard taken with bronchitis. Serious temperature, fitful sleeps.

21st. Leonard restless during early hours of morning, Popp practically up all night looking after fire and drink for Leonard. Leonard a little better in evening. White now, yesterday very flushed. Maud frightened.

DEC

20th Got the rabbit sent for me to Mr. K.

21st. Ted moved to 56 Chaucer Rd., Forest Gate.

22nd. Had the rabbit sent up by John Gilray for dinner. Popp had fish.

23rd Got a lovely turkey from Palmer's Stores from Mr. Wormold. 9/3 bird for 7/6. He had it already trussed for me.

Woodgrange Road, Forest Gate, the Sibleys' main shopping street in the first decade of the 20th century.

24th Dena came in afternoon to stay until Thursday or Friday.

25th Morning spent in cooking and looking after Leonard. Dinner ready at 2. Ed & Li came 2.30. Children started on dinner before they came. However it was not quite cold. Turkey very nice and tender. Will came in afternoon... Gave Will some old clothes.

Sibley ends the year as he began it, assisting his unfortunate brother Will in both looking after his daughter Dena and supplying him with garments. As the aspirant brother Thomas ascends, so it seems the flawed brother is slowly sinking inexorably under the weight of drink and troubles.

1907

JAN

16th Bought clock at Saqui Lawrence. 2/-9 1/2d. Maud's clock.

18th Wrote to Mr. Heward concerning his general letter requesting knowledge of differences. Divine healing the theme.

27th Sunday. Mr. Mathers called for Kate & they took Leonard. Leonard good with them... (but) then missed his 'known ones' and burst into tears. I was near at hand so relieved him and them.

FEB

1st Will Halsey sent up rent £2. Mrs. Serviour paying better.

11th Harlesden &c. 9 orders. Heard that Mr. Hopkinson is a rogue and has cleared out of Wealdstone.

15th Catford. Whilst at Dr. Bletchley's a boy was brought - had been run over - cold sweat on his brow - hurt internally. Mother awfully upset. Taken to hospital. (Boy died next day).

MARCH

4th Spoke to Snowden's traveller at Southminster & Burnham at Shenfield Station. He is a Christian - Plymouth Brother.

12th ... (bought) a text for Will & Alice on account of their marriage. Leonard enjoyed himself with 'Wo-loo' & tins.

14th Popp went to Ridley, enjoyed herself. She was quite excited over women's ministry &c.

Met Harry in Shoreditch after 4 years or so; had lunch with him in ABC. Moore - a stock clerk at Millinsons - also there.

19th Had some tunes on gramaphone after I had done my writing. Leonard enjoyed the 'ding-ding.'

23rd. Ed went to DH&Co CC (cricket club) dinner. Prize received for batting.

24th Sunday. Went to College in evening - all four of us did not enjoy it. Breach seems widening.

26TH Dense fog in City - all lights burning.

Smog was a perennial feature of London life until the late 1950s but there were periods when its density became remarkable, one such being 1907, when even in midsummer visibility was wintry.

28th Called in John's and got my coat. Heavier than expected - not at all stylish.

29th Good Friday. Had early dinner and met Ed, Li & family at 1.30, went to Ilford. Visited Cranbrook Park with new extension (Valentine's gardens). Children enjoyed themselves.

31st Sunday. Dena & May - Harry's daughter - came to tea.

APRIL

2nd Called in at Morgans & Scotts to buy 'One of China's Scholars' but after selecting the book the chap wrapped up 'Pastor's House.' Bought some boxcalf boots in Queen's St. 12/9.

14th Sunday. Mr. H. missed us (Ed & I) on Saturday. Ed said he went to Ridley. Had tea at Ed's and went with Mr. Welch to Aldgate. Conversation was why we in part left College Hall.

Smog obscuring St. Pancras station, July 1907.

15th. In Stratford, purchase dining-room suite, stair-carpet, bedstead. £6, £2, £2. Experience. At 11.30 could not open door - Maud fast asleep. No answer to our knocking. Went through next door neighbour's house & after trying windows, had to get through her bathroom window into our own bathroom. So got in.

Furnishing one's home in 1907 was not a cheap enterprise: in today's monetary terms Sibley paid £577 for his dining-room suite and roughly £200 each for the stair-carpet and bedstead.

17th. Popp wanted to go to Exeter Hall but I could not afford it so would not. Furniture arrived. Dining-room looks nicer. Maud's bed large and comfortable.

25th Met Walter Potter in ABC Shoreditch. Conversed for some time on Campbell (RJ) or rather his theology. Potter unfortunately only a professor, a churchman with no 'life,' now running after the new error, which is very old.

26th. Popp had a bottle of Stone's Ginger Wine 1/- 1d. to bring up wind.

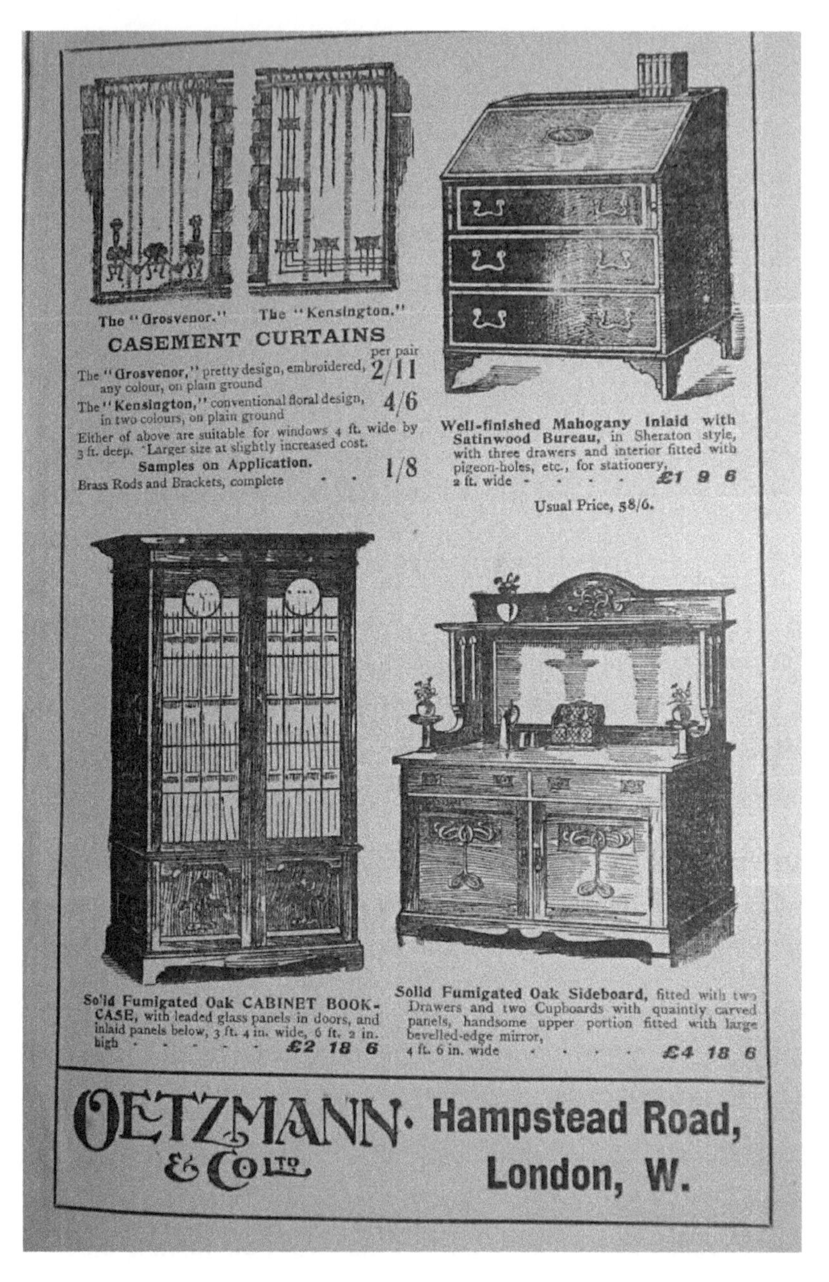

Furnishing one's home in 1907 was not an inexpensive enterprise.

MAY

11TH Caught 1.55 at Wanstead Park S. for Camden Rd. Walked to Camden Station and got bus to Zoological Gardens Gate. Had a look round, Leonard enjoyed the monkeys and the birds &c. Partook of some tea and bread and butter &c then finished our inspection. Saw the diving birds fed on live fishes. Caught 8 o'clock back from Camden Rd. Leonard a very good boy.

JUNE

4th John's to tea. Bob Carr there. Had a pleasant evening of spiritual conversation. Heard about a man who sees a blue light of permission and a red light of danger in his spiritual walk.

11th Mrs. 'Next Door' took our groceries in for us & waited for Popp to ask for them so she could have a jaw concerning Maud's mistake. Matters straightened a little so that was a blessing.

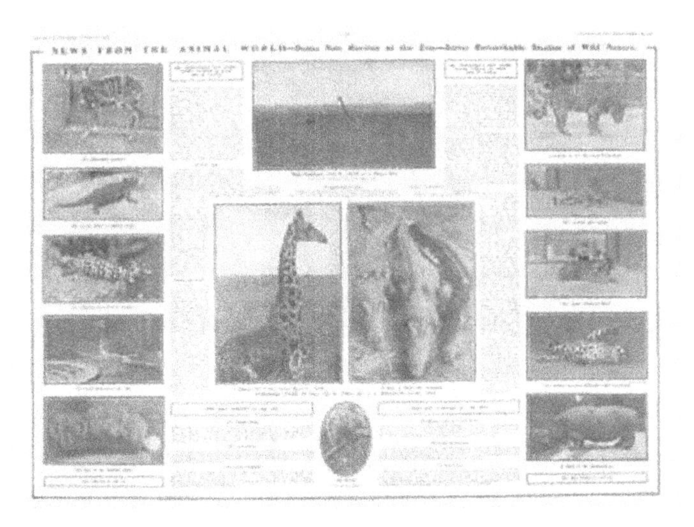

NEWS FROM THE ANIMAL WORLD

London Zoo underwent a huge reconstruction in 1907. Some of the animals Thomas & Leonard would have seen on May 11th of that year.

15th Saturday. Mrs Wallis & Kath went to Palestine Exhibition.

This was an exhibition organised by the London Society for

Promoting Christianity among the Jews at the Royal Agricultural Hall, Islington:

London Society for Promoting Christianity amongst the Jews.

Great.....

PALESTINE EXHIBITION

IN THE

Royal Agricultural Hall, Islington, London.

IN JUNE, 1907.

17TH Finished reading 'The Christian Leaders of the Last Century,' by J. B. Royle. Popp & I visited Ed's - had a game of cricket in garden with copper stick. ... much laughter & jesting.

18th ... Purchased strawberries at Hammersmith - the first of the season.

19th Weds. Made Rowlands my last call and proceeded by tram via Dalston Junction to Agricultural Hall. Had tea close by and wrote out my orders. Waited at entrance for 1/2 hour for Ed, Li & Popp. We then went over the "Palestine" exhibition. Too many people there to be pleasant. Inspected the different models and Eastern antiquities, also saw "life size" model of Tabernacle. Very interesting and useful. Spoke to Professor Rowse on Assyriology & Egyptology.

22nd Sat. Took Leonard for a short walk. Saw some bicycles.

25th Ed expects to be able to arrange my holidays for the last two weeks in September.

Met William Faulkner who I had not seen for about two years. He has a small business in Notting Hill.

26th Li is here all afternoon as Maud has gone to Palestine Exhibition with Esther Bowyer, Mrs. Wallis's servant.

29th Hornchurch & Grays. Mr. Carthy gave me £80 and gave me a good order.

Popp & I went round to Wallis and played lawn tennis. Popp enjoyed a game.

JULY

The summer continued with an awkward encounter with his old boss, W.J. Petty:

1st. Saw Petty at Wealdstone. He would not talk to me. I walked ahead of him to Harrow.

20th Took Leonard to have photo taken by Bob at Ed's. We were all talken in groups and Leonard on his own. Ed & I went to Wallis and had an afternoon of lawn tennis. Popp indoors - thinks she is 'carrying.'

AUGUST

3rd Popp and I went to Grays, High St. East Ham, where Popp was fitted for spectacles. It took over an hour.

5th Monday August Bank Holiday. Popp Leonard & I went to Wallis in morning, stayed until 1 o'clock. Played lawn tennis all the time. Had dinner at home then we returned calling for Ed & the family, & proceeded to Wallis. Played tennis, had tea, & played tennis. Left off because of darkness.

All greatly excited. Leonard not the least.

17th Holidays commenced. ... Caught 10.30 at London Bridge, arrived at Bognor safe & sound 12.35. Ed & I came up and heartily greeted us. They had found lodgings for us which we secured - very comfortable. Mrs. Wilson 27 Argyle Rd. 27/- 6d, 2 bed & dening-room.

Had a swim from bathing machine. Leonard enjoyed chee-chee (?) & sand.

Ed not wearing a cap, so I followed suit.

18th Leonard & I went round the back of Ed's at Gainsboro' Rd., and picked a blackberry. Ed & I walked to Selsey Bill and back (15 miles). Saw some warships firing. Secured a hut for bathing 6/- a week.

20th. 10.55 train to Littlehampton. Got a nice boat and started to row to Arundel about 12. After an eventful voyage with much hard work against the tide & ladies complaining - Li did not like water and Annie was not well - we arrived at Arundel at 3 o'clock. We had an exciting struggle to get under Arundel Bridge - quite a torrent, ladies scared. We had our sandwiches and looked for a short time at the scenery in Arundel Castle Park. Li & Popp returned by rail to Bognor; Ed & I took boat back to Littlehampton. Rowed with the ride and only an hour & a quarter for the 7 miles. Hands sore & blistered.

24th… hired a bicycle, for 2 hours 1/3d… I soon managed bike & Ed gradually began to get used to the balance. No accident.

25th Leonard had a ride with Eva & Winnie in a goat's chase. Wilfie & Ernie went on donkeys. Leonard had a donkey ride afterwards.

Bognor Regis, one of the jewels of the British south coast in the heyday of the seaside holiday.

26th. Ed & I started 12.5 for Goodwood race course, 10 miles. Arrived on course 2.30, & had a hurried repast of ham and tongue sandwiches. Lovely scenery. Pine trees especially fine, air lovely. Hurried for Duke of Richmond's mansion to get there by 3 o'clock. Arrived at 3.5 had to wait until 3.30 for a party. Went round and viewed the rooms and paintings, tapestries &c.

27th. Mrs. Wilson ill - poisoned by winkles - same as we had on Wednesday.

28th 2 o'clock train home. We filled a compartment. Arr. safely at Forest Gate at 5.30. Popp got some lovely pork sausages for tea.

29th Sunday. Ed & I with Mr. Law visited lodging houses in Stratford. Underground kitchen very unwholesome and stuffy.

OCTOBER

4th Sat. Took Leonard to buy some sweets before dinner, and after… bought an art bowl for palm which I had re-potted.

16TH Met Popp in Upton Lane. Wanted me to go to Town Hall in Stratford to see exhibition. Ed & I & ourselves went & spent two hours there. Found some things very instructive. Especially the lamp which burns all night showing one is alive.

21st … Had a gramophone out. Popp and I sang upon a blank.

29th… Went to the Conference Hall & heard Dr. H. Guinness on the Congo Inquiry. An opponent who had 5 minutes but created as much disturbance as possible & was turned out.

NOVEMBER

17th Ed & I went to the lodging house 'Oxford.'

22nd Heard that Dr. Herbert's wife had eloped with a young chap of 19. Dr. H. joyful.

DEC

22nd Ed & I went to Poplar workhouse, into young men's room. Rough lot playing cards.

25th Went to Ed's to dinner. Mr. Law there. Had games and generally amused the children.

26th (Ed & Li) went to Stratford Registry Office to witness the marriage of Mr. Ling & Miss Meecham. Ed, Li & family & Mr. Law came to dinner. Annie Cole came in afternoon & stayed to tea. Had some games &c & singing. Slept with Ed. Li & children slept at our house.

27th Called in John's & ordered underclothing. Palmer of Chapman's in a rage over receiving some bad whisky - threatened to close account.

Poplar workhouse, made to look somewhat attractive in these official photographs, was in 1907 a grim and forbidding place, where bad food and hard labour picking oakum (the fibres from old rope, used for caulking the seams of ships) was the lot of the inmates.

28th Gave notice to leave Whyteville Rd. Popp & I looked about for a house, discovered one - 20 Upton Avenue, 11/-. Paid off a deposit to Mr. Crocker, 270 Romford Rd.

31st. Mr. Hill said he had advanced my salary.

MEMORANDA

Income 1906-7 - £522.

As he ended the year. Sibley's income, in today's terms, was at this time nudging £50,000, a very respectable symbol of his aspiration and achievement.

1908

JAN

7th Evening spent in taking up lino & general preparation for departure.

Once again the Sibleys are on the move, remaining in the Forest Gate area of London and choosing a similar comfortable villa with the familiar layout of front parlour, dining room, back kitchen, and three bedrooms. They would have had a pleasant view across open undeveloped land - pristine meadows until the 1970s construction of a secondary school.

9th Went to 20 Upton Avenue and took some lino which I laid in the dining room. .. returned and put up bedroom poles. Maud brought some coals in pram. Ed came with her as one wheel was weak.

11th Saturday. Moved in at 20 Upton Avenue. Van came at 2 o'clock. Stemmings moved us, very satisfactorily for 12/6d.

His satisfaction was short-lived, and any euphoria at settling down in a new home evaporated very quickly on the night of the 13th...

13th ... About 11 o'clock the pipe just before upper cistern in loft burst, flooded passages etc. Plumber was supposed to have turned it off. Policeman came to our rescue & we managed to turn it off. Gave constable supper.

14th No water yet, plumber coming tomorrow.

FEB

2ND Sunday. Went to Poplar workhouse in evening. Had 2 helpers, and one upset some of the men through mentioning the atmosphere. Had my singing compared to breaking coke. Had a happy time.

12th Visited Stratford Town Hall and instructed Sanitary Inspector to inspect drains & Bay. He condemned both. Visited 42 Dunbar Rd., and saw nice house 13/6d. Gave notice to leave house. Wrote to landlord referring to the monthly tenancy &c.

14th Took five sacks of coal round to 42 Dunbar Rd. on a barrow. Laid down roughly dining room lino.

15th Saturday. Moved to 42 Dunbar Rd.

17th Informed Beverley (coal agent) that I had moved.

21st. Mr. Law brought around about 50 books for me.

MARCH

8th Sunday. We all went to lodging house. Unpleasant incident afterwards. Popp grieved.

His entry is cryptic but one can gently infer another miscarriage for the unhappy Annie (Popp).

9th Southend. 9 orders. Went on pier for a blow & walked to bottom and back, about 2 1/2 miles, and nearly lost train.

Undeterred by the criticism of his singing in the workhouse, Sibley and his elder brother Edwin persist in their attempts to instil a spiritual purpose and ambition in the inmates:

Sunday 15th. Ed & I went to workhouse. One man got up an argument afterwards which we partly parried but could not exactly avoid because of our invitation.

16th Had to have umbrella riveted on way home.

20th. Mr. Palmer in tears because he is leaving. Imbibed too freely.

21st. Ed went to Davy Hill cricket club dinner. He took prize but stated because of the Lord's work he would not play again.

30th Will came round to borrow some money. He took away a pair of boots and an old suit & l/-. He went round to Ed's who gave him 1/-.

31st Saw Bob at office. Desks &c on first floor as office is in builder's hands. Palmer late of Chapmans called at office to see me.

APRIL

1st. ... called for Ed and went to Rev. E.B. Samuel's abode.... conversed on Divine Healing, which Mr. Samuels cannot see as scriptural.

3RD... Ed came and we had some fun about Annie's home-made bread. Dena came this morning to stay a day or so.

6th Leonard has his birthday gathering. Ed's youngsters, Olive Wallis = 9. Dena & Maud played with them. Popp & I also Li amused them in the evening with parlour games.

7th Dena went home this morning.

8th Popp went to Wardales to have a tooth out and her stumps ground down in preparation for receiving false teeth.

13th Southend. Had 2 hours wait for train so walked to Pitsea, 6 miles distant.

17th Good Friday. Ed & I went for a walk. Wandered across some fields in the dark and had to climb fence into Wanstead Park.

That there were fields edging the urban park is a hint of the still-rural nature of parts of the growing East London-Essex suburbs. The huge building programme of the 1920s lay ahead, and the vast majority of houses were still Victorian stock.

MAY

1st Stanley Parker started for Liverpool this morning, sailing tomorrow.

3rd. Popp, Li., Ed & I went to lodging house. Mr. & Mrs. Abrahams there. Mrs. Abrahams greatly offended for some reason - best known to herself - & vented her spleen on Popp. Her coldness quite noticeable.

19th Viewed a few books at Farringdon Street but bought none.

25th George called in (Mr. Kettley) and had a little tea. Practised on the organ in the evening.

JUNE

4th Storms about 6 - huge hail stones. Storm burst upon me just as I got into West Ham tram car. Thankful for the shelter. Storm too heavy for car to proceed. Got wet only from going from car to house in Dunbar Road, so fast was the rain descending.

6th Saturday. Broadstairs holiday. Boat train Kingfisher to Margate then trammed it to Broadstairs. Lodgings - Mrs. Blackburn, Valdora, Prospect Place. 30/- for 9 days.

In today's monetary terms (2023) Sibley was paying £150 for a nine-day holiday. The classic landlady-run holiday lodging houses in seaside towns were a feature of the age, and would remain so for many decades as the forerunner of the Bed & Breakfast. In social terms they were a rung lower than the seaside hotel, and were a particular favourite of the lower-middle classes. The Sibleys preferred to choose different resorts every holiday, but many families would revisit the same boarding house every year. One recalls George and Weedon Grossmith's Charles Pooter in *Diary of a Nobody* making the same trip to Broadstairs with metronomic regularity, and indeed encountering his London friends Gowing and Cummings at the same establishment. They were more informal affairs than hotels, much like staying at someone's house as a guest.

9th Ed & I walked to Westgate after dinner.

10th Popp & Maud had a bathe from the public tents and the rest of us from our tent. Went to Margate… on the way we visited the (Freland?) Lighthouse.

11th Walked to Ramsgate. Leonard not in the least tired.

12th Had a good swim as far as pier steps where we had some diving. Had a walk to some tea gardens after inspecting St. Peter's Church.

13th Saturday. Ed & I walked to Minster. Viewed the old & interesting & also historic church. Had some cockles.

JULY

1st. Went to YMCA social garden party where Mr. - gave his address on his experiences of Singapore.

16th Went to Ridley in evening. Mr. Haslett spoke on 'faith.' Too much laughing. He spoke very sharply concerning some girls who tittle-tattle.

21st... A colonial recognised that I was a Christian from the book I was reading. Asked me to pray for him. He was desiring to get back to Australia. He belonged to the Salvation Army.

22nd Popp still very queer in bed. This time has been much worse than last through carrying.

28th. Had a swim in morning. Ed & John there. Gave John a lesson in swimming & had a ride on his bike. John sent round his dog & cat for us to mind whilst he is away on his holidays.

30th Went to Ridley. Mr. Haslett told me all about the burglary at Ridley Hall. Probably the man who was at the prayer meeting on Saturday previous.

31st. Visited Mr. Sluce and asked him for a loan of his bicycle.

AUGUST

3rd. Up at 6, had a ride around on the bike. Called for Ed. and with Mathers went to bathing lake and had a nice swim. Too crowded. After breakfast Ed had some lessons on the bike.

8th Popp & I went to White City. Had a good time although rather crowded. A wonderful exhibition. I went on the Scenic Railway. ... Saw the illuminations which are magnificent.

The Franco-British Exhibition was a large public fair held in White City from May to October 1908. The exhibition attracted 8 million visitors and celebrated the Entente Cordiale signed in 1904 by the United Kingdom and France.

The White City the Sibleys visited that day was pristine and newly built: only months before the whole area had been arable farmland. While Thomas, Popp and their son Leonard enjoyed the sights the Summer Olympics was taking place nearby in the gleaming new stadium nearby on the site of what was later to be BBC Television Centre, and ice-white marble buildings stretched as far as the eye could see.

13th Mr. Stevens sailed for Morocco.

17th Ed purchased Philip Coleman's bike @ 30/-.

20th Ed & I went to Wanstead for a ride and a swim. Ed able to ride across the flats alone.

25th. … Ed & I had some cycling. I borrowed Mr. Sluce's bike. Ed learning to mount.

SEPT.

8th Jack Blow came to Ed's and looked at his bicycle. They mended a puncture but the chain was worn and damaged. Ed took it to a man in Green Street. He practiced on Jack's machine. Popp & I went round and I was invited to try the machine, which I did. Very good, easy going ride: "New Rapid."

9th Ed had his bicycle seen to and a new chain affixed. I got on it but the wind blew the lamp out, so I discontinued my ride.

17th Box went off to Bexhill.

21st Popp & I went to St. Leonard's and walked around town.

24th Had an hour feeding ducks and swans in Egerton Park.

28th Went to Poplar to see Vinnie whom George told us was converted and suffering from religious mania. Couldn't speak at present as her head is bad.

29th Visited 3 bicycle makers and got their catalogues in Holborn.

NOV.

Had tea in Lyons 7.15, having had to come from Eltham by motor bus.

10th When I reached home I found a communication from Mr. Hill saying the firm was amalgamating with Heron Squire & Co. & Burns & Barron on Jan. 1st.

DECEMBER

1st. Li confined at 4.30pm. Li presented with a little girl.

25th Had breakfast 10. Prepared dinner. Popp able to cook it. Enjoyed our turkey, Christmas pudding etc. Took Leonard for a short walk in West Ham Park. Went to Li's for tea & had games with children. Came back 11.45. Will there to dinner.

26th. Mr. Law & Will came to dinner... Loaded Will up with food. He is staying at Rowton Lodging house in Camden Town.

Rowton House in Camden - now Arlington House - was a vast citadel in the back-streets of the north London district built as one of the network of lodging houses for destitute men by Victorian philanthropist Lord Rowton. Despite their obvious roughness as a place of last resort, they compared favourably with many of their squalid alternatives. In *Down and out in Paris and London* in 1933 George Orwell praised them thus: *'The best are the Rowton Houses, where the charge is a shilling, for which you get a cubicle to yourself, and the use of excellent bathrooms. You can also pay half a crown for a 'special', which is practically hotel accommodation. The Rowton Houses are splendid buildings, and the only objection to them is the strict discipline, with rules against cooking, card playing, etc.'* Whether Will's daughter Dena was still living in Hampstead workhouse is not known; if so, she was nearby, as Camden abuts Hampstead, and it is to be hoped that the occasional meetings between unfortunate father and daughter were positive ones. It is testimony to the frayed, yet not perished bonds of family that the Sibley brother Edwin and Thomas continued to reach out a hand of assistance to their fallen sibling.

27th Went to Poplar. Took the women's ward no. 44. They welcomed us and we enjoyed the meeting.

28th Went to office in morning and was introduced to some of H.S.J. travellers. They inspected our packed goods and we went to their warehouse and inspected theirs.

29th. Blizzard. "White Tuesday." Fearful earthquake in Sicily.

Rowton House, Camden Town, London. Similar vast hostels for unemployed or destitute working men were built across the capital.

31st. Went to Sluce's at 7.45. They had a small party of S.S. (?) workers. Had a meat supper, xmas pudding &c. One or two games and finished the year in prayer.

1909

1909 was a year of firsts. As the new year broke Britain's Liberal government took another progressive step forward when Prime Minister Herbert Asquith announced that everyone aged 7 and over would receive a pension; the first colour film was presented at London's Shaftesbury theatre, and Robert Peary became the first man to reach the North Pole.

Meanwhile, in a small house in Dunbar Road, East London, Thomas Sibley's career was inching forward.

JAN

7th Heard from Mr. Roger M. Harvey asking whether I could take certain towns. I replied yes but with one exception.

9th Tom Duncan & young lady - Beck Pycock - came to tea & supper.

12th Went to Barron Harvey's Co. in morning at 9.40. Had a long interview with the three partners. Mr. Howie showed me over the premises. Went to Albert Upton's children's party, Xmas tree. Popp, Leonard & Maud there. A noisy and not very pleasant time.

27th Fog. Had a most dark walk from Wood Green to Bruce Grove, quite an experience, could not see a pace in front. A man walked his horse on pavement very near to me.

FEB

5th Friday. Met Popp & Ivy Wallis at Westminster in Lyons. Ed there.... We heard D. Campbell Morgan on Zephaniah.

13th Saturday. Saw 3 doctors for BHC. Co., one doctor ordered Ticolex on my recommendation.

15th Popp & Ivy went to Mrs. Picks, 11 Mark Street Stratford, and took some groceries. She was overjoyed.

17th King & Queen opened Parliament today at 2 o'clock.

19th Had a Lyons Pie for dinner - after effects bad & painful.

MARCH

10th. Found that (Dr.) Ellery had flown from 367 Upton Lane & that the shop was closed.

19th Went to Westminster to hear D. Campbell Morgan and met Ed & Bob Carr in there. After lecture & as we were leaving Bob knocked his knee against a radiator which caused him to feel sick. Ed got him something from a chemist's as he was so faint.

APRIL

2nd. Balham &c 8 orders. Walked through Blackwall tunnel.

6th Had to make a special call and see Dr. Grieveson of Walthamstow between 7-8. He was at an auction sale which I visited but did not see him. I waited & he arrived soon after 8. I had dinner with him & remained until 11.30. Just managed to catch last post. Popp scared by my late return.

11th Ed & I went to West Ham Union, spoke to men in bed, 'N' block. A poor boy was there with hearts (sic) disease.

26th Crookham closed his account because we supplied Duggleby.

30th... Called in at George's and bought his bike for £2-10/-. George is agent for Harris of Coventry and purchasing their £37-18/6d machine for £13-10/- - a special offer.

Bicycles were still an expensive purchase: in today's terms (2023) George's proposed new machine - if he was to buy it new - would have cost him an extraordinary £3,500. Thomas' acquisition was a more respectable £200.

MAY

6th Called in at Morgan & Scott's & bought Torey's Ancedotes, & at another shop 'Billy Bragg,' & Luther's Sayings. George brought bicycle down for me.

10th Chemist's Exhibition commenced today. BDH had a good show.

16th Got up at 6 o'clock. Practised on bicycle.

20th. Got up at 6 o'clock and cycled to Whipp's Cross & back.

Lovely morning.

22nd We all went to Chingford and sat in forest.

27th F.H. James treated me contemptibly by leaving me in shop 20 minutes.

JUNE

4th Found that F.C. Kelly of Catford Hill had bolted.

21st Sent in income tax schedule 2, £168.

23rd. Popp & I went to Poplar. 2 men started fighting as we reached George's so we had to retreat until it was over.

25th Had brougham which I left at Bulmers.

29th Ed went to the 'Africa & the East' exhibition.

JULY

3rd. Cycled (abt. 36 miles), commencing 8.15, got to Davis 9.50. Wind against me on return, so had a trying ride home. Legs felt done up. Had hair cut in afternoon and bought Leonard a toy, 6d1/2d.

Long distance cycling was *de rigeur* throughout the Edwardian age and beyond, with many enthusiasts thinking nothing of travelling 100 miles or more on two wheels. With the country yet to experience the 'golden age of motoring,' the roads and highways still catered to the horse rather than the combustion engine, and roads were mostly still pleasant golden lanes stretching out towards a promise of fresh air and adventure.

7th. Called on Mr. Sluce. They gave us a tame bantam for Leonard which is laying an egg every other day.

For the Sibleys the first decade of the twentieth century ends on a high note both domestically and professionally. Thomas's career is progressing, and family ties with the unfortunate Dena remain thankfully still sound. With her workhouse-life behind her, the daughter of his reprobate brother Will spends a happy time at her Uncle Thomas's in Wanstead:

8th Dena came this morning & stayed overnight. She has developed into a woman - she is now 17 - quite plump. She went with us to Ridley and heard Mr. Cecil Smith give a missionary address. I gaver her Pastor HSI's conversion which I pray the lord will bless her.

10th Bought a little wood for bantam house. Made a perch in the dog kennel. Ed & I had an hour's spin on bikes round flats, Whipp's Cross &c.

11th. (At Ridley) Annie spoke to Emily about not coming to see her &c and found she was upset because she had been dismissed. Annie & I then had to act as mediator for Ed & Li's benefit.

13th .... Went to Farringdon St. but rain prevented me from viewing any books.

15th ... Called in at Paternoster Row and bought D. Campbell Morgan's no1 analysis of analysed Bible, also cookery book for Popp 1/-.

17th Saturday. Fleet anchored at Southend & Thames &c.

Built a light construction for bantam, with dog kennel in middle for shelter.

19th Monday. Southend, 7 orders. Went on pier about 5 and viewed the fleet. Saw 'The Dreadnought' & sister ships, with many cruisers. Torpedo Boats, Destroyers, Submarines. A magnificent sight.

This is a Tuck's Oilette published in July 1909 as a souvenir of a unique occasion in the history of the Royal Navy:

The commentary on the reverse gives a flavour of the occasion:

"Never before in the history of nations has there been so remarkable an assembly of warships as that gathered here together in the Thames, and stretching in one great pageant, the full extent of the river, some 45 miles, to the Houses of Parliament. It is practically in London itself, the very heart of the British Empire, that the fleet is foregathering, and nothing could be calculated more certain to arouse patriotic pride and Imperial enthusiasm than this unique display of a mighty nation".

In the week from Saturday 17th July to Saturday 24th July 1909, ships from the Home and Atlantic Fleets were moored along the Thames from Westminster Bridge to the Nore Lightship in the estuary, some forty five miles. The larger ships, the Battleships and HMS Dreadnought were moored near Southend and the smaller ships further upstream. The image shows Torpedo Boats moored at Westminster Pier, but there were also four submarines, two moored opposite the Houses of Parliament and two along Victoria Embankment. It was the first time there had been a Naval Pageant of such magnitude on the Thames. The timing of the pageant was thought by some to be linked with the vote in the House of Commons due on the 22nd July about the question of whether to build further Dreadnought class Battleships, happily the vote was passed and Britain was ready for what was to come in the First World War.

22nd John D. came round and we started for Grange Hill at 3.50 on our machines. Emily & Popp sent about 2 by rail & we met them at 4.30. Had a nice tea in garden. I had a puncture which after repairing we started for home, arriving at 7.35.

23rd Dena came in evening to stay a week.

AUGUST

2nd Bank Holiday Monday. Ed & I with 3 youngsters (Johnny, Ern & Wilf) went to Wanstead. Johnny came home on my bicycle step. Had a ride around the houses before dinner. … Played with the children until 9 o'clock.

5th Nellie & Dena came to tea. I had a ride to Loughton & back… a most enjoyable time.

6th John, Ed & I took Johnny Dowser who we carried on our bikes, (Ernie followed after with his hoop). Had our swim. Johnny went in water. I carried Ernie and John took Ernie & Ed his hoop, so we returned loaded.

11th … Had a side slip in Woodgrange Rd. when crossing tram-lines. Did not go down but bike did. Took Popp for a walk as far as the Laundry on Ramsey Rd. No likelihood of getting shirt & collars yet.

12th Hottest day for 3 years. 86 in shade. Ed & I had our usual swim, (getting changed) in the boathouse. The park keeper objected. Bought Popp a fancy bag & gloves at Hope Bro's.

21st. Epping 5 orders.... did journey on bike, & left machine for new inner tube & patches in Woodgrange Rd. on way home.

23rd Popp wrote to two addresses in Bournemouth, one out of Life of Faith & other Miss Priddy gave us.

24th Mr. Hicks and Mr. Clarke spoke to me about Glycerine - price &c. Spoke to Mr. Howie on telephone about D. Grieveson. Heard from Mrs. Birks of Bournemouth, 3 rooms £2.24.

26th Bought Leonard a 6/- teddy bear for the holidays.

31st Carmen collected bike box.

SEPT.

2nd Thursday... No trams available to had to walk to Plaistow Station. Arrived at Bournemouth West 12.10. Walked to our lodgings. Mrs. Birks, 'Coniston,' Studland Rd., Westbourne. Wrote to Ed asking him to get Popp's pince-nez, sending him our key. Had dinner (had steak) & went to Westbourne Marketing. The Chines are lovely, & scenery grand & natural. We are lodging on the side of Alum Chine.

3rd Mr. Birks offered us his tent 6d per week each person. An old military tent - we gratefully accepted. Had a ride to Bournemouth Central - a constable stopped me about riding on a forbidden spot. ... After dinner we hurried along front to pier and caught the 2.45 boat to Swanage. ... Had a glorious time at Swanage. Climb up hill... ovelooking bay. ... Had a tremendous dinner - Salmon, bass, chicken patty, custard & fruit &c.

5th Sunday... Richmond Hill Congregational Church... heard Rev. Jones. Church crowded. Lovely walk back through star-lit night. No moon.

6th Walked to Boscombe along the East Cliff. Had a few minutes *rest by Boscombe Pier then walked to the arcade.*

7th. … had a delightful swim. Had a companion in the shape of a stick which I practised diving under. Walked to pleasure ground in afternoon & Leonard put his boat in the bourne.

9th … walked through Southbourne. Saw relic of pier.

14th Popp & I gathered heather.

15th… went to Wanstead. Had a look over many houses. Some splendid ones for sale about £450.

Sibley's dream of home-ownership would take some years to fulfil, but in the meantime the family would content themselves with yet another rental. They chose to remain the up-and-coming suburbs of Wanstead, this time almost adjacent to the lush Wanstead flats in Harpenden Road.

16th … decided on 42 Harpenden Rd., if properly done up &c, £30 per year. Bicycle came and charge was only 2/- all the way. Mended 1 back wheel puncture, 5 front wheel punctures. (so far).

17th Cleaned bicycle ready for tomorrow. Filled in great holes and gashes with wool.

28th Inspected some carpet in Westbourne Grove. 2/11d 1/2 yd axminster. Wrote after considering, for 3 x 5 yd lengths, fawn coloured.

OCT

2nd. Repaired to Green Street, bought hall-stand, from Hummitons (Harringtons?). Also gas-fittings in Woodgrange Rd.

6th Wrote to Life of Faith ordering the Treasury of David, 16/6.

8th Friday. Lino laid and gas fittings fixed.

9th Moved to 42 Harpenden Rd., Wanstead Park.

12th House just upon straight except office & drawing room.

15th Wind broke a rib & bent another of my umbrella.

18th Left my umbrella at Adams to be repaired.

21st Collected my umbrella from Adams Upton Lane - 3/6 - & left my other to be repaired. Barber at Royal Free Hospital would not give me prices other (drug houses) were charging.

30th Mr. Ireland gave me about 2 doz. raspberry canes which I slung across my back.

NOV

20th Purchased a rhododendron 10/-.

30th Received Poor Rate & Water rate. Wrote for allowance for 2 weeks. House of Lords rejected the Budget, Maj. 350, Min. 75.

DEC

3rd. … The gale did a great deal of damage to fences and trellis work & arches in the gardens.

7th Bought Carlyle's French Revolution in Bayswater.

8th Took Popp for a quiet visit to Emily's. She (Emily) is still very poorly - mind in disorder, a blank, a wandering, a vacuum.

11th (At Stratford) bought Leonard an overcoat at Levy's 9/9.

14th Popp made some chutney. We had a bath at 11 o'clock and our cocoa in bed.

23rd. Made some purchases in evening - Leonard's train &c.

24th … Lunched at Lyon's Elephant & Castle, then went to SS.U. &

bought Leonard's book.

The 1909/1910 People's Budget was a proposal of the Liberal government that introduced unprecedented taxes on the lands and incomes of Britain's wealthy to fund new social welfare programmes. It passed the House of Commons in 1909 but was blocked by the House of Lords for a year, becaming law in April 1910.

25th Visitors came at 4.30, Ed, Li & children, Bessie, also Harris and Mrs. Davidson. Mr. Law came to dinner. Had some parlour games. Mrs. Davidson stayed all night, also Li & the children. I slept on couch.

27th... went to Emily's to stay a short time to see how she was. Had tea at Li's and then had some games. Emily came round for me in the midst saying Tom D. was barking like a dog. Bob took her to W. Poplar as her mind was reeling. I ran round to John's to find Tom D. groaning in a sort of trance. John & I had a strong talk and then he came out with me to look for Emily. John came round with Tom. Tom still chatting a little. Bob bolted. Popp very upset.

31st. Dr. Nicholls came & inspected Popp and said the trouble was functionary not organic. However, Popp would not take his medicine, being determined to trust the Lord. He sent a powder to cause sleep but the Lord answered prayer and Popp had a fair night's rest.

And so ends Sibley's first decade of the twentieth century. Like the British people as a whole he has travelled far, socially and economically, in his ascent from humble terraced house in a deprived quarter of the East End of London, to ample several-bedroomed villas in the growing suburbs. To a large extent his ascent has been self-engendered, through an adoption of the 'self-help' philosophy of the Victorian age in which he was nourished, and his later adoption of a style of Christian Methodism with a work-ethic at its heart. Yet this is not a selfish philosophy: in tandem with his self-drive he pays back to his community through visits to the humbler places in the districts from which he sprang - the workhouses, the doss-houses, the hospitals. He has lost his parents and begun to build a family. From the slightly wayward and fun-loving young man who rejoices in deceiving the railways of their fares and getting young women *'lively and saucy on wine'* he has developed into a rather stern young man, perhaps somewhat judgemental and self-regarding, but for all that confident in the efficacy of his adopted ideology. He is locked in to a deep cultural tradition of Protestant religion, a muscular Christianity that exercised the industrial-cultural power of a generation.

In the wider world Britain's capacity as a military imperial power to defend itself had been exercised to its fullness in the Boer Wars. Social progressivism proceeded apace with the Liberal timbre of the age, in particular the Chancellor of the Exchequer David Lloyd George and his young ally Winston Churchill - nicknamed the 'Terrible Twins' by Conservative opponents - who between them enacted the biggest redistribution of wealth in British history. No one doubted the momentousness of the achievement, least of all its chief proponents: on April 29th Lloyd George announced *'This is a war Budget. It is for raising money to wage implacable warfare against poverty and squalidness. I cannot help hoping and believing that before this generation has passed away, we shall have advanced a great step towards that good time, when poverty, and the wretchedness and human degradation which always follows in its camp, will be as remote to the people of this country as the wolves which once infested its forests.'*

In practical terms, land taxes and a super-tax on incomes greater than £2,000 were the fiscal foundation stones of the revolution. As the decade ended one could have been forgiven for thinking a new Golden Age was dawning. Few could have foreseen - except perhaps those deeply involved in the geo-political realities of the time - that Britain and the whole of Europe was facing perhaps the most menacing decade of upheaval and war in its history.

CHAPTER TWO

ZEPPELINS OVER WANSTEAD - 1910-1920

When the King died in 1910, a somewhat melancholy Admiral Fisher looked back at his short reign, then forward to the future, and wrote: *'I think we shall find the landmarks of life greatly changed. I am still dazed by the suddenness of it all.'* This elder statesman of the Navy could be pardoned for his slightly wistful tones. Calendar decades are by definition arbitrary, though their mental effects are very real: in the ensuing years British society was energised by events that gripped, galvanised, and traumatised the collective consciousness in equal measure.

In 1911 the Siege of Sidney Street dominated public discourse, a violent event in which a cadre of Latvian anarchists shot dead three policeman then holed themselves up in a hovel at 100 Sidney Street led by the semi-legendary figure dubbed 'Peter the Painter.' Winston Churchill himself, then Home Secretary, led the Scots Guards in an assault on these public enemies, along with more than a thousand police. The conflict ended in conflagration, with the perpetrators perishing in flames caused possibly by the Maxim gunfire Churchill ordered to be loosed on the building. This would not be the first time Churchill would use troops to quell civil disturbances - later that year the army was sent to South Wales to dampen miner's strikes (though no one was killed, contrary to later myths spread by anti-Churchill factions) - but troops did fire on Liverpool dockers the following year, killing two.

Abroad, the perennial Ireland question was bubbling to the

surface, culminating in the Easter Rising of 1916. Asquith had committed to Home Rule, Ulster was committed to the Union, and with two Home Rule bills failing, it took until the early 1920s for Irish nationalism to reach the boiling point of resolution. The Irish Question was undoubtedly the biggest political quandary of the age, with the assassination of Archduke Franz Ferdinand on June 28th 1914 hardly registering with the British public and gaining the barest of mentions in the House of Commons. Bernard Shaw's play *Pygmalion* had caused outrage in July of that year by its use of the phrase '*not bloody likely,*' and it was the common expletive that infused the gossip of the Season to a far greater extent than troubles in the Balkans. When Austria declared war against Serbia Britons still hoped the conflict would not drag this country in: but a complex series of Treaties meant otherwise. With Russia mobilising for Serbia and Germany mobilising against Russia, the catastrophe unfolded with dreadful inevitability. Lord Grey, the Foreign Secretary, had a frantic August, and apparently did not sleep for a month. On August 3rd he delivered a doom-laden speech to the Commons, then returned to Foreign Office with his friend the journalist J.A. Spender. As the sun set they looked out across St. James' Park where lamplighters were illuminating the greenswards with garlands of gentle flame. 'The lamps are going out all over Europe,' murmured the sanguine Grey, adding 'we shall not see them lit again in our lifetime.'

The war's outbreak spoiled a perfectly sunny Bank Holiday for many Britons, with the usual seaside holiday trains being full of troops and reservists. Throughout that month and beyond the War was the sole topic of conversation in shops and offices, and many times the streets of every city in the country were thronged. Not with protesters, but supporters.

Anti-German sentiment had been festering for many years; at Henley Regatta in 1914 an England four had beaten Germany to riotous cheering: in many ways, Britons looked on the War as a Regatta writ large. Newspaper and magazine articles, leader columns, even poetry with the patriotic verse of writers like Rupert Brooke and other 'Georgians' - all inculcated a sense of national solidarity that later critics have described as not so much patriotism as jingoism - a recasting of national confidence as something somehow distasteful. The War Office Press Bureau held a a tight grip on the national consciousness, censoring all negative counter-cultural expresssions, which fed into the perception of the times as one of tight-knit, solid unanimity.

Over the next four years, however, a sea-change occurred. With the shelling of coastal towns by German battleships - Hartlepool, Scarborough and Whitby, in which 137 civilians were killed, was a cruel shock to the national system. When the war reached a bloody stalemate in 1915 and Zeppelins began raining down incendiary bombs on London - in total 1413 civilians were killed by these monsters of the air - a gradual shift began in the tide of public opinion. The verse of Rupert Brooke began to be seen as fey and other-worldly, and tougher, more modern voices emerged - Sassoon and later, Wilfred Owen. American cultural figures such as Ezra Pound, who had settled in London and inculcated a surging 'modernist' revolution in literature and the arts along with figures like T.S. Eliot, James Joyce, Wyndham Lewis and Richard Aldington, led what amounted to counter-cultural reformation of old artistic ideals. Gone was Matthew Arnold's sense of classical beauty, and ushered in was a harsher, modern, more urban reflection of dirty actuality. In 1918 Lytton Strachey published *Eminent Victorians,* in which several heroes of the nineteenth century were subjected to the barbed wit and caustic satire of this new modern attitude - a sort of literary statue-toppling in which the idealised reputations of Cardinal Manning, Florence Nightingale,

Thomas Arnold and General Charles Gordon were unceremoniously besmirched. The Victorian Age had been summarily dismissed, and instead of a Tennysonian paean heralding the righteousness of the cause of the War, Pound's *'eye-deep in hell,'* and Owen's *'... the old lie - Dulce et Decorum est, pro patria more'* became the most powerful response to the international carnage.

So the War slayed many myths. Despite the huge growth of the state via the Defence of the Realm Act, in which the Government took control of many key industries between 1914-18, a certain unspoken contract between state and public had been broken. Not irrevocably, but one which permeated much of the educated classes and has done ever since; a cynicism towards the engines of a national leadership that led so many of its citizens to a brutal death. So while the Government increased its economic power over the country between 1910-20, it lost an element of its moral power.

Calendar decades being arbitrary, one must conclude then that it was 1914-18 that changed Britain forever. Not least, the role of women in the central economy was revolutionised. Huge Ladies Hostels were built in London to house women drafted in from the towns and cities of Britain to occupy clerical and factory positions of the men who had been sent to slaughter. Some historians state that Britain never fully recovered from the huge losses of its men, with the ensuing decades of the 1920s and 1930s having a paucity of expertise in the realms of politics and business. This is unquantifiable, but the socio-cultural effects were visible and vast. When the war ended in 1918 the total dead was 12 million, Britain's losses being 750,000 - 'half the seed of Europe,' as Wilfred Owen put it.

On the Home Front, the chief daily challenge was running a household without a man, and the daily dear of the Telegram from the War Office. Cosmetics firms exploited the anxiety of women: *'is strain turning your hair grey?'* queried on advert, while the manufacturers of Oatene skin cream promised to *'preserve the face he loved.'* Food shortages and hoarding became a daily reality, though rationining was not introduced until a few weeks before the armistice. Meat, butter and tea were then restricted - a small but grim foretaste of the 1940s.

The decade was to end with yet more national catastrophe - the Spanish 'Flu epidemic, as a result of which it is estimated that more people lost their lives than in the war.

Thus the macrocosm. As far as our family saga is concerned, as the years roll by the Sibleys will be seen to match these challenges with a resilience and fortitude that verges on the inspirational. Ahead there will be air-raids, evacuations, insecurity, terror and food shortages. But at each step the soul of Thomas Sibley seems to harden. He observes events with a cool, liberal omniscience, and a tolerance - notably, he refuses to go out with the others and see the smashed windows of German shops in the early part of the war. He continues to vote Liberal, he embraces a sort of personal Christian Science in his fervent belief in 'self-healing' through a positive mental attitude and prayer He describes the bombing of London with a detached strength that befits his role as husband, father and provider and - in this particular decade more than many - protector.

As the decade dawns, the international situation is not on his mind, but the health of his wife:

1910

Addresses:

Dena Sibley, 3, Frognal Parade, Finchley Rd.

He records the value of his investment, a small terraced cottage in Edgware, north London, which he rents out, with varying degrees of success.

Parish: Little Stanmore

Poor rate: 129.

Situation: Burnt Oak.

Gen. Estimated Rental: £10

Rateable value: £8.

JAN

3rd Nurse (Miss Fowler) came in the morning & Popp was looked after well. Put on special diet. Plenty of nourishment. Popp in drawing room. Dr. Nicholls came to see the patient.

4th … saw Mr. Hill… in afternoon who told me my expenses had been increased by 1/- a day, & salary £15 per annum. Praise the Lord for His provision.

6th Wrote to Dr. Nicholls saying it was not necessary for him to continue his professional visits.

7th Nurse stayed all night.

15th Free Trade or Tariff Reform General Election Commenced.

20th Took Popp out in bath chair nicely to Manor Park Station & back.

21st. Bought Leonard 4 horse soldiers in Forest Gate.

22nd Romford voting today. Bought a chicken and a blouse in Woodgrange Rd. Place alive with motors.

FEB

5th Saturday. Bought Leonard his white sailor's suit, 4/-6d, a hat, 1/6d.

14th Bought some metal animals for Leonard in Southend.

22nd Went to High St. Kensington Honiton Street Chapel, S.A.E.M. meeting. Popp was late as Met. train broke down at Baker St. Nice meeting, without gifted speakers. Speakers young and inexperienced.

MARCH

9th. Caxton Publications sent 'The Modern Physician,' £1-17/6d. 5 vols.

17th Took Popp & Leonard to Gamages and bought Leonard a fleet of 3 ships 1/9d.

Gamages, Holborn.

Gamages Department Store in Holborn was enamoured of children for its plethora of toys and games. Founded in 1878 by

Arthur Walter Gamage and his friend Frank Spain, it straddled High Holborn in splendour like garlands of tempting necklaces, and its Autumn Catalogue was a must-have item for lower-middle and upper-middle-class Christmas gift buyers alike.

19th Popp & I with Leonard looked over some houses on Lake Housing Estate.

Sibley was ahead of the race for the new suburban living. The post-war housing boom of the Twenties still lay ahead, when an ample three-bedroomed villa would cost £900, only twice the annual salary of the average professional man, but this ex-slum dweller had in a few short years cultivated a desire for the new dream of 'semi-rustic' living that housing developers promised. But we can see that house-building was already beginning to mushroom - Ruislip and Uxbridge on the western arteries of London, and in the East, Wanstead and ilford.

Lake House was one of grand houses of Wanstead, and its demolition in 1908 led to hungry developers parcelling up the land, with the local corporation flexing an early sense of conservationism in their insistence that the style of new housing was to be 'villas.' Between 1908 and 1914 a large estate of new housing was laid out offering vegetable plots, roses round the door, and bathrooms. This faux-'country' style of house was perhaps founded on the innate conservatism of the British people, who did not want to spoil the developed-on former meadows with rows of terraces, but rather detached houses that mirrored the mock-Tudor homesteads of yesteryear.

But housing is only one thing on the Sibley's minds, as the amorous activities of their live-in maid Maud are causing concern, as we learn that her beau, a certain Mr. Bob Carr, has been taking up more of her time than they'd like.

22nd. Received a letter from Bob Carr wondering at our restrictions & proposing to come little in future. Popp wrote to him and remonstrated with Maud, and generally upset herself. Nurse came and supervised the bread making.

25th Put new tyre on my bicycle. Found it more difficult than I anticipated. Bob Carr brought Leonard his fort.

APRIL

8th Filled in form for income tax - House Property.

18th Mr. Bryant called about purchasing a house through a Building Society. Left particulars.

27th Popp & Li out looking at houses on the Lake Estate.

28th Lords accept 1909 budget. Mr. Law waiting on doorstep. ... he had a fire on Tuesday and nearly burnt all his furniture, himself & the house in general. Firemen came in time.

29th I filled in form for abatement of £10 on account of Leonard, & sent to surveyor of taxes Newington Butts.

MAY

2nd Ed & Li went to Palestine Exhibition at Shoreditch Town Hall.

6th King Edward VII died suddenly at 11.45.

15th Sunday. Service for the late King in evening from Matt. V.

20th Friday. King Edward VII's funeral. Wanstead Park in afternoon - Ed, Li & children came after 3. Had tea on the lawn. Went and heard D. Campbell Morgan. Vast crowds saw the King's funeral - 6000 fainted. 9 kings present.

23rd. Went to Manor Park, bought garden shears and left bucket to be mended.

28th... I had a game with Aylmer CC. I made 23. Ed 10. Aylmer CC just won by 15 runs.

30th. Called in at the Creeds.... they have a nice house, 5 bedrooms, 3 receptions and a nice kitchen, £32.

Lucky Creeds - their five bedroomed house cost them £3,040 in today's (2023) terms.

JUNE

3rd. London had over 14 hours sunshine. Had a little star gazing before retiring.

7th Took Popp to Manor Park & ordered doormat, canopy 3/11 & another garden chair 1/9, pair of shirts.

17th JJ. Banyed Catford Hill has bolted.

20th Went to John D's, ordered cycling suit 25/-.

JULY

12th Hon. Rolls, the aviator, killed at Bournemouth.

Charles Rolls in his hot-air balloon, The Midget.

On 12 July 1910, at the age of 32, Rolls was killed in an air crash at Hengistbury Airfield, Southbourne, Bournemouth when the tail of his Wright Flyer broke off during a flying display. He was the first Briton to be killed in an aeronautical accident with a powered aircraft, and the eleventh person internationally. An Edwardian hero, he had founded the legendary Rolls Royce co. in 1904, and alongside his pioneering work in the automobile industry pursued a life of dare-devilry until cut short at the age of only 32.

23RD. Played cricket, Aylmer CC played St. Augustine's. Easy victory. I made 14.

31st. Bob Carr slept here this night.

AUGUST

1st. Popp believes she is carrying.

15th My bike began "chirping" so took it to Woodgrange Rd. to have it lubricated, also new mudguards and sticker for cyclometer.

18th Got up at 6.20 and had a swim round the lake. Swam round the island.

24th Went to office, borrowed £12.

25th Thursday. 8.36 to Ipswich. Arr. Felixstowe town station 11.5. Left bike at station and went on beach. Maud & Leonard stayed on front while Popp & I trudged for lodgings. Nearly everyone full up & very expensive - from 25/- 15/- a room. We were unsuccessful before dinner. Had dinner on beach (fresh rissoles & apple tarts). … managed to secure lodgings at 4 o'clock at Mrs. Stevens, Clovelly, Russell Rd. @ £2-5/- per week.

27th Had a spin on bike to Beach Station then Pier Station. Met Ed & family at Beach Station and they fixed up their lodgings at No. 9 Russell Rd.

28th We all went to Walton Church and heard the Dean of Colchester.

29th Enquired about a tent and searched for it round Undercliff in vain. Leonard cut his toe and had to be carried home. I bought him a pair of sand shoes 7d 1/2d. After dinner we had some cricket… and Mr. & Mrs. Haslett suddenly appeared.

30th. I had a nasty fall on back, full length, while trying to swing on pier. Went to Ipswich on the 'Norfolk' & enjoyed the overall scenery.

31st. Leonard had a bathe for the first time. After dinner we all walked into the country & finished near Landguard Fort. … Looked at some yacht racing on pond.

SEPT.

1st. Met Mr. & Mrs. Haslett and had a chat in a cornfield. Caught 11.25 boat to Harwich and walked to Dovercourt. Escaped the 2d toll by going along the rocks. Returned by 5.50 boat and had a fish tea. Met Mr. & Mrs. Haslett in Hamilton Rd. Mr. H. referred to a linnet's nest with 4 eggs in it which he found. A curious thing for this time of the year.

2nd Mr. Haslett came about 12.30 to our tent. His landlady suddenly died this morning. He will probably leave Felixstowe.

3rd. Saturday. … Ed & I hiked well into Suffolk on the way to Woodbridge, & got back 12.45. … Had a "blow-out" of duck and pickled pork for dinner.

4th Had a swim at 8.20. Mrs. Groom unexpectedly came on the scene. She had been looking for Mr. & Mrs. Haslett. Tent blew down and I had to go to the rescue.

6th Caught Belle Steamer 'Walton Belle' to Walton-on-the-Naze…

7th. Ed & I started for Woodbridge on our bikes at 9.40. Had a look round Woodbridge and came into contact with an entertaining man near his property by the river.

9th. Mr. Munro gave me a cock canary which I carefully brought home in a box. Maud bought a cage 3/3d. Had some trouble to get the bird from the box to the cage.

22nd. Heard that Mr. Sherwood had died suddenly yesterday whilst on his holidays at Lowestoft. Mr. Harvey gave me about 8 calls of Sherwood's to take over.

OCT.

12th. Called on Mrs. Shirtcliffe, Sibley Grove E.Ham. Practically engaged her £1-1/- per week.

18th George has purchased his shop & next door for £325.

21st Went to Forest Gate and bought at Penny Bazaar some plates.

31st Had tea - pork & pudding & kops ale. Went with George to Tabernacle Christmas Club to pay in his sub.

The Steamboat 'Walton Belle' at Walton Pier. The boat sailed from Great Yarmouth via Lowestoft and intermediate piers to Clacton, connecting with 'London Belle' for London.

NOV.

2nd. Bi-election (sic) result given at town hall. Sir Simon 2766 majority over Johnson. Great excitement in Walthamstow.

DEC

3rd. General Election. First pollings today West Ham started with a victory for Masterman (?). Popp & I went to Stratford in afternoon & purchased a bookcase secondhand at Boardman's, £3-10/-.

5th Liberals Winning

Burnham & Billericay. Stayed at Wickford for an hour so had a look at cattle market.

7th London returned 31 Liberals & 31 Tories. 3 seats for Labour.

10th Walthamstow polled today - Simon again.

12th 'Simply' Simon with an increased majority.

19th Sir J. Bethell was elected for Romford by 3000 majority.

20th General Election result. Liberals &c to have majority of 126.

24th Had our Christmas dinner, fowl & plum pudding. I finished Leonard's 'Pets Stores' & stocked it.

26th Went to Valentine's Park in morning, & kept goal for F.G.Y.M.C.A. Hackney team - we played Ilford YMCA - drew 1 goal each. Ed, Li & family came about 4 o'clock. Leonard & the children played with the Pets Stores. Had the usual parlor (sic) games. Had tea & resumed the Christmas festivities. After supper our visitors left us . I escorted them across the flats. It was raining with a high wind. They caught a tram all right. The rain was worse on my return and I got drenched.

29th Mr. Beck made me have a sample of his 'Yorkshire' Pork Pie.

22nd 3 policemen buried, service at St. Paul's. Murdered by aliens in Houndsditch.

In December 1910 the murder of three City of London Police officers and the wounding of two others was, and continues to be, one of the largest multiple murders of police officers on duty carried out in Great Britain. The three officers – Sergeants Bentley & Tucker and Constable Choat - were shot dead whilst trying to prevent a burglary at a jewellers in Houndsditch on the evening of the 16th of December. This incident and the events surrounding it formed the precursor to the famous Siege of Sidney Street in January 1911. Understandably the newspaper coverage was extensive and detailed.

1911

JAN.

3rd. Terrible affray with anarchists. Houndsditch murderers & anarchists found in 100 Sydney Street Mile End. Terrible fusilade - 1,300 policemen & some Scots Guards present. Guards fired at the house. House fired & burnt. 2 or 5 dead.

4th Leonard went to Lionel's party. Maud fetched him about 9 o'clock.

5th Paid rent to Mr. Cox 18 Kingly Rd. Forest Gate.

7th ... bought a nice eiderdown quilt at Boardman's 25/11 for 15/11d.

FEB

6th Went and heard W.J. Grenfell lecture on Labrador in Queens Hall.

7th Dr. Young came & saw Popp and reported it may be nearly a week. But nurse had better stay.

Gunfire on the streets of London.

8th Maud stuck her crochet hook in her finger and had to go to Dr. Stark to get it extricated. He had to cut and lance the finger.

10th. Doctor came and reported time short, so I prepared bike &c & got everything in readeness.

11th Irene born 1 o'clock.

Grays, 4 orders, arrived home 1.30. When I got home, found a fine girl - doctor had left 1.15. Popp got on well considering. Nurse looking after her well. Called in at Hyslop, and after Ed & Li. Met Mr. Haslett in Upton Lane. Bought some eggs and calf foot jelly. Mr. & Mrs. Wallis called in afternoon.

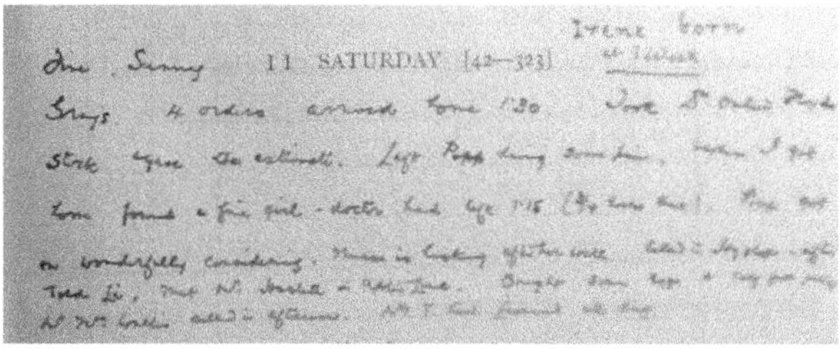

While in the wider beyond their door statesman conducted their affairs of international import, the Sibley family welcomed their daughter into their lives. Thomas takes one day off, then is back to work on the 13th.

13th Southend 11 orders. Called in and had lunch with Florrie Bittner (Etinger) Westcliff. Wrote to Will Halsey and told him to distrain on Seviour. Wrote to Seviour.

Paid nurse her £1-1/-. Leonard came home from school very poorly, stayed at home in afternoon then went to bed. Doctor saw him and sent some medicine.

14th Maud had a set back this morning. Bob Carr wrote to her breaking off their relationship. Maud broken-hearted. Had to try and soothe her. She wrote to Bob this morning proposing a meeting.

15th Maud waited for Bob Carr who did not turn up.

Heard from Seviour this morning who said Mr. Halsey would not take any rent. Replied to Seviour asking him to pay 2 week's rent and make arrangements for the remainder. Wrote to Halsey enclosing Seviour's letter. Paid 4/- to the Waverley Book Co. Ltd. Old Bailey for Bridges Bible Community, which is £3-3/-.

MARCH

2nd. Dr. McKettrick came and vaccinated baby. He had some tea with us.

Sibley does not record which diseases his young baby Irene was being vaccinated against, but as this was an extraordinarily early example of such practice it was almost definitely against smallpox. Vaccination against this deadly virus had been compulsory as far back as 1853 - it was not until after the Second World War that vaccinations against measles, typhoid and polio became commonplace.

20th Maud heard from Bob Carr definitely breaking off relations with her.

31st Cissy Williams here today. Stayed all night.

This is the first mention of Cecelia Williams, 'Cissy,' who would play such an important part for the Sibley family until Thomas' death in 1974.

APRIL

1st. Cissy, Leonard & Irene went to Mary Anne.

MAY

1st. Stayed indoors all evening as I have a nasty chill and ought to have been in bed. Baby not well…so doctor was sent for. No more Millins food. 63 Cow's milk & water (4+2 respectively) prescribed. Popp has a bad thumb - poisoned slightly.

4th. D. Lloyd George brought in his State Insurance Bill.

This momentous act, which came into effect in 1912, allowed Britons to claim unemployment and sickness insurance for the very first time, and created the bedrock of the later Welfare State. All schoolchildren were allowed free healthcare, and other healthcare was means-tested, meaning most of the poorer parts of the population received free healthcare from 1912 onwards. As a relatively high earner, Thomas Sibley continued paying his local doctor for all medical services receieved - and indeed, it was citizens like Sibley, the more prosperous lower-middle class, the middle class and the upper middle-class, who were the greatest advocates of a National Health Service, which was born from the wealthier elements of the population not being willing to foot the entire bill of the nation's health. It is estimated that by 1939 more than half the British population was already receiving free healthcare, the creation of the NHS being an economic and fiscal move to spread the financial burden to the entire population rather than just its middle and upper tiers.

9th. Popp very bad & extremely weak. Purchased a silk hat in Q.V.St. City Cork Hat Co. 12/6.

11th Went to Chemist's Exhibition, met a number of friends... Went part of the way home with Mr. Howie, who lives at St. John's Wood.

12th King & Queen open the Festival of Empire today at Crystal Palace.

16th Filled in Income Tax paper. £185. Leonard G.T.S. 24/3/1905 - 263 Monega Rd. Irene K. S. 11/2/1911 - 42 Harpenden Rd.

By 1911 Sibley was earning the equivalent of £17,577 per annum - a decent salary for its time, and as if to celebrate his tax return he goes out and promptly buys a further two hats.

18th Bought a straw hat 2/6 and collected bowler from City Cork Hat Co.

24th ... Dr. McKettrick called who confirmed Irene had measles. Kept her in our bedroom. Cissy looking after her.

The Festival of Empire at Crystal Palace (above) & the Coronation of George V in 1911 cemented Britain as the hub of imperial power.

27th King's birthday. Put some dahlias in.

JUNE

17th We all went to Blakehall Rd. & saw the return of the cyclists, some illuminated.

22nd Coronation of King George V.

23rd We all went to the School Coronation tea, and saw Leonard who went from school. Had a look at fireman's display. Leonard got lost, and found by Maud, by which time he lost his chance of running in the school race. It rained heavily about 7 so we returned in the wet. Read to Popp some of David Copperfield.

24th. Leonard & Ciss went to East Ham to see carnival. Popp & I had tea at Mrs. K's then went to City & to Buckingham Palace. Had some cocoa & pastries, saw many illuminated buildings. Got home 11.20.

29th King & Queen visited St. Paul's & Guildhall. Saw the King & Queen in City Road on the North London Way back to Buckingham

Palace.

JULY

9th Called in at Ed's & looked at his house, 12 Atherton Rd.

14th Heard that Maud intended leaving us at end of September.

19th Filled in forms for Dr. Barnados Homes, & returned it to Mrs. Godfrey, Lady Superintendent.

In search of a live-in maid to replace the heartbroken Maud, whose loss of Bob Carr in her life apparently led her to become disillusioned with the Sibley household, Thomas once again has recourse to Dr. Barnados to secure an orphan girl employment.

21st Tooting. 90 in shade. Lucky to get a brougham on such a hot day.

22nd Saturday. 93 in shade. Went to Valentine Park and played against Cranford Baptist C.C. who beat us hollow. I made 9 and got 2 wickets for 18.

27th Wrote to Mrs. Wilson Bognor to see if she had 3 rooms available for 1st week in September.

AUGUST

5th. Popp and I went to Stratford and purchased a rose bowl for P. Gray of Barking who had just got married, at Boardmans.

8th Popp & I had a look at the funeral of Rev. D.D. John of Romford Rd. Cong. Church who was drowned, and one of his boys, at Corton last week.

9th Dock Strike. Strikers were stopping all carmen and vans were being overturned.

10th Great Dock Strike proceeding apace. Called in office & found that strikers had prevented our vans from delivering to chemists and doctors, only hospitals. Trade will soon be at a standstill. Serious outlook.

The period 1911 and 1914 became known as the time of the Great Labour Unrest. Anarchist, Syndicalist and Communist thought had begun to ferment in the huge industrial populations, and while the economy was in a state of relative prosperity, when wages did not keep up with prices then protests broke out in places like Llanelli, Liverpool and London. What characterised these years was the relative ferocity of both the uprisings and the response from the authorities, with troops often being despatched to quell the festering civil disturbances.

11th Dock strike being settled. More vans out today.

15th Fierce rioting in Liverpool. Troops fire on mob - 2 killed, many wounded.

16th Fierce rioting in Liverpool & other places.

But ordinary life goes on. On the 17th Sibley hears sad news from a friend and colleague:

17th Ernie, Wilf & Winnie came saying Harry King's baby was dead. 6 months. Announced trolley with soldiers going about Liverpool. Strikers still rioting.

18th National Railway strike commences in earnest. Railway strike delays me a little. I was independent of Railway for most of the day. Many soldiers in London.

19th Rioting in Llanelly (sic). Soldiers shot 2 dead. Holiday travellers having a rough time. Very few trains on some lines.

20th Railway strike settled.

21st Wrote to Upsdale asking permission to move to 62 W.P.A. on 14th Sept. Wrote to Beverley ordering 2 tons of coals, 21/- a ton.

24th Bought 'Pickwick Papers,' 1/-.

26th Leonard lost his 6d because of going into 'Leg of Mutton' lake with some boys.

31st ... Took Irene to Dr. McKettrick's for ointment & physic. Eczema on back of head. Poorness of blood &c. Plenty of work to be done in preparation for holiday. Reckoned up cash. a/c £15 overdrawn.

Despite a financial setback, the Sibleys decide to escape strike-torn London and flee to Herne Bay for a rest in the September sunshine.

SEPT.

1st. Had no sleep with baby. Administered brandy. Up at 7. Hurriedly got ready & packed bag. Popp & I departed by 8.56 from Manor Park. Coachman did not turn up so went to Bank by motor bus. 10.4 to Tilbury. Caught Belle Steamer Tilbury to Herne Bay. … did some shopping on front. Went to pier with Ed & Li & enjoyed music by Cameron Highlanders. I was very sleepy.

3rd. Went on Downs after dinner.

5th Popp, Mrs. H & I walked along front to Whitstable.

6th Had a good row for an hour. Mrs. H. out of sorts so preferred to be alone. So we all essayed to get to Blean Woods. Walked too slow & only got 2 1/2 miles.

8th … Had a cold dinner as we were going to Canterbury. Decided to catch 2.30 motor. Ed & Li late so only found only room for one. Ed went, others to go by train. I went off on Ed's bike & got there in 45 minutes. Found no one there so went over abbey & ruins.

11th Caught 2 o'clock train for Margate. Left Mr. & Mrs. H on Margate Pier, & caught 3 o'clock boat home. Lovely voyage, arrived Tilbury 6.25, got to Wanstead 7.55. Got back very short of money - holiday cost nearly £9.

14th Moved to 62 Wanstead Park Avenue. Stemmings came soon after 10 o'clock... Paid Stemmings £1. Coal man delivered 2 tons of coals. Gas men fixed stove. Electric Light EH co. fixed electric meter. Got a lot done by 11 o'clock, when we retired tired out.

15th Popp & I went to Barkingside Village Homes to see Miss Godfrey. Saw a lady who stated that because of measles we could not have a girl for a month. Asked Maud if she could stay with us for a month.

18th Popp's head worse. Sent to Dr. McKettrick for a powder. Mrs. Shirtcliff came to see Popp. Read some of Pickwick.

25th George lent me £5, with advice gratis. Heard from Dr. Barnados, (warden Godfrey) asking Popp to go up Friday 2.30. I replied in the affirmative.

26th. Went to office. CAH introduced me to some new perfumes. Popp set the curtains on fire in the bathroom thro' a candle being placed too near. Did some damage and scared her.

29th Italy & Turkey at war over Tripoli. Popp went to Barkingside and saw intended maid. She will not be available before the17th. Popp sick with bilious headache.

30th Maud Grover left. Maud left 9 o'clock. I had a short chat with her about the spiritual. Gave her her money £1 6/-. Burglar caught in (Cloveney?) Rd. About 10 o'clock - great commotion.

OCT

3rd Popp very queer with neurasthenia. Rene bad with teeth - & ears troubling her. Cissy's face swollen thro' cold. Unhappy house at present.

5th Wedding next door (the Hunts), great commotion & hilarity. Maud Grover there helping with work.

9th Heard that Vinnie Upton (Popp's sister) had to go away - mind unhinged through neglect after confinement &c.

16th Leonard went to Mrs. Hunt's, had some tea, & then went & played round pond at parade. Got feet wet having been pushed in. He had a smack and sent to bed.

NOV.

2nd Bought a Voltalite 2/9.

4th Went to Edgware - found tenant out but saw W. Halsey. No money to be had. Seviour must go. Mr. Upsdale called for £1 for fortnight before quarter's day. Wrote strongly & pointedly refusing. An imposition.

13th Popp had a very bad night & morning and became so weak she seemed at death's door. Dr. McKetttrick came in morning... advised us to have a specialist. Nurse Shirtcliff came at 11.30. I got a bottle of brandy & Libergo's Meat extract. Nurse was frightened, also Mrs. Hunt. On my return I found Popp much better. Doctors sent a strong medicine to alleviate sickness. Popp was able to take some Liebergo.

16th Heard that Mr. Law was in West Ham Union Infirmary.

The practice of using workhouse hospitals for general healthcare was ubiquitous - the service was professional and free, and essentially constituted an informal free health service for the broad population.

While the Sibleys say goodbye to their maid Maud Grover and welcome Cecelia Williams into their home, Italy wrests Tripoli from the Turks.

29th Caught the 7 o'clock train to Southend… met the Southend Pharmacists & enjoyed the dinner with them. Sat next to Mr. Body, also J.J. Johnson… Had a good time.

DEC.

2nd. Hornchurch, Grays &c. Had tea in Lyons and went into Roberts Bazaar.

6th Carrie Carpenter buried today. Arranged to go to the YMCA dinner at Devonshire Hotel. Got on Manor Park Station at 6.20 to catch the 6.28 but no train came in so left and inquired about a tram. As it took between 40-45 minutes to get to Aldgate it was no use going, so I bought a chop and went home.

21st Maud came in evening and bought Leonard some soldiers and Rene a toy.

25th Popp busy all morning cooking 12 1/2lb turkey. Had a good dinner - ginger wine after it.

26th Ed & family, & Carpenters arrived about 3 o'clock. Had games. Plenty of romping. Pets Stores to the front.

29th Finished up turkey & ham (5 dinners off it).

The Sibleys end 1911 on a high - ensconced in their new house at 62 Wanstead Park Avenue, two young children, and Sibley's professional life going from strength to strength. He is spending much, but with a confidence in the certainty of prosperity. The 1912 diary is missing but as 1913 dawns we find the family still in Wanstead Park, and the company he works for, through a series of mergers and takeovers, has become the British Drug House.

Backing on to the Regents Canal in Graham Street, Islington, this company was an amalgamation of various old established

London firms of manufacturing chemists and wholesale druggists - Barron, Harveys and Co founded 1750, Hodgkinsons, Clarke and Ward founded in 1762, Hearon, Squire and Francis founded in 1714, Davy, Hill and Co, made up of A. S. Hill and Son founded in 1755 and Davy, Yates and Co founded in 1760; and played an immeasurable role in the growth of British pharmaceuticals in the twentieth century. The company was to be Thomas Sibley's second home for the rest of his working life until the 1960s.

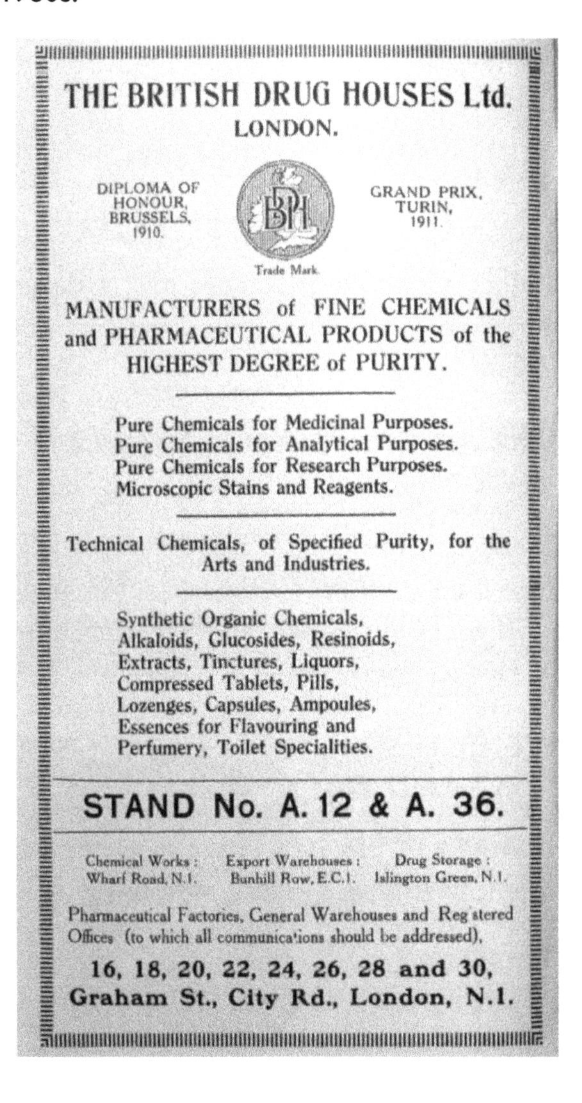

1913

Addresses

R. O. Sibley, 10 St. John's Terrace, Clay Hill, Enfield.

H. Sibley, 2 Holtwhites Avenue, Enfield.

With the journal for 1912 missing, the Sibleys begin 1913 with a customary restlessness, seeking to move yet again in their quest for betterment.

JAN

1st Paid Upsdale rent £8.

11th Popp & I went to Norwich Rd. and looked over No. 28. House too large & attics not becoming. Garden and conservatory in bad condition. A not-very-inviting house. Purchased at Boardman's a sideboard £8-2-6d.

14th Got to ABC Langham Place at 6. Mr. Warwick and Mr. Li arrived 6.45. I did steward's duty at Queen's Hall for E.U.S.A.

23rd Mr. Hill told me I was to have a £10 advance. Mr. Hicks told me I could have a double ticket for the Southend dinner. Met Popp & Li and took them to the CC anniversary meeting. Georgy Noakes in great form. Had a book presented as usual.

24th Popp wants No 16 Wanstead Pk. Rd. £33 per annum.

25th ... We walked over to Leytonstone and interviewed Mr. Yates the landlord of No. 16. He is a rather rough type of man but seemingly straight. We decided to take the house.

FEB

13th Popp & Cissy went to the Town Hall to view a dance.

MAR

1st Chrystall upset over our motorman's refusal to take away empties. I had to complain to the company.

15th Popp & I put our dustbin at no. 16, inspected house.

21st Moved to 16 Wanstead Park Avenue.

22nd Popp & Cissy had experience of joint catching fire in range oven, which was broken.

APRIL

Along with his new house, Sibley treats himself to a new coat.

17th Fitted on coat at Claytons but it was too big in front, too tight in arms, too long in sleeves. Had to leave it for attention.

25th … Went to Victoria by tram… heard Campbell-Morgan on John II. Popp, Leonard & most of the Sibley family went to Stratford Town Hall to the Sec(ondary) Schools Concert.

27th Sunday. Flower Dean St. Ed & I went as usual. A Jewish member of the C.C. there and he walked as far as Bow with us.

28th Popp & I went to Poplar in evening. Saw George & Mother. Tasted Lizzie's home-made wine.

MAY

8th Went to Caxton Hall Westminster. Church Jews Society - work in Jerusalem &c show by lantern. Motor Buses commenced running from Wanstead to North Woolwich.

London was changing. The sound of clattering hooves on cobbles that citizens had heard across the centuries since medieval times was giving way to the throaty noise of the internal combustion engine and the paraffin-fired steam bus.

Gradually animal power was yielding to mechanical, and mews houses, stable doors and horse-troughs that still linger today in towns and cities gradually became fading memorials to the lost supremacy of the horse.

15th Went to Queen's Hall EUSA. I acted as steward in the sofa stalls door B. Mr. Wallis arrived late, stewards not organised for his part. So arca ticket holders rushed the sofa stalls. Popp, Leonard, Cissy & Rene had been to the Sports Association with Ernie & Winnie's school.

The motor-bus was replacing the two-thousand year reign of the horse.

17th Went to Munro's and bought a large Invalid's Champagne. 4/-.

26th Developed some plates.

Sibley's burgeoning hobby of photography was typical of the age and an indication of his relative prosperity, for household cameras did not come cheap.

27th Popp & I had a walk into park before breakfast. I took two photos.

29th Popp, Cissy, Rene & I had a short stroll before breakfast. I took 2 photos & did a little printing. Developed negatives in evening.

JUNE

9th … did work and some photography.

12th Went to the Chemist's Outing… Arrived at Loughton at 3 o'clock. A goodly party - 3 brakes filled. Had a splendid drive through forest via High Beech and on to Chingford. We stopped for a short time at King's Oak Hotel. Graham and I took a photo. Had our tea at the Royal Forest Hotel & a good meal. Meat tea. Graham, Popp & I had an hour together afterwards. Graham took the plates - 3 plates. We had a sing-song afterwards - the expected artist did not turn up. I had to sing - 'When I was Single.' Caught a train about 9.40 to Wood Street & got home at 10.30.

14th … Purchased some photographical material. Took the tennis pictures on flats - spoiled two plates.

15th … Had some tennis & enjoyed ourselves. Did some photography in the evening.

19th Went to Poplar… took Mother's photo, also Bert's. George went to Ascot. Developed plates when I got back.

20th … bought some plates from Stevens.

21st Saturday. Called in at Graham's. Spent 14/- on photo. & medicines. Bought 5/- enlarger.

24th … helped Mr. Wallis to put some wiring across fowl house. Some animal had killed 16 chicks.

JULY

5th Beanfeast. Went to Margate with BDH by 10.30 Holborn Viaduct. 304 sat down to dinner at Queen's Highcliffe Hotel - we arrived about 12.30. Ed & I had a swim - dinner at 1.45. C.A.H. told us of the proposed Bonus &c. Ed seconded order of thanks. Returned in our saloon by 7.45.

12th Played my first tournament match. Miss Goff & I beat J. Warwick & Miss Way 6:4 6:3. Popp lost in hers.

18th. BURGLED. Loss - £5 & two cheap bracelets. Catford, Lee &c arrived home 8.30. Saw Popp at gate when I reached home talking to a policeman & I was informed that burglars had visited us. My desk as intact except for drawers other than locked ones which were opened and contents scattered. Our bedroom was in a state & bed turned over, & contents thrown about. Cissy's room ditto, but dening room was not entered. They broke in about 4 o'clock was disturbed by Leonard coming home from school. Popp & Cissy went to Mary Anne's about 3 o'clock, and returned about 5 o'clock. Popp & Cissy had a severe shock, & one of the men - a big fellow - was walking up & down opposite preparing for another entry. Police were fetched & the men watched - they decamped when they knew they were spotted. We were visited by a Detective Sergeant, Sergeant, & 2 constables - we (gave) the 3 latter some stout & cheese & biscuits. Poor old Popp did bravely but had a severe shock and was ill afterwards. God forbad the men to harm or destroy & did not permit their depredations. Money safe praise God.

19th Took Popp to Stratford and bought her a bracelet for her birthday 18/6, a rose bowl for Bernward Wallis, gun & doll for youngsters.

24th Burglars still on Popp's nerves.

31st Went direct to Linton & found the guests at Bernard's wedding. Popp went to church (West Ham Church) & came back in carriage. Over 50 guests. Bernard & Daisy went off to Jersey at 5 o'clock.

AUGUST

14TH Killed the cat as it was with kitten, and buried it. Men working at fence making it higher.

15th Friday. Popp, Len, Ren. & Cissy went to West Mersea. Got back at 8 o'clock. Cooked a chop and did work.

16th Too late for cycling all the way - was somewhat delayed. Postman brought a letter from Mr. Vaughan. Got to Colchester 9.45. Started for West Mersea 9.50. Had a fine ride to Mrs. Thorp's, arriving about 10.50. Popp & Cissy glad to see me. Borrowed a bathing box and had a swim. Had some oysters before the walk. Ed Harris arrived by Bus at 1 o'clock. Had a good dinner & played cricket with others in afternoon. After tea the "grown-ups" had a walk & then some oysters and some fun.

18th … Some of us went on board to have a sail to Bradwell.

19th After dinner we went to Sea View Road and on a very hard court played tennis. It produced more fun than tennis. Winnie came to tea. After tea they all assembled in our room. Warwick read some of WW Jacob's stories.

20th Went fishing. No fish about. Warwick & I caught a Dob each - only 2 for 3 hours fishing, and 7 lines going. Felt starving so had a fairly good dinner. Rode bike to tennis court, hard court & had 2 sets. They all gathered in our room and Warwick read some WW Jacobs.

21st The party went to Maldon by boat. I rode down on bike & saw them off - took 3 photos of them.

23rd … some had a swim. I did not venture on account of a rich dinner - duck, ham &c.

27th … Had some stewed mutton which upset both Popp & I.

28th. Had a painful night & morning - flatulence and cholic. Had some brandy, and afterwards a draft at Clayhorn's.

30th ... had dinner after a scene between Popp & Cissy.

SEPT.

1st. ... Had dinner and then went to Wilson's. Had my first attempt at retail.

2nd... Had dinner & then to Wilson's & served right merrily.

3rd Saturday. ... Popp & I went to S. Bromley... & saw Mother. She is very poorly & was in bed, recovering from a slight stroke... went to Wilson's & completed my week's work. Supper provided - beef sandwiches, tomato sandwiches, cake & milk.

After we had got to bed, a cab nearly outside our house had an accident - horse had a heavy fall. I went out to have a look - horse hurt.

10th. Wilson gave me £1 for my evenings work last week. Arranged to give him further service.

19th Popp still thinks she is pregnant.

20th Took nurse's photo. Had tea then went to Wilson's & worked until 10.30.

22nd Southend. Took sandwiches with me which I ate on the front. Went to East Ham by the 6.12. Went to Wilson's and worked until 9.40.

OCT

14th... Went... to West Ham Technical Institute & heard a lecture on Greek History - Egypt, Babylonia, Crete.

21st Nellie Buckley has not got syphilis - she has a non-contagious skin disesase.

NOV

8th Cissy took Leonard & Rene to Manor Park. Leonard had some fireworks, Rene some shoes.

18th Sent application to Farrow's Bank for 5 shares £1 each.

19th. I had to give Cissy a talking to. She is curiously dirty without understanding it.

25th Went to W. Ham Institute and heard a spiritual lecture on Socrates.

27th Met Popp at Liverpool St., walked to Ludgate Hill, met Gladys Wallis in St. Paul's churchyard. Visited St. P's hospital then took Popp by tube to Oxford Circus, then walked back to Piccadilly Circus looking for Lyons Pop'lr rest.

DEC

3rd Had dinner at the Middlesex Pharmaceutical Soc. Only one customer there of mine - Taggart of Harrow. Had some iced punch.

11th Met Mr. Hicks & Mr. Harvey, in consultation regarding journey, alteration, addition & reduction &c. I am to give up some calls - proposed to give up Hertford &c.

16th W. Ham Institute & heard a lecture on Aristotle.

18th Opened an account with Walker of Streatham. Did not get to office until nearly 5 o'clock. Mr. Hicks wanted to see me about journeys but I was too late for him. Mt. Harvey wants me to give up some of my calls. I wrote in evening proposing to surrender Chiswick & Shepherd's Bush rounds.

23rd Mrs. Chown gave us a tin of clear toffee, & Len & Rene a present each.

24th Walked thro' City… bought Len a book, Cissy an umbrella, Popp some spats, three shades for electric light &c.

25th … went to Ed's about 4 o'clock. Had tea & spent the time with parlour games &c. Warwicks there, also Miss Bennett. Left 10.45. Li did not offer to get supper.

26th. After dinner Ed, Li & family came. Had a good time with the usual games &c. They left about 11 o'clock but Popp saw that they had a good supper before leaving.

As the Sibleys partied on Boxing Day 1913 and the year ebbed, few were aware of the disturbing ripples of nascent conflict in the wider world. Family was the centre of human love, but ancient enmities had begun to surface once again, that perennial tribalism and hatreds between nations, regions, ethnicities. Dark forces were at work, but for the time being, as millions across Britain sang around their pianos or played parlour games with the young ones, the simple laughter around the fire was the greater truth.

1914

Income Tax

£216 - 16 - 8 12-9

+ 1/3 War Tax 4-3

JAN

8th Met Popp at Liverpool St. & walked to Farrows Bank and left pass book. Visited hospitals and took Popp to the 'Pop.' (LYONS) Piccadilly Circus. Bought a handbag 9/6d at Peter Robinson's for Popp's xmas box.

10th Popp & I went to Stratford.... brought back a sheepdog with us from the Dumb Creature's League.

14th Mrs. Pence sent Nellie Pepperall here from 607 Romford Rd. (Dr. Barnado's Homes).

17th Popp and I took back sheepdog and selected another.

The Dumb Friend's League - precursor to the present-day Blue Cross - was founded in 1897 by a group of animal lovers to care for working horses on the streets of London. The phrase "dumb friends" is thought to have come from a speech given by Queen Victoria.

21st We played 'Happy Family' in evening.

29th Spent the evening playing Happy Family & dominoes (paper ones).

FEB

5th Popp & I went to Sunday School Union and ordered a piano: Excella £25 4/- paid 14-6d a monthly installment.

19th Masterman lost his seat. Bethnal Green all excited over by-election. Bought some books at Paternoster Row.

21st Saw the two Misses Chowns on their way to a dance at E.H. Town Hall.

24th Dr. McK(ettrick) came & said (Popp) had gastritus, neuritus, neurathenia, anaemia, rheumatism &c &c.

MARCH

1st. Dr. Grenfell & Ed drove up in motor about 11.30. Caught me unshaven. Dr. G. examined Popp and said it might be a duodenal ulcer. Said he'd ask a specialist friend to examine Popp for me. Popp upset at the thought of an operation. Wrote to Ed & Dr. G. afterwards thanking them again for the visit.

2nd Popp had a restless night. Li came in afternoon, and did more harm than good.

4th Went and saw Dr. J.Y. Openshaw, at 16 Wimpole Street, 11.45. He wants Dr. McKettrick to write to him & he will then arrange to see Popp & examine her.

5th Cissy Baptised at M.P.B. church. Cissy went off to be baptised this evening - very excited.

13th Popp on ottoman. Better but nervy.

16th Popp all alone today. She started her usual trouble which made matters worse. Nurse ill, also Dr. McKettrick.

APRIL

2nd YMCA. D.Grenfell gave his lecture with pictures and dissolving views. Spoke to him afterwards. Accident & loss in Newfoundland of sealers caused sorrow especially to doctor.

10th Len & I went for a run with Fido before breakfast.

11th … bought Len a suit 7/11 & 6/- of music.

13th Bank Holiday Monday. Popp & I went to Great Portland Street Philharmonic Hall and saw 'With Captain Scott,' picture. Got back 11.30.

18th Started reading up Muller's 'My System.'

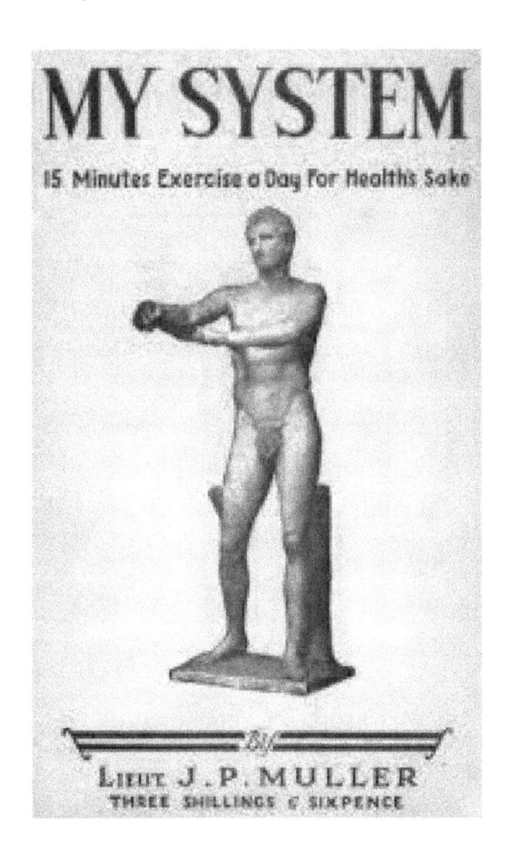

MAY

1st Catford & Greenwich. Poingdestre took me in his motor to his private house & I had tea with them, and he took me back to Greenwich. Had a very pleasant time.

2nd. Saturday. Went to tennis on bike. Lent bike to -... to go to YMCA for tennis balls but he only succeeded in dropping pump off machine & motor bus went over it.

28th Walked to Whitechapel Art Gallery & had a look around. Trammed it back to Manor Park.

30th Popp had been to Dr. McKettrick, and found he had been written to by Dr. Openshaw, and was greatly upset over not being consulted. Wrote to Dr. McK saying Popp would not be going to Openshaw's & wrote to Openshaw saying Popp would not be coming to see him.

JUNE

5th Fido taken back to Forest Gate. Had tea with Poingdestres - 15 Caterham Road. Popp enjoyed herself very much.

11th West Ham Chemist's Outing. 5 brakes at Loughton, 3 covered, 2 uncovered. At 3.40 it started raining hard & continued. Many got very wet. Had a splendid tea at Royal Forest Hotel & enjoyed a good concert afterwards. I sang 'The 3 Young Crows.'

14th Terrific storm in south London. 7 killed on Wandsworth Common.

20th. Eastbourne... Mrs. Britt, 44 Langney Rd.

22nd Went to a Pier Play in the evening, 'Arms and the Man.'

24th Popp & I went to Devonshire Park but did not enjoy the musical entertainment.

26th Very cold evening so had an experiment viewing some pictures, which were not greatly appreciated tho' some were good.

27th … a splendid swim… I watched a water-plane. Arrived Victoria at 4. … Went to Wilson's in evening… East Ham Carnival delayed me getting there until 8.30 - I was an hour & ten minutes on the tram.

JULY

11th Leonard got his Children's Encyclopedia from Smiths. 2/4d.

26th Austria at war with Serbia.

28th Russia mobilising. Serious situation.

29th War possible between Russia & Germany.

30th European situation critical.

31st Russia, Germany & France mobilising. Austria attacking Serbia.

AUGUST

1st. War declared by Germany against Russia & France. Len & I started for Mersea at 8 o'clock. Went on front, paddled with Rene, took 5 photos. After tea we had a rest then went on front with Mr. Meals, Warwick, Harris &c. Ed, Meals & I had a swim in the dark -

bright phosphorescence in the water. Harris, Warwick & the ladies had some fun over our towels being hidden. Carried Rene over to our lodgings at Mrs. D'Witt's.

3rd European War Commenced. We all went for a sail to Brightlingsea. Had a swim off boat - current very dangerous. ... Had a breezy tack back.

The Sibley's holiday to West Mersea in Essex as the German troops mobilised and the British War Cabinet convened to marshal its inevitable response, represents a counterpoint that was perhaps typical of the day. Edwardian prosperity and the imperial power of Britain had nurtured a self-confidence in the nation that brooked no disturbance of its sunlit certainty.

4th Ultimatum to Germany. Sir Edward Grey's historic speech. We are to stand by Belgium & France. Went on front, had a swim. Played hockey afterwards. Caught crowded bus at 6.10. I sat on step. Got to Colchester at 7.5. Caught our train about 7.20. Popp overdid it today at hockey & tennis so was hysterical when I spoke about giving provisional notice to Nellie. Ordered 1 ton of coal. Price up. Ed wired to return to office tomorrow. A rush of work. No hope

for peace now - Belgium invaded by Germany.

5th England declares war on Germany, 7 o'clock last night. Walthamstow &c, arrived home 6 o'clock. Everybody excited over war. People buying in provisions. Sugar 5/- a lb. Territorials embodied. Fleet & army mobilising. Ed came and stayed with us. Germany invades Belgium at 3 points. 4 battleships armed by Admiralty - 2 dreadnoughts, 2 destroyers.

Back from the seaside, Sibley, like millions of others, becomes locked into the rhythms of a changed world. In the first few days the war was a distant thing, perceived only through newspapers, but soon recruiting offices sprang up in every High Street, and crowds - not protesting but supporting the conflict - were a common sight in market squares and public places. The mighty conflict of empires was becoming a reality in everyday lives.

6th Great battle in Belgium. Germans repelled before Liege.

But alongside the epic clash of nations ordinary life had to go on, and Sibley's daily travels as a pharmaceutical salesman continued, albeit not without its own ructions.

6th contd. Chelmsford. Arrived home 6 o'clock. Drugs going up by leaps and bounds. Drug lists withdrawn. Great excitement over war. German mine-layer sunk in North Sea. German boats being captured. The plucky Belgians are keeping back the German hosts. Great courage. Bravo heroic Belgium. A great blow for the Kaiser. Popp jam-making.

7th 500,000 soldiers asked for. 100,000 at once. Woolwich. Wilson wrote saying trade quiet and he could do without me. Woolwich full of troops. Our troops being hurried quietly to Belgium. HMS Amphion sunk, 130 lives lost. 25,000 Germans killed and wounded at Liege in Belgium. Germany asks for 24 hours armistice. Ed turned up unexpectedly and stayed all night.

8th Saturday. Dr. Walker has sold his practice and moved to Dublin. Mrs. Walker in tears. I relieved her of some chloroform. Developed 4 photos which I took in Mersea. Closed account with Farrow's Bank. Two German cruisers being waited for in Med'tn sea by French & English fleets.

The staff of BDH Ltd. face an uncertain future.

10th French victory. 30,000 Germans killed & wounded. Too tired for tennis. French troops enter Alsace & defeated Germans, driving them out of their trenches... Liege still untaken. French declare war on Austria.

11th. Ed here for supper and stayed the night. Farrow's bank refused to close account - moratorium - offered 10% on £54. Germans attacking Liege with siege guns. Austrians to help Germans in Alsace.

12th North sea safer. Difficult to do journey on account of telling óur change in costs. Popp worrying until I arrrived. Ed came to supper and stayed the night. German army enters France. 100 spies shot in Belgium. 2,000,000 men facing each other in grim unrest for battle. The greatest battle of the world's history.

13th German detachment cut up by Belgians. Started first call 10.10, last call 5.10 without a break - no lunch. Had to get round because of change in prices. Ed came. Britain declared war on Austria. The great battle reported to have commenced over a 180 mile front. French capture 6 guns.

14th Called in Wilsons for a few minutes whilst meat was being bored and rolled.
French & Belgium victorious - many German casualties.

15th Another desperate assault on Liege forts. Belgian success in Alsace.

17th French advance. Japan sends ultimatum to Germany... to withdraw her warships. Poland promises to make Poland a nation again.
18th British Expeditionary Force lands in France - Boulougne. Greece warns Turkey. Germans seize a British frontier post in East Africa.

19th French victory and victorious march in Alsace. A serious rout in

Serbia. 3 regiments cut up.

20th Brussels in hands of the Germans. … government of Belgium in Antwerp. Germans cross the Meuse in great force. Russians defeat 3 army corps in East Prussia.

24th Fall of Namur. 2000 British casualties. British fought well.

27th Met Popp, Rene & Cissy at Cannon St. 2.45. Cissy went home and we went to Poingdestres. Had tea & then Poingdestre and I had a lovely motor drive to Chiselhurst and back. Returned and then motored to Woolwich Common. Left car at Greenwich garage then motored back. … Excited over marines being landed at Ostend.

29th Two Providential Insurance men came and inspected policies. I agreed to increase my insurance 1/6 weekly.
Great naval victory. 3 cruisers & 2 torpedoes sunk by our fleet in Bight of Heligoland. Bravo navy! Loussin destroyed by the modern Huns.

31st Kitchener's story of the 4 days battle - magnificent British behaviour. … our loss 6000 about.

SEPT.

2nd. Popp at Li's with Rene & Cissy & had some games in the forest with children.

5th Scene at town hall with a German who got run in. German naval mystery. Battered fleet arrives at Kiel. Premiere's great speech at Guildhall. Our troops maintain an unbroken front.

7th Pathfinder sunk. Also Wilson's Liner by mine. Germans advance towards south-east.

11th Mr. Asquith asks for another 500,000 men.

12th … wet prevented us going to Ed's blackberrying.
Glorious news from the front. German right wing in full retreat. Vigorous pursuit.

14th German armies in full flight in France. Great allies victory. 175 guns taken, 1000s of prisoners taken. Great Russian progress and victory.

15th. … Mr. Last there, who chatted about the Belgian refugees who were being put up in Aldersbrook Rd. Popp & I arranged to give 10/- a month towards their keep.

17th … went to St. Peter's Hospital then walked to Oxford Street. Bought Cissy & Popp a pair of gloves at Bourne and Hollingshurst (sic).

20th Sunday. Len & I went to M.P.B. chapel harvest festival.

29th … Went to West Ham Institute, heard a lecture on medieval history by Professor Shenstone.

OCTOBER

7th Saw Wilson after his return from France. He has a German helmet, forage cap, also pieces of shrapnel, which he has put in his window.

12th Stories of Antwerp, its siege & fall. 2000 mariners had to escape into Holland.

13th Rene in trouble this morning - threw a serviette in fire & got spanked.

31st Saw and chatted with Herman a big fat German. He expects to be interned any day. He does not sympathise with Germany.

Bourne & Hollngsworth Department Store, Oxford Street, in its Golden Age.

NOV

5th Mr. Milne at Chapmans gave me a kitten which I brought home in my bag.

6th Wrote to 'Daily Mail' to know where to apply for a Belgian refugee maid.

9th Wrote to Belgian Refugee Home Aldwych about a maid.

14th Finished place for fowls - wire netting &c.

DEC

15th Gertrude Smith came today. Quite a struggle to get Nellie Pepperill out of the house; as it was she was too late to see Mrs. Pierce and had to return to Forest Gate Home.

16th German cruisers bombed Hartlepool, Scarboro', Whitley this morning.

17th Leonard met me at Liverpool Street. Went to Wisbeys and inquired about a pram for Rene.

24th So foggy had to return via Green Street and Romford Road. Killed fowl this morning.

25th … Had a walk alone 3.30 -4.

29th Forest Gate round. Got to City soon after 12. Got to Armfields hotel 1 o'clock. Meeting of Travellers & Directors. Had a splendid lunch - 7 courses & coffee, wines, cigars &c. Business meeting after. Speeches, suggestions, hints &c.

1915

JAN

5TH… Len got into trouble for stealing some cheese. He was sent to bed.

6th Russians obtained a great victory over the Turks in the Caucasus. Enormous losses & captures.

11th Cissy went to Physical Culture.

12th I smoked a cigar given to me by Robinson of Walthamstow, one of four.

15th Killed fowl this morning - he seemed to have 9 lives. Chopped his head off to make certain.

Even in the cities many people kept food for subsistence in their back yards - chickens but also pigs and even sheep and goats. Until the 1950s and even 60s sheep and cattle would be permitted to graze in London's parks, and live animals were bought and sold in Fairs.

17th Sunday. Ed, Li & Winnie came to dinner - to taste our 'home-killed fowl.' Ed & I went to P.O. and heard a socialist.

There is no evidence in the diaries that Sibley ever gave socialism more than academic consideration born from curiosity, appearing to have been a lifelong supporter of the Liberal Party.

18th Popp went with Lenny to Mary-Anne's who is quietly upset about Ernie going into the army.

FEB

2nd Popp very poorly. Cissy had to lay about all day. Rene a little better. A house of sickness.

8th ... Went.. to East Ham Town Hall Police Concert. Two sketches, songs &c.

Graham had an explosion in his shop. His assistant was damaged & shop, through the mixing of KCSO3, thymol, borex.

10th. Heard all about Graham's explosion. His assistant is in East Ham Cottage Hospital. His eyes are injured.

11th Called in at Wisbey's and bought Rene a doll, 3/-.Went to W.P.H. & Co. dinner at London Tavern Fenchurch St. Sat next to Mr. K. Dodd. Had a good dinner, Mr. Miller in the Chair.

13th Saturday. Popp & Cissy went and viewed a dance at East Ham Town Hall.

18th German 'Blockade' commences - submarines and mines.

19th Mr. Reynolds would not give me an order because Sinclair has offended - Reynolds has been caught on Izal (?) by the Pharmaceutical Society.

25th Mr. & Mrs. Wilson here to supper. Played Mr. Wilson at draughts - which I bought in the City - & beat him. Mr. W & Popp went to East Ham Town Hall for an hour to view a dance.

MARCH

4th Went to office. Left child's magazines to be bound for Len.

11th Popp & Cissy went to a concert in aid of Belgian refugees.

It is estimated that between 1914-18 approximately 20,000 Belgians fled their home country to seek refuge in Britain. At the end of the war most of them returned.

APRIL

2nd Popp went to Town Hall Concert in evening in aid of Belgians. Very good programme - mostly sacred.

8th Took Len to the Tower in morning, inspected most of it. Popp & I went to Town Hall in evening, 'Within the Law,' - Belgium fund.

12th Spring Cleaning Commenced. Took Popp to Hyde park and walked through Kensington gardens. It rained consistently so we resorted to the 'Pop' & had dinner, 7/6, of some fish & sultana roll, coffee &c. Went to Selfridges and walked to Strand. Had tea in the Corner House. Slowly walked to Liverpool Street. Home at 7.30. Popp enjoyed her outing.

East Ham Town Hall today.

24th Went to Stratford, bought an oak chair, 11/6, and coal box 5/11. Rene enjoyed herself in Lyons at Stratford.

29th Took Popp to Town Hall to see 'Confusion' in aid of Belgians.

MAY

6th .... Went to Oxford St., met Mr. & Mrs. Wilson. Inspected Sale Rooms... Left Mr. Dalrymple of 176 Rye Lane, agent, to bid up to £8-8/- for a settee and 2 chairs. Bought an ornament at Bonhams 7/-. Had tea in Lyons & went to Philharmonic Hall & saw Professor Rainy's Pictures on animal life in their wild state - Africa. Lion hunt very exciting.

7th. Lusitania sunk. 1399 drowned. Went direct to Campbell Morgan. Do. Morgan said a timely word about the Lusitania being sunk and Germany's wickedness - positive defeat.

The *Lusitania* was briefly the world's largest passenger ship until the completion of the Mauretania three months later in 1908. She was sunk on her 202nd trans-Atlantic crossing by a German U-boat 11 miles off the western coast of Ireland, killing 1,198 passengers and crew. This wholesale slaughter of civilians by the Germans struck a new low in the brutality of the war. A few days later this seemingly new amoral tactic of the enemy, in which civilians were to be specifically targeted, was compounded by their use of Zeppelins to terror-bomb residential areas. As evinced by the unfolding events in London over the next few days, this created huge anti-German feeling among citizens, a feeling against which Thomas Sibley appeared to exercise admirable restraint.

8th Saturday. Popp & I went to Wilsons in the evening. Mr. Wilson's pianola arrived when we were there.

9th Southend bombarded by Zeppelin 2.30am.

12th Riots. Rioting took place against Germans. Shops smashed up & contents looted at Manor Park & most parts of London. Pop went and viewed it. I would not.

20th Tram strike. Somewhat delayed me.

31st London Zeppelin Raid. Whilst finishing my cash at 11.15-11.20 I heard muffled sounds from bombs. I waited until 11.20 & could hear no more so retired to rest. Popp nervous.

The Lusitania leaving New York harbour on May 1st 1915, its last voyage.

During the Great War there were 52 Zeppelin raids on England that killed 556 people and injured 1,357. Throughout 1915 and 1916, Zeppelin raids became a regular feature of life. These monsters of the air must truly have appeared horrific to citizens most of whom had never seen an aircraft of any kind, let alone huge bombers whose sole aim was to kill. Using the Thames as an ideal method of navigation, Zeppelins largely confined their missions to London, though other coastal cities in Britain also suffered. Eye-witness accounts attest to the terror felt by citizens: Londoner Florence Parsons recalled her horror at the sight of them: *'I was up in the city and it was a*

Saturday morning and I went to the street door and all of a sudden there was a, 'Ooh look at all that lot coming over, like a lot of birds'. And it was the new thing, aeroplanes they called the Gothas in those days. All coming along! Oh, and everybody panicked in the terraced houses all the way along. We'd see them coming over, so we'd run across that way and see them going over. They'd already dropped the bombs in the city, so I wasn't up there that Saturday morning, already dropped the bombs up in the city, the Gothas. Then they came at night. The city, as you know, was all bombed. I didn't go to work anymore up there, not then. It frightened you, because not one comes over, but a great flock of Gothas.'

There was no real system in place for civilians to shelter from the raids. Edwin Hiles lived in Hoxton in London. He was only three years old when war broke out: *'I was in the infant's class there, of course. And it was in the infant's class that I could well remember the teacher saying, 'Come, come children. We're going to play a new game.' And we were taken into a nearby cloakroom and there told to hide our faces in the coats – any coat – choose any coat you wished, but hide your face. Keep away from the windows. Later on, I discovered there'd been a serious air raid on London by German Gothas and quite a lot of children had been killed in the East End of London.'*

JUNE

1st. Zeppelins dropped 90 bombs, killed at least 4 & did some damage, mostly Shoreditch & N. London. Leytonstone had some bombs.

20th Took Rene to Manor Park Baptist Chapel in morning. Dena & her intended, Fred Bailly, came to tea & supper. Saw them off at MP station.

25th … Went direct to Campbell Morgan and heard his last address.

The very Zeppelin raid Thomas Sibley refers to in his diary of June 1st 1915, in which Zeppelins & Gotha bombers unleashed terror from the skies upon unsuspecting Londoners.

JULY

7th … retired after reading Gn. Ian Hamilton's despatch from the Dardanelles.

17th Saturday. Had some English lamb for dinner.

21st Gertrude Smith left us. Said goodbye to Gertrude, she was sorry to go. She was certainly the best girl we have had from Dr. Barnados Home. Sent her home to 509 Romford Road.

24th Cissy did some shopping, returned before us then went to Mrs. Nicholls. We tried to get in and ultimately clambered thro' Len's window as time was precious. Cissy could not see her fault - excuses as well as apologies as usual.

AUGUST

17th Air Raid. Harris came in evening and stayed all night. When we were about to commence supper about 10.40 a Zeppelin came over & dropped some bombs near by - one in Glenny's back garden. We were all a bit scared especially Popp. Rene was brought down

& Len... Nothing further happened. But I had supper at 12 & we retired at 12.30. Popp did not undress until 2.30.

This raid was the last of the night for German Naval Airship Division. Four Zeppelins set out but two, L 13 and L 14, turned back with engine problems. Zeppelin L 10, commanded by Oberleutnant-zur-See Friedrich Wenke, came inland near Sizewell and followed the Suffolk coastline down to Shingle Street where it turned inland. Near Ardleigh, northeast of Colchester, it dropped a parachute flare or incendiary, without damage, and followed the railway line as it passed through Colchester, Witham and Chelmsford, then turned west and headed towards Waltham Abbey. There, a couple of rounds from an AA gun sent L 10 on its way as it turned south towards London. After dropping most of its bombs over Leytonstone, in which ten were killed, it loosed its last incendaries onto Wanstead, which were the bombs the Sibley's heard that night. The greatest concentration of bombs dropped around the Lea Bridge Road where they demolished four flats at Bakers Almshouses and caused significant damage to tramlines as well as to the Leyton tram depot.

18th Could not easily do journey as Zepps had caused great damage in Leyton, Leytonstone &c. Several killed & injured. I saw more of the devastation in Mayville Rd., Bakers Avenue, Leyton Station (MR). Popp & Rene both upset. Popp very queer through the shock.

The Government imposed censorship on reports of air-raids but after the war evidence began to merge of severe and persistent symptoms of psychological trauma on the part of citizens: anxiety and restlessness being the principal after-effects. It is abundantly clear from the diaries that Thomas' wife Annie (Popp) suffered hugely, which led to Thomas eventually evacuating his entire family from London.

19th Popp & Cissie had a walk to find hole on flats caused by zeppelin bomb.

20th Did some photos. Velox printing.

To keep his mind off the regular bombardments from the skies Thomas threw himself into his hobby of photography, making glossy prints (Velox) of his subjects.

23rd Popp & Ciss went to Leyton to view some of the destruction by Zepps.

30th Harlesden. Had brougham... left it at Tottenham Court Rd. - it became wearisome riding home in it.

SEPT

4th. Saturday. We all walked to Wood St. then trammed it to Baker's Arms & viewed some of the damage.

7th London Zeppelin Raid. 56 casualties. Sound of bombs woke Popp & specials called up. Caused us to dress and stand at gate from 12 o'clock to 1.30. A good number of people about.

8th London Zeppelin Raid. Heard that Zepps - 3 of them, had been to New Cross & Woolwich, W. London, Ponders End, Milwall, Hornchurch &c &c. An areoplane descended in Flats this morning. Pilot (French) had lost his way. 3 or 4 Zepps bombed London. L'pool Street and other parts of London greatly damaged. We could see the shrapnel bursting near the airships but they were not damaged. Popp greatly scared. We all stayed in the hall.

9th Thursday. Saw some of the damage in Bishopsgate & L'Pool Street. Had to sit up until about 1 o'clock before retiring. Popp undressed about 3 o'clock.

10th Zepp scare still apparent. Retired about 11 o'clock but only to lay on bed. Got undressed at 12.30.

11th We all went to S. Woodford to Ed's. We then went to Loughton. Met Matthews family & some office friends & walked through forest to Copthill Farm. I left alone 5.40. ... I was preparing my lamp to go & meet Popp & Li when they came. A policeman told me to put my light out. Zepps reached as far as Epping & turned back. We got to bed about 2.

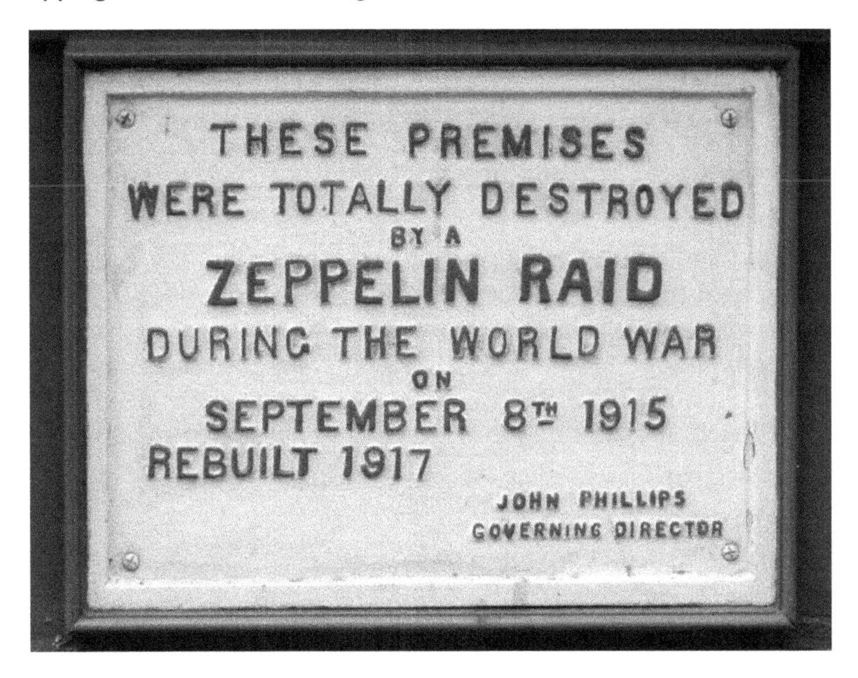

The Zeppelin raids in September 1915 were particular severe, as this plaque in Farringdon Rd., London, testifies.

13th Ciss & Winn telephoned for Bert Harris who came over about 9.30. Stayed to supper. Zepps reported so we all stayed up until 1 o'clock. Much fun before retiring.

14th Caught a little cold on chest thro' looking for Zepps.

25th British French offensive started.

27th Great Victory.

Had my first 2d1/2d cup of tea in Lyons Hammersmith. Great rejoicing over the allies great victory in France, over 2000 prisoners.

30th Got History of Nation 2/3 volume bound.

OCT

1st Dena came to dinner and stayed until 10.30 waiting for her husband who did not turn up. We saw her off at Manor Park station disconsolate. Heard afterwards that husband had lost our address.

Thomas' niece Dena's progress in life from the workhouse at Hampstead to married life was, we hope, a happy one, despite her husband's non-appearance at her Uncle's house. But what of her dissolute father Will? In the ensuing days we find out.

7th Popp made a cake for soldiers at East Ham Cottage Hospital.

11th Popp & Len went to Wood Green (102 Station Road) & visited Dena. I arrived in evening about 7 o'clock. Will turned up. He looked quite old - has lost most of his teeth.

13th Zepps. Just as I was finishing my writing, bombs started & firing. Zepps were in London E & W. We heard them go over our heads. We were startled again at 12 o'clock, some more of them. Woolwich attacked. One zeppelin was greatly attacked but did not come down.

14th 170 casualties. Saw something of the damage at Aldgate by Zepps. Could not get along the Strand - Kingsway damaged. Hertford got bombed - some killed & injured there. Bob saw some of the effects. Spoke to Mr. Hill about retreating into the BDH Munition Factory if necessary. Li came - full of trouble about Harry Thompson.

15th Went to Woolwich but saw no damage. Arsenal supposed to have been hit. Popp wrote to Miss Thompson & asked her to call &

see her.

17th Li & Popp broached the subject of Miss T to Ed when returning home. Ed refused to walk with us - in fact, ran away, & insulted Popp. We of course had to return home. I wrote to Ed in the evening. Ed acted like a guilty man or a spoilt child.

18th We were awakened this morning by an explosion. Becton engine works blew up. 1 killed, some injured.

19th Heard from Ed - a nice letter that smoothed matters over.

26th Received invitation from Lord Derby to join the army. Popp worried about the possibilities of conscription.

28th Thinking of going to Laindon to live. Arranged to go with Ed, Popp & Li on Saturday to Laindon to see if there were houses to let. Wrote to Yates saying we wanted to leave at Christmas.

29th... dense fog. Went down wrong turning. Got on a crowded tram that crawled to East Ham. Buses were going along a walking pace 5 & 6 in a row. Wrote to Ed saying we were not going to Laindon. Wrote to Yates cancelling notice.

31st Will came in afternoon, borrowed 2/-, & I gave him a pair of boots & socks. He had 2 teas and left about 8.

NOV.

1st. Dena, Fred Bailly & Mrs. Bailly came to see us.

2nd Started carrying perfumes.

5th Sold a good few perfumes.

11th Went by bus to George Wanstead & walked to Helena's in rain. Stayed until 10.40, arrived home about 11. 45. Had a big supper of home-made Brawn.

22nd. Sweep here... so we had meals in drawing room.

DEC

3rd Helena Ehninger died suddenly this morning.

4th Saturday. G.B. Wilson told me Mrs. Ehninger was dead. I rushed round to Gordon Rd. at once and found that Helena had passed away suddenly yesterday morning - found dead in bed by the servant (daily woman who came at 8 o'clock). Fred had left her after a faint & fall alone in the house, & went to business. Florrie there as well as Fred. Stayed half an hour or so - had a look at the body, & left Florrie in tears and great distress. Poor Helena - a good hearted woman with a bad son and much trouble. After dinner I had to tell Popp the news. She was greatly upset.

9th Funeral of Helena Ehninger at Manor Park. Coaches around 12.45. Went back in coach to 'Valencia.' Much trouble over affairs, Fred Ehninger untrustworthy. George Bittner took away jewellery.

10th Told Popp I should attest - the news gave much distress and many tears. Told Wilson I might not come tomorrow on account of the attesting delays.

11th Saturday. A soldier - Group 44 Home Service. Dr. Lowe examined me & enabled me to attest under Lord Derby's scheme without any trouble. All done in 1/2 hour. Did not get my 2/-9d as I was out of my district. Dr. Lowe found my legs slightly varicose & put me down for Home Service. Popp pleased at the news. Concert & drill display at M.P.B.C.

By mid-1915 the war was lasting longer than had been anticipated and the British military required more recruits; 'Derby's scheme' was a survey to determine how many could be obtained, via the use of appointed canvassers visiting eligible men at home to persuade them to 'volunteer' for war service.

Every eligible man, aged 18 to 41, who was not in a "starred" (essential) occupation was required to make a public declaration of whether he would enlist immediately or defer his service to a later date, to appear when called. When the scheme was announced, some went to the recruiting office immediately, rather than wait for the inevitable. The process began with each eligible man's registry card from the August 1915 National Registry being copied onto another card which was sent to his local constituency's Parliamentary recruiting committee. This Committee appointed 'canvassers' who they considered "tactful and influential men", and not themselves liable for service, to visit the men at their homes. Many canvassers were experienced in politics, though discharged veterans and the fathers of serving soldiers proved the most effective, while some just used threats to persuade. Although women were not allowed to canvas, they did contribute by tracking men who had moved address.

14th Sent to Ernie Williams France, cake, sweets &c.

17th Catford, Lee &c., arrived home 7.45. Had tea at Stevens as usual. Mrs. Stevens gave me a hand-painted matchbox for Xmas present.

12st. Bought a sheep's tongue for supper. It was sour, and Jeff (dog) had most of it.

23rd. Got my interim bonus 2 1/2 % = £6. Bought a turkey at Sainsbury's Islington 14/3d. Had dinner at Yeomanson's Aldgate.

24th. Erith - Woolwich. Waited 3/4 hour for a bus at Woolwich & then had to walk to trams. Had to watch the antics and afterwards punchings of some drunken men by ferry. Went to Wilsons. Had to walk all the way home - no trams after 11 o'clock.

25th Christmas spent at Ed & Li's at Woodford. Warwicks there, also Sid & Teddy. Had to walk all the way home at 11pm, because trams not allowed to operate owing to air raids.

1916

Sibley begins1916 by listing the names of his friends and colleagues away at war:

Gunner E. Williams No. 62280, C Battery 116 Brigade,20th Division R.F.A., British Mediterranean Expeditionary Force, Salonica

L. Corporal H. Williams, No. 15634 A Company, 7th Battalion DCLI, British Expeditionary Force, France

JAN

Sat. 1st ... Mr Wilson paid me & thought he could manage now without my assistance.

3rd. Paid income tax for Yates & self.

8th ... bought Len and overcoat at Levy's.

13th ... Popp & I walked to Ludgate Circus & had tea in Slaters. We then walked to St. George's Hall - Maskelyne & D... & spent a pleasant evening there. Plenty of laughter over the "Philosopher's Stone."

20th ... Popp & I went to the sale of Helena's furniture at Sim's 280 Romford Rd. Bid for many things - would not go higher than £2 for hall stand. Popp disappointed. I bought lot 108 - 4 rugs.

31st Zepps at East, N.E. & Midlands. City in darkness. L'pool Street pitch black. Find one's way by use of matches. Luckily got away on a train about 7.20 which took me as far as Forest Gate. Plenty of people in 'Tubes' for safety. Warning hooter went at 5 o'clock at

Harrow, warning Fire Brigade & Specials. Casualties. 54 killed. 67 injured. Birmingham, Stafford &c.

To strike terror into the hearts of the British by mounting a long-range nationwide attack the Germans launched nine airships on the night of January 31st 1916 to bombard cities from Liverpool to Loughborough. Sibley's record of the deaths is an underestimate - in total 70 were killed across the country.

FEB

7th Popp & Mrs. Wilson went to Police Concert at Town Hall. Cissy went to her Physical Culture.

12th Popp, Len & I went to Oxford Circus. Had some coffee in ABC, & then went to Philharmonic Hall & saw Williamson's Submarine Picture. Very interesting studies.

21st … Sent to Farrow's (bank) for Treasury note. 2 stamps sent.

24th The 'Star' gave the first intimation of married men's groups being called up - all probably by July 8th. Groups 43, 44 & 45 by

June 24th. Popp distressed but bearing up fairly well.

MARCH

2nd Len decided for Christ. Praise God.

4th Enquired at Grays about my attestation papers - they were sent to East Ham. First groups of married men called up.

11th Went to Ridley Hall prayer meeting - first time for over 2 years.

13th Had a p.c. from East Ham Recruiting Officer saying my papers were there at Town Hall & I was to call to complete same by 7 o'clock tonight. I did not go.

The Philharmonic Hall, Great Portland St., London

14th Went to EH town hall and got my armlet, 2/9d. Took 3/4 hour to obtain.

16th Called in at Farrow's bank and left my bond to be endorsed.

18th Had a walk in the moonlight with Popp.

19th Air raid on Kent coast. 4 Germans. 1 brought down. Took children's meeting at Leytonstone. Found Superintendent a peculiar conscientious objector to the war. Popp had a fright this morning over guns going off.

20th Walked home from Broadway with Lt. Higgins who lives at 27 W.P.A. He had been 9 months at the Front.

22nd Farrows Bank sent me a treasury note case. Paid in 356 at Ilford.

23rd Popp very concerned over the war. Constable told us to shade our hall light.

28th Worst gale for many years. Terrific gale and blinding snow. Fence down, numerous trees blown about.

31st Zepps near London & other places. One down in Thames estuary. Len sent to bed without tea for not getting home early. Len's school report worse than last year. He's going down. Many shots heard. Some shells bursting were visible from our estate.

APRIL

1st. I chloroformed the cat and buried it.

2nd Zepps at Waltham Abbey, Scotland &c.

3rd A terrible disaster occured in Faversham Powder Mills. 200 casualties.

At 14:20 on Sunday 2 April 1916, a huge explosion ripped through the gunpowder mill at Uplees, near Faversham, when a store of 200 tons of trinitrotoluene (TNT) was detonated following some empty sacks catching fire. The TNT and ammonium nitrate (used to manufacture amatol) had exploded. The weather might have contributed to the start of the fire. As it was a Sunday, no women were at work. There were 115 deaths of men and boys, including all the Works Fire Brigade, in the explosion and in subsequent sympathetic detonations. The bodies of seven victims were never found; 108 corpses were buried in a mass grave at Faversham Cemetery on 6 April.

13th Had my bonus £18 given to me.

24th Easter Bank Holiday Monday. Rene & I had a run on hills before breakfast. Went to City & walked to Piccadilly & had tea in 'The Cabin,' - Pop. overcrowded. Walked past Buckingham palace to Westminster & got back at 7.45. Enjoyed our ramble.

25th Zepps arrived 11.20. Annie & I had been to Poplar & been back about 1/2 an hour. Flats gun hard at it - deafening noise. We saw the zepp which was not far from Ilford. It did not risk coming further. Popp upset.

MAY

1st Wrote to Yates asking if I might leave in June. Wrote to Mr. Jaynes in Aylesbury about estate agent.

2nd. Irene started school. Mr. Yates sent down a board 'To let' to be put up.

4th Heard from Henley, Mr. & Mrs. Hamilton wrote referring me to Mrs. Wilson. I replied saying I would go down to Henley on Saturday.

6th.... went by 2.15 Paddington to Henley. Went over several homes and finally accepted one of Mrs. Wilson's, 'Belstone,' St. Andrew's Rd. £25. Mrs. Wilson gave us some tea & then we looked over the house - the people were out. Had short look at the town &

river & caught 6.35 home.

The Sibleys were not alone in fleeing cities as a result of the air raids. Full evacuation programmes were not administered the government as they were in WW2 but many families removed themselves from the cities to friends and relations in less-targeted and rural areas. Thomas Sibley's choice of Henley, then and now a pleasant market town on the Thames about 37 miles from London, was governed largely by its lack of importance to the Germans, and its railway links. For the foreseeable future Thomas would continue his commercial travelling in and around the capital, renting a room in London during the week while his wife and two children enjoyed the benefits of a new riverside home and he visits at weekends. Annie (Popp) was clearly suffering from PTSD as a result of the air-raids, and despite the dislocation of their lives, re-location seemed a good move. Thomas immediately plunges into the removal arrangements.

8th Wrote to Mr. Wilson confirming taking of house, £25 a year. Wrote for removal estimates from Harrods, Whitleys, Selfridges, Roberts, James Bro's. Wrote to Mr. Sluce saying Popp & I were calling tomorrow.

9th Popp & I went to Mr. Sluce's. We found that Mr. Sluce could not very well put me up.

10th Last groups called. Because of my group being called up for June 13th I wrote to Mr. Hill and asked him whether my situation would be kept open for me and what allowance & whether he would back my appeal.

11th Mr. Hill gave me a letter saying my position would be kept open for me - allowance under consideration. Filled in my appeal form. Trotter spoke to me about EFC.

12th Delivered my appeal to Town Clerk T.H. R. Dennis spoke to me about the EFC. Mr. Chown has offered to take me as a paying guest.

13th Len met me and I bought him some shoes 7/6 at co-op & some Blakeys. Popp & I visited Mrs. Chowns about 8.15… I was shown my room to be.

15th Wrote to J. Shaw Henley asking him to fit blinds.

16th Wrote to Mr. Wilson about moving in early in June.

20th Saturday. Very hot. A nice haze. Popp, Len & I went to Forest Gate and got a black dog 2/6. Had to go to the kennels Upton Lane.

26th Ed Tringham wrote asking me to take a morning's service - I wrote saying I was moving to Henley & was temporarily unable.

29th Sent BDH's letter to Chairman of Tribunal - Recruiting Officer had sent it back.

31st Naval battle at Jutland. Wrote to Stemmings giving date of removal June 15th.

JUNE

1st Rene had two companions in to tea. Ed called in the morning and interviewed me in the Bath Room. Ed's experience at the tribunal made him wonder whether I had better get firm to appeal at Finsbury. I said it did not matter. Jones only given a month. Ed & Li came over this evening. Ed thinks it (better) for firm to lodge an appeal at Finsbury if I can get my papers sent there. Popp and I called in at Stemmings & completed arrangements with him.

It would appear that Thomas is making attempts to volunteer for the Home Guard rather than join the regular army.

2nd. … visited in morning recruiting officer at Town Hall. No urgency - appeal not likely to be heard for 6 weeks. Groups 42-46 not going to be called for some time. Munition workers required 8 1/2 an hour. I.D.T. Daily Mail said conscripts are going to be called first - Groups last. Wrote to firm about my appeal and my interview.

3rd Papers gave account of the naval battle - our losses heavy. Germans more so.

4th Lord Kitchener (&?) staff drowned.

5th Sent £2 2/- for piano for Sunday School Union & asked about moratorium should I enter Army.

6th Heard about 2.30 that Earl Kitchener & staff had perished off the Orkneys, HMS Hampshire (?) mined or torpedoed. A terrible blow to everybody. Ordered 6 'beau' cups 2/9 from Owens. 10th Sent some gas brackets by post to Henley.

13th Dolly & Ada Chown called in to say goodbye to Popp.

14th Len & I took my desk & books to Mrs. Chown's. Had a lucky find - 14/-3d got lodged at the back of my drawer in desk & was temporarily lost.

15th Stemming's men arrived at 8.30 and commenced moving us out…. men got away at 12.30 well loaded. Len went (to Ed & Li's) and got a second dinner. I returned to Mrs. Chown's and wrote to Yates. Left keys at Mrs. Westways.

16th … Got to Paddington 11.45, went by 12.5 to Henley, arrived about 1.15. Ciss & Poppy went shopping, & I looked after youngsters & Jeff (dog). Had a walk and then about three had dinner. Mr.& Mrs. Wilson invited us to tea in the garden… Popp & I went into town to meet removal vans. Hurried back & helped to get furniture in - all in by 8 o'clock.

17th. Gas very dear, so we are using more fires. In the evening Popp & I had a walk along river - Berkshire side.

The street in Henley-on-Thames the Sibleys moved to in 1916 to escape the Zeppelins.

18th After dinner we all had a long walk along the river. Len & I went to Congregational Church. Popp & I had a nice walk in the country afterwards.

19th Caught 8.50 at Henley - they all came to see me off. The Chowns made me very comfortable, & I shall ultimately feel at home.

20th Re-examined for General Service. First morning at Mrs. Chown's; had hot water & shaving water… Went to Recruiting Office Medical Board & after a wait was re-examined and passed into 'class A.' Dr. took no notice of my legs. .. Went to Knightsbridge & viewed the Daily Mail Active Service exhibition. Trenches very interesting. Walked to Piccadilly & bused & trained home.

Following a growing hunger on the Home Front for knowledge

of what life was like for their loved ones in the trenches overseas, the Daily Mail organised an exhibition on behalf of the British Red Cross Society and the Order of St John at Prince's Skating Club and the adjacent Knightsbridge Hall from March 18 to April 8, including a realistic recreation of trench conditions.

Daily Mail Active Service Exhibition.—The Trenches.
(On Behalf of the British Red Cross Society and Order of St. John. 1916.)

21st. … wrote 1 each p.c. to Popp, Len, Rene. Had a letter from Popp.

Salmon & cucumber for supper. Jan-March returns down £1000 in comparison with 1915. Met Nicholson in Stratford - no need to worry about army yet awhile.

22nd Went to office. Mr. Hicks very friendly - showed me a pc of himself in uniform, N.G.

24th Saturday. Caught 1.20 (from Paddington). Popp, Ciss, Rene & L met met the train. After tea Popp & I had a lovely walk with Len. Retired about 11 o'clock. Popp had a good night's rest for the first time for a week.

JULY

1st … after tea Popp & I walked along river bank towards Hambeldon. Popp enjoyed it very much.

3rd. Wrote to Popp & sent Len some sums. Yates has let No. 16 W.P.A.

5th Paid £3-2-1 income tax.

8th Saturday. … Popp & I … had a lovely long walk to Shiplake & back.… Had tea then Popp & I went on a delightful walk together. One shower made us stand up awhile. Rene's arm must have been bad - it is better. Dr. said it was getting on nicely & gave her some more dressing.

9th Cong'l chapel. Mr. Tucker asked me to his house & invited me to take service at Nettlebed next Sunday evening.

14th Catford & Woodford. Gave up idea of biking to Henley. Took 2 Cambridge sausages to Henley as well as chocolates. Popp, Ciss, Len met me at the station. Had a good supper & retired with my old bobble.

15th … After dinner we all had a long walk towards Fawley. Went into some lovely woods - ferns as high as myself. After tea Popp & I had a nice walk towards Aston on the Buck'm side - a most delightful evening.

16th … Started for Nettlebed at 4.50, called in at Mr. Tucker's on the way… Pouring with rain all the way. Held service and started on the way home. Mr. McK caught me up on his bic. (sic) & rode slowly with me back. Mr. & Mrs. Tucker met us near Henley.

17th They all came to see me off this morning. Many kisses & goodbyes.

18th Shepherd's Bush. Lunch at ABC Praed St. Had some blanc mange & gooseberries & cheese for supper.

22nd Saturday. Directed & accompanied a Sergeant from Purfleet to Paddington. Got to Henley 1.30. Popp & I had a long walk after tea to Hambeldon lock & back by country route - most enjoyable. After a good supper I did some developing & retired.

26th British take Pozieres, Russ. Erzingan.

27th Left it late before returning on bike to my lodgings with the Chowns & had to risk being fined for not lighting up.

29th Saturday. Up at 4 o'clock. Had some cocoa & bread & butter. Got bike ready & started for Henley at 5.25. Had an excellent ride. Took Ham sandwiches with me which I ate near Colehook (sic. - Colnbrook?) *& read some of papers. Walked thro' Slough and had a soda & milk. Stopped in Maidenhead and bought some black cherries for Popp & then finished my journey arriving about 11.20. Enjoyed our tea in spite of the fact that Popp had lost her new brooch I bought her. Went with Mrs. Hitchins (Hitchman?) & Popp to get potatoes &c from a local garden.*

Sibley's epic cycle journey from Wanstead to Henley was a journey of 72 miles, completed in about six hours. From his journal it seems he took the Bath Road out of London via Hammersmith, Brentford and Twickenham, his pace growing to a tired stroll as he reached Slough in Berkshire. These were country towns in 1916, the Bath Road a pleasant westward highway fringed with cowslip-choked hedgerows and olde-worlde inns.

30th Zepps started early this morning, East Coast.

AUGUST

2nd Zepp again. 80 bombs - no casualties.

3rd Second year of war ended. Had a stroll along the Embankment about 7 o'clock. Did not stop to see German submarine mine layer.

Saw Nicolson at East Ham Town Hall - appeal likely to be heard beginning of Sept.

8th Chatted with Mrs. Chown about having a longer holiday as a paying guest.

11th Caught 9.15 Paddington. Pleasant company - soldiers chatty in train.

12th Took Len & Rene also Ronald Hitchman for a walk to bathing pond. Took the two youngsters on a punt after dinner & had 3 hours (3.30-6.30). Did some fishing when moored. Popp & Ciss got some tea and we had tea on the riverbank.

14th Holiday. Popp & I walked to Twyford. Had tea there then rode to Shiplake & walked home. Did some gaslight printing.

15th Len & I had a bathe in the swimming pond. After dinner we all walked to Reading. Took Rene's go-cart. Popp & I had some tea, Cissy & children milk, cakes &c.... returned by 8 o'clock train.

The Sibley's sojourn in Henley appears to be just the palliative and refuge it was intended to be, a quiet green world of country lanes, bustling market towns and small shops - a far cry from the soot-black din of London. Back in the city after his weekend with his family, Sibley is still engaged in appealing against his conscription into the regular army:

17th Poor chap lost his straw hat in Lyons and had to leave with a bowler. Wrote my letter to the Chairman of the Tribunal East Ham.

18th Arrived at '60' 8.5. Dolly here, others were at Pictures.

Popp, Cissy, Rene and Len would have paid a visit to the Picture Palace in Bell Street, still a cinema though now in a different reincarnation.

The Regal Cinema, Henley, in 1916 called the Picture Palace.

20th Sunday. Cycled to Nettlebed and gave service. Had a good dinner & did not go out. Cycled again to Nettlebed and gave gospel address which was appreciated. Got back in 20 mins.

24th Zepps visited East Coast. Went to Poplar & saw Mr. & Mrs. K. Ed, Win, Wilf there. Said goodbye to Howard Fleet who is going to France shortly. Mr. Haslett far from a conscientious objector.

25th Zepp visited London, Greenwich & Plumstead. Left brougham at Elephant… Bakerloo to Paddington. Poor Poindestre came back this morning to find a Zepp bomb had blown out his shop windows & done some damage. 8 killed 36 injured.

29th Bought fishing rod &c in Woodgrange Rd.

SEPT

2nd. Dr. McK. sent a certificate about Popp for tribunal.

3rd 13 Zepps. 1 brought down at Cuffley (?). Mr. Tucker called at dinner time and told us a zepp had been brought down in flames. Popp & I had a long walk to Peppard.

4th Called in Graham's on the way home. Heard all about the Zepp raid & the raiders fall in flames. Great excitement in London. Ernie turned up at Henley about 11.15. Had had a puncture. He was tired & hungry. Gave him a good supper and got him to bed. East Ham Town Hall Military Rep. wrote saying call-up to be re-examined medically.

Ernest Sibley is the son of Thomas' elder Brother Ed, and evidently as intrepid a cyclist as his Uncle Thomas. Taking advantage of their rustic surroundings, Thomas takes his weary nephew fishing.

6th Morning mostly spent fishing. Caught nothing except minnows. Had dinner then a long walk on the way to Peppard. We got some blackberries. Had tea then Ernie and I had a walk on the way to Hambeldon. Wrote to Captain Williams about my medical examination & asked whether Sept. 19th would do.

7th Replaced Ernie's puncture & got his bike to rights. We then had a ride towards Marlow. dinner at 1 o'clock and we (except Popp & Ciss) had a punt on the river. I took camera and managed 3 snapshots.

8th Ernie off for home. We started on bikes at 10.20. I left Ernie at Slough about 12 o'clock & rode to Windsor. ... Got back at 12.12 via Wargrave. Had a rest then we all went to Harpsden Woods blackberrying.

9th Len & I went fishing unsuccessfully. Had dinner. Popp & I tried to get onto 'The Venture' (charabanc) for reading - full up of booked passingers. We got over our disappointment & walked to Warren Row & on to the reading Rd. Had some tea at an inn, 1/6, and walked to Wargrave.

12th Popp & I went by charabanc to Reading for afternoon. Had a nice tea at the Talbot. Inspected ruins of Abbey &c. Went to Peppard & round pretty country.

West Street, Marlow, Buckinghamshire, along which Thomas Sibley & his nephew Ernie cycled one September morning in 1916.

13th After breakfast had a spin on bike to Marlow - looked about the town, went over bridge & then returned at 11.30. Rene & I walked to Warren Row. Lost Jeff on the way. Had a good dinner - got plenty of blackberries. Had a cup of tea - children had ginger ale. Got back 6.30. Jeff turned up all right & was waiting on our return.

Marlow in 1916 was a bustling market town some eight miles east of Henley nestling on the banks of the Thames. Wethereds Brewery was its industrial heart, a smart, broad prospering High Street, a small railway station linking the town to Maidenhead, and small villages and dairy farms dotting the surrounding hills.

15th. Went on bike after breakfast & interviewed the Head Master of Henley Royal Grammar School - Mr. Valpy. Had a nice chat with him. We all had another 'Pic Nic' and went to Bingfield Heath. Rene's leg was sore so had go-cart. 19th Tues. Received from Popp a note from East Ham R.O. to be examined at Stratford at 2pm. I went and all was well. Dr. Morrow examined me and was very friendly & put me down in C1 class. Home Service. The Lord worked for me - my prayer was Ps CXIX 17 & it was answered. Praise Him. Dolly & Ada are delighted over my success. Wrote to Popp and told her the good news. Mr. & Mrs. (Chown's) 24th wedding anniversary. They went to Boro Theatre.

20th. Tea at Mrs. Wilson's. Fresh herrings Yorkshire style; very nice tea. Had also an extra special supper - salmon & blanc mange and plums.

23rd Zepp raid tonight & early Sunday morning. 30 killed, 2 missing, 110 injured. 2 zeppelins brought down.

25th Harlesden &c. Heard all about Zepp raid. Bromley, Mile End, Leyton, Streatham & Brixton are the suffering parts of London. Two Zepps down. One at Billericay, one at Mersea.

26th Went to the Philharmonic Hall and saw the 'Somme' Pictures. Very realistic and absorbing. Creates a realization of the terror of modern war, difficulties to be overcome and the immense effort to succeed.

J.B. MacDowell and Geoffrey Malins's documentary was

intended to boost morale, but its scenes of wounded and dead soldiers, not to mention the contentious "over-the-top" sequence, make it a more complicated, thought-provoking and mournful piece of work. One of the "over-the-top" scenes was staged, but so much else is horribly real here – and the film was inscribed on UNESCO's Memory of the World Register in 2005.

27th Li & Win visit Henley. Good news from France. Combles & H'pool taken. (?)

28th Had a letter from Rev. W. Herridge 'The Manse' Hambeldon asking me to take his evening service on Oct. 8th. I wrote & accepted.

OCT

1st Air Raid. Another Zepp down at Potters Bar.

8th Sunday. Popp & I walked to the Manse. Congregational church Hambelden (Pheasant's Hill). Had tea with Mrs. Herridge & son. Took service & then Popp & I had a lovely moonlight walk home.

9th I called in at the Conference Hall for the last meeting of the Good Templars special annual gathering.

12th C class wanted at once.

13th Heard from East Ham that my appeal will be heard Monday next, 3pm.

14th .... Found Popp ill, crawling about & Ciss in bed with rheumatism & under Dr. Sussman. Popp in a bad mental state. Did what I could to help the situation.

16th Appeal Heard. Join the V.T.C. Got to town hall 3pm. My appeal was heard 4.30. 3 month's exemption with leave to appeal again. I had to join the V.T.C. I joined this evening. Saw Paget there - he is a sergeant major.

Sibley must have been thankful to have succeeded in his appeal against the regular army. By 1916 he was already 38 years old, a mature family man. His visits to the Daily Mail Exhibition and the *Battle of the Somme* at the Philharmonic Hall must in some way have been mental preparation for life in the army - had his appeal failed.

The Volunteer Training Corps (VTC) was a home defence militia, the First World War equivalent of the Home Guard. When war was declared in August 1914, there was an immediate demand for a means of service for those men who were over military age or engaged in important occupations. Combined with the perceived risk of a German invasion, this resulted in the spontaneous formation of volunteer defence associations around the country. By September 1914, a central committee had been formed. It was renamed the Central Association of Volunteer Training Corps in November 1914 and recognised by the War Office.The Volunteer Training Corps became more firmly established in 1916 after the introduction of conscription into the Armed Services in March. As a consequence of conscription, there was a necessity for Military Service Tribunals to hear the cases of men wishing to avoid service for a range of reasons. Some of these men were granted exemption on condition that they join the VTC.

17th Went direct to EVC, had a little drilling and a lecture on the rifle. Met Mr. Staines there.

18th Went direct to VTC and did some more drilling - more fun than work.

20th Trams 'all at sea' - breakdowns &c &c - so got out at Kennington Oval, & came home.

23rd Went direct to Drill Hall and put in a drill.

28th … Popp had had a sorry week. I cheered her up.

30th … Went direct to Drill Hall and did some evolutions in playground with Nos 1 & 4 Platoons.

31st. Proceeded to Drill Hall and did some shooting. Only 50 scored.

NOV

8th Musketry drill.

10th .... Had some tea at Abbot's Catford.

15th Bayonet exercises. Sent home early on account of Zepps about.

20th Platoon drill in sections in playground.

21st Went to Drill Hall & heard lecture from Lieutenant (late commander) Barker. Lecture on the trenches, soldier's life &c., was interesting.

24th Had some tea at Mr. Buckley's. Saw his friend just home from France and wounded. Went to Drill Hall and had some shooting. A friendly competition with 'cricket' cards. I got 14... and tied with a man. We had another shot each and I beat him so secured 2nd prize - a cup & saucer.

28th Mr. Chown met me at Drill Hall & handed me a telegram saying Popp was dangerously ill. I hastened off at once to Henley. Dr. Brownlow had been called. Gastritus through chill. I decided to get Popp back to London as quickly as possible.

DEC

5th Drilled with the Company on the Flats.

6th Wrote to Mr. Wilson of Henley giving notice to leave in March.

9th Had a chat with Mr. Valpy about Len being a boarder. Heard from Mr. Wilson - disappointed with short (3 mo.) notice.

25th ... took Rene over to Mrs. Chown's to see about Rene's skates. Had a glass of ginger wine. Had a scrumptious feed on Turkey, Ham, Xmas pudding (Popp's) & mince pies. Afternoon taken up mostly with gramaphone & music. Mrs. Bottomley came. ... Had parlour games, finishing the screaming consequences. I introduced the shopping consequence. Popp had all the work to do. Some unpleasantness between Li, Win & Popp. Spoilt the Xmas. Popp & I saw Mrs. Bottomley home to Crossley Rd.

27th After dinner Popp & I essayed to go to Wanstead in fog. Got mixed up on Capel Rd. Popp lost her bag. We were befriended by people at 37 Forest Drive who promised to look for it.

28th Left Ciss, Rene, Len safe in the train (Paddington) at 2.15.

Went to Drill Hall. Mr. Bohl gave us a lecture on Physiology, veins, and venereal diseases &c. Very interesting.

Popp's bag found by people at 37 Forest Drive. .... I gave them the silver 2/-.

1917

1st Popp, Ciss & Rene saw me off (FROM HENLEY) by the 8.50. Had 2 shots with my rabbit stew at Wembley & terribly luckily I didn't swallow them. Mrs. Chown had company, Mr., Mrs. & messrs Smith. I joined them and we had some singing. I sang the '3 Young Crows.' .... boiled beef, ham, Xmas pudding. Finished up with 'Cross - 2, C. Answers' & consequences.

2nd Went to drill - a short route march.

5th ....finished work and went to D. Campbell Morgan's for last time as he is going to leave Westminster on account of his health.

6th Found Jeff had been given away so did not need to kill him.

Popp & I went to Tuckers and arranged about Nettlebed. Bought tickets for Wednesday's children's entertainment.

12th Went to drill hall. Had a shoot & got 97 - 8 bulls - my best up to date. Sergeant Davis pleased.

13th Popp in a very serious mental condition occasioned by insomnia

& anaemia. Called on Girdles. He says our furniture will take 3 vans £15.

19th Great explosion in Silvertown. Woolwich, Erith &c. Had tea at Buckley's. While I was at Powis St. a great explosion took place - many casualties. Glass blown out all round me and quite a panic took place.

On the evening of 19th January 1917 a fire broke out in the melt-pot room of a vast munitions factory in Silvertown, on the north bank of the Thames near Newham, igniting 50 tons of TNT. The explosion killed 73, injured 400 others, destroying buildings and blowing out the glass from shopwindows for several miles around. Thousands were made homeless. Sibley was on the south bank of the Thames at the time, in Powis Street in Woolwich - such was the power of the blast that windows were blasted out of their frames as he stood attempting to sell his pharmaceuticals.

22nd Went into the ambulance class with Mr. Green.

23rd Some of the EVR went to Silvertown & kept guard.

29th Moved from Henley. Mr. Wilkins moved us from Henley by rail. When I had gone Mr. Wilson came round and some unpleasantness took place between Popp & him.

31st. … 3 month's extension. Appeared before the E.H. tribunal - Mr. Banks Martin in the chair. I obtained another 3 month's exemption - praise the Lord.

FEB

1st. Moved into 44 Clavering Rd., So. Wanstead.

5th Southend &c. Went to Central Park Picture Palace in case EVR were there but they were not so returned quickly to Drill Hall &

had a drill in playground in snow & bright moonlight. Called at E.H. town hall to see Captain Williams according to his request but he had turned up at 9.45 so I left interview for Tuesday.

6th Saw Captain Williams who wanted my request card, which is in the post. He said I was now out of the district and that West Ham would deal with my case in the future. Had drill - route march round Flats in the moonlight.

7th Landlord came round and had a look at house. He is going to have it done up immediately.

9th Went to Picture Palace - Central Park - with volunteers... Saw the Tanks.

25th ... dining room finished and looks very nice with red wallpaper.

16th Went to Mr. Ellis 3 Coleridge Avenue - ambulance class, & studied the lungs.

22nd Called in Follett & Co., 4 Victoria Rd., Bishopsgate St. to see about VTC uniform. Left it for next week.

25th Ernie Williams - back from Salonica - & his 2 sisters called in this evening.

26th Drill Hall - ambulance section. Had some practice in artificial respiration.

28th Had some musketry & then got my kit. Sergts Fitzgerald & White helped me get it on. Popp & Ciss met me at M.P. D Collins gave me a sample bottle of his home brewed stout.

MARCH

1st. Went to Pearl Ass. Co., High Holborn and was examined by their doctor for a War Loan Policy. Went to Follett's Bishopsgate St. & bought my volunteer's uniform 22/-. Popp & Ciss met me in

Empress Avenue with Mr. Chown.

2nd Bought some 'Kiwi' for cleaning belt &c.

8th I went to office and saw Mr. Halsey & Mr. Hicks. It was decided that I continue travelling for another fortnight.

9th Called in and saw George & Mother (MRS. KETTLEY). Mother hardly knew me.

10th. No Potatoes.

13th Sworn in & measured for a uniform. Was sworn in to serve until the end of the war. 14 drills a month until efficient, then 10.

The Voluntary Training Corps, VTC, were a National Guard of Home Front volunteers who assisted in many auxiliary actions in support of the regular army.

15th Popp & I went to see George & Mother. George gave me an old fashioned bomb on a mount & a stick of shaving soap.

16th Zepp raid S.E. coast. Popp & Ciss went to view St. Patrick's Ball & came home at 11.40 scared and alarmed because of air raid

alarms. Had to stay up until 2 o'clock. I got under the eiderdown.

17th Received 'calling up' papers from Stratford.

18th Went with ambulance corps. Did some stretcher drill. Got very cold.

22nd Took back my calling up papers to Stratford and produced my exemption card.

24th Last journey Pro Tempore. Spent afternoon in garden. Len helped and got some manure from meadow until man stopped him.

APRIL

6th I had 'calling up' papers again - this time from East Ham. Sent them back.

14th First Saturday in office.

It would seem that as Sibley has joined the VTC he is no longer permitted to work as a travelling salesman so is now working in the offices of the British Drug House - he is on standby so must be available at all times for the call to military duty.

21st Mr. Wilson Senior died today. Popp & Cissy went to Concert at East Ham.

22nd Rayleigh. Marched 3 miles to trenches (parapets). Half hour's digging, then dinner. I hour 10 mins digging then marched back with tools.

25th Went to Express Dairy Co. Angel for lunch. Got new season ticket 13/3d.

26th Did two drills at Water Lane. Got my calling up papers again - must get them endorsed.

27th Went to Town Hall and got my calling up papers endorsed by

Town Clerk.

MAY

6th Taube visited Stoke Newington about 1 o'clock this morning, 1 killed 2 casualties.

Despite its picturesque bird-like appearance, the Taube was a deadly mono-plane flown throughout the war as both a bomber and a guide for the Zeppelins.

7th Enquired about a hospital for Rene - adenoids to be removed.

8th Went to Wanstead Council Offices. Called before the tribunal 9.15 & got a month's exemption - final. Cannot appeal again except by permission of the tribunal. Popp rather upset. My hopes are still in the Lord. He will have mercy.

9th Told Ed about my month's exemption - he hopes that a certificate will come along for me.

14th Met Rene & Cissy at Liverpool Street & took them to Central London Throat & Ear hospital, Gray's Inn Rd. Rene was examined and arrangements made for next Thursday. Had a cup of tea in Lyons and Rene had a cake. Found that Len had been to my desk and attempted to get at my money & had stole some things. Had to beat him.

17th Took Rene to hospital. Rene went thro' the operation. Adenoids removed, tonsils cut & a tooth pulled out. Put Rene at once to bed - she is very collapsed. Went to drill at Water Lane Schools.

This was Water Lane in Stratford, East London, near what is now the University of East London. On the Home Front for the duration basic military training was taking place in schools, parks and drill halls up and down the country.

20th Terrific storms. Lightning startling & vivid. Len went with scouts to St. Gabriel's.

Ed, Ernie & Win came to see Rene in afternoon. Rene better but very poorly. She was brought down to tea.

21st … rode to Graham St., met Bob in the tram.

23rd. Had to send for Dr. Anderson who said Rene was dangerously ill - Septic Throat. Had to pour brandy down her throat at one time.

24th Zepp early morning Norfolk & Suffolk.

26th Dr. Anderson here, told us Rene had scarlet fever. We hastened after dinner to 'isolate' her - turned all furniture out of Cissy's room & put Len's bed in for Cissy, & Len in drawing room. Sheet well disinfected was hung over door &c.

JUNE

5th Washing Day. I gave a hand at scrubbing - Cissy not available for that interesting occupation.

6th Germans lose 10 aeroplanes out of 18 in Southend & Sheerness.

8th Saturday. Played tennis with Len after his tea. Sat with Rene for an hour.

Throughout their childhoods their father Thomas spent much time with Len and Rene, belying the received misconception that men did not engage in active childcare in this period; indeed the casual way in which he mentions it throughout his journals indicates that far from being rare, it was commonplace.

11th Dr. Anderson called. Gave him 10/- for last week.

12th Secured 2lbs of potatoes at Offord. Ordered some more for Saturday.

13th Great London Air Raid by 15 aeroplanes. Air raid took place at 11.30 today. I was at Barking - one bomb dropped near. I saw 2 of the Taubes returning. Hurried home and found Popp in a scared condition. Tried to mend punctures on bike but failed - had to buy new inner tube 5/-.

14th Casualties in air raid over 500 - 101 killed. Alarms of another air raid this morning which came to naught. Popp very ill - oh to be back in Henley!

15th Popp very ill - nerve breakdown & head bad. Had to make hurried arrangements to take her away... caught 1.50 to Littlehampton. Obtained good lodgings at Mrs. Scobie's 16 Clifton Rd., Littlehampton. Popp still a little weak but brighter. The Lord stood by us.

16th Saturday. Had a walk to Angmering. Bought some shoes for Popp.

17th Popp still very shaky. Had a walk towards Arundel - not very interesting.

18th Went to Worthing by 10.40 and... took unfurnished apartments at Mrs. Clare's 15 Hertford Rd. @ 10/- per week. Had some coffee at Kander's. Bought some oddments for rooms.... put a deposit down on a folding bedstead.

20th After breakfast Popp & I commenced our walk to Bognor. Portsmouth guns caused a distraction for a short time (we walked half a mile out of our way). Had some refreshment at Felpham then finished our walk to Bognor. Had dinner at Bognor - roast beef & yorkshire &c, 3/5d. Caught 5.30 to Arundel - broke journey and walked to castle grounds. Got back to Littlehampton at 7.10. Had a big supper - short walk, then retired.

26th A boy threw a stone and hit me on the forehead, fortunately on the hat first. I boxed his ears.

27th Wrote to furniture people Worthing, & Pickfords.

30th Did sundry jobs preparing to go to Worthing.

JULY

1st. Sgt of Police called to see why I had not joined up. My protection certificate prevented any trouble.

2nd. Mr. Wilson called... and took away 'Pinto' for 3 months.

4th Air raid on Harwich this morning 5.30.

5th Irene out of bedroom after 6 weeks. Rene had the two misses Cooper in to tea. She went out with them.

6th Packed bags & prepared to start early in the morning.

7th. GREAT AIR RAID ON LONDON. Took Popp & family to Worthing.

On 7 July 1917, London was attacked by 22 Gotha bombers,

which arrived over the east coast, formed up over Epping Forest and proceeded to bomb the East End and the City of London – in all 57 people were killed. The raid caused great anger about the lack of proper warnings and the lack of effective defences. It prompted another big anti-German riot, just as the sinking of the Lusitania had sparked off the mass rioting and looting in May 1915. The *Times* newspaper reported: *As a spectacle, the raid was the most thrilling that London has seen since the air attacks began. Every phase could be followed from points many miles away without the aid of glasses [i.e. binoculars or a telescope], and hundreds of thousands of people watched the approach of the squadron, the dropping of the bombs, the shelling of the German aeroplanes by anti-aircraft guns and the eventual retreat.'* The raid highlighted the exposure of London to attack by aeroplanes after the Zeppelins had been fought off in 1916.

The raid coincided with the Sibley's second flight from the capital, as they flee a city in turmoil.

7th July, contd…

Rainham arr. Barking 10.40. Watched fighting in the air whilst in the train when I got to East Ham. Popp & others at EH station under bridge in safety. Popp fainted and had some men look after her. Cissy found me just about to go to Wanstead. Went to London Bridge by VR - had an exciting time & a fearful rush. Just caught 11.50 - train packed, had to stand. Arrived safely at Worthing. Had dinner & put bedsteads up. A very exciting & tiring day, & we were glad to have supper and get to rest.

10th Guns distinctly heard from Belgium. Windows rattled.

11th Cissy had been rowing with the girl Clare over Rene and there was a bother with Popp, so things were not as nice as expected.

12th Caught 7.26 at Worthing. Popp saw me off. Arrived at office

9.45. .... Went to St. Peter's and had tea in Lyons, went to Water Lane & put in 2 hours with ambulance section. Arrived home 10 o'clock. Wrote to sanitary inspector about the bad smells.

13th ... Called in Offord's & borrowed his oil stove. He gave me an egg. Had tea. Picked some peas, turnip tops, mint & rhubarb. Cleaned straw hat &c.

The air-raid by Gothas on London on July 7th 1917. Eye-witnesses said the attackers resembled a flock of birds.

14th Popp & I had a nice walk & sat on front with Rene & paddled. Tea at 7 then Popp & I went to a pier concert.

18th. About 150 men & women went out on strike. Some of the warehouse staff went out on strike for union recognition and wages. Mr. Hill called a meeting and it was decided to carry on without them.

19th Office & warehouse closed now between 1-2.

21st ... Went to swimming baths and had a swim.

26th …. Had an hour in warehouse.

30th Spent morning telephoning for orders with much success.

31st I was not examined being sufficiently high in army classification.

AUGUST

1st. Joined library and had first volume 'Les Miserables.'

4th Saturday. Crowds of people going from London.

11th Had some coffee at Kandy's then Popp & I sat on beach & read.

16th Went to Richmond with West Ham Pharmacists. Steamboat to Hampton Court. Tea at Mitre Hotel.

18th Changed library book, selected 'Adam Bede.'

21st Distributing rifles. I did not have one on account of being in ambulance section.

22nd Air raid on Margate & Dover &c.

28th …. went to Philharmonic Hall and saw pictures 'An Ancient Evil,' & 'Where are my Children?' Real heart-searching. Very pathetic.

29th Caught 6 o'clock train to Worthing. Popp met me. We visited some rooms in Pavilion Rd. - many conveniences.

SEPT.

3rd Air raid on Chatham &c. - big casualties. Popp gave 3 weeks notice to Mrs. Clare.

4th Air raid at 11.30 20 aeroplanes (11 killed).

11th Let 4 rooms of the house (CLAVERING RD., WORTHING),

10/6. Mr & Mrs. Pollard.

Where are My Children? - a powerful anti-abortion film, 1916, starring Tyrone Power Sr.

Ed, Li & Wilf came over & helped me shift furniture from from dining room to drawing room. We damaged the gas brackets and caused some leakage. After some difficulty patched it up.

12th Went to Worthing by 6 o'clock train. Found folk in troubles and longing to get away.

For now the Sibleys decamped in the comparative safety of Worthing on the East Sussex coast, the only audible reminder of the conflict being the dull thud of heavy artillery from across the English Channel.

20th Up at 5am. Worked hard cleaning kitchen & scullery. Mr. Pollard moved in today.

22nd Saturday. Moved in to 'Symhurst,' Pavilion Rd. Mrs. Alexander lent us some furniture, a bedroom & a bedstead.

23rd Moonlight Air Raid. Harlesden &c. Had tea in ABC & met Graham from ambulance section in there. We went together to East Ham. On reaching West Ham - before station train in darkness was brought to a standstill because of air raid. ... air raid continued and bombs were dropped near enough to shake the train. Twice the raiders appeared. The third time was the worst. Heaven praise God I was kept safe.

24th … Just got indoors when the bombardment started. Twice the raiders tried to get through the barrage with only a little success.

27th Eight of us were despatched to go to Manor Park to fetch stretchers. Took stretchers back to 'Cedars.'

30th Sunday. Air raid on London by moonlight.

OCT

1st. When in the Woolwich bus the siren went so there was a general scattering. Tunnel packed. I went by GER to Custom House Station. Walked & trammed towards Plaistow Station where I had to stay 4 hours or so during a terrible bombardment.

6th Saturday. After tea Popp & I went to concert at Montague St., 'Zig-Zags.'

8th Got my season ticket… £6-5/- instead of £7.2.6. as former one.

19th Great Zepp raid. One got to London. Ed, Wilf & I went to Campbell-Morgan's - had tea at Hollybush Rest'nt. Warning given of air raid when meeting was half way thro.' We went down into the basement. We essayed out about 9.20 & got to L'pool Street alright. We had to stay there however until 2 o'clock. There was much humour to keep us from being miserable. I ultimately reached home 2.30.

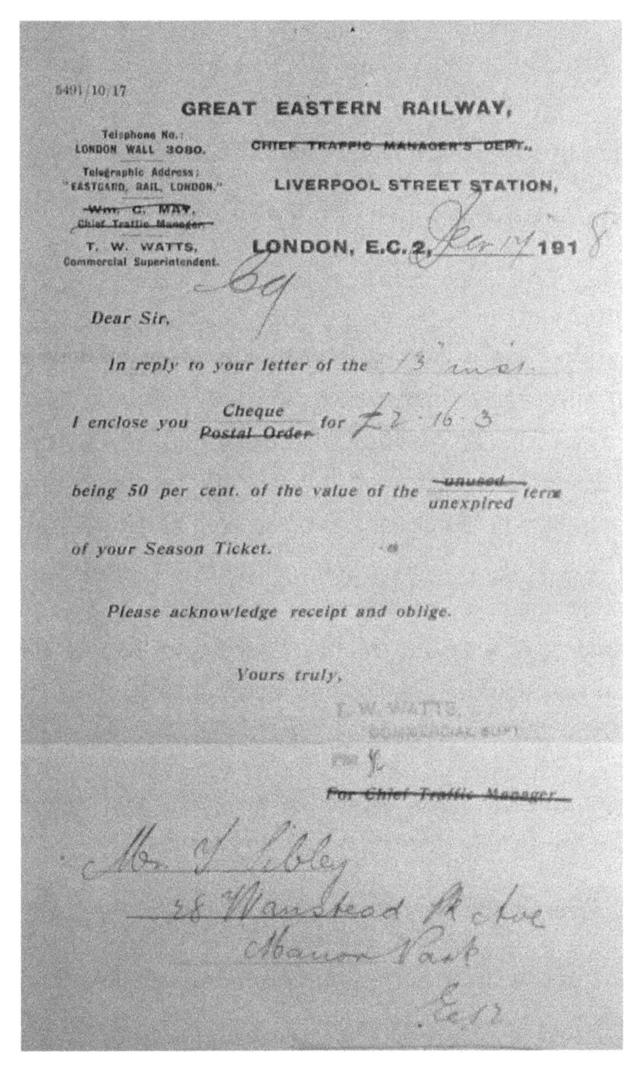

5491/10/17

GREAT EASTERN RAILWAY,

Telephone No.: LONDON WALL 3080.
Telegraphic Address: "EASTGARD, RAIL, LONDON."
~~Wm. C. MAY, Chief Traffic Manager~~
T. W. WATTS, Commercial Superintendent.

~~CHIEF TRAFFIC MANAGER'S DEPT.~~
LIVERPOOL STREET STATION,
LONDON, E.C.2, Apr 17 1918

Dear Sir,

In reply to your letter of the 13 inst.

I enclose you Cheque ~~Postal Order~~ for £2. 16. 3

being 50 per cent. of the value of the ~~unused~~ unexpired term

of your Season Ticket.

Please acknowledge receipt and oblige.

Yours truly,

T. W. WATTS, COMMERCIAL SUPT.
~~For Chief Traffic Manager.~~

Mr. J. Sibley
28 Wanstead Pk Ave
Manor Park
E.12

In a foreshadowing of WW2, many Londoners used the underground tube network for shelter, and the practice of humour and communal singing while the bombs rained down hundreds of feet above their heads was born.

20th … We went to Zig-Zags concert in evening.

26th Great Italian reverse by German, Austrian armies.

30th … Went direct to Essex V. Drill Hall. Signed next of kin form.

NOV

5th Lunched at Express Dairy Co. Golders Green.

8th Lunched at Veg. Minories.

12th Lunched at Veg. Rest. Jewin St.

Vegetarianism has a long established history in Britain, dating back to the early nineteenth century, culminating in the establishment of the Vegetarian Society in 1847. It has been associated with health for about as long, although in the early years that might be spiritual health as well as physical well-being. During the war vegetarians were subject to rationing in equal measures to those of meat-eaters - indeed, the war promoted vegetarianism as a result of blockades and supply difficulties; vegetarian restaurants boomed as a consequence.

23rd Made calls in Greenwich. Saw Poingdestre, who had just got over diptheria. Mr. Pollard helped me get couch up from cellar & to cover it & an armchair ready for GER on Monday.

27th Heard from Popp saying Len had Erysipiales.

28th Len's face a little better but his nose very much swollen & spotted.

29th Found that I had to do musketry. Arranged for Saturday.

DEC

1st Saturday. Called in at Ellis's for rifle but he had not cleaned it. Went to Purfleet Range & fired one round at 200 yards.

5th Air Raid by Goths. 3 killed in London, 11 injured.

6th Went to Cedars. Examination of some for Corporal & Lance-Corporal. I did not attempt to secure the stripes.

8th Broke up some of Mrs. Alexander's orange boxes to fit together as a sideboard.

13th Made 3 calls in Balham. Lunched in Lyons Clapham.

15th Lewisham &c. Gave Mr. Gregory (Sayers) his cigarettes (500 State Express), 5/6d.

18th Air Raid. 10 killed. Went on to Wilson, air raid warning whilst on the way. I just got to Wilsons when the air raid started. I took down his order and stayed with Mr.& Mrs. Wilson. All over by 9.15. ... Had to walk from East Ham station. Saw Graham at his door.

19th Left office at 6 o'clock. Extremely foggy. Air raid warning so rode by tube Met. to Bow Road. All clear then so trammed to Stratford & walked to Cedars. Did some bayonet drill. Saw 3 chaps home or nearly so as the fog was so dense. My torch came in very handy.

21st Rene nearly died with bronchitis. Tried to get some bacon but failed. Watkin brought me the fowl, 5/-11d. Called and saw George & Mother. George too poor to give us a Xmas present.

24th Finished making little sideboards. Stayed with Rene & then brought her downstairs. Popp & I went out in afternoon & evening... I bought her a fur necklace & Cissy some gloves.

25th Popp had a busy morning cooking. I did some odd jobs & amused Rene who was brought downstairs. Had a lovely dinner -

fowl & pickled pork, Xmas pudding &c. Len went to Morton's. Rene a little better but cough very troublesome.

26th After tea Popp & I went to concert - Jake-a-Loos, Canadians.

28th Lunched at Veg. Minories . Ed & I also Jack Dowsett & Wilf went to Campbell-Morgans. I walked with Jack D. as far as Hackney Station, and continued on bus until I reached Baker's Arms.

1918

JAN

5th Mr. & Mrs. Flower came into supper and stayed the evening. Mr. Flower came to Worthing today for his 6 months 10 days leave from the navy. He is an engineer.

6th Day of Nations Prayer.

11th … cleaned brass on uniform and equipment.

12th…. called in at Ivan Killetts & got some cheese and tea, also some brawn for supper.

14th Mr. Flower & family moved into 'Symhurst.'

15th Gwenny Flower had supper with us.

19th Had to stand up all the way to Brighton. … Popp could get no meat so my sausages came in handy.

21st Went to Whitehall Place in evening - First Aid.

24th ABC had no butter or marg.

25th Bought 2 pairs of kippers for 10d and a tin of army rations 1/10.

26th Saturday. Took Rene with me to library, changed books. Got all ready for Victoria if wired because of expected mobilization. Nothing took place so stayed in Worthing as usual.

28th Great Air Raid, 49 killed, 100 injured. Went to Whitehall Place Schools. Went through First Aid examination whilst air raid was going on. I easily passed. Stayed until a lull then went to Ed's. Ed, Ernie & Wilf out so kept Li company. I left at 1 o'clock and soon after the all-clear was given.

29th Great Air Raid. Bombs dropped on Kew gardens. … had a special prayer on account of approaching air raid. Ps 121 very precious to me. Air raid finished about 11.45 with a Hun letting all his bombs drop near Redbridge Lane & water works. They shook the house & me. Mr. Pollard & I try to ascertain what was done but it was too foggy.

FEB

1ST. Bought a watch from Offord then sold it to Bob 7/6. I thanked Mr. Hill for £10 advance. Ed arranged for more expenses for me.

4th Went to Whitehall Place and had my first lesson in roller bandaging.

5th Cissy 'phoned to me from Worthing saying Rene was very ill & would I come home. Caught 6 o'clock to Worthing and found Rene very bad, & Popp done up. We looked after Rene all night. … Severe bronchitis.

10th Looked after Rene who was in the dining room. She was a little better.

11th Lunched in ABC Oxford Circus.

12th Leonard started wearing glasses.

14th Went to St. Peter's Hospital and had tea in J.P's Strand.

23rd Saturday. Caught 1.20 to Worthing. We went to Pictures to see 'The Life of Lord Kitchener.' I did not enjoy it.

25th Meat, Margarine & Butter Rations Commenced. Lunched in Lyons Tottenham Court Rd. & used my first meat ticket.

26th Went round to Ellis - we presented him with a scarf-pin as a mark of our appreciation for his help in our 1st Aid Studies.

MARCH

7th Air Raid took place at 11.30, all clear went at 1.45. Stayed with Pollards and had some cocoa and cake at 1.30.

9th Popp & I had a walk & I then purchased 2 pairs of shoes for her and one pair for Cissy. Popp seemed very unhappy & generally dissatisfied with life and everybody.

10th ... Popp greatly upset over remarks misunderstood & said hurriedly &c which caused increased unhappiness.

12th Arrived at office 2.50. Heard from Popp - not well & terribly hurt in feelings. I wrote to her. Mrs. Wilson gave me a jam tart. Put some pieces on Len's boots & wrote up diary.

13th Left at 5.30 & Popp met me. We had a nice walk after supper and everything was as usual.

16th Popp & I had a walk along the front. Had tea - Pastor Crouch called in for a minute or two - & Popp & I went to Pier Concert. Not up to much. Popp a little better so more jolly.

21st Great German Offensive.

25th Lunched at Veg. Restaurant Furnival St., Holborn.

26th Hurried home and cleaned up my equipment & uniform for tomorrow night.

29th Ed, Ern & I walked to Goring, country route there & sea front back. Went to St. James Hall in evening and saw Mr. Henman's pictures on the Holy Land.

30th Ernie & I went to Museum & Library until 12.45. Ed, Ernie, Len & I played 'Blow Football.' Ed, Li, Ernie, Win, Popp & I went to the Pier Concert - heard a good company.

APRIL

1st. We went on the Front about 11 o'clock. The ladies intent on Khandys or Khongs, went alone. Ed & I stayed with the children. Rene able to enjoy herself on the beach.

2nd. … Went to St. James Hall concert 'Philip Ritz's company.' Very good, we all enjoyed it.

3rd Caught 6 o'clock to Worthing & read Chas Spurgeon's lecture on the Stockwell Orphans Homes.

6th Lewisham. Saw Mrs. Stevens who gave me a piece of cake. She was just off to a wedding. Mr. S. upset over a possible substitute taking his place to enable him to go into the army.

12th Had to make arrangement with Mr. Harvey about my work. He wants me in the office at 9 o'clock.

15th Caught 7.26 Worthing, arrived office 10 o'clock. After some trouble with Roger Harvey I left at 4 o'clock.

20th Went to pier concert - all women acted, & was very good considering.

30th Lunched in Veg. Jewin Street. Waitress saved me some marmalade roll, which I enjoyed.

MAY

1st. Bonus paid - £19-10/-.

2nd Willings & I lunched in JPs and talked over the contrasts of the 2 cities - Babylon & New Jerusalem.

3rd Called on Stevens. Mrs. S. out - Mr. S. & friend playing cribbage. Had army service rations for supper.

9th Sound of guns scared many people. All well however. Heard the nightingale.

20th Whit Monday Bank Holiday. ... about 11 o'clock we all started for country. Found our way to some nice woods where we had our dinner. Saw some German prisoners working on the land.

21st Lunched in Veg. Rest. Jewin Street - had to get our own dishes as 8 waitresses were absent. Received £15 loan from BDH.

JUNE

26th ... Popp and I had a nice walk along the front. Met one of the warehouse hands from British Drug House who is suffering from nervous exhaustion.

29th Saturday. Len earned 5.3d at Mr. Janalys - 5/- put by for bicycle.

JULY

1st Wrote to O.C. drill hall asking to be allowed to do 2 drills a week because of legs - legs bad today.

3rd. First experience of tending to boarders not good. Popp does not like Mrs. Shanadan. Saw the visitors. Had a chat during their supper. Cissy had to wait until 10.45 for them.

6th Popp dislikes Mrs. Shanadan & Mrs. Offord. They more or less treat her as a boarding house keeper, and want waiting on rather excessively.

7th Mrs. Offord & Mrs. S. not up when we started for tabernacle… Mrs. Offord upset at having to stay in & look after her baby. We talked her over after.

13th Popp getting on better with Mrs. Offord now she is alone.

20th Saturday. Whilst at Grays, air raid warning was given. 25 of our planes were up. 1 German plane attempted to approach the Kent coast.

24th Popp & I went to Steyne Gardens & listened to the Band. Retired early. Popp frisky.

25th … Made up drill-roll book for ambulance in orderly room.

29th Mr. Offord left our house.

AUGUST

2nd Just managed to get into the 9.10 (to Worthing) which was full 1/2 hour before its time. Train packed. 3 saucy girls got into compartment at Croydon who sat on their bags &c. Some fun between them and the young chap in the corner.

3rd Popp & I went to Connaught Hall with Mrs., Offord & the 2 boys.

7th Started back (from Lancing) about 5. We went by country road - bought some apples & chocolate on the way. Secured some Dabbs which fishermen had discarded as too small.

12th Had walk on higher esplanade… went on Pier and saw Say Joy.

21st Len won a first prize and Rene a second prize for running at the Sunday School treat.

22nd … on to Wanstead, calling on Davidsons DS to see if Mrs. D was in - opium wanted back.

26th Got smothered in mud by a motor bus & had to get a new collar.

SEPT

4th Popp saw Peg o' my Heart & told me all about it.

7th Met Bob and went by the 12.39 to Ware. Saw Mr. Dives & took over his house from 28th Sept. 15/- & taxes. 'The Limes,' Ware is the address. Went then with Bob to Little Amwell & had some dinner with him. Saw Doris, Lily - Nellie was in Enfield - & also his garden. Fowls, rabbits &c.

Perhaps wearying of the boarding-house accommodation at Worthing, the Sibleys now set their eyes on moving to Hertfordshire, north of London.

9th Wrote to Ware about coal, to Hertford about Len's school.

12th Wrote to Headmaster of Hertford Grammar School. Mr. Pollard decided to take another room, 13/- weekly.

19th ... bought some Digestive Biscuits - very good. Started to pull my room to pieces.

20th Went to Drill Hall. Returned with MacLawrin. He told me to transfer - discharge out of the question.

27th Got all furniture packed up by 1.30. Cabman refused Ware on acct. of Railway strike on GER. Called to pay account at LB & SCR and met Mr. Faires (of the Tabernacle) who is goods manager there. He arranged for my Ware lot.

28th Said goodbye to Mrs. Flower & family, also to 'Symhurst.' Went to Ware by the 12.39. Found place as I saw it. Mr. Dives had not had it cleaned. Bob, Nellie & the 2 youngsters came to tea.

Settled in Ware, Herts., not far from his brother Bob and his wife Nellie, Thomas sets off to place his son Len in a nearby school.

30th I did not put clock back and Len & I started for Hertford Grammar an hour too soon. We walked there. I interviewed Major Kinman & paid him the school fees - 10/- less on account of coming from Ware. Pottered about in the house… Popp & I walked to Hertford and met Len in afternoon.

OCT

5th … Had a good dinner of 'Bob's fowl.'

6th Popp and I had a long walk to St. Margaret's & back by River Lea.

10th Had a good dinner of pork & apple pie. Mr. Dives gave us apples & greens.

12th Bought Rene some war-time boots and put on an economite sole & rubber heels.

Their new-found idyll in Hertfordshire is shattered by a letter from their landlord from Worthing:

14th …a menacing letter from Chas. Alexander. I must pay for WC pan, charwoman's expenses & damages.

17th Ostend taken, also Lille. Popp a little brighter. Read a little Shakespeare to her.

Len had to walk and have lunch at school.

18th Bruges and Zeebrugge taken.

19th Bob had dinner at our place - we had the rabbit we got on Hertford Heath.

24th … symptoms of a cold.

25th Stayed in bed. Took some Sod. Sal. Popp worried over me.

Far away in St. Leonard's Road, Poplar, in her room above the little hairdresser's shop, Thomas' mother-in-law breathed her last as the final weeks of the Great War ebbed away.

29th Mrs. Kettley died this morning.

NOV

1st. Had tea in shop at Stevens. Mrs. Steven's brother back from sea, there with his sweetheart.

4th Went to office with Bob. Terrible rush on folders because of influenza. Ed not very well.

5th Very busy because of influenza. Ed away ill.

6th Ed away with influenza. I called & saw him. He was very poorly but fever seemed reduced.

8th Saw Ed, who is progressing slowly.

The 1918 influenza pandemic was the most severe pandemic in recent history. It was caused by an H1N1 virus with genes of avian origin. Although there is not universal consensus regarding where the virus originated, it spread worldwide during 1918-1919. It is estimated that about 500 million people or one-third of the world's population became infected with this virus. The number of deaths was estimated to be at least 50 million worldwide.

It was no consolation to the long-suffering British that the deadly pandemic wreaked far more widespread deaths in the United States than Britain, as this draconian US governmental response testifies:

HEALTH ORDER DOOMS LODGE HALL COBWEBS

Grip Ban on All Meetings Until Places Are Renovated; 21 Theaters Reopen.

GRIP VIGILANCE STILL NEEDED

Dr. Robertson Warns Against Relaxing Precaution, Despite Wane of Epid-mic

'OPEN-FACE' SNEEZERS TO BE ARRESTED

Orders to arrest any [illegible] indulging in the "open face" sneeze or cough [illegible]

POLICE RAID SALOONS IN WAR ON INFLUENZA; KEEP CHURCH WINDOWS OPEN

Stringent New Orders Are Issued for Preventing Spread of Epidemic; Police Ambulances Are Drafted; 100,000 Doses of Vaccine on Way.

1,613 NEW CASES SHOW DECREASE IN CITY; DOWNSTATE HIT WORST

FLU CURFEW TO SOUND FOR CITY SATURDAY NIGHT

Persons Not on Business Expected to Quit the Streets at 9 o'Clock.

The curfew will ring or, rather, blow in Chicago tomorrow night. Promptly at 9 o'clock the whistles of

DRAFT MEN TO BE FIRST INOCULATED FOR "FLU"

'NONESSENTIAL' CROWDS BARRED IN EPIDEMIC WAR

Churches and Saloons Exempt; Conventions, Athletics, Parties Hit.

FREE DOCTOR

Influenza victims unable to pay for a doctor can obtain one by calling Main 447, Local 108, day or night.

CHURCH WINDOWS MUST STAY OPEN, SAYS ROBERTSON

Health Department Gives Out New Rules in Fight on Influenza.

CHICAGO DEP'T. OF HEALTH - CUT 4CU

11th Armistice signed this morning. Went to office with Bob. Heard that armistice was signed. It was made public at 11 o'clock by Maroons. Great excitement. Many firms shut down. Lunch in Veg. - place nearly empty. Flags out, everybody excited. Popp excited over Armistice.

Much is rightly made of the huge psychological toll of the First World War but at its end there is no doubting the sense of relief and euphoria that swept through the nation. In their own small suburban way, the Sibleys partied along with the rest of the country.

12th Some of our old employees who left on strike in July 1917 came round and got drunk opposite our works and made a rowdy spectacle of themselves.

15th Paid in £28 for my Bond remittance.

16th Met Ed, Li & Popp. Tried to get into George's Hall - Maskelyne's, and Queen's Hall , but both were full up. We had a look at the guns in the Mall, and walked to Buckingham Palace, and then had tea in ABC.

17th Sunday. Rene in bed with cold and kidney trouble. Spent most of afternoon with her & Len. Told her some stories.

18th Mr. Hill said I could do my country journeys and could commence travelling next month.

23rd Popp very poorly and neurasthenic. Must get back to London. Popp wrote to Mr. Pollard to try and arrange to have part of the house for a fortnight or so. Cleaned bike and got ready to leave Dive's dug-out.

25th Took some crocks to 44 Clavering Rd. Mr. Pollard out so could not see him about taking 4 rooms for a fortnight. Mr. Pollard wrote to us - Popp had his letter when I arrived at Ware at 9.30. Pollard's letter insulting and foolish.

26th Took some more crocks to Clavering Rd. Saw Pollard about his letter & told him it was out of all reason, that his letter was badly received. I walked with Pollard to Manor Park station.

DEC.

4th Popp & Li went in to Selfridges. Afterwards Popp saw Mrs. Newlyn & arranged to move in to 28 Wanstead Park Avenue. I went to ABC Langham Place & had tea. Met Ed & Win. We went to the church at Langham Place. Second Advent Matins.

8th Got up rather late - had breakfast in bed with Popp. Spent most of the day packing 2 trunks, 2 wooden cases &c - a hard day's work - unfortunately necessary but not a happy day.

14th Moved to 28 Wanstead Park Avenue.

24th Made some ginger wine.

25th Splendid dinner - fowl & plum pudding, ginger wine &c. We all went to Ed's in afternoon. Enjoyed ourselves with music & games.

27th Popp & Ciss called on the Pollards and brought back our aspidistra.

30th Heard from Dr. Burness. Len would not be allowed to attend W. Ham Sec. School. Wrote to Headmaster Cooker's School.

Armistice Day celebrations in London, November 1918.

CHAPTER THREE

THIS HAPPY BREED - 1920-1930

Sibley's journals covering the years 1919 & 1920 are lost, but as we pick up his family saga from 1921 we see that while the world recovered from the seismic shock of the Great War, and economic tremors were added to the malaise, life in Wanstead Park continued much the same - one of self-determination. plodding progress, and stoicism.

By the end of 1920 there were more than a million unemployed, a setback fuelled by overproduction. Women were the first to be laid off, and ex-servicemen found it a challenge both mentally and economically to fit back into a society whose entire raison d'etre had been warfare for four years - one third of all former soldiers were without work.

It is glib to characterise the twenties as 'Roaring,' with a hedonistic, devil-may-care attitude of experiment and fun that was later to be truer of the Sixties. But there is no denying a greater freedom of spirit, with the old order of hierarchy and 'duty' beginning to erode. The trust between individual and state had been, if not destroyed, badly damaged. The franchise had been expanded in 1918, with men over 21 and women over 30 being granted the vote, and perhaps partly because of this increased empowerment, the Zeitgeist of the new decade was young. A new realism and frankness entered literature: D.H. Lawrence's Women in Love was published in 1921, portraying earthy emotions in the relationships between men and women; the first woman barrister in England, Dr. Ivy

Williams, was appointed in the same year. Films between 1920 and 1930 grew from being two dimensional entertainment to works of art: Chaplin's The Kid was released in 1921, a pioneering motion picture in not only being the first ever feature-length comedy but shot through with a social realism and a special pleading not seen on such a scale since Dickens.

In a further prefiguring of the Sixties, recreational drug use became so common in the 'Jazz Age' that Noel Coward chose it as the theme of his play *The Vortex. 'In lives of leisure the craze of pleasure steadily grows,'* crooned his flappers, while the reckless young sought heightened consciousness in the misuse of chloroform, opium and cocaine. The huge country piles of the Edwardian age were sagging under the burden of death duties and staff-shortages, and while the old aristocracy still turned out at the Races and Summer Balls, the nouveau-riche was beginning to encroach upon their fading grandeur.

The fun lasted until 1929. Ironically, the biggest musical hit that year was *Happy Days are Here Again, the* cheery tones of which were rippling out of wirelesses on Black Thursday, 1929, when the biggest financial crash in history wrecked economies across the world.

On a material, visible level, Britain changed: the motor car, the wireless, and mains water became not rarities for the common householder but commonplace between 1920-30. Indoor lavatories had not become de rigeur, initially because people thought them unhygienic, so many households retained the outdoor water closet right up until the 1960s and 70s, and central heating was not a feature of many houses for many years, the majority of families relying still on coal fires.

Shopping was a trip to the High Street, the market, and for wealthier citizens a telephone call to a grocer or other retailer for home deliveries. On Saturday nights in most towns, markets stayed open until well after dark, illuminated by naptha flares.

Most people had health insurance, paying 6d or so each week for free diagnosis at point of treatment. Those who could not afford it were still treated by their local doctor, who more often than not quietly 'forgot' the debt and covered the expense by those who paid.

With the explosion of new-build houses in the 1920s came a concomitant expansion in the need for maintenance: with new water tanks in the loft and new pipes conveying water to sinks and baths, plumbing issues were a burden of everyday life, as Sibley's diary testifies.

The extraordinary growth of housing in the 1920s created nothing short of a new way of living: Suburbia was both a physical reality and a state of mind, a dream fuelled by the partly-fictional lure of rusticity. It is perhaps one of the most significant social revolutions in British history, and the Sibley family was at its heart. Dream though it was, the cold reality underpinning its creation was the new-found relative prosperity of the lower-middle and middle-classes, and the financial liquidity and credit offered by the banks. Acres of green land was built over in an idealistic frenzy of construction that resulted in 1.5 million homes being built by 1930. It wasn't just London - Birmingham, Leeds and Manchester were similarly transformed. To the West of London it was as though an entire country was created, a fictional country made real, dubbed Metroland. People were sold a rural idyll that nevertheless possessed the civic characteristics of clubs, associations, railways and a driveway for your newly-acquired motor car. Public housing grew alongside private - fully one third of all houses constructed between 1920-30 were council built. Both slum-dwellers and aspiring middle-class benefited, with road-menders and agricultural workers joining the bankers, schoolteachers and civil servants, though in societal terms the change was sometimes too rapid, as evinced by the popular cruel joke of the time that the former occupier of jerry-built terraced houses would, when faced with an inside bathroom, promptly use the new bath to keep the coal in.

Metroland was a laboratory of taste, the housewife the laboratory rat. Furniture became more minimalist, the curtains less heavy and floral than those of their parents and grandparents: cleanliness, simplicity, and decorum became the order of the day, with the gentle curves of a wardrobe replacing the heavy-set dark oak of yesteryear. The latest domestic appliances became the sought-after status symbols of the decade - the Electrolux vacuum cleaner was the queen of labour-saving devices, with electric fires, toasters and kettles following close after. It wasn't until 1928 when the electric fridge began to replace the cool walk-in larder, but as early as 1920 the *Daily Mail* Ideal Home Exhibition was confidently predicting the all-electric house.

Ford, Austin and Morris were producing small family cars that powered the 1920s new commuting age. In 1922 there were 315,000 licensed cars on Britain's roads: by the end of the decade this had tripled to more than a million. Denby Motor lorries spelt the end of the horse-drawn load, with 334,000 vehicles flowing through the arteries of the nation by 1929. Southern Railway went electric in 1928 and Britain's first diesel train began operating in 1928, but it was still an age of steam, powered by the coal mines of Wales and the North. As far as flight was concerned, this was still the preserve of the rich; despite Alcock and Brown making the first non-stop flight across the Atlantic in 1919, passenger aircraft were still only able to fly in short hops; some had lavish comforts such as the

Bristol Pullman Triplane and the Handley-Page Flying Saloon, but more often than not commercial flying was trublesome, noisy and expensive.

In the Twenties, despite the colossal setback of the War, Britain was still a competitive commercial hub, evidenced by the Empire Exhibition of 1924 which took place in Wembley Stadium. Heralded by a performance of Elgar's Land of Hope and Glory, the exhibition boasted the largest concrete building in the world, the Palace of Engineering, as well as displays of an entire Hong Kong street and a Mughal Palace. This was confidence on a grand scale, culminating in the King sending a telegram to himself which whizzed around the whole Empire until it returned to Wembley stadium in a matter of 80 seconds. This confidence had been knocked, however, by the loss of foreign markets for the staple industries of Britain – coal, iron and steel, shipbuilding and cotton - during the war.

Industrial unrest, however, characterised the decade. Politically, the Labour Party replaced the Liberal Party as the progressive party in British politics. Governments widened insurance legislation to provide benefits for the unemployed and offered relief work, trying to avoid forcing the unemployed into the poor houses. Committed as they were to deflating the economy to strengthen the pound in the hope of returning to the Gold Standard, the symbol of international free trade that had made Britain great in the nineteenth century before being suspended in the War, successive governments failed to tackle unemployment. The Geddes Report or Geddes Axe of 1921/2, which brought cuts to government departments, worsened the chances of economic growth. Agitation from the unemployed was led by the Communist Party of Great Britain, formed in 1920, and the National Unemployed Workers (Committee) Movement (NUWM) formed in 1921. With Communist leader Walter Hannington, the NUWM organised many unemployed, and particularly ex-servicemen. The miners organised their own protest march. The Miners' March to London from Wales in November 1927 was supported by the NUWM, communist and socialist groups. The NUWM'S 1929 Hunger March, organised in January-February, saw marchers from nine areas of Britain march on London demanding better unemployment benefits and work for the unemployed.

War had led to Britain going off the gold standard and free trade, the hallmark of nineteenth-century Victorian economic prosperity. It was restored to the pre-war parity of $4.86 by Winston Churchill in 1925 when its value was only $4.40 to the £, hence British goods immediately became 10 per cent more expensive to foreign buyers. This added to economic decline and unemployment only to be heightened by the Wall Street Crash in 1929.

The continued policy of deflation, consequent wage reductions and unemployment, led to strikes and major industrial unrest. The coal miners struck unsuccessfully against wage reductions in 1921, largely because the Miners' Federation of Great Britain was not supported by the National Union of Railwaymen and the National Transport Workers' Federation or 'Triple Alliance.'

When the return to the Gold Standard led to further demands for reduced wages, the resistance of the miners in 1925 eventually led to the General Strike of 1926 when about 1,500,000 trade unionists came out in support of about 800,000 miners who were faced with wage reductions of 10 per cent and an increase in working hours. Although the General Strike failed, lasting only between the 3rd and 12th May, employers were afterwards more reluctant to try to reduce the wages of their employees.

Leisure in the Twenties was largely sports, communal activities, reading and cinema. There were public libraries in every town, and Boot's Circulating Library for book-lovers. Many evenings were spent mending clothes, making repairs. As Sibley's diaries show, family parlour games were routinely played at social gatherings, with names like Shop and Consequences, with rules handed down from generation to generation. For public entertainment, folk embraced the Variety Theatre, the larger, more modern version of the old music halls. In the 1920s every largish town in Britain had its own variety theatre and cinema, with the same building often offering both forms of entertainment. A whole industry of live entertainment sprang up to meet the demand, meaning that at any one time an army of thousands of performers from jugglers and magicians to comics and singers were traversing the country on the railways for their weekly residences at the Hippodromes, Empires and Palaces.

Against the backdrop of this national journey, the Sibley family, in true Voltaire-ian fashion, cultivated their garden, raised chickens, and tended to their daily needs…

1921

JAN

6th Returned to office with Bob in company's little motor van.

8th Moved chicken run to drier quarters. Len helped.

15th Had a game of 'Old Maid' in evening.

17th Farrows only to pay 3/- in £. Went to Lawn Tennis Committee meeting at Escott's house.

20th Brighton. Caught 11 o'clock Victoria arrived 12.30 at

Wilkinson's. Popp & I went on the Pier and listened to Lyall-Taylor.

21st Brighton, Rottingdean &c. Took Popp on West Pier for evening. Lt. Col. Rice (acct. in Ware office) is on the way to Mesopotamia for 3 years.

22nd Salary increased £25 & Farrow's loss taken over by firm.

29th Had to separate one of the hens as the others were pecking it. D. Anderson called & saw Miss Vipond. Popp & she had some upset about the unannounced visit. Miss V. offended.

FEB

1st Miss Vipond called me into her bedroom this morning and gave me a week's notice. Saturday's upset the cause. She bade me goodbye as she was leaving today. She left about 2 o'clock.

5th Claimed on Farrow's bank £104-13-3 - 2/- in the £.

8h Had two horrible scones at Bexley Heath.

18th Brighton. Popp, Mrs. Wilkinson, Hilda & Miss Madden went for a charabanc drive to Eastbourne. Popp & I went on Pier to orchestra.

In the 1920s Brighton was still the gaudy star of the south coast, attracting thousands of day-trippers and holidaymakers to sample its glittering wares and sample its waters.

23rd Mr. Gray has several tons of cheap scissors - German - so I took samples to sell some for him. Popp & I went to the Tennis Club's Concert at Manor Park Baptists. Quite professional - too much so for a place of worship.

25th Sold a gross of scissors to Milnes.

28th Li, Eva & Ruth came in evening. Gray sent some scissors. I gave them a pair each.

MARCH

1st. Cissy taken ill - probably influenza - severe attack on chest, lungs and throat.

Brighton, 1920.

2nd Popp taken queer with a bad influenza chill.

3rd Popp very queer with influenza cold &c. - had to fight for breath. Got their breakfasts - Cissy & Rene both in bed - and then sent Len for D. Anderson & sent him to 8 customers with a letter. Len brought back 7 orders and D. Johnson sent his on. Gave Len a shilling. He went on bike. Looked after patients and cooked their dinner &c. Telephoned to Ed & Mr. Harvey.

8th I have my limbs and back acting as with an influenza cold - but put up a fight against it, chiefly by prayer.

9th I have an influenza cold 99 temp. but I went out trusting the Lord.

But Sibley's mental resilience and self-healing, while powerful, required a medical nudge:

11th Too ill to go to bis - temp 101. .. took aspirin BDH.

12th ...stayed in room in dressing gown all day. I brought temp. down to normal.

17th Popp very poorly. Dr. McK came and said she was not to have Peptonised milk.

APRIL

1st Coal Strike.

6th Transport Workers decide to strike.

8th Eclipse of the sun 8.35-11. Dr. McK called and said Popp has a duodenal ulcer. Triple Alliance decide to strike.

9th Winnie gives birth to a boy.

12th. Strike of Triple alliance postponed until Friday 10 o'clock.

15th Strike cancelled.

Black Friday, in British labour history, refers to 15 April 1921, when the leaders of transport and rail unions announced a decision not to call for strike action in support of the miners.

28th No bonus this year. Saw Ed & Popp at office. Mr. Hicks presented with a cigarette case, and WH Naylor with a gold watch, on their retirement.

29th Had some tea at Buckleys. A youngster was brought in with a shocking scalp wound. The accident occurred after I had left the brougham - youngster jumping on back.

MAY

6th Mr. A. Walker sent a cheque for £35 for selling his business. I wrote and thanked him.

12th Taxi arrived 8.5., Popp, Rene, Ciss & I started for Brighton. (Madeira Place).

16th Took Rene on motor boat.

29th Took (Popp) in Remmington's Bath chair to Ed & Li's.

JUNE

6th Southend. Caught 8.35 which on account of bad coal could not get up steam easily and arrived at Tilbury Docks 1 1/2 hours late.

7th Motor came at 3 o'clock and I took Popp to see Dr. Henry Head Montague Square, £3-3/-. Motor 30/-.

18th Coal miners decide to continue strike. Filled in census paper.

23rd Had a spill at Stratford, damaged leg, trousers and bike but not seriously, praise the lord. Left a pair of goggles for Quinn at 37 Hatton Gdn.

JULY

2nd Another chick died - diarrhoea.

9th Saturday. Had dinner & went to tennis for an hour or so. Popp does not like me playing tennis.

12th Brighton. Had a splendid swim by Palace Pier. Lunched in Lyons. Met Hilda Wilkinson in St. James St. Dinner in L'pool St. Refreshment Room.

14th Wickford. Billericay. Spent an hour in the British Museum.

18th Southend. More trains now so caught my usual 5.30 fast.

AUGUST

1st Had a little cricket in garden with Len & Rene.

3rd Had another nasty letter from L. Matthews.

8th Ed & Li's Silver Wedding. Met Ed & Li in G.E. tea rooms. They had been to Madam Tussauds.

15th Went to Thorpe Bay . (Having holiday with Popp & children in Leigh-on-Sea, while he still does his rounds. Popp in bath chair).

17th We all went to Southend Pier. (Popp in her bath chair).

18th Wrote to Sec. London Hospital about getting (Popp) a private ward. Dr. Savia called & said Popp was better but must be removed home in an ambulance. Cissy… got St. John's ambulance to come tomorrow at 3 o'clock.

19th Ambulance came at 3. Took us safely home. Called at an Inn at Shenfield and we all had tea. Popp carried upstairs to bed. Cost, £4-10/-.

20th Chatted with D. Keats about a nursing home. He has a poor opinion of them. A nurse indoors is the best.

23rd Nurse Shirtcliffe came, also Mrs Graham & Popp was fed via rectum. Nurse S. came again in evening & I helped her to give the feed.

27th Heard that Wilson of So. Woodford wanted a barometer so I biked over with one about 8 o'clock.

SEPT

10th. Carried Popp into garden and took her photograph also nurses.

Wrote to E.E.Everest Ministry of Labour, Howard Hotel, about Leonard.

14th Nurse Davies left after dinner. Popp gave her a bottle of scent & handkerchiefs. She took my cheque for L. Hospital £9-9/-.

A momentous day in the Sibley family occurs in September when Thomas takes his sixteen year old son Len on his rounds.

15th Len & I went to City. Went to Norfolk St. and saw Mr. Everest about Len.

16th Popp trusting the Lord - threw all medicines away. Took Len to East Ham Technical College, signed on for shorthand & French.

17th Saturday. BDH Sports at High Beech.

28th Upsdale advised increase of rent £56.

29th Brighton. Another traveller was very insulting in Thomas', he came in while I was there and when I pointed out I occupied the ground he was abusive.

OCT

7th Bought Len a hat at Sainsbury's. Len up to Brown Bro's Ltd. Great Eastern St., and obtained the situation as junior Clerk, 19/- a week. Len delighted.

14th Len brought home his first week's wages - 19/- less 8 1/2d insurance. Len got his season ticket 19/-7d.

Len's annual ticket for rail travel across London cost him £39.00 in today's terms (2023).

21st Called round and saw Mr. Baines who had kindly recommended Len for a situation in Billingsgate Market.

Len's job search had been indefatigable; as this rejection letter shows he had already obtained an appointment elsewhere by the time it was received:

TELEGRAMS: GARSTIN, LONDON.
TELEPHONES: 4444 CITY (3 LINES)

159, Aldersgate Street,
London, E.C.1.

5th November, 1921.

Dear Mr. Sibley,

I had your letter last month, respecting your boy. I do not think I have replied, as I have been in ill-health and my correspondence has been slow.

I am afraid however, that we have no opening for such a lad as your's, but if there should be an opening we should be very glad to give him the opportunity. To that end he might when he is in London please call and see us. He could see me, or if I am not in the house ask for Mr. Burch. He should bring this letter with him in any case.

Believe me to remain,

Yours sincerely,
A.GARSTIN.

Mr. T. Sibley,
26, Wanstead Park Avenue,
E.12.

NOV

8th Popp being severely tested. Had a wonderful experience of the Lord's presence this morning. The Lord gave me 'Elijah' as an example to follow & broke me down to many sobs.

17th Went to Ridley Hall. Plenty of witnesses and testimonies of the Lord's wonderful healing at Notting Hill Gate by Pastor Jeffries - (Horbury?) Church. Blind in one eye, withered arm, very short sight &c &c.

19th Saturday. Popp, Ciss & I went with Ed, Wilf & Li to Notting

Hill Gate to hear Pastor Stephen Jeffries - no meeting, only a prayer meeting.

22nd. Went to Tennis Committee meeting at 48 H. Rd. Had a long chat with Desmond & Wilson. Christian, RC & Theosophist in arguments. Agreements and differences at times interesting.

DEC

8th Popp & I went to Mr. Bull's. He is not well - boils in arms. I anointed him. He anointed me on account of my varicose veins.

23rd Popp & I went out & bought a turkey - they were very scarce.

1923

JAN

31st Ed had been to YMCA Tottenham Ct. Rd. to see Ernie.

The famous YMCA building in Tottenham Court Road, built in 1844, demolished in 1971.

FEB

3rd. Popp & I went to Philharmonic Hall to see pictures of Mt. Everest expedition.

George Mallory and 'Sandy' Irvine, 1923.

A passion to climb the world's highest peak had been simmering in Britain since the 1890s, but it was not until in 1921 that the Royal Geographical Society and the Alpine Club formed the Mount Everest Committee. After prelimnary exloraitons and recce's, an attempt on the summit was organised in 1922. Members of the expedition were Brigadier General C.G. Bruce (leader), C.G. Crawford, G.I. Finch, T.G. Longstaff, George Mallory, Captain C.J. Morris, Major Morshead, Edward Norton, T.H. Somervell, Colonel E.I. Strutt, A.W. Wakefield, and John Noel. It was decided that the mountain must be attempted before the onset of the summer monsoon. In the spring, therefore, the baggage was carried by Sherpas across the high, windy Plateau of Tibet. It ended in disaster - nine Sherpas were swept by an avalanche over an ice cliff, and seven were killed. Mallory's party was carried down 150 feet

(45 metres) but not injured. This setback did not deter Mallory from making a further attempt in 1924, when he met his fate with fellow climber Andrew Irvine. Spotted by Noel Odell 500 feet below the summit - the last time they wre seen alive - it will never be known whether the climbers were descending, having reached the summit, or still in the process of ascending the last few feet.

6th Popp & Cissy tried to get into Ilford Town Hall League of Honour & Purity Campaign, unsuccessfully.

13th Went to C.E. Rev. EB Samuel spoke on 'Russia in prophecy.' Crowded vestries.

20th Went to C.E. & heard Rev. Boyd Morrison on Russia.

27th Went to C.E. Annual election of officers - I was re-elected Vice-President.

28th Cissy had her artificial teeth.

MARCH

1st. Went to British Industrial Fair Shepherd's Bush. Mr. Cocking was at our stand.

10th Wrote an article for 'Endeavourer' in evening.

15th Brighton. Popp & I went to Pavilion - YMCA anniversary. Mayor of Brighton - Mr. Parkhurst - in chair.

19th Popp & I went & heard Mr. Kensit on 'What I Saw in Rome,' & saw his limelight views.

22nd Workmen here putting in Inter-Oven Stove.

The Interoven Stove - 'two stoves in one' - was invented by Frank Pascall in 1911 and shown at the Ideal Home Exhibition of that year. The stove was still going strong many years later, when a reviewer warbled ecstatically *'I never cease to marvel at the multiplicity of conveniences of the Inter-Oven stoves.'*

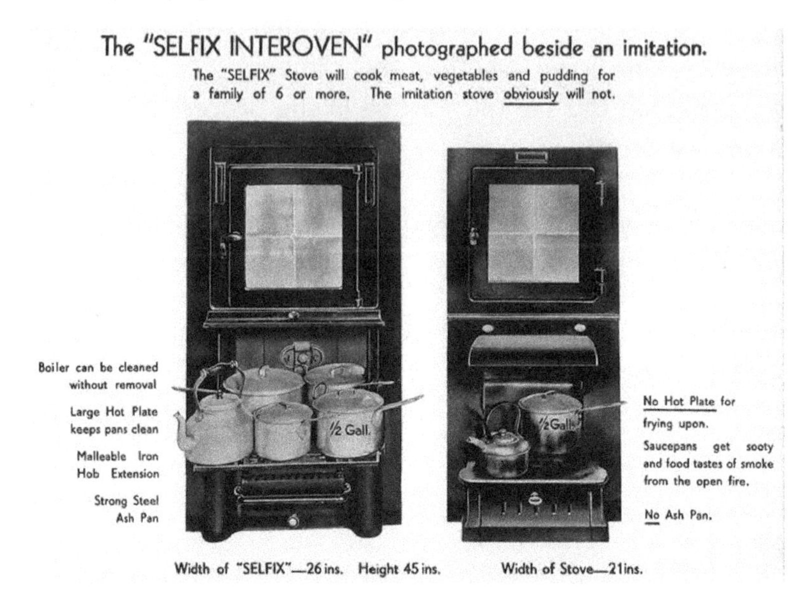

23rd Went to M.P.B. Mr. Hawkins replied to the Society's enquiry re. doctrine of Soc. & his letter admitted modernist tendencies. The committee decided to erase his name from the membership.

30th Spent most of time in garden. Rene helped me. Altered appearance of garden. Day was delightful for gardening.

APRIL

8th Irene accepted Jesus as her Saviour.

20th Len spoke to me about going to Australia.

21st So cold Rene & I had to make a fire in dining-room. Popp very much upset about Len wanting to go to Australia, and my giving him provisional consent. Len gave back his paper which I had signed. Popp left a letter which I replied to by letter.

25th Popp left another letter for me which I did not open.

MAY

18th Killed a fowl - greedy. She was egg-bound. Mrs. Griffiths kindly trussed it for me on account of it not keeping.

21st Len went off on his bike to Seven Oaks with Banks, 8.30.

26th Took Popp for a walk thro W.Park, Valentine's Park, to Ilford Broadway. Bought fish &c.

JUNE

6th Popp got her teeth from Jones & I gave him £2.

16th Special visit to Muswell Hill, (80 Sutton Rd.), Mr. York & Oakes (?) gave me his opening order. Spent afternoon with fowls and bicycle.

22nd 46 Today.

23rd Saturday. Went to Zoo. Had some coffee in Gt. Portland St. Rene fascinated by the monkeys.

30th Popp bought me a tie for my birthday, Len bought me a bicycle pump. Had lunch in ABC. Bought an ice-cream brick.

JULY

14th Took Popp to Loughton by bus. Had an enjoyable walk and rest in forest.

19th Met Popp at L'pool St. & went to Kingsway Hall. Heard Mr. Kensitt against Anglo-Catholics & confessional.

23rd Went to Church meeting. SS Building & funds generally discussed. Between £3000 & £4000 required.

30th Before closing meeting, Rev. J.G. Hipperson expressed himself forcibly about a letter written, & said many extravagant things not correct & made quite a scene. Will Wheeler had sent in his resignation & expressed about the unscrupulous methods being adopted by the church in raising funds &c. Mr. Hipperson acted unwisely.

AUGUST

3rd Mr. Hunter recently had a nasty accident - knocked over by a motorbike.

7th Hove, Brighton. Caught 7.25 back. Terrible crowd - racers. I had to stand all the way.

20th Went alone to prayer meeting. Mr. Moolenser (?) made a mess of things by his criticism of the wrath of God, and nearly wrecked the prayer meeting.

22nd Ley St., (Brethren's) & heard Mr. Fred Mace, (son of the prize fighter).

SEPT

Portslade. … Popp & I went as far as Hewitt's & Jeeves, then on front to Ciss & Rene.

6th Holiday. Went to Hassocks by train. Walked to Hurstpierrepoint. Went to prayer meeting in evening. Prayer for Japan.

The Great Kantō earthquake struck the Kantō Plain on the main Japanese island of Honshū on Saturday, September 1, 1923. The earthquake devastated Tokyo, the port city of Yokohama, the force being so great that in Kamakura, over 60 km (37 mi) from the epicenter, it moved the Great Buddha statue, which weighs about 121 tonnes, almost 60 centimeters.

Estimated casualties totaled about 142,800 deaths, including about 40,000 who went missing and were presumed dead.

7th Took Rene on 'Queen of the South.' 11.5 trip to mid-channel.

8th Packed box for Lyme Regis. Caught special train - fast - to Victoria 3.5. Len at home. Cleaned out fowl's house. Did some writing. Developed some photos. Everything & everybody well.

10th Caught 9 o'clock train (from Waterloo) to Lyme Regis, arriving at Mrs. Dollings, 38 Coombe St., at 1.15. After tea Popp & I had a nice walk on Cobb, & then walked home via a stiff hill at the back of town.

11th Popp & I got our deck chairs and went on beach. Swarms of wasps interfered with our chosen pleasure and rest. After manoeuvring about we gave up our chairs and retreated. Went into town and had some coffee at the Tudor.

12th After a fish dinner & some Devonshire cream Popp & I spent afternoon on East Cliff - lovely grassy cliffs & gorgeous scenery - yellow & slate coloured rocks. Cliffs with a mountain and dale prospect - a view stretching nearly to Portland - grand, majestic, picturesque & tranquil.

13th At 11.50 I started on my own for a walk to Landslide. A most wonderful walk full of ascents & descents, woods, ferns 6ft high, mighty hills, lovely dales, water springs and precipitous cliffs. Strikingly beautiful at times and quite awesome. Felt lonely at times, did not meet a soul for miles, only birds and field mice... The most entrancing walk of my life.

Saw carnival after tea & then had a walk to Cobb and back.

17th Got home 7.15. Praise God for his gracious care & a week's change.

OCT

11th Had tea in ABC Southampton Row & at 7 o'clock went to Church House & cross examined by the Committee of the London Baptists Preacher's Association. I was unanimously accepted on 3 month's probation.

16th Lunched in Sidcup. Made a special visit to Queen's Hospital. L.M.S. showed me over museum of facial cases operated on. Most wonderful alterations after treatment.

NOV

12th Gravesend. Had to go to Sidcup first as it was so foggy that ferry boats were not running at Tilbury.

24th Portslade. Popp & I went for a walk. Had coffee in Lyons then went to Museum & Art Gallery. Went to Royal Pavilion & heard a lecture on New Zealand with limelight views. Lecturer was very poor.

30th Leonard left Brown Bro's.

DEC

3rd. Leonard started in BDH's office as junior shipping clerk 30/- weekly.

9th Mizpah Mission... Dolly acted strangely and upset Leonard.

20th Ordered Rene an attache case from J.E. Mellish.

28th BDH luncheon at Midland Grand Hotel.

Sibley ends the year on a high by joining his local tennis club at the age of 43:

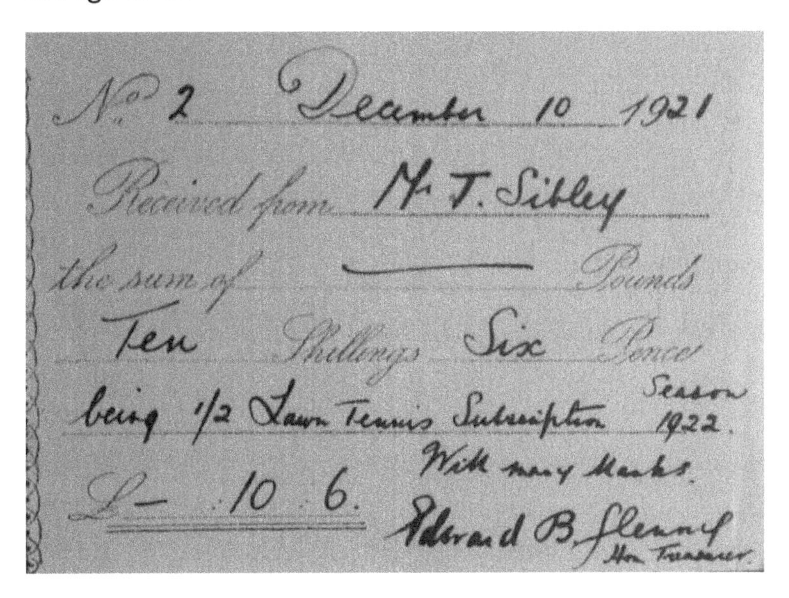

No. 2 December 10 1921

Received from Mr T. Sibley

the sum of — Pounds

Ten Shillings Six Pence

being 1/2 Lawn Tennis Subscription Season 1922.

With many thanks.

£ — 10 . 6.

Edward B. [illegible]

Hon Treasurer

1924

JAN

19th. Had a pleasant surprise - salary increased £20.

20th Railway Strike ASLEF started at midnight.

The period between the end of the war and 1926 was one of

industrial unrest, in which wages fell behind the rise in the cost of living for many workers. In 1923 the Railways Act 1921 merged about 120 of Great Britain's railways into four large regional companies. In December 1923, the new companies presented proposals that included some reductions in locomotive men's pay and conditions. Negotiations broke down and ASLEF ordered its members to strike, but the NUR instructed its members – including locomotivemen – to stay at work. After another nine-day strike, ASLEF was victorious, but the disagreement between ASLEF and the NUR left deep division.

21st Popp & I went to YMCA & saw limelight views and heard lecture on 'The Czar.' Only a few trains running.

22nd Got a train at 6.40 and got home 9.25 - splendid considering the strike & only a few trains driven by NUR men.

23rd Death of Lenin.

Despite being directly responsible for the Red Terror and causing the deaths of hundreds of thousands through famine or mass executions, by the time of his death in January 1924 Soviet leader Vladimir Ilyich Lenin had assumed the status of royalty. For decades, his murders were ignored or excused by both historians and writers on the left in Britain, with Russia's Red Holocaust being blamed solely on Stalin, whereby a neologism, *Stalinism,* was devised to shield Lenin from crimes against humanity and seal off his short bloodthirsty reign from later yet more horrific episodes. His cadaver still lies in state in Red Square in Moscow in a mausoleum modelled on Cyrus the Great.

24th Chelmsford. Returned by 3.30 bus. Raining heavily at Brentwood - struggle to get on - got front seat on top. A young commercial sat by my side under the umbrella & chatted on many subjects, mostly spiritual - he is a church goer but not a Christian.

29th Railway strike over.

MARCH

8th Took Popp to Kingsway. Went to Bloomsbury Baptist's Church.

15th (Brighton) Went to 'Dome' Pavilion & heard Requiem and Stabat Mater.

22nd Tram & Bus strike commenced. Had to walk from East Ham station on account of strike.

25th Walked with Popp to C.E. Mr. Barnes, a West Indian negro, spoke.

26th Called in at Midland Bank 658 Romford Rd., saw manager Mr. Pearce and arranged a current a/c, 21/-.

28th Bobby had a meal of bones which upset him, then he had a worm cake.

A group of "Old-timers" who will be remembered by many readers. Messrs. R. O. Sibley and A. E. Morgan (back row) are still with us. 1924

APRIL

1st. Trams & buses resumed.

2nd Bobby died early this morning. We buried (him) early this morning. We could not get him over acute gastritus. One of the fowls being frightened went over into cemetery & I had great difficulty in getting it back.

5th I chloroformed the cat (Peter) because of its unseemly behaviour & diseased skin. Its tail looked like coming off. Buried pussy. We have taken over Mr. Fotheringham's cat.

11th Popp & I went to Hove Town Hall & saw pictures & heard lecture on 'Romantic India,' - the same as we saw last year, 'Hindustani.'

12th Retired at 10.10 - putting clock forward it became 11.10.

JUNE

16th Popp thinks she is pregnant.

19th Popp & I went to Wembley. Visited BDH stand and looked about generally. Visited many interesting exhibits.

21st BDH Sports at Rye House.

23rd Popp gave me a walking stick and Len a bike bell for my birthday.

24th Popp had a shock but was graciously preserved by the Lord from being knocked down by a motor on 'Rabbit's Bridge.'

AUGUST

3rd. Upminster, Church outing. Most of us went for a walk across rather muddy fields to a church & then by road to some fields where we had our lunch.... Some of the girls went to view the

Garden City.

As early as 1904 the *Times* newspaper had bemoaned the expansion of the suburbs: '*...to surround London with acres of such streets is to produce a district of appalling monotony, ugliness and dullness. And every suburban extension makes existing suburbs less desirable ... It is the more necessary, if possible, to redeem the suburb from meanness and squalor.'* The Garden City' movement, inspired by Ebenezer Howard's *Garden Cities of Tomorrow,* 1898, resulted in Letchworth and Welwyn; but smaller pockets of idealised communities based on the principles of fusing the benefits of both town and country living were built in Hampstead, Brentham in Ealing in West London, and Upminster.

14th. Ordered lawnmower F.G. 29/11d.

SEPT

3rd Brighton. Boy fell into water from groyne and was rescued by a man who jumped in fully dressed. Rene & I went to Dog's Show & saw D. Prentis of Westcliff who was exhibiting a labrador.

5th Rene & I had a steamer trip to Seaford Bay. ... Had a good dinner then we all went by bus to Patcham.

6th Motor racing on Front engaged our attention.

9th Rene & I went by bus to Lewes. Enjoyed a walk on the hills. Visited Martyr's monument.

15th Rene & I went to Wembley... Visited Palace of engineering... coal mine, Palestine (Temples) &c &c.

The British Empire Exhibition took place in the newly built Wembley Stadium in Wembley Park, and was a bold statement of confidence from a Britain vying on the world stage with the

USA and Japan. A melange of international styles of architecture, the exhibition displayed pavilions from around the world from Burma to Kenya.

OCTOBER

29th Election. Voted for Edwards. (Clement Edwards?)

NOV

11th. Went to C.E. I spoke on 'Peace,' it being Armistice Day.

DEC

17th Explosion in Eastcheap. Len was blown up by a gas explosion in EastCheap. Mouth cut. Leg bruised &c, coat & trousers damaged. He came home 2.30. I wrote to Gas L. Coke Co. about it. Len went to Dr. Anderson.

25th. Excellent dinner. Geraldine Slicker our only visitor. Played several games.

26th. Len & I had a short cycle ride about 11 o'clock but rain drove us in. Evening had most of time in general knowledge.

1926

JAN

3rd Went to Walthamstow & took service. Len was convicted of sin, & went home alone & sought the Lord with tears & found Him - his saviour.

6th Went by appointment to office at 9.30 and arranged to give up my Woolwich & Eltham rounds to Mr. Proctor & take on 7 calls usually done by Clayhorn in Ilford district.

15th Friday… Went to MP Baptist Church. Only a few (5 + myself, 6) there so they went home without having a meeting. Mr. Fotheringham did not give his paper on 'Eternal Punishment.'

29th. Started to improve memory thro' a book on memory training.

FEB

12th Catford &c. Had brougham. Horse went lame & police stopped us.

13th Saturday. Rene went to Mersea with Li. Cissy grizzling because Rene has left her.

25th. … went to 'British Industries Fair,' White City. Left bag & hat at BDH stand & made a hurried inspection of the exhibition.

26th. Rene came back from Mersea. Li saw her in train at Colchester & Cissy & Popp met her at L'pool St. She is certainly better physically for the change.

MARCH

6th Grays & Tilbury. Just caught 8.34 by jumping into guard's van. Opened conversation over some wreaths and found him to be a stalwart Christian. Another Christian railwayman got in and we had a pleasant chat all the way to Tilbury Dk.

11th. Mr. Haslett leant me a book on Satan, L.S. Chafer.

16th Brighton. Lunched in Lyons - Lancashire hot pot not good so manager would not charge me for it - had steak pudding in its place.

24th Len's 21st birthday. Ed gave him £1. I gave him a Bible, 17/-.

27th ...took Popp to Ilford. Bought a bedroom suite of furniture £21 from Eastern Furnishing Co.

MAY

1st. Saturday. Len & Rene's Birthday Party, 21 & 15. Guests came from 3- 5 o'clock. Played in garden. Had a splendid tea (Popp & Ciss & I served & had ours afterwards). Parlor games - exciting charades - Marksman, Sailor, Mistake, Ailment. Mr. & Mrs. Dye called for a short time, also Mr. Stagg. (About 21 guests). Broke up 11.20. Retired 12.45.

In the pre-television age parlour games were, quite literally, played in the 'parlour' room of houses, where families and friends would gather of an evening in pursuit of collective amusement. Many of the games like charades or consequences had been devised in Victorian times, but new variations and games were being invented all the time, lasting well in to the 1970s.

3rd Everyone talking about the coming strike.

4th Tuesday. Great Strike Commences. Plaistow, East Ham &c. arrived home 7 o'clock. Cycled journey - no conveyances of any kind. Leslie Parrish borrowed Rene's bike & cycled with Len. Ed had to walk to office. Some ugly scenes on road - strikers refusing to allow men & women to work on lorries &c. Try to stop BDH van from taking staff home.

The fact that Sibley describes the industrial action of May 1926 as the 'Great Strike' is a measure of its significance in the consciousness of the ordinary British citizen. The withdrawal of labour lasted nine days, from 4th to 12th May, called by the General Council of the Trades Union Congress (TUC) in an unsuccessful attempt to force the British government to act to prevent wage reductions and worsening conditions for 1.2 million locked-out coal miners. Some 1.7 million workers went out, especially in transport and heavy industry.

5th Barking, Ilford &c... cycled journey. Lunched in ABC Ilford. Trade quiet on account of strike. Very little news through. A good deal of hooliganism at Poplar & Canning Town. Difficulty getting into City. Len cycled. Ed walked but did not return - stopping in City. Things looking very black.

7th Catford &c. Cycled journey. Stan Parrett overtook me on bike on way home from Woolwich. Strike ruffianism less apparent but effects being more realised. Govt. determined to win.

8th Dagenham &c. Cycled journey.

10th Strike news better. Govt. got matters in hand.

11th Strike going on unabated. Both sides winning but Govt. determined.

12th Heard at 1.30 that TUC had called off strike.

13th Prepared for Brighton but had to return as Railwaymen were not working. Cycled to Sidcup & Crayford.

15th Strike ending. Sundry troubles with men on railway.

30th Sunday. Took meeting at Mariner's Friend Society, Old Gravel Lane. Only 7 or 8 there. Saw Brocklebank (J.W.K.) Superintendent.

JUNE

12th Len returned from holidays (DEVON) at 4 o'clock.

17th Chelmsford. Spent 1 1/4 hours at cricket ground watching Essex v Somerset. Essex batting.

26th Twelve of us went for a pic-nic in Wanstead Park, stayed in the Glade & played cricket - tennis balls used.

JULY

3rd Len played for BDH cc.

6th Brighton. 2 Yanks - young gents - ret'd in carriage, & chatted during journey.

14th Received summons to act as juror on July 23rd.

17th Holidays at Southwold. Arrived Southwold 3pm. Had some tea - haddock &c at Mrs. F. Blowers, 14 Fieldstile Rd. Supper at 8 o'clock. We all had a walk afterwards. The 'buzzers' drove us from the cliffs.

19th... went for walk to ferry & back... played cricket on the green.

22nd Rene & I went on Southern Belle to Felixstowe... watched some swimming races. Had look at town, got back on pier 3.30, on board Yarmouth Belle 4 o'clock.

23rd ... went alone for a bike ride on a heath on the way to Dunwich. Country life lovely - partridges to keep me company.

26th After breakfast Rene & I cycled to Dunwich.

27th Cycled to Lowestoft.

28th Lovely swim - walked back with my 2 water companions - fat & thin. Rene & I cycled by easy stages - dodging the showers - to

Blythburgh. Visited church from outside, it being locked.

29th Took Popp around town - coffee & milk in Jellicoes.

31st Said goodbye to Mrs. Blowers… caught 12 o'clock train. Arrived home 5.40. Len & Leslie had been pillow fighting - feathers were all over the place.

AUGUST

3rd. Brighton very full of excursionists & busy.

7th Went on flats and played cricket with Len & others & finished with a split finger - one of Len's fast balls when I was batting. I was quite crippled. Len wrote out my advice cards.

18th England won the Test Match. Great excitement over test match - unexpected finish after Australia's collapse.

27th Cat upset round table in kitchen during night - several things brought down but only a plate broken. Cissy told not to use the table - no notice taken.

28th Leslie P., Alf came to tea. They took Rene on the lake for a canoe. Some splashing spoilt it.

SEPT

10th Catford. Lunched at Lyons. Had welsh rarebit which upset my stomach.

11th … Took Popp out to Forest Gate - first time she'd been out in 6 weeks. Bought her a birthday present - a woolly jumper.

16th Burnham-on-Crouch. Dr. Lander & Miss Wyatt had sent their order on so I only had Dr. Savage's to take. Dr. Lander gave me a brace of partridges.

18th Did a good deal of work in garden. Found an old medal: (W.M.

20th Fund. 'What hath wrought. The best of all is God is with us.'). This gave me a subject for children's address.

25th Len, Rene, Win & others went blackberrying at Hainault. They only got a few.

Foraging for food was a way of life for most Britons in the first half of the 20th century, along with the keeping of animals in one's back yard. The eye of the average person was more alert to the fruits, berries and nuts proffered by nature and available in the fields and woodlands.

OCT

2nd. Ed & Li went to St. Ives for a week.

21st … walked to P & I. (J?), bought a few books, then along the Strand. Had some tea in ABC Charing Cross & walked to Westminster Chapel. 'Baptist World Alliance' meeting. D. Lloyd George in chair. D.E.Y. Mullins & D.H.J. Rushbrooke were the speakers…

23rd Saturday. Popp & I went to Ilford to see some houses. Inspected suburban development houses, but did not like them. So' Essex Property Co. houses although only 6 rooms appealed to us, Popp acquiescing to a drawing-room/office in one.

28th Len started wearing glasses.

30th S. Essex Property co.'s clerk called & saw me about the house in Eastern Ave. - thought to be too noisy of traffic.

NOV

4th Forest Gate &c. Had to make a special call to see an Indian Doctor - Dr. Murchanderie, 56 Launston Rd. Forest Lane.

6th Wrote to C.A.H. about having a motor car. Rene, Will, also Len were taken with C.E. (Christian Endeavour) to Royal Albert Dock and went over a liner. Popp & I were taken over to Ilford, the Drive, Eastern Ave., by Mr. Robinson in his motor.... Inspected some houses and hope to set me in The Drive for £1045. Met Mr. W. Mallinson (Harry's governor)... he praised up Harry. U.M. Church is to be built on The Eastern Ave. & Drive. I saw plans.

12th Billericay, Southend &c. Lunched at Garons, Victoria Circus.

17th Motor Car granted by Board.

23rd Brighton. Accident on S.R. Train ran into lorry on level crossing at Hayward's Heath. Made trains very late.

DEC

4th Saw Mr. S. Robinson and arranged to buy 315 The Drive, £1085 freehold, no road charges. Signed contract. Sent him on afterwards £20 deposit & £2 survey fee.

The purchase of one's first home is always a momentous step; Thomas Sibley had to wait until the age of 48 until he achieved it, but one compensation was that he bought 315, The Drive, Ilford, for the equivalent of £53,000 in today's terms (2023). Exactly the same house is valued today at £700,000, meaning that as a multiple of earnings a house-purchase in 1926 for the average citizen was a far lighter burden.

6th Win has another boy. Both are doing well.

11th Saturday. Rene & Win went off at 1.5. to meet Len in City to see Dr. Grenfell's pictures &c. Polytechnic crowded and they could not get in. Looked in shops, visited British Museum, had a good tea in Lyons & returned home.

22nd Gave Mr. Upsdale notice to leave 28 W.P.A. Gave 3 mo's notice.

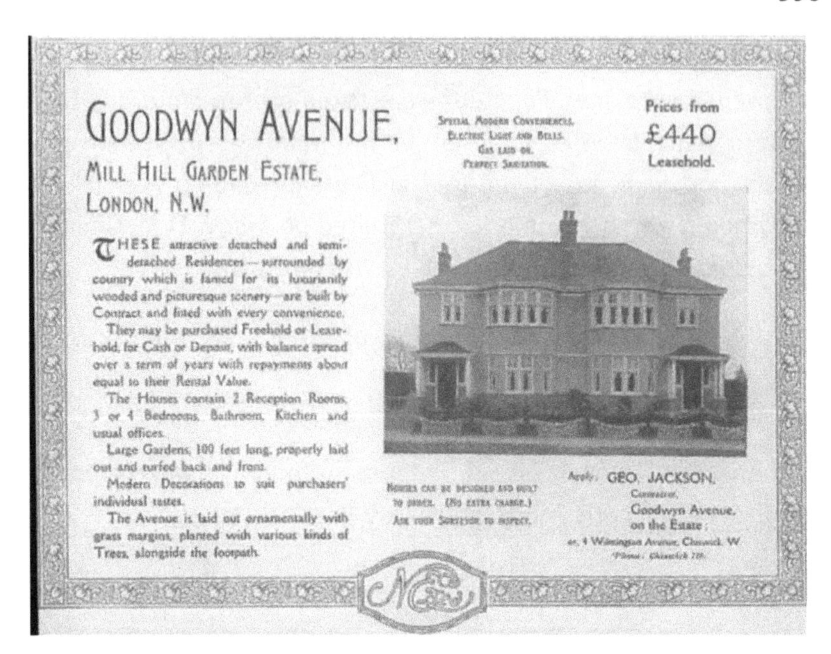

25th Haddock & poached egg for breakfast. Popp cooked dinner but could only eat whiting. Ed, Ernie, Len & I walked over to Ilford & inspected our new house. Back at 1.45. Ruth came from Winnie's. Turkey & ham splendid, also pudding & mince pies. Had some games in afternoon, 'Knowledge,' charades after tea, also 'Pit.' Broke up 11.55.

30th Caught 8.56 to City, went on to Graham St. Had cafe noir in Lyons. Mr. Carrr spoke on Vitamins. Had lunch in Food Reform Restaurant, Holborn.

The discovery of vitamins was a major scientific achievement in our understanding of health and disease. In 1912, Casimir Funk originally coined the term 'vitamine,' the function of each vitamin being ascertained through the work and contributions of epidemiologists, physicians, physiologists, and chemists. Rather than crowning scientific breakthroughs the reality was a slow, stepwise progress that included setbacks, contradictions, refutations, and some chicanery. Research on the vitamins that are related to major deficiency syndromes began when the germ theory of disease was dominant and dogma held that only four nutritional factors were essential: proteins, carbohydrates, fats, and minerals. Clinicians soon recognized scurvy, beriberi, rickets, pellagra, and xerophthalmia as specific vitamin deficiencies, rather than diseases due to infections or toxins. Experimental physiology with animal models played a fundamental role in nutrition research and greatly shortened the period of human suffering from vitamin deficiencies. Ultimately it was the chemists who isolated the various vitamins, deduced their chemical structure, and developed methods for synthesis of vitamins. Sibley's company The British Drug House was at the forefront of promoting vitamins as a major force in improving the nation's health.

1927

FEB

1st. Popp & Li went to Ilford to inspect 315 The Drive.

3rd Went to Stewart & Ardens & had lessons on gears and lubrications. Spent 4-5 looking about Bond St. & Piccadilly. Had some tea in Lyons Bond St.

Just as he was moving into home-ownership, Thomas Sibley's self-advancement was about to include auto-mobile driving, and he commenced a few lessons before driving his vehicle off from an Oxford street garage to his home in Ilford.

4th I went to M.P.B. Study Class. I spoke on Sin. An enjoyable evening.

10th Got to Stewart & Ardens 3.10. Stayed to 3 lectures - magnets, safety first, engine.

16th Visited Barclays Bank, signed forms for loan of £60. mortgage on Pearl Lessee (?) Co'y policy. Agreement on £25 shares. ... Drew out of P.O. Savings B. £19.

17th Received from Mr. J.C. Parson Conveyance & B. soc'y mortgage for £950 for signature. Read them in the train.

MARCH

1st. 315 The Drive now officially mine. Heard from Parson of Chelmsford. Everything completed. Got my driving license from E.H. Town Hall. 5/-.

3rd Mr. Bunting (only 21 years of age) gave me my first driving lesson in Hamilton Terrace NW. ... Went to Stewart & Ardens for further instruction on motor car.

10th Went to office then to Wharf Rd., saw car YE 8358.

Exciting though it was, Sibley's first ventures out on to the busy roads of London were not without their mishaps. It was the Golden Age of motoring, but the 1920s was a less policed age, in which drivers could perhaps be more reckless than today.

12th Saturday. Went to office 8.20, car not ready - had to wait until 9.30. Everything went well until I turned into Lea Bridge Rd. & turning too sharply ran onto curb and into LCC Section Box. Damaged box & car. After police had made usual notes I saw a motor agent about repair but decided to drive home. Arrived home 11.20, mishap occurred 10.10. Had something to eat - Popp scared. ... Took Rene in car to 315 The Drive, where I left it - drained out water. Paid Norman Stanley for electric work done, £4.19/-.

16th Popp very ill & Dr. Anderson said she must not be moved for several days. Had to cancel removal plans with Norris.

18th Went over to Ilford & bought curtain rods &c. Put up curtain fittings then motored over to W.P.Av. Had dinner. … took car to Smiths &c High Rd., Goodmayes for repairs - estimate to be sent to BDH.

23rd Removed to 315 The Drive Ilford. Back of washing stand broken. Norris took it back for repairs. Got to bed tired but thankful.

26th Saturday. Found car near garage all trim & new… Took Popp, Emily, Rene & Win to Beehive Lane & back, shopping, by car.

30th. Walthamstow &c. First journey by motor. Managed journey very well. A few blunders. Found I had gone up a hill with the handbrake on.

APRIL

1st. Laindon, Billericay, Rochford, Southend &c. … Car stopped on return for the reserve gallon to be put on - it took me some time to find tap in the dark.

6th … busy day and many delays. Nearly got into trouble at Barking - try to pull out from curb too quickly without signalling. Just missed another car.

7th … Went … to Stewart & Arden's & got some information on the Dynamotor.

8th Catford. Left car up up a side street some distance away. Two 'Ford' cars collided near my stationary car but fortunately missed it. A woman carrying a child nearly collided with my car on my way home.

9th Put clock forward.

14th Motored via Chelmsford to Walton-on-the-Naze.

16th Went alone to Frinton.

21st Window in Rene & Cissy's room smashed.

23rd Saturday. Helped on lawn - battening down grass. Winnie & Rene also worked hard at the lawn.

MAY

4th Saw Graham's new Singer 4-seater.

7th Took car to Mr. Cooper's, 27 St. Anne's Rd., & got some plants, which he had in excess. Spent afternoon in digging & planting. Sun gave me a nasty head. Oiled car. Mr. Robinson came in for a chat - he is trying to get into parliament - Liberal - he represented Chelmsford 1923-4.

15th Ruth (Ed's daughter) ill in bed. Sent for Dr. Beattie. He said it was a septic throat.

This is the first time Dr. Beattie appears in the Sibley family saga. As their trusted family doctor he would reappear at intervals for the next forty years.

16th Ed came twice. Li came here to look after her (Ruth).

17th Dr. Beattie called at 9 o'clock - Ruth rather worse & he said there were symptoms of Diptheria & endorsed Isolation Hospital. Li terror stricken. I phoned Ed for his consent for her to go to hospital. He said yes. She was taken away. Men came this afternoon and disinfected room, took away bed &c. - she has diptheria. Li hysterical.

18th Sanitary inspector called this morning and upset Popp by his behaviour. .. I met Li at Ilford Station at 3pm & took her to the Isolation Hospital to see Ruth.

The family troubles were compounded the following day when Thomas's son Len was fired from British Drug Houses:

19th Len has to leave BDH. B.D.H. told me to take Len away - month or 6 weeks. Poor old Len. Took Popp, Rene, Ciss for a ride into the country for about 40 mins - Chigwell &c. Wrote to C.A.H. & settled Len's time of departure - July 2nd. Told Len & asked him to trust God for another post.

At a time of increasing unemployment Len's 'letting go' was not unexpected, but with the Wall Street Crash and the Great Depression not far ahead, it was not a precipitous time to be job-seeking. But the apple never falls far from the tree, and the intrepid Len immediately sets to work in a quest for re-employment.

23rd Len wrote to several places after a berth.

JULY

17th Popp & I went to the Wesleyan Chapel and heard the blind preacher. Read two passages from S.S. from memory.

21st Came back for Popp, Rene & Ciss from Leytonstone and took them to Chelmsford. We had a delightful picnic 2 miles out of Little Walton. 25th Southend. … Had a Cydra at Woolworths.

28th Popp, Ciss, Rene & I started soon after 3pm for Childerditch by car, taking tea with us. Picnicked in St. Warley, forest lands where one is not allowed to camp or park cars. …Popp enjoyed the trip.

AUGUST

6th Saturday. … Departed for Childerditch & our pic-nic, Rene, Ciss & Popp in car and Alf, Cyril, Len, & Ada Bix on bicycles. Had an enjoyable time… Played for a time on Shenfield Common.

7th Len upset over spirt'l life.

8th Saw car blazing on Southend Rd.

17th Left car & had vectric heater put right at Lucas. Protested the 3/- charge and was let off.

27th Spent some time on car and a little time in garden. Did not have our usual joy ride.

SEPT

1st. Holidays.

2nd Put up tent in garden. Prepared for tomorrow's journey. Took car to Beehive garage - ammeters not registering, Dynamotor bushes dirty &c. 2/-.

In September 1927 the Sibleys set off on their first motoring holiday to the Essex coast:

3rd Saturday. Misty morning. Did not start until 8.15. Breakfasted a mile or two out of Chelmsford on a country lane. Arrived at Mr. L. Robinson's, Shore Farm @11.30. Left car at Simpson's Farm - Mr. Goslings. ... Drove into Dovercourt in afternoon. Back to tea 6pm, went on River Stour shores. Mr. Robinson got box from station.

7th Had a nice little drive by the Orwell into Shotley. A little boy nearly got killed by running in front of car - pulled up in time. Returning from Shotley I hit a fowl.

8th Went to Frinton in afternoon. ... visited Luffs, bought books & tea - 3/4 - a swindle. Got back to Wrabness (?) 6.30. Supper 8.30. Mr. Robinson told us some anecdotes.

12th Went for a drive past Harlow. Noisy rattle in engine spoilt ride. Showed it to Smith's RAC man on voyage & at Beehive Garage without success. No evidence at the latter.

17th Popp, Len, Rene, Win & I went for a drive to Laindon Hills. Picked a few blackberries. Speedometer went wrong - new cable?

21st. We all went, with the exception of Len, to Clementswood Baptist Social gathering to welcome back Dr. & Mrs. Beattie. Nice refreshments & several speeches, & 'visitings' from Fellowship Band. Popp & Rene preferred Mr. Duck's car.

22nd Len went to W. Mersea for a short holiday. Rene went to swimming gala and got sopping wet. Went to office - left car in Wharf Rd. ... Mr. Fidler said he would decarbonise car for me next Monday & Tuesday.

28th. Mr. Mathews told me he was now buying drugs from Stafford Allen.

29th Brighton. Started in car 8.5. Took Len as far as Blackwall tunnel. Arrived Edgar Jones 10.45.

OCT

20th Went to Motor Show at Olympia.

23rd Went to Mariner's Friend Society, Old Gravel Lane in evening. Only eight.

Despite having moved to the prosperous suburb of Ilford Sibley had not lost his missionary Christian zeal, and just as he had done in 1905 ventured into the dark pockets of a deprived London that still lingered in the late 1920s - the dockland area of Wapping and Poplar with its cobbled alleys, shambolic courts and decaying dark-brick sooty rookeries.

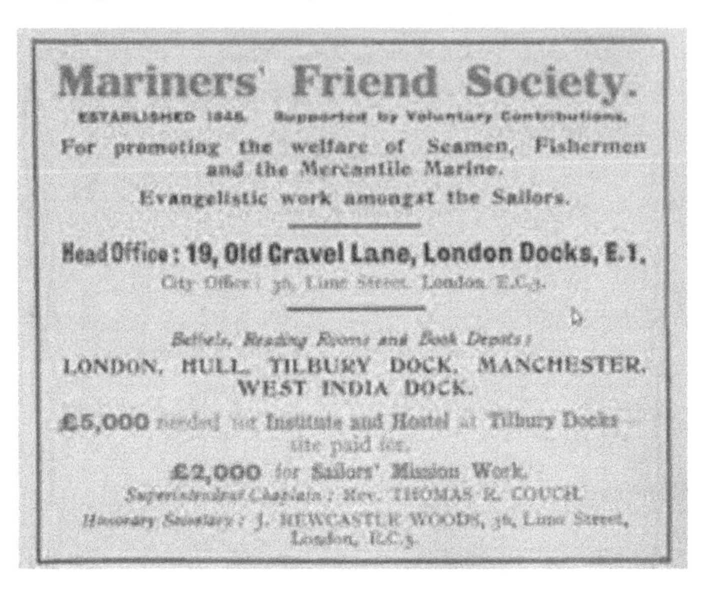

Mariners' Friend Society.

ESTABLISHED 1846. Supported by Voluntary Contributions.

For promoting the welfare of Seamen, Fishermen and the Mercantile Marine.

Evangelistic work amongst the Sailors.

Head Office: 19, Old Gravel Lane, London Docks, E.1.

City Office: 36, Lime Street, London, E.C.3.

Bethels, Reading Rooms and Book Depots:

LONDON, HULL, TILBURY DOCK, MANCHESTER, WEST INDIA DOCK.

£5,000 needed for Institute and Hostel at Tilbury Docks — site paid for.

£2,000 for Sailors' Mission Work.

Superintendent Chaplain: Rev. THOMAS R. COUCH.

Honorary Secretary: J. NEWCASTLE WOODS, 36, Lime Street, London, E.C.3.

Old Gravel Lane, Wapping, in the 1920s.

25th Popp & others (not Len) had been to Exhibition most of day.

26th Went to Exhibition for the first time & enjoyed lecture by Mr. Pearson.

29th Started on car 3.30, finished 10.30. Found a puncture which I mended. Popp & the others left for C & B about 6pm. I finished tyre and got ready to go, but car would not be persuaded. Looked overr magneto - Mr Duck helped me to push in car & then overlooked it. We managed to start it - self-starter not working. Had a run around to charge batteries - successfully. Disappointed at not being able to go to exhibition. NOV

7th Popp, Rene & Ciss went to C.Wood exhibition.

14th Had an alarming skid at Hadleigh.

15th Lunched in ABC Stratford. Had a chat with Pratt's assistant - a Jewess.

24th Len… went to his music lesson.

DEC

1st Put together wood for a cold garden frame tied on to tea chest for coke.

2nd … posted letter in new pillar box, Eastern Ave.

8th Burnham on Crouch & Chelmsford. … Another car stopped me and I was asked to take a young lady - a fine girl - of 18 or 19 - into Chelmsford.

21st Hundreds of casualties thro' slippery streets and roads.

24th … Rene & I went to Ilford in car, & bought cards &c, & towels, in market, & a game, 'Bombardo' in Manor Park.

26th Monday. (Sunday, 25th, spent in study and services)… swept snow from paths... stacked against trees. Snow quite 6' thick.

31st. Ed sent me a diary - refill.

1928

JAN

6th Car got stuck in a rut on Laindon Hill - 3 men helped to get me unstuck.

9th Two policemen held me up for having no lights. I had switched them off accidentally when switching off head lights at Newberry Park to let a van & bus pass easily. They took particulars &c.

10th Went to M.P.B. & heard Mr. Cutler the converted boxer. A stirring address.

14th Repaired electrical arrangements in kitchen. Pasted wallpaper on walls where it was coming off.

17th. Len & Rene went to M.P.B. & heard Mr. Cutler. Len decided to return fully to the Lord & His service.

21st Had puncture which was repaired at Grays opposite Dr. Tallick's. Had 'squeak' temporarily silenced at Beehive Gardens.

26th Went to office. Bayley meant to stop the squeak in car - gave him 1/- squeak however still there.

FEB

3rd Earl Haigh's funeral. Heard last part of Service on wireless at Barnes.

4th ... fined 10/- at court house Stratford for driving without lights on Jan 9th.

6th Southend. Had a dangerous skid on the way this morning - just missed a car & circled & was whirled on to the bank -... no damage. Car noisy coming home so had to return slowly.

7th Sent 2/6d & badge back to RAC for a nickel one.

During the First World War Field Marshal Douglas Haig commanded the British Expeditionary Force on the Western Front from late 1915 until the end of the war. He was commander during the Battle of the Somme, the Battle of Arras, the Third Battle of Ypres, the German Spring Offensive, and the Hundred Days Offensive.

11th Bought 5 sacks of manure. Shifted some trees &c.

23rd Voted for Compton Carr - Liberal - @Beehive Schools (1244).

24th Cons. got in at Ilford with much reduced vote. Popp & Rene had some excitement over two live plaice.

27th Brighton & Hove. Lunched in Lyons. Hard beef. Small rounded plate. Blunt knife. No enjoyment.

29th Rene started school again.

MARCH

3rd Saturday. Put spring on gate & numbers on gate.

6th Went to Cubitt Town, returning ran into a road block East India Rd., so escaped it down Crisp Street and Grundy (?) St. - home.

9th Catford &c. On my return I unfortunately ran over a dog in Greenwich - man wanted ny name &c - took my number. Said to be a police officer?

10th Saturday. … started on path in garden.

13th Bought 'The Motor.'

15th. Brighton. Cup of tea at Brighton Station. Bought 1st number of 'Wonderful Britain.'

17th Mr. Farmely came and went over car - put in new oil. … a friend of his called for him - a caterer at Lyle's Sugar Works where Ernie Sibley works.

22nd Went to Pickering & Inglis & Marshall Bro's. Bought several books. Cissy bought a large volume of Life of Shakespeare for Len & I a two version Bible.

24th Did writing in evening and typing.

29th Motored to Lawries with Len. A cyclist had a hair breadth escape & did not know it.

APRIL

5th Bought a new electric fitting switch & put it on bedroom wall.

19th Eva Sibley paid a surprise visit to dinner - she went on afterwards to meet Ed.

26th … called at Standon and saw Dr. Marriet at his sanatorium about Radio-Malt. Pic-nicked outside Little Waltham in usual spot. Popp very nervy in car at times.

28th Eczema on both arms troubling me. I feel very run down.

In the inter-war period incidents of nervous exhaustion, analogous to the late twentieth century's diagnosis of chronic fatigue syndrome, increased to a significant level, including an umbrella-term devised by medical practitioners of the age, *neurasthenia.* The condition was explained as being a result of exhaustion of the central nervous system's energy reserves, which was attributed to modern civilization. Physicians in the Beard school of thought associated neurasthenia with the stresses of urbanization and with stress suffered as a result of the increasingly competitive business environment.

30th Mr. Shapley bandaged up my arms for me - used Lolio Calamin.

MAY

12th Len took his motorcycle back to Lovett's, suggests he has a new one, a Raleigh.

17th Burnham-on-Crouch. Nearly had a collision at Romford cross-roads, had to brake down furiously. Had a cup of coffee in Burnham, talkative little child in room.

19th Saturday. Brought shed from Mr. Hardy's (next door). Leslie Parrish helped, also Len & I also Rene.

24th Spent some time in garden - finished path.

26th Len busy with Y.L.C. poster until 1.30am.

28th Whit Monday. Up at 6.45. A man broke into Davis' house - smashed glass in door. Seen by neighbour who acquainted Mr. Tilley. The would-be thief made a fight of it but was caught by the 'paper-boy' & his dogs. The boy - a sturdy lad of 18 - in spite of a blow in the jaw & a bitten hand - got him down and held him until help came. Man arrested. I bandaged the boy's hand. Mr. Duck & I boarded up the broken door.

29th. Southend. A lot of cars on the road. My 'Morris' going splendidly.

JUNE

6th Derby Day. Len busy with motorbike.

7th Brighton, Hove. Had dinner with Mr. Thomas & his wife in their Portslade home, 'Galen.' Left Brighton 5.45, arrived home 8.5 - a record time for me (2 hours 20 mins).

13th Len gave Rene a run on his motor-bike.

15th Filled up with petrol & prepared for Cromer.

16th Started for Cromer 6.50… breakfasted a little way outside Bishops Stortford… stopped for some tea at Thetford. Arrived at Cromer 1.50… staying at Mrs Watts, 'Tenby,' St. Mary's Rd. Mr. Watts (son) & Miss Watts (daughter) do all the work.

19th… Had some tea at Wells - peculiar old town.

21st Long walk before breakfast along the cliffs nearly to Averstead. 100's of rabbits & birds - lovely conditions & morning freshness. … Started for Sandringham, arrived there 4 o'clock, & paid 2/- to go into grounds. Motored into Hunstanton.

22nd. Cold bath. Sat on front to get brown. Motored to Lion's Mouth, Roman camp, Pretty Corner.

JULY

4th All disappointed at not having promised to purchase dog from Husbands.

12th 1 1/2 tons of coal arrived from Warrens.

26th Left Popp's teeth at Blackmores for repairs. Got back home 6.20. Took Popp for a run to Harold Wood, Gidea Park &c. & looked at some houses.

AUGUST

6th Motored to Brentwood & on to South Weald. Visited the church and ascended the tower. Lovely view. Popp climbed the steep stone steps. Two punctures on Southend Rd.- Cissy & Popp walked on while Rene & I repaired tyre. We got home first.

7th Southend. Roads crowded with charabancs & cars - passed them all, no car passed me.

14th Len got his Christian Endeavour Experts Badge & certificate.

18th Took Popp & Cissy for a ride nearly to Dunmow, round Harlow & home. Bought newly-laid eggs and apples from a country farm.

27th Started for Brighton in car 8 o'clock. Took Len, Rene & Cyril Lewington. Had to go through Rotherhithe tunnel, arrived 10.35. Put them down at Palace Pier. Met Mr. C.H. Wilkins at Royal Pavilion Hotel. … Met others 6.50 Madeira Place. They enjoyed themselves.

30th Brighton, Portslade &c. Left at 8 o'clock with Rene & Ken (lad of 11). Ran over a dog in Cherry Orchard Rd. - policeman said 'go on.'

SEPT.

1st. Sandgate Park (Storrington). Good reception. Put car in stable. Dinner 8 o'clock - prayers.

6th Charabanc & boat trip on River Arun to Littlehampton from Amberley.

8th Left Sandgate Park at 4.10 arriving home about 7.15. Len deserted us, motoring into Worthing arranging to meet the two misses Collys there. Mrs. Duck made us a nice tart.

OCT

4th Went... to Central Hall Westminster Medical Exhibition. Stopped at BDH stand for a time. Saw Mr. Shaw, Mr. Jewell & others. Later, we all except Len... went to organ recital by Sally Sellars at U.M. Church. Electric light failed during performance for a time.

10th A terrible accident on arterial road near The Drive 10.15 - a young man knocked down by motor bike and killed. He lived in Castle View Drive.

16th Special meeting at Cranbrook Baptists - Committee considered tenders for building. Lowest £4,320.

30th Two Accidents. ... at 1 o'clock whilst crossing the Barking Rd. a Ford van skidded into me - hit my offside mudguard. Constable took particulars & asked Ford Van man to back his car nearer - he backed into mine, doing damage to the back. Also, in Portway 2.30 a horse van in front of tram pulled out & I hit his wheel with my left onside rear mudguard, putting it out of shape - I did not stop.

NOV

25th King George very ill.

DEC

4th Spent evening putting pictures to perfectness - putting paper on their backs.

6th … A lad playing football jumped in front of car & got knocked over - mouth cut. Was able to stop without running him over.

8th Put some more gravel in front of garage.

14th Played a game at 'Touring.' BDH delivered cigarettes.

15th Played Rene & Len table golf.

25th Had a lovely dinner. Started for Leigh 1.55. … Sibley family all ok. Len & Cyril turned up about 6pm whilst at tea. Forgot to take petrol. Left car on Ed's garden, Will covered over. Had games up to 1.45.

26th Played table golf. dinner 1.30. Popp was ill & retching. Had to take her home at 3.5.

Got my tea by drawing-room gas fire and stayed there and read a little while Popp dozed.

Len & Cyril got back about 12pm. Xmas not a success - essentially not a happy one.

28th Lunch at Midland Grand Hotel 1.15. Mr. Sherrer gave the toast, very nicely and appropriately done. Usual conversations, nothing exceptional - quite a nice atmosphere of general good will.

31st 'Heard' old year out and new year in in bed.

1929

JAN

1st Billericay, Chelmsford &c. Mr. Thomas showed me over Dix's house - a large old-fashioned country house - shop - garden.

9th … left car in East Avenue whilst I had some coffee. Came out to find my car had flown. Reported to police at East Ham Town Hall. Wrote to firm &c.

11th Catford. Missed 10 calls. Wrote to them. Loss of car felt.

22nd Received fountain pen and bread knife from Ty-Phoo people.

24th Lunched in Homeley Rest. Bevis Marks.

29th Sent 3 snaps of car to HP insurance policies.

31st Lunched in Dartford… muscatelles & almonds.

FEB

2nd Saturday. Went into (the) Ducks for tea & evening's enjoyment. Mr. & Mrs. Crisp there, also Leslie Parrish came with Len. Played 'Pit.' Music etc. Left there 12.10am.

5th Heard from BDH - a saloon car to be ordered for me. 'What colour?' I replied at once - grey.

6th Rec'd cheque from BDH ex insurance co. HP policies £8 - personal property on car YE8358.

7th … Went off to Piccadilly & to R.Academy & saw the famous Dutch pictures.

11th Everyone frozen by the vicious East Wind. Taps hot & cold upstairs frozen.

12th Many people frozen out of water. No cold bath - force majeure - no water.

15th Went to works for new Morris Saloon VL5095. … Car very stiff & strange.

19th Car going well. I'm getting used to it.

22nd Mr. Brake called in and asked me from Building Committee if I would lay a stone. I consented.

23rd Farewell Bike.

28th Gravesend. Found rear light out - hurried to Garage near Pow(s?) St. Youth in charge could not help me - only wasted time. I ran the gauntlet of police & reached Bow Garage where a youth unattached to garage reconnected light for me - no charge.

MARCH

1st Petrol up 2/- 1/4 a gallon.

9th Stone laying ceremony Eastern Avenue Baptist Church. At 3.20 took Popp, Ciss & Leslie Parrish to Ashurst Drive - stone laying of

Baptist Church. 8 stones laid. I laid one on behalf of the Building Committee and rec'd an engraved mallet. A very good company - about 130 sat down to tea.

This church was to figure hugely in the life of the Sibleys; a modest, though ambitious building funded by the local people and driven by collective community enthusiasm. Hundreds of similar churches sprang up all across London and indeed the country, such was the persistence of the nonconformist movement. In 1929 the Church building and rear hall opened. The name chosen being 'Eastern Avenue Baptist Church'. In 1935, the church was renamed as 'Ashurst Drive Baptist Church,' with the Rev. F.S. Frape being its first full-time minister. Still going strong today, it played a dynamic part in the life of Ilford's community, and as a deacon for many years Thomas Sibley was a beating pulse of its activities.

16th BDH paying 8%.

21st Accident with stove - Popp's hair and woollen jacket alight.

22nd A careless driver nearly ran into us at 'Green Man' Leytonstone - just managed to avoid him by quick manoeuvre.

23rd Went by car to High Rd. Ilford Bazaar on behalf of Beehive Baptists.

29th Len & Leslie Parrish went off to Devon on the motorbike.

30th Filled up the hole in the garden - Mr. Duck put his rubbish in and I also emptied dust-pail in.

APRIL

6th New Gas Stove arrived.

11th. Brighton, Shoreham &c. Walked across bridge to see Mr. O.Jones at Shoreham.

Ashurst Drive Baptist Church, Ilford, founded in 1929 and still thriving today.

12th Will gave us a small grating to cover trap in front of garage.

19th Hooter giving trouble - refuses to hoot at times. Cissy accidentally put my letter down the car window.

MAY

4th Emily D., Rene & Popp went with me to BDH sports ground - opening ceremony by CAH - flag flown. I played cricket - Veterans XVII v. Present XI. V 75, P. 26. I got 1, and took 2 wkts. Had a pleasant time with old associates. Bob there.

13th Heard from Dena Slicker.

18th Dena Slicker came for a fortnight's holiday. Len met Dena at L'Pool St. and saw her into train. I met her with car at Ilford Station 8.45 & brought her home. Had a run to Ongar & back just to give Dena a drive.

Dena, Thomas' neice whose early life was fraught with so much trauma as a result of her dissolute father Will, with spells in the workhouse, has luckily found good fortune and a husband in Belgium.

23rd Pic-nic in Swancombe Woods. Rene picked some blue bells.

30th General Election. Voted Liberal. Dena departed for Belgium and home. She had a happy time and was loath to leave.

In the General Election of 1929, fought in the shadow of the economic difficulties caused by the Great Crash, the Liberals - led once again by the old lion Lloyd George - campaigned on a comprehensive programme of public works under the title *We Can Conquer Unemployment.* The election was often referred to as the 'Flapper Election', because it was the first in which women aged 21–29 had the right to vote. Despite gaining ground, the Liberals never recovered their former might, and Labour broke through. Even though it was a hung parliament, the two-party system in the UK, with the Conservatives and Labour dominating the political landscape, was born.

31st Labour winning.

JUNE

1st Labour won.

14th Ed on voyage to Ireland on SS Godwin.

20th Len is to have his holidays & goes on Saturday on his own - camping out.

22nd Saturday. Started for Southbourne 6.10. Len not ready so left him to catch us up. Nice drive thro- City & West End - Len failed to catch us up. Stopped a few miles from Basingstoke for breakfast. Someone like Len passed us and we thought it was him - Popp upset over it & we hurried to Basingstoke after him, & walked about there for a little while & had to go on with Len's breakfast with us. Stopped for an hour at Winchester & looked at Cathedral. Got to Mrs. Drummonds at 12.55 (I, Alexander Rd., Southbourne).

Walked on front. Photos were talken by Beadmans.

24th Dinner lamb minced, banana fritters. … Had a drive to New Forest, Lyndhurst and by Ringwood home.

27th … tramm'd it to Bournemouth. Went to Weymouth by 'SS Balmoral.' … Saw some warships in Portland Harbour.

29th Lovely dinner - chicken & pancakes. Bought Len a small attache case 7/6.

30th CID man called in afternoon about my last Morris.

JULY

2nd Accident just outside Crawley. Standard met Chrysler. Standard in ditch - I witnessed it.

3rd Met CID man at East Ham Police Station & took him to Hackney P.S. & identified my old car. It was a wreck to what it was when I had it. Many alterations. Several proofs for identification.

6th Saturday. Len went to City on bike - knocked over a man in Stratford - injured bike & self a little. Sold his bike for £11-5/-. Bought himself a new overcoat & shoes.

18th Tea with Lawton in his garden. Plenty of raspberries white & red.

24th Girl driver drive her Morris into a lamp standard, Gants Hill cross just after Popp & others had gone by.

25th Spent an hour… on Ward Lock's book on Burnham.

27th Popp's nerves now bad when motoring.

AUGUST

5th Len came back from his camping and went to Birmingham.

14th Went to Bowie's bible school in evening. Bade goodbye to Irish friends - Atkinson, Cook, 2 Weirs, also 3 Misses Beattie.

23rd Heard that Len may be out of working thro' Kimber losing his contract.

SEPT

5th Len has secured another job - Hay's Wharf, so will not be going with us to Burnham-on-Sea.

7th No view of beautiful Bucks in fog. Caused a collision between a Morris & a lorry on the way. Henley 9.45 where we had breakfast near Golf links. Got to Reading abt 5 mins before Ed. They all went to get something to eat, I looked after the cars. An hour wasted. Ed's car going badly, smoking horribly at back. Lunched on Bath Road. Got to Bath 4pm. Ed & I left the others and inspected the Celtic & Roman baths. Arrived (Burnham) 5pm.

10th … Went to Cheddar's wonderful gorge & caves. Only visited Goff's cave. Ed & his car party were behind us and we met in the cave. Cave crowded… Went afterwards to Wells Cathedral.

11th Took Rene for a drive before tea to Bream, & Ciss for a drive after tea to Breat Knoll. Walk on front then they all came to our place & sang choruses and read 'Ole Biscuit.'

14TH Started at 9.15. Very pretty ride. Stopped at Stonehenge. Picnic lunch near Whitchurch. Lost one another near Ealing. Found one another again on G.W.Rd. Lost Ed's car at Wembley. Li prefers my car.

25th Signed agreement as guarantor for loan of £1000 for Baptist fund.

28th Saturday. Grays &c. ... got to Walton 2.35. Had a swim... tide very low... windy, shallow, choppy.

'Ole Biskit' - a series of popular comic tales published by Herbert Jenkins

OCT

17th. Interviewed A.F. who went into the matter of our corresp-ce over 'Gentian,' & assured me no offensiveness should have been read into it - I expressed regrets and we shook hands.

19th Wilf returned from Australia after 7 years.

28th Haines & Warwick painting house.

30th. Went to P.M. (?, sic). Rev. M.C. Bowie threw down a bomb - this is my last prayer meeting here, and Sunday my last Sunday. Bandeni upset and nearly had a fit. Brake, Dilling & myself got him out & after, he came round & had prayer. Bowie laboured for half an hour on Rev. III-7, and afterwards was persuaded to remain with about a dozen for prayer and guidance... I went on to Dr. Beattie's.

NOV

1st. B.D.H. interim dividend 3%.

2nd Rene & I painted window sashes of bathroom & W.C. Cissy called on Dr. Beattie who asked her to ask me to preach Sunday morning 7 at Clementswood Fellowship 3 o'clock. Had to do some preparing at once.

3rd Sunday. Took service at Ashurst Drive B.C. At the close Mrs. Reiderman spoke to Mrs. Beattie about Mr. Bowie & Mrs. Beattie broke down in tears. Dr. Beattie preached in evening.

4th Len started night work - 8pm - 5am.

7th House painting finished.

17th Sunday. I helped Dr. Beattie by taking the service, leaving him to preach the sermon.

18th. Brighton. Popp & Rene went with me. (They) went to Mr. & Mrs. Ward's, 41 Lansdowne St. I got there to lunch - boiled bacon & syrup pudding. dinner at 6.45 - beef (well done) & macaroni pudding.

23rd Visited market. Took Beautiful Britain vol. iii to be bound.

DEC

9th Southend &c. Popp, Rene & Ciss went with me and I left them at Li's in Leigh-on-Sea. Fish tea. Left there at 9 o'clock. Sing most of the way home.

11th Spoke to Dr. Henry of Barking about his soul. Left him with tears in his eyes.

13th Wrote to Exeter for 5 'Ole Biscuits.'

25th Len went with Row, Brake, to see West Ham F.C. Got to Ed's 3.35. … Len pulled a hassock & let Popp fall on ground injuring bottom of spine. A pleasant ride home 11.50.

Despite Popp's tumble, the Sibleys ended the decade on a high; in relative prosperity, they had ridden out the tribulations of perhaps the biggest economic crash in Britain's history, become home-owners, and established themselves physically and spiritually in their community. Annie (Popp) had journeyed from far-off Poplar and the grimy streets of London's docklands, Thomas had extracted himself from a family beset by dysfunctional pressures. By all appearances they were a comfortable, stolid, hard-working family. But troubles lay ahead, and the survival of the family in the strange, unsettled decade of the Thirties is a potent lesson in durability and stoicism, as they faced turbulence, struggle and war.

CHAPTER FOUR

THE LAST DANCE - 1930-1940

The 1930s began brightly with the discovery of Pluto by Clive Tombaugh, and ended in a global conflagration the likes of which had never been seen before. In between unfolded a decade of hard desperation, a cold nexus of economic hardship and extremism, the two things intertwined perhaps and creating a sense of dread inevitability that dragged all in its slipstream. For those who escaped the Depression - such as the hero of our story, commercial traveller Thomas Sibley - it was a continued saga of suburban prosperity and self-improvement, marred by the everyday challenges of family health and happiness that nibble at the contentment of all humans.

For much of the working-class in the 1920s, poverty was the grim face at the window. By 1931 unemployment had passed two million, and the Dole became a permanent reality for many. Life became a routine of make-do-and-mend, scavenging, soup kitchens and the black market. This landscape was one shared by much of Europe and beyond, and it is testimony to the suppleness of the British state that unlike several of its European counterparts, the country never fell prey to the false resort of fascism or communism.

Not that we didn't come close. The Thirties was a time of marches, when simple strikes morphed into calls for social and political change. The most famous of these, the Jarrow March of 1936, became legendary, with the cloth caps of the unemployed joined by the bowler hats of Jarrow's mayor and Councillor Riley. It achieved nothing except to ignite the imaginations and empathy of the nation, for despite the National Government being swept to power in 1931 in a landslide pledging to wrench the country back from an economic precipice, by the end of 1933 40 per cent of miners and a full 60 per cent of shipyard workers were unemployed. This cold fact is sufficient to explain the appeal of Oswald Mosely's New Party, a British fascist movement that sought to ape the totalitarian nationalism of its victorious counterparts in Italy, Germany and Spain. Mosely failed, but extremism on both left and right bubbled to the surface throughout the decade: with Stalin's monstrous crimes uncovered or simply ignored, the British Left maintained a strange misplaced devotion to the 'shangri-la' of Soviet Russia.

But Britain did not collapse, perhaps largely to the nourishment and growth of suburbia: by the end of the decade an extraordinary 30 per cent of all Britons described themselves as 'middle-class.' It is to the flexibility and social mobility of Britain's class system that we must look, perhaps, to the survival of our democracy in this unstable decade. As the Hollybush Lanes and Mulberry Gardens were thrown up, so too was a concomitant contentment that stifled the desperate urge to destroy. In this decade of contrasts, consumer goods especially for the home had never been more abundant - electric cookers, vacuum cleaners, fridges, luxury furniture, all became the goals of the British family rather than the Soviet Committee or the Collective Farm.

It was the golden age of the Cafe. The growth and popularity of the Lyons Corner House that we have noted in the early decades of the century continued unabated: Maison Lyons, which opened in 1933 in Marble Arch, London, seated an extraordinary 2000. But even this was dwarfed by the Coventry

Street site, which fed 4000. Public entertainment was never perhaps so fruitful; Variety theatres, Cinemas, cafes, pubs - all offered either recreation, discourse or simple escapism.

Others escaped to the countryside. Physical health became something a cult movement in the Thirties, not only in Britain. In Nazi Gemany it possessed a somewhat unsavoury undercurrent, that of creating the 'master-race,' but in Britain it was thankfully more of a hobbyist's enthusiasm. Railway posters urged citizens to 'Hike for Health,' (the word *hiking* being invented in the 1930s for the purpose), Keep Fit Classes sprang up in town halls, and the passion for the countryside became so overwhelming that city-dwellers, frustrated by being kept off land belonging to the old order of the gentry, staged periodic 'invasions,' - rebellious rambles across hitherto sealed-off fields and hills. The most famous of these became known as 'The Kinder Trespass,' when 400 hikers from the British Worker's Sports Federation roamed freely but illegally across Kinder Scout, moorland owned by the Duke of Devonshire. Five were sent to prison, but the dream of an 'open countryside,' fuelled by the knowledge that our ancient landscape was criss-crossed with green lanes, footpaths and routeways carved out by our ancestors long before the Normans parcelled them into estates, persisted, championed by the Council for the Preservation of Rural England, founded in 1926. Further evidence of the 'democratisation' of the countryside can be discerned in the growth of membership of the National Trust - 1,700 in 1929, and 7,100 by 1939. Its acquisitions of stately homes doubled across the decade from 141 to 175.

For the aristocracy the decade was perhaps the 'last fling,' and many were probably grateful to hand over their piles to the state, burdened as they were by the dual hammer blows of death duties and the Great War. Contrary to much received opinion, the officer class had been all but wiped out by the

1914-18 conflict, decimating the British upper-class and sentencing the great houses of the landed gentry to an inexorable slow decline. The rituals continued - the passing out of débutantes, the gentlemen's clubs, the hounds at hunt, the grand country house weekend parties - but there had grown a weary sense of unease and relative hardship among the former higher tiers of British society. The lower and middle-classes had entered parliament and government, and already Evelyn Waugh was becoming wistful at the passing of an age in his eulogy to the golden age of aristocracy, *Brideshead Revisited.*

When Chamberlain broadcast his fateful declaration of war in 1939 his words bore the heavy stamp of regret, failure and gloom; this was no triumphal speech shot through with the bellicosity, eagerness and enthusiasm that had characterised the beginning of the First World War. *'You cannot imagine what a bitter blow it is to me,'* he sighed, his words pregnant with memories of the trenches and loss. As a member of the older generation he had the painful foreknowledge of what lay ahead. It took Churchill, of course - an elder statesman too but made of sterner stuff - to turn, almost alchemically, the dread and fatalism of the nation into something stronger. *'Be this the whetstone of thy sword,'* wrote Shakespeare in Macbeth, *'turn grief to anger; blunt not the heart, enrage it!'*

1930

JAN

6th Len started at the Tunnel Cement Co. West Thurrock.

At a time of growing unemployment, the Sibley son Leonard's acquisition of a job at the Tunnel Cement Co. in Thurrock was a godsend. The raw materials of chalk, clay and water in this area, together with transport links to the Thames and railway made Thurrock a thriving centre of cement production, and Len was riding the wave. The Tunnel Cement Co. was established in 1874 and endured until 1968, when foreign production took over. His workplace was a landscape of dystopian bleakness - scarred with quarries, criss-crossed with railways, heady with the din of huge drills as the chalk was extracted, and the furious flame of kilns.

Alternatively called Tunnel Works, this was the parent plant of the Tunnel company, and was named after Tunnel Farm, on the lands of which it was situated, and which had been so named since the mid 18th century. From 1911 the plant grew to become the largest in the country, between 1920 and 1940 becoming a maze of rail track, boasting at its peak 20 km of private track. The jetty remained in use for receipt of fuel.

After 1968 the site was rapidly redeveloped and is now covered with light industry and warehousing. The jetty is used by an oil and chemicals transporting operation. The main chalk quarry is now the Lakeside Retail Park.

But as Len started work, there were changes afoot in his father's job as well, as he changed his routes for the British Drug Houses.

10th Farewell journey (Catford). Most of my customers are very sorry I'm going off the round.

16th Last Brighton journey. Returned by 5.35 - Southern Belle.

17th Billericay, Southend &c. Plenty of whiting to keep me going to bed time.

20th Saw Ed. He said I was foolish in giving up Brighton - CAH did not like it.

21st Wrote to CAH about the changing of ground, reminding him of the possible loss of returns.

22nd Rene grieving over Victor not writing.

24th Spent evening with further considerations of new grounds. Received a letter from CAH saying my salary had been advanced £10 - an excellent reply to mine.

27th First Maidstone journey. Managed new ground fairly well - got 9 orders.

FEB

3rd Went by train to Wharf Rd. & took away a new car (cracked window), GC 4490.

6th Visited Mint. Met Popp, Cissy, Rene & Mrs. Pettigen in

(Stratford) ABC. Had hurried lunch then journeyed to the Mint. Phoned Ed in morning & he said he would come - he was there waiting for us. Mr. Barnard took us over - it took 2 hours, & we were most interested. Quite an education. .. We visited P & I (Percy & Inglis?) & we all bought some literature.

11th Telephone wires put in 6.55pm.

By the 1930s, it was common for affluent homes in the UK to have their own telephones, with networks spreading far enough for calls to be made across several cities.

A typical office of 1930, with blotter & telephone.

18th Len home. No fire or dinner.

19th Telephone completed.

20th Used 'phone to BDH.

22nd Collected car from Stewart & Ardents.

25th Arranged to let Len have money to purchase motor-bike.

28th Lent Len £26 5/- for motor-bike.

MARCH

1st Sibley Party. Len bought motor-bike. Took Len to West Thurrock in car. Ed, Li, Win, Ernie, Wilf, Roy, Alan, Eva, Ruth, (Bert in Germany), came to tea & spent a jolly evening with us. Mr. & Mrs. Pettigen & Leslie Parrish also came & joined in the fun. Len got motor bike from Mitcham.

The high spirits and camaraderie of the Sibley family party at 315, The Drive, were soon to be shattered by a nasty incident the following day:

3rd BURGLARS. Len got home 9.30 only to find door bolted. On investigation he discovered burglars had been in thro' scullery window. Phone police - no trace of miscreants. Got Len's clock, & Rene's, my watch, Popp & Cissie's best dresses etc. Desk drawers broken. No sleep for Popp, Rene & Ciss. Got to bed 1 o'clock.

4th CID man came at 9 o'clock. Suspicion fell on two men selling plants. Len got them round and CID brought them into house and cross-examined them. Mr. Duck saw one of them in our garden. Could prove nothing however & they were let go. Mrs. - of Castle Drive called in & said what she knew about the men who went to her house. 'Phone dbank as cheque book stolen. Phoned Eagle Insurance Co'y. Started for work and Len at 11 o'clock.

Crime in the 1930s was rising, very probably as a result of the economic downturn and huge unemployment.

10th Claim sent in to Eagle Insurance Co. for £31-6-6d.

13th Lunched in Dartford - baked beans &c.

20th Assessor 'phoned in evening. Len answered as I was out. Assessor offers £26.

21st. I 'phoned and accepted £26.

APRIL

5th Started to whitewash ceiling & strip off paper in kitchen. Worked to teatime.

14th Gave Wilf (Ed's son) 5/- and said goodbye to him. He sails for Canada tomorrow. Percy Harding, San Pedro Mission, going by the same boat.

21st Bank Holiday Monday. Read 3 stories from 'Chimley Corner.' Len went to Hastings on motor bike and returned with Vera on pillion.

23rd Rev. Mr. Bowie here to tea. Vera Hardway also here. Vera, Len, Rene & Victor had some games in the evening.

MAY

9th Went to Committee Meeting at Dr. Beattie's at 8.30. Rev. F.H. Smith in the chair. All went well until the S.S. was mentioned. Dr. Beattie referred to what happened at Monday's T.M. D.B. threw down a challinge - if certain men continued he would resign. Mr. Brake really censured thro' asking. Selly, Leach to become teachers. Mr. Brake resigned, which was accepted. Meeting closed at 12.15.

13th C.E. meeting. I was elected Vice -President, Len Sec.

18th Sunday. Children's Day at Ashurst Drive.

21st Went to Ashurst Drive. Church officially formed. 52 members - praise the Lord.

JUNE

4th Derby Day.

5th Popp went with Rene & Mrs. Petigern to Livingstone College

Leyton in afternoon.

6th Len preparing for his camping out.

7th Dena Slicker came to spend a fortnight with us.

9th Whit Bank Holiday. Rene, Dena, Cissy, Gladys D. & another went to Lambourne End to meet Len, Horace & others. They had a good time. I stayed in garden all day.

14th S.S. Excursion. Theydon Bois. Helped with their races. Played cricket.

16th Heard that Len Phillips, Herongate Rd., had been killed in Eastern Ave. Chadwell Heath. Knocked from his bike by a motor.

17th Went to C.E. ... Leslie Parrish came in unexpected - he returned from Canada as his employer had discharged him.

Margate 1930.

21st BDH outing. Started for Margate 7.10. Parked near bathing pool - Rene & I had a swim. Hurried alone to Dreamland where BDH had their dinner. CDH in chair. I sat at principle (sic) table with the head next to Proctor &c. Spent afternoon on Cliftonville sands with Ed & others. Home by 4.15 boat to Southend.

JULY

1st England loses second test at Lords.

5th Saturday. Up at 5.10 & prepared for journey, left 7.10. Breakfast in Cobham Woods. Continued to Strood & thence to Snodland. Arrived at Tenterden 10.45. ... by car to Camber Beach. Rene & I had a swim.

7th Rene & I motored to Folkestone. Saw times of boats to Boulougne. All had a walk to 'Little Scotland' and rested & read among the bracken.

8th ... went on 'Friend of Kent' for Boulougne, 28/-. Changed £1 into Francs - 123. An inglishman working at Chatham Hotel met us and we lunched at his place 42 francs, 4 courses. Walked over town - St. Peter's Church, Notre Dame, ramparts &c. Bought a bottle of Lily of the Valley - 22 francs - for Popp. Sat on beach. Sent off 3 cards. Took a few photos. Risked a few words in French - sometimes all right. Had tea near Casino grounds. Gave a beggar 25 centimes. Boat left Boulougne 7.20.

9th .. all had a car drive to Boxlen (?) Castle & back via Hawkhurst.

11th ... drive round by Appledore. Popp & I had a walk to St. Michael.

14th Got a puncture and changed wheel in Blackwall Tunnel.

21st Southend. Had a delay with car - needed water - filled up at a wayside Refreshment Room (empty) from a water butt & bottle.

AUGUST

4th Bank Holiday. (They're in W. Mersea) Policeman woke us up at 12.40 to ask us if motor outside belonged to us. Popp & girls scared.

7th Popp, Ciss & I started out for Tilbury Docks, arrived at Mr. Lavercrook's 3 o'clock. Mr. L... took us into the docks and showed us ovrer the P&O Liner 'O.....' He also took us to the great dry dock & he and I inspected the new landing stage.

23rd Rene went to Victoria to meet Victor Esher (?) who is staying with us a week. Vic & Rene went to see Len play cricket, & Len brought back Freda Pettifer, a girl he is going out with from Manor Park.

30th Len & Freda called in for half an hour in evening.

SEPT

11th Boulougne. Went by old-fashioned tram to Wimeraux (?). Women conductors. Lunched in Wimeraux. Bought a bottle of eau-de-cologne for Popp 26 francs. Had some cafe au lait 5 fr's.

12th Had walk through town (Folkestone) & down zig-zag path &c. Had some coffee in the Sugar & Spice Restaurant. Had a walk as far as band. Watched performing cyclist.

OCT

1st R101 passed over - a good view.

5th R101 down in flames - 45 dead, only 7 survivors.

The R101 was one of a pair of British rigid airships completed in 1929 as part of a British government programme to develop civil dirigibles capable of service on long-distance routes within the British Empire. When built it was the world's largest flying craft. The terrible crash in Beauvais, northern France on October 5th was probably a case of too rapid technological advance. On its final flight, R101 departed from Cardington in Bedfordshire on the evening of 4th October 1930 for its intended destination of Karachi, via a refuelling stop at Ismaïlia in Egypt, under the command of Flight Lieutenant Carmichael Irwin. Lord Thomson, Secretary of State for Air. As it flew over Essex and the Sibleys gazed up from their garden in Ilford at the majestic sight drifting silently hundreds of feet above, one cannot help but imagine if their minds journeyed back to the Zeppelins of the Great War. At first the cause of the disaster was unknown. Later investigations revealed the probable cause was a spark from the electrical system igniting the hydrogen.

GREATEST DISASTER IN THE HISTORY OF AVIATION: THE TORN AND TWISTED SKELETON OF "R101": AN AERIAL VIEW OF THE WRECK ON A HILLSIDE NEAR BEAUVAIS.

14th Popp & Rene visited Boardman's about employment. Len had another spill - bike skidded - gave him a shaking & torn trousers.

24th … refreshments in 'The Crumpled Horn,' Upminster.

NOV

17th Took Rene to Boardmans and waited for her in evening.

20th Funeral service in Ashurst Drive on Master Howes 5 1/2 years. Primary School.

23rd Youth Campaign. I preached at Ashurst Drive. Left off at 7.35. Many hurried to Super-Cinema.

DEC

4th Lunched in the Blue Bird, Dartford.

8th Hurried to High Rd. Ilford Cong'l church & heard part of Mr. Fletcher's address. They gave him a rousing send off. About 200 sang and cheered as he drove off in Mr. Duck's car.

25th … Motored round to Will Warwock's and left him a book - he & Em were having breakfast.

Len went to Freda's after dinner, & Rene & I motored to Leigh with our presents.

26th Victor Usher came about 12pm & Freda about 1.30 just as we were commencing dinner. Rene & Len decorated the dening room in morning. … resumed our games… after Popp & Ciss had retired, with ghost stories. (I made up three, and told the Spec'd Band). Retired 12.20. Freda & Vic sleeping here.

31st Went to Graham St. & said goobye to GC 4490. Tour of new building and part of Wharf Rd. Luncheon at Midland Grand Hotel. Mr. Birnie read a nicely written eulogy to BDH. & CAH replied.

1931

JAN

3rd Went to Wharf Rd. for car (GK 8048) which was ready waiting for me. Romford, Dagenham &c. Lunched at Crumple Horn.

5th Southend &c. … Ran into a dense fog past Rayleigh & crept home by the curb with windscreen open (it was covered in frost) eventually arriving (home) very very cold at 9.40. Had a good meal & gradually thawed & did writing until 11.30.

19th Saw the results of a fearful smash in the arterial road - one telescoped beyond recognition. 3 taken to hospital.

22nd Tea in Hills, Ludgate Hill. Went to Ecclestone Hall. Valedictory Meeting RBMU(V?).

FEB

19th Popp & I went … by free coach to B.I. Fair Olympia. Saw CMH & D. Carr at BDH stand.

MARCH

17th. Hurried to C.E. Mrs. Brinnie sang a hymn in Chinese.

25th Popp & I went to the Baptist Colonial Society Rally at Seven Kings B.Church.

APRIL

2nd Len took Freda to Brighton.

9th… Hurried to the Lighthouse, Poplar, & took chair for the Prize-giving Social for their S.S.

18th Saturday. Car parade, 3.30. Tied on placards & cars & bikes &c paraded for an hour around Ilford, "Come to Church April 19th."

MAY

23rd. Victor Usher came for weekend. Popp & I went to Albert Hall. ... 2 splendid seats in #14 Box (Loggia), C.E. Jubilee Convention. Duke of York & Chairman of L.C.C. spoke - a good meeting.

25th Bank Holiday. Popp scalded her foot with hot rhubarb which prevented us going to the Albert Hall. Vic, Rene, Len & Freda here to dinner. Motored the youngsters to Beehive Lane & got some ice cream.

JUNE

7th. Earthquake 1.26am. Some damage - a few hurt. Popp felt the shaking.

The Dogger Bank Earthquake, as it became known, began at around 1:30 am on 7 June 1931 with its epicentre located at the Dogger Bank, 60 miles (97 km) off the Yorkshire coast in the North Sea. The effects were felt throughout Great Britain as well as in Belgium and France. The earthquake resulted in damage at locations throughout eastern England.

22nd 54 today.

28th Rochester Pageant finishing tonight.

The Rochester Historical Pageant of June 1931 was a grand affair attracting thousands, and depicting the history of the city from Roman times via Chaucer to the present.

JULY

4th Grays &c. Mr. Laverick had a case of Colgates Shaving Sticks to sell. I took a dozen boxes 4/-.

9th Len had a fall running for bus in morning and badly grazed his hands.

Actress Sybil Thorndike as The Spirit of Rochester, June 1931.

11th Saturday. Up at 4.30 and started for Sheringham at 6.5. Coffee at Holt, and arrived at Mrs. Reeder 11.45. Sat on front and wrote 9 pc's (postcards).

18th King George at Ilford opened Hospital.

25th Len came from holidays at Branscombe Devon (camping) with Freda.

29th Went to Barnard's and gave Phyllis an hour's tuition on motor driving. Run on the curb once in The Drive. Kept to bottom gear and went round the houses.

AUGUST

5th Got Mr. T.H. Wilson who is now at G. Harris as optician to test my eyes. We chatted for half an hour or so on Theosophy against Christianity.

20th Popp & I went to the City. Visited Pickering & Inglis then went to the National Gallery (had some coffee in ABC Cheapside).

In his never-ending quest for education and self-improvement, Sibley takes his wife to a lecture on mammoths at the British Museum, but is sorely let down.

22nd Popp, Victor & I went to British Museum… Mr. Skint'M.A. lectured on mammoths, 4.20-5.55. Disappointing - not sufficiently interesting.

28th Victor & Rene home. They had had a very unhappy time. Eva & Winnie very unkind and insulting. Rene very upset.

29th Holidays.

31st …dinner at 1 o'clock then we all motored to Dunster… then on towards Dulverton.

SEPT

3rd Rene & I motored to Gare (?), going up Porlock Hill. … motored to 'Lorna Doone' farm. Had a thrilling walk - glorious views - moors & forest, rivers, waterfalls.

4th Steamboat trip to Barry. Blue Anchor for an hour or so.

5th Dined in car on Salisbury Plain - visited church near Amesbury. Had coffee at Stonehenge. … Had to skirt London via Wembley.

11th Budget news - poorer by quite £15 per a.

21st Fall of the pound sterling.

OCT

3rd. Went to Ilford. Went in - electric showroom and bought an electric stove.

7th Mrs. Barnard presented me with a pair of slippers for teaching

Phyllis to drive.

8th Popp, Ciss, Rene & I went to Harrow Green Baptist Church and heard Ruth Chilvers on 'The Congo.'

25th Ernie Williams died of septic pneumonia.

27th General Election. National Govt. returned, overwhelming majority. I voted for D. Russell Thomas - Liberal.

NOV

2nd Ernie Williams' funeral.

4th Win & Phyllis Barnard called and used our 'phone just before 8pm.

9th I studied Christian Science in evening.

13th Fog kept Len home from Freda, who 'phoned for him. Vic 'phoned up to Rene.

14th Vic came in his father's car (1926 Morris Oxford Coupe).

16th Motored to St. George's St. Wapping, C.E.F. Headquarters Scarman Institute. Howard Hind in charge. … I spoke on Christian Science.

DEC

5th … Called in Tunnel C. (cement) Co. Offices for Houghton's list - wireless, which Len had taken to show one of the clerks, at 12.45. … Ordered a Pye £17-17/- wireless, got through Bayley's Dagenham.

14th Bought Xmas presents at Hope Bro's & Pickering & Inglis.

18th Southend &c. … Ran into a dense fog by Wickford…. followed a 'Sunlight Soap' lorry at walking pace thro' Romford, Chadwell

Heath to Ilford. Fog so thick I was over 3 hours behind that lorry, taking in the exhaust fumes & fog. I got dizzy especially when by Romford & missed the lorry. I turned car into Clements Lane by Post Office - locked it, and walked home. Felt sickly…

25th Rene decorated dining room. Ginger & Rene helped in D.R. Played in garde tennis 'Come-Back' in afternoon. Len went to Freda's 5pm.

30th We all went to the Midland Grand Hotel 1.15. Luncheon a very good feed. I proposed the toast to the BDH. M.D. & D. C.A.H. pleased and said it was the best toast yet proposed at our luncheons and gave him 'food for thought.' … I was overwhelmed with congratulations on my speech… Rene was sent home from Boardman's.

31st. Went to office 10 o'clock. D. Carr spoke for an hour on Vitamins. Said goodbye to Mr. Watkins and Mr. Parsons who are retiring after 50 years service. More congratulations on speech - one from RRB.

1933

JAN

4th Took Popp & Ciss to 1. V. Gds.

7th Saturday. Removed to 1 Vaughan Gdns.

14th Met Mr. Harvey at 315 and we discussed the needed decorations.

The Sibley's have decided to let their house on The Drive and move elsewhere. And judging from their purchases in the ensuing days from Whiteleys, a grand department store in north Kensington, his prosperity was going from strength to strength, as he and Popp set out to spend the equivalent of £2,828 on furnishing their new residence.

23rd Popp, Rene & I motored to Whiteleys. I ordered a dining Room Suite, Bedstead & Gents Compn., £49.7/-6d. Had some tea there.

25th Freezing. Skating in many parts of London suburbs &c.

28th Car accident - boy knocked down. Motored to Tilbury to catch D. Godfrey and while going down Calcutta Rd. a boy - Billy Moore, age 8 - ran in front of car and got knocked down with face injuries. Car did not stop dead when brake was jammed on, on account of road being affected by the frost. A man, Edwin Sullivan, 5 Montreal Rd. took the boy in his arms and hurried off to the Tilbury Hospital. Parents came along afterwards and I chatted with them. Took them all home after the boy had been bandaged up & examined. Policeman... took my statement - signed. Whiteleys sent furniture - Comp'n too large so sent it back, otherwise dining room looked nice with new suite. Our new bedstead - mahogany - looked less imposing than our old brass one.

1933 advert. Clean lines, curves and geometric design - art deco dominated the look of the 1930s.

FEB

3rd Wrote to Mr. Moore about Billy. Wrote to Laverock and asked him to send Ovaltine & Sweets to Billy. Posted a large book to Billy.

5th Went to 315 and saw that the place was in good order. Jack cleaned and scrubbed it out.

8th Had another letter from Mr. Moore of Grays.

While Adolf Hitler was settling in to his new role as Chancellor of Germany, things were happening in the Sibley family as Doris, Bob's daughter, gets married to Mr. Bulley.

20th Motored to Hertford Heath and saw Mr. Bulley & Doris Sibley married. Bob & Nellie 'lose' their eldest daughter. Mr. Bulley - baker - peculiar in looks, shy & not talented - did not look happy. Lily is now a fine girl - Bob's 2nd daughter. Mr. & Mrs Harris, Ciss & Aunt Polly, there, also Bertha & Stanley - Harry came later. Stayed to the reception.

24th Heavy blizzard all over the country, especially Wales & N. England.

25th Sent Billy Moore some Radio Malt and sweets thro' Laverock.

Radio Malt - a compound of vitamins A,B & D and advertised as a safeguard against 'depleted reserves through 'lack of sunshine.' It was one of the biggest sellers from the British Drug Houses.

MARCH

5th Motored to St. George's in the East and took the service at the Seamen's Christian & Friend Society. Had a happy time.

11th Rene met Vic and went to Tolocombe for weekend. Rene had dinner and departed for the Ushers for the weekend.

14th Rene returned from Brighton looking better.

21st Bought 10 ordinary shares of BDH @ 15/-.

28th Borrowed Mr. Barnard's car. Rather strange to drive the old pattern again. Took it back to Barnard's 6.30 - looked at his wireless set.

APRIL

1st. Farmely came and saw to car. Introduced him to Mr. Barnard to service his car.

14th Mr. Iszatt motored here and showed us his Riley 9; took Rene & Ruth Hammond for a short run.

17th Victor & Gracie Usher came about 8.30pm. I had supper with them. Wireless & knitting occupied the evening.

20th … spare wheel stolen - strap cut thro' with a knife.

21st. Reported loss of wheel to police - (Ilford Tel. 1111) who told me of a wheel found in Melbourne Rd. I went there and found it was my wheel without tyre.

MAY

11th Mentioned Aberystwyth to Percy Iszatt who jumped at the idea of going away with us.

20th. Popp went with me to Mr. Barretts to have a lower set of teeth fitted. Impressions taken. Sent 2/-6 to News Chonicle for next 4 vols of Dickens.

24th Got Ward Locke's book on Aberystwyth.

25th Elected again as Deacon.

JUNE

3rd Saturday. At 2.40 we started for Good Easter. A short walk and rest then we motored back to Leaden Roding Woods & there had tea. Rambled about for a little while - took photos.

8th Terrific storm in Manchester.

10th Car decarbonised, Farmery.

17th Saturday. Started for Tring 3pm. ... enjoyed the meeting. Two beautiful duets.

20th Went to C.E. Mr. Tyril of L.C.M. gave his experiences among the bargees.

23rd. Did work and motored to '315' & saw Mr. Harvey. He surprised me with reference to Miss W's TB, which a neighbour had informed her & Mr. H. Visited Dr. Moody who said there may be danger. House should have been disinfected & redecorated &c top to bottom. I advised him to see Dr. Beattie or Dr. Yell.

24th Percy Iszatt came round in his new Riley 12.6. He let me drive it from Newberry Park to Gallows Corner - very powerful but held it in to 30mph.

JULY

1st Thorpe Bay, arriving 1.30. Popp. Ciss, Mrs. Pettigern & Derek our party. Sat on front in deck chairs. ... Went to South Shoebury Poultry Farm for tea.

3rd Southend &c. … Had a swim in Eastern Esplanade swimming pool.

13th Ernie (Sibley) came to tea, arriving at 7pm in his Austin 7. He took Rene for a drive at 8.20, got back 10.15.

22nd. Holidays. Started for Aberystwyth at 5.15. Met Iszatts in Woodford Ave. Stopped for breakfast between Thame & Oxford. Stopped at Oxford for a look around but not for long. Went through Cheltenham, Glos., and on to Ross-on-Wye where we had dinner. Had a look at Wye Valley, Whitchurch & Symonds Yat. Arr. Aberystwyth 7.40 - very tired. Had a fish tea. Put car in garage in Queen's Rd. (Savage & Co.) Had a walk then we all got into bed very tired. We're at Mrs. Edward's, 3 Elm Tree Ave.

24th … motored to Aberaeryon (sic). Popp upset at a hill.

25th Tennis on grass courts UCW sports ground. Len, Rene, Harold & I went to Devil's Bridge & had some fun and thrills - exciting climb & marvellous scenery - took 12 photos.

Mrs. Edwards… complained about mess on stairs & room after bathing - small stones &c from beach. After tea Popp & I had a walk alone. Sat on seat in castle grounds.

26th Prince George came to Aberystwyth and opened the Agricultural Show.

28th Read a little of 'Wild Wales.'

Wales had become a tourist destination in Victorian times, with the English upper and middle classes affording it the same romantic image as they did the Lake District and, later, Cornwall. Spa towns like Llandrindod Wells and Builth Wells grew up, with grand hotels full of wealthy visitors lured by the crystal fresh mountain waters and spectacular scenery. By the 1930s with its culture of physical health, Wales had become a magnet for the middle and lower-middle classes: with the foreign holiday not yet in the purview of most, the boarding-houses of Aberystwyth in West Wales sufficed for the Sibleys to experience a taste of wilderness.

31st Percy, Harold & I went for a blow on Const'l Hill - 50mph gale. Went for a drive to Tregaron - hilly. Returned another & more precipitous way but raced away from Percy and got home 9 mins before him.

AUGUST

3rd Len, Freda, Rene, Harold & I went by motor-boat to Aberdovey. A very enjoyable voyage - lovely sands.

4th Sang with YL campaigners outside Alex. Hall.

5th Departed 8.40. Lunched between Winchester & Chipping Norton.... Percy went round a corner too fast and nearly upset. Went thro' Oxford in mistake - Percy went wrong too but we met at Aylesbury - had some tea. Lost Percy at Edmonton so had to wait for him at Gants Hill. Arrived 6.50. Len rather nervous in Percy's car.

7th Bank Holiday. Len & I went for a swim in new baths - very crowded. Rested in garden half-clad. Freda came to dinner then went off with Len to tennis. I started on my model. Pye box being connected. Tea - hosed garden. Had a short walk at 8.40pm with Popp in Valentine's Park.

9th Harold Iszatt came and brought me some drawing paper. Heard about the exodus of Alan Francis.

11th Called at Iszatt's and brought away some paints.

15th Popp, Ciss & Rene walked home and got scared because Len had come home early and gone straight upstairs. The 3 stood in street shaking - Ciss told man opposite but Len's appearance caused things to have a happy ending.

The nature and cause of this curious incident is not known; very possibly Len had had some trouble at work.

19th Spent evening painting for my children's address.

20th Took service at the Victoria Park Cong'l Church (Church I used to attend Band of Hope when I (was) about 10 years of age).

22nd Len passed on to Rene that Victor was asking to get rid of her - he did not want a girl. Rene upset.

26th Rene had a letter from Vic and went to rest more contented.

28th Southend. ... had to hurry back at 50mph - Popp upset, Rene liked it.

SEPT

9th Finished my model, Darkness & Light, for children.

10th Worthing Pier burnt.

Designed by Sir Robert Rawlinson, Worthing Pier was opened to the public on 12th April 1862. Described as an *"elegant pier of iron, 960 feet long, for promenaders only"*, it was constructed of wooden decking laid onto the iron framework and was about five metres wide with seating down both sides. A conflagration destroyed it in 1933 but it was reconstructed and opened again in 1946.

13th Rene & I went to Goodmayes - Lecture Hall & saw Morris Cinema Pictures - Rene enjoyed them very much.

OCT

5th Heard that Mr. W. Thomas, BDH rep. for Birmingham District, had died suddenly. (suicide).

12th Rene did some roller-skating in afternoon.

14th Went to Galway Hall Woodford Green & heard D. Northcott Dick & saw his lantern pictures on 'The Solomon Islands.'

19th Rene went to skating rink and had a fall and hurt her back. Rene has notice to leave Boardman's.

Having got over her rejection by her former suitor Victor, October 1933 sees the first appearance of Cliff Ringwood into her life.

22nd Cliff Ringwood came to tea & supper. Rene too poorly to go out.

28th Cliff Ringwood came in evening.

29th Sunday. Rene went & and saw Vic Usher in West End & went to Kath. Usher's.

31st. C.E. Sealed orders. Cliff Ringwood went alone but did not stay till the end as Rene was not there. Popp's head bad over a 'silly' woman at Chelmsford.

NOV

11th Cliff came to tea & spent the evening. I stayed some time in the dining room.

18th Cliff Ringwood polished the dining room table.

21st Hurried over to Southern Rd. Mission and spoke to the 'Sisterhood,' about 150. A good meeting. I enjoyed it - cup of tea afterwards.

25th Cliff Ringwood here as usual.

DEC

22nd Heard about young Henson being waylaid and robbed in his car near Colchester.

23rd I had to go and buy a ham - 8/1 - as Will Warwick had not sent me one this year.

24th Rene put up decorations in dining-room. ... Cliff turned up at 11pm. Rene & Popp had commenced to worry. Tied up presents for Xmas.

25th Len & Cliff got a barrow and collected Rene's bookcase. ... Ernie brought over Ed & Li from Bert's, - Eva & Wilf came later by bus from Mersea. Had a good dinner. ... Len went out to dinner, returned about 12pm.

31st Len came in at 9.30 and soon went to bed. The rest of us sat around fire & heard the service on the wireless the service - passing of the old year. Cliff stayed all night.

1935

JAN

18th Went to Mr. Draper's housefor tennis club committee meeting at 8.10, left 9.15. took Holt, Galdys B., Phyllis B. in car.

27th Did not go out in morning as back was very painful. Bible Class on 'Love.'

28th Southend &c. Lunched in Garons - Chicken in casserole which was very nice. Tea in James Westcliff. Went by rail as roads were dangerous. Back's still painful so left bag behind. Had to miss Vange, Pitsea, Benfleet & Thundersley.

Garons cafe and cinema in the heart of Southend-on-Sea in Essex played a big pat in Sibley's travelling life, and would feature heavily across the years.

Garons Cinema & Cafe stood in the heat of Southend for many decades, until demolished in 1962.

It was a grand establishment, typical of the Edwardian taste for providing a touch of aristocratic splendour to the middle and lower classes. On 29th October 1910, local businessman Harry Garon announced his plans to build a cinema and café in the High Street. Garons Imperial Bioscope duly opened on 27th July 1911, with 600 seats. The panelled walls of the auditorium were painted white. The screen was 18ft square. The large café seated 300. In 1921 a two-manual Estey organ was installed, mounted below stage level (not on a lift). This was played by local sisters Ena, Celesta and Florence Baga (Ena and Florence - as Florence de Jong, following her marriage to band leader Harry de Jong - later became famous as cinema organists). Rita Legget and her trio played in the café during afternoon teas. During 1920, a fine ballroom was added above the cinema, which was renamed simply Garons Cinema. In 1929 the cinema auditorium was extended, increasing the seating capacity to 916. Sound equipment was installed, the first 'talkie' being *'The Wolf of Wall Street'* starring George Bancroft and Nancy Carroll, on 14th October 1929. During the intermissions, at each side of the screen, fountains would send up jets of water about three feet high, illuminated by coloured lights. These survived until 1956, when a wider screen (though not CinemaScope) was installed.

The Garons complex closed on 4th May 1963, the final films being *'Atlantis, the Lost Continent'* starring Anthony Hall and Joyce Taylor, and Clark Gable and Sophie Loren in *'It Started in Naples'*. The building was later demolished and shops and offices built on the site.

30th Heard from CAH that my salary had been advanced by £10 - an unexpected pleasure.

FEB

1st. Bought loaf & nerve food from Ogdens.

2nd Popp's Party. Got renewal of license for wireless, 10/-.

At ten shillings - the equivalent of £28.00 in 2023 - the BBC licence fee had not changed since the inception of the broadcaster in 1922, only rising to £1.00 after the war in 1946 to fund the expansion of television.

Popp very poorly but got downstairs. Party commenced to arrive 5.30. … 16 sat down to tea. Had several games. Parish Priest, Coffee Pots, Hospital. Len & I gave a charade (Longshoreman). Party broke up 11.55. Rene did her cooking well - cakes, sausage rolls &c.

6th Called in for another 'volume up-lift.' No good. Mrs. Carrell Colemans gave me 2 photos of self & car and Mrs. Carrell.

9th. Popp & I motored to Barnards - Tennis Social.

11th Southend. Lunched Garons, Victoria Parade - (Casserole chicken &c).

Later in the week the courting habits of Rene his daughter and her beau, Cliff Ringwood, causes some paternal concern:

16th Had to have a word with Cliff & Rene about stopping after 11, which upset them. Popp ill, Cissy with bad cold, yet they thoughtlessly stop as long as possible making everyone late to bed.

23rd Mr. G.J. Williams of the Inst. of Psychology now on BDH's staff.

27th Popp about the same, crying all day about going to die &c.

MARCH

2nd Did work then burnt my letter in incendiary in garden - rescued part, had to write orders again.

4th … took Popp & Rene to Dr. B.T. Leggett 353 Romford Rd. for x-ray at 11 o'clock. 5 films had to be taken. He finished at 5.30 and gave us tea & biscuits. … Report satisfactory as to gall stones - none to be distinguished. (extinguished?) Popp went thro' the ordeal well.

5th Took Popp with Rene to Dr. Leggett's who took an x-ray of colour at 10 o'clock.

8th Paid Dr. Leggett his bill - £5 in notes.

12th Dr Beattie came & had a 'rough and tumble' over x-ray results.

15th Called in at '315,' & saw fence which has been blown about in gale.

18th Mr. Harvey called about fence & offered £750 to buy house but I said £825 was my price.

Now clearly selling their house at The Drive, the shrewd Sibley was holding out for an equivalent (in 2023) of £47,625.

21st Popp in drawing room all day. Still in much pain and terribly depressed.

23rd. Popp in pain crying & Ciss foolishly brought in my dinner in drawing room, and I could not partake in such a case - I went without - had some nuts &c afterwards.

28th Address written… G. King & Son, 3 Gabriel's Hill, Maidstone. Mr. C.J. Harvey came about the sale of '315' and offered £800, which I accepted. We agreed to have one solicitor, Hillarys of Stratford.

29th Dr. Beattie called in unexpected and cruelly upset & abused Popp for nothing - objected to technical terms, and there was an argument, big baby. Said he did not mix Christianity with his profession.

30th Len obtained his Hoover from Freda and went over our carpets - he had the morning off. Ran Len & hoover to Measly Rd., - he and others are going to Tunnel Sports dinner at Grays.

APRIL

1st Paid electric bill £5.0.3.

8th Had to have a pink tablet for neuralgia in night.

9th Mr. H.J. Stanley rang me up to thank me for the particulars of the Kent journey given to him - had quite a long chat on 'phone.

10th. CE Anniversary. Mary Anne operated on - breast taken off - cancer?

13th Clocks put forward.

14th Cissy went to Hampstead Gen'l Hospital. Left 12.40, returned 6.30. Went to Mizpah in evening. Took my clock - had for marriage 32 years ago - to Mr. Skeffington.

16th Mrs. Robinson came to work here. ... did a hard day's work cleaning.

20th Bert, Win, Roy & Alan visited us 4-8. Had tea and a few gramaphone records - Sandy Powell.

21st Went by car to Hampstead Gen'l Hospital & saw Mary Ann. She was glad to see us and was getting on. I gave gluco mints, bottle of L-spirit. Chatted to a patient who had no visitors. Returned by N. Circular Rd.

22nd Inspected 'Hoover' & tested it on carpets. After dinner & listening to the wireless, another hour in the garden. Took Popp out in Valentine's Park in bath chair.

MAY

4th 315 The Drive Sold. Hillary's sent me cheque £94-18-10.

6th Silver Jubilee Day - 25 years reign. (George V).

21st Went to CE. Col. Geering, ex British Syrian Mission, spoke.

Hampstead General Hospital, demolished in 1975.

JUNE

1st Len moved his furniture to Grays by Tunnel lorry. Driver had dinner here.

12th Ed bought Len a nice tea set (or told Li to get it).

A momentous weekend in June saw Thomas & Annie's son Len - who all those years ago in 1910 had been told off for running into the municipal pond after his toy boat - married to his sweetheart Freda Pettifer, to start a new life in Grays, Essex.

15th Saturday. Len & Freda Married.

Up at 7 o'clock. … gave car a good clean. Took Rene & Canteen & tiered cake-stand &c to 107 Mearley Rd. Saw Mrs. Pettifer for the first time. Bob rang up about Nellie but was too late for her at Ilford Station - she caught an earlier train. Bought a hat at Dunn's & returned just in front of Ernie (Alan & Roy), Will W(arwick) & Ruth. Li & Eva here & Ed & Bob came later, also Elsie. Had a good lunch and started for St. Michael's at 1.40. .. Len went with Ernie - the best man. A good crowd at the church. I saw to the button-holes (white carnations). Nellie brought a home-made rug for Len. .. After ceremony photos were taken. … & we motored to Anderton's Hotel. A very good reception. Mr. P(ettifer) proposed toast to bride & groom and Len & Freda both replied. Ed proposed toast to bridegroom and I replied. As Mr. & Mrs. P had not been toasted I proposed their toast, which was heartily responded to. .. Len & F. went off in Ernie's car to… Ryde. IoW.

17th Mr. Blackmore 'phoned through saying radiogram was at his place. I went at 9.30 and got it. Mr. B. put in light for AC and showed me how to work it. Ciss helped me to get it out of car. Got it going. Popp likes it.

21st Paid electric bill £18-18-11, and Mr. Blackmore for radiogram £11-12-6d.

22nd Had to run out to get a white loaf. As I returned Len & Freda appeared. They looked well. … I took them by car to Barking Station.

28th Strange sleeping alone. Popp did not sleep well with Li. (He's at Ed's at Mersea).

29th Ed at L'pool (Llanfarfachan for weekend).

JULY

2nd Radiogram not functioning. 'Phone to Blackmore.

Made with polished wood to blend in with the furniture of the time, in the 1930s a radiogram was a stylish addition to any prosperous household.

4th Trouble over our "acid" aq dest. & orders @ Livingstone Hosp'tl.

5th Took Aq. Dest. to office & it was tested. Quick decision made to send out no more jars with aq. dest. Len called in and brought plates kindly given by Mr. Pettifer.

6th Had a puncture - a gramaphone needle got in.

12th Syringed rose trees.

13th Saturday. First visit to Len & Freda's. Popp, Ciss & I motored to Len's house. Len & Freda both glad to see us - got there about 3.45, going via Upminster. Len had booked a court at Claughtons, so after calling at their place and then at the park, found them by the bathing pool. We had 3 sets and I was in the winning set each time. Had a good tea and left about 7.30. …Freda had her dog, a thoroughbred terrier, just a wee puppy.

14th Very hot. 83. Too hot in garden so laid on bed with Popp. Went in garden for dinner & tea. Shaved Popp under arms to cool her.

15th Popp worse so had to 'phone for Dr. Moreton. He said that Popp had brought it on herself by eating solid food. Had to go on slops for 5 years.

18th Dartford &c.... Tea in Williamsons Gravesend - spoke to 3 Sweedish (sic) lads on a visit - at my table.

20th I phoned thro' to Dr. Leggett and arrangd with him about a TIP x-ray for Popp. Ordered soem TIP meal from BDH for him.

22nd Popp went to Dr. Leggetts at 8.45 & took a BDH TIP meal & lemon juice water. Popp has TIP x-rays.

23rd I paid (Dr. Leggett) £4-4/-. No gall stones for Popp.

27th Visited Dr. Barrett's who stopped a tooth and pulled out 2 front teeth which left a nasty gap & a sore feeling. Goodbye after 50 years service.

28th Carried her downstairs into drawing-room about 4.30. Had some music in the evening - gramaphone records & service.

29th Carried Popp downstairs in morning and upstairs in evening. England meet USA in Davis Cup tennis at Wimbeldon.

30th England drew with S.A. but won Davis Cup 5-0.

31st Visited Mary Anne and took folding bedstead for Cissy.

AUGUST

3rd Holidays at Mersea.

4th Spoke in open air tho' minus two front teeth.

10th Went to Colchester to meet Ciss - Popp & Eva with me. Eastern Counties bus half a hour late. Popp & I had some tea & biscuits. Heard that the canary had died.

Ed, Eva, Poppy, Miss Leach (from Barnados Home) & self went for a sail with Albert on his yacht. Had a pleasant time - nearly stuck in mud - got back about 9.

13th Went to Mrs. Theobald's, 3 Shop Lane East Mersea. … Left car outside the 'Dog & Pheasant' for the night.

16th Had a walk with dog on chain - she is such a fighter. … motored to village & called on Dr. Beattie & chatted… for an hour. Sibleys at 11.45… got to Li's about 3pm and found that all except Li had gone on Albert's yacht. Yachters came back.. Ed Popp & I went to Dr. Beattie's for tennis. Back to Ed's at 8.20 and had oysters.

17th Ed & Albert went to conduct some sports near Sudbury (Suffolk).

18th Rene & Cliff came back from IOW riding on bikes in rain all night.

19th Rene & Cliff got back safely yesterday… Cliff here all the evening talking over their Isle of Wight experiences.

20th CE. Miss E J Lowry told us about the work of the Spitalfields Lodging House Mission Band.

22nd Chelmsford. Got photos from Armstrong. We inspected the houses in Park Estate - Lord's Houses - Lord Ave. £1095. Popp thrilled.

The Sibleys' Ilford was expanding. From its village beginnings in the nineteenth century it was now becoming a feeder suburb for the capital. By 1903 the area between Wanstead Park Road and the Drive had been built up as far north as Seymour Gardens. Farther east most of the streets between Cranbrook Road, Ley Street, and Valentines Park had been laid out, though not completely built up. On the opposite side of the High Road, the main built-up area, between Ilford Lane and Gordon Road, extended south to Mortlake Road. West of Ilford Lane development was less continuous. At Seven Kings and Goodmayes most of the building was north of the High Road, between Aldborough Road, Meads Lane, and Barley Lane, but there were also a few streets running off Green Lane. By 1910 a few more streets had been added between Wanstead Park Road and Cranbrook Road, along Green Lane, and at Loxford and Uphall, but the pace of growth was slackening, and between 1911 and 1921 the population rose by only 7,000, to 85,194.

In 1921 the London County Council started work on the Becontree housing estate. The Ilford portion of this, mostly completed by 1926, comprised only 10 per cent. of the whole, but it was a substantial addition to the town: some 2,500 houses and 11,600 people, in the Becontree Avenue area. Private building also went on rapidly between the World Wars. The urban area was extended north through Gants Hill and Newbury Park to Barkingside, and there was also development in the south of the town, around Loxford Park, farther east near South Park, and at Chadwell Heath. The population was 131,061 in 1931 and was estimated at 166,900 in 1938.

23rd … Got particulars of 12 Beaufort Gardens (3 yrs agreement £70).

24th Barnet took out another tooth, and adjusted top dentures.

25th Had a look at 12 Beaufort Gdns - house to let. Mr. & Miss Robinson - very nice people. Took Cissy and we went to Park Hill estate and had another look at £1095 house. Deposit £110, balance £1-9-5 a week 20 years.

27th Nurse Finch stayed with Popp all day. … Popp likes her nurse, who is 32 and well trained.

29th Electric clock came - set it going, and then thro' having to undo connections, I could not get it to go again. Fuses?

31st Told Mr. Robinson, 12 Beaufort Gdns., that we would not take the house.

SEPT

5th Pitsea, Ongar & Epping. On the way home I motored along the Clayhall Estate as far as Barkingside. Looked at several houses and bungalows.

7th Decided on 35 Lord Avenue, Ilford. Popp, Nurse Finch & I motored to Barkingside and looked at a house then on to Lord Ave., & decided to buy £1095, paid £2 to secure no. 35. Had a little music.

And so on September 7th 1935 Thomas Sibley, that youngster from a humble terraced working-man's house in Victorian Bethnal Green, buys a substantial suburban villa in the brand-new Lord Avenue estate. Though much was to change over the years, both happy and tragic, he would remain there until his death in 1974.

11th Len & Freda, also their puppy 'Rex' came for the day. After dinner - Popp carried down by Len - I took Len & Freda to look at the houses on Lord Avenue. Freda enraptured. Went to Smiths (Motors) and saw some of Morris 'Sound' Films.

12th Bought dressing set from Odell's - £1 - and when I got home found that the comb had a tooth out. Wrote to Mr. Simpson about it.

14th Went to Grays and got my lower dentures from J. Barrett (Barnett?). £2-1/-. Can now speak better. Sent comb back to Simpson (Odells).

16th Went to office 9.45. Special meeting of the representatives, Autumn programme. Lunch 12.50 (went to Food Reform Rest., Holborn).

19th Mr. Iszatt came in afternoon and Percy came in evening. Had a nice chat & prayer. A brotherly kiss at the door.

23rd Dr. Moreton saw Popp & told her it was nerves - she was starving to death. … rallied and ate some chicken, and became excited and better.

30th … motored to Bow Rd., left car in garage and railed it to S. Kensington & walked to Albert Hall. Heard Rev. G. Groggin (?), McCullogher & Lionel Fletcher. Lyndsay Cliff in chair. A great meeting.

OCT

1st. Miss K.M. Savage lent me 'Mending Your Nerves' from Hickman.

3rd War - Italy & Abyssinia - begun. Took Popp & Mrs. Fisher to 35 Lord Avenue. … chose fireplaces. Mrs. Fisher likes the house. Sat with Popp for an hour or so in the dining room, listened in to the news &c.

4th Heavy fighting in Abyssinia - many casualties, Abyssinians being worsted.

13th Had a good service on wireless. Rene & Cliff considering marriage expenses.

26th Heard from Payne that Huddersfield B.S. would give me a 15 years mortgage.

NOV

1st Len & Freda came… Len does not look well. Freda putting on weight.

12th Went by car to Humphreys, Paternoster Square, & W. Lewis showed us carpets. Bought a Wilton stair carpet, Body carpet & runner (about £20).

14th General Election. Nat. (Cons) Govt. returned.

17th Rev. Townley Lord on wireless, ex. Bloomsbury chapel.

23rd Went to 35 Lord Avenue, did a little digging. … Had a chat with our neighbour, no. 39. Builder &c, plenty of money.

25th Ran into fog at the 'George,' Wanstead, and took an hour to get to the Drive.

30th On my way to Grays a lorry swept a stone up into my windscreen. Afterwards it fell out like small crystals. .. Met Len in Grays and we had coffee in Williamsons. Len came home with me - had dinner and went off to hockey at West Ham Park. Bert came and we dug up two apple trees and planted them in Lord Avenue.

DEC

10th 35 Lord Ave. Went to Grays Inn - Payne & Co. - by car to Bow Rd., & tube to Temple. Signed deeds, paid fire ins. 17/-6d. from Xmas.

11th Went to 35 Lord Ave., obtained keys for house. Shed had come from Thompson Bayliss. Paid a p.d. cheque for £20-19/11d &

arranged for laying of the carpets. ... wrote to Mrs. Evans about leaving on the 4th.

14th Called & saw Freda - I took back a number of 'History of War.' Too early for Len.

17th Gave Bert instructions about planting the trees.

23rd Lunch at Euston Hotel - not so elaborate as formerly. Mr. Brown gave the toast. ... Left about 4.30 for Wharf Rd., attempted to take home new car but fog was too thick so returned. Sent off 40 Christmas cards.

24th Went to Sainsbury's and bought 1/2 ham, afterwards went for Cliff's green slippers. Had a good deal to do. Cliff staying here over the holidays.

25th ... afternoon spent playing 'Sorry,' & whist. Ham forgotten & overcooked.

26th Got car and we tied on 'railways,' & we went to 35. Cliff put one up in 'lounge.' Returned for lino... tied on to car 3 rolls of lino, Len & Cliff held on to it. Listened to 'Scrooge' on radio. Len & Freda left about 11.30.

27th Cliff & Rene at 35 putting up 'railways.'

1936

JAN

4th Moved into 35 Lord Avenue. Workmen took away broom so Bert could not sweep place. Popp burnt her hands badly, got a bad head and nearly collapsed.

8th Trouble with Ideal Boiler flue - cement got in.

11th Had a hot bath - too hot, no cold available. An experience. Cliff

& Rene had a day's work at Boardman's Sale.

17th Popp enjoyed a hot bath.

18th King very ill, on danger list. (GEORGE V).

19th George and Dolly Slicker came to tea.

22nd News full of the late King & present King. Edward VIII proclaimed.

23rd King George V's body brought to Westminster Hall to lie in state until Tuesday next.

26th Bertha Sibley died today.

28th King George V laid to rest at Westminster.

Shops all shut - a day of mourning. Wrote to Harry (husband of Bertha).

30th Bertha buried Edmonton cemetery.

FEB

8th Called on Len and took back remainder of War books. Len gave me 5 wallflowers. Had saveloy & pease pudding for supper.

9th Called on Mr. & Mrs Wall, 13 Lord Avenue. They belong to the Brethren.

14th Ordered small heater 9/6 for Cissy's room.

22nd Popp & I motored to Thomas', changed bell for chromium letter box.

MARCH

1st Sunday. Listened to King's speech, message to the Empire.

The millions that huddled round their wireless sets on March 1st 1936 to hear, for the first time, their monarch addressing them, could not have foreseen that only a few months later he would be making a far more portentous address - announcing his abdication.

3rd Popp very poorly. Took her & Ciss to Dr. Burnett Rae, 93 Harley St., started 2.30, got there, via Euston, 3.15. … Popp with him quite an hour & I interviewed him afterwards - £3-3/-. A nice man, kindly, gentle, searching.

14th Dressing table made by Cliff bought by Mr. Ringwood.

20th Cliff commenced work at Lewis, Green Street. Davies men laid grass.

21st Paid Mr. Davies £3-5/- for trees etc. He had 4 men waiting on him for money. Davies is either a fool or a rogue. Roses came from Norwich which I put in garden. Finished mostly front garden except 'rockery.' put in 'box' plants obtained in Woolworths.

26th Win Barnard died yesterday. Wrote to Mr. Barnard.

27th Popp went to Dr. Dr. Beatties & Dr. Moreton gave her a (UV Ray on her back. Rene had her photo taken at Bodgers. Ordered rustic arch from Andrews Ilford Lane.

APRIL

4th Grays &c. Listened to Oxford Cambridge boat race in Graysbridge Pharmacy.

10th … Hours digging. Rested 11.30, cup of tea & heard part of service on wireless. More digging. Relaxed in evening. Music on radiogram. Rene & Cliff went pic-nicking on bicycles. Not a very happy outing.

11th Warren delivered crazy paving and rockery stone. … Bert re-concreted path to bird bath. Did some more digging preparing sunken garden.

JUNE

1st SS Queen Mary arrived safely at New York on her maiden voyage - listened to the account on the wireless.

It was now the golden age of radio - most people now obtained their daily news not from newspapers but the wireless. And in many ways it was a golden time too for Thomas Sibley - his children had grown up, his job was flourishing, and as he approached his 58th year, he launched himself into home improvement and work on his garden. But as he tuned in on that June day to hear the good news that the SS *Queen Mary* had safely landed in America, there were also rumblings of international tension: Italy, fascist since 1922, had launched a disastrous invasion of Abyssinia in an attempt to carve out a 'second Roman Empire,' the Spanish Civil War was to break out in a matter of weeks, and in Germany Hitler was implemented a ruthless programme of oppression and anti-semitism. Tension vibrated in the air like an approaching storm, though in the summer suburbs it was hard to descry.

15th Cissy bought two love birds for Popp.

JULY

1st Called on Nurse Cornwall 126 Richmond Rd. who came along early.

Rene arranged with Rev. Chamberlain about wedding.

6th Told a man about his danger in turning into main road too uncautiously - he resented it. Too big.

13th Tenderness under the shoulder-blades, indigestion worse. Only weighed 9 stone 6lbs - lightest yet. Decided to trust the Lord rather than doctors and medicines.

18th Carried Popp into Rene's room and put bed by the window so she could see the garden.

AUGUST

3rd Monday. Bank Holiday. Rene & Cliff went out for the day on bikes.

5th Rene & Cliff settled on a flat in Gants Hill Crescent.

8th Called at Len & Freda's and brought away his Vol. on Gen'l inform(ation).

13th Ashurst Drive. Ed & Li came - going to get a flat in Ilford for

Winter & retain Mersea 'Chilambi' for summer.

21st Rene had a present from her colleagues - jug & glasses.

Yet the seemingly idyllic summer in which Rene had announced her marriage and Thomas, Cissy & Popp were settling in to their new home in Lord Avenue, international strife was mirrored in the appearance or re-appearance of mental problems for Annie, and the hysteria that she had first experienced back in the first decade of the century began once again to afflict her.

26th Popp had another nerve storm - hysteria. I had to be angry.

27th Poor Popp. Had no sleep until 4am until 7am. .. Prepared to go to Sidcup. Popp dressed about 8.35. She suddenly screamed and temporarily lost her reason - must kill herself. I held her down and prevented her from throwing herself downstairs. Had to get Doctor... hyosine (?) injected into her spinal column.

28th Able to go to Brentwood. Rene & Ciss with her. Suicidal tendencies remain. Had to be kept in bed, sometimes by force.

29th Slight improvement. Nurse with Popp - most hideous to Popp, whose eyes enlarge and distort.

31st Popp slowly improving but eye vision and distortion greatly troubling her. Only one or two troublesome moments - less violent.

SEPT

3rd Rene & Cliff helped by Mr. Ringwood moved their furniture into their new abode.

5th Rene married 1.30 St. Andrew's Church. I bought a bowler from Dunn's, 21/-. Put ribbon on car. .... Happy ceremony. Curate married them and gave a nice exhortation. ... All the Sibleys, Bob & Nellie &c. Returned 5.30. Poor Popp drugged, came to 5.30.

7th *<u>Holidays.</u>*

13th Read D. Grenfell 'The Master Mariner, a life Indeed.'

14th Cissy missed the 9pm Bus.(iness) post.

16th Did (Popp's) nails.

29th Wrote to Huddersfield Building Society to give formal notice to let '35.'

As the owner now of two properties, Sibley prepares to let out his former home.

OCT

In early October the health problems of Popp were temporarily forgotten as the first Sibley grandchild was born.

3rd Freda gave birth to a girl - both doing well. Mr. & Mrs. England, Editor of 'Cycling,' viewed property with view to renting.

14th Wrote to Mr. & Mrs. Lord about concreted sideway.

16th Southend. Lunched at Thorpe Bay. Motored along front and saw illuminations.

17th Called in at Len's and saw grand-daughter for first time. 'Anne Sibley,' - a fine child. Freda wonderfully well. Took back Len's book, Household Words. Cissy got Rene & Cliff's photos at wedding.

19th Heard of Emily Duncan's death. I started on an all fruit diet - Monday to Friday - apples, pears, oranges, grapefruit, grapes, dates, raisins, figs.

20th … continuing my fruitarian diet.

In his never-ending quest for physical and spiritual improvement, Thomas Sibley launches into an all-fruit diet. It doesn't last long.

21st Had some tea and bread & butter as fruit was turning my stomach to acid.

22nd Had a partial fruit breakfast but ordinary dinner.

23rd (Popp) had 'imperial' drink. … Best sleep for weeks.

25th Cliff baptised by Mr. Frape.

Rev. F.S. Frape, Minister at Ashurst Drive Baptist Church 1932-1938.

29th Popp had a poor day tho' she ate well - rabbit & pork.

31st Did a football competition & crossword puzzle and sent same up to get the prizes.

NOV

6th Rene here, fried the fish - brought me some of her date pudding. I bought Dr. Hay's book, cookery recipes.

7th Will Warwick sent me a munificent gift, as from the Lord. £20 cheque.

14th Ed wrote... saying he did not expect any more money for 'Chilamber,'- a gift of £3 and electric costs. Praise the Lord.

18th Got petrol from Pettifer's and chatted about grand-daughter and windscreen wipers.

This was clearly Mr. Pettifer Senior, Freda's father in Len's father-in-law.

25th Ed sent D. Hay's book 'Building Better Bodies.' Heard that Mrs. Smith (Castle View Rd.) & Mr. Paget were dead.

30th Heard on wireless that Crystal Palace had burnt down. Flames & glare seen 27 miles away, & by aeroplane 50 miles. Popp talking about Emily all day long.

For nearly a century the Crystal Palace had been a familiar landmark for Londoners and visitors alike, whether in its original location in Hyde Park or when it was moved to Penge Place in 1854. It had been an extraordinary history - opened by Queen Victoria in 1851, home to that monumental display of Britain's industrial power the Great Exhibition, and latterly housing cultural and geographical displays.

On the evening of 30 November 1936, the manager of the Palace Sir Henry Buckland was walking his dog near the Palace with his daughter Crystal, named after the building, when they noticed a red glow within it. When Buckland went inside, he found two of his employees fighting a small office fire that had started after an explosion in the women's cloakroom. Realising that it was a serious fire, they called the Penge fire brigade.

Although 89 fire engines and over 400 firemen arrived, they were unable to extinguish it.

Since the Festival of Empire in the 1920s the Crystal Palace had been in decline, but Sir Henry had turned its fortunes around with its current exhibitions. Sadly he was forced to watch as his life's vision literally went up in smoke.

900 firemen could not extinguish the conflagration of the night of Nov. 230th 1936.

DEC

3rd King Ed. VIII wishes to marry Mrs. Simpson of USA. This would be her third husband.

4th Everybody talking about the King & Mrs. Simpson.

6th Wrote to Mr. H.J. Green resigning as Vice President of Christian Endeavour.

9th Paterson's Aburnethy (?) biscuits came to hand thro' Chrystalls -

Popp liked them.

10th Prince Edward broadcast on his abdication at 10 o'clock. ... Duke of York proclaimed King George VI.

It was not just the power of the church in the British state that led to the Abdication of Edward VIII; every leader of the Empire disapproved of his marriage to the divorcee Wallis Simpson. Only Winston Churchill and one or two other allies attempted to find a solution, largely involving the denial of Ms. Simpson, or her heirs, any titles. In the end this proved unacceptable, and lifelong exile awaited the couple.

12th Dr. Nevin - neurologist - specialist of Harley St. - came. .. Nothing wrong with Popp's nerves organically... Injections of polynaturitus - psychological persuasions for mind trouble.

16th Rene came home early from Boardmans - with bad head, sickly temperature.

21st Started work on the 1937 journey book.

22nd Walked to Food Reform Rest. for lunch. Lectures and demonstrations at Wenlock Bldgs. Back home to tea in new car. DMM 558, Blue-black.

Food Reform in the 1930s was a continuation of a movement that had begun in the nineteenth century hand had been accelerated by the First World War: a movement founded on the encouragement of wholesome, economic cooking. Reignited by the reduction in food imports that had occurred between 1914-18 and had continued during the Twenties, it was by and large a Liberal organisation promoting voluntarism in increasing the quality of one's diet - as a result, several 'Food Reform Restaurants' sprang up in the capital.

25th ... had games with Rene & Clif, 'Sorry,' 'Smash Up,' Lexicon

&c.

26th Len, Freda & Anne came 1.45.

30th Fair amount of 'flu about keeping Dr's and Chemists busy.

1938

XMAS PRESENTS

Gave Ciss Material, Brooch. Received gloves.

JAN

5th Elsie & Ethel came about 3 o'clock... Had a look at Rene's house.

29th Cheque came from BDH for £68-16-10. Praise the Lord.

FEB

7th Winnie called to see how we all were. Rene here - Cliff called in - did polishing next door.

12th New curtains from Roomes of Upminster put up.

14th Bought Popp a thick pink dressing-gown, £1-1-9d, hot water bottle, pink corset.

21st A. Eden resigned Foreign Office.

Eden resigned as a public protest against Chamberlain's policy of coming to friendly terms with Fascist Italy. Eden used secret intelligence reports to conclude that the Mussolini regime in Italy posed a threat to Britain.

22nd Mr. Page paid Cliff £2 for his polishing.

MARCH

4th Cissy gave Popp an upset as she went out with Rene without saying so in afternoon.

11th Miss Spencer… came & saw us at 11.30. Popp liked her and she will be coming to stay with us in 3 week's time £1-5/- weekly.

19th … Chatted with Cissy about leading a true Christian life.

24th New electric fire arrived from Thames Board Mills via Percy Iszatt. Rene gave a party in honor (sic) of Cliff's birthday.

25th Friday. Ernie & Louise Dean came about 8.30 & stayed until 10. They had a little supper. Louise 'adored' many things. She is 'superlative' & gushing & boisterously natural. Popp got excited and could not sleep for some time.

26th Put in a lot of work in garden. .. planted 12 standard rose trees at back. 2 clematis & a mountain ash in front garden.

APRIL

Looking after the sickly Popp was becoming a challenge to the staff employed by the Sibleys, and sometimes was too much, as the ensuing days would prove.

2nd Nurse Ralston departs, Miss Spencer appears. … Popp rather worried over Miss Spencer. Does not like her & feels unhappy over her.

3rd Exit Miss B. Spencer. Whilst I was having my bath Miss Spencer hurried out, going to her sister's. .. Could not stop here. She returned with her brother-in-law and took away her clothes. Job too hard for her - made many excuses. Popp & Cissy both had a shock.

7th Mr. White brought Mary Purkiss aged 16.

11th Nurse Pritchard came this morning at 9am…

18th I sat with Popp - cleaned chrome fittings in lounge.

29th. Nurse Cox left at 5 o'clock - everyone glad to see the back of her.

MAY

27th Mrs. Fisher here for tea. Brought her King Charles spaniel with her. Read a little of 'Citadel.'

JUNE

6th Whit Monday Bank Holiday. Booked courts for tennis 11.40. Had two sets with Cliff - won one each.

Cliff Ringwood and Rene are now happily married and living in Leigh-on-Sea in Essex.

9th Len sent word that he had obtained the new berth for Tunnel Cement at Brentford.

Len's company, Tunnel Cement, had a warehouse on the Grand Union Canal at Brentford, an old Victorian warehouse once used by Jupp's Malt. It was to here that Len, Freda and their young daughter Annie decamped in 1938. The building still stands today (2023, though under threat of demolition.

16th Had to shave with a safety razor - first time.

Some form of 'safety-razor,' as an alternative to the more dangerous 'cut-throat,' had been in existence since the seventeenth century, but it was the invention of the removable blae by Gilette and its becoming standard issue to the US military that popularised the item for mass domestic use.

JULY

1st Listened to tennis final, Budge & Austin. Budge won easily 6-1,

6-0, 6-3.

6th Made a special call to Matthews Wanstead. Mr. Leonard Matthews grumbled about prices. Visited Barclays and signed document - on shares - for overdraft £45.

13th Miss Jubb introduced me to Mrs. Joseph - general help & nurse 25/-. Told Popp who wanted to see her so I went to 146 Wanstead Park Road but she was out - left a note. Mrs. Joseph came and saw Popp and we engaged her.

Staffing problems aside, things were happening again in the Sibley family, as Thomas' daughter Rene gives birth to a son, Graham.

14th Rene confined early this morning. Cliff came round 9 o'clock saying Rene's baby boy was born 7.30 - only 6 hours labour. Everything satisfactory. I went round at 8 and saw the babe and Rene. Mobile Police spoke to me by Wanstead Flats.

16th Exit Miss Arnold.

22nd Popp 61 today. Bishop's Stortford. Popp & Ciss went with me. Over 2 years since Popp went with me on this journey.

AUGUST

6th Stuck some of Popp's photos in her album.

18th Cliff put up new railway in drawing room.

24th Australia collapsed & were beaten by an innings & 579. Bradman & Singleton both injured and unable to bat.

25th Dr. Moody called. Mrs. Joseph told him we did not want her any more - paid her 17/6. She was nasty especially against me for not giving her a full week's money.

27th. Ed wants to keep on 'Chilambe,' Li does not. Usual quarrel making things unpleasant.

Despite the domestic difficulties between Thomas' brother Edwin and his wife Li, he and Popp spend a little holiday at their house in West Mersea, Essex.

29th After breakfast too Popp & Li to village. Afterwards Peter Wallis went with me to St. Peter's Well for water. Got a dozen eggs from Wallis. Amused myself morning, afternoon & evening with Clock Golf to keep warm. After dinner took Li, Eva & Popp for a motor drive around country, visited Layer De la Haye Church, curtains allowed of some hide & seek (?). We were interested in 2 sows and 16 sucking pigs. After tea played Li & Eva at clock golf. Ha 1 1/2 hours of lexicon. Supper and some hearty laughter. Retired happy - thus ended a perfect day.

31st Chatted with Mr. Bernard & Phyllis. They have a new car - Morris X 1936.

SEPT

2nd Ed came about 8.40. Li & he at loggerheads. Unpleasant atmosphere.

3rd Saturday. Packed bags and started from West Mersea 10.45. Len & Anne came to tea. Rene & Graham here until 7pm.

12th Hitler's speech at Nuremberg. I had usual coffee at Lyon's in Milford.

As Sibley sipped his coffee in the Lyons Corner House in Ilford Hitler was addressing the Nazi Congress. His speech was a grim foreshadowing of war; on the surface merely decrying the supposed oppression of Sudeten Germans but in reality preparing for the invasion of Czechoslovakia. To this end, he engineered the Munich Agreement of a fortnight later in which

Britain, France and Italy in a blindingly un-prescient act of appeasement signed away Czechoslovakia's border and unleashed the menace of Hitler on an unprepared Europe.

Hitler leaving Nuremberg after his speech on Sept. 12th 1938.

13th Popp enjoyed the wireless programme this evening. Great problems with the Germans & possibility of war.

14th Czechoslovakia & German menace of war disturbing country & general trade.

16th Heard from Bob & wrote to him. N. Chamberlain flies home - hopeful, & going back to Germany.

17th Popp about… got my tea for the first time in 2 years. Praise the Lord.

19th Mrs. Sapte came and took up residence here this afternoon. She is 65 - rather old for the post. Has been good looking but now rheumatic and little energy.

20th Broke spring of specs. Mr. Gruttock at McCarthys put a new one on - 6d.

23rd Mrs. Sapte not too well. War news very bad. Hitler truculent.

24th Chamberlain back in England. War news very black.

26th Hitler's speech broadcast at 9.40 - threatens Czechs. Told Mrs. Sapte if war is declared it would be better for her to seek a safer place. She agreed.

27th. Mrs. Sapte preparing to leave. Popp very poorly - air-raid & war &c causing her to worry. Rene upset too. People, especially women, scared over war possibilities. Trenches being dug in parks &c. Neville Chamberlain broadcasted this evening.

28th Popp more cheerful over possibilities of there being no war. Meeting of British, French Prime Ministers, Hitler & Mussolini arranged for tomorrow. Made things appear more hopeful. Cissy got her gas mask.

29th. Exit Mrs. Sapte 10.15 - glad she has gone.

Mrs. Sapte went and we were all relieved - she really was in many ways a wicked woman. Stemmings brought bed, 2 chairs & folding bed from 'Chilambe,' - they moved Ed's goods from West Mersea. ... Chamberlain, Galadier, Hitler & Mussolini met at Munich today - had three meetings. I went and got gas mask - large.

30th PEACE. Great excitement over peace news. Chamberlain back about 7pm. Wonderful scenes, cheering &c. Agreement with Germany ended approaching strife. Czechs accepted terms & evacuation of Sudetenland German territory to begin tomorrow.

Popp very happy about it and listened to the news.

OCT

3rd. German soldiers marching into Sudeten territory.

7th Bought Graham a piece of Orris (?) root as he is teething and suffering. Hair dresser came and did Popp's hair for tomorrow.

8th Went round for Rene & babe. Motored to Ernie's & got there about 12.30. Louise & Ernie made us very happy and comfortable. Their present from Ed & Li - an ultra wireless set - had just arrived. … They have a very nice house and Popp was enraptured with it, and furniture.

"My good friends, for the second time in our history, a British Prime Minister has returned from Germany bringing peace with honour. I believe it is peace for our time... Go home and get a nice quiet sleep."

14th Popp & I had tea & coffee in the thatched house Cafe in Harlow.

15th Heard from Miss Sapte who has waived her claim for £2-1-8d.

16th Popp went to Ashurst for first time in over 3 years.

19th Rene upset at Cliff not getting home until 10 o'clock - he went to his Mother's.

Popp not too great - hurt her left wrist trying to lift a saucepan.

20th Popp not too well but went to Spirella demonstration.

The Spirella Corset Company offered women a made-to-measure demonstration, usually in their own home.

21st Popp, Ciss & Rene went & bought a winter coat for baby Saxon. Popp cooked dinner.

22nd Saturday. Prepared for Twickenham and departed for Rene 11.5, left then for Len's 11.10. Found our way without much trouble to Tunnel Wharf - had a look round then took Len on board and went on to 322 Staines Rd. Had a good dinner - Graham got frightened and cried a lot which hindered dinner. Except for walking to the corner time was spent with Mothers and babies. Saw Saxon Frederick for the first time - six weeks old, a good babe and little trouble. Freda rather round shouldered.

23rd Popp upset - money affairs - marriage discord.

25th Fog very thick near Wanstead waterworks. Popp & I sat by fire and listened to wireless.

322 Staines Road, Twickenham, today - Len & Freda's home in 1938.

27th Chelmsford &c. Mr. Baugh a R.C. very upset at BDH making & selling Volpers (?), threatened to close his account.

31st A dog - a red setter - at number 42, is proving a nuisance. Scared Ciss on her way back from Rene's. Popp wrote them a letter.

NOV

1st. Mr. Potter from number 42 called to apologise and explain about his dog. He is a very nice man. I called in at Barkingside Police Station and told the Sergeant about the dog. He 'phoned to number 42 and told them to keep their dog under control.

5th A quiet evening with wireless. Finished reading Tom Sawyer.

9th Heard Chamberlain's speech at Lord Mayor's Banquet.

16th Bought 4 fancy perfumes for Xmas presents.

DEC

3rd Took Popp, Rene & babe to Roomes, Upminster. Bought 7 jelly glasses & a few little things. Graham had a cry when being taken round - upset Popp & Rene a little.

9th Lady Anne Grenfell died at Brookline, Massachusetts.

11th Wrote to Sir W.J. Grenfell a letter of sympathy.

21st Roads slippery with show so proceeded with caution. CMH spoke to us on sales of medical products. ... As it has been and was still snowing all day I did not wait for Ed & came away at 4.45pm.

23rd Luncheon at Euston Hotel 1.15. Went with Price & Gregory - train. A very good luncheon - I sat next to Richardson. I went to office with Turnbull and we got our cars. I took away GMM 814. Nasty slippery drive home.

24th Went shopping. Visited Woodmills, Scotch Bakers, Prentises, Ogilvies, Sainsburys, Harris & others. ... Ed & Eva came round. Got presents packed and gave them. Started on decorations. Put up fairy lights.

26th Went for Len & Family 12.30. Back 1.30. Had a taste of Pettifer's special hawthorn wine - 7 years old.

1939

JAN

5th Heard from Dena.

13th Had photos of children from Len. Lent Rene my camera for Cliff to take Graham.

18th Rene took babe & had photo taken in Beehive Lane.

26th Barcelona taken by Franco. Tea in Williamsons, Dartford.

Now in its third year, the Spanish Civil War was coming to a head. Barcelona was captured on 26th January 1939. The Republican government headed for the French border. Thousands of people fleeing the Nationalists also crossed the frontier in the following month, to be placed in internment camps. Franco closed the border with France by 10 February 1939.

FEB

8th Bought electric shaver from McClouds of Barking. Electric Shavemaster - £2-10/-.

23rd … dressed with difficulty in evening shirt &c. Popp all ready in new dress - Rene did her hair. Called for Mr. & Mrs. Everett, 91 Grosvenor Gdns, Woodford & after 15 mins wait took them to the Waldorf Hotel, Aldwych, arriving 6.10. Took car to Drury Lane Garage 2/6d. Dennis Desmond, President West Ham & E.D. Association dinner. Met many friends - J. Milner & Mr. Mortimer & daughter (married to a Dutch lawyer). Had a splendid dinner. Fruit Cup 5/-, Ginger Ale 1/8d, Water 2/-, Benevolent Friend 2/-. Stopped until 10.15 and chatted with friends whilst looking at the dancing. Popp enjoyed herself - could not do justice to the dinner but tasted most dishes.

MARCH

2nd Bought some crocks at Marks & Spencers Southend.

10th Gas mask boxes brought round this evening.

11th (Popp) had 2 doses of Birch Juice.

16th Popp's bowels troubling her now. Hitler takes possession of Czechoslovakia.

18th Neville Chamberlain spoke against Hitler in Birmingham -

appeasement dead.

APRIL

1st I spent 2 hours or so in garden - put in carrots, parsnips, tomatoes & lettuce seeds. Hitler greatly upset over Britain siding with Poland.

Waldorf Hotel

West Ham & Eastern District
Association of Pharmacists

(Founded March 1903).

Annual Dinner
DANCE and CABARET

THE WALDORF HOTEL,
ALDWYCH, LONDON, W.C.2.

Thursday, February 23rd, 1939.

PRESIDENT :

DENNIS A. DESMOND, Esq., Ph. C.

Hon. Secretary : JOSEPH REED.

6th Departed for Misses Bates, 1 Brierley Avenue W.M. Had a comfortable journey, arriving at 7.5.

7th Got some water from Peter's Well, Ed going with me. Got Popp Bovril. Ed & I visited Wallis, who has to keep to his bed, or nearly so. Heart tired but still his cheery old self.

10th Went with Ed to front 6.30, measured his ground and interviewed a prospective buyer.

11th Started for home 8.15am. Put Ed & Li down at 16 Mornington 9.55.

14th Roosevelt gave a good speech, jacketing the Dictators.

15th Dictators distinctly checked - less tension now.

20th Cissy left pudding and rhubarb - two saucepans, on electric stove this morning & went out and forgot them - burnt up. Hitler's birthday, 50.

22nd A young Irishman called & I agreed to his cutting barks of trees for the health of the sap and to fight against 'Big Bud.' Wanted 25/- but did them for 12/-6d.

24th Budget.. Conscription.

MAY

3rd Phoned plumber to see pipe leaking above kitchen. A workman dropped dead away (no. 31) - commotion, police, ambulance &c.

24th Watered garden. King George spoke to the Empire from Winnipeg, Canada.

25th I had unmistakable signs of rheumatism in joints &c.

26th Got to Misses Bates, 1 Brierley Ave., (W. Mersea) 9.5pm.

27th Saturday. Ed & I went to village for water & papers, called at Fairhaven Ho., & saw George & Ciss. Met Wallis and had a chat. .... Went to Front and got some chairs & ice cream and sat on shore for an hour or so. Wilf came up also Grace and baby Sheila. After tea (5pm) Ed & I went to Wallis's and had 3 sets of tennis.

JUNE

3rd (Popp) sat in garden with Rene. Took 3 photos - Dufaycolor film.

7th Walthalmstow &c. 89 degrees F. Had orangeade in Lyons & tea in Williamsons. Found it difficult to get round as quickly as usual - too warm. Mr. J.T. Merriott of Rayleigh sent me £1-1/- for helping him get locum work - most unexpected.

17th Arrived in Brighton 11.15. Ushers, 12a Salisbury Rd. … Popp. Ciss & I went on West Pier and saw 'Molorado' or 'Dodge 'im.'

20th Had a swim off pier - too cold. Hot coffee on pier then motored to Eastbourne.

21st King & Queen returned from America. Took Mrs. Usher on pier. She gave us pier tickets and I paid for band seats. Child there caused annoyance.

22nd. 62 . Went for a country drive in afternoon. Had tea in Cowfold. Enjoyed the country (drive) which was very beautiful. Dinner 6.30 - gooseberry pudding as a birthday present.

30th Fishmonger's man was noisy & insulting this morning, so went to shop and made a complaint - he returned and apologised to Popp.

JULY

14th Bunny's birthday tea. (Graham) Lots of presents and cards.

18th Six month's return gave 9% increase - Praise the Lord.

19th Took Popp & Ciss to Mr. Fisher's, "Bellegrove," Woodford Rd. E.18. … Mr. Fisher showed me over the flat (3rd storey).

20th Popp in chair, Ciss, Li & girls went to P.D.S.A. fete & baby show.

22nd Bought Popp a birthday present - cork tablemats.

AUGUST

12th Cliff, Rene & Bunny went to Hove for a week's holiday. Bought Grace Bates a brooch at Heath's, 3/-.

14th Len rang up this morning - on his own. Freda & children at Manor Park. Len not at all happy.

17th Southend &c. Lunched at Thorpe Bay in car. Had a lovely swim.

22nd German Peace with Russia.

Rene harping on Hove & Ushers. Russian pact with Germany - non-aggression caused consternation. War seems probable. May the Lord forbid it.

23rd Barking, Ilford &c. … everyone talking about possible war. Papers full of the crisis. Parliament recalled. King returning to London. Our envoy flies over to Hitler. Ribbentrop flies to Moscow. All is in the Lord's hands.

24th News very bad. War imminent. Parliament reassembled. King in Council. Chamberlain speech broadcast.

25th "War" news very bad but hope still remains. President Roosevelt wrote to Hitler & Poland as well as the King of Italy.

26th Saturday. … Got to Len's wharf 12.30 but he was too busy to come home with us, so he gave me a plan and I motored to 322 Staines Rd. … Len turned up about 3.15.

27th Hitler still talking and threatening but news more hopeful.

28th Detailed preparations. Hitler stubborn for Danzig corridor. Japan's Govt. resigns. World upheaval. Lovely day.

30th Hitler striking out for Danzig. Chamberlain and Hitler still corresponding.

31st. Evacuation of children decided on for tomorrow and onwards.

SEPT

1st Germany invades and bombs Poland. Rene very upset over news. Germany started war with Poland 5.30 this morning. British & French ultimatum to Hitler. Parliament met at 6pm. Full mobilisation. People mostly determined to fight and smash Hitler. Wonderful speech by Chamberlain. Blackout tonight.

3rd Sunday. War declared on Germany 11 o'clock am. Popp very poorly - had had no sleep, traffic noise, Bunny crying & worry took sleep away. Britain and France declared war on Germany. Popp's head so bad we motored to Undercliff and sat on sands until 12.30. dinner 1pm then sat on sands again taking tea with us. Sat there until 4. After tea went to Rosebery Rd. Bapt. Church... solemn service. Popp nearly frantic. Took Popp & Rene for as short run (drive) afterwards. Changed bedrooms with Ciss & Rene.

On Undercliff Sands in West Mersea today there are still remnants of the war: defences built such as concrete blocks to deter landings, pill-boxes, look out stations. That stretch of the Essex coast, though they might not have known it at the time when they sat gazing out to sea as war was declared, was an ideal location for a German invasion.

Thomas and Popp were now in their early sixties. They had journeyed from the Victorian East End to the leafy suburbs, raised a family, seen bombs raining down on their city only twenty years ago: and now, their world once more was seemingly being threatened by another great clash of nations. They were philosophical yes, but not defeatist; there was a strange flame of obdurate will in the British people that, although many over 40 would clearly remember the last war, there was very little sense of exhaustion or cynicism, despite the strange air of melancholy in Chamberlain's speech. *'You cannot imagine what a bitter blow it is to me,'* he spoke to the nation. Well, they could imagine, but they did not warm to such self-indulgence. They had a bigger battle to fight than Chamberlain's own self-doubt or awareness of his own mistakes. There were gas-masks to distribute, children to evacuate, recruitment offices to visit. Meanwhile, though, for the middle-aged couple seated on an Essex beach, there was a greater need: that of quiet mental preparation, and a reminder to themselves perhaps of the things their country would be fighting for: the simple things - swimming, sunbathing, a fish dinner.

The sands at West Mersea, Essex. Here Thomas & Popp sat as war was declared on Sept. 3rd 1939.

4th Went on Undercliff Sands. I had a swim & sunbathe. Coffee & tea. Enjoyed a happy morning. Fish dinner and apple pudding. No band on pier now. … News of SS Athena sunk by submarine. Poles fighting bravely.

5th Tuesday. Proceeded to Undercliff Dune & sat on sands. Had a lovely swim. Rene and I had a short walk. Cliff's letter concerning joining A.F.S. worried her - especially being left at night. Popp got upset over possibilities. I read some of Treasure Island. Fighting is mostly in Poland.

The Auxiliary Fire Service (AFS) was first formed in 1938 in Great Britain as part of the Civil Defence Service. Its role was to supplement the work of brigades at local level. They were to play a major part in the Blitz. For now, though, the 'phoney war.' As Thomas wrote, '*the fighting is mostly in Poland.*' So there is time to read, time to escape into *Treasure Island.*

6th 'U' boats active, some sinkings.

7th Popp full of fear. Rene & I had a walk towards country. Finished Treasure Island.

9th Popp done up. Very poorly. Ready to collapse.

11th Bought some black paper. Miss Kirkpatrick gave some black crepe paper. Did some more black outing. War News: French advance, Poles retreat. U Boats sink 3 of our steamers.

12th Chamberlain in France. British troops landing. Poles holding back the Germans.

13th French hammering the Germans. RAF helping. Poles resisting with some successes.

14th Southend &c. ... Southend had an air-raid warning 1.30. I stayed with J.A. Sharpley by his 'refuge.' All clear 1.45 (accidental warning thro' some mishap).

16th Up at 7, packed cases & called for Li 10.30 (Had a look at Brook's dug-out, very good and strong. .. Arrived 'Earlston,' East Rd.,

12.30 (W. Mersea). Grace there. Had some lunch and started blacking out - put up paper we had brought & managed to get some more and completed work before dark. ... Cissy unhappy. .. Retired at 10.30 after prayer to our hard beds.

17th Aircraft carrier 'Courageous' sunk by U boats.

18th Popp a little better, and Cissy brighter - she got some blackberries - at thoughts of going back to Ilford. Russia marches on Poland.

22nd Filled right up with petrol. Rationing tomorrow.

Cliff came round and fixed some blacking out paper on wood.

26th War Budget. Warsaw capitulates to Germans.

29th Registration Day. Grermany & Russia peace proposals.

OCTOBER

4th Rough night. Very dark. Had to use torch to go to post.

6th Had some wireless - still more peace alterations. Hitler's speech - so called peace terms.

8th Could not concentrate on reading.

12th Chamberlain spoke in answer to Hitler's peace propaganda.

13th Hitler greatly upset over Chamberlain.

14th Battleship Royal Oak sunk by u boat - great loss of life - sunk at Scapa Flow.

16th Edenburgh had an air-raid - no damage - Germans lost three planes.

17th Air raid warning at Dagenham.

19th Turkey signed pact with Britain and France.

25th Anthony Eden spoke after 9 o'clock news.

NOVEMBER

4th Spent evening reading Churchill's History of War.

8th Bomb attack on Hitler.

Johann Georg Elser was a German worker who planned and carried out an elaborate assassination attempt on Adolf Hitler and other high-ranking Nazi leaders on 8 November 1939 at the Bürgerbräukeller in Munich.Elser constructed and placed a bomb near the platform from which Hitler was to deliver a speech commemorating anniversary of the Beer Hall Putsch. Tragically, unknown to the assassin, Hitler had cut his speech from two hyours to one hour, so left earlier than expected. The timed bomb went off thirteen minutes after he had left, killing 8 people and injuring 62.

16th Mobile police in Canning Town accused me of going across an uncontrolled crossing endangering the life of a pedestrian - took all particulars. (K159).

23rd Heard from CDH and Ed about the death of Frank Brooks. Ed went to Bournemouth to represent BDH at his funeral tomorrow.

25th Received summons to appear at West Ham Court on Thursday.

30th Russia invades Finland.

DECEMBER

1st Finland bombarded from air land and sea. Popp's wart on eyelid troubling her.

7th Fined £1 at West Ham P. Court. The AA defended.

14th Finished Churchill's first volume.

18th British submarine sunk German cruiser.

19th Books came from Kingsgate Press.

20th Bought two records and some fruit in Prentises.

24th Turkey giblets and pigs trotters for dinner.

25th Went round for Cliff, Rene & Bunny. … Thick fog. Cliff walked in front of car. Ed, Li, Eva, Ruth, Ernie, Louise, Ciss, Cliff, Rene, Popp & Bunny were the party. Bunny slept in pram all evening.

CHAPTER FIVE

THE ENDURING FLAME - 1940-1950

When Prime Minister Neville Chamberlain called the first year of conflict with Germany 'the strangest war,' people quickly re-dubbed it 'phoney.' Since 1936 the public had seen the might of the Nazi Luftwaffe on newsreel footage from the Spanish Civil War and Stanley Baldwin had issued the grim forecast that 'the bomber would always get through,' so the first act of the British Government was to establish a nationwide network of Air Raid Protection wardens - the ARP - and from that point on the sound-scape of the home front became dominated by the regular mournful scream of the siren and the scramble for cover. Street lamps were extinguished, blackouts fastened in every window. Britain's cities became places of darkness, so much so that by the end of 1939 4000 people had died in 'blackout accidents,' leading the government to urge people to 'wear something white at night' to avoid traffic.

But the precautions were premature, for it was not until 1940 that Hitler rained down his fury on Britain's cities. By then there had been an outward flow of children from the cities to the countryside. At the stroke of a pen thousands of city children were suddenly offered a view of another side of Britain they had only glimpsed in books. Dislocating, yes, but not all negative. A young boy wrote to his parents from the heart of rural England: 'Dear Mum, I am learning to be a poacher. Mr. X takes me out at 4 in the morning. It's great.'

The first few months then were preparation, a steeling of the national spirit. No one quite knew what was to happen, or how to act. It was only when the British Expeditionary Force was rescued from Dunkirk by the Royal Navy and an *ad hoc* fleet of 'little boats,' that the national soul of the 1940s was forged and defined - that of the heroic, plucky islander, both military and civvy, pitching in to defend our ancient homeland.

First the Battle of Britain, then the Blitz. The ariel bombardments began on September 7th, in truly a baptism of fire. Indeed, the flames burned so bright in Bethnal Green, Thomas Sibley's childhood stomping ground, that people said you could read a newspaper by the firelight in Shaftesbury Avenue.

The war on the Home Front became a war of volunteers, from the auxiliary fire service to the Home Guard. Would the Local Defence Force, a mixture of old-timers and inexperienced youngsters, have made a difference in the event of a German invasion? 'As a military force,' we were a gigantic bluff, said one volunteer, while another more quixotic Home Guard soldier insisted 'We know we were needed. We were sore needed.'

Much has been said and written of the tenacity of Britain under siege and its fortitude in the face of hardship. Myth must be untangled from reality - there was still crime, the black market, selfishness, exploitation - but the resolve of the people, while anecdotal, cannot be doubted. When 500 tons of high explosives fell on Coventry on September 14th 1940, within five days 21 key factories in the city were back in full production a mere five days later, with a Trade Unionist remarking '*the factories were covered in tarpaulins... the only heating was coke braziers, yet they stuck at their machines for 12 hours at a time.*' This resolve reached the very top of society: Princess Elizabeth refused to be evacuated to Canada, and her father King George

VI practised firing a Tommy Gun in the grounds of Buckingham Palace. The entire Royal Family stuck to standard rations, and painted a black line round the bath at the permitted amount of water.

On the less visible Home Front the intelligence services chipped away at the German war machine twenty four hours a day, from Bletchley Park and the birthplace of Churchill himself, Blenheim Palace. Many of Britain's stately homes became hives of spying, eavesdropping and decoding for the duration - Woburn Abbey, which housed Britain's 'black propaganda,' Southwick Park in Hampshire, and Wilton House in Wiltshire. Not since the dissolution of the monasteries had so much property had been seized by the state.

The social changes effected by the war were swift, profound and long-lasting. Women filled the factories, from Woolwich arsenal to the steelworks of Sheffield, and suddenly the Women's Auxiliary Air Force was full of women able to strip and rebuild Spitfires; WAAF member Nina Hibbin remembered *'Suddenly there was this whole new field of work and thought.'* Economically, the impact was seismic: as overseas imports plunged as a result of both the German plan to starve Britain into submission and the British government's own need to conserve cash reserves, rationing was not confined to food and drink. While the population was restricted to 4oz of bacon and ham, 8oz of sugar and 4oz of butter, so too was clothing: President of the Board of Trade Oliver Lyttleton issued the grim pronouncement *'I know all women will look smart, but we men may look shabby. If we do, we must not be ashamed,'* as each man, woman and child was issued with 66 clothing coupons per year.

The Germans never invaded but the Americans did, in an Allied conquest characterised by glamour, chewing gum, and sex. While Tommies struggled to provide for their women, British female eyes were turned by the Yanks, who seemed like film stars made flesh to those who had been raised on the American accents of the stars of the silver screen. It wasn't just Americans who altered the social landscape of the 1940s - thousands of Poles became temporary or permanent Britons as they fought for the liberation of their nation. People's eyes were opened to the relative exoticism of foreigners - many of them had perhaps never before seen anyone from overseas in their lives.

The harshness of life was tempered by entertainment: many theatres closed and the fledgling BBC television service was shut down for the duration, but dance-halls and impromptu pop-up musical events were the order of the day. There was an urgency to life - a work hard, play hard ethic suffused the nation, with the background fear that every day could be one's last. The Lion Churchill sensed this default consciousness, refusing to ration fish and chips and proclaiming that *'the people's will was resolute and remorseless. I only expressed it. I had the luck to be called upon to give the roar.'*

Did life get better as the war dragged on? The answer is no, for it was darkest before dawn: from 1944 the British people were subjected to new kinds of deadlier air attacks from the dreaded V1 rockets, an early cruise missile launched in June by the Wermacht as terror bombs from the shorelines of France and Holland. These were followed by the even more brutal and unstoppable V2's, the world's first long-range guided ballistic missile. Britain's only counter to these menaces was the issuing of bogus intelligence reports as to the results: when they missed their metropolitan targets British Intelligence would claim they had been successful, and vice-versa. This led to the Germans recalibrating the guidance systems, which thankfully resulted in more than half of all V2's landing in rural Kent.

Despite this, 1,754 Britons were killed between 1944-45.

The stoicism of the people was tested further by the tightening of rations as the war came to its close, and an understandably prudent governmental approach to wages which led to a miner's strike in 1943. Coal production fell so alarmingly that Ernest Bevin, minister for labour, implemented a policy of one in every ten conscripts being consigned, by lottery, to the mines, and the 'Bevin Boys' were born.

With victory in sight after six long years, the war that had begun with Churchill's roaring lion speech *'we will fight them on the beaches,'* ended with a far humbler beast accepting his defeat with dignity at the ballot box. *'They have had a very hard time,'* admitted the outgoing Prime Minister, adding *'I thank the British people for many kindnesses shown towards their servants.'* The celebrations that tore through the country like forgotten laughter, with many experiencing a sense of *deja vu* as they hung up bunting kept since 1918, were tarnished by the sadness of loss - many a husband and son and brother and father had not returned home - not for them or their families the street-parties or the bunting.

In 1945 the new Prime Minister Clement Atlee knew the British people needed rewarding. They were not be rewarded by an alleviation of rationing - that would continue until 1947 - but by full employment to returning servicemen, a welfare state, and a National Health Service. Hungry and colourless those immediate post-war years might seem, jobs were plentiful. And not just at home - the Australian government offered £10 to all those eager to make the journey across the world to start a new life there. Between 1946 and 1949 well over one million Britons settled in Canada, Australia and New Zealand.

As far as recreation was concerned, an end to war meant the

rediscovery of the British seaside. Long entombed in barbed wire and anti-aircraft guns, the sandy resorts began to open up. Ice-cream kiosks removed their hoardings, boarding houses pulled down their blackouts and opened their curtains to let the sunshine and guests in. The big holiday camps like Butlins and Pontins began to create a new Golden Age of the British holiday. With the threat of ariel bombardment removed, cinema-going boomed - a survey in 1947 revealed that two out of three young people went to the 'pictures' two or three times a week. With television yet to make inroads as a form of mass entertainment, crowded dance halls, pubs and 'the flicks' were the major outlets for a joy-starved population.

The perception that the National Health Service, finally established in 1948 after fierce opposition from doctors up and down the country, was the first time free health care and medicine had been provided to the British people is of course erroneous - people who could not afford insurance had been receiving free healthcare for decades; it was the tax-paying middle-classes and upper classes who benefited most from the NHS, as overnight it was free at the point of need for all.

Britan's postwar reconstruction, like Europe's, was financed by the USA and its Marshall Plan. It was both welcome and essential, though not quite sufficient for the ambitions of the new Labour Government, who had to go to the Americans at the end of the decade for a top-up in order to meet the cost of taking over all of Britain's previously charity-run hospitals. It was a huge bill - even the prime architect of the NHS himself, Aneurin Bevan, admitted later that '*we should never have nationalised the hospitals.*' It was a bill Britain only finished paying back in 2006.

As with health, so with homes - as soon as the sirens fell silent aeroplane factories turned into centres for housing as a huge programme of homes-in-kit-form was implemented, churning out family accommodation that could be built in 4 hours. These aluminium-framed prefabs were aimed not only at those families made homeless by the Luftwaffe but for demobbed soldiers, and for many the amenities and space they offered compared favourably to the cramped, filthy lodgings they had been used to. With separate indoor bathroom and toilet and running water, it was a glimpse of a postwar dream: 'It was gorgeous,' said Renie Lester, 'you could have a party: next door neighbours wouldn't be knocking on the wall because they couldn't hear you. You had a nice little garden, and birds of a morning. You'd have your windows open.' They were intended to last ten years, but some families stayed in their prefabs way beyond their proposed lifespan.

Such were the achievements, but not all were happy with the efforts of Atlee's Labour Government, largely because some of their promises were over-reaching. Ernest Bevin's pledge to build five million homes 'in quick time' proved rash and frustrating, leading to demonstrations in Leicester Square and a famous squat by communists in Duchess of Bedford House, a luxury block in Kensington. The answer was council houses, with one million being built by 1951. They were quality, too, the minimum size being laid down at 1000 square feet and three bedrooms. Qualification for re-housing was by a strict points system, based on the number of children and whether or not one had a bathroom. Competition was fierce, with mile-long queues forming at council offices.

Life is too vast and complex to be subjected to any reductive adjective but if pushed, there is one defining characteristic of the postwar years, and that is the overweening hand of the state in everyday affairs. From health to town planning, the government was in charge. War had established the role of officialdom in people's lives, and that did not change. If anything, it expanded. Today it is difficult to comprehend the reach of the state in those years: the canal network was nationalised, all lorry transport was nationalised, and water, coal, steel and the railways fell under the aegis and control of civil servants. Britain became one of the most collectivised societies outside the Soviet Union. Sibley's diaries reflect this - his encounters with 'officials' become an almost weekly occurrence, whether it is a problem with benefits or an application for compensation for war damage. The bowler-hatted civil servant became a *bete-noir* of everyday life, and one can see it in the films of the era, in which these brief-cased tinpot dictators, bristling with new-found power, often had their comeuppance in a fictional dream-fulfilment on the part of the put-upon hero. The decade ended with perhaps the ultimate comedic cock-a-snook at the New Authority, Ealing Studios' *Passport to Pimlico,* in which the residents of a small London Borough celebrate a new-found freedom from the tendrils of a Socialist State.

Perhaps Ealing films had their eye on Europe. In this wider world, Stalin's conquest of eastern Europe cemented communism across vast swathes of the continent from Poland to Czechoslovakia, a system enforced by a ruthless network of secret police and spy networks. The Cold War was born. While Britain was aping in its own milder way the collectivisation of British society and power of the state, cultural warning shots were being fired against the dangers of this concentration of power - allegorically in George Orwell's *Animal Farm,* published in 1945, and his *1984* of 1948, and philosophically in Karl Popper's monumental paean to liberalism, *The Open Society and its Enemies,* released in the same year.

The tone of literary and cinematic culture in the postwar years struck a sombre note: it was the age of Graham Greene, *film noir*, and Existentialism. The horrors of the Holocaust was a lance piercing our faith in human nature, and this ghastly disillusion rippled through poetry, art, philosophy and the novel. Some artists became wistful for a former age, like Evelyn Waugh who bemoaned the decline of aristocratic England in *Brideshead Revisited,* while others thought change was not coming fast enough, like the early Kingsley Amis who, along with the later *Angry Young Man* movement, took satirical pot-shots at the lingering class-system and snobbery of the times.

Uncertainty, change, and idealism tempered by cynicism: the postwar age was a complex soup. It was an age in which the Town Planner was King: people watched as developers finished off the work of the Luftwaffe and changed towns forever before people's eyes, with bypasses and the wholesale demolition of medieval centres, transforming the built environment. As Thomas Sibley resumes his rounds in the Home Counties as a travelling salesman, he sees a very different daily landscape emerging out of the rubble. Hemel Hempstead, Stevenage, Letchworth - Garden Cities that promised a new commuting life to the postwar worker, and a better life with a garden and a bathroom. It took the 1950s to consolidate this New Britain, but the foundations were being laid in the Forties.

But that change lies ahead. Back at the beginnings of the war, as we lurch from the macrocosm to the microcosm, in Ilford our hero and his family are engaged in a battle for survival. Sibley's 1940 journal is lost, but we meet him in 1941; they had endured a year of the Blitz, and now were struggling with shortages and the everyday challenge of trying to heat his house.

1941

JAN

1st Ordered coke & coal. (No coke for some time). Got diary from paper shop, 3/-, and paid bill, 2/9d. R.A.F. over Bremen. Germans bombed Eire.

2nd No day alerts in London but short one in Chelmsford. Evening siren 7 o'clock. Popp had a bad head. They called to Coutts Frimley for lodgings. All clear about 11 o'clock. Germans bombed Cardiff. RAF dropped 20,000 incendiaries on Bremen.

3rd Southend &c. Quite a blizzard at Shoeburyness. No sirens today. Four alerts during night but no bombs near.

4th Saturday. Hurriedly packed car and Popp, Rene & Bunny started for Frimley 3.35. Unpacked car at Mrs. Edwards. Same cold & draughty room - couldn't get warm. Popp & I slept downstairs in 'shop.' A rat disturbed us in night, but I was unable to frighten it away. 2 alerts at Frimley. London had a small raid. Australians took some 5000 Italian prisoners.

5th Great British success. Bardia (Libya) captured.

6th Two land mines dropped last night in Goodmayes & S. Kings - great damage. Wrote to Popp - no alerts last night.

7th Alert & guns going all day. Heard Burgoyne's were hit, 2 killed.

8th Ciss & I had wireless. RAF over Germany.

9th RAF over Ruhr. Great Greek successes - 4 Germans brought down last night.

13th Got rations from Sainsbury's. Plymouth bombed by Germans.

18th Saturday. Heard from Rene… she wants her wellingtons sent to Mr. Weston's, 4 Council Houses, Weybourne, Holt, Norfolk.

20th Posted off wellingtons to Rene. Paid Home 18/11.

22nd Tobruk taken. 20,000 prisoners.

The British capture of Tobruk was a major first step on the road to eventual victory, with British successes in North Africa joining the US and Russian victories in France, Poland and ultimately Germany. The Battle of Tobruk in Libya was fought between 21 and 22 January 1941 as part of Operation Compass, the first offensive of the Western Desert Force (WDF) in the Western Desert Campaign.

23rd Italians in retreat - Libya, Sudan, Abyssinia. Poles in daylight raids over France.

24th Lord Halifax went to USA in our latest battleship, the King George V.

29th Death of Greek Prime Minister - Gen. Mataxus.

30th Bombs dropped in Chelmsford - I heard the bombs. Wrote to Dane.

FEB

1st. Bought biscuits and food at Sainsburys.

4th Popp fell downstairs, injuring herself severely. Dr. Beattie came. Injection. Popp slept on and off with help of nembutals.

14th Scones & Coffee in Central Cafe Bishop Stortford.

All lives were being dislocated. As Thomas continued his rounds, his son-in-law Cliff had been called up and posted to Scotland.

20th Cliff phoned from Newcastle. On the way snow drift held up train for hours. Cliff did not arrive - train in snow. Swansea got most of bombs.

21st. Cliff phoned from Kings Cross. At last train had arrived - over 40 hours of travelling.

BISHOP'S STORTFORD
SAWBRIDGEWORTH
and DISTRICT

War Weapons Week

March 9th--15th, 1941

OUR AIM £75,000 : OUR DETERMINATION TO DOUBLE IT

LEND TO DEFEND
YOUR RIGHT TO BE FREE

Money saved is Money earned. Remember, you are not asked to give—you are asked to invest. Good interest is paid on National Savings, your Money is safe.

Go to your Bank, the Post Office or one of the Selling Centres in the town. Buy Defence Bonds, Savings Certificates or Savings Stamps and help to buy Weapons to defeat Hitler.

Let your Money Fight.

Herts & Essex Observer, 1 March 1941

24th RAF bombed invasion ports.

26th East Ham & Manor Park got several land mines. Graham lost his front window. RAF bombed Cologne.

27th Rene, Cliff & Bunny went to Scotland this morning, c/o Mr. Jamieson, East Aberdour, Fife.

MARCH

6th Bomb dropped before alert. Popp upset. Cut some of the front roses.

7th New Zealand warship sinks Italian raider in Indian Ocean.

9th Much damage in London districts. Popp upset.

11th Heard from Rene. Cliff may be invited to take a commission. Widespread raids over the country. Shipping losses very heavy.

15th Grays & Tilbury had bombs last night. Both Jordans shops had narrow escapes. Popp comes down into the drawing-room and stays until tea-time. I received my cheque for commission £165-7-2d. Commission now suspended because of war conditions.

As above, so below: all national tragedies are personal tragedies writ large. As the bombs rained down on London a larger tragedy was unfolding in 35 Lord Avenue, Ilford.

16th My poor wife Popp died suddenly, painlessly. Heart attack. Was sitting in armchair. Just had a good tea. Became ill, & in half an hour was dead. Died about 7.15pm.

Death of poor suffering Popp.

Married 29/1/1903

Died 16/3/1941

Known one another 43 years.

Went to Ashurst in morning. Dr. Beattie preached. Lord's supper followed - large number stayed. Rested in afternoon. Nurse came twice. Dolly S. brought 6 eggs. Mrs. Hurst came to see Popp. Wrote to Kings Cross about trains. Popp taken ill - 'phoned Dr. Beattie who came and pronounced Popp dead. 'Phoned Len, Rene, Ed, Mr. Iszatt, Nurse came 9 o'clock and did needful. The Lord gave, He has taken away, blessed be the name of the Lord. I had no sleep thro' night altho' I took 2 aspirins, and was burning hot. Went upstairs 5 times - result of shock.

After a lifetime of illness and anxiety ameliorated by love, Annie Sibley gives up the ghost at the age of 63. That girl who Thomas courted in the far off days of Poplar at the turn of the century, whom he kissed in Ullin Street, Bow in their youth and who he devoted his life to, fades in the darkest days of the war. Perhaps the terrors of life had finally proved too much - twice in her life she had faced horror from the skies. The Edwardian age had promised so much, a never-setting sun. But in the end humanity let us down, dragged us twice into conflict of such magnitude that it scarred a generation. Popp was never perhaps strong enough for the world, and Thomas Sibley had cast himself in the role of empathetic protector who guided her through the turbulence. But he could not prove her ultimate saviour.

17th. Did not go to business. Saw Dr. Beattie for Death Certificate. Went to Registrar. Midland Bank, Prudential. Gave up Popp's ration book & identity card in afternoon. Will Warwick out. Ciss and I had dinner. Ordered 2 wreaths, one for Len. £1-1/-. Len came to tea & stayed until 8 o'clock. Percy and Mr. Holt called. Rene 'phoned. … Popp laid in her coffin (6') this afternoon. She looked lovely in death, a peaceful and restful smile. Wrote to Harry & Dena. Had a quiet night, no raids. Cissy and I had a good sleep.

18th. Did not go to business. Up at 7.30. Had breakfast & motored to Ilford. Sent £6 off to Rene by wire. Drew £10 out of bank. Mrs. French, Prudential agent, took away policies and death certificate. Bought black tie & socks - Cissy got me a band for sleeve. Cissy bought black hat & coat & stockings. Spoke to green-grocer's boy about his soul - he used to go to Roding Hall but now goes to a Catholic Club.

19th … Cliff, Rene & Bunny came at 11.45. Rene greatly cut up. Brought Cliff & Bunny back to 298 & I returned to 35. … 8 wreaths arrived.

Big air raid started about 8.40pm. Land-mine on parachute landed in park, damaged roof severely. A big piece of clay came right thro' roof & fell on landing. Soot smothered dining room. 2 panes of glass out. Ciss had a narrow escape as she went to the door as the bomb exploded. Mr. Holt called in at midnight. All clear 1 o'clock. Ciss & I cleared up indoor mess. I then went to sleep.

A/20 Nº 09368 —18

NOTICE TO INFORMANT.

I hereby give notice that I have, this day, signed a Medical Certificate of the Cause of Death, of Mrs Annie Sibley deceased

Signature [illegible]

Date 16/3/41

This Notice must be given by the Certifying Medical Practitioner to the person who is qualified and liable to act as Informant for the purpose of the registration of the death. As to the person liable to act as Informant, see back.

DUTIES OF INFORMANT.

The Informant must deliver this Notice to the Registrar of Births and Deaths of the Sub-District in which the Death took place, bearing in mind that the Death cannot be registered until the medical certificate has reached the Registrar. Failure to deliver this Notice to the Registrar renders the Informant liable to prosecution.

The Informant must be prepared to state accurately to the Registrar the following particulars :—
(1) The Date and Place of Death, and the place of Deceased's usual residence (2) the full Names and Surname (3) the correct Age (4) the Occupation and (5) whether Deceased was in receipt of a naval or military pension, an old age pension, or other pension or allowance from public funds.

The wider world is indifferent to our personal tragedies, and in an act of supreme ill fortune Sibley's house is bombed just has his wife is lying at rest in their front room. No part of London was immune to the Nazi onslaught during the Blitz, and between 1940-45 Wanstead was the target of 110 High Explosive bombs, 4 Land Mines, 8 VI Flying Bombs, 7 V2 Rockets, 8 Oil Bombs, plus 19 other unexploded bombs, 1 unexploded Land Mine and innumerable incendiaries. The biggest onslaught had taken place in September 1940 but the air raids of March 19th 1941 were brutal. Fortunately a record of the entire civil defence of Wanstead was kept by a warden Stanley Tiquet, in his account *It Happened Here*. Remarkably, it contains an account of the precise events of that night, in which the civil defence volunteers in the borough experienced the most dreadful fatalities of the war - no less than 4 wardens losing their lives:

'The wail of the siren opposite the Post announced at 8.15 p.m. the arrival of the raiders. The Post personnel saw a startling sight. The Flats were a sea of flame. Thousands of incendiaries were burning on the open space. The guns roared. It was obvious that the enemy was making a concerted and determined attack. Bomb flashes stabbed the black-out. Planes droned overhead. The batteries on the Flats joined those further away in putting up a terrific barrage. At 8.50 p.m., three H.E. bombs fell in Lake House Road, damaging a number of houses and partly demolishing Nos. 14 and 31. A few casualties resulted, one being a man who was trapped in the doorway of No. 14. Wardens heaved on the obstruction to release him. Gas escaping in the same house caused a fire. This was quickly dealt with and the flames smothered. A nearby barrage balloon had burst into flames, illuminating the scene with glaring brilliance and revealing the widespread damage. At 9.20 p.m. this first incident appeared closed, and Services were awaiting the result of a final search and check-up before being dismissed. Then a parachute mine landed. It exploded a few yards from Aldersbrook corner on the Leytonstone side. Houses in Lake House Road, already badly damaged, tottered to destruction. Number II caught fire and was

destroyed. Loss of life would have been heavy but for the fact that most of the inhabitants had by now taken refuge in the Aldersbrook public shelter, and those who remained were in their own dug-outs. The attack died down. Wardens returned to their Posts; but the number for Post 41 was sadly lacking. The two boys' cycles stood in their usual place. "Busy somewhere" said the Chief. But the absent ones did not return, and a search was made. They were found in the mortuary, three of them. It was known that two others had been taken to hospital. Warden Barnett was one of these. He died next morning of his injuries. Just before the mine exploded, the Messengers had been giving assistance in one of the less badly-damaged houses. Broome, although officially not on duty, had rushed out to lend a hand. Warden Hutton was endeavouring to turn off the gas at No. 14 when the mine fell. So the four from Post 41 died doing their duty on the Home Front. The two boys, pals in the Service, sleep in one grave in Old Wanstead Churchyard. The two men lie close by, in Ilford Cemetery.' ('The Story of Civil Defence in Wanstead & Woodford 1939 – 1945,' Stanley Tiquet, 1946).

Yet life goes on, ceremonies undertaken to impose pattern and dignity on the chaos.

20th Funeral of my beloved wife, Grave No. 109648, Chapel Avenue, City of London Cemetery. There were many lovely floral tributes of affection. Up 7.15 & found the mess in both gardens terrible. Spent 1 1/2 hours, also Ciss, clearing up the tiles, clay etc. Had to hurriedly get ready for funeral. Mr. Adams arrived 11 o'clock (under difficulties of raid). Hearse & 3 cars of mourners - Len, Rene, Freda & Cliff; Ciss, Ed, Li, Eva, Win, Bert, Ernie, Will Warwick & self (13). Percy Iszatt, Holt & Ashbolt, Rev. A.E. Pope from church, Mr. & Mrs. Hunt (Ethel & Elsie at cemetery). Rev Pope took service at Ashurst. Popp buried in Chapel Avenue, C.L. cemetery, 12 noon. The Lord gave me strength to give a short testimony. Len, Freda, Cliff, Rene, Li, Ernie, Bert, Winnie came back for tea and sandwiches. …

Visited Town Hall regarding damage to house. ... Len & Cliff did what they could to patch roof. Mrs. Ringwood looked after Bunny. Evening alert about 8.30 - all clear quite early, & we had a good night's rest. Thanks to the Lord for his wonderful grace & strength.

The very crater in Clayhall Park, Wanstead, from an exploding landmine, that caused the fall-out damage to Sibley's house on the night of March 19th 1941.

21st Ciss & I cleared the tiles &c from sideway & back garden and placed muck in road. R.W. George 'phoned up about my journeys which he would take over.

23rd National Day of prayer.

26th Sent letter by Cissy to Town Hall about my roof. Bought felt for roof, spent 2 hours in loft. Heavy rains caused us a lot of strength. Prudential paid £47-1-6 for poor old Popp.

27th Yugoslav revolt. Council men started on roof.

28th Council men repaired much of roof. Cleared loft of pails, baths, paper, wool &c. Took some time. Cleared some tiles from garden. Had a hot bath before tea.

31st Dolly Slicker called in whilst at tea and stayed talking to Ciss.

APRIL

1st. RAF using a new bomb - 5 times explosive power - poor Bremen!

2nd Inspected a suitable gravestone at Druits, £28-10/-.

3rd Banghazi recaptured by Germans & Italians. Went to Druits and booked gravestone. Gave wording. Wrote to Clerk of Frinton for permit to take car to coastal towns.

5th Rec'd cheque £1-8-3 from council - returned amount paid for shelter. Dena & Joan arrived about 3 o'clock & stayed until 6.30. I took them to Ilford Station. Gave Dena 2/6 towards expenses. Dena has had facial paralysis and shows it slightly. Joan (14) quiet & delicate. 2 boys Dennis & Freddy in forces. George will soon be called up.

8th Coventry greatly bombed again.

9th RAF bombed Berlin.

10th Wivenhoe, Brightlingsea, Manningtree. Lunched in Manningtree - White Hart (Staying at Rd Lion Colchester) - soup, steak pudding &c - 2/-. Had a walk after dinner until 8.30. Had a read & got into bed 9.45 & was soon asleep. No night alert.

And so life goes on - a mere fortnight after his wife's death and the partial destruction of his house Thomas Sibley is back on the road as a commercial traveller.

12th … Heard from Rene - she is still poorly and Bunny not quite fit yet.

14th Easter Bank Holiday Monday. … spent most of time repairing shed roof and putting on roof felting. Len, Freda, Anne & Clive came 12.30. I finished work. Len had ricked his back so could not help. Dinner 1.30, soup, beef, chicken & fig pudding (Cissy did very well). We all went to Popp's grave & saw the memorial. Quite satisfactory. Freda Len & I played Kan-u-Go for an hour. Tea 5.30 and I took them to Barking station. They enjoyed themselves. RAF at Brest &c.

16th Paid A.R. Adams bill for funeral & grave, £40-4/-. Sent for petrol rations. Air-raid started 9.10 and continued until 4.50. Terrible bombing of London and districts - by 500 bombers. Worst raid on London yet. Great damage and many casualties. I laid on bed until 5.30 and then got into bed. Eva & Ciss went to bed 12.30.

17th Yugoslavia gives in. Will Warwick sent and had new pan put in outdoor W.C. Berlin bombed by our latest devastating bombs.

19th Went to Conference at Victoria Hall. Stuart Hine & Watson were the speakers. Very good. Had a chat with Stuart afterwards. Air raid started 9.25. A terrible raid on London & districts. Longwood (?) Gdns hit, several houses down - some casualties. All clear 4.50.

21st Tripoli got a tremendous bombing. I put in 7lbs of Majestic potatoes.

23rd Greeks giving up. British still fighting well in Greece & Libya.

25th Put some surgical spirit No. 2. in petrol tank.

MAY

3rd 150th anniversary of Poland's Constitution. Winston Churchill broadcast.

5th Pearce's journey No. 2. Dedham, Hadleigh, Lavenham & Long

Melford. dinner at White Horse Hotel Sudbury (steak, bread & butter pudding, cheese &c). Only a small place. Mr. & Mrs. Pearce at Dedham so had a chat with them. RAF bombed Mannheim.

6th White Horse Hotel Sudbury, up 7.15. Finished 6.30. Had a 4 mile walk - bought 6 eggs. Chatted with 3 other commercials in C. Room.

7th Dinner at Abbey Hotel 6.30 (Saffron Walden). Had a long country walk, about 6 miles & came back tired. Had a little read in Commercial Room & retired about 10.30.

11th R. Hess flew to Scotland, landed by parachute. Bunny not well - gastric trouble.

13th Rudolf Hess seems to have flown to Britain to escape some dissension in the Nazi Party.

14th Great speculation on Hess and why he came to Britain.

15th Vichy practically at war with Britain. Gravesend &c. Had a soldier, afterwards an air-pilot, for passingers. Germans using Syrian aerodromes.

16th Sollum again in British hands.

19th Southend & Shoeburyness. Lunched in Garon's, Victoria Parade. Mrs. Appleyard in bed, sprained ankle.

20th Germans making a tremendous attack on Crete.

21st A great fight for Crete - thousands of Germans landed by air.

23rd Fight for Crete still raging. German convoy smashed by Navy. RAF bombed Cologne.

26th Bought a 20/-6d savings certificate at Becontree. Cissy painted window-frame in back bedroom. We lose 6 warships off Crete.

Terrific fighting in Crete.

27th German battleship Bismarck sunk by our navy. Got photo prints from McCarthy's for Popp's album. 'Hood' revenged by sinking of the Bismarck. Great rejoicing. Cissy got some oranges today - she went to East Ham and saw Elsie. RAF bombed Cologne.

31st Ciss went with me to graveyard and I put some plants on Popp's grave. Crete evacuated 15,000.

JUNE

2nd. Whit Monday. Bank Holiday. Mr. & Mrs. Iszatt come round and we play Chinese Marbles. RAF bomb Berlin.

5th Clacton. Had to go by bus as permit had not arrived. Called in Frinton Council Office and got one. Permit had been posted to the Red Lion. Splendid lunch at Walton Cafe - Beef, York., spam, & Baked potatoes.

8th British and Free French invade Syria.

9th Bought tickets for Aberdour - 2 x £4-3-7. Bought cabin trunk at Moultons, £2-9-11. Packed trunk. Invasion of Syria going smoothly - not much resistance.

10th Ciss heard from Rene. Cliff going to W.Scotland, Rene upset.

Family first: and the Sibleys travel north to see Cliff, their son-in-law, who has been posted to northern Scotland.

14th Up at 6am. Ciss & I departed for Aberdour, Fife. Met Ed & Li at K'Cross station. Started 10am and reached Edinburgh at 7pm. Had a nice journey and pleasant people travelling. Rene & Bunny met us at Edinburgh and got to 'Beulah,' Aberdour at 8pm.

15th Sunday. Had to shave with safety razor - no electricity after breakfast. Went to Scottish Kirk Com'n service. Ed & Li did not stop stop.

16th Ed & I caught 10.35 to Edinburgh. Went to Picture Gallery. Caught 2.35 back and went on sands - paddled with Bunny & took photos. Nice day.

19th We all went to the woods, taking our tea. Stayed & enjoyed the surroundings until 7pm.

20th Ed Li & I went to Edinburgh by 10.35 train. Walked down Princes St. then to High St. & along to Heywood Palace & Abbey. Argument with an attendant about spiritual things - he was a canny unbeliever, one time Elder & SS teacher. Lunched in Brown & Derbys. Sat in gardens in afternoon and saw electric clock made of flowers.

22nd Germany invades Russia. 27 German planes down. 64 (SIBLEY'S BIRTHDAY)

24th. Caught 11.45 to Edinburgh. Alighted in Haymarket and took tram to Zoological Gardens. Spent afternoon looking at the animals. Bunny liked the monkeys best.

25th After tea Rene & I had a lovely walk on Donny Bs estate.

26th Went by 2.20 bus to Dunfermline and spent afternoon and early evening in Pittencrieff Glen where we had our tea.

28th Packed bag and caught 8.18pm - they all saw me in train at Aberdour. Put bag on bunk (No. 15). Had a young negro soldier and young soldier 20 as sleeping companions.

30th Country journey No. 2. Witham then Dedham. Arrived White Horse Hotel Sudbury 5.40.

JULY

1st. Sudbury. White Horse Hotel. Had a 5 mile walk. Chatted with an old soldier in his garden.

5th Took Cissy to Ed's and saw Ernie & Louise & baby. It is a fine child. Harvey, 6 months, 24lbs. Ed took our photos.

Sudbury in the 1940s, the sleepy Suffolk town Sibley would have known.

8th Germans being held by Russians - heavy casualties on both sides.

9th Visited grave, tidied it up of weeds &c. Russians fighting well. No London raids. Coasts visited by raiders.

11th Fighting still going on in Syria. Russians holding up Nazis.

14th RAF heavy bombing over Bremen & Hanover. We lost 5 bombers.

15th Ciss & I went to C.E., my first appearance for 5 years. Speaker did not turn up so I was pressed into service. Spoke on Ps. XXIII.

16th Heard from Cliff.

18th No letter from Len yet.

19th Saturday. Went to the 'Chase' fields with Sunday School. A very short innings - made 4 bowled off legs. Tea in Baptist Church. Rain kept children inside - played games. I gave round some sweets &c. Took some children part way home in car - 2 lots - then the Buggys home.

26th W. Mersea. Walked to Fairhaven House & chatted with owner of bungalow built on Ed's ground. Ed'd hut missing.

28th Air raid on London. Heard alert & three rows of planes go over, & all clear at Mersea. One bomber down at Wivenhoe. Russians showing great fight against Hitler.

30th Went for paper and posted Cliff's letter. Chatted to young lady who is getting married next Saturday, & gave her Mrs. Green's address (W. Mersea) for the weekend. Had a short walk thro' Castle grounds.

AUGUST

1st. Left Red Lion Hotel 9.20, Colchester, paid them £2-8-10. … got home… Ciss had been poorly, had a day in bed on Wednesday at Mabel's. Sent form to Huddersfield for part payment of war damage.

The War Damage Act of 1941 allowed for victims of air-raids to apply for compensation for the rebuilding of their homes. By all accounts the system was very rigorously policed, and it was no easy thing, as the longevity of Sibley's claim testifies, for it drags on until after the war.

2nd Called in a Li's and got 3lbs of blackcurrants. RAF bombed Berlin (heaviest yet).

4th Bank Holiday Monday. Wrote to Dena, who desires a loan but I did not agree the need was sufficient. After dinner at 6.30 Ciss & I motored to Clayhall Bapt. (?) Field. I played cricket.

5th Romford &c. Had to go on foot - no petrol.

7th Sidcup &c. Went by bus (first time for over 14 years). Coke delivered.

12th Big RAF raid on Berlin. We lost 20 bombers.

Sibley's recording of British losses proves that, despite the strong hold the Government exerted over morale and propaganda, by and large the BBC did not sanitise the negative fall-out of the war.

14th Hon. Atlee broadcasted (sic) that Churchill had interviewed Roosevelt on his yacht. Important declaration. Rene wrote to Ciss. Still in trouble - both she & Bunny are unwell & had to have doctor.

16th After dinner Ciss & I went to Len's via Barking & Richmond. No. 90 bus to Fountain (fares 8/6d). Freda got us a nice tea. Had a look at Len's allotment. ... Enjoyed our visit.

17th Sunday. Mr Holt came round abt. 3 o'clock, &c Cine, and took some photos of us - we had some laughter.

20th Rec'd £1-5-4d from Huddersfield - War Damage Act 1941. Wrote for Supplementary Coupons.

22nd Got shrapnel helmet.

25th C2 journey, Dedham &c, arrived White Horse, Sudbury, 5.15pm. Rm No. 6.

26th Lunched in Halstead - (Mutton, Yorkshire, marrow, apple tart 1/11d). 3 other commercials here. Had a walk by the river. Found Brethren's Hall for future attendance.

27th Got to Saffron Walden 12 o'clock. (Abbey Hotel). Saw Cresswell then lunched at the Copper Kettle Cafe. Finished calls then went to room No. 14, (attic). Not very nice. Mr. Bennett

(Carr's Biscuit Co.) there, very chatty & pleasant. Museum for 1/2 hour.

Saffron Walden, Essex - High Street & Abbey Hotel.

28th Back to Braintree & White Hart Hotel.

28th Cissy home, not up to much. She had been to Bursell's & was found to be blind in left eye. He is making her two pairs of glasses.

31st Sunday. Took service at Tottenham Baptist Church, High Rd. Went to Ashurst in evening... Brought home an airman (ex Fairlop) to supper - Harry Bainbridge.

SEPT

1st. Rene telephoned Ciss for certain documents - worried over house & mortgage.

4th Workmen spent evening on ceiling & wall. Ciss & I took some earth from next door, on permission of new tenant.

5th Workmen here doing kitchen. ... Met Mr. Newbolt on bus and spoke to him about the earth in 'Page's' garden.

6th Saturday. Went to Victoria Hall and saw Stuart Hine giving a lantern lecture on Czechoslovakia.

7th Ashurst. Ciss received into membership, transferred from Clementwood.

8th Workmen here. Decided to have kitchen painted light blue.

10th Mr. Long finished painting kitchen, paid him £2-10/-. Italy got the bombing.

15th Ciss & Li turned up, they had been to see Ruth off to Norfolk & to Selfridges &c.

19th Mowed lawn before having tea. Germans take Kiev.

20th Saturday. Ciss & I caught 1.21 to L'Pool St., & went by 2.28 to Broxbourne. Bus 342 to Hertford Heath. Bob met us. Nellie glad to see us. Bob Jr's wife Iris there - she is living with them. Doris & daughter, Lily, husband & daughter came and we had a good party. Got home 8.55.

22nd C1 journey, Danbury, Maldon &c, arr. Colchester 5.30. .,.. went to Grosevenor Hotel Maldon Rd. Had supper - cold lamb, veg., trifle & tea. One other there. … Had a walk in Castle grounds & got back to hotel 8 o'clock. Too much of a pub about it - plenty of noise. Wrote to Len then had a read.

23rd Got back to Grosvenor Hotel 6.30, had fish &c. Two others here, had a nice chat. One gave interesting war experiences in East 17/18.

25th … Got back to Grosvenor 5.15. … went for a walk and met Mr. Moss who was going to Albert Town Hall to see Repertory Party. I thought I would go and have some music but when I got in I found it was a comedy - 2/- sheet. Quite harmless & better than the music & noise at the Grosvenor.

The Albert Hall, Colchester

26th Left Grosvenor Hotel 9.15. Gave girl 2/-6d. Not very good food but comfortable room.

27th Saturday. Len, Freda, Annie & Clive came to dinner. Took fruit & flour round to church. Len came with me. Len mowed the lawn while I spoke to Mr. C.E. Potter about painting front of house - £6. Eva & Li came just as Len and I went to church. Eva was offended because I said Ed could of (sic) come if he had wished - he went into the park - tired. Took Len & family to Barking. Guns woke us up 1.30.

28th Harvest Festival, Ashurst.

OCT

11th Ciss & I both had a hot bath before tea. We forgot all about the BB Social at the church.

13th Heard from Rene - troubled about mortgage. Will be coming to Ilford and not going to Shetland Islands.

22nd Abbey Hotel (Saffron Walden?) Rm. 6. Sat in lounge. Bennett came in and we talked to the ladies & then with Col. Johnston, late of Indian Army until 11.20.

23rd Got to White Hart Braintree 5 o'clock.

24th Rene's M.O. sent to Leeds has not turned up. Workmen have finished ceilings, and paint the outside of house. No electricity upstairs yet. Heard from Cliff, also from Len, giving me C.V.

29th Visited cemetery for a few minutes. Thunder, lightning, snow & sleet. Quite a blizzard for October.

30th Mr. Thorpe called about the damage to my desk but professed no responsibility. Dolly Slicker came round to tea.

NOV

9th Charles & Molly Honey came for an hour or so in afternoon. Painter finished my room and started on bathroom ceiling and Cissy's room.

12th Went to Town Hall for ration books (pink).

13th Aircraft Carrier Ark Royal sunk in Mediterranean.

19th Colchester. Lunched at Jacklin's - jugged hare &c. with Mr. J. McBride also owner of a Picture Palace in Mersey Rd.

20th Went to Albert Hall and saw Annie Christie - did not enjoy it.

27th Mr. Kefford died this morning.

28th Gondar (?) surrendered. Mussolini's Empire gone. Desert war (Libya) continuing unabated.

DEC

3rd Filled in war damage form for CA & sent to Potter for signature.

6th Got some paint from Thomas for Morrison's Shelter. Started painting shelter in garden but rain and darkness did not allow me to do much.

7th Japan declares war on USA & Gt.Bn.

8th Dagenham. Everyone talking about Japan entering into war. Russia doing well and British forces attacking Germans in Libya. Put a few books straight in bookcase.

10th HMS Prince of Wales & Repulse sunk by Japs. Broke news from the East of the sinking of our newest 35000 Battleship and 37000 Battle Cruiser.

11th 2000 (about) saved from sunk battleship.

17th Abbey Hotel (Saffron Walden). Went to Baptists - no meeting. Met a young RAF pilot (USA) who is a Baptist. Had a chat... hopes to go into mission field.

18th Left Abbey Saffron Walden 9.30. Said goodbye to Mr. Bennet (Carrs) as I am not likely to see him again.

19th. Received 1942 Car Licence and wrote off for supplementary petrol allowance.

20th Took Bunny & Brian to S.S. Christmas Party, also Ciss who helped. Came home and painted shelter. Len rang up for a chat - he may be going into army.

23rd Brought a soldier from Woolwich to Ilford Lane (he lived on Woodlands Rd.).

24th Tried to buy diaries unsuccessfully. Ed gave me one.

25th Japs capture Hong Kong. Played records until 1 o'clock. Had turkey, bacon, sausages, Christmas pudding, mince pies, Ginger Wine, a real good feast. Went to Ed's about 4. Ruth, Win & Bert,

Ernie & Louise, & Margaret (one year). Motored to Iszatt's - had some games. Harold took photog's. 18 guests there. Spent a happy evening. Len Moulton cycled back to North Weald.

Morrison's shelters were the indoor versions of the more familiar Anderson shelter, named for the Minister of Supply for the National Government, Herbert Morrison; Basically robust metal cages with reinforced roof acting as protective sleeping spaces.

26th Len, Freda, Anne & Clive here. Had a good dinner - cold turkey &c. Len Freda & the three children paid a visit to Li's - I took them in car. Back at 5.15. After a small tea Len & family departed abt. 6.10. I took Rene & Bunny to Barking Station.

27th Rene went to bed with toothache & glands painful.

31st I.T. £2-10/- for excess over mortgage - sent on cheque. No alerts.

And so ends the second year of the war. 1942's journal is missing but the folllowing year proves to be a big one for the Sibleys.

1943

Marriage Arrangements (for) 17th April 1943:

Two years following the death of his wife, Thomas and his near-lifelong companion Cecelia Williams, the former Barnados girl, have decided to marry.

Thomas, financially astute as ever, does the accounts:

Rev. G.R. Beasley-Murray - 3/6d.

Ashurst Drive Bapt. Church Caretaker - 5/-.

Registrar - £1-8-1d.

Co-op, Reception - 50 @ 5/-.

2 carriages Cosben £3

Reception invitations cards & boxes (Wilson) - £1-16-1.

Cake £2-15-6d

Ring - thro' greengrocer girl, Fisher Leytonstone - £6-6/-

Dress - Richards - £41-10-8.

£41-10-8d.

Bob & Nellie

Mr. & Mrs. Warwick

F.H. Bursell.

P. Iszatt & family - Eiderdown.

Deacons - Bedspread.

Ethel - teapot.

Mabel - cake stand.

Len - fish knives & forks.

Mr. E.M. Young - Coffee set.

Mr. & Webb - teaspooons and pastry forks.

Mr. & Mrs. Hunt - Table Runner.

Mr. & Mrs. Petigern - Tea cosy & cushion.

JAN

1st Russians have great victory, take Leliki Luki.

6th Russians still continuing their magnificent advance.

7th Got 400 tabs of saccharine from Simpson of Dartford.

11th Bombs dropped in East Anglia.

16th Berlin bombed.

17th Evening raid on London.

18th Leningrad freed from Germans - terrible fighting - Germans everywhere defeated - German losses 250,000 men.

19th Eltham &c. Mr. Moss (Millin & co, Eltham) kindly lent me his Remington electric shaver. My Shavemaster petered out this morning - I'd only half shaved.

20th Daylight raid - 11 down. Visited grave. London and So. England had a heavy raid 12-1.15. 50 children killed in So. London - school hit. I went to Iszatts - Deacons meeting. Left hurriedly - air raid. Holt & I walked thro' the 'gunfire.' All clear 11.10. Ciss found a pekinese dog. Stayed all night.

The German attack on south London was part of a raid by 28 Focke-Wulf Fw 190A-4U3 fighter-bombers escorted by Messerschmitt Bf 109 fighters. The bombing of Sandhurst Road School on Minard Road, Catford. A German fighter-bomber dropped a single 500-kilogram (1,100 lb) bomb on the school at 12:30 pm, killing 38 children (32 killed at the school and 6 more died in hospital) and 6 staff and injuring another 60 people.

22nd. School that was hit on Wednesday was Sangley Rd. (sic) Catford. Unhappiness still reigning at 16 Mornington Rd. (Ed & Li's house), Ed staying at Hoxton for weekend, Li & Eva going to Ernie's. Peky still here. Tripoli taken.

26th Mrs. Browning had a letter from Mrs. Bist (Montreal) saying her son was alive, wounded, and a prisoner of war in Germany.

30th Germany had two day raids on the Nazi's 12th anniversary. RAF bombed Hamburg at night. Fence blown down.

FEB

2nd Cologne bombed. Stalingrad - all Germans surrender.

Most historians agree that the victory at Stalingrad energized the Red Army and shifted the balance of power in the favour of the Soviets. The battle was a key turning point in the war, siphoning as it did many German divisions from France, thus opening up room for a liberating invasion from the allies. Stalingrad was strategically important to both sides as a major industrial and transport hub on the Volga River. Whoever controlled Stalingrad would have access to the oil fields of the Caucasus and would gain control of the Volga. Germany, already operating on dwindling fuel supplies, focused its efforts on moving deeper into Soviet territory and taking the oil fields at any cost. The city's loss to the Nazis was a pivotal engine of their eventual defeat.

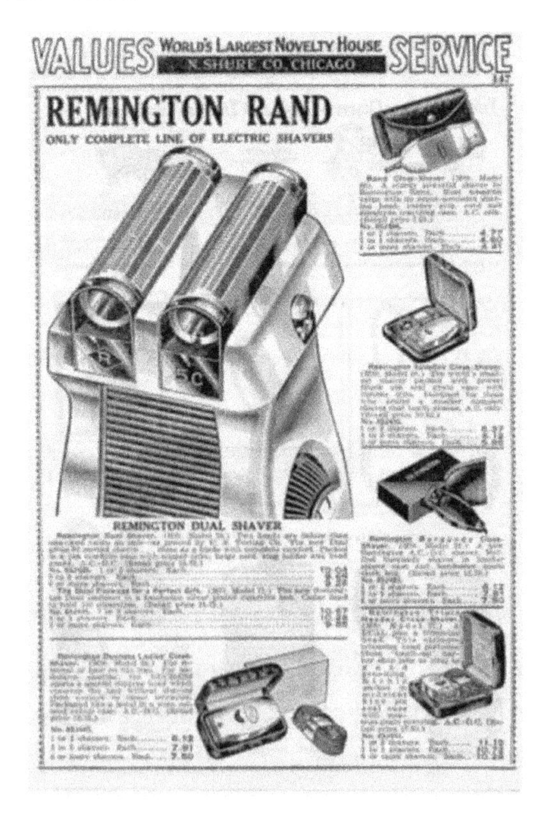

Back on the home front, pressing problems was the growing scarcity of food; even Sibley's beloved Garons in Southend was having trouble meetings its customer's high expectations:

5th Southend. Went to Garons for lunch but menu so poor went on to James, Westcliff, where I had lunch with Mr. Smedley. Wrote to Co-op about catering.

8th Ciss wrote to Registrar and arranged for April 17th. Wrote to him tonight giving names of our father's, occupations &c. Heard from Rene. Russians take Kursk - large and important town.

11th Wrote to Co-op accepting Buffet for 5/- (a head) for April 17th 2 o'clock.

12th Greenwich. Lunch in ABC Lewisham. Saw Victor Reed in bed (downstairs) and gave him a large propelling pencil. He loaned me 6 clothing coupons.

13th Met Ciss who had been to Clementwood 'talkies' on Wm. Carey. Remainder of French Fleet going to be repaired - many now in USA already - in fight against Axis.

16th Karkov taken. (Krakov?) Ciss and I went to C.E. 'Brains Trust.' Addikin in chair. South Wales was bombed.

17th Co-op 'phoned up and I agreed to 2 carriages, 2 journeys for £3. Americans suffer a nasty setback in Tunisia.

23rd Halstead & Sudbury. Lunched in British Rest. Halstead - soup, lamb & date roll. Heard that Mrs. A.I. Ritchell, widow of D.A.H., committed suicide - selfish, miserable woman. Nobody loved her and she loved no one.

24th Lunched at the Abbey (Rm 3) on calf's head.

27th Rec'd £125 from BDH.

MARCH

1st Berlin had a terrific bombing this evening - 19 bombers lost.

3rd Raid on London. 3 raiders down. Great USA & Australian victory over Japs in New Guinea. A big convoy of warships destroyed by bombers & fighters.

4th Terrible catastrophe at an underground shelter. 178 dead. 60 in hospital.

11th. Gravesend. Met Mr. Barnard in Dartford, who did not at first recognise me.

12th Ilford - also Romford - had a bombing & machine gunning this morning. Ciss & I were in bed. We hastily went downstairs. Damage in High Rd., Eaton Rd., &c. Several killed. Co-op burnt out.

13th After dinner Ciss & I went to see Ben Lewis & Rose Spreadbury married - about 80 there. Ciss & I then went to C.E. Social - about 60 there. We had games and a good spread. Warning went at 9.10 so we broke up. Ciss & I left at 9.30 when all clear went.

14th Sunday. Walked to Ashurst. Mr. Murray preached on 'Are you a lost sheep?'

15th Germans have Kharkov again.

21st Ashurst. Mr. M. preached on 'Have you a Wedding Garment?' He referred to my approaching marriage as illustration.

23rd. Took aspirins to Mr. Iszatt. He gave Ciss & I from the family a nice eiderdown quilt. He also gave us a bottle of sherry & port.

24th Setback for eighth army in Tunisia.

25th Heard from Len who sent me £2-2/- for a present.

26th Ciss went to Town Hall for extra rations for 35 Wedding party ,

40. Piano tuned by Mr. Dawkins 6/-.

27th Berlin bombed.

28th Ciss wrote to Board of Trade for household coupons. People expecting reprisal raids because of Berlin being bombed.

29th Coggleshall. Arrived Red Lion Hotel (no. 4 room) 5.30. Had dinner, jugged hare.

30th Lunched at British Rest., Walton - not so good - had to have spam.

British Restaurants were communal kitchens created in 1940 by Winston Churchill to help people who had been bombed out of their homes, had run out of ration coupons or otherwise needed help. In 1943, 2,160 British Restaurants served 600,000 very inexpensive meals a day. They were disbanded in 1947.

31st Dinner - Pigeon &c.

APRIL

1st Lunched in Dovercourt. As wind was so cold & strong I had an hour's shelter in the Pictures. Nothing worth seeing - Donald Duck clever but for children.

2nd Heard from Harry - not coming to wedding. Heard from Rene, expected home Monday morning.

4th Double Summer time.

5th When I got home I found Cliff, Rene & Bunny waiting for me - they arrived about 10.30am. They had a rough journey on the boat. Rene was just getting over sea-sickness.

7th Took Ciss with me to cemetery - put flowers on grave - then to Caves taking the old coat to be made into a new coat for Bunny.

Cliff, Rene & Bunny called in - paid her for calf skin rug 25/-. She took away Valpers Radio Malt. Filled in form for next 3 month's petrol allowance. Another victory by Eighth army over Rommel in Tunisia.

8th Ed 'phoned up about holidays - July 3rd - Minehead?

A British Restaurant in Woolmore Street, Poplar, London, 1942.

10th Ciss has a chest cough and nettle rash. Fire guards practice and stirrup pump. Sfax taken by Eighth army.

Led by General Montgomery, the stunning victory over the Axis forces in the re-capture of the Tunisian port of Sfax was a major turning point for the allies, leading to the invasion of Sicily.

The Regal, Dovercourt in the 1940s, when Thomas Sibley took shelter there.

14th Heard from Petroleum Officer - wanted to know the area I covered. Had a 'phone call that wedding cake for us would be sent tomorrow ex Petergern. Raid brought us downstairs at 12.40. All clear 1.25.

15th Mr. Petigern sent us a lovely wedding cake - 2 tiers & ornaments, £2-15-6d.

On 16th April war was forgotten as the Sibley clan gathered at Ashurst Drive Baptist Church for a family wedding:

16th MARRIED TO CECELIA WILLIAMS. Len best man. Rene maid of honour. Up at 7.50. Had hair cut and shave & called in for our meat - butcher let us have a tin of corned beef. Ciss and I were busy all morning. Mabel, Arthur & Win came about 11.30. Len, Freda & children arrived at 11.55. Carriages came 12.30 & we went off at 12.40. They brought Ciss & Arthur at 12.45 - too early. Smuggled Ciss & Arthur into vestry. Pastor came 12.50 & registration. We were delayed on account of cake not being brought in my carriage. Len went back for cake in D. Young's car & got back to church 1.5, when we were married. Ciss & bridesmaids looked pretty in their dresses. About 50 sat down to reception. Co-op did the catering very well indeed. Cake was good. Ed proposed toast of bride and Percy of bridegroom. Evening spent with music. All departed by 11.45. Ciss & I got into bed at 12.30am.

18th. Did not get up till 9.20.

24th Holiday. Had an hour or so in garden - put in potatoes, peas, scarlet runners, onions, marrows, & a few turnips.

In the face of growing food shortages the Government had promoted a campaign of The Dig for Victory campaign was launched in 1940 to combat food shortages by promoting the planting of allotments in gardens and on public land. The aim was to make Britain as self-sufficient in food as possible. People were encouraged to turn their flowerbeds into vegetable patches and grow fruit and veg anywhere that could be cultivated. Dig for Victory helped evoke the Great British spirit and build the sense that all members of population were involved in the war effort. Before the war Britain imported about 75% of its food. By 1945, 75% of food was produced in Britain and allotment numbers rose from 815,000 to 1.4 million.

30th Spoke to Ed on the 'phone - he has fixed up for Minehead July 3rd-17th.

MAY

2nd. Win. Head married to Ft. Sgt. D.P. Enns, R.C.A.F. Ciss & I went to Ashurst in morning, stayed and saw Win & David married. Ciss & I went to Arthur Head's house & reception. About 30 there.

3rd Heard from Dena.

7th Bought a dozen mounts ex. Arnetts for photos.

8th Ciss looked after Mrs. Webb's baby in afternoon. Bombs dropped on Purfleet.

11th Bishops Stortford. Li came with us. Bought silver plate entrée dish £2-10/-, 1 doz. tomato plants, 7 seed potatoes, soap flakes 5/-, large bottle of malted milk food 2/9d, half a calf's head &c., rhubarb. Had a cup of tea at Haymeads and another with Kennington. Li enjoyed herself. Took her home. Tunisia now cleared of axis except prisoners. Von Arnim captured.

12th Greatest raid on Germany as yet - Duisbourg. 34 bombers lost.

14th Charles (Tom) Parker (BDH) dies in his 69th year.

18th Ciss & I went to C.E. Brains Trust on general biblical subjects.

19th Mr. Churchill made a great speech to the USA Congress & Senate. Deacon's meeting at Iszatts. Everyone except Buggey and Buckingham were there. Berlin bombed by mosquitoes. No losses.

21st One alert but short one. We went downstairs but did not go into shelter.

23rd Ed lent me War & Peace, Tolstoy, vol. 1.

24th Listened to wireless - Empire Day programme. Terrific bombing of Italy, Sicily &c.

26th Wrote to Mrs. Saunders - expressing sympathy at the death of her son Frank - killed in Tunisia with the First Army. Ciss & Elsie went to cemetery taking roses.

JUNE

2nd Raid on East Coast - one brought down, some casualties.

12th Lampedusa falls to the British. Italy loses her three islands.

14th King in North Africa.

25th King back in England.

28th Journey No. 2. Arrived Red Lion Colchester 5.15. Room 57. dinner, beef - not much for 5/-. Had a good walk in Castle Grounds.

JULY

1st. Rowdy lot of Yanks in hotel - probably at dance.

3rd Holiday at Minehead. Train was filled but we got comfortable seats. Pleasant company. A major & his wife had depended on a restaurant car and had brought no food, so had some of our coffee and tarts. We arrived about 4.30 and walked to Mrs. Farrier, Sunnydene, Blenheim Rd.

5th Walked along front and had a read. I bought the Daily Worker.

7th We all went swimming - pool. Swimming gala. We could not get tea so returned to Oakfield. Ciss asked for tea instead of coffee - Ed & Eva disapproved.

8th We all went to Taunton. We took sandwiches but as they were paste Ciss & I went to Moore's Restnt. for lunch. Ed, Li & Eva had the sandwiches near the Museum. Afterwards we met at library. Went to Picture Palace (early closing in town).

9th Walked to Front and sheltered under a tree in heavy rain. Went to North Hill. Ciss & I climbed to the top. Walked about North Hill until 10 o'clock. Eva & Ruth went to the pictures.

10th Invasion of Sicily.

11th Ciss & I had a walk along front, country path through Alcombe to Sunnydene, arriving 10.45.

12th Heard from Dena.

14th 2 motors came 2.30 - Ed, Li, Eva, Mrs. Gifford, Ciss & I went in the large one - a Buick 36 hp Straight Eight. ... We were taken for a lovely drive. Stopped at Luccombe Ch., Homer Woods, Battiscombe, where we had tea in gardens. Visited Silworthy Ch. & cottages.

RED LION HOTEL, COLCHESTER.

The Red Lion Colchester: a 15th century coaching inn, still a working hotel today.

17th Packed bags. Got seats in a Pullman at 9.50. Chatted most of the time - everyone dozed except me. No papers so we mostly talked. Paddington 4.5. Met crowded.

18th (Ashurst) Church 14th Anniversary. Ciss & I went in evening. Ciss had to go without stockings - leg so painful. 1/3 of Sicily in our hands.

23rd Wrote to P.O. A.C. Bist (Germany).

24th Played tennis with Dorothy Maskelyne - 2 singles. Cavalieri Benito Mussolini Resigned.

26th Found a hedgehog in garden by the rhubarb. Wrote to Mrs. Bist, Montreal, & to Mrs. Sutherland - sympathy at the loss of her husband. Hamburg has a terrific bombing.

AUGUST

1st. British start offensive in Sicily. USA bomb Rumanian oil wells.

2nd. Ciss heard from Rene - Cliff left Shetlands last Wednesday.

Hamburg bombed by RAF (4th in 10 days). Berlin being evacuated by women and children.

4th Had to line up for 50 minutes at Romford for bus to get home. Cliff turned up unexpectedly at 10.30pm. Got to bed at 12.5. Ciss 'phoned Len about Saturday and Kew Gardens.

5th Catania taken by Eighth Army. Good war news from Sicily & Russia - Germans having to retreat.

6th Lunched at cafe in Brentwood - rabbit.

7th Kew Gdns 1.35, Len, Freda and children met us. Went over gardens, afterwards to Len's for tea. Cliff came along about 6.35. Cliff left us at Charing Cross to meet a friend.

9th Cliff returned to Shetlands. Ciss & Anne saw Cliff off at Ilford Station, Cliff heavily loaded with fruit &c.

14th Saturday. Len, Freda & Clive arrived 1.25, dinner was soon served. Spent afternoon in garden - took photo. Gave Len photos of wedding.

15th So. coast raided - 6 down. Milan bombed.

17th 50 bombers came over - 11 down. Sicily cleared of Germans.

Our forces commence bombing mainland.

19th News of great victory of USA over Japan - 250 or so aeroplanes destroyed to 6.

22nd Rene sent a box of haddocks - 2 dozen - which we distributed. 8 to Mabel, 6 Holt, 2 Webb, 4 (No. 29) & 4 for ourselves.

23rd Berlin had its heaviest bombing - 700 bombers. We lost 58.

24th Wilf came at 9.15 to Ashurst & went across to Mrs. Browning, & discussed Wilf's children & going to court on Wednesday week.

30th White Horse Hotel (Sudbury). Went into dining room & had a chat - 3 other reps there - one Christian, one R.C. & one man of the world.

SEPT

8th News of Italy's surrender. Ciss's legs getting worse - like phlebites. Ankles swollen &c. Heard that Italy had capitulated - much rejoicing.

10th Rene busy packing for Wales. Germans capture Rome. British & Americans land near Naples.

11th Rene & Bunny depart for Llandidnrod Wells. Germans free Mussolini.

20th Mr. Churchill's return from Quebec. Mr. Churchill spoke for 2 hours & 7 mins in Parliament. dinner 7 o'clock.

26th Smolensk in Russian hands again.

27th Red Lion Hotel Coggleshall (?). Rm 55. dinner at 7 - lamb & stuffed squash - sort of marrow.

28th Met Mr. Luff coming out of the British Restaurant Walton where I had lunch. Had tea at Southgates who gave me some apples. Mr. Penney of Dr. Barnados was there - he had given a lecture & film on the work - lobster &c. Finished 1st vol. Peace & War (sic) Tolstoy.

30th C.A. Hill resigned office of Managing Director. DFH Carr now Chairman, & F.Cozen Shaw managing director.

OCT.

1st Naples in Allies hands.

4th Spent two hours writing to CA Hill, DFH Carr & F.Cozen Shaw.

7th. Ashurst. We had to walk home with a raid on. Longest raid for 18 months. 60 raiders - 15 got through to London. A bomb we heard coming down - did damage to South Woodford.

12th Ciss went with Eva to Jubilee Hospital to have x-ray for gall bladder.

13th Ordered a coat from Caves for £6-6/-, & a suit for myself £8-8/-. Had a nice letter from Miss E.F. Krako on behalf of C.A. Hill. I answered her letter. Did a little writing and destroying letters ex. BDH.

17th Cis & I had a lie-in & got up at 12.15pm. Cis' cistitis (sic) needed warmth & rest.

18th Early morning raid 2.20am-3.10am. We had to get under shelter. Bombs dropped at Highams Park & Hornchurch. Another raid - heavier. Some damage and casualties. No raider down - bad shooting.

23rd Cis went to Seven Kings and registered. I met her outside High Rd. Baptists and we went in and heard D. Graham Scroggie.

29th BDH have imposed on sales reps a form to be filled in every week declaring every call made.

30th Cis & I went to Will Warwicks 6 Wayside Close, Petters Lane & spent afternoon and evening with him and Alice.

NOV

1st Russians have cut off Crimea.

3rd Heard that Ernie was ill again and going away for treatment.

Germany had her biggest bombing - hundreds of American bombers in the day and hundreds of RAF at night - terrible damage.

5th Cis & I went to Pickering & Inglis.... spent £1.0.4d. Rene 'phoned up and said they were returning tomorrow by 10 o'clock train. Kiev taken by Russians.

7th Sunday. Bomb fell in Putney in a dance hall near 2 picture palaces. Several hundred killed.

11th Lunched in Woolworths Bexley Heath. Bunny very poorly - possibly result of immunisation vaccine. Cliff had gone to Market Harboro' - L.A.A. - he is greatly annoyed. Had to get up at 3.45am - terrific gunfiring, no warning - firing at one of our planes. Warwick's men repaired pipes to Ideal Boiler.

18th Cis & I started for Ashurst but distant alert sent us back. Left Cis at Lord Ave. and I started out for Ashurst but local warning caused me to return. All clear so got a bus. Lantern lecture by W. Morogowski, a Russian Jew - spoke on gospel among Jews in Germany.

19th Cliff rang up 11.30 and said he was at L'Pool St. 48 hours leave - he came along about 12.20 & squeezed in with Rene.

29th Sudbury. White Horse. Rm. 6. A pro-Russian here was a peculiar individual in conversation - spoke for nearly an hour.

DEC

1st Graham St. Presentation to C.A. Hill by 600 or so employees of gold cigarette case, & an illuminated address. Mr. Monk, oldest employee under Mr. Hill, gave the present.

8th Rene took Bunny to council school and saw headmistress who arranged for Bunny to go on Monday. Bunny delighted.

9th Cliff went back to Market Harborough.

10th Molly moved into '298.'

23rd 1000 tons dropped on Berlin - 17 lost.

24th Cis & I went round to Rene's - Cliff had a day off but had to leave 3.30pm. Played with Bunny - plasticene &c. Put up fairy lights in dining room, trussed turkey.

25th Went to Rene's with Bunny's gifts in a pillow-slip. Cis & I then went on to Iszatts, usual family circle there. Played 'sorry.' Home 11.45.

27th Rene & Bunny came 12.30 and Len, Freda, Anne and Clive about 1.30. They all enjoyed the turkey, xmas pudding, mince pieces, ginger wine (Freda had sherry). Played with children until 4.30, and Win & Dave came. We six had chinese chequers in the drawing room.

29th Ilford & East Ham. Lumbago still bad but managed journey.

So the Sibley family's 1944 ends with a happy Christmas: he has three grandchildren, Annie, Clive and Graham ('Bunny'), good relations with his son and daughter Len & Rene, and he is close to his elder brother Ed. He has lost his beloved wife of four decades but is still doing his rounds as a travelling salesman, albeit at a reduced rate. His journals of '44 & '45 are missing so the family's celebrations at VE Day are not recorded, but it can be surmised that on May 8th of that year, when German guns fell silent and relief and joy swept through the towns and cities of the nation, that the Sibleys joined in the euphoria of both those who had fought and those on the Home Front.

1946

Certificates of post-war credits

1941-42 - £29-17.

1942-3 - £28-10

Tax payable - £146-17-3.

Preaching engagements - 1946 - 26

JAN

2nd Cis very poorly with Erysipelas.

VE Day, Piccadilly Circus, May 8th 1945.

3rd Went to Severalls Asylum and had a long chat with Morris.

Severall's Hospital opened as a County Asylum in 1910 and was renamed the Essex and Colchester Mental Hospital in the 1930s. In August 1942 the hospital was bombed by the Luftwaffe and 38 patients killed. Closed in 1997, the main building is Grade II listed.

17th Southend. Lunched in Garon's Victoria Parade.

Happily, Sibley is still dining in one of his favourite eateries of the Kent coast, Garons in Southend, the old majestic deco cafe having survived the war.

22nd. C.E. Farewell service for Dorothy Appleby who is going to So. India.

23rd CMH wrote - no more commission, basic salary £580 - £430 + £25 + £125. Heard from Stunt & Sons, & sent them £2/2/- for deeds to be posted to me.

29th Said goodbye to Suffolk men. 6 reps at White Horse.

FEB

1st Polling - Cinemas opening Sundays?

2nd Result of Poll for Cinemas:

For opening on Sundays - 15,613

For not opening on Sundays - 6429.

4th Took House Deeds to Midland Bank.

MARCH

7th Had to spend evening with journeys - I have to continue most of my Kent rounds.

Now aged 68, it seems that the British Drug House has finally seen fit to reduced Sibley's rounds: he no longer roams the Sussex coast, but focused on the home counties north of London - Hertfordshire, Cambridgeshire &c.

25th Mr. Brown came... with electric fitting and got electric clock going. I gave him 10/- for his trouble.

27th Put in new bar in electric fire in bedroom.

30th Saturday. Ed, Li. Eva, Percy Lyle came to tea & spent evening with us. Had 2 games of chinese chequers - Mr. L won 1st, Ed won 2nd.

APRIL

1st Country journey No. 3. Hemel Hempstead. Had a cup of tea Woolworths Harpenden. Got to Old Cock Inn 1945. Room 6. Had a long walk over golf course. dinner 7 - wild duck.

3rd Radlett, St. Albans. Called & saw Mr. C.J. Lewis, 4, The Grove, Radlett. He is 88, wife 86 who was in bed unwell. Mr. Lewis wittery & poorly.

4th Letchworth. ... arrived at Sun Hotel 5 o'clock - room 12.

5th Arrived home 4.30. Everything all correct.

17th Mrs. Hawkins left Rene's. ... got a taxi and deserted Rene leaving for her sister's in Ealing. A blessing in disguise - she is a wicked woman.

18th Cis queued up for fish and kept me waiting for 3/4 hr.

19th Ciss & I went to pictures at Ashurst at 8 o'clock. Crowded. Pictures scenes of Palestine and religious film on Barabbas.

22nd Easter Bank Holiday Monday.

Cis & I went for Rene & Bunny & they came to us for dinner &c. dinner then Bunny & I worked in garden, so that path thro' by shelter & cover was put up. Len, Freda, Anne & Clive came 3.30. Romped in garden. Good tea and a finish at Leg Ball. I took them to Barking Station. Rene & Bunny slept here. A good day's work.

29th Colchester. Arrived Red Lion Hotel (room 35) 5.45. dinner 7 o'clock (Pheasant).

30th Clacton. Had lunch on Frinton front. Had a look at the sea. Tea at Mrs. Southgate's. Mrs. S gave me two cauliflowers. Wrote 5 letters to BDH. 3 changes - D. Moody for Powdell's, Co-op for Privett, Mrs. Knight for Leach.

Frinton on the Essex coast had been at the front line for the duration of the war.

MAY

1st … went to Brethren's meeting. Fred Hock there, builder, who is going to Germany to work in Control Commission.

2nd Gave a ride back to Colchester Mr. Gooch's assistant who lives in Colchester.

The postwar baby-boom is upon us and the Sibleys are no exception to this demographic trend, with Thomas receiving a fourth grandchild, Howard, on May 8th - VE Day - 1945.

8th Rene has a boy. Ruby called in 5.20am and said Rene was in labor (sic). Cis went round at 8.30 and I motored round 9 o'clock and saw Rene & baby. Brought back a few things for Bunny. Bunny here for 2 or 3 weeks. … Dr. Beattie delivered Rene using chloroform. Nurse Guy there.

11th Bunny went to a local party, a Victory Party. Bunny disappointed in having a toothbrush for a present.

12th Cis & I went on to Ashurst. U.N. Witness Team took service. 9 there, one at piano, & 8 gave testimonies. An airman gave a splendid evangelical address. 4 army, 2 naval, 2 airmen.

15th Ilford &c. Took Cis as far as Health Stores. Cis went round to Rene's. Nurse still behaving wickedly. She is either an amazing hypocrite or mental.

16th Cliff demobbed.

At the end of the Second World War, there were approximately five million servicemembers in the British Armed Forces. The demobilisation and re-assimilation of this vast force back into civilian life was one of the first and greatest challenges facing the postwar British government. Aside from the institutional problems of release, returning service-men and -

women faced all kinds of personal challenges on their return to civilian life. Britain had undergone six years of bombardment and blockade, and there was a shortage of many of the basic essentials of living, including food, clothing, and housing. Husbands and wives also had to adjust to living together again after many years apart. One indicator of the social problems this caused was the postwar divorce rate; over 60,000 applications were processed in 1947 alone, a figure that would not be reached again until the 1960s.

Mr C, Stilwell returns to his home in Farnham, Surrey, after being demobbed and is greeted by his wife.

17th Bunny saw his father this afternoon - very excited. Came here in early evening - box of soldiers &c.

18th Cliff sacked Nurse Guy. Went round to Rene's... Cliff gave me a pair of German boots which were not large enough for him.

19th Rene getting on - she came downstairs.

20th Rene's pay book missing.

21st Country journey No.2. … Arrived White Horse Sudbury (Rm. no 3) 5.30. Had a 3 mile walk into country & back.

22nd Abbey (Thaxted). Had a stroll in the park & read some of the 'Fortunes of Nigel,' until 6 o'clock. dinner 6 o'clock - cold beef, spam, salad, marmalade roll & coffee. Had a walk to Audley End in evening - birds, trees & country enrapturing.

25th Met Len, Freda, Anne & Clive at Kew Gdns. … Went over 'Palace.' Went to Len's for tea. Len gave me some rhubarb.

28th Hemel Hempstead. … Had a long walk to a park near Verulamium Museum.

29th. St. Albans & Radlett &c. List of hospitals turned up so I ventured to call at Hill End Hospital and Cell Barnes Mental Colony (difficult to find).

31st Clifff & Bunny came round in evening. Cliff has bought a Jowett £98.

JUNE

1st Dr. Barnados Garden Party & tea afterwards. Cliff left his car in my driveway. Mr. Hunt cannot find my garage key and I have lost the pocket torch Eva gave me years ago.

2nd Found pocket torch.

6th Cis & I went to the Big Tent (94 Romford Rd.) and heard the famous negro spiritual Jubilee Singers - Mr. A. Lyndsay-Gregg preached. Very good meeting.

8th Victory Day.

10th Whit Bank Holiday Monday. Cliff, Rene, Bunny came to dinner. In afternoon we desired to have a drive in Cliff's car. Two punctures, one changed wheel, then the other Cliff had to mend. It rained hard during the performance. Cis & I returned home from Chigwell by bus, Cliff Rene & baby by car.

The Jowett Javelin was an executive car produced from 1946 to 1953 by Jowett Cars Ltd of Idle, near Bradford in England.

12th Wrote to petroleum officer for an allowance of petrol to go to Swanage.

15th Holiday at Swanage. Went via Frimley, Aldershot, Winchester, & saw some of the old spots. Rained hard going through the New Forest. Arrived at 'Centra'… 5.30. Bedroom large & comfortable, next door 'Cranbourne.' Dr. Brookes late of Rainham here & many nice Christian people.

19th Played bowls for the first time in my life. Party of us went out for coffee then went on electric cars - dodgems. Beryl & I partnered and we enjoyed it.

20th Long walk to Studland and back. Had a drive to Lulworth Cove - Cis & I and Mr. & Mrs Scudder. It pelted with rain and we went straight into the tea-place. I borrowed Mr. S's berry (sic) and Cis borrowed Mrs. S's umbrella and we walked to the Cove and had a look. Drove back in the rain and it left off as soon as we reached Swanage. I had a game of darts.

21st I had a swim - 9/- beach hut. The girls gave us a farewell supper in beach hut (No 38). Sandwiches & orangeade. Happy party.

22nd 69 I had many presents which caused a lot of fun. Len sent a card. A very happy birthday.

JULY

26th Heavy storm at home. Terrible damage.

29th Hertford & Ware. Ciss, Rene, Bunny & Howard went with me. Had coffee & lunch in car near Ware Park Sanatorium. Visited Nellie in afternoon. Doris came in. Bunny enjoyed looking at rabbits.

AUGUST

1st. Ed moved to West Mersea.

2nd Sent letters to Two Brewers (Chipperfield), Peahen & Sun (Hitchin).

5th Bank Holiday. Had a driver to Theydon Bois & sat in the forest. Walked about the forest. Bunny captured a frog and took it home.

10th Bunny's birthday. Len, Freda, Anne & Clive came 3 o'clock. Cliff, Rene & babe about 4 o'clock. Cliff took Len & children to '298' to see Bunny's toys &c. Bunny had his birthday cake and cut it himself. Played in garden until 7.45. Had a read of Martin Chuzzlewit.

The shadow of war had not faded as we find Thomas still pursuing his compensation under the War Damages Act of 1941. The wheels of postwar bureaucracy were grinding slow, but there was a happy outcome:

14th Ministry of Works Inspector came to view damage with respect to war damage - passed most of estimate.

18th Cis & I took some flowers and a milk jelly to Mrs. Dilling. She is getting on.

20th Country journey No2. Took Mr. Cole a Parker Pen. Arrived at White Hart Braintree (Room No. 12) 6.30.

21st. Lunched near Thaxted. Scarmer let me have 4 bots. cider. Mr. Porter here, ex-schoolmaster at once grammar school - friend and schoolfellow of Kaper of Dunmow. Schoolteachers from Ipswich here - Miss Jolly &c.

24th Grays & Tilbury. Cis & Bunny went with me. We went on to Thorpe Bay and joined in with the Sunday School on beach. We went on Pier after Tea - rode there but I with Maureen (one of Dr. Barnados girls).

SEPT.

3rd Heard from Council & Ministry of Works passing estimate for war damage - maximum £200.

4th Spent afternoon bringing down books to dining room.

5th Mr. Burite White called and took away licence to get material - at 8.30am.

11th Went to Brethren's meeting. Miss Hobbs going to Congo.

16th Cis went to Town Hall - York Room - about War Damage payment. Unsatisfactory - must go to Leadenhall.

21st Went to Ashurst - debate - 'Is Christianity reasonable?' - agnostic Mr. Bowman, Christ'n Dr. R.E.D. Clark - Editor of Ilford Recorder in Chair.

23rd Take Pat's photo in garden. Pat has put on 4lbs.

It would appear that a certain Patricia Sibley, the three year old daughter of Grace Sibley, has come to stay with Thomas and Cissy. The full story of the child's placement with them is not clear, but it is evident that there is some family dysfunction at play, when the child's mother pays a visit a few day's hence. What is clear is that the youngster is in need.

24th Mrs. Webb gave Pat some of Helen's left-off clothes.

26th Mrs. Heard (Greengrocer) gave Cis for Pat several garments.

30th Cis & Pat went to Ashurst to help with the Harvest Festival. Most went to White's Homes.

OCT

1st Nuremberg sentences started. Doom for some of the leading Nazis.

Paying for their crimes. Nazi Fritz ter Meer receives his sentence at the trials at Nuremberg.

2nd Sent cheque to Eagle Insurance advancing amount to £750.

22nd White Horse Sudbury, Room 5. I sat alone and started reading 'She.'

NOV

12th Ed here for 3 days. Cis & I went to City - bus to Bow Rd., DR to Blackfriars. Visited Pickerings, Morgan & Scott & Evangelistic Crusade Book Salon. Had tea in ABC Ludgate Hill. Past at Rene's. Sent 10/- to British Sailor's Society & King Edward Institution.

21st Grace Sibley & her mother & 2 children came to see Pat, and only stayed a few minutes. Li had come at a moment's notice & Mabel was here. A few unpleasant words between Li & the mother.

Just how Grace Sibley is connected to the main branch of Sibleys is not known, but family discord over the welfare of young Patricia is the chief characteristic of this episode. Perhaps the disruption of war has been the culprit:and absent or dead father, or marital fracture.

24th Pat four today.

25th Whites men started on our bedroom. Filled in forms for Pat's sheets, mattress (Officer in charge - Utility Furniture Office, Board of Trade, Kingsway, Southport, Lancs.).

26th Went as far as Brentwood when I was told my boot of car was open - lorry driver shut it for me. I then discovered my towel & bag was missing. I motored back home thinking it had been stolen but found it in the dining room. Got to Coggleshall 11.30 after stopping for a cup of coffee in car.

29th Mr. E.C. Holt has bought a Vauxhall XII.6. £350. Wrote to Ministry of Family Allowance about Pat's claim.

DEC

1946 ends for the Sibleys with the sad departure of four year old Pat Sibley:

7th Patricia taken away by her mother & Grandpa Pullen. Arrived home 1.10. Grace Pullen with Pat just going as I drove up - little more than goodbye - poor Pat very unhappy. Cis upset over her going.

9th The Board of Trade Inspector called & saw Cis and took away Pat's clothing coupons.

12th C.M. Hill asked me to carry on - no successor yet. Wrote to CMH saying I was willing to continue until a successor is found. Wrote to Bob in reply to his letter - he is retiring. Bought an electric blanket from Smedley & Ralph - £6-5/-.

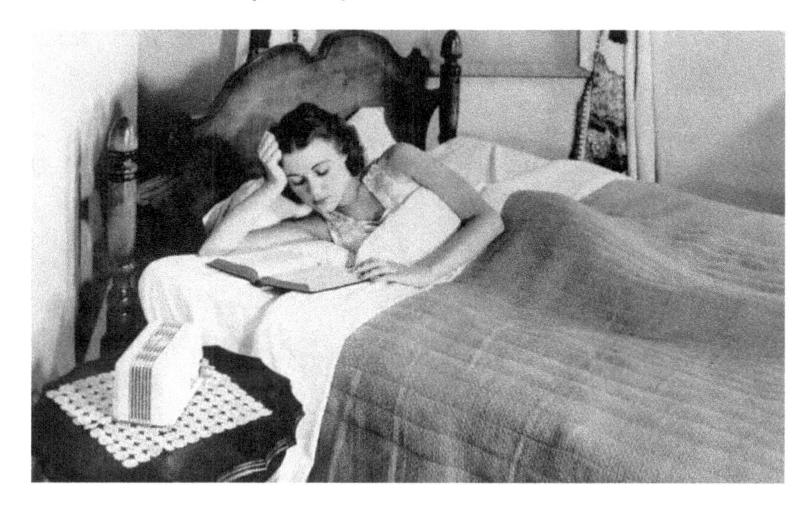

In 1936 the first automatic electric blanket was invented but took off in 1946 in the cold postwar winters.

13th Fog compelled me to walk to Broadway.

19th Ed presented with gold watch& cheque for £62-7/- from BDH.

Traveller's gifts received - I had a silver wristwatch and wallet. Cafe Royal for dinner, 7 o'clock. Very good food - plenty of wine, champagne, whisky. Oscar Shaw gave a good speech. Artistes - singing, Miss Vera Florence & Mr. Walter Midgley. Broke up 10.35.

20th Burites finished war damage.

23rd Cis and I called for Bunny and we motored to Aldridges, Sainsburys. Cliff put up shelves in my room.

25th Cis & I went to Rene's to dinner. Mr. & Mrs. Ringwood came too. Charlie, Molly, Honey & Anthony came to tea and stayed all evening. Had several games and finished with Chinese Chequers. Cis & I walked home about 12 midnight.

MENU

Pâté Maison

Médaillon de Saumon
Braisé Chambord
Petits Pois Clamart
Pommes Persillées

Biscuit glacé Royal
Poire Belle-Hélène

Café

SONGS
by
MISS VERA FLORENCE and MR. WALTER MIDGLEY

O Lovely Night — London Ronald
Arise O Sun — Maud Craske Day
The Flower Song from Carmen — Bizet
Macushla — Dermott Macmurrough
Lovely Maid in the Moonlight from La Boheme — Puccini

30th Hertford. Had puncture in Hertford and changed wheel. Took wheel to Triangle for puncture repair.

31st Cis & I went to Watch Night Service at Ashurst 11.5-12.15.

1947

<u>Retired but still carrying on.</u>

JAN

2nd Cis not very well so didn't go to Ashurst for the Central Asia Pioneer Missionary Trust lantern lecture. Mr. White 'phoned up - wanted cheque £38-5/- for private work. I put him off for a week.

4th Southend. Had coffee in Lantern Cafe, Leigh.

6th Country journey No. 1. Arrived Red Lion Hotel Colchester room 54 5 o'clock. dinner - soup, fish, lamb, cheese on toast.

7th Clacton. Roads not dangerous so went by car. No snow in Clacton. Tea at Southgates. Mrs. Southgate soon going for an operation - cancer in bowels feared.

14th Cliff & Rene went to hear Chopin played at C.E. GRB-Mornay.

17th Went to YLC. Mr. Horace Thackeray's farewell - he is going to Sidmouth (Devon) to live. Olive Simmonds will carry on secretarial work.

20th Red Lion St. Albans rm no. 3. Hotel cold.

21st Had a long walk before dinner to build up circulation to ward off serious cold.

22nd Chatted with husband and wife from Stowmarket in lounge. They went to the pictures& I went to lounge and read.

23rd Hitchin. Arrived at Sun Hotel 5 o'clock - room no. 5. 27th Walked from Gants Hill to Greengate to get warm.

29th Roads frozen and dangerous. Water pipes leading from cistern frozen so we had no water for upstairs.

30th Cliff round and brought fire to thaw our pipes. After he went we discovered the hot water tank was leaking. .. Went round, Cis & I, to Mr. R.S. White, 2 Mellows Rd., (Wanstead), who came later & inspected damage, & promised to come in morning and repair it.

FEB

3rd White, plumber, turned off water from hot-water cistern. New cistern necessary. Got in touch with Haines & Warwick about chimney stack.

12th Electric current cut off from most places between 9-12 & 2-4. Fuel restrictions imposed. Put miner's lamp in loft this evening.

Clacton 1947.

On February 10th 1947 Winston Churchill stood up in the House of Commons to ask Britain's relatively new Prime Minister Clement Atlee why he was imposing power-cuts on the country. Atlee replied: *'Shortage of coal has led to a critical position every winter for the last five years owing to insufficient stocks. During the wax the drastic closing of non-essential industries, the blackout and the imposition of double summer time curtailed demand and enabled the crisis to be overcome.'*

17th Hertford. Cis came with me. We called on Bob and saw Nellie & Doris. Bob keeping busy mending watches &c.

20th Car accident. I knocked over a cyclist on crossroads, Dunmow-Ongar-High Easter. Nose and bike injured of cyclist, mostly deficient. (?) Took him to farm, Dr. Priestly. Reported by letter accident to Dunmow Police. Wrote to CMH about Yarman who is after my job.

MARCH

3rd. Country journey No. 1. Arrived at Red Lion hotel Colchester 5.40 - room no. 60. Town very dark and miserable looking. Hotel fairly comfortable.

4th. Had coffee in Clacton. Bought 'Kidnapped,' R.L.S., 1/-. Mrs. Southgate had had her operation - not cancer. In bed 10 o'clock, read Nicholas Nickleby.

5th Colchester. Lunched in Lasts/ Tea in Regal.

6th Much snow. Snow too thick - so went by bus to Manningtree.

7th Haphazard drive to Brightlingsea at 8-10 miles an hour. Thawed water in tank and we had hot water first time for several weeks. Filled appln. For Suppl. coupons.

12th Called at Electricity Rooms and ordered Hotpoint £4-13-6d, and for man to come and bring new hot plate for stove.

13th Queen's Hotel Grays - attended the Romford Chemist's dinner. Good number there - Wilson of the Pharmaceutical Society was the Guest Speaker, Kemp, late of BDH, now May Baker. Too much speaking. Lady & Gent singers.

17th St. Albans, Red Lion Hotel, rm. 28.

18th Breakfast porridge, kipper - no marmalade. dinner poor - soup, steak pudding, sole, cheese. Sat in lounge - fire out. Gas fire in bedroom.

20th Hitchin. Sun Hotel, rm 16. dinner - minced beef and sultana sponge.

Rec'd petrol coupons for April-July.

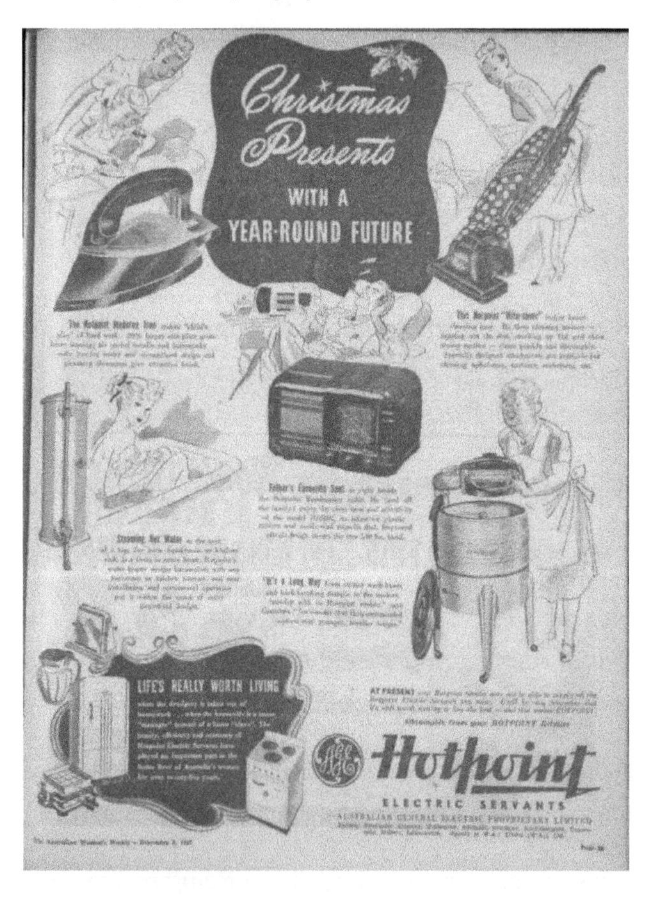

Even though British households were still labouring under rationing and powercuts in the postwar years, they were eager to transform their kitchens into the clean, electric paradises promised by the advertisers. An Australian advert for Hotpoint, 1947, boasting the 'electric servants' of the future.

27th We had sweep for kitchen 3/-.

29th 50 of us went to R. Albert Hall by private bus. Took some sandwiches & cake. Tom Rees - one of his giant Youth Rallies.

APRIL

2nd Mr. Ed. Smith, Romford, came and looked at chimney (41, Hillfort Ave. Romford). 'Phone Romford 5067. War Damage Commission sent me £100 on account.

8th Tired after exertions of yesterday, and we overslept ourselves. Cliff woke us up at 8.50. Smiths men came to do chimney. White Horse Hotel Sudbury 5 o'clock.

14th Commando Campaign starts for Greater London.

21st Mr. MacGregor called about War Damage… He said the War Damage Commission had not given consent & had not passed my claim on. He was writing to Burites.

22nd Mr. MacGregor sent in chimney stack claim, £8-10/-.

24th Rene & Cliff went to Park Hill School - Graham (Bunny) taking part in play - Hiawatha.

MAY

3rd Cis & I went to Ashurst and heard Pastor A.E. Pokovny (Austrian) give his life talk on his conversion from Nazism. Mr. Porkovny came back with us.

5th Mr. Prokovny did not leave here until 10.50am. We went to bed early, 10.20. When undressed Mr. Porkovny 10.30 came to stay the night. Cis went down and got him some tea & biscuits, and got his bed ready. Cliff called at 11pm & Mr. P. opened the door as Cis was in bed.

6th Mr. Porkovny left about 10.30am and went to Dr. Beattie's.

8th Cis went to Barkingside and bought 22/- of sweets for Rene and ourselves. Rene washed Cis's hair. Cliff brought four live fowls.

10th Successor BDH appointed. Heard from CMH that Mr. Ronald E. Benz has been appointed as my successor. Cis & I motored to Mr. & Mrs. Scudders. Had an enjoyable afternoon. High tea - spam, blanchmange and peaches.

13th J.P. Dunbar - BDH - died after an accident in the Royal Surrey City Hospital.

14th. Radlett. Braised steak and had a walk along Harpenden Rd. Petrol up tomorrow.

19th Rene going to move to Leigh. Cis went to to Dr. Beattie's and got a certificate for travelling by car. Cliff went to Leigh-on-Sea and fixed on a house.

20th Wrote to Regional Petroleum Officer, Acton, for coupons for Swanage (300 miles).

26th Bank Holiday Monday. Len & family came 2.50. Children went to park and saw Red Riding Hood.

31st Dena & Freda Overalls went to Rene's from Belgium.

JUNE

7th Dolly Slicker married.

8th Went to Ashurst - Dena, Freda, Cliff, Bunny.

9th Hertford. Called in at Bob & Nellie's. Lily's daughter Jacqueline there. Bob inspected some of Cis's watches.

Blood is thicker than water, and Thomas lends his son-in-la £110 to buy a house in Leigh-on-Sea.

12th Lent Cliff £110.

22nd 70. (years old). Len 'phoned thro' 3pm. Had a great day.

24th Women's outing to Broadstairs.

28th BDH outing to Margate. Ed & I motored to BDH, left car at Wharf Rd. ... 30 coaches - we were in coach 21. Bob and many old friends there. .. Lunch in Dreamland Cafe. Roast beef - not first class. Ginger beer. Four directors did not arrive - accident to car. Ed, Miss Philbrick, Thompson & self went to Birchington, sat on front and had tea. Ed paid. Caught first coach back. ... A fine day.

JULY

1st. Cliff gave me the £110 which he borrowed.

2nd 'Phoned Salari about Mr. Benz - I am to start taking him round. Paid in £50 to Post Office.

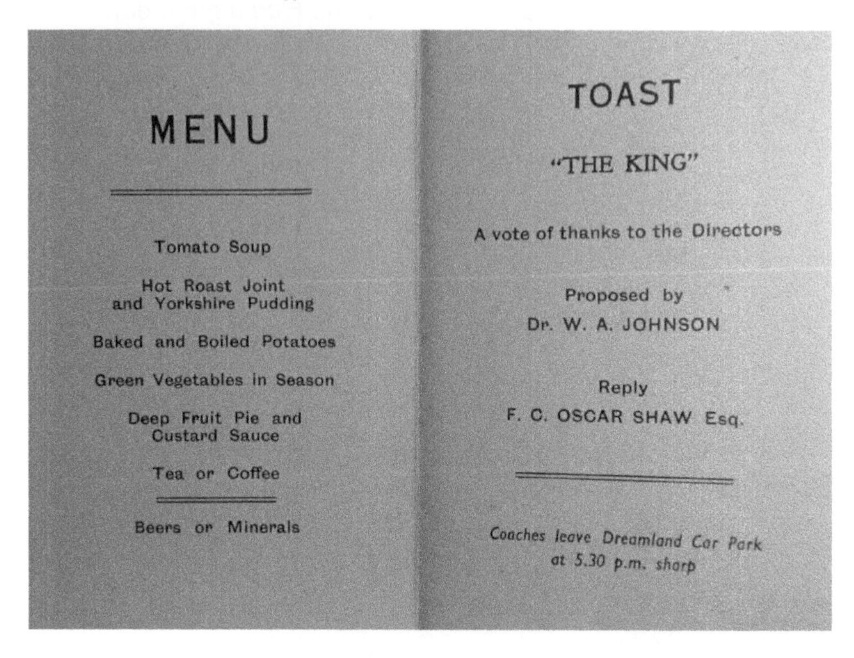

MENU

Tomato Soup

Hot Roast Joint
and Yorkshire Pudding

Baked and Boiled Potatoes

Green Vegetables in Season

Deep Fruit Pie and
Custard Sauce

Tea or Coffee

Beers or Minerals

TOAST

"THE KING"

A vote of thanks to the Directors

Proposed by
Dr. W. A. JOHNSON

Reply
F. C. OSCAR SHAW Esq.

Coaches leave Dreamland Car Park
at 5.30 p.m. sharp

4th Last journey on my own for BDH. Mr. Benz came to see me and stayed 2 hours. I motored him to his home 73 Aukland Rd., & had half an hour's chat with Mrs. Benz.

5th Holiday.... Swanage. We are sleeping at 30 Alexander Rd.

7th 48 of us went by coach to Poole Harbour then by motor launch round to Mess (?) Island to Poole Harbour and back. Wind boisterous and cold but otherwise enjoyable. Had refreshments at Richmond Cafe.

8th Cis & I motored to Wimborne. Had a look over Minster then had a raspberry tea. I bought Cis a green mac - Christmas present. 39/-11d.

11th Cis & I walked past Tilly Whim caves.

13th Motored to Weymouth. Lovely but crowded.

19th (Home). Lots of correspondence. CMH told me to finish up July 31st.

21st Wrote to Insp. of taxes about certificate of post-war credits.

28th Ernie brought Margaret to stay with us for three weeks.

30th. Called for Benz 9.45. Left him at King George Hospital. We had to consult a skin specialist.

31st Last official journey for BDH. Called for Benz 9.10.

AUGUST

1st. Retired. Called for Benz 9 o'clock and took him round. Benz's first day. Introduced him to some old customers.

And so Sibley's final day as a commercial traveller for the British Drug Houses arrives, a job he has been doing since 1909.

2nd. Epping &c. Called for Benz 9.30. Saw all but one customer. Had cheque for £10 15/- for war damage.

3rd. No Sunday School on account of Infantile Paralysis.

4th Spent whole day clearing out shed and clearing out garage. Mr. Drew came round this morning and arranged to have garage at 10/-, allowing me to have steps in it &c.

5th Holiday in Leigh-on-Sea. 5, Canonsleigh Crescent.

6th Took Graham & Margaret on beach. Cliff finished putting the roof on his car. Cliff took Rene & I for a ride round Shoebury and back, also visiting their 'next' house *in Walker Drive.*

7th We had an RAF rubber dinghy, so what with a polo ball, 2 motor tyres and dinghy we enjoyed our swim. Finished reading Edgar Wallace's Room No. 13.

11th Southend by bus. Took children to Play Fair. Mgt. Graham & I went on Jigsaw Railway, Margt on Zoo Railway, and Graham on Dive Bomber.

19th Finished clearing Shutter Cabinet. Study in too much disorder to commence studying for Sunday evening.

SEPT

9th C & I went to Westminster (bus to Bow Rd.) Walked thro' St. James Park to Piccadilly - looked at shops. Tea in Kardoma - quite good.

10th Edgley's van called for shutter cabinet and left cheque for £8.

15th Cliff took us to Leigh.

17th Bought 'Coral Island' for Bunny also birthday card for Clive. Called for Bunny and went on to Walker Drive but had no key.

18th Coffee in Rectory Grove Cafe.

19th Went to JH Parkes (old customer in Leigh), taking 1.4 of tea, he gave me 2oz Sugar. Benz was there yesterday in a car.

25th War damage repairs commenced by C.E. Potter.

26th Mrs. Drew paid 4 weeks for garage - £2.

OCTOBER

2nd I have a poisoned left thumb.

6th Gordon Harris came round to verify tomorrow's motor trip.

7th Went to Halstead - bought 4 ciders. Went on to Cambridge & then Parminster (?) - Mrs. H's sister, looked over factory. Had a high tea of apples and cabbages given to us.

8th. Mrs. M. Brown, Percy Ward, Grosvenor Hospital for Women, 2.30. She is getting on & very cheerful. 4 other beds - 3 occupied. The Hospital is in St. Vincent's Square, off Horseferry Rd. Had cup of tea in Express Dairy.

10th Cliff bought kitchen cabinet, £10 & took away broken top and sheet of asbestos.

11th Mr. & Mrs. Benz and baby came at 4 o'clock… Mr. B. took away car oil, stationery, duplicate key FYX255.

15th Ernie Ringwood, wife & baby called, said Cliff was in trouble over house.

22nd Potten finished decorating.

24th Mr. Potten bought in receipted bills - I paid him £6-19-5/-. War damage £63-19-5, and private work £20. Cis worked hard until bedtime as Rene is coming tomorrow.

NOV

3rd. Went to East Ham, got frying pan from Trading Stamps shop.

14th Farewell to my remaining teeth. Went to CH Blackmore and had my remaining four teeth out. He used cocain (sic). Walked home thro' park and got home before Cis.

15th Mr. & Mrs. Benz came for us at 3.00pm. .. Chatted until 8.30 then we had two hours television.

We do not know if this was Sibley's first taste of television, but at 8.30pm on November 15th 1947 when they settled in front of a set in their friends the Benz's front room they were treated to a star-studded 'review of twenty five years of television,' with Frank Muir, Doris Hare, Vera Lynn and the Windmill Girls. Whether the Windmill Girls appealed to the confirmed Baptist in Sibley is not clear, but this cavalcade must have made an impression: resisting the purchase of a TV - a rarity in 1947 in any household (in 1947 only 15,000 sets existed in the entire country), they succumb in the years consequent to the Coronation in 1953.

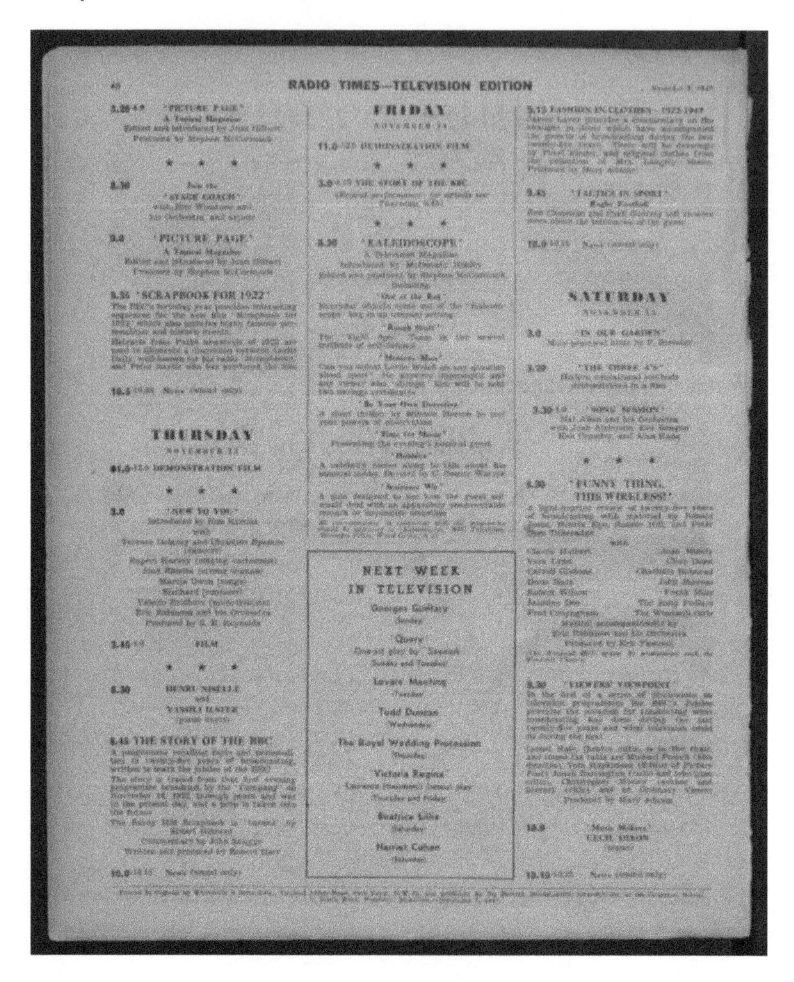

RADIO TIMES—TELEVISION EDITION

'PICTURE PAGE'

'SCRAPBOOK FOR 1922'

THURSDAY

FRIDAY

'KALEIDOSCOPE'

SATURDAY

'FUNNY THING, THIS WIRELESS!'

NEXT WEEK IN TELEVISION

Georges Guétary

Query

Lovers' Meeting

Todd Duncan

The Royal Wedding Procession

Victoria Regina

Beatrice Lillie

Harriet Cohen

17th I padlocked outside lavatory. Heard from Ed - Fred Warwick very ill.

18th Potten's plumber fitted Burlington cistern in lavatory. Wrote a letter to GPO about Xmas employment.

20th Princess Elizabeth married to Lt Mountbatten.

Picture - Brighton photo - fell off wall but did not break glass.

22nd Re-elected Deacon.

28th Got on with fence. Posts were placed and cemented in.

It is clear that Sibley is not easing into his retirement with stoicism: a certain restlessness characterises his early 70s, in which he keeps himself busy with physical activity:

29th Finished fence. Cleaned old mangle.

DEC

4th Visited GPO and I was accepted for some P.O. work from Dec. 15th. I refused night work.

5th Len 'phoned up this morning. I took Mabel's mangle to pieces and thoroughly cleaned it.

14th Gants Hill Tube Station open.

23rd I made a claim for £10 on Eagle Ins. Coy for burnt eiderdown quilt.

25th Cliff & Rene gave me braces.

27th Cis, Graham & I went to Southend. Searched about for bread and got some in a Jew's shop in York Rd. Bussed it back. Dinner goose & Christmas pudding. Tea, consequences. Listened to play on the wireless.

1948

Income Tax (E.G.George & Co.) 52.54 High Holborn WC1. Tel. CHA 514.

M. Insurance No. ZH364191

This mention at the top of the diary for 1948 of income tax relating to employment with 'E.G. George' indicates that far from slipping into old age and retirement with acceptance, Sibley's drive has impelled him to go back to work.

JAN

3rd Stayed in bed with Cis who was not well. Cis went to The Drive and saw Dr. Beattie who gave her some sulphonamide (?).

5th Cis & I went from Gants Hill - Cis did not like the escalator - to Cannon St. Walked along, looking at shops, to Kardoma, Piccadilly. Went to Westminster Cathedral for meeting of W.E.A. Dean of St. Paul's in chair.

7th Potton put in loft tank.

9th Did little worthy of note. Rene wanted to come on the 17th but Len cannot manage it.

13th Read 'David Copperfield.' Heard from Ed.

21st Cis & I walked to Barkingside - Dr. Barnardos Homes, & interviewed Miss B. Cole (Trefoil: Village Homes) for church membership. Ed came at 8.30 and we played Kan-U-Go. Did not reach bed until the morning.

31st Fred Warwick died.

FEB

6th Wrote to Montpelier Hotel New Brighton for 2 rooms Feb 28/29 for Tom A. & I.

11th Ash Wednesday. Mr. Hall, solicitor, 'phoned up about putting up a locum, Mr. Wakeley, who is living in Dorset, for six weeks. We said yes. Had pancakes. 13th Cis busy preparing tarts & jellies for tomorrow.

14th Saturday. Cliff, Rene, Graham & Howard. Len, Freda, Annie & Clive. Fish pie and Xmas pudding. Played 'Stations.'

16th I started walling up the shelter. Not an easy job.

Across the country people were now bricking up their old air-raid shelters. Once an ubiquitous sight in many a back garden, overgrown with brambles or walled up to stop infestations from rats, it is now an extreme rarity to spot the remnants of the old Andersons.

23rd G.R. Beasley-Murray farewell (Ashurst).

26th Mr. Wakeling came to stay with us. He brought some rations and emergency card. He was a major in the army. He is a solicitor's clerk doing locum work for Mr. Hall solicitor who is going into hospital tomorrow.

The Sibleys were not alone in postwar Britain in taking in lodgers or 'paying guests.' This was a larger demographic spike. With hundreds of thousands of war widows populating the suburbs and the cities, vacant rooms in one's house became the norm, and lettings agencies seized on this vast pool of accommodation for tenants.

27th Wallasey by ferry & then to Montpelier Hotel New Brighton. Egremont B.Church. Room 14, very cold.

MARCH

23rd Sent Len his birthday card. Cis & I went to Barking Tabernacle. Saw film 'Palestine 2000 Years Ago.' 'The Day's Work.'

25th Arrived 7 Walker Drive (Leigh - Rene & Cliff's home) 4.15. Cliff finished making up our bedstead (divan) & I had a long walk all the way to East Leigh Bapt. Church.

27th Saturday. Cliff went to work. Cis, Rene & I went to Broadway.

Graham went to his Cubs, Cis to Food Office & I to Atkinson. Met Cis - she got meat & Bermalen loaves.

APRIL

1st. Visited Blackmore, got new set of teeth, plastic, £30.

2nd Cliff 'phoned this morning saying Rene was very poorly, symptoms of appendicitis. Cis 'phoned and fixed up Dr. Beattie for tomorrow morning.

3rd. Cliff, Rene & family came at 9.15. Rene very poorly. Dr. Beattie diagnosed appendicitis & arrangements were made for operation. Cliff & I & Howard took Rene to Maycroft Nursing Home. Rene had her operation 9.30. Satisfactory.

4th Cis & I visited Rene at Maycroft 3-4pm. She is fair - taking nothing yet, lying flat &c. Cis & I and Wakeling went to Ashurst. About 200 there.

6th Cis went to Dr. Beattie's and got her milk permit. Had to take Howard with her.

7th Took Graham to Sth. Kensington. Nat. History Exhibition. Geological & Science Exhibition. We both left at 3.30 with 'thick' heads. Had a cup of tea in Lyons - Graham left his. He wanted lemonade but there was none. Got home 5 o'clock. Cliff was here - he'd seen Rene who was making progress.

14th Rene came out of nursing home.

16th Cis went to town hall and got Rene's emergency form and lost it (stolen in Sainsbury's). Had to fill in another form for another.

22nd Mr. A.G. Wakeling left for Verwood. We were sorry to say goodbye.

24th Rene, Graham & Howard went home.

27th Leigh. Sat on seat (on front) for 2 hours and read 'Bandy Loo,' C.E. Roberts.

MAY

5th. Len 'phoned through - he wants our mattress, £2-10/-.

8th Howard Two Years (old). Cis went to Gants Hill & sold flags for Princess Elizabeth Children's Day.

Children's Day is a commemorative date celebrated annually in honour of children, whose date of observance varies by country. In 1925, International Children's Day was first proclaimed in Geneva during the World Conference on Child Welfare. Since 1950, it is celebrated on June 1st in many countries. Now somewhat faded from consciousness in Britain, it is still celebrated in other countries, particularly Japan, Russia and Turkey.

10th Len 'phoned about lorry calling for mattress.

11th Tunnel Cement Co. came with some cement and sand from Len & took away mattress & plaques. Heard from War Damage Commission - Potten had not included license.

14th Spent all day in garden. Cis went shopping in afternoon & treated us to ice cream which we had in garden with our tea. Evening spent quietly. Had hot bath.

22nd Cis NHS payment to date £1-4/-.

26th Cis & I went to Geary's (?) school and witnessed Boy's Brigade Display.

27th Cis received first payment under new scheme of NHI Sick Benefit.

31st Holiday at West Mersea.

JUNE

3rd Ed and I played billiards. A nice change altho' I know nothing of the game.

7th. Bus to Colchester. We went into Castle grounds. Ice cream & banana in Refreshment Rooms. Tea - Eva (Ed's daughter) again very offensive - gave a bad atmosphere.

The Boys' Brigade was founded in Glasgow on 4th October 1883 by Sir William Alexander Smith. From this one Company formed in Scotland the BB has grown in to a worldwide movement having worked with millions of children and young people for well over a century.

Finally in June of that year Sibley received some good news from the Government:

12th War Damage paid in full, £63-19/-5d.

14th Heavy storm. Cis at home making my birthday cake was scared.

16th F.C. Oscar Shaw's funeral (BDH).

22nd 71. Still going strong.

23rd Troops unloading ships with perishable goods.

28th Cis went to Town Hall for new ration books. Picked sufficient peas for dinner.

30th Dock Strike over.

JULY

2nd Heard from Ernest J. George & Co. Ltd.

3rd BDH office outing. Lovely day at Eastbourne. Lunch - the Devonshire Lagoons. Tomato soup, roast goose, strawberry melba). Short speech by GM Guthrie - veterans called up by name and clapped. Went to Beachy Head, played cricket (tennis ball). Tea at Beachy Head Hotel.

5th New Health Act. Cis & I went to Ashurst Drive Women's outing to Felixstowe. Messrs Adams, Ashbolt, Fraser & self were the males. We had a good lunch at the Alexandra Cafe on the front. Cis & I had a long walk looking for town - missed it and came back by seafront.

The National Health Service Act came into effect on 5th July 1948. The Act provided for the establishment of a comprehensive health service for England and Wales. There was separate legislation produced for Scotland and Northern Ireland. The first Minister of Health was Aneurin Bevan MP.

9th Cis & I went to Victoria Station and saw Edwin off to Jamaica. At Samuelson's Garage, Southdown coach took the ship 'Jamaica Producer' company to West India Docks. Cis & I waved him goodbye. Took 2 snaps.

14th Graham - 10 Years. Engaged by E.J. George & Co. (Pharmaceuticals). Got a bag and went off to E.J. George's 329

High Holborn & interviewed. They put my name down for stock-taking and engaged me for some propaganda work doing whole of Essex commencing Sept. 6th. Went to BDH and had lunch with Casswell. Saw some BDH outing photos.

Tired of retirement, Thomas Sibley went back to work on 14th July 1948, for a company founded in 1926 and which still exists today - E.J. George Pharmaceuticals, specialising in the stock-taking for pharmacies.

17th Visit to Len. We purchased a fish & a tie for Len's birthday. Arrived at Len's 12.55. We all went to the London Areodrome. Saw some planes come and go. Rain drove us in to the Marque Pavilion for tea.

The growth of the airport at Heathrow from a rural lane mentioned in 1410 to the world's largest airport was almost complete, though by 1946 The passenger terminal was still an area of army tents and duck-boarding next to the south side of the Bath Road. Its expansion was largely a process of demolition and encroachment, with compulsory purchases by the Air Ministry causing controversy and some resistance. Some relics of the old village of Heathrow lingered well into the 1980s, such as the Bricklayer's Arms pub, but several farms and whole swathes of houses fell under the wrecking ball in the pursuit of progress. Its history had not been without human tragedy of a more dramatic nature - on 2nd March 1948 a Douglas DC-3C of the Belgian airline Sabena crashed at London Airport, London, United Kingdom, killing 20, the airport's first major disaster. By the time of the Sibley's visit in July Runway 1 was ready for use but the old Heathrow village area's country lanes were still visible, and Perry Oaks farm and some houses along Hatton Road were still there.

20th War damage completed except gate. Dug up potatoes, put in

Brussells, Broccoli & Savoys that Len gave me.

24th Cis heard from BMS.

25th Sent periodicals to Len.

From farmland & hamlet to military airfield to passenger airport - a Bristol Brabaxon comes into land at London airport in the late 40s.

AUGUST

6th (Holiday in Leigh). Wrote to Ed - 11, Cargill Ave., Halfway Tree, P.O. Jamaica.

9th About 3am I got up but because dizzy fell back on bed and then on chair and hurt coccis (sic). Cis frightened.

10th We all went to Leigh Station and saw Freda Averals off to Tilbury to meet George Slicker who lives in Snodland. Cis, I & Graham played Chinese chequers. Graham had a lovely win which excited and thrilled him.

12th ... all went by bus to Chalkwell. Nothing doing, so we sat about, looked at bowlers, & returned by tram to Leigh. Had a read of R.Bruce Lockhart's 'Come the Reckoning.'

13th I had nice walk skirting Belfair Woods. Afterwards we all went to Leigh Broadway & I bought some socks, (Rene treated me to one pair - birthday present), & Cis & I bought Rene a cup and saucer, a breakfast cup for ourselves and a perspex tea-strainer from Woolworths.

14th Had a read of 'Treasure Island' before passing it on to Graham.

20th Cis' leg paining so I gave it a massage. Heard from Ed in Jamaica.

24th Holiday in Cornwall. Paddington - pleasant journey to Truro. Mr. & Mrs. Mason met us. Went by car to Mrs. Blarneys, Carne Farm, Veryan. Went to bed 10pm. Separate beds.

25th No electricity. Carne beach in afternoon. Climbed up 'Goat's Path' on homeway. Supper own cured bacon - too thick for us and we could not eat much and felt sickly. Mr. Mason lent me some books on Cornwall. We are back to oil lamps and candles.

26th Captain and Mrs. Lang came by car from Prothcatho to tea - very nice people. Capt. in army in India, and then a volunteer missionary.

29th Went to beach and read The Roadmender.

SEPT

1st Blackberrying… filled out biscuit tins. dinner - rabbit pie and apple tart. Gave Mr. Mason The Roadmender, & Quiller-Couch short stories.

2nd End of Cornwall holiday. … Got final payment of War Damage £11-9-9. Income tax rebate £19.

3rd. Got form P46 for E.J. George & Co. Got a Ribena at Finlay's. Spent afternoon and evening considering E.J. George's businesses for sale, & 'stock-taking' calls and journeys &c.

6th Started for E.J. George. Barking, Ilford. … Dr. Foster gave me a pleasant interview & stopped about 40 mins. 4 orders.

9th About 2am a girl opposite (Phillips) cried out - molested by a man. Cis went to Barkingside, had lunch with Mabel, and for her ration of sweets.

11th Cheque from E. J. George - £5.18/-.

14th Southend, Shoeburyness. Had a pleasant day with old friends.

15th Laindon, Canvey Island &c. Had a good lunch at a cafe in So. Benfleet. Got to Rene's about 4.15. Cliff… delayed by getting out of petrol and pushing car for some distance.

20th Colchester journey for E.J. George. Met Benz at Newbury Pk. Garage. And went with him to Ingatestone. Got 2 orders. Arrived at Red Lion Hotel - room 54 - at 5.20. Benz & I had dinner. We adjourned to lounge. I read and he did some BDH work.

21st Lunched at Walton, Portobello Hotel.

28th Dorking. Took stock with Mr. Wynne at Mr. Frith's shop.

OCT

3rd Anne Twelve (Len & Freda's daughter).

4th Edgware, to Derek Clark Ltd. 73 Station Rd. 4 stock takers. Cis got me 1949 diary.

7th Oval & on to Wyndham Rd. - McConnell & Bretts where Wynn and I took stock. Lunched at 'The Horns,' Kennington.

8th Edgware, Derek Clarks. Lunch at Green Man. Wynn played bar billiards.

12th Blackheath. Grimwade and Hayward, 43 Shooters Hill Rd. … Badly blitzed pharmacy, drafty (sic) and wants pulling down. Mr.

Hearne... phoned in afternoon saying they did not want me to help in stock-taking at present, & I could go travelling again.

15th Cap'n P.N. Correy sentenced - 5 years.

Brentwood. Chat with Langley. Jim is in college tho' not officially demobbed. Cis visited Dr. Heston (Beattie out - possibly in court for Captain Correy).

18th Ed's return from Jamaica. Ed arrived safely home in SS 'Eros.'

24th C.A. Hill died - 74.

The death of Charles Alexander Hill in 1948 was the end of an era. This remarkable tribute in *Nature* magazine from 1943, the year Hill retired, bears testimony to this giant of 20th century British industry:

MR. CHARLES ALEXANDER HILL has retired from his position as chairman and managing director of the British Drug Houses, Ltd. He has been succeeded by Dr. F. H. Carr, who becomes chairman of the company, and Mr. F. C. Oscar Shaw, who becomes managing director. Mr. Hill represents the third generation of a family of wholesale druggists, his grandfather's firm dating back to the reign of George II ; he has done perhaps more than anyone else to establish a sound and progressive fine chemical industry in Great Britain and can look back on a business life of outstanding achievement. He was the moving spirit in an amalgamation of drug firms some thirty-five years ago, thus forming an organization large enough to undertake scientific research which led to the development of the manufacture of fine chemicals in a state of high purity for use in medicine. Hill actively encouraged this development on its scientific side, and among other things introduced during the War of 1914-18 the manufacture of pure reagents for use in analysis, microscopic stains, etc., and went on to supply chemicals of high quality for research purposes, displacing

Kahlbaums from the position they had hitherto occupied. For this alone British science owes him a debt of gratitude. Later, the progress in medical science led to the introduction of pure hormones, vitamins and chemotherapeutic products. The production of these by British Drug Houses, Ltd., and the spirit of adventure shown by the firm, have won for it as the leading firm in the fine chemical industry a world-wide reputation.

- Nature, 16th October, 1943.

26th Col. Ralph Key Harvey died aged 83.

NOV

4th Benz waiting for me at Hatfield. Had a pleasant trip round Hitchin. Got to Cock Hotel 5 o'clock - rm no 3, comfortable. Had a pot of tea in the Cinema.

8th E16, E13, E15 journey. Had nice chats with several old customers.

11th E1 journey. Mixed reception. Met no one I knew, mostly Jews. Had coffee in ABC Whitechapel. Lunched in ABC Holborn. Visited E.J.George & Co. & had a chat with Mr. Hume. Mr. Dixon (acct) referred to his son who was killed in war and was at BDH.

14th Princess Elizabeth has a son, 7lbs.

15th Ed came for night. Gave him 'World Chaos & Remedy' and Li Desk Calendar for Xmas.

16th Ed spoke at Victoria Hall on Jamaica.

19th Finished up for the time being with E.J. George & Co.

28th Started coal fires.

30th From 4-6.30 I spent on sticking 1944 photos in album.

DEC

1st. Visited GPO and fixed temporary work. Sorting 1-9pm. 2 days at Clements Rd. and 5 at Horns Rd. Visited Bodgers. Millets - gloves, 19/11, socks 3/11. UD co. for brown loaves. (United Dairies). Walked from Gants Hill. Stuck in some photos from 1945. Read 'World Chaos Root & Remedy.' SS Queen Elizabeth sailed after 13 days delay.

4th Tax Rebate for £10-5/-.

8th Phone Mr. Rushton (E.J. George Ltd.) for NH Insurance card.

15th Ed & I went to Church House, Kingsgate (Press?), & I bought 'Recovery.' Ed & I went to Foyles and bought a few books. Went to BDH & chatted to Casswell. Held their meeting in a church room where Ed spoke on his Jamaica visit and work. Had a good lunch in canteen - lamb and jam pudding. Saw fellow-travellers who are having their meetings this week. Ed saw film, 'Atom Bomb,' at Church Ho.

18th E.J. George & Co's dinner. Cis & I went to… Beale's Rest., 368 Holloway Rd.. 5 toasts. Home 10.50. A very happy evening. Some remained to dance.

20th Started for P.O., Drill Hall, Horns Rd. Had quite a busy day,. sorting, facing, tying up &c. Supper & ret'd rather tired at 11 o'clock.

24th Went to P.O. Horns Rd. and finished work for this Christmas. The Post Master made a little speech thanking the auxiliary workers.

25th Had a letter from CMH objecting to me calling for E.J. George on my old ground or mentioning BDH. I wrote to him. Cliff, Rene, Graham & Howard arrived about 12.45.

27th Cliff met Len & family at Gants Hill. Usual excellent dinner. Played games with children in afternoon. 10 little nigger boys, House &c. Len, Freda, Anne & Clive left at 8.30.

31st Finished reading The Deerslayer, Fennimore Cooper.

1949

JAN

3rd Went to John Harley Ltd., 25 Queensway, Bayswater. Helped stock. Lunched in Express Dairy Westbourne Grove.

5th Heard from CMH. Quite cordial but he insists I give up travelling. I replied.

10th Went to JS Tunicks Homerton. Lunch in workman's cafe, steak pudding 1/8 - not good enough.

11th Tunicks. Lunched at The George, Glyn Rd.

15th Heard from CMH - had permission again to call on customers.

22nd Heard from Hume - nothing for me now for some weeks.

26th Cis & I went to Selfridges. Went on 4th floor for lunch.

27th Cis & I went to the auction sale of Mrs. Brown's furniture & house. We did not buy anything. House went for £3000.

31st Cis paid rates £18.7.4., & coal bill £2-6/-.

FEB

11th Finished cutting out Cis' Chinese girls for Sunday School. I stuck wood on the feet of three Chinese girls to make them stand.

15th Cis & I went to C.E., saw a film 'David Livingstone.'

19th Charrington delivered a ton of coals, £4.

MARCH

2nd Wrote to St. Ives booking holiday June 4-18.

4th Went on special journey for E.J. George - NW district. Snowed or rained all day - cold and cheerless, got feet wet. Lunched in ABC Golders Green, a lot of walking and waiting for buses & could only make 7 calls - one order.

23rd Spent evening by fire. Read some of 'Our Mutual Friend.'

APRIL

1st Went to Lawrence's Camberwell Green and helped Wharton & Parkin to finish the stock. All done except windows. Had a fine lunch at the Leopolds - Italians.

6th Budget - only disadvantages.

7th Went to McEwen's, 17 Craven Rd., and helped Orme take stock. Had lunch in Italian cafe opposite.

16th Southend. Had ices at Rossi's.

18th Bank Holiday. Thorpe Bay, sat on beach. Finished reading 'Water Babies.' Cis, Rene & Graham played Old Maid.

22nd Mabel said Arthur has TB - lung to be inflated.

In Britain in the 1940s 80,000 cases of pulmonary tuberculosis were diagnosed each year. treatment for patients suffering included little more than prolonged bed-rest and fresh air. In 1943 Selman Waksman discovered Streptomycin, first given to a human patient in November 1949, but it still remains the world's deadliest infectious-disease killer.

24th Went to Mansfield Rd. Nursing Home to see Arthur Head -

Mabel there. Arthur getting on nicely.

MAY

4th Cis went out in evening selling flags for Princess Elizabeth Day.

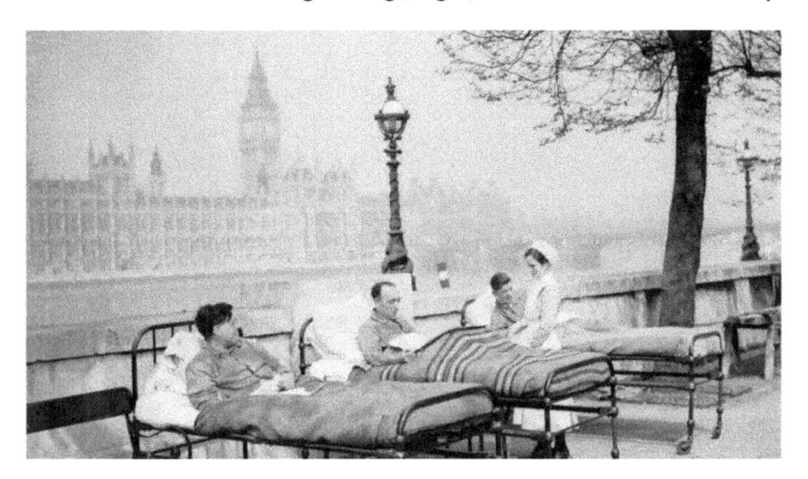

28th Outing to Clacton.

JUNE

4th Holiday at St. Ives Cornwall. Arr. St. Ives 5.45. Taxi to Trecastle Hotel.

St. Ives' transition from remote Cornish fishing village to seaside holiday resort began in 1877 with the opening of the branch line of the Great Western Railway that threaded, and still threads today, for it survived the Beeching Cuts of the Sixties, through the gorse and rock of the Cornish cliffs from St. Erth to St. Ives bay. Its reputation as an artist's colony had not begun with Ben Nicholson and Bernard Leach in the 1020s, for Turner himself had discovered the town as far back as 1811; and when supreme sculptress Barbara Hepworth settled there in 1939 and the *troika* school of pottery was founded, the artistic character of St. Ives was fully formed. Quite remarkably, art historian James Fox has described this 'mid-century renaissance' thus: the St Ives artists *'went on to produce some of the most exhilarating art of the twentieth century... for a few dazzling years this place was as famous as Paris, as exciting as New York and infinitely more progressive than London.'*

St. Ives Harbour, by Sidney Lee. At the time of the Sibley's visit, the Cornish town was already a thriving artist's colony as famous as Paris.

10th The Country Kitchen, Zennor. Bus packed.

11th Went on the sands and played cricket.

12th Dove St. Hall Brethren. Hall full. Went on the Island to see sunset. Very enjoyable party - back 11.5.

5th Zion Church, Countess Huntingdon Connexion. Cis & I sat on hot sands in the afternoon.

13th Cis & I went by bus near to Penzance & walked to Mount St. Michael. Went over the Castle and Chapel. Went by motor boat to Penzance. Some of the girls made me an apple-pie bed. Much laughter.

14th Lizard's Head. Bought ice cream and stone lighthouse for Rene. Walked to Kynance Cove. After tea and photos by Mr. Sleigh in lounge we played a court case. I was the defendant, accused of wandering without visible means of support and deserting wife, and searching for angel face. Much laughter. Mr. Darke was Judge.

16th Porthminster Beach. 2 rounds on putting green.

22nd 72. (birthday). Cis bought a cow's heel near Caves & when home found that it smelt sour. Took it back - shop shut.

23rd. Victoria Station and Cis & I walked to Tate Gallery and spent 2 hours looking at the paintings. Went by d. Rly to Temple and there to Kardoma where we had tea.

25th Church Anniversary - 20th.

A nostalgic revisiting to the poppy fields of Cromer evokes a rare foray into emotion for the ageing Sibley.

30th (Norfolk journey. Royal Hotel Norwich). Crowded bus to Cromer - standing all the way. Was able to have a look at Cromer, full with many memories - poppy fields glorious in colour. Made me think of 1902 when Annie became Poppy. West Runton, where I had lunch. Sheringham - had a long chat with Mr. & Mrs. Jordan.

JULY

6th Went to Diss. 3 calls, all very pleasant. Shopping week. I was stopped & informed that I was 'Mr. This Week' and given 10/- voucher.

7th Back to Norwich, 'Heathcote.' Railway Mission - 7 there, I made 8. Old railwayman gave a rambling statement on the Resurrection.

13th Wells. Saw a chemist - Kingborn - who knew me at Tilbury 36 years ago. Bus to Burnham Market. Another rep - Clements, Gillette blades, had lunch there and took me to Hunstanton. Mr. W. Clements, 22 Broadhurst Gdns., Thorpe Bay.

AUGUST

8th Had a walk on front near old Leigh Station. Graham and I went on pier and had a good view of the Viking boat. Stayed on pier until 9.15. Beautiful illuminations.

12th Cliff & Rene went off on their own to Hastings and Cis looked after the youngsters.

13th Took Graham out, went over the Golden Hind replica of Drake's famous ship.

15th Cliff sold his camera, £9, and decided to have a few days holiday so they went to Fairlight Glen, Hastings. Booked seats for Herne Bay tomorrow. Wrote to Len.

17th Walked to Hadleigh Castle through woods and back.

18th I went by bus to A.J.J. Bakers, Thundersley & had a chat with him. He has no relatives - 74 - just lost his son Jack who was killed in a motor accident, and is on his own with heart trouble.

19th Home again. 22nd Cliff came 8.50 bringing Graham to stay a week or so. Cis did her washing and Graham went next door with the children, also in the park.

24th No 8 bus to British Museum arriving 2.5pm. Spent 1 1/2 hours there. Went by bus to Marble Arch & walked to Madam Tussauds, spent 1 1/2 there. Chamber of Horrors 7d each. Graham enjoyed it. Home 7.45, tired thirsty & hungry.

25th Graham went to play with Maureen Smith (103 The Drive).

27th We started for Twickenham 10.20 (Len's). We all went to London Airport for 2 hours.

SEPT

7th Women's outing to Felixstowe. Coach misdirected to The Drive and we started at 9 o'clock instead of 8.30. I had a swim alone whilst others went to lunch. Water lovely. Had a motor boat trip round the bay which was delightful. Tea in cafe near cinema, very good.

9th Wrote to William Collins & Co. 10-12 Bow St., & sent back 'Mr. Midshipman Easy' which had the wrong pages bound in it.

15th Cis 55.

17th Cis & I went to the Mildmay Centre and saw the coloured film 'Peruvian Pilgrimage' by Morris & Levett.

20th Ed & I went off to BDH's 11.15. Saw several old BDH friends.

21st Walked from Ware to Little Amwell and spent 1/2 hour with Bob & Nellie. All fairly well.

22nd Bishop's Stortford. Lunched at XVII century cafe. Wrote to Howards, 49 Broadwick St., W1 for 2 "Biro" pens & refills.

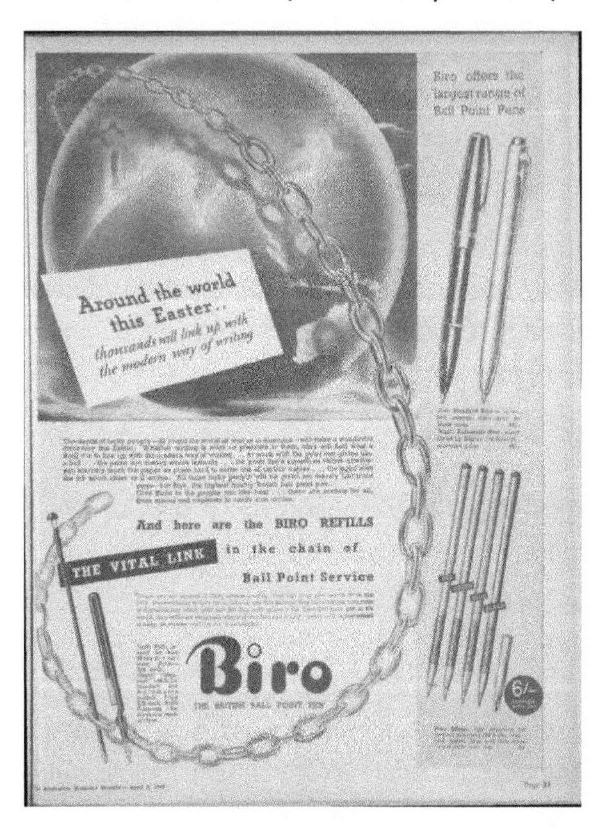

The switch by Sibley from fountain pen to ballpoint was a momentous day: although invented in the late 19th century the 'Biro' exploded internationally after 1945 when Hungarian Lazlo Biro developed the use of a viscous, smudge-free ink. Thereafter the lives of offices and schools the world over were transformed as the ubiquitous inkwell was banished from history.

OCT

5th Bonus from EJ. George - £5.

24th Mr. Attlee's Economy Cuts.

After increasing health spending from £2 billion to nearly £11 billion, using money largely borrowed from the Americans, Attlee's paradisal vision was beginning to dissolve, and the reigning in had begun, resulting in rationing continuing in Britain for some years. A certain Mr. Winston Churchill was waiting in the wings...

25th Princess Elizabeth visited Ilford.

Princess Elizabeth visiting an Ilford home in 1949.

NOV

1st Barbara Shaw's funeral.

2nd. Mr. A.O. Ling dies. Miss Arrow died.

DEC

2nd Went to Boardman's & Roberts. Howard enjoyed the escalator.

Howard saw Father Christmas in both places and got two toys.

6th Cis, Rene, Howard & self went to Hamlet Ct. Rd. Looked at many shops. Bought Howard a tortoise and a balloon. Got back 12.20. Played with balloon until it burst.

13th Electric Power Station's Strike.

18th (Sunday) took service at Old Gravel Pit Mission.

22nd Went to E.J. George's and took part in sales rep. Conference.

23rd Went to Sainsburys and got an Irish Turkey instead of the Hungary bird reserved for us. Phoned Len - he was at home suffering from neurasthenia.

24th Plenty of cooking & preparing for Tuesday. Ernie & L. sent... handkerchief for me from children and brooch for Cis from children.

27th. Up at 8.30. Prepared to receive company. Started coal fires. Cliff came 11.30 and brought a home-made Punch & Judy Show. ... Cliff went to Gants Hill and brought along Len & family. Len & Freda pleased with the cosy and teapot. dinner incl. home-made bon-bons. Dancing 'Charlie Chaplin' amused them, also Punch & Judy Show. Blow-football &c. Good tea, & the 'house' presents gave excitement. All enjoyed themselves. Len & family left at 8.45, Cliff &c left 9.30. All tired but happy.

INCOME TAX YEAR 1948-49
CERTIFICATE OF PAY
AND TAX DEDUCTED

T. Sibley
(Name of employee and Works No., if any)

Code No. at 5 April, 1949 (Enter "E" if an Emergency Card is in use at 5 April, 1949) 69

District Refce. (if any) 145/11630/33

	Gross pay			Tax		
	£	s.	d.	£	s.	d.
1. Pay and tax in respect of previous employment(s) in 1948-49 taken into account in arriving at the tax deductions made by me/us						
2. PAY AND TAX IN MY/OUR EMPLOYMENT ...	106	14	-	-	-	-

I/We certify that the particulars given above include the total amount of pay (including overtime, bonus, commission, etc.) paid to you by me/us in the year ended 5 April, 1949, and the total tax deducted by me/us (less any refunds) in that year.

THE BRITISH DRUG HOUSES LTD. Employer
31 MAR 1949 Date

TO THE EMPLOYEE. Keep this certificate. It will help you to check any Notice of Assessment which the tax office may send you in due course.

P60

CHAPTER SIX

BRAVE NEW WORLD - 1950-1960

When on May 3rd 1951 King George VI formally opened the Festival of Britain, in director-general Gerald Barry's words it was planned to be a *'tonic for the nation.'* With 8.5 million visitors swarming into London to experience the party, it is difficult - despite some grumblings by the penny-pinching press - not to agree. Welsh poet Dylan Thomas who attended the event wrote of the *'gay, absurd, irrelevant, delightful imagination'* of the whole affair, combining as it did funfairs, modernistic sculptures, theatre and singing.

The whole thing was, in Archbishop Fisher's words, *'...a family party,'* designed to give a boost to a nation exhausted by six years of war and further years of continued rationing. State-run shindigs are more often than not wryly considered mere bread and circuses thrown to a populace with the hidden intention of distracting their minds from more pressing, real problems of everyday life, a policy oft-seen in the playbook of dictators. But in Britain's case this was not so, for economically the country was sharing in the postwar boom enjoyed by most Western nations, spearheaded by the powerhouse of the USA.

In this decade Britain gave away much of its empire but retained a sense of its own heroic place in the world; mentally perhaps it still had one foot in the Edwardian culture, extolling individual achievement. When in 1952 Winston Churchill was re-elected Prime Minister and Labour was swept out of power it was the beginning of a Conservative decade in which full employment, affluence, and rising exports culminated in Prime Minister Harold MacMillan declaring in Bedford in 1957 that the British people had *'never had it so good.'*

The remarkable bounce-back of the British economy can be demonstrated with some simple yet staggering statistics. In the 1950s the UK exported 75% of the world's cars, and between 1950 & 1965 people's incomes in real terms rose by 40%. This latter fuelled both the material well-being of the nation, with more households owning goods like fridges, washing-machines and vacuum cleaners and so on, and also the cultural life of the nation. Consumption was king. More people had disposable incomes which in turn created demand for Rock & Roll and the Beatles. It was this symbiotic nexus that fed into social change: money meant not just consumption but empowerment, louder voices. Social mores and the class system was first gently mocked, then openly challenged, the culture of the 1950s in many ways being a dress-rehearsal for the tectonic shifts of the Sixties. From Kingsley Amis' *Lucky Jim* to the films of Norman Wisdom, in which his 'little man' character poked fun at the snootiness of his superiors, the timbre of the age was decidedly - if not revolutionary - then gently rebellious. In 1960 when the satirical revue *Beyond the Fringe* made its debut in the Edinburgh Festival, the public had been prepared for its barbed assaults on the military, the establishment, and the government.

The defensiveness of the West in the 1950s was no mere paranoia - as the decade began British traitors Guy Burgess and Donald McLean fled to the Soviet Union and a ring of Cambridge spies was revealed, so called after their recruitment at Trinity College. Three more were added - Kim Philby, Anthony Blunt and John Ciarncross. The damage done was perhaps more to US confidence in the British Secret Services than in the value of the intelligence they were passing on, but there was no doubting the effect it had on the establishment:

for a swathe of the educated classes in Britain to have turned its back on liberal values and embraced the totalitarianism of Marx, Lenin and Stalin, was a ghastly hammer-blow. The establishment absorbed it, but the reaction was swift: during Winston Churchill's premiershp of 1951-1955 he announced that Britain had developed an atomic bomb. The iron heel of the communist empire was solidified in 1955 when eight eastern European countries, their puppet Soviet governments firmly in place, signed the Warsaw Pact. Thirty years of Cold War lay ahead, featuring sporadic suppressions of democratic uprisings by the Stalinists in Hungary and Czechoslovakia, and intermittent roarings of the imperial British Lion in Suez and Kenya.

But the spirit of pre-war Britain did not buckle. Where we could no longer conquer territory, we conquered mountains and broke speed records; Edmund Hillary's ascent of Everest in 1953, Roger Banister's smashing of the four-minute mile in 1954, together with the Coronation of Queen Elizabeth and Crick & Watson's discovery of DNA - all these were sources of a nationalistic pride no less potent than the imperial achievements of previous years. And in many ways Britain has trundled along in more or less the same spirit ever since, a twin-tracked culture containing both traditional conservatism and radical cynicism. As we looked forward to Harold Wilson's *white heat of technology* of the 1960s, in which we were at the forefront of scientific advances that would shape our economy and society, many were nevertheless persisting in standing up for the old values - mourning the market towns of pre-1939 which were being demolished or transformed before our eyes in the wake of the huge growth of car production, the rows of independent shops that were being replaced by mighty superstores, the Victorian terraces from the rubble of which were rising brutalist tower-blocks. One such figure of nostalgia was the comedian Tony Hancock, whose TV sitcom *Hancock's Half Hour* was a weekly cultural phenomenon attracting many millions of viewers and which captured people's sense of dislocation at the changes of the 1950s. His character railed against modern cafes, teddy boys, contemporary art, the power of the state. Each week he marched against the council who were trying to cut down his oak tree, tried to emigrate, attempted to secure himself a knighthood. This was comedy of frustration, an everyman suddenly surprised by the swiftness of the changes going on all around him, and in many ways the character of Anthony Aloysius St. John Hancock sums up the social history of the decade: British citizens had emerged from the war and stepped, as it were, onto a fairground ride that sped them off into a Brave New World of scientific change, social change, musical and artistic change. At times it was bewildering and dizzying, but never less than exciting. Few could have predicted that it was propelling us towards even greater and faster changes in the Sixties.

That lay ahead. Meanwhile, in a small corner of England, our family the Sibleys were facing their own changes; Thomas had stepped down from his role as travelling salesman after four decades, and had become a stock-taker. Ten years more work lay ahead, but also tragedy.

1950

JAN

13th So. Harrow. R.C. Franks (stock-taking). Lunch in 'Nip-In' cafe - boiled beef & carrots. 2/2d. Orme had tea spilt over him - collar, jacket &c. his fault - he knocked the waitresses' hand. Caught train to Leicester Square. Walked to Orange St. then into National Gallery for 1/2 hour.

18th Bought Cis a fur coat at Redmayne's Ltd., 366 Oxford St. £19-19/-.

20th Cis met Len at Gants Hill. Len much better. May buy my Harris Tweed suit for £8. Len had a quiet evening with Cis.

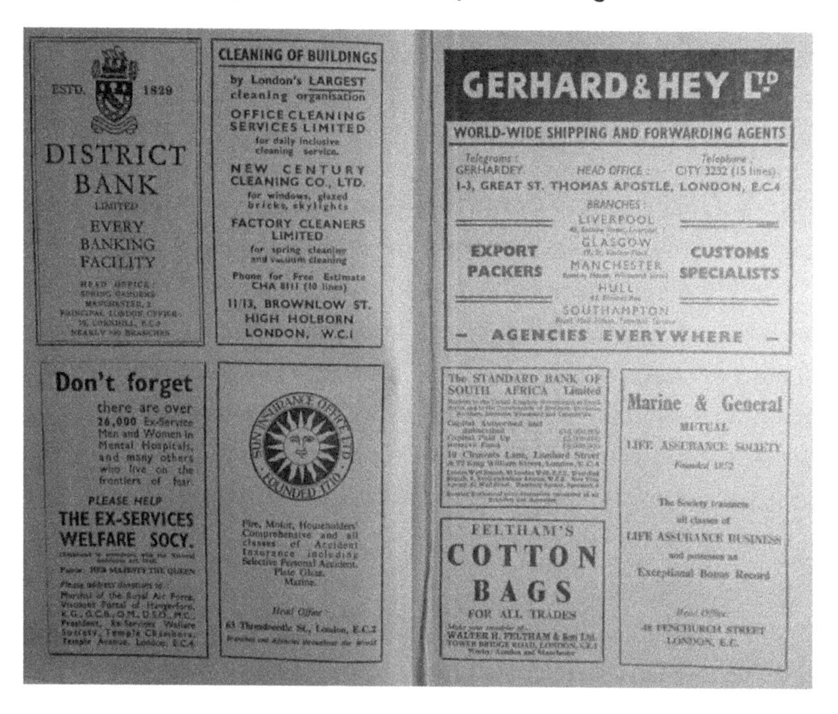

These are the first hints of Len's illness; he's been working for the Tunnel Cement Co. for several years, and in the ensuing months it becomes evident that his health is beginning to deteriorate.

21st. Len got up at 11.30 - he had breakfast in bed. Cis's fur coat arrives.

22nd Rested in afternoon & Len had a doze. Went to Ashurst in evening. Hurried to High Rd. - Cis & Len there. Listened to D. Warren Walker (USA) who gave a brilliant address. Home 9.45. Len stood it well.

23rd Len bought flowers. Had dinner and we went to High Rd. Len 'phoned Freda.

24th Len had a rest all afternoon.

25th After lunch and a rest Cis & I saw Len on his way home going as far as Mile End Station with him. He took my Harris Tweed with him. Len showed a wonderful improvement, both spiritually and physically. He was happy and would like to have stayed longer.

This poignant entry shows a deep concern filtering into the pages of Sibley's diary: a certain special pleading in *'Len showed a wonderful improvement.'* The son he had raised since 1905 has perhaps started to fall prey to the many thousands of health problems caused directly by the era's ignorance of the poisonous effects of industrial products. Asbestosis, caused by the fibrous material used in building construction for nearly a century, was only fully banned in the UK in 1999.

FEB

6th Cis phoned the police as 2 suspicious men were loitering about. Nothing happened - possibly plain clothes police.

12th I wrote to Len.

13th Southend. Coffee in Rossi, High St. Finished Westcliff, got back to Rene's 5.15. Listened to radio, Dr. Hill. Commenced reading Great Expectations. Rene taken up with Labour.

16th Said goodbye to Rene & Howard - left Rene 10/-, and promised Howard 5/- towards his scout hat.

23rd General Election. West Ham Chemist's dinner. Bush House Aldwych. Saw many friends.

24th Labour in again. Small majority. Listen to the 'coming in' election results on the wireless.

The government's 1945 lead over the Conservative Party had shrunk dramatically, and Labour was returned to power but with an overall majority reduced from 146 to just 5. There was a 2.8% national swing towards the Conservatives, who gained 90 seats. Labour called another general election in 1951, which the Conservative Party won.

MARCH

1st Cis & I went to the Methodist Ch. The Drive and saw the films The God of the Atom and The Voice of the Deep.

2nd. Ashurst. Had words with Mr. & Mrs. Brown over going to cinema - he goes now and again, no harm? I felt disgusted with him.

7th Cis very poorly (leg gave way a few days ago). I stayed in bed with her. Read some Great Expectations.

10th Dr. Beattie rang through - came at 10.20.

I went shopping 2.15 - Harris, Bank, Ben Barnes, Grapes in Clements Rd., fish in Eastern Ave., Top Hat loaf, meat in Aldridges, & Harris for medicine. Back 4.10 - made tea in Heatmaster teapot.

20th Took stock at J.B. Tillots, 94 Marsham St. SW1. Lunched in the Westminster Tavern, 2/6d.

24th Len 45.

APRIL

4th Stock-taking W.C. Fords (73 Camden Rd., Camden Town) again. Mr. Herbert upset over my trying to 'convert' him from Roman Cathm.

18th Budget.

29th Arsenal won cup, beat Liverpool 2-0.

MAY

14th Went and took service at the Seaman's Chapel, 27 The Highway, Shadwell, E1. (London Docks).

JUNE

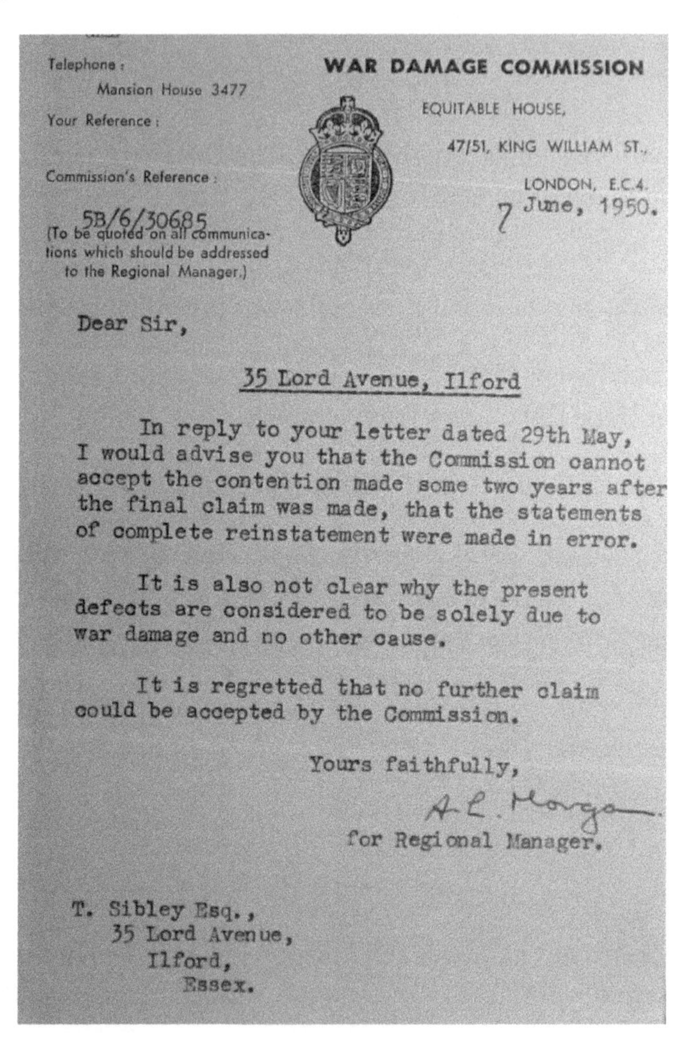

Telephone:
Mansion House 3477
Your Reference:

Commission's Reference:
5B/6/30685
(To be quoted on all communications which should be addressed to the Regional Manager.)

WAR DAMAGE COMMISSION
EQUITABLE HOUSE,
47/51, KING WILLIAM ST.,
LONDON, E.C.4.
7 June, 1950.

Dear Sir,

35 Lord Avenue, Ilford

In reply to your letter dated 29th May, I would advise you that the Commission cannot accept the contention made some two years after the final claim was made, that the statements of complete reinstatement were made in error.

It is also not clear why the present defects are considered to be solely due to war damage and no other cause.

It is regretted that no further claim could be accepted by the Commission.

Yours faithfully,
A. L. Morgan
for Regional Manager.

T. Sibley Esq.,
35 Lord Avenue,
Ilford,
Essex.

10th Holiday, Weston Super-Mare. Mrs. Yeoman's, 10 Grove Park Rd. High Tea 6.30. Only 3 old ladies here.

12th Went to Marine Lake. I had a swim.

13th Wrote two more pc's - Len & Bob. Another old lady came = 4.

14th Nice walk - old pier, toll gate. Walked to Sanatorium and back.

15th Walk on Front to Clarence Park.

16th Went to Cardiff by 9.45 boat, (PWS), arrived at Cardiff 10.35. Bus to centre of town. Walked to Castle. Lunched in Kingsway Cafe. Went to Clifton Street 'Boats' to find Ernie Smith but he had gone.

17th 5 or 6 mile walk - woods, toll road.

20th Went to Swimming Baths and saw exhibition diving and acrobatics. Had tea opposite Town Hall. In evening Cis & I went to Madeira Cove and listened to orchestra.

21st Len sent me a birthday card.

22nd 73.

24th Holiday over.

29th Len 'phoned up.

30th No meat this weekend owing to Carmen's (LONDON MEAT DRIVER'S STRIKE) strike for 18/- increase. Only corned beef. Cis & I went on Essex tour with Contact Club. Stopped at Greenstead Church, High Lawn Church & Blackmore Church. Mr Pincher gave us a little history.

This strike was a knock-on effect of the dockworkers dispute with the Labour Government, which had been ongoing from 1945 and which drivers refused to transport meat unloaded by troops.

JULY

1st. (Saturday) Went to Midland Bank to get £15 & found it had closed at 4 o'clock. Visited Harris who let me have £15.

3rd Bell Hotel Norwich, room 45.

7th 20 mins in Norwich Cathedral. Photos arrived from Willcocks and Williams.

10th Bell Hotel 5.20. dinner goose & pear bitter Helene (stewed pears, ice cream & chocolate).

12th Could not get an Evening Standard so got Evening News.

13th Went to Full Gospel Hall, St. Stephen St. (Norwich). I thought it might be P.B. but it was 'four square.' Prayer meeting instead of Bible reading. It was discordant and noisy, several praying or groaning together. 3 spoke in tongues and one interrupted (no real value) excitement with shouting and repetition. No reverence or spiritual questions. Got back to Bell 9.10.

17th Duke's Head Hotel. Kings Lynn. Rm 20. Read for half an hour Old & New London. I had to ask man in next bedroom to lower wireless.

27th Heard the tragic news of John Drew's accident. He has both thigh bones dislocated, his girl killed and friend concussion. Terrible blow to the Drews.

28th Did odd jobs rather than gardening. Strengthening door to shelter.

The Bell Hotel, Norwich, said to date from 1485, later one of the city's leading coaching inns. During World War II the top floor was turned into a dormitory for the American Women's Army Air Corps.

AUGUST

1st Ed and I went to Oval… and saw Surrey beat Middlesex by 10 wickets. Surrey the better team. Took sandwiches with us and had tea on the ground.

2nd Cis & I had a little outing to So. Kensington. We visited Geology & Science Museum, also King William & Mary Exhibition, & Constables' paintings. Walked along Knightsbridge in Hyde Park to Piccadilly, & had some tea in Kardoma Cafe.

4th Cliff 'phoned and came to lunch. He offered me a black suit for 25/- which I accepted. I gave him 20/- and put 5/- to his credit.

9th Took Graham to L. Zoo. CLR Gants Hill to Tottenham Ct. Rd., N. Line to Camden Town, 74 bus to Zoo. Graham had 2 ice creams and I had a cup of tea. Returned by trolley-buses via Camden Town, Manor House, Woodford.

11th Went to Leigh for a fortnight.

12th Took Graham to Funfair. Crazy Cottage. Won a 'dog' at a catch-ball show. Had tea in Cinema, High St.

14th Cliff and I went by car and inspected 2 bungalows - Thundersley, and Dawes Heath.

16th Cliff polishing caravan, so I took Graham on the pier.

17th Cliff and I went on a hard court opposite Tudor Cafe and had an hour's tennis.

21st Wrote to BDH (ordered Livergen for Len). Len 'phoned - he is coming to Leigh on Saturday for a week.

23rd ...went to Southchurch Park and saw Essex playing West Indians. Sat next to French girl who was with a family & had a little chat & looked at her French magazines. Cis & I went to Pier, listened to orchestra.

25th Back from Leigh on Sea. BDH Pensioner's Open Day. Ed & Bob there with about 56 others.

26th Harold Morgan & family came to stay.

SEPT

2nd Eastbourne holiday.

15th Cis 56. Spoke to Len on 'phone.

16th. Cis got eight birthday cards.

18th Bedford. Swan Hotel (room 42).

20th Bus to Luton, arriving Red Lion Hotel 2.30.

21st Did Luton - 19 calls, 3 orders. Lunched in cinema. dinner, chicken, chatted with old chap who'd been in Indian army.

25th Len went into Springfield Hospital Upper Tooting.

Len's admission into Springfield was a grave development. The hospital opened as the Surrey County Pauper Lunatic Asylum in 1840, became Wandsworth Asylum in 1888, and Springfield Mental Hospital after the First World War. Although his illness seemed only physical, its mental effects were evidently perceived as dominant, hence his admission to psychiatric care.

Springfield Mental Hospital, Tooting, South London.

OCT

17th Heard from Len.

18th Cis went to Springfield Hospital Tooting Bec & saw Len. Did not see him until 4 o'clock as he was in the grounds. He is getting on slowly, is hopeful but very weak.

24th Went to Trafalgar Sq. and had tea in ABC Charing Cross. Went to C.I.M. autumn meeting. Mr. Mitchell in chair. Film on China.

26th Cis and I went to church meeting. Not as stormy as might have been. Church voted for Percy and Tom to reconsider their resignations. I said I would not stand for Deacon again. I created a scene, upset Farthing.

29th Sunday. Took service at Custom House Baptist Church. No heat so we all had to wear our overcoats.

NOV

1st Cis and I went at 12.35 to go to see Len at Springfield Hospital. Trinity Rd., Tooting Bec. Arrived 2.30. Freda & Anne there. Len looked so thin and haggard but eyes better and normal. He chatted quite easily and intelligently and seems to be making progress. Cis took him a cake, milk and butter &c. He was glad to see us.

3rd Bernard Shaw died. Bought Nostromo, J.Conrad.

8th Heard from Ed - Li seriously ill.

14th Cis phoned to Freda - Len might have Infantile Paralysis.

Polio was a highly infectious virus, later called *infantile paralysis* owing to its propensity to affect children. Symptoms were usually mental fog and low fever but occasionally developed into full-blown paralysis and brain infection. Whether this diagnosis was correct in relation to Len Sibley is not known, but judging from his symptoms in the following days it would seem that he was suffering more from a respiratory condition, perhaps exacerbated by polio.

15th Started out at 12.30 for Springfield Hospital. Len in bed with a bad cold. He seems much worse - weight 7 1/2 stone. Breathing difficult - breath bad odour. Complains of chest stomach & back. Inclined to vomit up food (he vomited up the tea Cis helped him drink - I helped him to the lavatory). He looks like a dying man. Cis 'phoned to Freda - she was upset. I spoke to the Orderly about his condition. Wrote to the Medical Superintendent of Springfield about Len suggesting another hospital.

16th Up at 6.45. E1 & E2. Arrived home 4.50. Heard the sad news of Leonard's death - died in the miserable cheerless ward with no loving attendance or comforts. However he is now safe with the Lord - out of all pain & suffering.

Remarkably - though perhaps not so when we have travelled with Mr. Sibley across the decades and witnessed first-hand his indomitable drive and conquest of his own emotions - he sets out to work as normal on the very day after he has lost his only son.

17th Made 13 calls in Walthamstow.

18th Heard from D. France, physician at Springfield, saying Len was dead and Inquest necessary. I replied.

19th Took service at Lighthouse, Bromley (Devons Rd?). Spoke on Romans 1.1.

20th D. France of Springfield rang up to tell me no time to see me - no useful purpose served. I wrote to Dr. Beccle, medcl supt., about Len's treatment.

Whether Sibley's anger at his son's treatment is justified or not we cannot ever fully know, but the offhand nature of the medical authorities in the face of his enquiries gives grave cause for concern.

23rd. Funeral of poor dear Len. We started off for Twickenham 11.10... got to 322 Staines Rd. at 1 o'clock. Ernie Sibley came at 1.30. Many wreaths, beautiful and costly. Funeral 1.35 at Twickenham Cemetery. Baptist Minister Rev. Morgan of Twickenham Baptist Church officiated - very kindly middle-aged man. I spoke to him afterwards. Freda, Ernie, Mr. & Mrs. Pettifer, Cis & self were chief mourners. Several from Tunnel Concrete Co. came.

25th Heard from Dr. H.C. Beccle of Springfield hospital and replied.

DEC

6th Met Mr. L.A. Black at Perkins & Co., 99 Piccadilly after nearly 20 years, we recognised each other - had a nice chat. Had a cup of tea in a milk bar near Piccadilly Circus.

A Milk Bar, Barmouth in Wales, 1950.

Milk bars were an international phenomenon, founded in Australia but very quickly spreading across the US & Britain after the war. Initially their purpose was to encourage young people to consume non-alcoholic drinks, but their real success was as social hubs, later taken over by fast-food outlets.

7th Cis went to Tribunal re. Sick Benefit but nothing doing.

8th Cis made inquiries about unemployment &cc with no result.

13th Shepherd's Bush. Saw Mr. Windwood, 96 Askew Rd., for the first time in over 40 years - he recognised me, he is living at St.

Leonard's & often sees Percy Gray.

15th Went to Dr. Beatties. He added to my script… but is non-plussed for treatment.

16th Read 'Jungle Doctor,' Paul White, bought for Percy Iszatt.

19th Mrs. Holt called in at 8.20 and brought some old clothes for the displaced persons of Europe.

21st Went to BDH's. All the representatives there. Had some pleasant chats. Lunched in the canteen and forgot to pay.

23rd Cis phoned up Freda.

25th Rene, Cliff, Graham & Howard. Cider, Tizer & bon-bons. Chinese Chequers. A Happy Christmas.

29th Cis went to Labour Exchange - more forms to fill in.

1951

JAN

4th Dawkins tuned the piano - 5/-.

6th Win Enns returns to Canada by Plane No. 201. Went to Feltham via Gants Hill, then by bus 90b to London Airport (Heathrow). Comfortable waiting room - had coffee and tea. Said goodbye 4 o'clock. Plane went off 4.25. We saw it taxi away but not rise - too dark, wet and windy.

12th Finished West London districts. Lunched in Odeon Kensington High Street (tripe &c). Spent an hour in the National Gallery.

17th Visit to West Mersea, last look at Li.

Cis & I went to West Mersea by 9.50 coach - Mill Rd. Li has cancer of the liver and cannot last long. She was pleased to see us.

18th Cis & I went to Charing Cross. Went over Civil Service Stores. Walked to Oxford St. via Charing Cross Rd. and went to Bourne & Hollingsworth. Went to C&A's and bought Cis a mac, 59-11d, & a hat 25/11d. Had tea opposite - Italians, very good, but expensive.

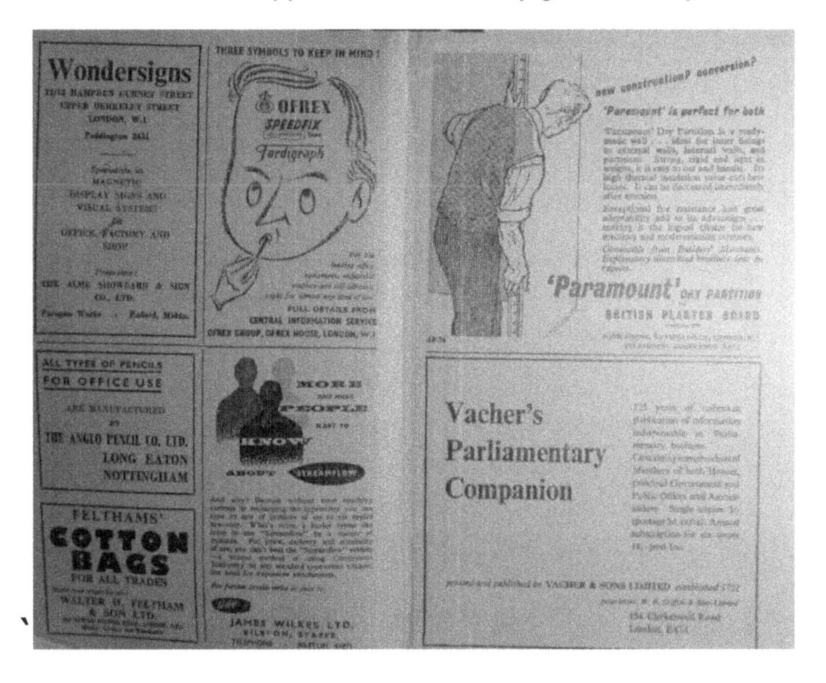

21st Wrote to Mr. Lewis & Rev. Chilvers about Len.

31st Leslie Wright called in and booked rooms as from March 10th. 30/-. His young lady is French living in Strasbourg. He teaches scripture and history at Council School - Wenlock St. City Road.

FEB

5th Went to Percy's P.M. Utting there. I borrowed for Cliff a volume of Shakespeare.

8th Osterley. A lot of walking. Sole of boot became unstitched.

14th Holborn. Went to Church Ho. bookshop and bought 'Jungle Doctor's Enemies' by Paul White. Went to Foyles & bought The Rosary, Barclay, & Last of the Barons, Lord Lytton.

23rd Cis & I went to Town Hall and saw Fact & Faith films - 'God of Creation' and 'Dust of Destiny.'

26th Listened to David Copperfield on wireless.

This production, adapted by Philip Wade and starring David Endera in the eponymous role, was so successful it spawned a TV series a few years later:

MARCH

9th E.J. George's office. Lunched Fortes. Found Mr. Isaacs to be an agnostic - cannot believe as nothing is proved. Had a little argument over dinner table. No value.

17th. Ilford. Visited Bodgers and had our photos taken for passports.

24th Oxford & Cambridge Boat Race. No race as Oxford nearly sank.

30th Li died at West Mersea 8.45am. Went to F.G. Wells, Battersea Bridge Rd., & finished stock-taking at Parsons. Tea in Lyons Sloane Square. Bought a French phrase book at Smiths.

APRIL

3rd. Leslie and Marlise Wright arrive.

10th Budget. All a little poorer. Read a little Uncle Tom's Cabin - Li's bequest to Graham.

17th Cis heard from NHS. Appeal granted.

21st Cis recieved a cheque from NHI for £20-18-8d.

23rd Aneurin Bevan resigned, also Wilson.

MAY

3rd The King opened the Festival of Britain.

4th Spent some of evening upstairs with Leslie & Marlise, Mr. & Mrs. Wright.

22nd Went out about 2 o'clock & proceeded to Temple - too rough for Lords so walked along Embankment to Charing Cross Bridge. As it was 10/- to get into the Festival of Britain Exhibition I went into Waterloo Station & had a cup of tea & then walked to National

Gallery, & had nearly 2 hours with the paintings.

The Festival of Britain on the South Bank of the Thames.

23rd Mabel & Arthur Head came in evening. I showed them how to make out will.

26th Rec'd statement from B.H.F. - £91-17/-.

27th Visited Smiths Gants Hill and ordered a guide to the Riviera.

28th Lowestoft, Suffolk Hotel, room 12. Braces broke when talking to Miss Woodcock, had to buy new ones, 7/-7d.

31st Did Beccles, lunched in Co-op. Walk along the front. Boisterous and cold.

JUNE

1st Paid Suffolk Hotel bill, went to Oulton Broads and back.

7th First test match in So. Africa.

12th Woodbridge and Wickham Market. Chatted to a young Canadian, Gordon Poppy, (23) about Canada and the Lord.

16th Holiday in Menton (So. France). Marlise came to bus and helped with bag. Got to Victoria 12.5. Met party 1 o'clock. Good company but no youthful people. Pleasant trip to Calais. Tea on boat and tea on S.F. Riviera train. Stopped in Paris a little time. We all tried to sleep.

17th 1 1/2 hours sleep. Difficult - 8 people in 8 seats. Arrived Floreal Hotel Menton safe and sound. Went to C of E church - St. Johns - poor. Had an enjoyable walk on front. In bed 10.30. Slept heavily.

19th Went to town and got D. Express. Went by motor boat to Monaco - 400 francs each. Had a look at the Casino & saw the roulette tables - elderly Scot got me through the grounds. Had a bottle of light sweet wine. In bed 10.40.

20th Visited caves at St. Cesare. Had some tea at Cannes.

21st Mr. Bates has legs sunburnt. I put on some Tanna-Flame.

22nd 74. Visit to Italy. Coach 9 o'clock, greeted by Happy Birthday to you. Card - 20 signatures. Cis gave me a card. Went to Ventimiglia.

23rd Visited St. Michael's Church and chapel of the White Penitent.

30th Home from France. Boulougne for breakfast. Home via Victoria & Gants Hill 4.45 - everything in order, praise the Lord for bon voyage and a lovely holiday.

JULY

14th Graham 13. Cliff & family came 12.45 and stayed to dinner and tea. Arthur and Mabel came 4.30. Cliff, Howard and I went into the park & played cricket - Graham came afterwards. Leslie & Marlise also had tea with us. 10 to tea - a very good one. Rene left 8 o clock and Arthur 9 o clock. A very happy day.

23rd. Kings Lynn, Dukes Head Hotel, rm. no.18.

24th Saw Queen Elizabeth drive in from Sandringham to open the Old Guildhall. ... Walked towards Town Hall & saw the Queen walk from the Town Hall where she had tea with the Mayor. I waited near the church and saw the Queen come out & enter the Daimler and was driven away.

25th Bus to Hunstanton, made 2 calls and had a look at the sea. Burnham Market, Snettisham... Watched the youngsters play cricket. Sandringham Flower Show made the buses busy.

29th Sunday. Took service at the old Gravel Pit Mission.

AUGUST

1st Got 'Monopoly' from Iszatts.

2nd Cemented coal bunker and mended some of the path that took me all afternoon.

6th Bank Holiday Monday. Rayleigh Carnival. It rained heavily so we returned somewhat wet.

7th Went by car to Chalkwell and sat on front.

9th Back to tea. Cliff lost his temper and was offensive so I said I would not come again and stop. Rene upset. Cliff went out in car for 2 or 3 hours.

10th Cliff & I went to Chalkwell Park and played tennis - all in Cliff's favour. Motored to High Street and bought Graham's school blazer and badge. Cliff took us to see a bungalow to view.

12th Cliff motored us to Cong'l church & Cliff took service. Cliff's first attempt at local preaching. Quite good but a little short (3/4 hr).

14th Took Cis & Graham to pier and listened to Ben Oakley's orchestra.

17th Packed up ready for Cliff. We all got in car - well wedged in with luggage. Arrived at 35 around 3.10. Leslie on holiday. Rene & Cliff had a cup of tea and Cis got some beans and cabbages from next door. Went thro' correspondence and read that Percy Jordan had died. Cliff Rene & Howard left about 4.30 - Graham stayed with us.

21st Had a game of Monopoly. A police officer came round and asked Cis about the accident she witnessed.

22nd Graham & I took sandwiches and & went to the Festival of Britain Exhibition, South Bank. ... Stayed there until 4 o clock (arrived 11.40). Lunched on steps. We went by bus to the Pleasure Gardens and stayed until 5.15. We were both tired and Graham got a headache. We both went into the 'House of Fun' and Graham won an egg-cup on the shooting but nothing from rings. Got home... Graham had a headache and was sick so went straight to bed.

The Festival of Britain, 1951, on London's Southbank.

30th. Cis had to go and get some fish as the calf's head we had Tuesday and Wednesday had turned sour. We went to 30 Kent Rd., Winchmore Hill... & saw Harry also Win. Harry looks well but fat and rheumaticky, has not been out for two years.

SEPT

1st. Cis & I went to Westminster W.E.R. Festival of Britain Campaign.

11th Clive's birthday - 13. Arthur & Mabel departed for Canada.

12th Ashurst Drive. Women's outing by coach to Hastings.

19th ... bus to Luton where I put up at the Red Lion Hotel - room 2. Had a cup of tea in Lyon's with another traveller - for Stonham's, fabrics &c for furniture. He went off to the Pictures and I went back to the hotel.

20th Had a read of 'Old Mortality.'

24h Tring... where I had lunch, half an hour walk, and an hour in the Museum. Hemel Hempstead... Midland Hotel, top of Midland Rd. - bedroom no. 11. Sat in lounge alone before electric fire. Some gas in room.

25th Had some dinner with Mr. & Mrs. D - Cyril and Gladys - then some TV - a play and newsreel & Paris Dresses Exhibition at the Savoy.

28th Bus to Welwyn. Had lunch at 'Sundeck' cafe, Welwyn Stores. Cis not very well - went to Dr. Beattie's - heart at fault, must go steady.

OCT

2nd. Heard from Rene - she said Mr. Ringwood had died on Sunday. Sent Anne a birthday card. (Anne - daughter of Len & Freda).

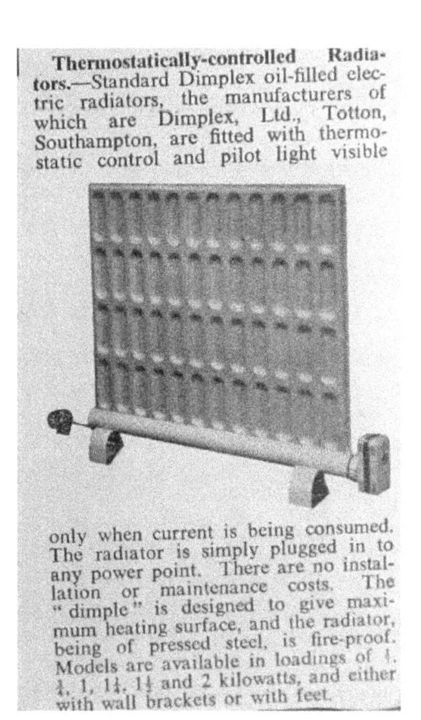

Thermostatically-controlled Radiators.—Standard Dimplex oil-filled electric radiators, the manufacturers of which are Dimplex, Ltd., Totton, Southampton, are fitted with thermostatic control and pilot light visible only when current is being consumed. The radiator is simply plugged in to any power point. There are no installation or maintenance costs. The "dimple" is designed to give maximum heating surface, and the radiator, being of pressed steel, is fire-proof. Models are available in loadings of ½, ¾, 1, 1¼, 1½ and 2 kilowatts, and either with wall brackets or with feet.

3rd Anne's birthday - 15 years.

4th Ed went to see Harry at Winchmore Hill. .. Ted Pike (Australia) also paid an unexpected visit to Harry.

5th 12.50 Ed & I set off for BDH Pensioner's Open Day. 69 old friends there - Bernie, Roberts, Gregory, Jones, Turnbull, Burr, Symons. Bob, Ed & self - family together.

6th Leslie Kerridge started painting house.

Phoned Bursal - he is giving up his pharmacy and optical practice and going near Colchester - pig farm.

15th Timmins & Kirks, 183 High Street, Beckenham. (Stock-taking).

19th Cis went to Dr. Beattie's for certificate.

24th Read some Shakespeare.

25th General Election. Conservative victory.

26th Read some Shakespeare (Timon).

27th W.S. Churchill Prime Minister.

29th Train to Reigate and helped Jones & Green & Speight take stock at Baldwins, 34 High St., Reigate.

NOV

2nd Cis & I went to Holborn and we visited Church Ho. Book Room & I bought 3 books & ordered The Death of Christ by Denney. Walked to Scripture Book Crusade Ludgate Hill and bought 2

books, 3 calendars, 24 Christmas cards. Tea in Kardoma Fleet Street.

9th Freda 'phoned - unable to come tomorrow, Mother still unwell.

10th Freda rang thro' saying she could not come or children. I spoke to her. Cliff, Rene, Graham and Howard came 4 o'clock and stayed until 6.30.

15th Harwich. Walked to Dovercourt. 24 bus to Kings Arms Ardleigh & walked to Dedham. Sibley of Burgoines (?) at Gooch's. Red Lion. Ret'd to my room 9 o'clock. Ball in dening room disturbing.

DEC

12th Cis went to London Hospital and spent an hour with Timothy Hipkins a Dr. Barnados boy & Sunday School scholar.

13th Dense fog in most places. Ilford escaped.

17th E.J. George's dinner at Beale's Restaurant. J. George are taking up Fentosan as a selling line. Cis & I went to Beale's Rest. Holloway Road. Soup, fish, turkey, ice pudding & strawberries, port and fruit cup.

19th Tied up parcels for Ernie, L & Ruth.

22nd Freda & Anne came and Clive - who helps his Grandad Pettifer. Good tea, fish cakes, and played Pit until 8 o'clock. Exchanged presents - I had socks and Cis stockings.

26th Cliff, Rene & Howard came 12.35… Cliff tried the iron with electric connection - broke lighting fuse and then oven fuse. Played games with Howard. Occasional chair broke away from back. Happy day.

27th Cis, Graham & I played Monopoly until 10.35.

28th Went to Godwins. Mr. Jarvis went over Cis's eyes saying hardly any change since 1948.

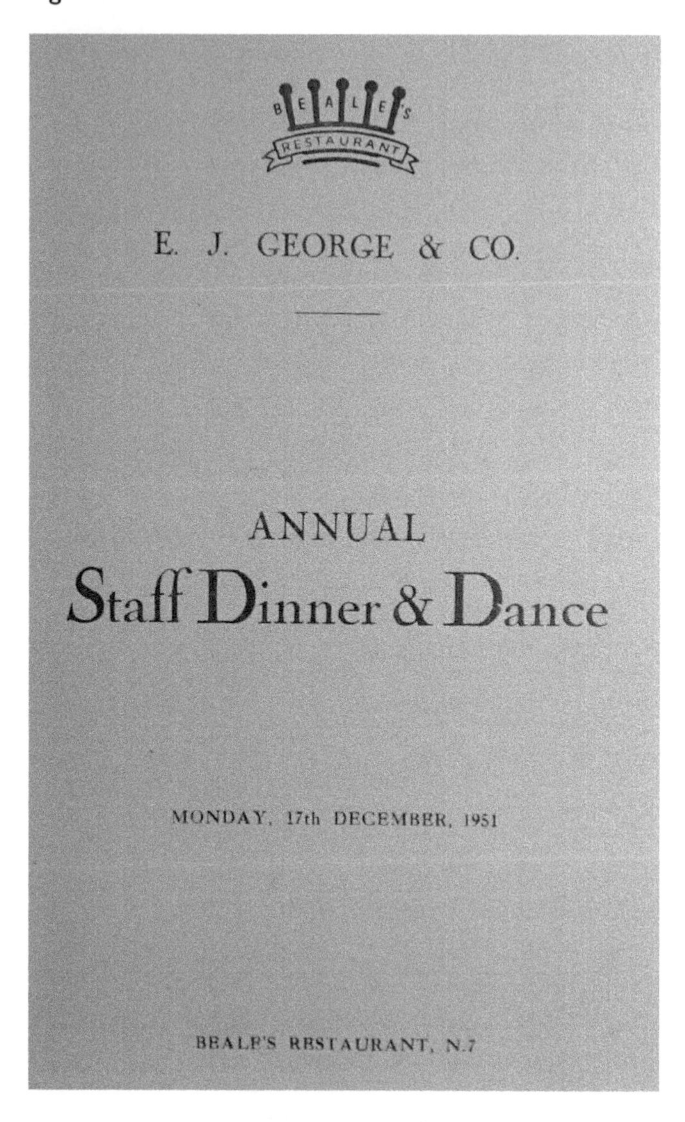
E. J. GEORGE & CO.

ANNUAL
Staff Dinner & Dance

MONDAY, 17th DECEMBER, 1951

BEALE'S RESTAURANT, N.7

1952

JAN

3rd Flossie Thompson rang up and said she, Ed & Eva were going to Algiers.

4th Cis rang up Louise & had a chat, & I had a talk with Ernie.

5th Percy & Mrs. Iszatt brought Mr. & Mrs. Utting. Leslie & Marlise joined us at 4 o'clock. Had a fish cake tea and cakes & jellies - very good. After tea we settled down to parlour games which brought much hilarity. Drawing consequences - what would we do? What shall we give him? Imitating which caused roars of laughter. Giving a sweet blindfolded &c. Party left 10.45. A happy New Year's evening.

6th We overslept so could not go to church.

7th Went to E.J. George's office & helped entering transfers in the DDA Register. (Dispensing Doctor's Register). Walked back with Utting. Gave him a jar of marrow and ginger.

9th Went to Orient Line office, 9 Kingsway & enquired about boat journey going to Algiers. They do not go. .. Rail to Marseilles and boat to Algiers.

16th Miss T., Eva & Ed are staying in Tangiers in 2 months.

23rd So. Woodford. Had a nice chat with E. Willcocks. Saw Reg Offord, then called on Tommy Offord, 97 Capel Rd. He had had a stroke but was getting better. Saw his daughter Win & two grandchildren Ivonne & Mary.

26th Marlise went to hospital. Long service certificate received (47 years). Marlise had her baby boy - 8lbs - Paul.

30th Ed rang up, saying steamer 'Dunnottor Castle' leaving from Tilbury, they must be there by 10.30am on Monday Feb 4th.

FEB

1st. Baptist Holiday Fellowship Reunion at Conway Hall, Red Lion Square. Entertainment until 9 o'clock - music hall ditties, colour films on Norway & So. France. Two plays. Recitations, solos by Mrs.

Ingles.

6th Death of King George VI.

The reign of George VI - real name Albert - had probably been one of the most eventful in recent history, with its extraordinary unexpected beginnings following his brother's abdication, to the necessity of falling in line with Chamberlain's appeasement of Hitler, to the struggle of maintaining unity in a dividing British Empire bubbling with Nationalism (India in 1937 held no formal celebrations of the Coronation, citing excessive expense) to his sudden death from lung disease at only 55. But In 1945, it was clear that the British people had warmd to him, and he had acquitted himself as a well-liked, respected monarch. Crowds shouted 'We want the King!' in front of Buckingham Palace during the Victory in Europe Day celebrations. In January 1946, George addressed the United Nations at its first assembly, which was held in London, and reaffirmed 'our faith in the equal rights of men and women and of nations great and small.' His growing ill-health in the last year of his life meant that Princess Elizabeth had begun to assume more and more Royal duties, but nevertheless when his demise came it was still a shock to a nation still feeling the after-effects of war.

7th Queen Elizabeth & Duke of Edinburgh arrive in England from Kenya.

9th Opening of Roding Lane Free Church Free Hall.

11th King's body brought from Sandringham to Westminster Hall.

12th Westminster Hall open to 3am to see memorial and coffin. Marlise home from maternity with baby Paul.

13th Queue 3 1/2 miles long to visit King lying in state.

14th Benfleet. Lunched at Restawhile Cafe.

15th King George VI's funeral - buried at Windsor 2pm. Two minutes silence. I sifted and shifted some coal & chopped some wood.

18th District Officer called & saw Marlise and baby.

20th Cis went with Marlise to the Clinic. Report better than expected on baby Paul.

28th West Ham & District Phamacist's Association founded 1903. Cis & I went to dinner, Bush House Rest., Aldwych.

MARCH

7th John Cummings of BDH dies of pneumonia.

8th Leslie & Marlise bought a pram.

18th Read some of 'A Late Lark Singing.'

20th Charringtons deliver 4cwt of coal - remainder of ration.

22nd Took part of electric stove to Howes for new parts. Met Cis at Wyatts and we walked home together.

23rd Roding Hall in evening. Col. Thomson (War Office) spoke on Christians behind the Iron Curtain. A long and interesting address.

24th Heard from Rene - Howard has scarlet fever so cannot stay this weekend.

APRIL

17th. W.C. Ford, Camden Town. Lunched at Station Hotel. Cis visit to MOH for examination.

25th. BR Fellowship at Bloomsbury, anniversary meeting. Cis went to Dr. Beattie's and saw film on Billy Graham's book.

29th Central Hall Westminster. Dr. Bob Pierce, Don Devos, & Herman Vos - all American. Terrible acct of the war, Christians suffering martydom in Korea.

MAY

2nd Cis went to have further examination under the NHS at Gants Hill.

4th Finished reading Ed's 'Prickly Pear,' - Eric Fisk.

7th British Sailor's Society Annual Meeting. It was overcrowded in the Egyptian Hall.

14th Lowestoft. 11.29 to Southwold. .. Read on front of 'The Golden Ass.'

15th Finished reading The Golden Ass.

16th Cis had been in bed all yesterday - pleurisy, cystitis & ear trouble.

21st. Had a read of Chevalier de Maison Rouge.

24th Marlise dropped milk bottle in our glass dish full of apples.

28th Suffolk. Had a look round Bry's stalls, it being market day.

29th Sudbury. Four Swans. Bought R.L. Stevenson's The Master of Balllantrae from stall in market.

JUNE

4th. 3 mile walk to Sahan Toney (?). Rested in church & enjoyed some meditation.

11th Norwich. ... Went to Assembly House next to the theatre & saw... film on the rescue of a cripple from a witchdoctor thro' eclipse of the sun.

12th Cromer. Salad lunch opposite church. A pleasing and good looking Glasgow girl served me.

13th Norwich, Bell Hotel. 6 calls - the Unthank Rd. district.

20th Ed gave Cis a heat-resisting basin which he bought in N. Africa.

22nd. 75. I had 3 birthday cards.

30th Holiday in Brittany. Cis & I went to Gants Hill. Bought American short shirt in mistake, D. Telegraph at Smiths &c. ... Waterloo... tea-rooms.. bread & butter & strawberry milk. Southampton... SS Falaise.

JULY

1st. Arr. St. Malo 8.30.

3rd. Stopped at Dol - cathedral where several kings were crowned. Mont. S. Mich. 11.30. Went over the abbey. Cis would not go as there were many steps. Guide spoke poor English. Chatted with some Americans.

7th St. Brienne. Visited cathedral - virgin and child, special image in costly array was being visited, & garment kissed - dreadful superstition.

12th SS. Falaise sailed 9.30.

16th Cis washed my dressing-gown and went shopping. I spent most of morning getting 1/2 ton of coal in coal shed.

17th Coach started at 9.7. Stopped at Stanton-near-Marks for refreshments, arrived Dr. Beattie's house W. Mersea 11.30. Dr. Beattie working hard to get tennis lawn usable. Other then helped get grass cut, marked out and net up. Had lunch and then I played 3 sets. Had to leave Dr. Beattie's with Cis and go to Ed's. He was in bed - pleurisy. Did not stop long and got back to Dr. Beattie's

4.30.

21st Went to Lord's. Game commenced 10.30. Middlesex v. Surrey. D. Compton failed (18). Graham came unexpectedly in morning - Cis was out so Marlise cooked him some lunch.

24th Went to Lods and watched Gentlemen & Players match.

28th Oval. Surrey batting against India.

AUGUST

4th At Rene & Cliff's, Leigh-on-Sea, Fairmead Avenue. Graham & Howard went to a neighbours and saw television. Cliff took us to Eastwood and showed us the bungalow he might possibly buy. Then we motored to Rochford and had a look at the aerodrome.

12th Cliff and I went to a car breakers in Downham and he bought a headlamp. Went to Chalkwell Park and played tennis. Rene & Cliff went to Southend for the evening.

16th Tremendous damage in West Country thro' storm - 13 killed and 25 missing in floods - at Lynemouth - half the town destroyed.

25th Ed 'phoned through - he is better but Ernie is ill in hospital, nearly expired.

SEPT

9th Wrote to Ernie Sibley - Harrow-on-Hill Hospital. Cis got a birthday card for Clive. Read some of Wuthering Heights.

10th Coach to Seaford. Stroll along the front in sunshine. A very pleasant day.

11th Clive's birthday.

17th Invitation to BDH Pensioner's 'open day' 24th October.

29th Ware. Walked to Bob's. Sign posts misleading & went out of my way. A woman with her bike showed me the way. (Full of woman's troubles). Had a cup of tea with Bob & Nellie.

Thomas had never lost affection for his younger brother Bob. Many years had passed since they had 'mouched down the Bow Road' and imbibed together as young men-about-town in Mile End or at Holborn Town Hall. They were both approaching old age now, Bob settled in the county of Hertfordshire with his wife Nellie.

OCT

1st Cis heard from Ministry of Health - all claims disallowed. Must frank own card - self-employed person, 4/5 a week. Ed came about 8.30 and stayed the night.

6th Bought R.L.Stevenson's St. Ives at Rodney St.

8th Great railway accident at Harrow. 109 killed, over 190 injured.

On the morning of October 8th 1952 an overnight express train from Perth crashed into the rear of a local passenger train standing at a platform at Harrow & Wealdstone station. The wreckage blocked adjacent lines and was struck within seconds by a "double-headed" express train travelling north at 60 mph. The crash resulted in 112 deaths and 340 injuries, 88 of these being detained in hospital. It remains the worst peacetime rail crash in British history.

9th Cis went to needlework class. She lost my church key among the cabbages so had to go without.

21st Cis 58.

22nd Marlise and Cis had a dispute over use of electric kettle. Leslie gave flowers, china, basket & violets for birthday.

24th BDH Pensioner's Open Day. Envelope given to me - 10/-. Photos taken.

The scene looking south over the aftermath of the Harrow and Wealdstone train crash on 8 October 1952.

NOV

10th Louise phoned thro' saying Ernie was in Middx Central Hospital, Park Royal, on danger list.

11th I phoned Middx Hospital - must see Ernie before 10 o'clock. Louise phoned later - Doctor does not want anyone to see Ernie.

12th Went to Guiterman, 37 Soho Square and took back Shavemaster Elec. Razor for repair. Slippers from Dolcis 25/9d. Bus to Gamages and we walked to Ludgate Hill. Had tea at Kardomah Rest. Fleet St. Walked to Oxford Circus and trained to Notting Hill Gate. Some difficulty in finding Talbot Street and Tabernacle.

14th Louise phoned - Ernie slightly better.

27th Went to Middx Central Hospital. Ward C4. Only Ernie and another in his room. Louise there, Rev. Methodist Minister called in ward. I stayed there until 4 o'clock and returned with Louise to Harlesden Station.

30th Wrote to Freda and sent 10/- to Sailor's Society.

DEC

2nd. Louise 'phoned to say Ernie was much better and that Win would like to see me when in Watford.

3rd Louise 'phoned to say Ernie would be coming out of hospital on Sunday.

12th Cis & I went to Westminster Central Hall and enjoyed the evening with the L.E. Choir.

16th Went to Victoria Dock Mission and spoke to The Grandfathers.

18th Went to High Rd... bought a locket for Cis from Freit.

22nd Beale's Restaurant - EJ George Christmas dinner.

Dancing commenced 9.30.

25th Leslie ill. Dr. Beattie came. Cliff, Rene & Howard came 1.30. Afternoon spent rather quietly, as Howard was not well. Dr. Beattie gave Graham a script for cough. A few parlour games. Cliff & Rene & family left at 9.30.

26th Leslie still very ill - temp. 105. Called emergency doctor who was here within the hour. Cis & I had a quiet day on our own - the quietest in memory. We had baby downstairs to relieve (sic) Marlise.

1953

JAN

25th Dr. Beattie has pneumonia.

26th Paul Wright one year old.

27th Pension increased by £15 a year.

31st Princess Victoria sank near Ireland - 128 drowned.

FEB

1st Terrible disaster from storm and flood last night. East Coast devastated, Lincolnshire to Kent.

The 1950s seemed beset with memorable extremes of weather. The 1953 North Sea flood was a major flood caused by a heavy storm surge that struck the Netherlands, north-west Belgium, England and Scotland. Most sea defences facing the surge were overwhelmed, resulting in extensive flooding. The storm and flooding occurred at the end of Saturday, 31 January 1953 and in the morning of the next day. A combination of a high spring tide and a severe European windstorm caused a storm tide: in the Netherlands 20% of the land was below mean sea level. Such land relies heavily on sea defences and was worst affected, recording 1,836 deaths and widespread damage. Most of the casualties occurred in the southern province of Zeeland. In England, 307 people were killed in the counties of Lincolnshire, Norfolk, Suffolk and Essex, and 28 people were killed in the north of West Flanders, Belgium. Nineteen were killed in eastern Scotland. In England, from Lowestoft to Canvey Island the effects were felt; homes were swept away, boats wrecked.

11th I fixed up our repaired electric fire in lounge, put heels on shoes, adjusted lock on lavatory door, & took out and dusted books in dining room. Read two battles from my 'Battles of the 19th Century.'

23rd Walked to Piccadilly and saw Trocadero.

MARCH

24th Queen Mary died 10.20pm.

On the night and morning of Feb 1st 1953, 326 people lost their lives in the North Sea Flood.

25th F.G. Wells, 80 Battersea Bridge Rd. … went to the Prodigal and had a good lunch.

26th F.G. Wells. I upset Strachan by not agreeing with him about stranger's partners - single men - being invited to firm's dinner, also his loose language. He would hardly speak afterwards.

28th Cis and I went to Royal Festival Hall… enjoyed evening with London Endeavour Choir (E.T. Shepherd). Guest speaker Rev. Alan Redpath.

APRIL

8th CL Railway accident (central line), Stratford. 9 killed, abt. 50 wounded.

About 6.30 an Epping train ran into a Hainault train.

17th Cis went to Soho hospital to see Mrs. Ringwood and got home before me.

23rd Wembley Pharmacy, 40 Harrow Rd., Monks Park. Mr. Davenport gave me a rubber 'teddy' for Paul.

30th Levison's, 84 Fulham Palace Rd. (stock-taking).

MAY

11th Went to Oval, saw Surrey v. Australians. Poor Surrey in a hopeless position, 46-6, so left at 1.30 and went to Lords... saw Middx batting against Hampshire.

13th Cis & I went to Mansion House, 135th anniversary of the British Sailor's Society. Lord Mayor (Sir Rupert de Biere, MA) in chair, Her Royal Highness the Duchess of Gloucester. Speakers - Sir Fred Sykes, Capt. the Rt. Hon. Lord Teynham, Sir Kenneth R. Swan. Buffet tea. Rev. Dempster put us in reserved seats. Egyptian Room crowded, many standing. Home 5.00pm.

18th Suffolk Hotel, Lowestoft, room 54. In bed 10 o'clock. Pulling of WC water next door disturbed me thrice.

21st Loddon. Had to spend 2 hours there. Had a nice country walk - sat down and had a read.

23rd Saturday. Louise phoned and said we would be met at Kenton Station. Margaret met us at 3.40. Had a pleasant afternoon and evening with Ernie, Louise, Margaret & David. Sat in garden. Tea & left at 9 o'clock, got home 10.20. Louise & Margt. saw us to Preston Rd. Station. Had a pleasant time. Ernie much better.

25th Bank Holiday Monday. Cis & I went to Furrows Hall. Two sets of tennis. Tea in grounds 4.15. High Tea 7pm. Had photo taken. Saw film - Norway, and story of answered prayer for child.

26th Ilford, 8.20 train to Harling Road. Had my usual 1 1/2 mile walk to East Harling. Flowers, birds, trees and rabbits all interesting and lovely. Visited church and had a chat with a workman or caretaker. Went to Brandon and then to Thetford. (Bell Hotel).

31st Coronation Services. Dr. Beattie preached a Coronation sermon.

JUNE

1st. Cis left at 5pm for Royal Albert Hall. Had 3/6d seats Sec. Tier no. 71. United Service Prayer & dedication - W.E.A. London Endeavour Choir sang. Dr. W.E. Sangster gave principal address. Dr. & Mrs. Beattie there, and they walked to Oxford Circus - decorations, illuminations, & 1000s of people squatting all night for tomorrow's event.

2nd. Showery. Very cold. Queen Elizabeth II crowned. Cis & I went next door to Mr. Curtis & watched the crowning of Elizabeth II in Westminster Abbey (10.46-1.15). Returned for lunch - egg salad. Went back to Curtis and stayed to the end 5.10. Evening so cold we sat by the electric fire. Curtis had coal fire all day.

PHARMACIST LEADS IN COUNTRY FAIR: Miss L. M. Humfress, M.P.S., Lavenham, Suffolk right, is seen with other ladies from Lavenham in traditional costume who are to hold a country fai on Coronation day in aid of children's tea party. Miss Humfress is shown representing an apothecary

3rd Central Hall Westminster. A fine address by W.E. Sangster. Crowds in West End to see illuminations &c. extraordinary weather for June - coldest on record - 53, down to 45. Fires and hot water

bottles again.

5th Dr. Beattie has the offer of Mildmay's organ but wonders where it will go.

13th Holiday to Newquay. At Paddington Cis stumbled on escalator going up & nearly fell down. I was in front. But an inspector following helped her and took her luggage, but she bruised her hand and ricked her neck and got a shock. Arrived at 7.00pm at Mrs. Scroggie's and McKendrick's.

14th David (Griffiths) & I had a five mile walk past St. Columb minor.

16th Had a look at Port Isaac. Visited King Arthur's house & Tintagel Castle - good climb up steps. A film was being made about King Arthur's knights of the Round Table - men dressed accordingly.

18th Went to Polperro and stayed 40 mins. Cis bought a sketch by H.V. Morton, 1/6d.

20th Finished reading 'King Arthur's Knights' which I bought for Graham.

21st Cis & I went to Roding Hall. Rev. Cyril Noad took service. Rev. Noad represents the Worker's Christian Fellowship.

22nd. 76 (yrs old). Had 2 birthday cards - Rene, Cis, Leslie.

24th Wrote to G.R. Lane, Gloucester, for a 6/- book, Common Sense Eating for Rheumatic Sufferers.

27th Paid elec. bill, £5.6.2d - Leslie's portion £2.5/-, which Marlise thought too much. Left unpleasant feeling. Graham came and spent the day with us. Rene & Cliff went to a party at Browning's.

JULY

1st Pleasant time at Diss - sat 1/2 hour by lake watching ducks and reading.

8th Bury St. Edmunds. Four Swans Hotel. Had a read. Finished Bulldog Drummond.

9th Sudbury. Had lunch in cinema - roast beef, 3/2d.

10th Tea on lawn. Paul running about garden.

11th Keswick. 30 Helvellyn St., (most unsociable woman). Comfortable bedroom but lavatory conditions poor.

12th Cis & I went to Methodist Church (Keswick) and heard Mr. Leith Samuel.

25th Leslie, Marlise & Paul left for Mr. Wrights after 2 years 4 months & going to Strasbourg on Wednesday. Said goodbye. Cis sorry Paul is going. Cis has a painful gland in her neck. The wear and tear by Leslie & Marlise was considerable.

26th Plenty of dirt left behind by Leslie & Marlise.

28th Wrote a long letter to Leslie Wright. Lady 'phoned up about rooms. Coming to see them.

29th Started creosoting garden clothes pole but rain prevented me finishing. Mr. & Mrs. Dipper of Seven Kings came to see rooms (35/-).

30th Leslie sent 10/- and a bitter letter saying he 'hoped he would not hear from us again.'

AUGUST

5th Mr. Holt & Mr. More came and saw Cis and earnestly desired her to return to Ashurst Drive S.services in spite of Brown. I joined in the conversation.

7th Arrived at 7pm at Rene's. .. Had a look at TV as Rene & Cliff went out for the evening.

10th Evening spent with TV. extraordinary whirlwind at Westcliff this evening.

12th Went in car to Ed's and had some tea with them. Cis & I had a read but the others resorted to TV.

15th Saw cricket on TV.

19th Cis & I went on pier and heard Ben Oakley's orchestra.

SEPT

10th Pottered about mostly in my room, going through old papers and documents.

11th Clive - 15 years.

14th Ordered refrigerator from Astral Gas Co. £41, £43 installed.

18th Cis & I had a day in Brighton. Had lunch on Hove front. Went to Thomas' Sackville St. but he was on holiday, and to Mrs. Stevens 7 Braemore Rd., but she had removed. Got to Grace Hackers 4 o'clock, had a cup of tea, chatted with Mr. & Mrs. Jack Hacker and Mrs. Ball who is 87 - well but memory failing.

23rd Cis went to Electricity Demonstration at Morisford Schools. I went to Mission to Lepers mtg. at Friend's House Euston Rd.

OCT

3rd Anne's birthday (Len & Freda's daughter). Rene 'phoned thro' - wants to stay for a quiet week's rest - rest or operation, gastric ulcer.

5th Leicester. Grand Hotel tonight, tomorrow Diamond Jubilee Hotel. Dinner calves tongue and biscuit glacé.

6th Diamond Jubilee Hotel, 123 Belgrave Gate - small affair. My bedroom a single bed - head near window, a dressing-table & one chair, no hooks for clothes & no towel. One bath for all and lavatory for six persons.

16th BDH Open Day. L'pool Street, walked to Graham St. Saw many friends - over 70 there - Bob & Ed there. I went over Wharf road and saw the livestock and heard about the new insulin. Photos at 4.30 and high tea, ham tongue.

17th Mr. & Mrs. Harvey came and saw rooms and decided on them right away. He had been a member of Duke St. Richmond for 10 years, only married to his second wife 4 months. He was very volatile, rather eccentric. Prayed. They stopped for tea & cakes. He is a tool tester and his wife works in a laundry.

21st Cis 59. A strike of petrol men in Essex affects whole of London. Cis got several cards - and a £1 from Ed.

24th Troops used to bring petrol to London.

NOV

2nd Having to wait for Hume, had a look round Gamages for 3/4 hour, which was crowded (half term for children).

11th Benfleet. Lunched in 'Restawhile Cafe.' Coach to Eastwood. Got to 'Longview' 4.55. TV, Children's Hour. dinner & TV.

18th Arrived at Ed's 6 o'clock. ... Pleasant evening with Ed & Eva.

DEC

2nd Engineers had 24 hours strike for 15% wage increase.

7th Ed taken to hospital.

11th Ed hurried to Black Notley hospital. Ernie also rang thro'.

13th Ernie rang thro' saying no hope of recovery - complications.

14th Bus to Braintree and 2 mile walk to Black Notley Hospital. Ed better than we expected - kept alive with glucose solution going through nose.

17th Eva phoned thro' late saying Ed was to have another operation.

19th E.J.G. sent me £19 bonus.

20th Ernie phoned - Ed a little better.

22nd New stove put in kitchen, 'Taygo.'

25th Rene, Cliff & Graham to dinner. Mimic guessing game.

28th I am not wanted for stock-taking in January, possibly in March.

30th Bus to Black Notley Hospital. Ed looks much better.

1954

JAN

14th Gardener came and put gummy substance round trees.

20th Rang up Louise. Latest report of Ed not good - no appetite &c.

27th Caught 1.30 bus to Black Notley Hospital - Mary Ruck ward. Ed was sitting in n easy chair by bed. Gave him the grapes - skinned and stoned in jar - and tulips. Eva came around 2.30. Had a pleasant 1 1/2 hours with him - he was glad to see me.

30th Cis & I did not go to the L.B.P.A. annual meeting as it was too cold and did not merit the expense. We stayed in the warm and played Kanugo.

FEB

5th Dr. Beattie gave me a 'coal priority permit' for Mr. Harvey.

6th Cis & I went to Y.L.C. Squash at Co-op Hall Ley Street (opposite Victory Garage).

7th Cold affected kidneys so did no go out in morning. We both went to Roding Hall. Dr. Beattie preached on Eternal Bliss.

8th Having to lend Mr. Harvey coal and coke as they have none.

9th Went to Roding Hall. Wedding bells for Miss Edna Bibby and Mr. Vincent Craven of Canada - their present was an hors-d'ouvres dish.

15th Ernie rang thro' saying Ed was leaving Black Notley on Wednesday.

17th Ed back at West Mersea. Ed left Black Notley Hospital this morning in ambulance and arrived safely at West Mersea at 1.30. Ernie and Eva were there & soon made him comfortable. He was very weak but soon able to eat his dinner. Nearly ten weeks in hospital - 3 operations.

23rd Had a short time with wireless, listened to 'Jane Eyre.'

24th Cis & I went to Northwick Park via Oxford Circus & Baker Street, arriving at Eernie's at 4.00pm. Spent evening with Ernie, Louise, Margaret & David. Had tea. Ernie came in about 6.00. We left at 9.00 with Ernie's dress suit which he lent me again.

25th Went to Worldwide Missionaries Exhibition, Waldegrave Hall, Duke St. W1. Saw Kodak-slides on Egypt Today.

MARCH

4th West Ham District Association of Pharmacist's Annual dinner. Trocadero Rest. Joan Cloud toasted, J. Heseltine responded.

5th Roding Lane in evening. All prayed especially for Morris & Levett and Billy Graham.

16th Cis & I went to Mansion House 62nd annual gathering. Lord Mayor in chair - Alderman Sir Noel Vansittart Bowater. Tea at Kardoma Fleet Street... Harringay, arriving 6.5. Had a good seat in Arena. Fine meeting - 11,000 there - some unable to get in. Splendid singing and a fine address by Billy Graham - 'Loneliness.' Several hundreds declared for Christ.

17th Spoke to two bus conductors about Billy Graham.

26th Mrs. Birke of Eastwood had an accident from which she died, leaving Rene the bungalow 'Longview.'

APRIL

3rd Oxford won the 100th Boat Race, 20 mins 23 1/2 seconds.

5th Went to Bank & got £5 and will & 2 books of National Savings Certificates.

8th Sowed runners, dwarf beans and sweet peas.

15th Cis & I went to Eastwood. Rene very poorly with gall bladder or liver trouble as well as her duoDenal ulcer. Took Howard to Southend and had a breath of sea air.

19th Cliff got Mrs. Birke's wireless set which I bought for £4.

24th ... went to Haringay. Queued up... and was told there was no room in the arena so we went into the annexe - very unsatisfactory. Cis & Graham very disappointed and upset. After the service we found the party from Eastwood & Graham went back with them, taking blazer & raincoat.

Billy Graham was an American evangelist and an ordained Southern Baptist minister who became well known internationally in the late 1940s. He was a prominent evangelical Christian figure, and according to a biographer, was "among the most influential Christian leaders" of the 20th century. Graham held large indoor and outdoor rallies with sermons that were broadcast on radio and television, with some still being re-broadcast into the 21st century. In his six decades on television, Graham hosted annual crusades, evangelistic campaigns that ran from 1947 until his retirement in 2005. He visited Harringay Arena in London in March 1954: beginning his sermon with: '*We've not come here to the city of London to save England. We have not come here with any great ideas that we are going to tell you how to do it. We haven't come here to try to reform you. We have come here at the invitation of these churches to help lead you in a Crusade to win men to Jesus Christ and help promote the kingdom of God in Britain.*' More than

2 million people attended the historic three-month Crusade, with nearly 40,000 commitments to Christ.

Harringay Arena, March 16th 1954.

MAY

4th Finished cataloguing books in dining room.

5th Heard from Ed - he has been downstairs.

17th Went to E.J. George and continued the entries into DD.Reg. Had to sit in the typist's office.

19th Queen's visit to Mansion House. Went to E.P. Caine's, 2.v. Street (2 Victoria Street?), & opened shop and cellar for E.J. George on behalf of Grossman of Aldgate who has bought shop but affairs not yet settled. I had to wait for the fitters and shop front fitters to take measurements. They finished at 1 o'clock but the crowd was too dense for me to see Queen or Duke. Lunched in ABC Ludgate Hill, & opened cellar door for young Grossman who would work among the W.V. stock - dirt & dust during afternoon. Number of house may change to '39.' I wrote to Mayor in protest.

20th E.J. George may not want Suffolk & Norfolk done this year. Mr. S. Maynard, 32, Lord Avenue, getting up a petition against re-numbering. Cis & I went and got many signatures. We got good receptions.

22nd Billy Graham's crusade, final two meetings. Coach to White City 1.15 where we heard Billy Graham & some of his team speak & sing. Some of our party went on to Wembley - about 120,000 attended for the final meeting of the crusade.

27th Had an afternoon of cricket in Valentine Park - Essex & Kent batting, followed on.

JUNE

9th Women's Outing to W. Mersea. Arr. 12.45 'Lilybank.' Heard that numbers here are not to be altered.

10th Cis told many (about) the victory at the council over the numbering. A few were disgruntled because of the expense they went to in altering their numbers. (17 altered their numbers, 110 did not). I wrote to Ed about lady who wishes to buy land in West Mersea.

11th Wrote to BBC and did Baptist Times crossword and sent it up.

12th Holiday at Sea View, Isle of Wight. Springfield Court, Springvale - just a small town.

Mr. & Mrs. Allshurst at our table - retired Govt. Official, 20 years in Kenya.

23rd Had a birthday card from Rene.

26th End of holiday. Cost approximately £35. Got home 6.50. Mr. Harvey had mowed the lawns. 'Air' letter from Mabel - coming back - to us.

28th Sent off film to Gratispool, Glasgow, and 2 films to W.W. for D&P. Cis sent an 'air' letter to Mabel.

Gratispool - literally meaning 'free film' - was arguably the first, and certainly the most famous, of the UK photographic film processing companies that dealt directly with the public via mail order. In various guises they operated from the early 1930s through to the early 1980s, whereafter the company was sold to a succession of new owners over the next 20 years, during which time the Gratispool brand name disappeared.

30th W.V.S. promised to lend us a bedstead for Mabel.

JULY

1st. Cis & I went to Spurgeon's College via Gants Hill, L. Bridge & Norwood. Speech Day. Chairman H.C. Janes of Luton. Diplomas & prizes.

8th Cis & I left about 2.00 for Ernie's. All fairly well. Played with David - toys. Ernie got in 5.45. Tea & afterwards 'putted' on the lawn. I had 3 games with Ernie, 2 with Mgt., 1 with David, 2 with Cis. (Clock golf). Happy time. Louise suffers with thrombosis of the leg. Ernie's skin fairly good. Children well.

9th Cis 'phoned Canard... and found out that the Empress of France arr. L'pool 8am Monday morning.

14th Return of Arthur & Mabel Head. Arthur very weak but voyage did him good. Sleeping in lounge for time being. Cis & Mabel very happy to see each other.

15th Arthur sat about much of day. Cis & Mabel went shopping in afternoon. Mr. & Mrs. Harvey went to Kew to see some rooms.

23rd I signed my will with Wakeling & Mabel witnessing. Cis did not sign hers as she wanted it altered again.

27th Cis signed her sill, Wakeling and Mabel witnessing.

28th Dr. Beattie called and examined Arthur. Much of the trouble now his heart.

AUGUST

6th Got a recorder for Cis. Cis & I caught 2.55 coach to Southend, 4/6d return, to Jones Corner. Garden so very wet could not go out except for a look round. Rene now has chickens, dog, cat and budgey sic) also garden to look after. Cliff transforming kitchen. Additional room being built on to lounge. After tea played cricket with knitting needle and table-tennis ball.

7th After tea we had TV until bedtime.

13th Cis went to Rayleigh, Hadleigh, & Leigh-on-Sea finding NHS employment bureau.

14th Cliff took us to Canvey Island. Read a little of Dombey & Son.

18th Went to Ed's. Ed walking about with a stick.

27th Arthur not so well - weak and despondent. Had to help shave him with my electric razor.

Seemingly a staple of every child's schooling in the postwar era, the humble recorder experienced a renaissance in the 1950s and 60s.

SEPT

3rd Cis & Mabel went to King George Hospital & the x-ray was done. I made tea for Arthur & myself. They returned after 5.00pm. Mabel very brave.

6th No operation - too far gone. Would have to go to London Hospital three times a week for radio-therapy.

10th Sent Clive a card.

11th Clive 16.

19th (Sunday) Listened to Radio Mission Service, Rev. S. Windwood.

31st Entered up some more books from lower bookcase. Arthur had a visitor from Beckton Gas Works.

OCT

1st Sent a card to Anne.

3rd Anne's birthday.

4th Arthur taken into Hermon Hill Hospital for 02 (oxygen)... On the danger list. Cis went with him and stayed till 10.00pm.

6th Luton. Left case at George Hotel, room 51...Had a walk around and found Baptist Church. A poor Irishman begged coppers - I gave him 3d and a gospel message.

14th Dock & Bus strikes worse.

15th BDH Open day. Hardly any buses in the City. Bob & Ed there, and 75 others.

16th Bus strike.

NOV

5th Saffron Walden. Coffee in Copper Kettle.

7th Grove Rd. Missionary Church. Reverend White preached from 2 Peter III - element dissolved - fervent heat - atom bomb.

8th Mr. Harvey started work at Plesseys.

12th Central Hall, Westminster. Great Radio Rally. L.E. Choir took part. Eric Hutchings, John Grant gave a special replica broadcast.

12th Signed Barclays Guarantee £100 for Cliff.

On Nov. 16th domestic tragedy strikes, as the Sibley's lodger, Arthur Head, falls ill.

16th Arthur Hubert Head died, aged 72. Mabel & Cis went to hospital. Cis rang thro' saying she would be back later as Arthur was worse. Minutes later he suddenly died - myochardia infarction. Mabel & Cis were back 8.50. Mabel very brave but greatly upset, and Cis.

20th Undertaker brought Arthur's remains this morning and placed in lounge.

22nd Funeral, City of London Cemetery.

DEC

2nd Brother Harry died this morning, aged 84. Win. Sibley 'phoned through saying Harry passed away this morning. I 'phoned to Ed & Eva and told them. Harry died in Enfield hospital, sudden heart attack.

6th Cis enjoying the making of a wool dog.

8th Harry buried. 144 to The Cambridge, 34 to Green Lanes, and trolley bus to Winchmore. Arriving 11.45. Bertha's sister Annie's daughter Dolly - lives at Westcliff - was on bus and guessed it was me and we went together to No. 30. Harry's son (Stan) & May & Win, (Grace in W. Africa), Bo & son Bob there, with Stan's daughter Carol, & May's son Peter & daughter. Funeral 12.15, & grave in Edmonton Cemetery. Despite heavy rain & wind, everything was carried out well - C of E. dinner provided - meat pie & lemon curd tart. Bus to Turnpike Lane & Picadilly tube to Holborn. Went to Stoll Theatre and saw 'Souls in Conflict,' - Billy Graham's film. 3/- seat. Very good.

The older generation of the Sibley clan is fading. Thomas is now 76, and entering the age when friends and relatives are passing away.

9th Central Hall Westminster. Cis brought two macaroons.

Christmas Carols.

18th Tied up parcels for Louise, Ed & Freda.

20th E.J.George's Christmas dinner, Beale's Rest. Cabaret & dancing 9.30.

Richard Beale's Resturant in north London was coming slowly to the end of its life as a heart of fine dining and entertainment. It was to be reborn as a hotel, and indeed Beales Hotels still exists as a family business dating back to 1769, when master baker John Beale opened a shop in Oxford Street. Remarkably one of their advertsing brochures from the 1950s survives, so we can enter the restaurant with Thomas and Cissie and the staff of E.J. George's Pharmaceutical stock-takers on the evening of December 20th 1954.

23rd I went to Ilford and got a desk calendar for the Harveys. Went to Woolworths for lamps. Cis got a tongue from Aldridges. Ed sent 'Albert Schweitzer' & a scarf for Cis.

25th Cliff, Rene, Graham, Howard, & kitten - Felix - came 12.45… Played 'House,' & 'Pit.' Left 9.30 for Romford to collect Mrs. Ringwood.

1955

JAN

4th Helped Cis with her 'Pictorial' prize attempt. Warmed myself by sweeping snow away.

12th Called in at 97 Capel Rd. and had a chat with Tommy Offord who is 84, also Winifred (Popsie), the daughter & her 2 children, also Stanley who travels for Morney's - he was in bed with a broken arm and gout. Had a cup of tea with Tommy who wanted me to play him a game of chess. Mabel kindly said she would give me £50 towards the trip to Italy in August.

14th Cis & I went to Ilford. I bought Cis a mack at Fairman's, High Rd., £3-13-6d.

17th Leslie Wright wrote a nice letter - regretting his former letter, and desires to be reconciled. Went to Caves and got (Arthur's) overcoat which had been altered.

18th Bought 'What to Say in Italian,' from Smiths, Barnet.

20th Wrote to Margaret and David, and Leslie Wright.

21st Bob 76 years.

29th Bob died. Robert Oldren Sibley.

And so Thomas's companion and brother from his childhood and youth was gone. But after one day's mourning the indomitable travelling salesman is back on his rounds and off to Hemel Hempstead.

31st. Hemel Hempstead - Midland Hotel.

FEB

1st. Harpenden, Mrs. Dillings. Cyril & Gladys came in about 6.15 and we had High Tea. I did writing in dining room and they looked at television in lounge. Cis rang through saying Bob had died on Saturday. Funeral on Thursday at H. Heath. This was a sudden blow and so unexpected. Cyril & Gladys went to a local social & Mrs D & I chatted until 10.40.

FAIRY SNOW HOT WATER BOTTLE OFFER

20 YEAR GUARANTEE

This Hot Water Bottle is made from polythene and has been carefully inspected and tested. Should this article prove to be defective or unusable because of rot of the materials used in its construction within twenty years of the date of this offer, we hereby guarantee that the article will be replaced without cost to you, if it is returned to the address below accompanied by this certificate.

This guarantee does not apply to parts (including the cap washer).

THOMAS HEDLEY & CO. LTD. GOSFORTH, NEWCASTLE UPON TYNE 3.

November, 1958

2nd Gladys showed me their new car, Ford 'Consul.' St. Albans for lunch at Thales - waitress wanted to charge 3/6d. 341 bus to Newman's, bus stop at Oakwood Drive, arr. 5.30. Chatted with Mrs. Newman while pressure cooker cooked vegetables. Margaret and Mr. Newman arrived soon after 6 o'clock when we had dinner - chump chop, peas, potatoes, plums and custard - very good. Mrs. N. & Margaret had to attend classes so Mr. Newman washed and I wiped. We had a long chat. Mrs. N. & Mgt returned soon after 9 o'clock. Mgt retired (she is 17, plump & tall), and Mr & Mrs. N & myself had CSSM reading & prayer. Cis sent Bob's letter and a black tie.

3rd Funeral of poor old Bob (companion of early days), aged 76 years. Breakfast at 8.15 - cornflakes & bacon. 9.10 bus to Hertford & 10.32 bus to Hertford Heath. Bob's funeral 11 o'clock. Poor Nellie was in a sad way and did not attend funeral altho at local church. All Bob's family and most of Harry's there. Ed, Eva & Cissie Harris motored from West Mersea. Service at the church very nice.

Doris played the organ. We all returned to Bob (Junior's) house - modern, & all had a cup of tea and hot dinner - stewed steak and apple tart. Bob redeemed my case from Sheffields and left it at P.I. where he works. Ed's car took me to Hertford on his way back to W. Mersea. Bus to Stevenage and was at Cromwell Hotel at 5.00 - room no. 10.

9th Mabel had the welfare officer from Beckton Gasworks visit her. Phoned Mr. Cooper about Italian Grammar.

11th Rene 44.

16th Cis 7 I went to Ernie's… Northwick Park. Had to walk thro' the snow. Welcomed by Louise & David (who is better from his meningitis). Ernie came in at 6.00, Margaret abt. 5.00. We had tea 6.00 - cheese &c & rice pudding and apple tart.

17th Mabel had an early visit from Beckton Gasworks who paid her £2.

22nd. Some study of Italian. Still reading 'French Revolution.'

23rd. Mr. Pledger came round and inspected dining-room wall - damp.

28th Finished cataloguing my books. I have about 1,300 bound books.

MARCH

7th Mrs. Harvey went to Roding Lane and Mrs. B lent her the 'Life of Amy Carmichael' which she wanted me to read first. I started on it.

21st Spent afternoon making a nesting box and nailed it into the wall above the kitchen window.

22nd Started for Northampton - F.C.F.C. 59th Congress. Arr. 2.17, *had a look around town, left case at Community Centre - Methodist Church. ... Back to Community Centre 4.30. Mayor arrived & we had tea. Speeches afterwards. Rev. Copland Simmons very witty. Met Mr. E. Dickens who took me to his house in his Rover car. Met Rev. E.H. Roberts who is to share bedroom with me and we returned to 17 Abington Pk. Crescent.*

23rd Visited Philip Doddridge's Church and saw relics and curios.

25th 10.5 to Euston. Had a young soldier in my carriage and I was able to talk to him about his soul. Went to T.C. Rd. Station and visited Foyles. Started entering up my report on the Conference.

26th Packed electric blanket away for the summer.

APRIL

14th Rene came to dinner and stayed until Cliff & Howard came for them. Cliff took Howard to Central Hall Westminster to see mechanical engine train and models &c. Finished reading Madam Bovary, Flaubert.

19th Tommy Offord died - aged 84.

21st Newspaper strike over.

MAY

10th Went to Eastern Avenue Methodist Church Rally. Induction of President Rev. Norman Upright.

14th Graham & Howard came to dinner 12.30. Howard brought Dinky toys to play with.

23rd Dock Strike commenced in London and several ports.

26th Ipswich. Had coffee and a chat with Mr. Hale in his office. He asked me to say grace. He had saccharine & brandy in his coffee (for his heart).

28th Great Railway Strike commenced at midnight.

JUNE

22nd 78 - praise the Lord.

27th Kings Lynn. Dukes Head, room 36. Lunch at Regent Cafe - mutton & coffee, 3/-, & 3d. Little Italian.

JULY

6th Eggs, porridge, bacon. (Uova, tegame e pancetta).

7th Cromer. Walked to Hipperson's, 34 Mill Rd. Mr. J.S.H. had been away in a mental hospital and unlikely to work again. I left my card.

18th Oval. Surrey v. S. Africans. The Queen came & was introduced to the S. African players & the Surrey team.

21st Brookes (opposite) moved out and newcomers moved in.

22nd Leslie Wright & Paul came to lunch. Paul the same only bigger.

23rd I went with Graham to Euston and saw him on to the 10.40 train to Grange-Over-Sands. Fearful crowd.

28th Sudbury. Lunch in Tudor Restaurant - fish and gooseberry tart. Sudbury Market Day - very crowded. Bought 'Count of Monte Cristo.'

30th Paid rates at Westminster Bank. Went to Euston and met Graham at 3.46 on his return from Grange-Over-Sands. He enjoyed himself - had spent all his money. Got back to 35 where he had a good meal - he'd had nothing since 8 o'clock. Graham went home on the 6.45. coach.

AUGUST

2nd Cis got another deck-chair canvas which I nailed on. Dug up the remains of peas and reset the brussell sprouts.

4th Had a look round Foyles and got a small book on Italy 8/-6d.

8th Oval. Surrey & Middx. Lunched there - chatted with a young man from the Civil Service (Intelligence Dept.).

11th Got French & Swiss francs & Italian lire and 2 x £5 traveller's cheques. Ordered Myatt refills from Smiths Gants Hill & bought 5/- book on birds. Lunch then I spent afternoon in Valentine's Park watching cricket match - Ilford Thursday versus Mayor's team. Cup of tea on the lawn. Had a read in the evening.

12th Cleaned up case for records - case given to Cis by Mr. Curtis.

19th Holiday in Italy. Cis saw me off on train. I met Rev. G.R. Beasley-Murray at Victoria 11.45.. our party only 15 as one fell over and broke her leg so could not go. Calais by the SS Cote d'azur. Smooth crossing.

For the ordinary Briton foreign travel was still very much a novelty in 1955 - the days of the affordable package holiday was some years away but the international coach trip was in its ascendency; so for Sibley to vacation abroad in his Seventies was both pioneering and an adventure.

20th Lovely journey through Switzerland. Milano, Hotel Locarno, room 14. We went as a party to the Chiesa della Grazie, and saw the original painting on the wall, The Lord's Supper by Leonardo da Vinci. Visited Cathedral, went on roof.

21st Up at 8.5, overslept. Lock jammed and had to be forced before I could get out. Most of us went to Baptist Church. Wrote to Cis, & 3 cards - Rene, Graham & Howard, and Mabel. Rambled round by use of maps. Very enjoyable - loving people.

22nd Went on to Verona. Lunched at the Hotel Rivas Lorenzo - a fine place. Lunch was spaghetti, beefsteak, peppers & grapes. Had a look at the arena, climbed the steps. Had a look at notable houses and balcony where Romeo & Juliet met. Coach, then went on to Venezia - steamer along the Grand Canal to Calle dei Fabi - Hotel Servizia .We all had a Gondola trip along the Grand Canal - wonderful sight and experience. Coffee in Piazza S. Marco - band playing.

23rd. Up at 7 o'clock. I had to ask the woman attendant 'che ora e?' - otto meno la dieci. Miss Bridgstock had her handbag stolen from her bedroom - money, passport &c. D.B. Murray informed police. Poor Miss Bridgstock upset. We all contributed something for her immediate use. Bought penknife. Visited Doge's Palace - magnificent marble rooms, paintings, walls & ceilings by the great masters. Also went over the prisons, and glass-blowing manufacturers. Had a look at Lido and returned to the Servizia 7.30.

24th Ferrara and Ravenna for lunch, a very beautiful place. Hotel

Capallo, Casa Francesca da Rimini. Had a look at Dante's memorial. Florence 7.00 - Hotel Medici. Wrote to Rene & Cis. Hot in bed but not as bad as Venice.

25th Walked on veranda and stood in the sun - fine view. Coach to Palazzo e Galleria Pitti - guide took us to a wonderful art gallery and museum, (some of the world's best painters).

26th Visited il Duomo. Pisa. Climbed tower.

27th Arezzo, lunch at hotel Subario, Assisi. Hotel Ginerva, via della vita 29, Rome. An American lady took us to the fountain and to

King Emanuel memorial.

28th Went over George Boardman Taylor orphanage.

29th St. Peter's, catacombs, coloseum, pantheon.

30th 8.23 to Naples. Guide took us over Pompeii.

31st Left Hotel Ginerva Roma. Lunched at Hotel Milano, Aquapendente, where Princess Margaret stayed in 1949. Tea in Siena and hurried visit to Cathedral. Bought a book on Florence, 400 lire. Packed for journey.

SEPT

1st. Milano station 4.15, left at 5.35 for Calais. Trouble with Italian office through Miss Bridgstock not having her passport, wanted to turn her out. D.B. Murray managed to keep her in the train.

2nd Home 5.30. Gave Cis pendant, neckerchief, purse, Mabel powder, soap and pretty glass vase, something for Cliff., Rene, Howard & Graham.

6th 10.15 coach to Jones Corner (Leigh-on-Sea). Met Rene on way to butchers. Howard came in from school.

13th Cambridge. Cherry Hinton Rd., Glengarry Hotel. Proprietor's wife knows Italian, had a chat with her. dinner again at the Scotch House.

14th Ely. Bell Hotel.

16th 10.42 to L'Pool St. An elderly, educated, loquacious & somewhat loquacious lady was in the carriage with me.

26th Bedford. Swan Hotel - room 46. Coffee in snack bar and viewed the illuminations on the riverbank.

29th Heard from Cis - poor old Graham had his first operation last

Tuesday.

OCT

4th Harpenden. Dalkieth Rd. - Mr. & Mrs. Dilling. Mrs. Dilling went with me to the post, and we sat over the electric fire talking until Glady & Cyril came home. Had some supper and sat talking until 11o'clock.

5th Gave Mrs. D a doctor's book, 'Doctor to the Rescue.'

Welwyn Garden City - Cowper's Arms Hotel. Rm No. 7.

6th Stevenage. Cromwell Hotel. Duck & apple crumble.

12th Cis & I caught the 1.18 Ilford to Rochford. Met Rene & we went to Rochford Hospital - Victoria ward. Saw Graham. He was very cheerful and looked fairly well. I took him 9 records for his gramophone.

14th BDH Pensioner's Open Day. Ed there, about 87 assembled. Had a chat with Oakley in the Galenical Dept. who now lives at Billericay. A short highly dressed actress woman sang several songs - Marion Sanders.

15th Trotter said yesterday that Tommy Offord had died. He died April 19th.

19th Caught 1.8 train to Rochford. Rene met us and we visited Graham who was cheerful in spite of being on diet (no sugar, sweets, biscuits). Food must go to the bones and not to make fat. Cis took him pomegranate, apples, pears, grapes, bananas, but no dates.

20th Started fires in new grate.

21st Cis 61.

24th Colchester. Cups Hotel rm 42. Moot Hall meeting. Crowded. Had a chat with Bill Bathman (USA).

26th Arrived Ed's 5.00. Evening spent in reminiscences. Caught 9.30 bus from Seaview Avenue. In hotel by 10.10. Mabel & Cis went to London Hospital.

NOV

2nd Cliff has bought the Ford car for Graham.

3rd. Cis & I went to Blackfriar's, Script. Lit. Crusade. Cis bought me a grey thick washcoat (?) for Christmas.

15th Pitsea. Had a long wait for Brylcreem's rep at Tarpots. Lunched in 'Restawhile Cafe' - not good enough now.

16th Cis went to see Graham - Rene & Cliff there. Cis gave Cliff Mabel's £45 - loan until Eric gives his to Cliff.

30th Walthamstow. Lunched in ABC Hoe St.

DEC

3rd. Ilford. Went to Bank, and Mrs. Thomas's for Andrews, Ribena, Steradent, and Bile Beans.

5th South Woodford. Lunch at Robinson's (stewed beef).

8th Cis & I went to Holborn ... Cis... and a mask outfit for Howard. Walked to Oxford St. And Cis bought a red coatie from Peter Robinson's. Went to Picadilly and had tea in Kardoma. Walked to Westminster and listened to L. Emmanuel Choir. Very good - Victor White and Mr. W. Challen were excellent.

13th Snow and ice in many parts of England.

14th Wrote a letter in Italian to Sugarino Santo, Acquaclepente, enclosing colonial stamps & a Christmas card - put John III.ch 16 in Italian on letter.

20th Tied up parcels for Ed, Eva, Ernie, Louise & family. Did some Christmas cards and book for Paul Wright.

21st. Cis & I went to Rochford Hospital and saw Graham who is in a wheelchair. We gave & received presents. I received a Fonopad, (Cliff & Rene), desk blotter (Graham), & 2 handkerchieves from Howard. Mabel all right with Mrs. H. Mabel has a small wireless in her room.

26th Bought Cis a 4/- ice cream cake.

I rang up Freda and had a chat with her and Clive. Clive is over 6ft.

28th Cis went to hospital and saw Graham - he is on crutches.

30th Went to Mrs. Thomas' for Andrews, Ribena, & Yardley Gift set for Cis. Nurse came about 12 o'clock and gave Mabel a blanket bath.

1956

JAN

4th Saw Graham in his wheelchair. Gave Rene some of my Cassell's history books.

5th AA - 'worst fog ever.' The Automobile Association were not entirely correct - officially the Great Smog of 1952 was the worst onslaught of pollutants, that killed in excess of 4,000 and was the impulse for the Clean Air Act of 1956, which reduced the use of coal-fired furnaces.

6th Not certain of fog, so did not venture out.

11th Cis went to Rochford Hospital for the last time (we hope). Graham has had to go home on account of his bed being required. He was pleased and yet sorry as he was liked by both patients and nurses. Cliff took him home in the car.

12th EC2 & EC3. No orders. A tiring day in the rain.

13th Called in Dewhurst's on Bishopsgate St. and got an Irish chicken for 7/6d.

London smog in the 1950s was a way of life until the Clean Air Act of 1956.

18th E2 journey. Half an hour in B.G. Museum. (Bishopsgate?)

23rd Wrote to T.L. Ireman (?) MP to vote against the small lotteries & gaming bill, and to Dimplex Ltd. Totton about their oil-filled radiators.

25th Sent off to Daily Sketch with Baby Competition selections for prize of fur coat.

28th Bob (author's note: his brother Bob's son) *'phoned through saying his Mother Nellie had died.*

FEB

1st Ellen Elizabeth Sibley buried, aged 70. Funeral 11am Hertford Heath Church. Arrived Bob's house, 55, Woodlands Rd., 10.20. Doris, Lily, Bob & Joe, Stan & Iris, were the followers.

8th Ambulance came at 8am and took Mabel to London Hospital.

11th Rene's 45th birthday Reunion Party. Prepared for visitors. Freda, Anne & Clive arrived 4.15. (Clive over 6ft - a fine lad). Cliff, Rene, Graham & Howard about 4.30. Dinner, special menu (which I wrote): turkey, ham, sausage, peas, Banana Splits. Honey mould jellies, petit-four, fruit cup. Pleasant time in lounge. Graham played the gramophone, Howard did some magic. Had a mime, and 'What would you do?' Freda left at 9.30, Cliff 10.30. A very happy reunion.

At a dance hall in Twickenham in the mid-1950s, Clive Sibley smokes while his mate makes an obscene gesture. This was the age of the jitterbug, the birdy hop, and sticking two fingers up to the older generation.

This was a memorable family gathering of three generations of the Sibleys; a rare visit from Len's widow Freda, and her children Anne and Clive. They were still living in Twickenham, proof being that we have a photograph of Clive at a dance hall in the 1950s.

13th W8 journey. High St. Kensington, lunched in Lyon's Earl's Ct. Rd. Bussed it to Charing Cross, had an hour in the National Gallery, walked to Oxford Circus.

14th Wrote to J.E.B. - 1955-56 travelling ended.

15th Had just a quiet day. Glad of a big fire.

22nd Had a real lazy day. Cold seemed to sap energy and initiative. Cis thawed out our frozen basin - froze during the evening. Frightened out a bird in the 'house' near the window sill.

25th About 6 o'clock Cliff, Rene, Graham & Howard drove up - Graham driving. Cis managed a good tea for them. They left about 9pm taking mattress.

MARCH

2nd Helped Cis make a model tree for her Sunday School class.

5th Heard from Ed - he told me Mr. Barkey had been killed in Algiers, Mrs. Barkey injured. Ambulance came 3.5., took Mabel with Cis for examination. Fluid wa drawn off chest - Cis was told by a doctor that she was dying. Mabel seemed none the worse for her ordeal - a little pain on the chest during the night. Nothing more can be done for her.

7th Mr. Harvey gave me an enlargement of Mabel. He was upset when I told him Mabel did not like it.

8th Trocadero Restaurant, WHDA Pharmacist's Dinner and Dance, 53rd year. Miss Joan Cloud President Home 10.45. Mabel all right.

12th Mabel quite unable to get out of bed. Looked thro' and destroyed some of Arthur's old gasworks magazines.

26th. Mabel still alive, difficulty breathing. Went to YLC meeting Clementswood & saw the film 'Driftwood' by London Embankment Mission. Heavy rain when we came out. I walked through the rain with Mr. Croyston. Arrived home and found that Mabel had died 9.10. Cis in tears. Mr. & Mrs. Harvey sat with her until I returned.

Mrs. Stewart came by taxi and laid the body out. Cis helped her. She charged £2-2/-. Mr. Curtis took Mrs. Stewart home at 11.20 - she couldn't get a taxi.

27th Went to 70 Aldborough Rd. and got the usual death certificate. C-op men called this evening with a coffin. Mabel's remains placed in it and layed in lounge. They did the work well.

28th Cis & I went to Ilford and Cis bought a navy blue coat, £8-8/- from Fairman Ltd., High Rd.

30th Several wreaths arrived. Mr. & Mrs. Harvey went out for the day in Buckinghamshire.

31st Mabel Ellen Head buried 10 o'clock. Co-op came, funeral C.L. cemetery.

APRIL

2nd. Bank Holiday Monday. Cliff, Rene, Graham & Howard came in the Ford car. Graham took me for a drive around. Rene had many things to take back.

3rd Went to Co-op and ordered lettering for the gravestone, £4-12/-.

9th Discovered hedgehog in garden still. He woke up and went to Curtis' fence.

13th Made a small black 'bedouin' tent for Cis.

This craftsmanship was for Cis' Sunday School activities - earlier in the week he had bought some lead animals from Woolworths.

6th Cis collected from '37' old glazed tiles to make crazy pavement path in garden.

21st Gas Co. sent Mabel's death allowance £6.

28th Saturday. Went to Beal Grammar School NYLC Rally.

MAY

10th Trip to Worthing. Walked to Mr. & Mr. Sobey's 37 Queen St., & stayed about 45 mins. Visited Mr. & Mrs. Child at no. 11 - nice house. Home 10 o'clock.

23rd Cis found a tortoise in the park - brought it home, given to her by the park-keeper. Went to cemetery and put lilacs on Popp's grave and on Mabel's grave.

JUNE

2nd TV set fixed up. Had to hurry to Mr. Hall's to complete Mabel's affairs. Everything signed and sealed. .. I got my balance, £102-0-3 leaving Win £906-9-2. Alf Partridge and his girl came and he and Cliff came and helped fit up TV set, and aerial in garden. Paid Cliff £18.

4th Woodbridge. Wickham Market. Booked in to the Great White Horse Ipswich, room 12a. Dinner at Queen's Hotel.

9th Holiday Isle of Wight - Seaview.

14th Bowls in Pucknall Park.

JULY

7th TV fire. Put on another connector. Vocal all right but vision noisy, and then caught fire (connexion broke and burnt out). Cis & I got the set in garden. Cis 'phoned Cliff who will come over for it. Mr. Pledger helped us in with it as it was so heavy.

16th Thetford. Changed at Harling Rd., walked to East Harling, got a lift back. Station master (at Harling Rd.) was 'fishing' his keys left on office desk - he had shut himself out. He had a long hook which he was using through a window. My case & lunch was in the office.

Had lunch in waiting room, went to Brandon then back to Thetford, Bell Hotel, room 14a.

25th Mixed cement and finished off path. Hot work! Rene rang thro' saying Cliff & Alf were coming for TV set. Alf examined set and said it was badly burned and estimated damage at £20. They left the TV set for the insurance co. to inspect it - all in pieces.

The White Horse Hotel, Ipswich.

AUGUST

7th BDH increase of pension £18 p.a. Income tax refund £19.

8th Cis & I went to Thorpe Bay and visited the Newmans at their chalet (No. 17).

11th Alf Partridge came with another table TV - he wants £19-10/- for it. Wrote out for Eagle insurance - total loss.

15th Cliff & Rene came about TV, and Cliff managed to get it going. Aerial mostly at fault.

16th Mr. Hall 'phoned. Can we put up an assistant solicitor for a time? Cis said yes. He will be coming October 1st.

20th Dickins & Co. Assessor's representative called and looked at remains of TV. Passed claim for £20. Called in Woolworths and bought socks and book, Mutiny on the Bounty. Cis met Howard at coach stop W.B. Rd. 11.45.

21st. Took Howard for a day's outing. Visited Tower of London. Looked at river and Tower Bridge. Walked to Fenchurch Street Lyons. ... went to Chancery Lane and took Howard to E.J. George's office. Went to Baker Street, Madame Tussauds. Chamber of Horrors.

24th Swiss Holiday. Wengen. Alpenrose Hotel.

SEPT

11th Rene pleased with her musical cottage and the boys with their Swiss caps. Howard at school, Graham at work.

30th Mr. K. Lloyd came to stay for a time.

OCT

1st. Bedford, Swan Hotel.

2nd Visited museum near Swan.

4th Did most of Luton. Red Lion for dinner - service bad, they were teaching a young Spaniard to serve who did not know English - had to order in French. Back to the George and had a chat with the Swiss friend who is attending to some chemical insulations. Had a read of Mutiny on the Bounty.

For 200 years Luton was a thriving, beautiful industrial town founded on the hat industry and, in the 20th century, aviation and car manufacturing; both Vauxhall and Electrolux were leading manufacturers of the locality. The town had a tram system from 1908 until 1932 and the first cinema was opened in 1909. A Carnegie Library opened in the town in 1910. By 1914, the population reached had 50,000. It is accepted by many today (2023) that Luton is in a state of managed decline; as of 2022 the unemployment rate is higher than the regional and national rates, 6.1 per cent in comparison to 3.8 and 4.4 per cent respectively.

5th Cliff, Graham, Rene & Howard brought my TV, got it fixed up. They didn't stay long. Looked at TV. David Copperfield &c.

13th Tried out TV 5.20-6pm. Ok.

14th Cis put tortoise, 'Joey,' in box, leaves and old blanket, in hall cupboard.

19th BDH Pensioner's Open Day. Ed there, also Willings. I did not stop for the singing, only the conjuring.

Luton in its nineteenth century heyday as a prosperous semi-industrial market town - now in a state of managed decline.

21st Cis 62.

31st Colchester. Lunched in Last's - beef. 4.15 to W. Mersea, had fish tea with Ed & Eva. Ed imparted some serious news about Eva's behaviour to her father in spiritual things on account of Flossy Thompson. Ed going to leave Mersea and marry Florence. He is greatly upset over Eva as well as Ruth & Winnie.

Just as the Suez crisis was fomenting, at home there were domestic ructions as Thomas' elder brother Ed seemingly has a fling with the housemaid, Flossy Thompson.

NOV

1st The English & French bomb the Egyptians.

2nd Israelis got Gaza and took many Egyptians prisoners.

5th Russians still slaughtering Hungarians.

6th British and French take Port Said.

9th Put TV on for Cis to see David Copperfield. Ed rang thro' and told Cis it was all off because of Eva. Cis rang up Louise - Ernie had been to W. Mersea for 2 nights.

10th Dug up carrots and limed some of ground.

16th Leigh-on-Sea. Went to Kent Elm Corner and walked to Rene's where I saw Cliff & Rene and had a cup of tea and cake.

17th Cis & I went to Mile End, the opening of the East London Tabernacle new building - about 1000 there. Captain Jack gave a stirring address.

22nd Lunch in Wells. Expresso coffee in milkbar.

DEC

11th Wrote to Mr. Blackwall. No more travelling until after Christmas.

15th E. j. George send me £25 bonus.

19th Ernie & Louise send us a 'Daily Mail' Calendar.

20th Discovered a painful stiffness in my left side.

22nd Saturday. Cis went to Sunday School party 3.00pm. taking her manger model - cakes, presents. She is to be Old Mother Hubbard and she took a toy dog with her.

23rd My side affected but not whilst walking.

24th Went to Sainsbury's for turkey - tremendous queue but I got mine quickly as I had paid for it, 32-11/-3d. 50 Christmas cards received. TV not working properly - no use as it is.

25th Cliff, Rene, Graham & Howard arrived 12.30.

Evening spent with games. They left for Eastwood well-loaded. Started electric blanket.

1957

JAN

6th Wrote to Ed, Ernie & L., Margaret & David.

9th Lunch in ABC Lower Clapton Rd.

11th I finished E. London rounds for E.J. George & Co., going to Poplar first and then on to Bow, St. Leonard St., and saw Mr. Bell with whom I had a cup of tea and got his S/T order. Lunched at Lyons, Hoe St., & saw Mr. Williams (W & W) & had a chat.

15th Took electric clock to LEB Gants Hill for adjustments. Heard from J.E.B. who wants me to do some of W.End.

17th Dave & Win sent Cis & I pullovers for Christmas presents.

24th Cis went to Princess Louise Hospital St. Quinin's Avenue Ladbroke Grove with Graham.

FEB

11th Spent evening with old photos.

12th Got TV & Wireless licence, £3.

14th New 'phone installed and new bell. Pedestal one old and out of date.

27th I ordered a 'Westamac' cape from George West Ltd. 443

Oxford St., encl cheque £2-19-6.

28th Louise 'phoned through, stopping us coming tomorrow - David has mumps.

MARCH

6th Said goodbye to Mr. Kenneth Lloyd (LODGER) who is moving to Theydon Bois.

7th Trocadero. West Ham & District association of Pharmacists Annual Dinner.

9th Cis put tortoise out.

13th Mrs. Drew paid up to 30th March and gave notice to quit.

22nd Rene had thieves in afternoon when she and Cliff were out.

25th Heard that Mr. E. Sage of BDH had died. Mr. Wood - 30 Lord Ave - came over about car - too small, will try his other car. He is director in engineering firm.

27th Mr. Wood came round and said garage was too small - left a bottle of sherry for the trouble we took. Engineers to strike in London - Harvey will be out.

28th Cleaned out garage and got it ready for new tenant - Mrs. Balcombe of 13 Lord Avenue.

APRIL

3rd Cis had a fall - leg gave way, and she fell in road in Healey Drive.

16th Went to Winchmore Hill N21, called at 30 Kent Rd. House looked gloomy and uncared for. Left a note for Winnie who was out. Ed went out about 10 o'clock and returned 5 o'clock - spent day with Florence T., much to Eva's chagrin.

17th Cliff & Alf motored here about 7.30, saw to TV, which seems in good order. They took away the old TV frame.

28th Went to the Brickfields Congregational Church Stratford & took service.

MAY

1st Went to Westminster Chapel... Rev. Douglas Stewart. Walked thro' Hyde Park - stopped and had beef sandwiches there on park chair - to Piccadilly station.

ILFORD Pictorial

AND GUARDIAN No. 3214 3d.

Thursday, December 10, 1959

PALAIS OPENING

Three lovely models with scarlet-plumed headdresses, figure-hugging costumes, and black nylon fishnet stockings stole the hearts of many Ilford men on Friday night. Where were they? At the dazzling celebration ball which marked the opening of the new Ilford Palais. Photographer Arthur Kaeller found them in the Tudor Room there. Palais opening, report page 17.

2nd Cis won a £36 carpet in Ilford Pictorial. Great excitement as we read in the Ilford Pictorial that Cis had won a carpet in Burn's competition. Cis started to take some dining room stuff into lounge for expected carpet to go into dining room.

9th Dr. Beattie sold his farm at Chigwell - retains 3 cows, chickens etc.

11th Wrote a letter to the 'Pictorial' thanking them for their gift of a carpet. Went to Ernie's 609 Rayners Lane Pinner. Margaret and David met us near to their home. Had a pleasant time, nice tea. Saw their 'new home,' much smaller than the Kenton one but very suitable for them. Had a walk after tea in the adjacent park.

13th Lowestoft. Suffolk Hotel, room 46.

16th Dinner soup, chicken & pear melba. Had a long walk along the front and had a talk with a semi-blind man about his soul.

JUNE

5th Leslie, Paul & Mrs. Wright came to see Cis & had dinner. Paul now 5 years.

10th Heard from Mr. Button. He needs help but that is a problem. Packed our trunk for Seaview.

22nd 80th Birthday.

JULY

4th Cis received 10/6 from Pictorial & pillowslip. Saw on TV Test Match & Wimbledon.

7th Roding Lane. Some of Wycliff School of Languages there.

29th Cis & I played a game Cis bought this morning - 'Speed.'

AUG

9th Read 'Don't Open the Door' by Anthony Gilbert. (Not really worth reading).

14th Howard went to Leigh to buy a toy soldier. Played Monopoly with Howard who won.

17th Cis & I picked 22 lovely big peaches off our tree.

20th Howard went with Curtis in the car to see the lights.

21st Took Howard to West End. Madam Tussauds, Marble Arch, Hyde Park, Serpentine Buckingham Palace.

26th Holiday in Austria. Dover, Cote d'Azur.

27th Innsbruck. Seefeld. Hotel Lamm. We are all housed in chalets, mine no. 17 attic. I protested against it.

28th Went to Mittelwald (Germany). Had a good look around this 'violin' town.

30th Wrote cards to David S., Howard, Cis, Eva & Louise.

31st Started for Cortina (Italy). Had a wonderful day. Dolomites and lakes made splendid views.

SEPT

7th Arrived at Calais abt 11 o'clock, crowds of people, the SS Cote d'azur full so had to wait 4 hours for the next boat. Waffle & apple on board ship. Rain sent me below. I was late getting off boat but got into Golden Arrow with others. Cis met me.

29th Neuro-dermatitus. Stayed in bed all day.

30th Day in bed. Glands still swollen, beyond recognition. Percy Iszatt came and stayed about 20 mins. Ernie Holt came and chatted for over an hour. Bought some fruit from Ashurst Harvest festival.

OCT

3rd BDH open day. Ed there. He stayed the night. My complaint is better.

7th Did not get up all day. Dr. Beattie came in evening.

11th Cliff, Rene & Howard paid a surprise visit to me in evening. Anxious about me.

12th I am mostly on a fruit & vegetarian diet. Cis made herself a meat pie.

16th Eva & Win 'phoned from Watford enquiring after my condition Ed rather disturbed about me.

NOV

2nd Opening of new Cranbrook Rd. Baptist Church at Marks Gate, 26 Eastwood Rd. Could not go.

4th Great loss in country thro' gale. Aluminium roofs in Hatfield New town blown off.

14th Cis & I went to Rene's. Howard & Cliff there but Graham not back in time to see us.

18th Made several calls for EJ.G. in Ilford. Eight orders.

DEC

1st. Percy rang thro' to Cis. My name for Deacon was not put through by Holt. Short walk through the park.

25th. Rene, Cliff & Howard came by car 1.20pm. Graham at home in bed - flu? Howard turned up sickly. Not a merry Christmas.

30th Did nothing all day but sleep, or near to it. Cis 'phoned Ernie and inquired about Ed.

31st Had letter from Ed, who is getting on better.

1958

JAN

Sibley's year does not begin well, with no entries for the first three weeks of January as he labours under the weight of illness and the deleterious effects of medication.

22nd Danger. Got out of bed, could not get back in. Too much dope taking its course. Dr. Beattie came, got me back in. Temperature 104 - danger. Cis did not take her clothes off, watched me all night. (Did not take her clothes off until Feb. 4th).

24th Very ill. Under dope.

26th Temp. 104 - danger list. Cis greatly upset.

27th A black day. Still confined to bed. Temp. 105 - danger list.

28th Dr. Beattie came and said he had arranged a bed at Isolation Hospital, Chadwell Heath. Ambulance came 7 o'clock and was taken to Ward B, room 12. Cis broken-hearted. The Lord watching over me & Cis. I was soon tucked up in bed. Examined by Indian doctor. Lights out 10 o'clock. Cis wept most of the night.

29th Cis made her first call - 7.30-8. A short and happy interview through window. Will be glad to have me back home again - return very shortly?

30th Cis doing much phoning. Too foggy to come and see me. Rail accident at Dagenham - several casualties.

FEB

1st Cis & Percy came... and we had a pleasant hour, with prayers. Lovely hour soon went.

3rd Dr. - said if I left tomorrow it would be against his advice, as the report on the culture had not come through. (Going in the name of the Lord). Had a walk around the room. Shall be glad to get home from this prison. Sat in corner of room. Daily Telegraph. Dinner - beef, greens, milk pudding. Left on my own - so strange no one to speak to. Walked about the room and read. I was permitted to go to outside lav - what relief! Signed paper of release for tomorrow. Cis came at 7.30 and brought my clothes. Cis and Percy will be here at 9.30am. Night Nurse bad tempered with me for putting teeth out on table.

4th Cis and Percy came at 9.30 and I said goodbye to Matron. I was so glad to get away.

14th Bought a Viceroy Dry Shaver from Mrs. Thomas £5-6-6d.

MARCH

1st Dressed ordinary, first time since Christmas.

3rd Walked to Gants Hill where I got my Savings Certificate cashed.

6th Rene came - Cliff brought her in car, then went to Prudential meeting in Cranbrook. Cliff returned 12.50, had a lot of work to do.

Cliff not too well - nerves.

14th Read some of Bleak House.

29th Heard from Freda. Freda going to get married on June 21st. Mr. Pettifer died Jan 1st. Anne at work. Clive at sea - frigate Torquay in Mediterranean. I wrote to Freda.

APRIL

12th Cis & I had a walk to Mrs. Colletts, got Radio Times and paid bill.

18th Started reading Lorna Doone.

24th St. James Park. Prophecy Investment Society meeting.

28th Mr. Wood's servant brought over 56/- for garage.

MAY

3rd Cup Final. B.W. 3 MU 0.

8th Mansion House, British Sailor's Society 140th anniversary.

10th Cis & I went to the opening of L.B.C., 19 Marylebone Rd., opened by J.Laing OBE. Over 2000 there. Walked to Oxford Circus, macaroon in ABC.

19th Suffolk Hotel, Lowestoft.

23rd. Cis met me to carry my case.

JUNE

4th Sudbury. Left case at Black Boy, - room no. 2 - very fair,. Lunched in cinema cafe. Steamed plaice and date pudding. Sat in lounge and read some of Tale of Two Cities.

12th Went to Felixstowe and made some calls. Mrs. Cook sprung a surprise by accusing us of not trying to sell Springers of Ipswich business.

14th Holiday at Minehead. Cis & I set off for Minehead in Newman's car, 'Humber Hawke,' 8am. Went via Staines. Bagshot, arrived at Westhulme 4 o'clock. Room No. 10.

16th Letter from JEB saying EJ George had died in Glasgow Hospital.

Another old lion of British industry had gone - Ernest J. George, who founded his pharmaceutical stock-taking company in 1926 and which still exists today, and had taken on Thomas Sibley when Sibley was at the ripe old age of 67.

19th Saw Reverend Fraser and family off on their journey to Tasmania. Bought a pocket mac. Cis & I had expresso coffee in Avenue.

21st Freda married. Second marriage - now Mrs. Wallis. I am 81.

27th Concert. Laughable sketches and mannequin parade. I was in it.

JULY

10th Norwich. Bell Hotel. Had a good read of 'A Woman in White.'

12th Went to Valentine Park and saw Ilford 2 v. North Poly.

21st Cis could not do her washing as sweep was coming to sweep kitchen chimney.

24th Cis & I started for Watford 11 o'clock. Went to Watford High St. & walked to 77 Rickmansworth Rd. Win received us warmly. Ed in bed & Eva helping generally. Ed got up at 3, had a walk in garden. Photos taken. Bert played some records. Bert & Win motored us to Watford Junction.

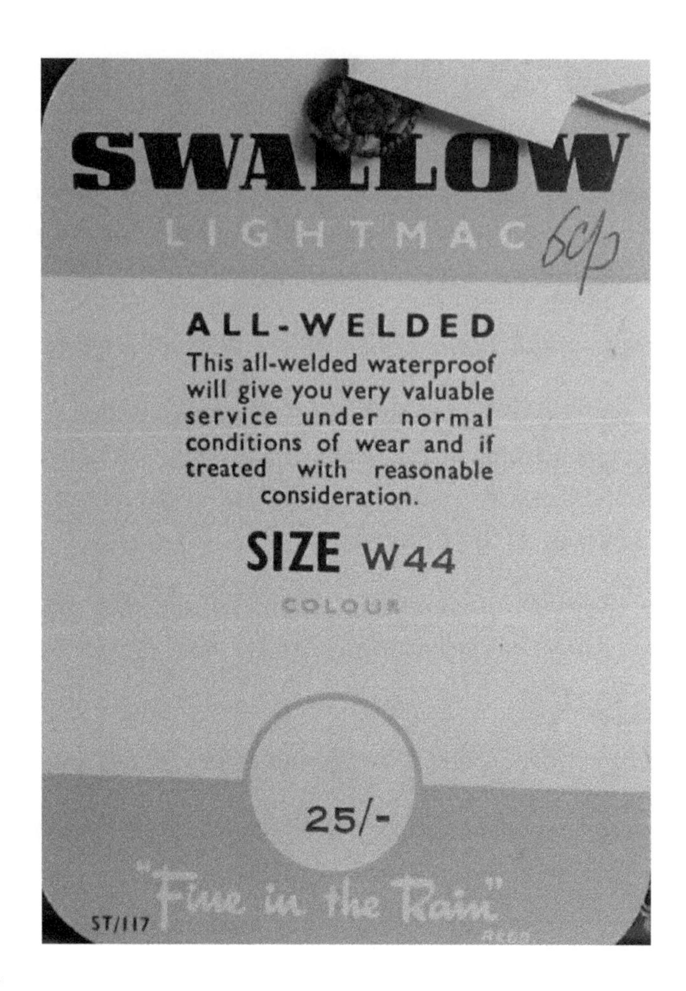

AUG

6th Howard came about 4 o'clock. Howard went out with Curtis after tea.

7th Howard out with the Curtis boys.

8th Howard mostly next door.

SEPT

5th Terrific storm. Great damage.

9th Seaview, IOW holiday. Cis & I walked to Ryde.Had coffee in

Union St. I played my tournament, putting - and won, beating R.Hicks, (19 yrs)

17th Lamb, Ely.

22nd Bedford, Swan Hotel.

27th TV not working but had 'Jack Warner' on sound.

Dixon of Dock Green was a BBC police procedural television series about daily life at a fictional London police station, with the emphasis on petty crime, successfully controlled through common sense and human understanding. It ran from 1955 to 1976. The central character, George Dixon, first appeared in the film The Blue Lamp. Dixon is a mature and sympathetic police constable, played by Jack Warner in all of the 432 episodes.

OCT

10th BDH Open Day. Ed missed. Mr. Williams gave us the welcome speech and I replied. Stopped for a little while to see a music-hall-type lady.

15th W. Mersea bus from Coates and was at Ed's before 5 o'clock. Ed in bed, fairly well but weak, no appetite - can read but cannot write. Had a good fish tea with Eva. George Harris called in - Cissie Harris in St. Mary's Hospital - diabetes - leg amputated. Spent most of evening with Ed & Eva in bedroom.

18th Graham and his friend Bill Smith (16) came in car and brought back our TV. Cis heard from Brazier saying she had been struck off the roll of membership.

21st Cis went to Ashurst Women's Anniversary meeting. Holt spoke to her about the letter and told her to forget it.

25th Pledger finished cementing runaway. Percy Iszatt is engaged to Mrs. Frape.

31st Went to Harlow New Town. Had a light lunch in hair-dressers. Visited Marsh Green Line to Epping. Long chat with Stebbing who flies his own plane and takes aerial photos. Mr. Holt came round and protested against my letter to Brazier. He was very cross. However we finished with prayer and good friends.

NOVEMBER

5th Dr. Beattie rang and said he made an appointment for me at Jubilee Hospital to see me on Friday 2.30.

7th Jubilee Hospital. Dr. Thompson. He said I would have to go to hospital for 3 weeks to be cured. Did not go out in evening. Cis upset at me having to go into hospital.

8th New Television set. Portable, £57-15/-. Alba ex-A.J. Balcombe

Ltd. It gives a beautiful picture with full lights on. Watched Remembrance Day programme from Albert Hall.

10th Could not get ATV sound.

17th Southend. Called in at Bellfair & Joys.

22nd. TV. Looking at 'Nurse Cavell' made us late for bed.

24th Don Mason came round at 9 o'clock - he came to tell Cis that the church had erased her name from the roll. She could no longer be a teacher but would she stay on until New Year.

27th Cis & I went to Chancery Lane and visited office - saw Blackwell, Jenson & others. Hurried to Salmon Ody and got my new truss. We went to Lyons Corner House Marble Arch for tea.

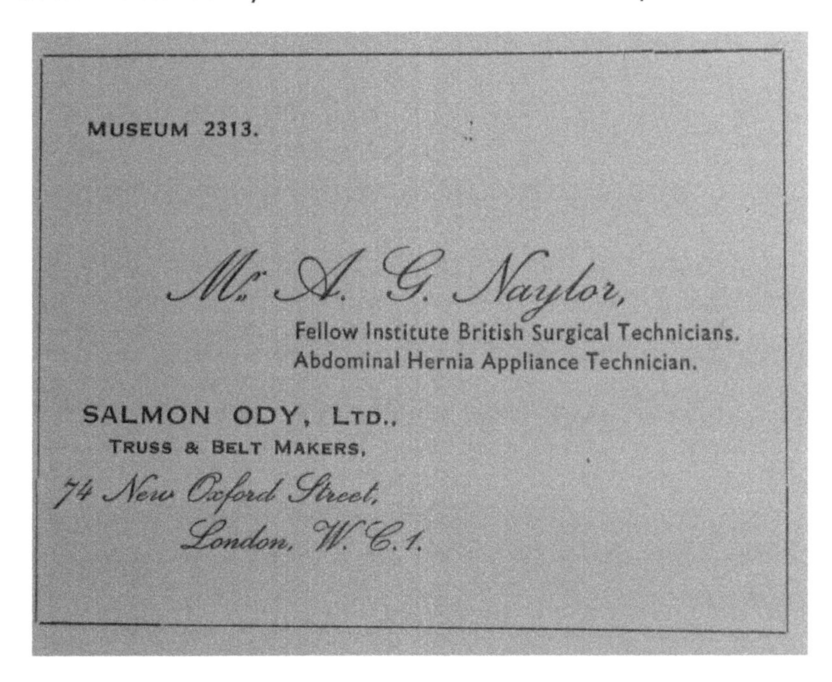

MUSEUM 2313.

Mr. A. G. Naylor,
Fellow Institute British Surgical Technicians.
Abdominal Hernia Appliance Technician.

SALMON ODY, LTD.,
TRUSS & BELT MAKERS,
74 New Oxford Street,
London, W.C.1.

DEC

2nd. BBC not going well. ITV all right.

10th Taub came and took TV away for inspection. Heard news on wireless.

13th Edward Janner brought back TV. No real improvement. We may have to have an aerial in the loft. EJG sent me £25 bonus.

25th Rene, Cliff, Howard & Graham arrived about 1.00pm, Rene & Cliff in their car and Graham & Howard in 'van.' Swell dinner and tea. Played 'Black Magic,' consequences and Shops. Rene went home loaded, even with some wood. I had boot-trees, collars &c.

29th Heard from Ed - very poorly, right lung affected.

30th Sent cheque to lepers.

31st Don called in at 7 o'clock and wasted much of Cis' time - wants Cis to give up her Sunday School class. Cis refused.

1959

JAN

1st Mr. Brazier 'phoned Cis in evening - no useful result, only argument and unpleasantness.

7th Did journeys No. 14 & 3. Heard that Mr. Poulton had died (he called me the 'wonderful gentleman.' Lunched in Lyons Whitechapel - waitress took my umbrella to manageress, who returned it to me - I had to sign for it.

15th Rev. Moon called and saw Cis - her name will soon again be on church roll.

16th BHJ Reunion at Conway Hall. Good programme. Films, dances, accordion player.

21st Percy's party. A happy evening.

FEB

7th Had 'Abraham Lincoln' on TV.

11th Rene 48.

18th Got new suit from Cissens. Got home and found one pocket short to order, so Cis 'phoned them.

20th Council men came and removed huge honeycomb (wasps) nest.

25th Joey (TORTOISE) awake and had walk in garden. Stayed out all night.

MARCH

5th Got on new suit. West Ham & District Pharmacists Annual Dinner & Dance. Trocadero Restaurant - Empire Suite.

APRIL

2nd Went to Caxton Hall - Prophecy Investigation Society's meeting. Professor F.F. Bruce, M.A.D.D., paper on Antichrist in the early church.

6th Howard came for the day. He played with Geoff & Philip Curtis for most of the time.

23rd Mansion House. Council of Spurgeon's College invitation. Shook hands with Lord Mayor, Sir Harold Gillett M.C. Good tea in Egyptian Room.

MAY

2nd Wembley Cup Final, Luton 1 Notts. Forest 2.

6th. W. Mersea. Ed confined to his bed but little stronger although asthma still with him. George Harris there for dinner. Eva got us a good meal - cold chicken pie and milk pudding.

7th We both went to poll and voted Liberal.

9th Cis busy getting room ready for Jones.

11th Lowestoft. Suffolk hotel. Lunched at B. Home Stores.

12th Yarmouth. Coffee in Milk Bar in arcade.

22nd Charringtons sent a ton of coal.

JUNE

Isle of Wight holiday.

JULY

9th Wymondham. Rain very heavy so took refuge in Woolworths. Missed my hat which I'd left in the bus station restaurant. Got it back.

13th Kings Lynn. Booked in at the Duke's Head. Looked over museum.

15th Heard from Cis. News about Graham is disconcerting.

29th Mr. Jones left us for 110 Collinwood Gdns.

AUG

3rd Cis rang up Louise, Margaret answered. Ernie in hospital, pain in chest.

13th Dusted dining room & lounge. Ernie, Louise, Margaret & David came in their Austin car at about 3.00pm. Cup of tea. Happy chat. Tea 5.00 - ham, tongue, salad, mousse. Rene 'phoned and said she and Cliff were coming over - arrived about 7.15. Pleasant evening. Ernie left about 9 o'clock and I gave Margaret and David Egypt books. Louise brought box of sweets. Cliff left 9.30. Louise phoned through abt. 9.30 saying they had all arrived safely.

14th Cis & I picked 29 peaches. Only 5 left now.

SEPT

1st Holiday in Minehead.

OCT

14th W.Mersea. Ed very weak. Last visit to Ed.

15th Colchester. Tea & toasted scones at Lasts. Went to 19 Cambridge Rd., and had 1 1/2 hours with Warwick. Had a dandelion coffee.

21st Cis 65.

30th BDH Open Day. Spent nearly all time talking in reception room. Had photo taken with Mr. Treves Brown. Most of the old ones there except Guilles. Tram to Elephant & Castle, met Cis outside the Metropolitan Tabernacle (Spurgeons College night).

NOV

1st Wrote to Ed. My last letter to him.

5th Cis & I went over St. Paul's Cathedral. Walked slowly to Kardoma. Cis bought two ties & a scarf for Dave & Win. Had our usual tea and brown bread & butter in Kardoma. Walked slowly along Kingsway to Chancery Lane. Waited on station for crowd to thin. Home 6.45.

18th Ernie 'phoned through about 12.15 saying that Ed had passed away this morning - 9.30. Bert & Win 'phoned later.

21st Saturday. Ernie and Louise called for us in car at 8.20 and motored us to West Mersea. Will Warwick took service in Beachy Head. Will read service over grave. Tea & sandwiches. Bert, Win, Ernie, Louise, Ruth & Dave, Cis & Eva chief mourners.

22nd Watched service, ITV, Baptist Church Coventry.

30th Mr. Harvey's first day out of work.

DEC

4th Mr. Harvey got a job at Mica factory, Hainault.

11th Mrs. Harvey went to So. Woodford & Lewis, and got back at 6.25. Mr. H. got back at 5 o'clock - very angry at being left alone so long.

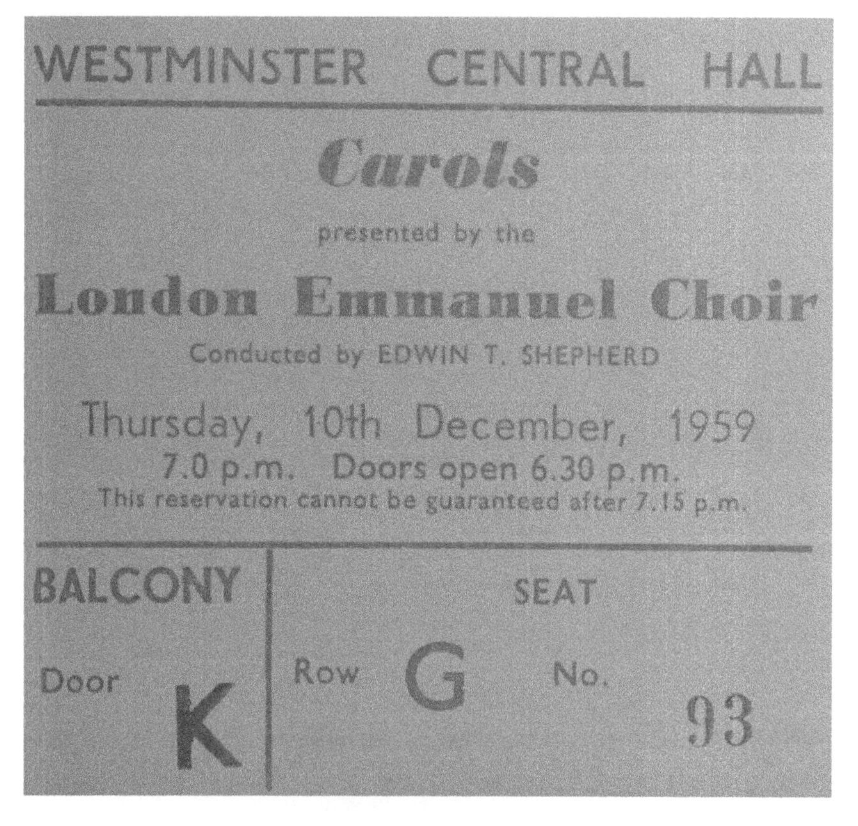

WESTMINSTER CENTRAL HALL

Carols

presented by the

London Emmanuel Choir

Conducted by EDWIN T. SHEPHERD

Thursday, 10th December, 1959

7.0 p.m. Doors open 6.30 p.m.

This reservation cannot be guaranteed after 7.15 p.m.

BALCONY | SEAT

Door K | Row G | No. 93

15th E.J. George's dinner. Beale's Rest., Holloway Rd. Got there early so looked at shops. Cis bought Mrs. H. a pair of gloves. Had 2 sherries to ease bowel pain. Tomato soup, fillet of sole mornay, turkey, chipolatas. Goodly company.

21st Cis took Geoff & Philip to Moultons to see elephant.

22nd Went to Richards and chatted with his temporary asst. Jackie - going to Oxford next Sept.

25th Rene, Cliff & boys came 1.00 (2 cars). Afternoon spent in games - 'What' and 'Jackstraws.' Dave & win sent me a book, 'Klondyke.' We had nearly 60 Christmas cards.

31st Heard from David Sibley & Margaret Turner. Tried to mend electric fire in bedroom - no good. TV in evening. Heard a little noise from the passing of the year in bed. About 20,000 people in Trafalgar Square.

CHAPTER SEVEN

BLUE SUBURBAN SKIES - 1960-1972

The bald facts underlying what historians now call 'The Golden Age' of the international economy from 1955 to 1973 was a stable exchange rate, year on year growth (in Britain of 2.8%), low unemployment, high wages, and low inflation. More importantly these dry figures translated into an era of human happiness and improvement not seen in perhaps the whole of human history.

In the Sixties Britain led the way in almost every field of human endeavour - science, technology, art, music fashion. The Americans and Soviets might have their space programmes, but it was London that film director Michaelangelo Antonioni described as the 'liveliest city in the world.' From a small underground club in Liverpool in the late Fifties a group of young men transformed the music scene - fan Shelagh Johnston remembers '*... the pulsing beat, the thumping bass... We'd been into the American High School scene, then suddenly there was this sound, the harmonica, the real rhythm and blues bit. It was so different.*' The Beatles were later to say 'we reconnected people with their bodies.' At the outset the liberation was sexual, a continuation of the eroticism of the 1950s with its rediscovery of the buxom blonde bombshell. In the 60s both skirts and relationships became shorter: when Enoch Powell introduced the contraceptive pill in the NHS in 1961 he may not have foreseen the profound social changes that would result - the decade did not invent sex before marriage, far from it, but the Pill facilitated an increased freedom particularly among women.

These were years of confidence, ambition and a certain heady euphoria, when it seemed the West could do no wrong, but was reaping the harvest of its acceptance of free market capitalism tempered with liberal welfare programmes and Keynsian management. When Russian leader Nikita Krushchev flew over Los Angeles, looked down and saw swimming pool after swimming pool in the gardens of hundreds, thousands of Americans' homes, he turned to his companion and said *'communism cannot compete with this.'*

Thomas Sibley lived, of course, in Swinging London, but clearly he was only a witness to the spectacle, not a participant. Perhaps he's seen it all before - the 1920s we know had been 'roaring,' with the same loosening of social mores, expansion of the idea of how women should 'be,' and the same invasion of foreign genres of music and dance, with the proliferation and popularity of jazz. The wisdom of his age might have taught him that these thing come in cycles, and by the time he was coming to end of his life in the early 1970s the frenetic party that was seemingly the Sixties was indeed about to crash upon the rocks of the oil crisis, strikes and economic downturn, leading the Seventies themselves to assume the nature of a next-day hangover.

Not a participant in the cultural scene, then, but certainly in his capacity as a traveller - remarkably he continues his role as a commercial salesman right into his late eighties - a spectator of the profound changes being made to Britain's built environment. By 1960 already 600 miles of motorways had been constructed, and more were to come as Labour introduced the dreaded Beeching cuts of 1963-65, as a result of which a staggering one third of all railway routes were closed down by 1970. Overnight much of the West Country and north and central lost all rail travel. The Sixties was assuredly the decade of the car, and it might seem that the interests of the individual were ignored as flyover after flyover, motorway after motorway, criss-crossed the country and bisected old towns like scars caused by the slashing strokes of swords. People stood and gaped as the towns and cities they'd grown up in were smashed to bits around them in subservience to the automobile. In the western reaches of London residents emerged from their Victorian terraces in Brentford to witness a growing daily shadow moving not-so-silently above them as the M4 was raised up into the sky from Brentford to Hammersmith. The city of Stockport was literally cut in two. Towns like High Wycombe, once entered by a single ancient route laid down in Roman times, now stood as if besieged by an abstract network of roundabouts, bypasses. In the Sixties the Ring-Road became king. Ancient streams and rivers were built over, and pedestrian shoppers were consigned to dingy underpasses.

Thus the downside of progress. While London partied and hedonism caught the eyes of the papers and television, the majority of the British people continued life as they had always done, in the daily grind of work. This is not to say they were immune to the epicurean celebratory nature of the New Young Culture: when the Beatles played their last performance on the rooftop of the Apple HQ in Savile Row, their audience contained not a few spectators who had been born in the nineteenth century, and to a man and woman they praised the event to the film camera. *'Lovely talented bunch of boys.'* While radical politics fomented, it was nevertheless a decade of remarkable affection between the classes, where bowler-hatted commuters walked alongside mods and hippies, where toffs were - while being sent up rotten in films and TV comedy - not *despised,* but the source of gentle amusement. The older generation were dismissed as 'grandads,' as in *'leave it out grandad,'* and mocked as 'squares,' but the temper of the age lacked the ferocity of the 21st century's seemingly deep, visceral hatred of the Senior Citizen, as in environmental activist Greta Thunberg's famous denunciation *'How dare you! You have stolen my dreams!'*

While the modern world sped along around him Sibley plied his trade, cultivated his garden in his suburban home. He did participate in the new technology, endeavouring at all times to buy the latest household goods - electric fires, electric kettles, while stubbornly persisting with coal fires as he had done since 1900. He worked, holidayed, watched television. His favourite programme of course was *Songs of Praise* but he also enjoyed *Dixon of Dock Green, Coronation Street,* and *Charlie Drake.*

A quieter decade, then, for the Sibleys, and as his diaries reveal, the domestic flavours of the age seep in: green shield stamps, premium bonds, television. Further tragedy would unfold for the family, balanced by the collective euphoria of the Moon Landings of 1969, but as 1960 dawns we find 82 year old Thomas venturing out on a cold winter's day, as he had done when he was 22, to sell his pharmaceuticals. His world has grown smaller: but he still travels his rounds of the Home Counties as doggedly as he did at the beginning of the century.

1960

12th Started on journey but returned as roads too slippery. Did not go out all day. Mr. Curtis came in to borrow tacks and hammer. Reverend L. Moon 'phoned in evening asking as to our welfare.

24th Both had restless night. Couldn't have service in bedroom (wireless) as it was R.C.

27th Wrote and accepted Sir Cyril Black's invitation to the House of Commons on Feb. 18th.

FEB

1st One day rail strike.

3rd Cis treated me to a pair of shoes at True-Form, 69/11, and a slippers for Rene, and I bought a black hat at Dunn's, 60/-. Very early this morning there was a fire in the High Rd. - Richards. £50,000 of damage.

14th Cis & I in bed all day.

18th Went to Westminster, House of Commons, and joined Sir Cyril Black and Spurgeons Tea reception. About 300 there. Home 7.00pm. Enjoyed our outing.

19th Queen Elizabeth gave birth to a son, 3.30pm, Buckingham Palace.

23rd Walked to golds, Beehive Lane, and had a chat. Found a purse on the way that belongs to Mr. Tykin, 103 Glenwood Gdns.

MARCH

15th Graham paid an unexpected visit.

16th Evening with TV and one of my old diaries.

As the future shrinks, Sibley returns to his past:

18th Couldn't dress until 2.45. Read some of diary 1901.

APRIL

3rd Cis & I went to Ashurst Drive. Rev. Moon peached on 'Weep for yourselves,' - not a great message.

6th Sent off card for Cliff's birthday.

7th Louise 'phoned through saying Ernie had been taken ill and was taken to hospital on Monday - pulse and temp. very low - cause not yet determined.

11th Mr. Bayliss of Amplivox, 80 New Bond St., W1, called and saw me about hearing. Postponed decision until Oct. or Nov.

13th Went to Sousters, and chatted with Mrs. - ? - nee Souster, who worked at Boardman's with Rene.

19th TV - saw House of Lies.

22nd Went to Blunden's about truss. Went to Oxford Circus in mistake for T.Ct. Rd., and walked through to Euston Rd. Saw Mr. Green who adjusted truss and still thinks it should suit me better. Home 5.00. Truss did not keep its place. Changed it several times - no use.

MAY

7th Watched Wembley Cup Final on TV - Wolves 3 Blackburn Rovers 0.

10th Cis and I went to Broadstairs by Lacy's coach from Ilford Lane

(Mayville Rd.). Lunch on front. Went to Griffiths, 33 Swinburne Avenue, & spent afternoon and had tea. Return coach 5.30.

16th Lowestoft, Suffolk hotel, for EJG.

18th Hotel 6pm. Watched some continental football - Real Madrid.

JUNE

Seaview holiday, IOW.

28th Thetford, Bell Hotel, Rm. 6.

29th. Watton. Lunched in Green Lion.

JULY

1st Watched Wimbledon on TV. Saw final of men's singles. Neil Fraser beat Rod Laver.

2nd Watched TV. Tennis - Miss Bueno, winner of of Ladies Wimbledon.

7th Sheringham. Expresso coffee and biscuits in High St.

11th Bell Hotel, Norwich. Read 'Gorillas were my Neighbours.'

AUG

4th Went to EJ.George's and saw Blackwell & others. Mr. Jensen let me speak on his Dictaphone and I heard my voice for the first time.

Sibley is mis-remembering here, for in the early 1900s he and his wife's family the Kettleys found much amusement in listening to their voices on a wax cylinder phonograph.

15th Mr. Curtis came in with Philip and picked some peaches, 50, high up using high steps.

25th Cis & I went to Rene's. Cliff was there - he does not work

Thursdays. Mr. Parrott, aged 79, was there.

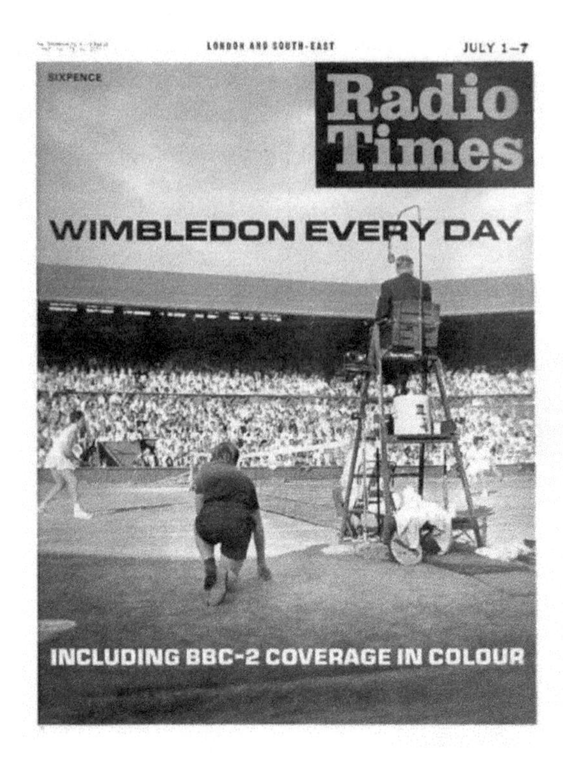

Throughout the 1960s & 70s televised coverage of the tennis at Wimbledon became a national pastime.

27th Most of our peaches (about 300) now picked, and many pears off tree fallen. Packed our case for Minehead.

29th Cis & I commenced cleaning out 'Tall Boy.'

31st Graham called in about 6.45 on way home - had lemon & barley drink and biscuit. Took away some fruit.

SEPT

1st. Cis hoovering room. Sat in dining room. Could do nothing, so wet and stormy. Floods in country.

2nd Pledger went on roof to repair damage.

14th Started for Ernie's 2.40, arrived Pinner 4.30. Played darts in garden with David, Ernie, Cis. After tea Margaret paid us a surprise visit.

29th Eric Ringwood sent for our dining room suite - settee and two armchairs.

OCT

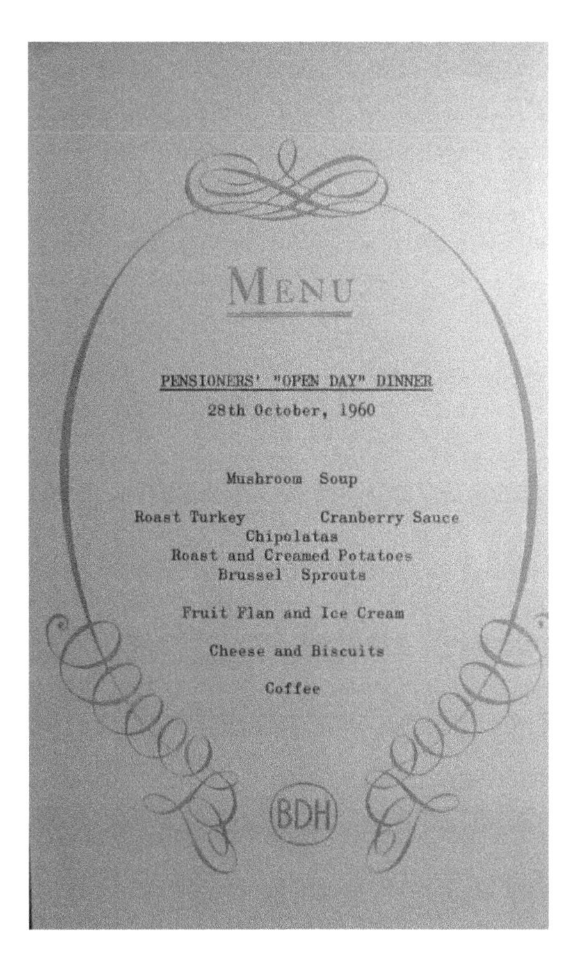

MENU

PENSIONERS' "OPEN DAY" DINNER

28th October, 1960

Mushroom Soup

Roast Turkey Cranberry Sauce
Chipolatas
Roast and Creamed Potatoes
Brussel Sprouts

Fruit Flan and Ice Cream

Cheese and Biscuits

Coffee

BDH

21st Cis 66.

23rd Went to Ashurst - converted a teddy girl, Sylvia Smith.

The Teddy Boys or *Teds* were a mainly British youth subculture of the early 1950s to mid-1960s who were interested in rock and roll and R&B music, wearing clothes partly inspired by the styles worn by dandies in the Edwardian period, which Savile Row tailors had attempted to re-introduce in Britain after the Second World War; though with the boom in second-hand clothes' stores during this period there was a plentiful supply of genuine Edwardian attire to satisfy a fashion-conscious youth. The Beatles were later to adopt Edwardian garb as a part-nostalgic, part-ironic stance. Teddy Girls, while rarer, aped the fashion and attitudes of their male counterparts in their rebellious stance against authority and the 'old order.'

Teddy Girls of the 50s-60s rebelled against the social mores of the age.

DEC

20th Cis went to Taub's and had her hair done. Beale's Rest. 6.15. Usual happy reception. Cabaret 9.30. Stayed until 10.30. Too late for 123, so got as far as waterworks, walked to Grove Rd. and got

11.35 bus. In bed 1.00am.

23rd Dr. Beattie sent round the Tonic.

26th Rene, Cliff, Graham, Howard came 1.15. After presents we sat down to a feast. Played usual consequences, drawings, animal alphabet etc. They departed about 10.00 by Graham's motor.

29th Terrible fire in Barking - timber wharf.

1961

JAN

4th Wrote to Louise & sent her Warwick's fathered notes on Romans. We went to Percy Iszatt's at 4.00pm & had tea with them - tongue, ham, egg salad, cheese-filled celery. Percy showed us his cine-pictures of USA & Canada on screen.

17th Journeys 8 & 9. Lunched in ABC Mare Street.

MARCH

13th Too cold to do anything but sit by the fire and doze. Cliff & Howard in to dinner 12.30. Cliff finished work in evening.

25th Horns given up milk round to Hitchmans.

28th Cleared a place for old coal bunk.

APRIL

12th Russia sent a man into space, and safe return. A great historic event.

24th Census paper collected.

MAY

1st Sent cheque to Gamages and Telephone manager.

3rd Westminster Chapel. Stirring and excellent addresses.

6th Cup Final Wembley. Spurs 2 Leicester 0.

Man in space. Thomas Sibley, who had been born in the Victorian era, had lived to see space travel.

16th Webb & Mount Southwold. Mount upset over E.J.G's charge letter when he purchased business. Had a walk on Front. Had lunch at Restnt. 5/6d.

18th Suffolk Hotel Lowestoft. Paid bill of £7-5/-. I was charged for a coffee and lunch which I did not have. Cashier made a fuss when I did not pay.

JUNE

8th Lowestoft. Did work and watched some of wedding at York Minster - Duke of Kent and Miss Katherine Worsely.

17th Holiday at Seaview (IOW).

22nd Perks & Llewellyn, chemists, Hitchin, closes down.

30th Fancy Dress Competition - I was one of the judges. Cis got 2nd prize for putting.

JULY

1st. End of holiday at Springfield Court. Delayed at ferry for an hour. Had lunch in a shady spot under pine trees. Had a clear run to '35,' arriving 4.30. Could not find Joey. (Tortoise).

2nd. Norwich. Bell Hotel.

17th Kings Lynn. Booked in at the Duke's Head room No. 20.

19th Brandon Market, Snettisham.

20th Fakenham. Dinner lemon sole a la portugal, banana sundae. Saw Boyo (?) QC on TV.

AUG

1st Watched England's losing game against Aust. Australia won by 54 runs.

3rd Hurried to office, saw Blackwell. Left office, got home 1.15, Graham & Bill arrived at the same time, they had refreshments and stayed to dinner (Rene, Dina, Norah, Howard). Howard helped Curtis' gardener pick peaches. Rain caused Cis to 'phone Cliff for car as the girls were lightly clad. Whilst waiting for Cliff we played Chinese Chequers. Rene won.

10th Charringtons delivered 1 ton of 'Excelite' coal. Graham called in and had a little lunch. Private car, not lorry.

16th Ernie's via Baker St., got to Pinner 3.20. Waited on station for David who came 3.30 for us. Had a game with David - clock golf.

Ernie came at 5.40 and we had tea. Louise, Margaret and David had a walk around their park.

SEPT

6th Ely. Booked in at the Lamb. Had a long chat with Malkin who was doing locum work for Sutcliffes. Lunched in another cafe - had a chat with a man on six month leave.

11th Bedford. Booked in at the Lion, room 20. No wardrobe or place for clothes except hanger on back of door. ... On the way back to the Hotel it rained heavily so I had to stand up as I had no coat or gamp.

16th Louise 'phoned in evening to say Ernie was in hospital. Stomach?

17th Ward C4, Central Middlesex Hospital.

21st Stevenage, Cromwell hotel, room no. 11. Did New Stevenage City Centre. Cooper & Maguire. Had pot of tea, scone & butter at Co-op. Big fair at Stevenage, taking in both sides of road. Been in operation 800 years - cannot alter it except through Govt. action. Very pleasant Scottish receptionist.

25th Joey out of his box in shed.

30th No TV after 'Dock Green.'

OCTOBER

2nd. Chelmsford. Cis carried bag to bus stop. Got Burgess order at Danbury. Rupture came down, (hernia) so went to Gents & put rupture back. Witham. Cups Hotel, room 36.

4th Colchester. Went to Brethren's meeting. A good number there. Mr. Grant from Scotland spoke, but too softly to gather all the points - chiefly about the forgiveness of God. Saw many I knew.

10th Hatfield. Had to wait to see Nina Barnes - she had a complaint over a broken scent bottle.

11th Bill Pledger finished painting, now awaiting paper-hangers.

12th Remained in bed until 5.00pm.

13th Remained in bed until 5.00pm.

14th Cis & I went to High Rd. and bought carpet from Albert Hall A. King, gave cheque £26.

15th 32nd Anniversary. (Ashurst Drive Baptist Church).

18th Motor Show.

24th Bought electric fire, £7-7-9 (16/5d a month). Read Jane Eyre.

27th Mrs. Clara Dilling died, 80.

NOV

1st. Funeral of Mrs. Clara Dilling, Barkingside cemetery. Rev. Moon officiated at the grave. Saw Gladys Olden, Hetty & Madge Horwood.

2nd Chelmsford. On returning I had a fall on concrete, turning. Injured knee and hands, went home with handkerchief covering wounds.

4th Finished reading Jane Eyre.

6th Cis went to Trebor with party from Ashurst.

11th Had TV - Remembrance Day.

13th Strike on ITA caused cancellation of certain items.

16th Chatted with Mr. Curtis (next door) partly about his back arch and rear gate, and Geoff's Batmitzvah on Saturday.

18th Cis & I went to the Jewish Synagogue for Geoffrey's Bar Mitzvah (sic). We had to sit separately. I had a worshipping shawl given to me. Mr. Rubie sat with me and helped me to find the place in the prayer book. A friend motored us to '37' and we had refreshments. A large gathering. Had a little cherry brandy & pineapple. Left them at 2.00pm.

21st Mr. Harvey's nerves troubling him.

The Sibley's long-standing lodger, Mr. Harvey, falls ill.

28th Mr. Harvey not so well - head strange this morning.

30th Mr. Harvey came down and did chest exercises.

DEC

1st. Southend. Got home 6.30. Mr. Harvey felt ill & Cis 'phoned Dr. Beattie who came at 9.25. Dr. Beattie says there is nothing wrong with Mr. Harvey.

2nd Cis disturbed most of night. Mr. Harvey died suddenly at 2am. Cis 'phoned D.B. and told him. Cis 'phoned Nurse Stewart , 29 Sunnymede Drive, CRE 4601. who came round about 9.45 & layed out body (sic). Body must go away on account of being fat and full of food and rapid degeneration. Dr. B. put it in hands of Coroner for autopsy. Coroner came 1.30. Body taken away at 4.00 for post-mortem. Mrs. Harvey used lounge. Mr. Utting came and saw her and had a chat with us. Mrs. Harvey sleeping in her same bed.

3rd Reverend W.J.C. called this morning and interviewed Mrs. Harvey.

5th Mrs. Harvey's sister Eva came to stay with her until after funeral.

7th J.J. Harvey's funeral, 67. Mr. H's relatives, and son & daughter, came in morning for his funeral. Barkingside Methodist Church for service. Rev. White preached at grave.

9th Cis made her Christmas cake.

12th Lunched in Shoreditch, 'Rendezvous Cafe,' - poor.

19th E.J.G's annual dinner, Beale's. Mr. Rushton toasted 'staff' and paid me a gracious tribute. A very happy evening.

22nd Mr. Wood sent a bottle of sherry. I decorated cake for Christmas.

23rd I attempted to dust dining room but rheumatism in back muscle crippled me. Heard that Olive Fleet had died.

25th Rene, Cliff, Howard & Graham arrived 12.00. Some played 'Budg-it.'

Tea 6.30. Graham left first to go to a party. Rest left at 10.00pm to go to Eric's. Cis & I had 70 Christmas cards.

29th Cis & I played Lexicon.

1962

JAN

1st. Had a card from Dina (Belgium).

8th Letter from EJGs posted to me on the 4th arrived this morning. Postmen working to rule.

9th Benfleet, and Canvey Island. Had a long chat with Venables, who is fond of Sandow and his system.

17th Cis bought Tom Brown's Schooldays, posted to Paul (Strasbourg).

29th Did not go out as underground on strike and some buses out in sympathy.

FEB

1st. Received 5 Readers Digest condensed books.

5th Finished East Anglia for E. J. George & Co.

10th TV, football results. Finished Tom Brown's Schooldays.

13th Went thro' some old magazines. Threw away some mags.

14th Sent 12/6d to Billy Graham for 'Decision.'

16th Went to barber's (Archers) and had hair cut by Italian assistant. 3/3d. Went on to Cassen Bro's and got suit - £13-6/-

17th Looked at 'Wonderful Britain' for Lavenham.

18th Cassen's suit not satisfactory.

20th Cis went with me to Cassens & took back suit for alterations.

25th Cis not well enough to face the snow and cold. TV (BBC) - from Cardiff 6.15-6.45.

MARCH

1st. W.Ham & dist. Pharm. Dinner, Colonial House, EC3. Started out 5.25, arrived Baronial Hall 6.20. Welcomed by Mrs. C.R. Stein & Miss M.A. Burr (Vice-President Pharm. Soc). Only good speaker Miss Burr.

2nd Gardener came, 10/-.

4th Neither Cis nor I felt up to going to church tonight, so had 'Praise' service on TV.

6th Mansion House. London City Mission 70th annual gathering. Deputy Lord Mayor Sir Denis Truscott in the chair.

7th Read some of 'The Soul of London' by Wrintmore, and some history of England.

8th Gale and destruction, Cornwall, Devon and South Wales.

13th Bennett cleaned windows, 4/-6d.

20th Margaret Sibley came at 5.30 and spent the evening with us. We had hot dinner, lamb and 'Cis' pudding,' - baked sponge. We had the evening together chatting, and looked at some photos. She left 9.30 for her nurses home near Oxford St. Had a happy evening. Margaret, who is 21, is a very fine girl, refined and stately.

30th Wrote to Hi Fi Hearing Clinic, 1, Grand Bldgs, Trafalgar Square.

APRIL

2nd Dr. Beattie still very poorly, only able to do morning surgery.

7th Cis & I played Lexicon - no programme worth watching on TV.

8th Songs of praise from Edinburgh.

9th Budget. TV - Great Expectations.

12th Tortoise awake - Cis let him out for a walk. Mr. Curtis' kittens growing and looking very attractive, 2 white & 2 tabby.

19th 'Phoned Mr. Blackwell to wish him Bon Voyage for his trip to the Mediterranean. Bed-table delivered this morning.

28th Ipswich top of the league. Great excitement over Ipswich winning league trophy.

30th Finished Great Expectations. Posted April 'Crusade' to Graham.

MAY

2nd. Westminster. Glanced at pictures on embankment.

5th Tottenham 3 Burnley 1. Queen presented cup to Spurs players.

10th Cis & I walked to polling station. Went to Blackfriars and went to Kardomah and had tea. Walked to Crown Street Royal Commonwealth Theatre, (Commercial) TV room. Very crowded. Questions. TV Review time. Some prizes given but not our way.

23rd Suffolk. Watched Coronation Street, also sport, England & Peru.

25th Cis met me 12.30 at bus stop. Cis had been sending letters to next week's hotels.

BDH taken over Woolley of Manchester.

26th TV - Lone Ranger.

30th Lowestoft. Had a walk in Abbey Gardens. Little TV - Coronation St. And 'Tago Secret.'

JUNE

8th Mrs. Harvey had her hair bobbed.

12th Gants Hill. Went to Smiths and ordered a suit £18-18/-.

13th Cis took my suit to be altered at Elmers, 385 Eastern Avenue.

16th Holiday Seaview IOW. Springfield Ct.

22nd 85.

27th Cis & I had a walk to Prickpool Park, had a round of crazy golf to warm us up.

JULY

4th Norwich. Bell Hotel. Got film & took it to Howard for DP (PROJECTOR). Cis wrote to me and said Howard was ill in bed.

16th Kings Lynn, Dukes Head Hotel.

18th Up 7.00am. Breakfast, porridge, egg & bacon. Caught 8.50 bus to Hunstanton. Went to Wells by 10.00am bus. Saw Jaggers. Burnham Mkt - saw Mr. White. Bought 2 bananas - sat in church. Docking - saw Kettle. Had a short walk in country then sat on seat outside Roy's. Hunstanton - saw Mr. Malkin. Walked to station, train to Fakenham, then walked to Bus station, and Bus back to King's Lynn, Duke's Head. Spoke to two very tall constables about way to Magdalen. Had dinner in Chinese Restaurant, 6/-6d. Had Chinese dish - fried chicken and almonds. Did work. Wrote to Cis. Posted letter 8.20. Entered up diary - in bed by 10.35.

20th 9.33 to L'pool St. Chatted with an American who is over here lecturing on literature.

24th Went to BDH via Angel. Cassell out, also Causer. Guthrie has left. Had a chat with Davies in the buyer's office. Walked to Angel and train to EJGs office. Had a chat for an hour with Blackwell. Walked to Reader's Digest office, said I had not paid my 25/- for the monthly RD. Went home, turned up cheque for Reader's Digest.

27th Mr. & Mrs. Curtis started for New York - SS Canberra.

29th Couldn't put collar on so couldn't go to church. Had singing from Wales (TV).

AUGUST

11th Curtis's return home from their trip to New York.

16th Leslie Wright 'phone to say he, Marlise & their three children were coming over tomorrow for tea.

17th Leslie, Marlise & children came in car 4.15. Played in garden - photos taken. High tea - tongue etc.

27th Cis & I went to Rene's by 11.25 bus. Cliff and Rene went off to

East Mersea. Watched Yorkshire & Surrey cricket. Howard let at 3.15 to go to aerodrome. Graham showed us his films on projector - his trip by aeroplane to France.

31st Howard & his chum on motor bikes went off to E. Mersea to meet his mum & dad at the caravan site. We left 'Longview' about 11.30.

SEPT

10th Bus to town centre and I booked in at the Blue Boar hotel - room 35, quite good. (Cambridge). Made calls at Cherry Hinton - Evans very pleased with our stock-takers. Went to Scotch House.

11th 2.30 bus to Burwell. Saw Rivers - having a shop and house built next door. (At home) new fireplace put in by Pledger.

22nd Put some lino down in the bathroom - quite a job - not well done - difficult material.

OCT

8th Half an hour or so in garden. Brought some books from the lounge. Had a read of 'England in the Middle Ages.'

12th Cis & I went to Blackfriars & walked to Christian Literature Crusade, bought Christmas cards and 3 books. Walked to Pickering & Inglis and bought a few booklets. Walked slowly to Kardoma and had tea. Walked slowly to Holborn. Bought Cis a birthday card. Caught 6.30 train home. Met Utting in queue and he walked with us. He got his recipe for skin trouble.

13th Cis and I went to Dunns for a fancy waistcoat - ordered one for next Thursday.

21st Cis 68.

NOV

2nd. Got a gift from Ilford Market - 3 aluminium saucepans.

12th Shoeburyness. 6 orders. Had letter from Eva.

14th Dinner cowheel and leg of beef.

15th Southend. Coffee in Rossi's, High St.

The first Rossi ice-cream parlour opened along Southend High Street in the 1930s, run by Massimiliano Agostino and his wife Anna Rossi. Two other shops were opened between 1931 and 1933, with the three sites being located on the High Street, Marine parade and Western Esplanade. Rossi is still thriving today.

16th I called in at 11 Pavilion Rd., and was told that Mr. Petigem was dead and that Mrs. Petigem had gone away for 3 weeks. Cis had long conversation with Louise over the 'phone.

28th Heard from Margaret Sibley announcing engagement.

Things were once again happening in the Sibley family, as Thomas' brother Ernie's daughter Margaret becomes engaged to a young ancient languages scholar Alan Millard, later to become Rankin Professor Emeritus of Hebrew and Ancient Semitic languages, and Honorary Senior Fellow (Ancient Near East), at the School of Archaeology, Classics and Egyptology (SACE) in the University of Liverpool.

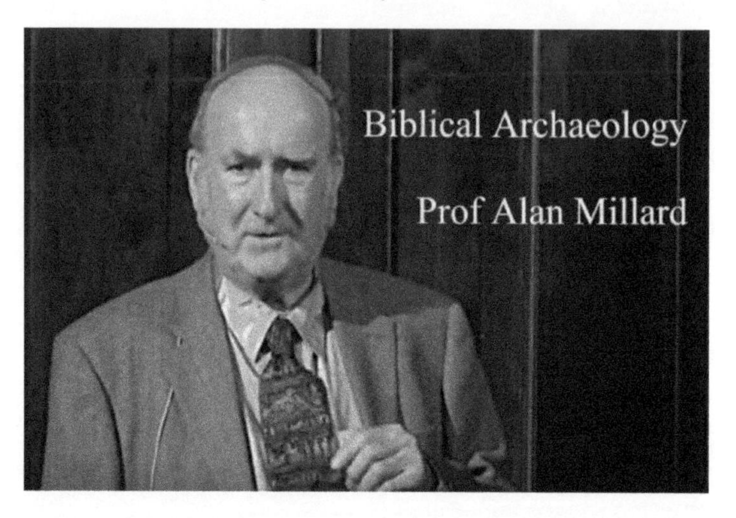

Professor Alan Millard, who married Thomas Sibley's nephew Margaret.

Other tiers of society were similarly celebrating:

29th Princess Alexandra engaged to Angus Ogilvie.

DEC

4th Mrs Harvey went out for my letters did not catch the post - the milkman posted them later. Dense fog over most of country.

6th Heard from J.E.B. saying I must not venture out this weather.

11th Called and had a chat with Eric Ringwood.

25th Rene, Cliff, Graham, Howard.

28th 74 cards altogether.

1963

JAN

8th Mrs. Harvey broke my 'Lorna Doone' cup & saucer and replaced it with one from Australia.

11th Conway Hall BDH reunion.

17th Just finished dinner when electricity was cut off. Lost 'Double Your Money' at 7 o'clock.

19th Death of Hugh Gaitskell - 56.

26th TV out of order (partially). Could not watch 'Dock Green.' Put on sound for News.

FEB

1st Water pipe in garage burst and flooded the garage, and ran into road. Pledger came round and cut water off, and left us with only warm water in kitchen and no water upstairs. Mr. Curtis told us about the burst - water swamping place.

4th We welcomed at 5.00pm Margaret Louise Sibley & Alan Ralph Millard. We had a high tea of cold turkey, ham salad, peaches & cream. They left for Barts, and Alan home, at 9.30. A very happy time.

11th Had a read of Barchester Towers.

18th Charringtons deliver 6cwt of coal for Mrs. Harvey.

19th Pledger got a fluorescent strip light for kitchen.

28th Heard from Alan Millard, who enclosed a book on archaeology which he had revised (('Archaeology Gives Evidence,' A. Rendle Short).

28 Days FEBRUARY, 1963 2nd Month

Snow, Ice Very Cold 4 MONDAY (35—330)

Up 8.30 breakfast in bed. Dressed about 12 o'c Lunch soup &c. Had a rest in afternoon. Changed about 3.30. We welcomed at 5 o'c Margaret Louise Sibley & Alan Ralph Ballard [Bible museum] &c. We had a high tea cold turkey, ham, salad &c peaches cream &c. Had a long chat afterwards finishing with Chinese Checkers. They left for 'Barts' & Alan home 9.30 Had a very happy time. (No water except main)

MARCH

6th E12 & E6. Lunched in Lyons Ilford - Lyons in East Ham shut down.

13th Did most of journey No1. Lunched in Lyons Aldgate. Made some calls on Commercial Rd. Rain, fine but threatening, drive me home along the Mile End Rd. Brazier was in train but no recognition. Belling Zenith Convector delivered today.

14th Mr. R.W. Cooper came round on his bike and brought 'Lessons in the Italian Language.'

20th Listened to Dr. S.R.B. Murray on radio - Resurrection.

29th Pledger took away TV and wireless for inspection.

APRIL

19th We used our Zenith convector heater.

24th. Cis carried up TV, so we had the view of the Royal Wedding in the bedroom - Princess Alexandra & J.B. Ogilvie at Westminster Abbey. Crowds of people.

25th Read History of England.

27th Some TV - poor programmes.

29th Geoffrey borrowed my pick-axe - no good for him to knock down a wall. A brick fell on his finger and I had to bandage it up.

30th Joey the tortoise dead - the severe winter killed him.

MAY

10th Went to Argies twice for haircut but other people there. Went to hairdresser in Maybank Rd. Put in scarlet runners. New electric cooker delivered and fitted: LEB 'Trimline,' £40.19.0d.

14th 'This is Your Life,' - Gladys Alward.

15th Yarmouth. Quite sunny here for a walk. Had a cup of tea at a *milk bar.*

JUNE

7th Cliff & Rene came for an hour. I gave Rene the rest of History of England, and Cliff some 'Readers.' Mrs. Harvey started her holidays - went to Nottingham by coach.

12th Bury St. Edmunds, Suffolk Hotel. Bought Josephus' Jewish Wars, 5/-, Penguin.

22nd 86.

JULY

14th Songs of Praise from High Wycombe.

15th Kings Lynn/Swaffham. Had a look round Woolworths - very large, new building.

Woolworth's, Kings Lynne, opened on the High Street in 1922.

AUGUST

8th Visit to Watford. Bert met us in car. Dinner, lamb, sherry burgundy. Win's arthritis very bad for getting about.

16th Rene & Cliff came for surprise visit with Howard. They'd had lunch at George, Loughton. Howard was driving his Ferrari.

17th Cis saw Pledger about roof still not being done - many excuses.

28th Hedgehog made a nest at the back of our shelter, opposite lavatory. Cis gave it some milk.

SEPT

2nd Rain still coming through roof. Did a little preparing to vacate my room.

5th Peaches did for stomach. Took some peaches in to the office for Blackwell, also Rushton, Hume, Issaacs, Jensen and Russell.

6th Heard that George Slicker had suddenly died. Cid 'phoned Rene - Dina there.

7th Took some peaches to Wilson, Maybrook Rd.

9th Cambridge, 8.30. Cis walked with me to bus stop. Booked in at Blue Boar - room 15. Finished at Evans, Cherry Hinton. 2 orders.

11th Ely. Lamb Hotel. No. 2 room.

15th Mrs. Harvey's sister came from Slough for the day.

16th Fast train to Luton and Bedford.

18th Leighton Buzzard, Dunstable. Hurried to Luton - George Hotel. Ham salad in Lyons. Bus to Dunstable and made 5 calls. Rev. Baker came for me and I went with him to Beechwood Green. Called at Marge's - Kath was in bed, pregnant 2 months. I stayed to Harvest Services.

28th Cis & I went to St. Andrew's Church, marriage of Helen

Christine Webb & Ian Hawksby. Mr. B took us in his car to Harrison Gibson's Room at the Top.

29th Mr. Sawood put his new car in garage - Maserati.

OCT

6tH Some TV in evening - Dixon of Dock Green & Charlie Drake.

10th Welwyn Garden City via Gants Hill & Kings Cross. Cup of coffee in Wimpy. Bus to Hatfield - no cafe so had nothing to eat until I got home at 6.45. Returned via Barnet and Archway - bus delayed so made journey tiresome.

Sibley's journeyings are apparently starting to get him down. He is now 85, though not averse to sampling the new Wimpy bars that were beginning to bloom in every town in Britain, bringing a taste of the American diner to the High Street.

Though there are still 67 Wimpy bars across Britain, its heyday was in the 1960s & 70s, taking over Lyons Corner Houses as the staple cafe of the High Street.

11th Bus to Spurgeon's College - stone laying, new wing.

13th Ashurst Anniversary.

18th BDH open day. Gants Hill to Old Street. Walked to Methodist Rooms, bought birthday card for Cis. Got to BDH 2.40pm, usual 10/- gift for expenses. Saw many BDH pensioners.

21st Cis 69.

24th Had coffee in Wimpy, Grays.

28th Too tired to go travelling today.

NOV

6th My skin very bad.

7th Went to Blackfriars and to the Christian Literary Crusade shop. Walked to Kardoma and had my usual tea and toasted teacake.

12th Cis got her fur coat from Co-op.

15th Rain still coming into spare room.

17th Could not go out so Songs of Praise in evening.

22nd Assassination of President Kennedy.

Bus to Southend. Lyons for lunch. TV full of news of death of President Kennedy. One man arrested.

24th Sunday. Cis & I went to Roding Lane. American preacher. Service on U.S. in mourning.

30th Went to Ernie's, Harrow-on-the-Hill. Spent afternoon and evening with them - chatting, laughing. Margaret and Alan came later. Tea, toast, cheese etc. Sundaes. Louise motored us to Harrow Station.

DEC

8th Could not go out in evening, so watched Songs of Praise.

13th Electric blanket in use.

25th Rene, Cliff, Howard & Graham came 1 o'clock. Dinner turkey, chips, Christmas pudding, manchester tart, ginger wine etc. Graham showed his cine-pictures - (continental - Italy, Austria, & aerodrome etc.). Also cine pictures of ourselves last Christmas. Tea & games.

30th Howard looked in and left his car in our driveway while he went off to the West End and met a friend.

31st Dancing and stupidity in Trafalgar Square.

Special offer—to introduce you to the ease and fun of personal movies! Low price includes 8mm camera, a roll of KODACHROME II Movie Film, and an informative idea book. BROWNIE FUN SAVER

1964

JAN

2nd Cis & I walked to Selfridges and had tea in the Jungle Room.

10th Did part of E11 but had to leave ground at Leystonstone - wind chilled me, especially back.

13th Searched me desk and found paying-in book. Drew cheque for rates and Reader's Digest.

14th Mr. Blackwell from E.J. George's wrote to me warning about going out in this weather.

18th So cold we did not go out in evening.

19th Went to Roding Lane - D. Fry took service. I could not hear much.

24th Sweep for Ideal Boiler arranged to come 10-12 noon - he arrived around 4pm. Cis received 2/6d Postal Order and 2 Heinz Soups.

27th Became sickly over breakfast. Had nothing to eat or drink except a sip of soda water. Was very giddy. Had to keep in bed all day. Head too giddy to read.

28th Could not go out today - still giddy. Breakfast grapes and an apple. Cis 'phoned office.

30th Bennett cleaned windows. Electrician came round to look at electric light in kitchen - starter broken, must get new one. Lunch Bovril and toast.

FEB

1st E.J. George's announced change of address - 278-282 High Holborn.

13th Pledger came round to say he could not work on the bathroom taps as the boil on his wrist was too bad. Cis, when taking something round for Pledger's dog, had a nasty fall on pavement - badly bruised knees and hands. I put on a dressing and washed her with Dettol. Cis had a rest and some tea and felt better, but the fall had shaken her.

22nd. Bloomsbury - L.P.B.A. annual meeting. (London Baptist Preachers Association). Mr. John G.J. Hough became president. Tea 4.30 - good ham salad, eggs, tomatoes, cakes etc. President gave address. I could not hear it.

25th Went to Maybrook Rd., to have haircut at the Cypriots - 3/6d.

27th Graham called in about 1.00 o'clock, picked up a few things from Cis. We saw him off to the aerodrome.

28th Did E5 and part of E8 & 9. Lunch at ABC Mare Street.

29th Princess Alexadra had her first baby. Mrs. Harvey went out for the day to Egham.

MARCH

3rd. Did journey E1. Lunched in Lyon's Aldgate, & returned home via Burdett Rd. & Mile End. Mrs. Harvey (LODGER) is staying with Mrs. William, who is mentally affected.

4th Mrs. Harvey returned from Mrs. Williams, who has lost her reason.

5th Cis went to Ilford and had her hair done for dinner tonight. Started for Oxford Circus, walked to Cafe Royal, arriving 6 o'clock. Braised beefsteak. Fruit salad, coffee. Toasted the Queen. Mr. Woods gave us a lift to Gants Hill. A steady snow.

6th. I dressed to go and see Pennington who has had to have his leg off, but it was so cold that I stayed by the fire.

9th Lunch lentil soup.

12th Pledger came and took away TV for adjustments. Hade to be content with ordinary wireless.

13th Income tax refund £5-2/-. Cis mended fuse.

18th Wrote to Lowestoft (Suffolk Hotel) and Ipswich (Crown & Anchor) booking rooms for May-June.

20th Went to City and did some of EC1. Called in at BDH and ordered multi-vitamins, codeine etc. Saw Casswell, Davies &c. Went to E.J. George's new offices, 278-282 High Holborn. Went to Lyons for a light lunch, made a few calls.

23rd Cis and I went to the Salvation Army Citadel - an evening of sacred music.

26th Went to Wilsons and got the new Ronson's Cutter, 10/-2d.

APRIL

2nd Too bad to go out. Spoke to Louise on the 'phone.

7th Chest very wheezy. Taking tablets for bronchitis.

9th Cis and I went to the polling station and voted.

10th I am a little bit livery - felt lifeless.

16th Louise 'phoned saying David was getting on nicely (no sports for a while).

23rd Cis & I started out for Rene's at 10 o'clock on the 251 bus, 6/- return. We arrived at Jones Corner 12 o'clock. Howard in car met us and took us to 'Restormel,' the new chalet. We took five bags full of stuff. Cliff came in. Dinner lamb chops. Cis & Rene went shopping. Heavy storm.

MAY

1st. Went to Watford. Bus to Croxley Green, bus to Rickmansworth, and saw Miss Summer. Bus to Burr and Berry Lane, then bus to Chorley Wood. Fast train to Marylebone, home 5.50.

2nd Watch Cup Final on TV. West Ham 3, Preston 2.

5th W.J. Jewell (BDH) dies.

7th Cis & I went to the School and voted for our 3 candidates (Liberal).

11th Lowestoft. Suffolk Hotel. Lunch at British Home Stores.

12th Bus to Kessingham & 11.3 to Southwell. Saw Munt and had a nice chat. Mr. Webb has sold his business to Mr. Bloomfield.

14th Saw three chemists in Beccles.

15th Arrived back at Lord Avenue 12.30. Cis was waiting for me - carried my case.

21st Inspected trunk and found it in doubtful condition, and rusty, to send to Minehead. Cis got Pledger's mower to try out - mowed lawn. Rain fell.

25th Ipswich. Crown & Anchor. Did work and wrote to Cis. A friendly and chatty rep. at hotel. Dinner chicken and lemon souffle. Saw TV - 'No Hiding Place.'

26th Walked to Normans and station and went by 10.50 to Saxmundham and to Aldeborough.

JUNE

2nd. Bus to Lavenham. Saw Miss Humfries in garden and was invited in to tea. Stayed chatting until. 2.15. Saw successor Mr. Taylor & chatted about Brighton. At hotel, half an hour of TV - 'Meet My Wife.'

11th Cis & I went to E.J.G's office, and saw JEB Jensen and others.

We went to Gamages and Cis bought a pair of shoes suitable for the seaside.

13th Cis & I started for Royal Albert Hall. Festival of Evangelical mixed choir music.

16th British Railway van collected our luggage for Minehead.

19th Waited all afternoon for Mr. Bond of Severans, who fitted earphone hearing aid. Total £41.

20th Minehead. Arrived Westholme 2.30 - room no. 17. Pleasant fellow passengers on train - Mr. & Mrs. Tyson, ex. So. Africa. Had a walk along the Avenue. Our table is with Mr. & Mrs. Tyson.

22nd Birthday. 87. Happy Brithday sung at breakfast. Cis, Rene, Howard & Graham sent cards, and Mrs. Harvey.

23rd Cis & I walked to Mrs. Jewells and had some tea and a long chat. She is very lonely after Williams' death.

25th Very warm. Had a chair on front, strawberries and cream.

29th Cis giddy and stayed in bed. Had no breakfast.

JULY

3rd Cis and I had a walk to the lifeboat station. Did not join the Concert Party.

4th End of holiday. Paddington by 10.54. Compartment was filled wih Westholme friends.

6th Norwich. Bell Hotel, room 46.

7th Went to North Walsham by 10.33. Had lunch in Grammar School Rd.

9th Went to Sheringham, saw Shewell. Sat on front, watched putting and bowls.

10th Train to Ilford. Met Cis at bus stop 12.40. Lunch tongue and salad. A Reader's Digest Sterephonic Record Player brought here by a man, 28 - ex-navy - who demonstrated it.

16th Hingham. Found Horsburgh in hospital - knocked over by motorcycle.

No letters as postmen on strike.

20th Kings Lynn, Duke's Head room 18. Did not write to Cis because of strike. Some TV - No Hiding Place. Painful sitting so returned to my room. Practiced fitting in hearing aid, wrote diary.

29th Bought Cis a dressing-gown at the Co-op in Ilford, £2-3-6d. Mrs. Harvey's sister bought Cis a lovely box of carnations at Romford market.

AUGUST

11th Cis started on spare room - a difficult task, much waste but may be serviceable.

19th Cis 'phoned Rene to say I was not fit enough for a long bus ride.

22nd. Cis & I started out for Pinner at 2.15. Ernie & David came in a car for us at Pinner Station at 4.25. David made us a cup of tea while waiting for Louise, Alan & Margaret. Nice chat and then tea - cheese, peaches & custard, cake &c. Mr. & Mrs. Millard, and Hillary, 61/2, came in evening. We had a nice time together. We left at 8.30 - Louise rook us in her car to Harrow-on-the-Hill station. Home 10.20.

24th Bill and Pledger came over and started on back room. Trudy got locked out - 'phoned to shop. Cis showed her how to get in window. Rene 'phoned 6.40 saying Graham would come over on

Saturday.

25th Went to office with many peaches which I distributed. (Blackwell was away so I left 4 for him). Home 4.45. Cis in the midst of her peaches. About 400.

27th Rene, Graham and Mrs. Ringwood came about 3.30. Mr. & Mrs. Wilson came about 4.30 and took away dozens of peaches - they saw the garden and peach tree. Mr. Dennett and son Roger - 6ft., 20 - also saw the peach tree and took away about 3 dozen.

28th Had my ear syringed by Dr. Beattie. Took DB some peaches. Cis took Percy & Wynne some peaches.

31st Mr. Herbert came about 5.30 and took away some peaches.

SEPT

1st. Had to go to Gants Hill to see Mrs. Lee. Took some peaches. Mr. Wood motored here with his son for some peaches.

3rd Cis & I went to Southend by the 11.38 train and took 25 bus to Thorpe Bay. We were in plenty of time as Newman was having a swim. Had lunch with them in Hut 72. After a rest Victor, Terrance, Cis & I had a 'putt,' 18 holes. Friends of Newman - Bill & wife - came to join us. Victor took us to Southend Station and we returned by 8.45, home 10.5.

7th L'Pool Street to Cambridge. Booked in at Glencarry Hotel, room No 1. Dined at Scotch House, Haggis - 9/-. Had a lot of walking, probably made my skin worse. Had a restless night.

9th Bus to Soham and back. Coffee in Bonnets. Made three calls. Looked round cathedral. Had lunch in Bonnets - beef & apple pie.

12th Marriage of Margaret Louise Sibley to Alan Ralph Millard. Breakfast in bed. Mr. Sayers of Chigwell called at 10 o'clock and motored us to Belmont Hall in Harrow-on-the-Hill for marriage of

Margaret and Alan. Simple and nice ceremony at 12 o'clock. After service we were taken to the West House Reception Rooms for Wedding Breakfast 2.00pm. Started with reception of bridegroom and guests - drank and chat on lawn in reception ground. I became Uncle Tom to many - was treated bountifully. Breakfast was soup, chicken and peach melba. Walked around recreation ground - many photos of happy pair and others. We went home to Ernie's and had another meal. We were motored home by Sayers. Home 10.15.

Thomas Sibley at the wedding of his niece Margaret to Alan Millard, 1964.

14th Bedford. Swan Hotel. Did most of Bedford. Dinner at Lion Hotel. Saw some of 'No Hiding Place.'

16th Luton. George Hotel, room 54.

17th Mr. Waddesdon of Houghton Regis invited me to lunch - 3 lady assistants, his wife and babe. Liver and bacon and rice pudding. Mr. W's mother a minister - very stout. Knew Ed and several Mersea men.

18th Cis waiting for me. Peter Jones called to see if we could put up John Elwin whilst he searched for a house. We said yes - Cis hurried to get the bedroom ready for Monday week.

21st. Chelmsford and Danbury. Lunch in cinema restaurant. Colchester - booked in at Cups, room 66, third floor. On my objection they moved me to room 52, second floor. BBC TV only so missed No Hiding Place.

22nd Went to Walton. Saw Miss Derry - very nice girl, married to a builder and going to Australia.

23rd Wivenhoe. Young rep., Sanders, motored me back to Colchester. Smiths frep. motored me from Moreley to Cups. Went to Coats, Mersea Rd., then back to Beeleys near station.

Had motoring chocolate in place of dinner. Went to Maldon Rd. Brethren's meeting and listened to Mr. Pike of Ipswich, but did not have my hearing aid with me so did not hear much. Had a pleasant time with the Misses Davies, Knock, Bishop &c. Back to Cups, had a read.

24th Dovercourt & Harwich. Bus to Colchester. Met Eva outside Cups and had dinner. Walked her to the bus station and she went by 8.45 to Mersea.

26th Cis & I started out for Spurgeons. Extension of premises. Gants

Hill, London Bridge, fast train to Norwood. J.A. Spurgeon of Coventry Chairman. After meeting, gathered company pronounced building open.

27th Cis has bedroom ready for John Elwin.

28th. St. Albans. But to St. Peter's Streeet and booked into Red Lion Hotel.

OCT

3rd. Income tax £6-10/- - first time it has changed since 1947.

6th Cambridge - made 5 calls. Finished at Mrs. Bedwells. Home 6 o'clock.Mr. Elwin had his first hot bath.

8th Welyn Garden City. Coffee in Wimpy. Mr. Johns took me over his premises. Motoring choc. and coffee for lunch.

9th Maybank Road and had haircut. BDH. Saw plenty I knew - 4 reps, Harry Thompson, Matters, Casswell &c. I only spoke to Ralph & Parker of Directors.

12th Tokyo - Olympic Games.

15th Cis & I went to Poll Station and voted Liberal. Election - Labour Victory.

19th Called in at Co-op and inquired about TV for Cis.

21st Cis 70 (born 1894).

23rd Co-op sent a new TV set.

28th Ventured out but rain drove me in so I only got 6 orders - unlike last week when I had a record day.

30th Cis & I dressed and went to Percy's to dinner 5.40. Mrs. W. Shuttleworth and Mrs. Reynolds. Had a Chinese dinner and Percy showed us his pictures of Jersey on screen.

NOV

2nd. Elwin here - still looking for a house.

4th Cis started fires.

11th Labour Budget.

16th TV - Crime and Punishment.

20th Cis & I went to Blackfriars to Christian Literary Crusade and bought calendars and Christmas cards, £2-14-6d. Walked along Fleet Street to Kardoma and had some tea and toast - Cis had chocolate cake.

21st Cis & I went to Ilford. Cis bought a raincoat - £9-19-6d., and shirts for Graham and Howard.

26th Went to Barnet and forgot it was early closing. 144 bus to Turnpike Lane and underground to Cockfosters - long walk to Simmons, then Innes. Hurriedly made my calls. Mr. Blood kindly motored me to Southgate… 144 bus to Lord Ave.

DEC

4th Cis went shopping and got back to find place flooded. I was asleep when Pledger was told and water was coming through the garage ceiling. Bill soon attended the trouble and got into loft - they got through window as I was asleep. New piping was necessary in airing cupboard.

10th Westminster, Central Hall. Our seat in balcony. Programme very good - 'Night of Miracles' - JLS Peterson, and xylophone solos by Ken Cushing. Fog on the way home.

11th Elwin had his bath before dinner which upset the usual arrangements. He went to his Firm's place - party - and got back at 12.15am.

12th Went to Wilkin's farewell dinner - he's going to Toronto. He got a silver salver.

16th Charringtons delivered 4cwt coal for Christmas.

24th Tried to get Stereo-gram to play Christmas records but could not get it to work.

25th Cliff, Rene, Graham and Howard came in two cars at 12.30. Had usual turkey, ham, sausages, Christmas pudding. Ginger wine. Cliff & Graham got stereo-gram going and we had several records. They departed for Ernie's at 10.00 and took one of our chairs.

29th Had nice letter from C.H. Wilkins in Toronto, who is retiring. He was managing director of BDH for 32 years. Cis 'phoned Percy in evening - up but not getting about.

31st Stayed up and saw the Old Year out and the New Year in.

1965

JAN

4th I attempted to clear my desk but only looked through old letters.

5th Forest Gate, Journey 7. Lunched at ABC Green Street.

12th Bus to Basildon. Lunch in Wimpy.

15th Win & Dave sent Cis a brooch and me a wallet. I dropped my hearing apparatus and broke connector.

16th Cis' finger and hand worlse so she went to King George Hospital with Mrs. Harvey and had to have an injection in her finger. Any further delay and she would have lost her arm.

18th Went to Scrivens, 245 Regent St., had a repair to my hearing aid. Lunched in Lyons Drury Lane. Bus from Ronson's, 352 Strand. Cis's finger throbbing and painful.

19th Forgot to send cash sheet to EJG's.

24th Death of Winston Spencer Churchill, aged 90 years, caused many to go to churches.

After three days of lying in state, Sir Winston's Churchill's funeral was held on Saturday 30th January 1965. At 9.45am Big Ben was silenced and Churchill's coffin placed on a gun carriage, which was escorted by military bands to St Paul's Cathedral. This lion of British history, who had carried his people forward through the most testing of times, was laid to rest.

27th Lying-in-state of W.S. Churchill commences. Thousands parade past in Westminster Hall.

29th Thousands still passing catafalque of Churchill.

30th Winston Churchill's funeral. Procession started at St. Paul's, and continued via Tower Pier, launch. Festival Hall. Train left Waterloo 12.25. Haddock for tea.

FEB

1st. Bethnal Green. Lunched in Lyons Whitechapel.

2nd Mile End. Lunched in Lyons Aldgate.

Feb. 27th was a significant day in the lives of the Sibleys, as their family doctor for many decades, Dr. Beattie, finally hung up his stethoscope and retired.

27th Dr. Beattie officially retired. Huston takes over.

MARCH

4th. West Ham & District Pharmacist's Annual Dinner. Cafe Royal Napoleon Room. Long chat with Evans and family, and many I knew. Cis sat next to an unmarried couple. Girl very young.

30th Harlow via Epping. Had a chat with Mr. Stebbing and his father. Had coffee and a sandwich in Harlow town centre.

APRIL

3rd Oxford won by three lengths.

8th Heard from Mr. Blackwell (from E.J. George) referring to my leaving at the end of the year. I wrote to him. Cis and I went to Westminster Central Hall L.E. Choir Spring Festival. Good Salvation Army Band.

10th Mr. Large jumped from the window of his shop in Thetford. I wrote to Mrs. Large. MAY

1st. FA Cup Final - Liverpool 2, Leeds 1. Evening TV - watched Sherlock Holmes.

5th Watched England v Hungary.

6th Cis & I went through a walk in the park and paid a visit to Mrs. Marks, 47 Lord Avenue.

10th Lowestoft. Suffolk Hotel, room 16. Made several calls. Lunched at British Home Stores, 3/-2d. Went on to Packfield, saw Laing. Grossmith's rep. took me to Moretons in car. Saw Lewis and others. Long wait at Coles with no result. Long chat with Mr. Smalls who knew a lot of BDH reps.

13th Two hours on front. Saw 'Survival' on TV.

17th Ipswich, Crown & Anchor room 9.

19th Saw some football - West Ham beat continental team TSV 2-0 - great excitement.

26th Theobald's bus to Sudbury. Arrived at Four Swans. Had lunch in Market Hill Cafe.

Had letter from Cis. She had had letter from Rene - Rene has given up smoking.

JUNE

3rd Visited E.J. George's. Said goodbye to Mrs. Gray who has to leave on account of having a baby. Mr. Curtis' car caught fire - a short caused the trouble. Mr. Kettle put it out. Fire engines came. Cis & I had tea on the lawn.

12th Mr. Elwin came round with his 2 girls, 3 & 4. Watched some tennis, GB v. S.Africa - Sangster Drysdale.

13th Fred Browning brought round flowers from the church for my birthday.

17th Mr. Moon came round and gave me some grapes for my birthday. I have him a book - Andrew Murray's.

19th Started for Bexhill-on-Sea at 8 o'clock. Had to get a taxi to Covington House. We arrived 1.30. Mr. & Mrs. Codman and girls have us a good welcome. Mrs. Codman took us to Bexhill town and bought me sandals for a birthday present.

20th Mr. Ireland took us to Baptist Church.

21st Breakfast of porridge, eggs, bacon, Heinz Beans, coffee. Played croquet and lost. Watched some Wimbeldon tennis. Had a walk to Cooden. Played Beetle gasme in evening. TV - Our Man at St. Marks.

22nd. 88. Bought shirts in High Street, then had coffee in Dela Ware. Mr. Codman gave me a beautifully decorated sponge cream cake Cards from Rene, Cliff, Howard, Graham and Mrs. Harvey.

28th Norwich. Bell Hotel. Bus to Hunts then walked to Larders. Called on the two in Prince of Wales Rd.

JULY

1st. Stayed in Cromer until 6.15. Had lunch in Tudor Restaurant 8/6d - beef, Queen pudding. Sat watching bowls most of afternoon morning I went on pier. Bus to Norwich, got back to Bell 7.30, watched some TV but couldn't hear much, so dozed through The Saint.

3rd. Saw some tennis - Women's Final. Margaret Smith beat Buano.

4th Fire at Curtis's - electric blanket caught fire. All the upper part *of the house burnt.*

5th Norwich. Made usual Aylsham Road calls, then went to Eaton Village and saw chemist. Saw No Hiding Place on TV.

17th Herne Bay Court.

19th We all played bowls. Newman and self played Curtis and Noble. They won by one. Had a good time. Back to lunch. Cis & I went to the sea and we had tea and cake.

AUGUST

2nd Heard about Curtis and Pledger's quarrel.

3rd Went to Percy's. Carol Iszatt was there - she is 20 years old and getting married in November to Peter. Rev. Moon came round and chatted. After Mr. Moon had gone Win came down - she has a ricked back and is under an osteopath. Percy looks very poorly - he is very glad we came.

7th Received £100 bonus, less income tax.

12th Curtis passed about 40 books on to Cis.

16th Cis & I caught bus to Jones Corner, 6/9d each. We took our beef, and bacon, which was hotted up for dinner. Cliff here to dinner, and Graham and Howard came about 5.15. Rene went out 8.15 with us to bus stop - had to wait 40 mins for our 257. Got home 11 o'clock. No water.

21st Cis wrote to Win & Dave about sleeping here part of time.

23rd Posted cheque for £1-1/- to Pioneer Mission.

24th Called in at Smiths and ordered suit, 23 guineas.

27th Went to Smiths to have suit fitted. Got shoes re-soled.

SEPT

1st Leslie Wright and Paul (from Strasbourg) came to visit, by air. Only stayed an hour. Took away some books.

6th Cambridge. Went to University Cafe and had dinner. Spaghetti. Chatted with two men at table.

10th Win and Dave at home. Glad to see me and I them.

18th Battle of (Bulgaria?)

22nd Colchester, Red Lion Met Eva. Evan and I chatted until dinner. Wilf came and collected her.

OCT

2nd Mr. Pledger brought in Pott gas stove.

8th Went to Morrison's of Stepney Green and got his orders. Sent off my orders with Mrs. Harvey. Pledger still here working on gas heating.

9th We went to Win & Berts in Moor Park. They have a very nice house - large and nicely fitted. After lunch and looking over garden Bert put on some soft music and I sat in lounge with a cup of tea. We had tea - Win & Bert had a light French wine.

11th Pledger still working on Potterton gas heater.

13th We had hot water.

22nd BDH Pensioner's Open Day. Cis & I went to Gamages and Cis bought shoes £1-12-6d.

26th Had a cup of tea at Percy. He's very will and weak as looks as though he is ready to pass away.

28th Pledger worried about the new Redundancy Act. He sacked Bill, only to take him on again later.

NOV

1st. Percy Iszatt, our old friend, passed away. Pledger, Bill and also Kettle cut down our privetts. Bill Thompson 'phoned through at 8 o'clock saying Percy had passed away. Evermore with the Lord.

5th Percy Iszatt laid to rest, Ashurst Drive Baptist Church, 3.00pm. I dressed (new suit) for Percy's funeral. GR Beasley, Murray & Moon officiated. We did not go to the grave or stay for refreshments. Walked home then went to Victoria Halls WC1 for LBA Celebration dinner.

6th Cis went down at 7.30 and found leakage in kitchen - water flooding. We had no water or warmth in radiators. Pledger came round and did inspection. Filled in some information for Hume about customers.

11th Cis and I went to Ludgate Hall and bought Christmas cards and calendars. Had tea in the Golden Egg, Fleet Street.

13th Had 'Jack Warner' and usual British Legion Remembrance

festival on TV from R. Albert Hall, and 'The Working Man,' - Charlie Drake.

14th Cis commences fires.

DEC

2nd We did up Win & Dave's parcel for Canada. Scrivener's called and inspected hearing apparatus - ok.

8th Westminster L.E. Choir, Central Hall. Very good programme: soloist Miss Bette Stalnecker - reciter Nigel Goodwin.

11th Bank sent statement - £247.19.4d.

18th Margaret Millard's birthday - 25.

23rd BDH sent me photo of self with Reeves Brown & Griffin.

24th Saw 'Pickwick' on TV in afternoon.

25th Prepared for company. The Witherington twins came for half an hour's chat. Cliff & others came about 12.30. Dinner 1.30. Ten of us - played Consequences - much laughter. Cliff &c left about 9.30.

27th My cold very severe. We had dinner in dining room but lived in lounge where we had a good fire. Rug got burnt from cinders.

1966

8th Booked for Bexhill June 11-25th.

13th Was ready for Doughty. We went to Ingatestone and Chelmsford.

Finally, at the age of 88, Thomas Sibley faces up to his age and begins training up his replacement, the keen Mr. Doughty.

14th Leigh-on-Sea, lunched in Lyons Southend.

18th Doughty came at 9.30. I could not go with him because of illness. He went off alone to do Saffron Walden.

19th Cis 'phoned Doughty to say I would not be going out.

20th Burst pipe caused water to flow into airing cupboard, toilet and garage. Mr. Witherington came and turned water off.

Cis 'phoned to Pledger in Bournemouth - he will come back earlier tomorrow.

21st Harry Pledger returned from Bournemouth and was able to repair pipes.

24th Did E$ and E17. 'Wet atmosphere,' - affected my skin.

25th Doughty came in car and we did E7, E15 & E10.

FEB

1st RETIRED - at 88 years of age. Left school 1891. Started travelling May 1900.

2nd Went to see Mrs. Thomas to see about valuing her business. Went to L'Pool Street and got my hair cut. Went on to office and saw Russell, Hume, Jensen and others. Left word with Jensen about Mrs. Thomas' business.

8th I did not go out all day.

As the 1960s became noisier, Sibley's life becomes quieter.

11th Bus troubles and threatened rail strike has affected shopping. Lots of illness - many cases of influenza.

14th I wrote to the Borough engineer about No. 9 being converted into a betting shop.

28th I had an officer from N.A.B. come to see me about income. I could not obtain a supplementary grant. General election announced for March 1st.

MARCH

1st Heard from Margaret who said she is expecting a baby in August. Louise 'phoned Cis later in morning.

2nd I wrote to Margaret and Alan.

5th Trudy had a special party - engagement - at No. 37.

7th Arrived at Mansion House 2.30. Lord Mayor arrived and opened meeting. Egyptian Hall filled - good meeting; Sir Lionel Denny &c., Judge Ruttle, G.W. Holland, Rev. Canon &c.

10th Doughty called for me at 9.30 and we went to Watford. We did part of Watford.

11th Watford. Accident on N. Circular caused some delays. Doughty brought a gas ring.

12th Cis & I went to Salmon Lane. Opening of New Hall by Mayor of Tower Hamlets.

27th Mr. Taton (opposite garden) nailed up our fence.

31st General Election. Much excitement.

APRIL

1st. Labour Victory - Labour 363

Conservatives - 252.

Liberal - 12

Republican Labour - 1

12th Had a hunt for my life Policy - unsuccessfully.

14th Snow. Blizzards. Coldest day this century. Went through old papers & letters.

21st Queen opens parliament. Cis washed and put up curtains.

22nd TV in evening - exciting piece.

28th I 'phoned Hume to say I would be ready to help Doughty when he is ready.

29th My side getting worse. Trouble getting in and out of bed. Cis is helping me wonderfully.

MAY

3rd. Budget.

7th Dixon of Dock Green has finished until September.

20th Had a nice letter from Margaret in Cambridge.

JUNE

2nd Pledger and Bill started on our wall and gate in back garden. USA reached the Moon.

4th Went downstairs and watched cricket. England hopelessly outplayed by West Indies. Eng. 167, W.I. 277.

6th Malcom Browning called for milk bottle tops.

11th Bexhill holiday. Collington house.

13th Had a walk to Little Common and bought some cards.

14th Cis and I walked to Bexhill shops and had tea & scones opposite Woolworths.

16th Too wet for putting but had a round with Cis before dinner.

In the 1950s & 60s recycling was a way of life, with both glass bottles and metallic bottle-tops being re-used.

17th After dinner we watched dancing and prize-giving. Mr. Ireland won two prizes.

JULY

1st. Went to bank. My bank balance is disagreeably small. Watched Wimbeldon - Santana won.

16th Football. England 2 - Mexico 0.

26th England 2, Portugal 1. Great enthusiasm over England win - Bobby Charlton scored both.

30th Great excitement over World Cup final. England 4, Germany 2. A great victory. The Queen, Wilson, and other big men there.

AUGUST

8th Mr. Witherington died in Wanstead Hospital.

12th Three policeman shot dead by criminals.

18th Cis & I started out for Moor Park, Win & Bert's. Bert met us in car. Lunch cold fillet steak, tea & biscuits. Sat in armchair and *garden. Bert motored us home, arrived 9.30.*

22nd Cis 'phoned Co-op about TV not behaving itself.

24th Clare Millard born 4 o'clock. Margaret well. Cis and I went to Ilford and ordered Mrs. Harvey's coal from Charringtons.

25th Alan rang through and told us of the birth of a daughter. Another policeman shot - 2 men caught, one injured by police truncheon, in hospital.

Daily Mirror **MASSACRED**

4d Saturday, August 13, 1966 No. 19,483

IN THE LINE OF DUTY

After the massacre . . . one detective lies dead in the road while a policeman pulls up a screen to hide the scene of the killings. In front of him is the Triumph 2000 Q-car under which can just be seen the head of another dead detective. The third detective was shot dead in the car

18,000 JOIN HUNT FOR KILLERS OF 3 POLICEMEN

TWO dead detectives lie in a street . . . still, silent symbols of the worst crime London has known this century.

More than murder. It was a massacre. Three policemen savagely gunned down in the line of duty when, unarmed, they ran into three gunmen.

Keener

Continued on Back Page

THE GREAT MANHUNT
Story and pictures on Pages 2 and 3

THE VICTIMS - Back Page

Story: Mirror Crime Squad Pictures: Mirror cameramen

The 1960s was marred by a rise in violent crime, particularly amongst urban criminal gangs.

26th Police still hunting for Roberts.

SEPT

5th Cis & I went to King George Hospital and I had my hearing tested.

7th Graham drove up with Pat to see us. We all went to the Town Hall to get form for Rates Rebate. Went to Woolworths and got bookbinding material.

8th Cis getting room ready for Wakeling.

OCT

6th Got ready for transport to Royal N. Throat Nose & Ear Hospital. 4 others in ambulance, & we went via London Hospital & Royal Free, and got to RNTNE 10am. Hindu Doctor saw to my ear, and got me a hearing aid etc. Cis & I had coffee and cake in hospital. Abulance came for us at 12.15 and we were home at 12.45.

7th TV making a shrill noise. Had an hour or so with Mrs. Witherington - had a sherry.

14th BDH Open Day. Went to our office (EJG's), and saw Russell & Hume, then walked to BDH. Too far. Went to Pensioner's Dept. and got my 10/6d. Chat with Robins, Cresswell, Gerald and others. Sat at Top Table.

17th Gad a nice letter from David Sibley - becoming a librarian.

20th Wrote to David Sibley who has started work as a librarian in Reading.

21st Cis 72.

Terrible calamity in South Wales - Aberfan. Many children buried in mountain collapse.

A child is rescued. The Aberfan disaster was the catastrophic collapse of a colliery spoil tip on 21 October 1966. The tip had been created on a mountain slope above the Welsh village of Aberfan, near Merthyr Tydfil, and overlaid a natural spring. Heavy rain led to a build-up of water within the tip which caused it to suddenly slide downhill as a slurry, killing 116 children and 28 adults as it engulfed Pantglas Junior School and a row of houses.

27th Heard from Will Warwick.

NOV

5th Had a letter from Margaret from Cambridge. I may go on Nov. 25th or 28th.

15th Ernie & Louise visit.

18th Ambulance sent, took me to King George's Hospital. Could not get rupture back - operation necessary. No food or drink. Ford Ward.

19th Saw Cis for half an hour. Very weak.

20th Long dose of morphine. Had visitors - Cis, Cliff, Rene. Lad next to me aged 14. Polan Ramsey.

21st Cis cancelled choir seats at Westminster.

22nd Intravenous injections. Cis stayed with me until the bell rang.

23rd Was told I could now drink anything. I ventured on to Horlicks. Had a card from all at EJG's office - get well quick.

24th Hospital times. This makes for a very slow day. I was told I could get up and walk the ward. Had a poached egg. Shaved without difficulty.

25th Another fortnight here possibly. Visitors at 2 o'clock - D.B. Murray, Cis, Graham, Bill Thomson.

29th Doctors told me I could go home tomorrow afternoon. Exit, praise the Lord.

30th Went home. Soon got back to normal.

DEC

1st Cis phoned Murray Moon, electrician, about leakage in electric cooker.

5th Bill Thomson called and brought me a diary.

14th Trudy took us to hospital. Saw Mr. Park who was very pleased with my recovery, and I need not attend hospital again without fresh need.

15th 'Here Comes Christmas' on TV - mostly negro spirituals.

19th Rep. from Wanstead council called and enquired about our means re. Rates.

24th Received 80 Christmas cards. Dixon of Dock Green finished for season.

26th Rene, Cliff, Graham, Pat, Howard. Dinner, games. Company left 10.30.

28th Cis & I played 'Donkey.'

29th Had Nicholas Nickelby in evening.

1967

JAN

3rd Ernie, Alan, Margaret & babe arrived 11.15. Clare a lovely girl of 4 months. Had dinner - shoulder of lamb. We had a pleasant time together... I gave Alan an old missionary book - The Remarkable Jew - and he borrowed Baron's Zachariah.

4th TV in evening - strike prevented us seeing College Contest and Coronation Street.

9th Cis got paraffin stove for lavatory from Halfords.

12th Council gave me rebate on rates, £17-12/-.

19th Read some of 'Old & New London.'

31st. TV - Double Your Money, and Mrs. Thursday.

FEB

10th Read some of 1902 diary. Very sad and gloomy. Passing of Mother and Father.

11th Rene's birthday. TV Charlie Drake.

12th I wrote to Will Warwick.

MARCH

2nd. Cis and I dressed for evening. Taxi to Gants Hill, train to Oxford Circus, Walked along Regent Street to Cafe Royal, Napoleon Room.

Received by Mr. Mrs. A. W. Newberry. Dinner 7.00pm. Cornets de Jambon, Oef a la Russe, trout & lamb chops, Peche Montreal, petits-fours. I had a sherry with Mr. Evans.

10th Reading Old & New London, & History of 1914-18 War, and Madam Gurgon (?).

15th Dr. Merriman came, sounded out my chest - very satisfactory.

21st Record warmth for this date.

23rd Cis & I had a walk through the park.

APRIL

4th Heavy attack of dermatitis. Goodbye to Monica Rone (?) in Double Your Money.

8th Neuro-dermatitis very bad. Little sleep at night.

26th Eva paid us a visit - came about 8.30. I sat on lawn with her. Dinner, chicken, then at 5 o'clock, tea on the lawn. She left us at 6.20. Cis saw her on the bus.

MAY

3rd. Had my walk. Cold, cheerless weather. Dinner - boiled belly of pork & pease pudding and carrots. Sent hearing aid to Scriveners for adjusting.

17th Mrs. Harvey had a fall at the Laundry and injured her leg.

18th Sweep expected at 7am but came at 9am. Left 10am. Cis had a very hard day's work.

20th Cup Final, Sputs 2, Chelsea 1.

24th Read some of Dr. Grenfell's autobiography.

26th Egg-man left me some mushrooms. Mrs. Harvey went to her sisters in Slough.

30th Boy left wrong paper so Cis went to paper shop and got Daily Telegraph.

31st Wimbeldon - Santana v. Davidson.

JUNE

2nd Saw some tennis - Taylor & Cox, Surrey tournament.

3rd Paid telephone a/c - £3-15/-.

7th J.E. Blackwell sent a card, remembering my birthday. War, Israel & Egypt, Syria &c.

8th Israelis beating Egypt - Israel has taken all Jerusalem.

9th Tennis from Eastbourne - Sangster versus Sultana.

12th Cis' eyes bad so she 'phoned Dr. Merriman, who gave her ointment.

13th we sat on lawn and Cis protected her eyes with umbrella. Carin Pledger brought me some grapes from S. Africa.

17th Holiday. Pledger took us to Clements Rd., and we got in coach. Nice ride to Hastings.

22nd 90.

JULY

1st. Coffee in Longley's, walked to front. Mr. Codman took us to Fallaise Street for the coach to Clements Rd. Taxi home, 10/-. Everything as we left it, safe and sound, praise the lord.

3rd Watched Wimbeldon. Taylor beat Ruffles.

5th Wimbeldon - Newcombe v. Pizie.

6th Mrs. Anne Jones beat R. Casals (only 18 - USA).

8th Billie King beat beat Ann Jones and got shield for winner presented by Princess Marina. Mrs. King won three firsts - women's, women's doubles and mixed doubles.

9th Heard Billy Graham 6.35-7.00. Fred brought flowers from Ashurst. A lad brought eggs from Roding Lane.

10th Ernie only making a little progress.

13th Ernie rather worse - Louise on 'phone.

19th Graham and Pat came to tea.

21st Tried to repair back fence but had not the nails.

24th Cis up early as she has to get to New Barking Hospital about her eyes. She got to Hospital by 179 bus. She was seen by several doctors - specialists.

27th 1 ton of coal from Co-op - £13-1-8d.

AUGUST

5th Cis has kidney trouble and blood pressure.

8th The dog from no. 31 getting through fence and causing trouble.

21st Cis went to Upney Hospital. Picked some peaches.

22nd Had a card from Graham who is in Cornwall.

23rd I had an attack of gastroenteritis. Cis could not deal with me so 'phoned Mrs. Pledger who was out, so D. Houston came and lifted me on to bed. All I wanted to do was sleep. Re. Moon came round to visit during my plight. I felt weak and lifeless.

SEPT

17th Rene 'phoned to say she and Dina would come tomorrow. Cis 'phoned Louise - Ernie is having to have a new kidney - on danger list at Halton Hospital, Bucks.

18th Rene, Cliff & Dina came 6.45pm. Cis made a high tea for them - tongue, ham salad &c. They stayed until about 8 o'clock. Dina is very thin and not very fit (smokes a lot).

23rd Dressed for Ashurst Drive Women's Guild event. Bill Thomson came for us at 5.00pm. We had a good meal. Entertainment followed - brass band and Holt Primary singers. Many old friends.

24th Bill Thomson brought us some flowers - Harvest Sunday.

OCT

2nd Louise 'phoned saying Ernie had died yesterday.

16th Dock strikers fighting. Communists at fault.

18th I wrote to Will Warwick.

20th Cis finished gilding the painted metal trolley.

21st Cis' birthday - 74.

NOV

4th Mr. Benchley of Kings Lynn about my books, and bought what I offered for sale - £13-13/-. Mike and his young lady -Sheila - brought Christmas cards, and I bought some, and some calendars.

22nd Cis did her shopping. I was going to meet her in the park but I mistook the time, so she came home on her own.

24th I went to meet Cis in the park who was late, and missed me. She went home alone, then returned to the park for me.

30th Pledger put up new gutters at rear. Gas Co. sent man to clean Potterton stove &c.

DEC

1st Saw Daktari on TV, and then Mrs. Thursday.

2nd Rail workers working to rule.

6th Went to Westminster Carol Festival. L.E. Choir. Good programme.

11th Dr. Merriman wants me to be x-rayed at his place at Chadwell Heath.

16th Did up parcels for Louise, Margaret, Clare, Alan, David.

21st Mrs. Phyllis Pledger has left her husband Harry for good. Gone to Brighton taking the cat and dog with her.

22nd Mrs. Harvey collected our turkey.

23rd Cis took capon to C-op butcher for putting in his cold safe.

24th Harry Ppledger called in and said he was off to his father and sister's in Bournemouth.

25th I had an attack of gastro-entiritus. Cis could not help so the milkman got me back in bed. I slept and could not get up for Christmas dinner. Graham and Pat arrived first, then Rene, Cliff, Howard following. Cis looked after them.

28th Did not get up and dress - stayed in bedroom all day. Sherry going rapidly.

30th Harry Pledger carried me upstairs - fireman's hold. Mostly in bed all day.

1968

For the first fortnight of 1968 it would seem that the 90 year old Sibley, who began to suffer from illness for the first time in his life during the previous year, is confined to bed.

JAN

14th Had Songs of Praise from St. Martin's in the Field. Able to shave out of bed.

15th Bert Green came around and had a coffee. Had no lunch until Doctor had been. He said I was getting on well and should get on my feet.

18th 'Phoned Dr. Durham to say I was not able to come to be x-rayed. 22nd Louise 'phoned offering to pay for 'phone in bedroom. Invitaton to West Ham District Pharmacist's Association Annual dinner March 1st - declined with regrets. Unable.

26th Mrs. Harvey doing our shopping.

FEB

1st Dr. Greenhalse came 3.30 and went over me. Not satisfied with progress of healing.

3rd Had letter from Eva who has thrombosis in leg.

7th Doctor's arrived about 12.30. Dr. Price recognised me and gave me a thorough examination, and pronounced my wound an H.W.B. burn.

His old building pal and neighbour Mr. Pledger pops in with perhaps a welcome visit, including work and a chat. Sibley's world now in his final decade is closing on on the small realm of his home, friends and neighbours.

9th Pledger is in putting in a new wash basin. Bert Green came round - after the old wash basin and piano. Re. Moon called in. I was soon exhausted with talk.

11th Rene's birthday - 56.

12th Rene & Graham came. I sat out pleasantly all the time. Pledger got me a qtr of brandy - 18/-.

15th Pain in my chest kept me a prisoner for most of the day.

16th Received some lovely carnations from Mr. & Mrs. Blackwell.

20th Mrs. Irene Browning called and a had a cup of tea.

26th Death of Dr. N. Beattie, Worthing General Hospital. 51 years medical practice at Ilford, pastor of Roding Lane Evangelical Free Church.

28th Did nothing particular.

MARCH

1st. Wrote to Mrs. Beattie (Cis did the writing).

13th Read more of Oliver Twist.

14th I wrote to Eva and Margaret and Alan at Cambridge.

15th Read a little David Copperfield - print too small.

18th Read some of Boleham's Cliffs of Opal.

24th Finished David Copperfield.

APRIL

5th Read some of Reader's Digest July '66.

10th Dr. prescribed Synalar cream for neuro-dermatitis.

13th Wrote to J.E. Blackwell and David Sibley.

15th Mrs. Harvey returned from Nottingham bringing Cis a cardigan and 1/2 a dozen eggs.

16th Got a/c balance from Midland Bank - £157.00

21st Went downstairs for the first time this year.

25th Watched tennis - Laver & Cox, Cox beaten.

MAY

28th Had a walk round garden in the sunshine.

JUNE

1st Got dressed for the first time since Christmas.

3rd A little TV. White City Sports.

4th A short walk with Cis round to Pledgers - saw his garden, fuschias &c.

5th Just heard that Robert Kennedy, brother of late President, shot - died. 10 children.

12th Sat in garden in afternoon. Ice cream and strawberries. Walked round to Pledgers with Cis. He was entertaining a Mrs. Pearce. Evening - Coronation Street.

22nd Birthday - 91. I had a surprise gift - Codman sent a box of carnations. 8 cards. Heard from Eva.

27th Will Warwick wrote, sending a book, Residue of Days by Hugh Redwood.

JULY

2nd Bank account - £153-18-1d.

29th Had a read of Churchill's History of the War.

AUGUST

1st. Finished reading Churchill's The World Crisis, 1911-18.

9th Cis went shopping. I went to meet her with umbrella as it was raining heavily. Met her by the bus stop. I had to change into another suit.

23rd David's birthday - 21.

24th Clare's 2nd birthday.

27th Princess Marina died - tumour on brain, aged 6.

28th Cliff and Rene had serious 'words,' - rowing &c.

29th Cis had 'phone message from Rene telling her about Cliff. Sad news - Cliff has deserted Rene and gone away with Mrs. Turner.

This seismic family ruction comes out of the blue; the marital break-up of his daughter Rene and son-in-law Cliff Ringwood. There follows desperate 'phone calls, meetings, those rare but intense huddles in front parlours that all families have over the years and which rock the sense of certainty and safety within the domestic nest. As an ordered man of drive, purpose and control, this event must have rocked Thomas Sibley.

30th No news of Cliff and Mrs. Turner.

SEPT

2nd Rene, Graham & Pat came about 7.30 and had a little talk about Cliff's desertion - sorrowful.

5th Heard from Mr. Blackwell and David Sibley.

11th While Cis was downstairs getting tea, I fell, banging down chair and table, cutting and bruising forehead. Cis 'phoned 999 for hospital. Ambulance soon came. I was in King George's Hospital. Forehead bandaged, and had x-ray and tetanus. Took blood pressure. I was taken home at 1.00pm. A very black day.

12th Read Barnaby Rudge.

23rd TV - Sherlock Holmes' Dancing Men.

27th Visitor from Hospital to see how I was getting on. Mrs. J. Willcox, H.V. & Co., Kenwood Gardens CRE 4541 (Health Welfare Dept.).

OCT

2nd The Avengers.

3rd Read some of Study in Scarlet.

Sibley's own health concerns are exacerbated by his daughter Rene's troubles. Her problems would soon worsen, but for now a fall is being treated in hospital.

4th Bank - £153-13-11d. Rene had a fall.

5th Rene in hospital.

6th Graham 'phoned about Rene who is in Rochford Hospital.

7th Graham 'phoned through about Rene who may leave hospital and come here. Rene brought here by Graham and Pat - to stay here until she is better.

8th Cis looked after Rene who had a good night's rest and some breakfast.

9th Cis went shopping. Rene and I met her in the park.

11th Filled in Election form. Included Rene's name.

13th Rene went back with Graham and Pat.

14th Rain came through roof. No news from Rene.

15th Louise 'phoned through - general news. No news from Rene.

The following day, there is a shock 'phone call from his grandson Graham.

18th RENE DEAD AGED 56.

Up 8.45. Graham 'phoned through saying Rene found dead in bed.

'Phoned again in afternoon saying Rene being cremated next Thursday.

The loss of his son Len in 1950 had been tragic enough, but to lose his remaining daughter Rene, whom he had raised since 1910, was beyond sadness. The cause of her death is not known.

21st Cis' birthday, 75. Had letters from Eva and Margaret Milward. I had a walk in the park in the sunshine. Graham and Pat came about 9.45 - talked about Rene &c.

25th Funeral of poor Rene - 56. Graham 'phoned. Funeral went off satisfactorily. Several came to church.

NOV

1st. Cis went to bus stop and met Eva about 11.30. Had a general talk. Eva not in good fettle. Mr. Blackwell rang thro' asking about our welfare.

2nd Saw some tennis - Dewar Cup. Mrs. Court & Mrs. Wade - Mrs. Court won. Hewitt won.

7th Pledger and Bill round here working - putting new fireplace in Mrs. Harvey's room.

8th In bed all day. Aftermath of shock of Rene's death.

11th I have recovered from Saturday's 'knock-out.'

13th Harry Pledger and Bill here working on the water system. Leakage at join of lead and copper pipes. Bill painting back of house.

14th Wrote to Mr. & Mrs. Lamaitre - accepting invitation to Graham and Pat's wedding.

17th Sunday. Young people from Ashurst came at 3 o'clock, and Rev. Moon. They took the service and I chose the hymn. Cis gave them a hot drink.

20th Graham and Pat came round and spent evening with us. They brought several coats of Rene's.

27th Anne Hamley & baby Robert, 14 months, came at 3.15 and stayed until 4.30 - tea & cake. Kenneth at school in Dagenham.

28th Pledger sent in his bill - £94-8-6d.

DEC

4th I had an attack in the night and was compelled to stay in bed all day.

7th Made out cheque to BDH, made out to A. Neville, Staff Shop.

12th Mrs. Witherington moved from her house, 33 Lord Avenue.

14th Cis had to thaw pipes in Mrs. Harvey's room. Our pipes ok - pipes in No. 33 frozen up. Did up parcels for Eva, Louise, Alan & Margaret.

16th Mr. & Mrs. Blackwell sent a Christmas parcel from Selfridges. Alan & Margaret sent a large photo of Clare and a nice letter. Cheque for £5 from E.J. George's,

18th Wrote to David & his wife who are on furlough.

24th Rev. Moon and Mr. Pipkin came and we four broke bread. Watched some TV - 'On Way to Moon.'

25th Graham, Pat & Howard came by car about 12.20. Quiet afternoon. The Lord was with us to give me health and strength for the occasion.

27th Louise 'phoned, also Alan & Margaret, and Clare spoke.

28th Heard from Mabel Fleet - 79. She still takes a class at Mark's Gate.

31st No fun or noise at the passing of the old year.

1969

JAN

3rd Cis and I went round to Pledgers for an hour or so in the afternoon and had some music.

7th Had a read of Pledger's book, The Scourge of the Swatika.

9th Wrote to David Sibley about his wedding, 1969.

After family tragedies come, of course, family celebrations. Such are the seasonal ebbs and flows. Not only his nephew David but his grandsons Graham and Howard are all due to be married in the ensuing days and months.

11th Graham's wedding. Graham came for us at 11.00 and we motored to he and Howard's house, 50 Green Lane, Eastwoood, Southend. St. Andrew's church. After marriage ceremony we went to the Roadhouse for reception. Nana, Jim Ringwood and others there. I stood the ordeal well.

14th Finished reading The Scourge of the Swastika by Lord Russell of Liverpool.

17th Sent the Foot-Painting Artists a monthly 10/-6d.

20th Heard from BDH Chemicals, H.E. Davies, about the 1949 trust fund. 6-12 Clarges Street, W1.

25th Howard's wedding. Graham came for us 11.45 and we were motored to the church of St. Lawrence and All Saints, Eastwood Lane, Southend. Howard was married to Laura Beverley. Graham was best man. After ceremony we were taken to the Civic Centre. Sherry, sandwiches, cakes, fruit cup &c. Said goodbye to Ringwood family - Jim, Roy & wives.

27th Read some of the Tartan Pimpernel.

FEB

8th Had a letter from Winnie Sibley who has moved to March.

13th Had £30 sent to me by BDH Trust Fund. Harry Pledger came in for a chat.

28th Louise rang through saying Margaret's baby had arrived. Stephen Dudley Millard born 1.45pm.

MARCH

5th Had a card from Mr. Blackwell from Portugal - raining.

10th Will Warwick has changed his address - 78 Drury Rd., Colchester.

15th Mrs. Harvey nearly set the house on fire. Towel burnt with great hole in it. Said it wasn't her. Jews fighting in number 27 - bloodshed - a party?

APRIL

5th Had a nerve attack.

6th Workmen came next door - no. 33. Noise all day, from knocking down wall and partition wall.

7th Got out of bed and fell. Could not get back up. Laid on floor. Workmen next door came and lifted me onto bed.

10th I was quite unable to get about.

15th Entered up diary with Cis' help.

Still scarred by the recent death of his daughter, as if to

reassure himself that tragedy is baked into each successive generation, and to process that fact, Sibley turns to his diary of 1900 and reminds himself of the domestic tumult between his own mother and father:

16th Read more of diary 1900-1901. Sad reading. Poor mother suffered from a drunk husband.

24th Harry took away our dining room electric stove for repair.

30th. Cis went shopping. I met her in the park and sat on the seat with her. It was a very nice morning. Mr. Brigbourne came in and had a chat about our wall damage. Harry wanted the job but we gave him until Monday.

MAY

2nd Wrote to W.P. Mullen, (Irish Republic), new director of Glaxo. Sent £1 to RNM to DSH, and £1 to Soc. DHS for Jews.

5th Cis had to go to Upney Hospital about eyes. Broke journey back and bought a wheeled carrier from the Green Shield Stamp Stop.

13th Had a nice letter from Howard. Trudy Curtis is to be married next year.

16th £25 sent to me by '49 Triangle Fund.

22nd I wrote to Gorings and told them I intended to call on my builders of work if not done within 7 days (damage to house from neighbouring work).

26th TV - Coronation Street and a play 8-10pm.

JUNE

2nd Graham on 'phone who told Cis Eric had met Cliff in Bournemouth on Sunday. I wrote a letter to Goring's (Romford) saying all building work was now in the hands of H. Pledger.

The Triangle Trust helps people of the Pharmaceutical Industry

The Triangle Trust 1949 Fund is an independent charitable trust whose main purpose is to give assistance with education expenses or to relieve hardship or distress for people, and their dependents, working in the pharmaceutical industry in Britain and the British Commonwealth.

The Trustees will consider sympathetically any applications for assistance, beyond the scope of an employer's responsibilities, concerning education or training at recognised centres of study for general or special subjects, including music and the arts.

For additional information, or to apply for assistance, write to:

The Secretary, Dept CD
The Triangle Trust 1949 Fund
Clarges House, 6-12, Clarges Street
London W1Y 8DH

4th In the evening Graham, Pat & Mrs. Ringwood came to see us and had a good meal. Graham told Cis about Eric finding Cliff in Bournemouth.

JUNE

16th Bexhill. Bussed it to town and went to De La Ware for coffee. Walked to Woolworths and then to Ware's and Cis bought a jacket, £8.19.6d.

22nd 92, praise the Lord.

24th Mr. Codman took us to Eastbourne and we had coffee at the Grand Hotel.

28th Saw some good tennis - Ashe beat Gonzales.

JULY

4th. Mrs A. Jones beat Mrs. King.

5th Watched final. Laver beat Newcombe. Went to Roding Lane. Organ recital by Kenneth Goodman. A wonderful display of talent and memory.

7th Wrote to Mr. & Mrs. V. Sawyer declining invitation to David and Wendy's marriage.

14th Strike robbed us of Coronation Street so we had some BBC - Royal Tournament, Canadians.

17th Watched tennis. Cox beat Mand of S. Africa. Some rowdies came and sat on court - police came and removed them.

18th Howard moves from Eastwood.

20th Lost Songs of Praise through TV going to the 2 men entering and going on to the Moon. Most wonderful happening this world has seen. Most of evening taken up with men getting to the Moon.

For Thomas Sibley, who had been born in the fullness of the Victorian age, when Jack the Ripper was roaming the streets and manned flight was only the fancy of fantastical authors, to live to witness the setting foot on Earth's satellite must have been an extraordinary event of numinous power.

21st Had TV. More about landing on Moon.

23rd. Dr. Adigo came round. Deep breathing helpful.

24th Watched arrival and descent of astronauts. 3 Americans arrived safely from Moon adventure and achievement - wonderful.

AUGUST

2nd David's marriage.

5th Trouble with next door - workmen burning garden stuff. Dinner delayed. Council men and medical officer came 2 o'clock. No more fires.

Buzz Aldrin on the Moon, photographed by Neil Armstrong. For one born in the fullness of the Victorian age, this sight must have been stirring beyond measure.

6th Jonathan Paul born. Bruno had trouble with water tank.

12th. Mr. Pledger will not accept offer of £12-10/-. Court case? Bruno Bagione came in and saw us about cost of damage to dining room. Offered £12-10/-.

13th Harry Pledger sent in a letter for me to sign and copy and send to Biagione. He wants £25 or will go to court.

16th Cox played Nastase.

18th Letter from H.S. Rolfe (MD) about Open Day at Poole, Oct. 3rd.

19th Bruno Biagione sent in a cheque for £25 for wall damage.

28th Rec'd repayment of Income Tax, £44-1/-. Wrote cheques for telephone, and Co-op coal.

SEPT

11th Pru returned my policy for Annie Sibley's death.

17th Portable TV not working properly.

20th Louise, Alan, Margaret, Clare & Stephen to dinner. All well. Leg of lamb and plum pies. Went to Park. Clare enjoyed swings. Sat on seat and had photo taken. Visitors departed 3.30 after a jolly time.

23rd Policy for Popp's death £95. Quite unexpected.

OCT

3rd Bank Statement - £264-8-2d.

7th Park closed because of dustmen strike.

8th I paid in by transfer £50 to Deposit account. Balance £100.

21st Cis 76. I had an attack at 1am in garden. Pledger came round and helped Cis get me back into bed. I remained like this until Wednesday morning. Poor Cis and on her birthday too!

NOV

18th Graham & Pat came 8 o'clock. Graham not quite fit.

19th. Wrote to BDH for Glaxo News. Also asked for negative of our photo in Glaxo News.

22nd Sent birthday card to Laura Ringwood, 37 Gainsborough Court, Station Av., Walton-on-Thames, Surrey.

The Good Old Days, a BBC TV series recreating the heyday of British Music-Hall, ran for an extraordinary 30 years. For Sibley, who had lived through the actual heyday, it must have warmed the heart to see his childhood re-enacted on the small screen.

DEC

3rd Women from 33-31 quarrelling over their side entrance.

10th Westminster Hall, Choir. Had refreshments in Lyons. Met Ivy Moyes and Joan Sills in there. Louise came and met us in the hall. Louise gave us the taxi fare from Gants Hill to 35 Lord Avenue - £4/6d.

25th Howard and Laura here, also Graham and Pat. After dinner - presents and chat. Guests went at 10.15. A happy Christmas.

30th TV - the Good Old Days - very good.

1970

JAN

1st I was quite helpless in my bed all day. Dr. (locum) came and prescribed tablets for congestion of chest. Had some of Mrs. Harvey's sherry.

2nd In bed all day but able to take food - beef tea.

9th TV - Wheel of Fortune. Finished reading 'The Gospel of the Life Beyond,' by Lockyear.

10th Cis 'phoned Gertie Fennell who may be able to call for us on Saturday and take us to the Manor Park re-union.

12th Postman brought six copies of photos from BDH at Poole - six enlargements.

15th Rose Cherry 'phoned and invited us to go to Manor Park reunion in their car.

17th Mr. Butcher and his wife came for us and motored us to Manor Park Baptist Church. Rev. Bernard C. Moore took service. Saw old friends - Reynolds, Pastor Stump (3 children), Rosie Parrett, Rene Wightman &c.

21st Decided not to send 2 photos to J.E. Blackwell.

24th TV - Vanity Fair.

27th Searched for 'Vanity Fair,' - unsuccessfully.

28th Pledger called in for his book. I lent him an article on Dickens - The Sunday Companion.

FEB

1st. Looked through diaries 65, 66, 67, 68, 69. No approach from Ashurst.

3rd. Triangle Trust 1949 Fund allows me £15 for fuel in April and £15 for fuel in Oct.

7th Some TV - Jessie James.

19th In bed all day. Unconscious to all around.

MARCH

2nd. Cis phoned Bob Sibley, Hertford, who will come tomorrow.

3rd. Trudy from number 37 has discarded some items which we could find useful.

12th Trudy Curtis. WE went next door and saw the bride. The bride left home at 2.30. I had a sherry, Cis a soft drink.

13th Wrote to Eva, also to Brentford Nylons, 19, Great West Rd., sending cheque for 29/11d for 2 pairs of nylons, blue and pink.

18th Cis booked Grey Green coach for Torquay June 6th-20th.

28th Geoffrey Curtis (next door) in bed with a temperature over 100.

APRIL

6th Did a little sweeping. Some pain. Stooping with handbrush was not good for me.

8th. Went to bank and got a/c - £186-2/-9d. (Equivalent of £2,500 in 2023).

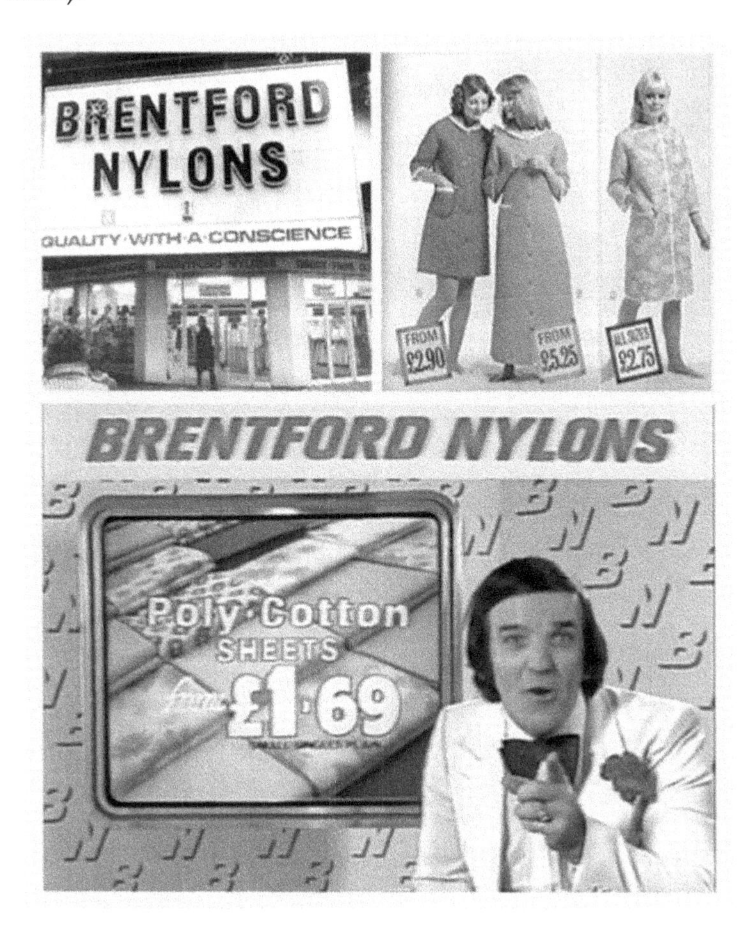

Brentford Nylons was a highly successful purveyor of nylon bedding, shirts and slacks, famous for its iconic TV adverts starring Alan Freeman. Operating out of Brentford, West London, the company went into administration in February 1976.

11th Cup Final, Leeds v. Chelsea, 2-2 draw.

14th Men on way to the Moon - excitement and great danger.

16th Lent Graham 'Battles of the Nineteenth Century.'

20th Wrote to Foyles, Holt Jackson, regarding selling books.

26th Went to Ashurst - Minister from India. Too long for me and I got a headache.

MAY

16th Graham came for us at 10.30 and motored us to Shoeburyness - 12, Whistler Rise. Had coffee, dinner, little walk in afternoon.

22nd Trouble over S. Africa cricket.

29th Had a read of Lewis Carrol.

JUNE

2nd Mr. Curtis helped to mow our lawn.

6th Holiday, Torquay. Up at 6 o'clock, got ready for journey. Had a plesant trip, break for coffee 11.30, and another break for tea. Cis nearly lost handbag, leaving on coach. Box arrived in good time and in good condition. In bed about 11 o'clock, tired and sleepy.

9th Very warm. Had chairs by the sea. Wrote cards to Win Sibley, Bob, Eva, Pledger, Alan & Margaret, Louise, Mike & Sheila.

11th Walked to putting green and had some rounds.

25th Rates bill arrived, first instalment April-Oct. - £37.17-1.

JULY

7th Letter rec'd from Margaret and Alan - Alan promoted to lecturer in Hebrew and Semitic languages.

AUGUST

3rd Pledger here. Bill putting in outside toilet, painting lavatory door

&c.

6th Graham & Pat here. Graham & Cis picked some plums.

10th I wrote to J.E. Blackwell, sending Glaxo Quarterly.

12th Geoff Curtis home from States - 3 weeks holiday. I cut some of lawn.

15thHoward and Nora motored up and stayed an hour or so. Had coffee, looked at garden, and left for Nora's mother.

18th Victor Newman died suddenly in his garden. A shock for Mrs. Newman, who was out shopping.

SEPT

2nd Filled out form for men aged over 88 - pension.

12th. Cis picked some greengages and made some jam.

17th Garage empty - tenant wanted.

18th Rec'd £15 from the Triangle Trust Fund '49.

25th No papers - strike.

26th Bill Thomson came and took us to church for the Harvest Supper. Poor number - about 60. Quite a nice entertainment. Good meal - turkey salad. Got back home 8.30.

27th Bill Thomson took us to church, and Mr. Cunningham brought us back. He has a German car.

OCT

2nd BDH Open Day in Poole, Dorset. Alf Curtis came for us at 8.10 and we went to Gants Hill - train to Waterloo via T. Ct. Rd. 10 o'clock train BDH Special to Poole. Dinner good, very professional class. Weather was so bad we were glad to sit in lounge while some went on coach trip to the New Forest. Coffee and sandwiches in train. Returning home, TV was out of order so no late news.

5th Dolly Slicker (Richards) came to see us - surprise visit.

6th Cis 'phoned Daniel Slicker.

17th We went to Roding Lane Free Church for Thanksgiving. Mrs. Beattie came from Angmering. We were made welcome - many of our old friends there.

The last known photograph of Thomas Sibley & Ciss, taken in Poole 1969.

29th Louise 'phoned thro' about Nurse Milcah coming to Ilford to finish her training in midwifery.

NOV

25th Louise 'phoned - she had been to Margaret's in the Wirral. Post Office workers on strike thro' sacking of Lord Hall.

26th Had a read of 'David Livingstone' in Great Lives.

DEC

7th Power cut - darkness for most of the day.

8th Power cut of electricians.

9th Power cut.

14th Electricians strike ended - on go slow? Some gains for men.

15th Edwin Shepherd taken ill and died suddenly.

21st Cis looking after Harry Pledger's bird. Cis iced the Christmas cake and I ornamented it.

25th Snow prevented me from having a walk. Cis busy making sausage rolls and mince pies. The tap in Mrs. Harvey's room leaking.

26th Mr. Curtis brought us some tarts. Visitors arrived - Graham and Pat, Howard and Nora. Presents given and received - Nora gave me 'In the Steps of the Master.'

1971

2nd Disaster at football match - 66 died. Mr. Blackwell 'phoned thanking us for a gift of flowers for Mrs. Blackwell. He is a little better.

3rd Read a good deal of The Monk Who Lived Again.

8th Cis bought two budgies and a nice circular cage from lady at 482 Eastern Avenue near Odeon. Tel. 500.

12th Cis had a letter from her brother Harold in Cornwall. They are all well. Cis took down Christmas cards - 68.

13th I wrote to an address in Bexhill - Dunselma, 25 Marina.

18th Postal strike.

20th Read some of Mayhew's London.

24th Mrs. Harvey went to her sister's in Slough and brought me back a bottle of sweet sherry.

28th Mr. King of Scrivens came about 7 o'clock and tested my hearing aid. Bill - £60.

FEB

7th Serious earthquake in Italy.

17th Cis went to the bank for me. Unhappy with the new money. Balance £190.50.

18th Michael Miles died in Spain on business.

22nd Pledger brought round some small cut wood.

23rd Graham and Pat came to see us. Supper - chicken and tart. Had a pleasant time. Graham is not very fit.

Housewives grapple with Decimal Day, as Britain says goodbye to the imperial system on Feb. 15th 1971.

27th Prepared for the evening meeting: Eliz. B. Murray, lantern slides and a long lecture on the Congo. Home 11.20. Stayed up for football special and tennis.

28th I was congratulated by Ken and others on being elected Honorary Deacon.

MARCH

1st Had a read of Warfare in England by Hilaire Belloc.

2nd Rod Laver beat Nikki Pilic.

18th Had an accident over trunk. I got it out of garage and pulled it on to myself. Had to be helped up.

22nd Dr. Chowdrhy came and examined me - no injury through fall. Quite fit - care needed - some bruising.

26th Croydon suffered a raid on bank.

27th I had a walk - posted 3 letters and walked thro' park. At the door I became giddy and fell. Cis and Mrs. Harvey got me up after the bruising and shaking. Rested in afternoon.

28th Cis 'phoned Bill Thomson saying I would be able to go to church, but my back got worse, so Cis 'phoned again saying I could not make it. Read the London City Magazine, Jan-Feb '71.

30th Good deal of talk about Budget.

APRIL

2nd Ford going back to work.

27th I drafted a letter to Eva and one for Bert.

MAY

3rd Great football match - Arsenal 1, Spurs 0.

8th Tremendous battle - Arsenal 2, Liverpool 1.

21st Cis went shopping at 11. I met her near buses. Chatted with a lady who wanted to loan me a chair to rest.

25th Graham and Pat motored here - new red car. Pat needs an operation for spine trouble.

JUNE

12th Bill Thomson called for us and motored us to Spurgeon's College. Enjoyed the first part and tea. Speech Day.

19th Packed box and labelled it.

22nd 94 today. England v Pakistan - draw.

26th Coach to Bexhill-on-Sea. Arrived Dunselma 3.30. Mr. Cole welcomed us to our room.

30th Coffee at Langley's. Spent morning on first floor.

JULY

3rd Sat on front. Coffee at De La Ware.

4th Rev. Edmund Heddle came for us and took us to the Baptist Church Buckland Rd. Glad to meet there Barbara (ex. Saville), special reference and memory of the late Mr. & Mrs. Charles Saville of Ilford & Ashurst Drive.

10th Got back safe and sound. Glad to get back to Ilford.

11th Margaret sent us a photo of the children, Clare and Stephen. Very good.

30th Trouble in Scotland - Clyde.

AUGUST

5th Watched some dog training.

22nd Teager came and took us to Ashurst and brought us home again. Teager now a citizen of the borough.

SEPT

5th Mrs. Holt had to be carried out of church - fainted.

11th C&D announced that Orridge & Co. and E.J. George had joined hands. Regent House, Regent St. W1R 8SV.

27th Had a letter from J.E. Blackwell - he is not at all well, and has resigned from E.J. George.

OCT

1st. Bournemouth, BDH Open Day. Met our many friends. Went to the Potteries, West Quay Rd. Train to Waterloo. Had a mishap on the way home - fell and damaged my patella, kneecap.

2nd. Rested. Bill Thomson came for us and we attended Harvest Supper.

19th Had a read of David Copperfield.

21st Great gas explosion - great loss of life in Glasgow.

28th Had no food all day. Wrote no letters.

30th Circus -? - trouble between two actors.

31st. More explosions by gangs of ruffians.

NOV

18th Dinner, cow-heel. Paid gas & telephone.

19th Read some of King Solomon's reign.

21st Was dozy. Cis anxious over me so she 'phoned Bill Thomson and I decided to stay at home.

28th Good deal of fighting between India and Pakistan. Cis & I went to Pastor Thomson's after the service, where we had coffee and biscuits. A very pleasant hour or so with Mr. & Mrs. Thomson, Dr. Leone and wife.

DEC

12th Heard about Lowrie Bennett - his fall from his high pedestal.

19th Special candlelight Christmas Service. Church crowded - good service. Carols.

21st Finished reading David Copperfield.

23rd Cis went to shops and got our turkey. Lovely in appearance - white and plump, 14lbs and 8oz. I was able to meet her and help a little at the end.

25th Visitors came about 12 - Graham & Pat, Howard & Nora. Lazy afternoon. Had games - consequences &c. Guests went home around 11 o'clock.

28th Read some of Notre Dame de Paris, Victor Hugo.

31st Wrote a cheque for Reader's Digest - £4.50, and Brentford Nylons, £3.20.

1972

JAN

3rd Sent a booking cheque to Mr. & Mrs. Cole Bexhill, £8.10th TV - Opportunity Knocks.

11th Midland Bank sent a/c - balance £239.38.

15th Trouble over taxes - income &c.

19th Cis called at Tax office & saw Mr. Ward - Tax is correct.

FEB

2nd Alice Warwick died in nursing home.

4th Baby Jonathan Ralph Millard arrived at home 3am. Weight 10lbs.

5th Alan 'phoned thro' 6 o'clock.

6th Will Warwick in hospital.

14th Strike. Miners doing their worst. Hughie Green - Opportunity Knocks.

18th Heath saw miner's leaders. Miner's strike still on but picketing off.

22nd Mr. Pledger came in and spoke about the increased value of my house and property.

23rd We had cuts again midday and between 6-9. Had to manoeuvres over tea.

27th Strike - blackouts 6-9pm.

MARCH

1st. Louise 'phoned - unable to come tonight as she is on duty.

2nd Read some of my diary, 1900.

3rd. Tea - lovely strawberries from Palestine.

4th Read some of old diary from 1900.

As Sibley's future wanes, he turns to the past, and collects clippings of his old days in the early decades of the century.

Some of the Office Staff, about 1916

13th Rec'd from Glaxo Trustees, £24.60 per annum, Clarges St.

14th Cis found the missing cheque book - in book-case.

16th Wonderful day for March. I sat in garden and read paper.

31st Bank balance £224.27.

APRIL

2nd. Cis rang Bill to say I was too unwell to go to church. Church sent us flowers.

10th Will Warwick sent a card saying Mrs. Hoare had suddenly died.

11th I felt giddy and unwell - took 2 aspirin. Wrote to Will Warwick.

17th Rail strike. Chaos at stations.

MAY

1st. Keith and Sheila came to dinner. Keith clipped the hedge. Said goodbye to them - off to Canada.

4th Did not have my dinner. Feeling sickly.

6th Cup Final. Leeds - 1, Arsenal 0. So the Cup goes Midlands.

13th Saw a great rugby match - St. Helen's and Leeds. Leeds won. Railway strike still on - upsetting for passengers on Southend Railway mostly. Cis washed her hair - used hair-dryer.

14th Sunday School Anniversary. Pageant. A fair number attended. Half hour hymn singing - very good.

18th Went into King George's Hospital. On danger list. Uncon…

19th Fine and sunny. Had a rest in lounge.

24th In hospital. Getting better.

25th Sunny and warm. In hospital, surrounded by young ladies, who cut my hair.

26th Pledger came to hospital.

28th David Teager visited, Bill Thomson, Pastor Thomson, Graham, Pat, Laura & Howard.

29th Fine and sunny. Prince of Wales' death at 77. Sat out in a chair.

30th Cis brought some shopping. Cherries, and a towel.

JUNE

3rd Warm.

5th Still in hospital, King George's. Waiting to see doctor today.

24th Holiday.

This was a forlorn entry he'd made at the beginning of the year recording a pre-booked holiday to Bexhill. He and Ciss never made another of their beloved seaside excursions. The end was near. Now for the first time in his chronicle there appear huge snowy gaps in his journals, swathes of vacant time that passed in a quiet hospital room, accompanied only by sunshine through the blinds and the cool tick of the hospital clock. There would have been more visitors - his beloved Cissy, and nephew Graham. Sadly it was not to be that his son Len & daughter Rene passed by, for they had long gone.

SEPT

28th Breakfast, grapefruit, porridge, fruit, bread & butter and marmalade. Nurse Crump came at 2.30. Washed, sat in chair. Lunch, veal, beans, rice, baked custard, baked apple.

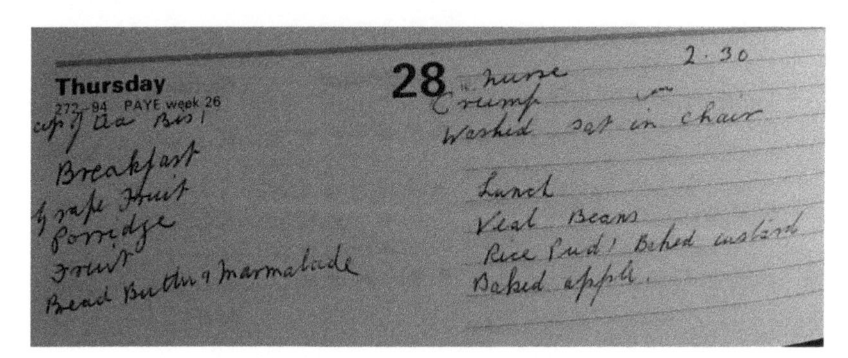
Thursday
272-94 PAYE week 26
Breakfast
Grape fruit
porridge
fruit
Bread Butter & marmalade

28 Nurse Crump 2.30
Washed sat in chair

Lunch
Veal Beans
Rice Pud! Baked custard
Baked apple

Thomas Sibley was to live for another two years but this is his final diary entry. His last twenty four months went unrecorded.

As for his century, it had not passed in the blinking of an eye but in the long travails of a humanity confronted by challenges and pressures not hitherto seen. Historian Andrew Marr, in his *'Modern Britain,' (Macmillian, 2009)* diagnosed the twentieth century as one in which *'ideologies were replaced with consumerism.'* It is certainly true that in Britain and across the West the post-1945 economic recovery was one in which the physical needs and comforts of a population deprived of such things by war and financial crashes became the focus of governments of all colours. The experiments of communism and fascism failed. And Liberalism, too, despite Thomas Sibley voting for them all his life, failed too in Britain, as the economic philosophy of Keynesian interventionism replaced *laissez-faire* and created the postwar welfare consensus that lasted until the 1980s.

The wider story is of a Britain that shifts, quite quickly, from being the world's largest imperial power to a northern European social democratic state uneasy in its relationship with both its former colonies and the wider world. Time will tell whether its leaving of the European Union in 2016 was a seismic re-alignment with the old Anglo-sphere it had created two centuries previously, and that its relationship with the USA, Canada, Australia and New Zealand was a more natural and comfortable coalescence than a fractious assemblage of European nations many of which had been Fascist in our lifetimes and which proceeded to overcome and destroy Britain's manufacturing base.

It is clear that from the second half of the twentieth century Britain has seemingly been in a state of managed decline; its manufacturing eroded, its imperial markets cauterised, its identity fractured and questioned by an increasingly cynical culture within. The success of the *counter-culture,* if not engendered in the Sixties then certainly accelerated during it, is evidence of a country turning negatively inward, and we are still perhaps living with the fall-out of this iconoclasm.

Sibley of course was immune to such counter-culture - we can see from his diaries that his attitude towards popular culture was most certainly an observer rather than a participant. He stuck ruggedly to the old order. So we must infer from this that he represented millions of like-minded Britons - ones who still stood to attention at the flag, attended Royal visits, ran Sunday Schools, held church fetes, preached self-help to the inmates of doss-houses and sailor's homes. What is evident from weaving our story from the diaries of one single individual and tracing the impacts of national and international events upon three generations of a single family, is that although the participants in the drama of life react, they also *act.* The heroes of the small drama of one family are not puppets blindly responding to vicissitudes: the central story of one's life is written not by outside events but by the mental map one incorporates as a guiding force. Sibley's life can be seen as almost antithetical to the philosophic demands of the age. While thinkers both scientific and philosophical demoted or abandoned the notion of God as a potent phenomenon in the mental life of a people, Sibley doggedly went against the grain of his culture and adopted it, with a vigour and vitality that never left him.

His was a life that not only responded to the social glue that kept Britain together - that freemasonry of everyday affairs in a community that binds people together like clubs, churches, charities - he *created* that symbiotic force, by dint of his moral actions, his ceaseless engagement with the flow of life and community and work. The philosopher Paul Tillich wrote that ones value in life and belief in God is measurable by examining one's *extent of concern,* that is, one's simple level of participation and belief in a purpose-driven life. Life as a self-fulfilling prophecy - if one gives it meaning, it has meaning. In the seemingly crazed patchwork of British life in the twentieth century, Sibley's, while seeming at times austere and stubborn, can be described, in more simpler terms, as possessing *grit.* The same 'grit' that saw us through two world wars, and while the world around us collapsed under the barren weight of ideology, never allowed us to doubt our belief in democracy; a nation that gave away its empire and moved gently into a new era of nations, like a ship setting out to sea from the docks in Poplar where Sibley took his sweetheart at the turn of the nineteenth century, with their whole lives ahead of them.

The author with David Sibley, Thomas Sibley's nephew, returning his Great-Uncle's diaries.

THOMAS SIBLEY FAMILY TREE

William Sibley 1844-1902 m. Susannah 1840-1902

|

Thomas 1878-1974 m. Anne Kettley 1878-1941

|

Len b. 1905 m. Freda   Irene b.1910 m Cliff Ringwood

| |

Anne b .1938 Clive b. 1939   Graham b. 1938 Howard b. 1945

Milton Keynes UK
Ingram Content Group UK Ltd.
UKHW040420071023
429907UK00012BA/128/J